BINDING THE STRONG MAN

BINDING THE STRONG MAN

A Political Reading of Mark's Story of Jesus

CHED MYERS

> No one can enter a strong man's house and plunder his goods
> unless they first bind the strong man; then indeed they may
> plunder his house.
>
> —Mark 3:27

ORBIS BOOKS

Maryknoll, New York 10545

Tenth Printing, December 1997

The Catholic Foreign Mission Society of America (Maryknoll) recruits and trains people for overseas missionary service. Through Orbis Books Maryknoll aims to foster the international dialogue that is essential to mission. The books published, however, reflect the opinions of their authors and are not meant to represent the official position of the society.

Manuscript editor and indexer: William E. Jerman

ISBN 0-88344-621-9
ISBN 0-88344-620-0 (pbk.)

To Phil and Liz
and Ladon

For every 10,000 words
there's a deed
  floating somewhere
head down, unborn

Words can't make it happen
They only wave it away
    unwanted
        Yet Child, necessary one
        Unless you come home to my hands
        Why hands at all?
Your season your cries
  are their skill
      their reason
                              —Daniel Berrigan

Contents

PART TWO
READING THE FIRST HALF OF MARK

PART THREE
READING THE SECOND HALF OF MARK

Foreword

by Daniel Berrigan

Long before publication, this work by Ched Myers accreted a remarkable history. West Coast to East, section-by-section, revised repeatedly, the manuscript made its way.

Here indeed, we quickly agreed, was a scriptural study to reckon with. It invited (and shortly received) serious pursuit: reading, meditation, passionate discussion.

Through Myers, Mark spoke, as the Quakers say, to our condition. It spoke most powerfully to those whose condition seemed remarkably akin to that of the early communities: those for whom, we are told, Mark's Gospel was first written.

Those of us who were so lucky as to come on the Myers manuscript saw our lives being both honored and beckoned. For some time we (like Myers' Mark; indeed, like Mark's Jesus) had been testing our mettle on strenuous terrains. Many of us who gathered for retreats and study, a current version of *Binding the Strong Man* in hand, were incurring the wrath of the titulary gods: those daemons who guard the impassible borders of empire, the multicorporate lairs, and nuclear sanctuaries.

Such Christians, coming together to catch breath and pray and reconnoiter, tend to regard ourvselves as a species of occupied people, striving to free ourselves from the yoke and lash of the culture.

And then, through Myers, we met the early Christians called the community of Mark.

•

You could see it in their faces, these children of a greater God, the God of refusers and renegades and resisters. Their look tended to a wide emotional range, from near despair to set purpose, to—now and again—near ecstasy.

Their set purpose was a different "way." Different with regard to work and its nature and rewards, with regard to children and women, with regard to the rights of humans—and the all-but-universal and official contempt of such rights. A highly different view of the law; especially of laws whose manifest aim was to keep people ignorant, fearful, or numb.

•

The tools and weapons of the "Strong Man" were a kind of demonic litany of the culture. The Christians knew it by heart: appetitiveness and sanctioned violence and the strut and lying and straining and achieving that were all the rage (in more senses than one).

And they refused to incant the litany. Not for them the slots, perks, ripoffs; nor the soft or hard fascism of the main mode of church and state, as currently practiced.

It was a small matter to them that the culture had, in fact, geared itself, been designed, in their favor. (Or so they were rather frequently assured by priest and parent.)

You grabbed and ran; that was it. And whatever devil (whether city shelter or welfare docket or mental hospital or city morgue) took those who were hindmost. It was a "style" straight out of the jungle, it made straight for the jugular. It was straightfaced, up front; it was the classic American "way" in the world.

Well, why not run with it? You had "class," were born to the manor, born to a market sometimes bullish, sometimes unaccountably sheepish. Born to free enterprise, to nuclear "security" and noisome political myth.

Born, if truth were told, to live and die, predestined to your slot; metronomes, clones, well-mannered and impeccable parasites.

Destiny, it was called. And on the grand scale, the imperial scale, manifest destiny.

But something else, Someone else, intruded. Vocation.

•

Some, those troublesome Markans, walked out on it all, "declassified" themselves in the Marxist sense. They would take no part in current social or sexual or economic idiocies, incompatible as such were with passion, imagination, faith, the work of one's hands.

•

Beginning in the civil rights days of the late fifties, Christians broke the mold. They broke iniquitous laws. They went to court, they went to jail. And many of them came out on their feet, intemperately asking for more.

If there was fault to be found with them (they found plenty of fault with themselves), it surfaced inevitably as time showed the true face of things—as it became apparent that America, having learned little or nothing from Selma to

Hanoi, was hell bent on its perennial obsessions: greed and violence. Indeed, that these were shortly to be imbedded in politics; high crime in high places.

It came home. Resistance was to be the uneasy tenor and rhythm of life itself.

•

Were we prepared for this? We were not.

Our plight was a serious one. How was resistance to endure, to show itself lasting and consistent in this land of Nid and Nod and Maybe and Mañana?

We were like amputees determined on a strenuous athletic contest. The prize was a noble one; the means were in serious question. How continue the arduous quest, the long haul toward the realm of God?

•

Our need could be thought of under a double image.

A map that would point us, straight as a discharged arrow, in the direction of sources. Important beyond words, the need to know, vividly, concretely, where we came from, what symbols, words, events, communities had lived the gospel, in fair weather and foul, from the beginning.

And then another image. We needed a handbook brimming with encouragement: stories, instruction, discipline, reproof, irony, hope, valiance in the breach; we needed the beckoning hand—out of another time and place (but not really another)—of Someone to be trusted. Someone to indicate the way to go.

•

The Myers manuscript, meticulous in scholarship and daring in scope, landed among us. And things have never been quite the same.

What a gift it was, and is! Myers plays mediator to Mark, in somewhat the way Mark had mediated Jesus. Pondering the manuscript was like entering a classic recognition scene, weighted with irony and hope, seizing the imagination, shedding light in dark places, challenging assumptions. We met our true ancestors, and learned and listened. We breathed the bracing air of new starts, we were introduced to the Way of Jesus, announced and lived out in the midst of conflicting ideologies and frenzies, the itch toward collaboration and violence.

What Jesus verified for the first disciples, Mark verified with disconcerting directness for his community, whose position vis-à-vis society proved very like that of the first disciples.

Like ours as well.

Which is to say, a community under fire.

•

Under fire we certainly were, and are; but who can describe a fire, who stem it, control it? Fire is the image nearest our situation; it burns, it destroys, it changes as it destroys.

The tinder is deeper and subtler by far than the decay and rubbish, the lethal landfill that smolders and mutters away under the thin crust of culture, under the murderous bonhommie, the nuclear installations, the cruel guarded borders, the lackey courts and jails.

In order to walk the fiery landscape, we had to know—whether our resistance were a mere curiosity or perversity (it was frequently stigmatized as both). Or whether, maladroit as we often were, and much given to backward glances and fear and trembling, we might still, in virtue of a summons beyond reckoning, might qualify as—disciples.

•

The culture came down hard on such aspirations. During the preceding decades, a kind of Procrustean arrangement, sometimes subtle, sometimes brutally direct, was put in place. Christian resisters against racism and war were persuaded to "fit in"; secularism was all the rage. Declarations of faith, whatever their form, were regarded as ill times, all but ill mannered.

A "religious left," a "Catholic left"? If that was all, if the tags matched the facts, we were in trouble indeed.

Procrustes and his bed proved to be a ruse, and a tormenting one at that. To fit the cultural measure was to die.

The rules of the game were strait and narrow indeed; there were few choices. Some who spoke up or acted up were judged inordinately forthright, too spirited. They must be cut down to size; only so would they fit the pygmy resolve of the age. Jail would do; so would exile.

Others, it was judged, were infected with an unseemly modesty; they must be persuaded to assume the guise of technological superman. So it was done; they were destined to "fit in," to join the culture, good, sensible, solid, taxpaying, in sum "disappeared."

•

Thus the method was clarified in the act. One measure allowed, one version of the human; a forced growth, a forced "coming to terms." In any case, spiritual mutilation, a violent alteration in nature. Homo Americanus emerged; from the point of view of spirit, a biological mutation, recessive, selfish, belligerent.

•

Eventually (we were slow learners in this merciless school), the Christians came to a measure of understanding. Did one wish to be human in an inhuman time? If so, it would never suffice (if ever it had) to describe, tag, identify oneself as simply American, to conceal or downplay one's faith (the adjective "Christian" appended, an afterthought, a personal devotional matter; a kind of grammar of the hangdog, uttered with an air of vague diffused apology).

The lesson came home, hard. We must have at our disposal other, far different resources than the tormenting uniformity of the rack. The resources must be older, less questionable, more thoroughly tested than the times would allow—or could possibly grant.

In such a time, Mark's Gospel and the stunning insights of Myers came together, a happy conjunction indeed, a life line woven. Many of us would not hesitate to name the event providential. And to grasp and hold on, with all our might.

•

A phrase occurs: Myers' work is marked by a "new authority."

Of the older scriptural authority we had learned something in universities and seminaries; it proved, alas, of little help in the world we must walk, the fires underfoot.

Too abstract, too specialized, chary of the times and their questions, a game of artful dodgers and academic isolationists. The method worried the text, held it up like a dead specimen, turned it this way and that in one hand, in the other a dissecting tool. Words, words, words.

The inference was clear; at hand was a given text, foreign and undoubtedly venerable. And then there were other texts, equally venerable, of pagan origins.

And was there a difference to be noted, even passionately noted, between, say, the text of Mark and the text of Cicero or Sophocles? And if so, what, to a dissecting mind, might the difference be? Might it be a matter of faith, of an unmistakable (sometimes abrasive) style in the world, of that "way" to be confused with no other, either in direction or source or end? Might it be (horrors) that unpleasant matter of the cross?

Such questions were often brushed aside. The gospel text was gingerly passed along, honored by dispassion. Its words might flare into life, in the awakening of this or that student. But all such matters or events were outside the purview of class, study, method, plod—and the inevitable day of reckoning, the examination.

Such professors as we suffered under! Some would consider an expression of faith or passionate agreement or recoil or the shaking of the text into life—as a breach of academic politesse. To be winced at, ignored, in accord with the code of the officers' club or the university commons.

The scribes took no chances, or very few; and the truth suffered, for the truth demanded chances, the chances the Truthteller had taken, and suffered for the taking.

But the truth, never.

●

Myers took chances, dared to be passionate or indignant or ironic or loving. He renewed the sap of the text, the zest, the risky start, the hope of finishing. He drew the text into life, our lives—where indeed, by supposition, the text was meant to lodge, to discomfit, ennoble.

His method makes of the Gospel of Mark a veritable tract for the times. Mark announced the "new authority" of Jesus: an acute sense of tradition and an equally vivid respect for experience.

Tradition—a community intent on its task, its faith a drama and crisis. This, according to Mark, was the will of Christ, as it had been the will of the prophets before Him. Like a dry tinder the annunciation set his people, beleaguered as they were, occupied by a merciless power, humiliated and bereft of power, set them ablaze with hope.

And experience—life and its facts, it headlines, its unknown, ignored, anonymous victims. What of them? Who speaks for the speechless? Today, today the gospel must speak! Must discern the political realities and subterfuges, must proclaim the despised truth, defend the victims, judge the executioners, hold them accountable. This, or the gospel is a closed book, and we the betrayers of the hope of Christ.

And then what? The principalities, the weapons, the lies, the idols and their votaries, the spurious strength of the Strong Man—these have all the say and sway.

●

Myers refers in his first pages to the absurd presumption that scholars (or anyone else) come to Mark's Gospel as a tabula rasa, pure nous applied to the text. As though no special interest or passion or skin or economics or gender were intervening or brought to bear.

The presumption is by no means toothless; in fact it dictates the method. Exegetes become a species of "objective reporters."

We are only beginning to see, in the main through women and Third World theologians, not only the absurdity, but the arrogance that underlay the presumption of "objectivity." This while the heavy hints and the heavier facts, such realities as male, capitalist, white, pressed down on the scholarship, a nudge here, an innuendo there; in any case a coloration and bias.

In contrast, as Myers points out, biblical scholarship, rightly understood, is heavily and rightly indebted to—life. To its fury and injustice, its divisions and politics, follies and crimes.

•

Myers of course brings his own bias to the text; he is quite forthright about it. The "bias" amounts in his case to an attentive analysis of the politics of Jesus; to that Way of defiance, loving, albeit courageous, toward the worldly powers that in His time and ours ravage the world and legalize high crime.

Iniquitous authority, lawless and spurious, must be cast from its illegitimate throne; justice must be enthroned. This is the work of Jesus. It proceeds in the community of Jesus.

Love, defiance. Instinctive affection toward persons, even the worldly powers; defiance toward their power, its malfunctioning and maleficence.

•

One senses in Myers' work a Jesus who would be accounted a stranger by many biblicists of the Western world.

But hardly new to the resisters of our lifetime, the base communities, the Christians hailed into courts and jails here and elsewhere, that noble "third world" that has invaded our own with its sublime evangel of liberation. A Jesus witnessed to in art and music and poetry and dance, the noble testimonies and testaments of the tortured and disappeared.

The glance He casts, that Jesus of Mark!, upon the world, in our direction too. A glance that takes much into account, that is both merciful and courageous, that ranges where it will, upon outcast, woman, child, the half-hearted, and the hero; upon harvest, coin, lurking scribe, snoops and parasites and betrayers, soldiers and their vainglorious superiors. A glance that rests with equanimity upon the powers that will destroy Him.

The glance rests on the disciples—nursing their pride, only half understanding, half wilful, boastful in good times and fretful and childish in the breach. All taken in, and taken into account.

And then the end, or the purported end, the showdown.

But on the third day. . . .

•

And what of the "meantime," our own time, that long sighing hiatus between Now and Then?

Let it be said that through Myers, we know our task better, and will perhaps set about it more resolutely. Entering the house of death, binding the Strong Man in the name of the Stronger! And seizing those larcenous goods, loosening that overbearing claim and clutch. Reclaiming our world, in the name of a far different Master. For hope renewed, for "beauty and valor and act," this word of gratitude.

Preface

This book is situated within a still young North American exegetical tradition, which emerged in the late 1970s under the inspiration and guidance of Hebrew Bible scholar Norman Gottwald. This new approach to Bible study has been referred to variously as "political hermeneutics," "sociology of the Bible," "liberation reading of scripture." Gottwald summarized it as:

> A fundamental effort to interconnect aspects of Bible study that have been split apart and treated as unrelated, even antagonistic, in academia and the churches. . . . Many yawning chasms presently separating the several integral aspects of political and social hermeneutics must and can be soundly bridged by critical reflection and practice [1983:2].

Binding the Strong Man endeavors to carry on this tradition by carrying out the "bridging" task in a reading of Mark's Gospel.

Gottwald identified the major "chasms" as those between (1) thought and practice; (2) biblical academics and popular Bible study; (3) religion and the rest of life; and (4) the past as "dead history" and the present as "real life." As for the first chasm, this book stands apart from academic commentaries in its fundamental commitment to a contemporary practice of radical discipleship, and the place of Mark's Gospel vis-à-vis that practice. I accept the axiom of liberation theology that practice must lie on either side of reflection. In adopting the model of the "hermeneutic circle" (below, 1,A), I have made explicit my own partisanship concerning the grave questions of our own time. These issues form the "lens" through which the text of Mark is read; the text, in turn, answers right back with disturbing questions of its own. I wish to take both sets of questions seriously, maintaining simultaneous allegiance to, as Karl Barth put it, Bible and newspaper, Word and world.

Bridging the second chasm I have found to be a most difficult task. This book is pitched half way between the deeply alienated camps of professional biblical scholarship and "lay" Bible study. I have proceeded in the full awareness that many in the latter camp will find this book too difficult, whereas some in the former camp will dismiss it as insufficiently dispassionate, or nuanced, or sophisticated. But the field of biblical interpretation has become so technical that the average reader, unfamiliar with the in-house literature, can quickly become discouraged. The scholarly guild, for its part, has largely abdicated its responsibility to make the Bible more, rather than less, intelligible.

It is true that these ancient texts are cultural artifacts, not easily or accurately interpreted without historical and critical tools. Yet as scripture, they are not *merely* artifacts, for they continue to shape the world as documents of a living ideology and practice. Moreover, the Bible understands itself to belong to the people of God, not to the scholars—Mark himself reserved his sharpest criticism for the scribal classes. This, however, does not give us license to simply settle for novel ways of extracting instant "relevance" from the text. We North Americans are particularly susceptible to our media-saturated culture's propensity for immediate gratification. Persons should be urged to work harder with the difficult issues of interpreting biblical texts (below, 1,B).

Conversely, more serious exegetical work should be directed to a popular audience rather than to the self-referential world of scholarship. As an activist trained in the biblical academy, I am conscious of the enormous wealth of insight that is locked up there, wealth that activists are too often content to disdain. This only impoverishes our own efforts at critical reflection, to which we are allegedly committed. I think it a lesser evil therefore to risk oversimplifying complex but important concepts than to abandon popular study to platitudes. Whether I have been successful in this attempt to plunder the scholars' house on behalf of the people is of course up to the judgments of both parties, but especially the latter.

To overcome the third dichotomy I have refused to abide by the typical distinction between "religious" and "political" modes of discourse. The reason for this is twofold. First, the distinction is simply inappropriate to the study of biblical antiquity, indeed to most premodern cultures (below, 2,A,iii). Secondly, in our own time the wedge driven between theology and politics has only resulted in the domestication of the former and the sacralization of the latter. In the North American context this has clearly been articulated in the writings of the late William Stringfellow. My book endeavors to carry on his great work of uncovering both the political character of theological discourse and the theological character of political discourse. To this end I have employed the unified concept of "ideology," critically examined to yield its liberating or oppressive social functions (below, 1,C).

The fourth chasm is the most treacherous for students of the Bible. A good example of how historical and present meaning are strictly segregated can be seen in most intepretations of biblical apocalyptic literature. Ever since E. Käsemann rediscovered that "apocalypticism is the mother of Christian theology," there has been something of a renaissance in the historico-critical study of this ancient genre. Few scholars have dared, however, to risk a "translation" of apocalyptic ideology into our own day: "There is no doubt that the old apocalyptic currencies have been negotiated by the various versions of modern theology at a very low rate of exchange" (Braaten, 1971:482). Those endeavoring to read the Bible politically (i.e., liberation theologians and Marxist interpreters) have also tended to avoid apocalyptic discourse. It seems the only ones who *do* attempt to find relevance in apocalyptic symbolics are the popular "profiteers" of doom, huckstering their gratuitous timetables of the future.

I believe the ideology of apocalyptic holds the key to an accurate political reading of Mark—indeed, of most of the New Testament. In order to translate that ideology into meaningful terms for modern readers, I use the Gandhian notions of *ahimsa* (nonviolence), *swaraj* (liberation) and *satyagraha* (truthforce) as a "heuristic" hermeneutical key (explained below, 2,A,iii). This is not an entirely novel approach, having been already tentatively proposed by both biblical scholars (see the works cited by J. and A. Y. Collins) and theologians (see the works cited by J. Douglass), though it goes far beyond previous attempts to portray Jesus as a nonviolent revolutionary (e.g., Yoder, 1972; Trocmé, 1962; below, Appendix, A). A full explication of this thesis concerning apocalyptic ideology and revolutionary nonviolence, however, as well as other hermeneutical connections that I hint at herein, are beyond the scope of this book.

Though my reading of Mark tries to maintain a synoptic view of what the Gospel *meant* in its own socio-historical context and what it *means* in ours, these two necessary tasks of interpretation are not identical, nor can they always be carried out simultaneously. Thus I wish the reader to know that this commentary is only the first of a two-part project on Mark and radical discipleship. It concentrates on the former task, though never outside the purview of the latter. My reflections concerning the shape of Mark's call to radical discipleship in our own context must—because of the already daunting length of this book—here be kept general and brief. They will be explored in depth in a forthcoming companion volume, the second part of my political reading of Mark.

A few words about how this commentary proceeds are in order. For better or worse, if we wish not only to avoid but to *overturn* the kind of simplistic Bible readings that are everywhere used to justify aberrant Christian ideologies, from the White House to the Crystal Cathedral, we must deal with the numerous procedural difficulties of methodology. "Simple Bible-believers" who disclaim the need for hermeneutics are the most suspect interpreters of all. On the other hand, socio-political studies of the Bible today are notorious for their tendency to overwhelm the reader with methodological apparatus (e.g., "semiotic theory," "modes of production," etc.), so that he or she cannot even get past the preliminaries! Yet to do away with methodology altogether only serves to make the reader dependent on taking the author's word for their interpretation, which only perpetuates a hermeneutic of "dependency."

Obviously my study is not exempt from this problem. In chapter 1 I define, in popular fashion, the salient terms and characteristics of my "socio-literary reading strategy." A detailed treatise of the methodological issues involved would make rather dense reading, especially for those unfamiliar with the fields of sociology and literary criticism. I believe my generalizations concerning "text as ideological discourse" will suffice for purposes of reading Mark, into which I am anxious to get the reader as soon as possible. I refer to other scholarly works where the issues have been treated at length, leaving readers free to explore further if they so wish. I hope this eliminates a psychological obstacle to this commentary for those who are less concerned with methodology than its fruits. Readers who yet find part 1 slow going are encouraged to start right in with the commentary, which begins midway through chapter 3, and return to the introductory material if and when questions concerning method arise.

The reading strategy I propose skirts between the twin errors of contemporary biblical criticism. To port lies the Scylla of historical criticism's dismantling of narrative texts; to starboard the Charybdis of the new literary criticism, which divorces narrative signification from the historical world (below, 1,D). I insist upon both the literary *and* the socio-historical integrity of the whole text. I call my approach "socio-literary" in order to distinguish it from three current schools of criticism, each of which I draw from in part but none of which I fully endorse: sociological exegesis, narratology, and materialist criticism (below, 1,E,iii).

The length of this commentary is due to the demands of depth and breadth. A socio-literary method stipulates that the gospel narrative must be interpreted whole, not in isolated parts. As for political hermeneutics, it has tended either to rely upon exegetical generalizations or limit its investigations to select texts. If the long-range task, however, is to reclaim the liberating Bible, we must offer systematic commentary on texts in their entirety, and not just the ones that seem at first glance to lend themselves to a political reading!

This is not so much a verse-by-verse commentary as an "episode-by-episode" exposition, studying the meaning of each literary unit and its relationship to the other units and to the overall ideological strategy of Mark. I have made every effort to avoid getting bogged down in details of exegesis or narrative structure, as is so easy, and apologize in advance for those places the reader may find inappropriately sclerotic. I have also tried to preserve a narrative style in my own writing, as opposed to the usual detached prose of commentaries. Still, this is a book for Bible *study*, meant as a tool and reference work. Needless to say, it must be read with the text of Mark at hand, for I have not reproduced it herein. In my biblical citations I stay close to the text of the *Revised Standard Version* (RSV) except where otherwise indicated; the RSV remains the best study text in English. I have included the transliterated Greek where necessary for clarity.

Because so much work on Mark is available, I have steered away from well-established insights, and concentrated instead upon texts, themes, or socio-literary characteristics that I believe to be underappreciated. My thesis about the whole of the Gospel is as important as my treatment of any specific part, and the reader is invited to take issue on both levels. Because my method is eclectic and cross-disciplinary, it has all the attendant assets and liabilities. Although many of my conclusions are original, I have borrowed freely from a wide range of the traditional exegetical literature, as well as from the newer sociological and literary fields. Indeed, one of my intentions has been to expose the reader to some of the exciting exegesis being offered in contemporary Markan studies. To avoid cluttering the pages with secondary references, however, I decided against all but a very few footnotes. Instead I have preferred to guide readers to sources that I have found particularly helpful, in the event they wish to pursue something through further investigation.

It is my hope that this commentary might stimulate further work along similar lines, in Mark or other biblical texts. But above all it is offered, as the Gospel itself is, to discipleship communities, however discouraged and weary, as part of our ongoing search for renewed direction and hope in our struggle to follow the way of Jesus in difficult times. A true reading of Mark compels us to come to terms afresh with our faith and most certainly our lack of faith (Mk 9:24). I pray that this study might help Mark to speak, and the reader to have "ears to hear," the good news that promises yet to overthrow the structures of domination in our world.

Acknowledgments

Mark's Gospel was written both to and on behalf of a circle of discipleship communities. The same is true of this book. It is a reflection upon actual (not imagined) praxis, growing out of a decade of living, organizing, and acting with sisters and brothers around the country and around the world, struggling to envision and embody a different way of being human and Christian. The primary soil of germination was eight years in a community in Berkeley, California, which took its name from Mark's blind beggar-disciple, Bartimaeus. The material that eventually became *Binding the Strong Man* was first tested there through teaching and preaching, and subsequently in other communities. Such sites remain the most important crucible.

The method and much of the exegesis for this study was originally worked out in a master's thesis at the Graduate Theological Union. Gratitude goes to several of my teachers for their input and encouragement: to James McClendon, who taught me theology; to William Herzog, who introduced me to literary criticism of the Bible; to Athol Gill, who has faithfully taught Mark to several generations of radical disciples; and especially to Norman Gottwald, who aside from being a pioneer in the field of socio-political hermeneutics, is the model of a "people's scholar," and a key supporter of this project. These friends of course bear no responsibility for whatever errors of judgment or exegesis may be found here.

This manuscript took shape over the space of three years and two continents after I left Berkeley. For me it was a time of itinerancy, reflection, self-confrontation, healing. As Jung said, "The right way to wholeness is made up of fateful detours and wrong turnings." Several communities have helped along the way with hospitality and support. On the U.S. east coast, Sojourners in Washington, D.C.; Jonah House in Baltimore; and the Covenant Peace Community in New Haven. On the Australian east coast, House of the Gentle Bunyip in Melbourne; Avalon Baptist Peace Memorial Church in Sydney; and the House of Freedom in Brisbane. A considerable part of the writing took place in southern California (truly the entrails, yet roots still), where I received deeply appreciated emotional and financial support from my parents and the Spurgin family.

Many Pacific islanders are borne in this book without knowing it: Julian, Darlene, Roman, Hilda, Rev. Welepane, and especially old man Kabokal, who will never read it but whose words that steamy jungle night of Holy Week 1985 remain deeply within me. Countless others who struggle for justice and peace in the world and fidelity to the gospel have contributed to whatever is worthwhile in this book. Like Siddhartha by the river, I see the faces of so many loved ones flow by: John and Carol, Sandy, Sandra, Libby, George and Jocelyn, Chris, Skip and Margaret, Katy and Dean, Dan, Bill and Jeanie, Jim and Joyce, Danny, Gene and Faith, Richard, Neil and Denise, Scott, Bob and Janet, Giff, Jim and Shelly, all the good friends of Pacific and Atlantic Life Communities . . . and above all Maggi, my companion on the road for all those years.

> Though your lips can't recall now
> all the joy and all the pain . . .
> dream on, sweet dreamers. . . . (Peter Campbell)

Words are not the way to liberation. Insofar as this study offers any clarification or inspiration, it is done on behalf of all those nonviolent resisters presently in jail because of their witness against the imperial Goliath. "May we become the wind that diverts the oncoming storm!" (Bernard Narakobi).

Binding the Strong Man is dedicated to three persons who stood with me one cold morning at the Pentagon, Thanksgiving 1976, a time that I look back upon as my own second call to discipleship. They have helped me, and help me still, with that long, ongoing catechism in reality, in which the truth of imperial America, with its vast disparity between rich and poor, its permanent war economy, and its institutionalized racism, is laid bare. To Phil Berrigan and Liz McCallister, who have with their lives exegeted the meaning of apocalyptic radicalism in our day. And to Ladon Sheats who gently called me (and so many others) to follow Jesus, and who has been there every time I have, like Peter, broken down and wept in the face of my own betrayal and that of my companions. Mahalo, friends; by your discipleship I continue to measure my own.

Abbreviations

A.M.	Assumption of Moses
Ant.	Josephus, Antiquities of the Jews
BibTheoBul	Biblical Theology Bulletin
BJRL	Bulletin of the John Rylands Library
CBQ	Catholic Biblical Quarterly
HTR	Harvard Theological Review
JAAR	Journal of the American Academy of Religion
JBL	Journal of Biblical Literature
JSNT	Journal for the Study of the New Testament
JSOT	Journal for the Study of the Old Testament
JSSR	Journal for the Scientific Study of Religion
LXX	Septuagint (Greek translation of Hebrew Bible)
NedTheoTijd	Nederlands Theologisch Tijdschrift
NovTest	Novum Testamentum
NTS	New Testament Studies
SBL	Society of Biblical Literature
TDNT	Theological Dictionary of the New Testament (10 vols. G. Kittel and G. Friedrich, eds.; Grand Rapids: Eerdmans)
TheoZeit	Theologische Zeitschrift
War	Josephus, War of the Jews
ZAW	Zeitschrift für die Alttestamentliche Wissenschaft
ZDPV	Zeitschrift des Deutschen Palästina-Vereins
ZeitNTWiss	Zeitschrift für die Neutestamentliche Wissenschaft

BINDING THE STRONG MAN

Part One

Text and Context

CHAPTER ONE

A Reading Site and Strategy for Mark

Hermeneutics seems to me to be animated by this double motivation: willingness to suspect, willingness to listen: vow of rigor, vow of obedience. In our time we have not finished doing away with *idols* and we have barely begun to listen to *symbols*.

—Paul Ricoeur (1970:27)

During the 1984 U.S. presidential campaign, Ronald Reagan repeated over and over his singular interpretation of the historical moment: "America is back," he extolled, "and walking tall." The campaign strategy of the incumbent administration was simple: to feed the people and the equally credulous press a steady diet of blithe reassurances about America's divine anointing and world dominance, and contemptuously brush aside all social and political evidence to the contrary. It was clear that (yet again) Reagan had identified and was successfully exploiting the mood of that significant part of the electorate anxious to suppress the deepening contradictions of empire.

There were of course some who took strenuous exception to the president's assessment. During the last two weeks of the campaign, some of them gathered daily outside the White House to register their dissent. They, like Mr. Reagan, chose the language of metaphor and symbol, but theirs contrasted starkly with his. Some erected a tent city in Lafayette Park, across the street from the White House, to dramatize the reality of America's burgeoning ranks of the homeless poor. Others fasted, a public reminder of the millions who starve as a direct and indirect result of the administration's brazen preference for "bombs over bread." And still others entered the White House grounds each day, throwing blood on the portico, and then kneeling and praying. Citing the Hebrew scriptures, they insisted that the blood of the innocent, victims of Reagan's policies from Central America to southern Africa to South Korea, was crying out from those whitewashed pillars.

But the spell woven by the president's carefully honed images of imperial pride and piety prevailed: he was swept into office for a second term. Protesters, for their trouble, were thrown into jail. But the contest of metaphors

3

raging across the White House lawn on the eve of election day 1984 represents a phenomenon that will occupy the central concern of this book: it was a "war of myths." The evangelist Mark, too, enlisted into the war of myths in his day; he did so by writing his Gospel, by retelling the story of Jesus of Nazareth and his struggle with the "powers" of Roman Palestine. Today, how we interpret that Gospel depends upon our reading of, and engagement in, the war of myths that still continues.

1A. WHY A POLITICAL READING?

i. *The Hermeneutic Circle*

Any serious study of a biblical text must begin with a discussion of "hermeneutics." This term, like most of the technical vocabulary of professional theologians and philosophers, is intimidating to lay readers. It refers to the art (or "science") of interpretation, especially of written texts. No text "speaks for itself," argues Ricoeur; it is vulnerable, dependent upon an interpreter to restore its voice:

> Written discourse cannot be "rescued' by all the processes by which spoken discourse supports itself in order to be understood—intonation, delivery, mimicry, gestures. . . . Henceforth only the meaning "rescues" the meaning, without the contribution of the physical and psychological presence of the author. But to say that the meaning rescues the meaning is to say that only interpretation is the "remedy" [1977:320].

Obviously, a text produced in a time, place, and culture distantly removed from that of the interpreter—such as the Gospel of Mark—is all the more vulnerable.

Given this, the etymology of "hermeneutics" is germane. Hermes was the "messenger of the gods" in the Greek pantheon; it is easy to see why they derived their word for "interpreter" from his name. Hermes was also, however, the patron god of invention, cunning, and theft (Kealy, 1982:236). The lesson for would-be exegetes is evident: the critical task of *restoration* can all too easily turn into *robbery*! It is for good reason, then, that contemporary hermeneutics is preoccupied with "suspicion."

In historical criticism, hermeneutic suspicion has meant the task of creating critical distance between text and interpreter. Readers attempt to suspend their assumptions, so that the world and voice of the text can be understood as much as possible in their own linguistic, cultural, and historical terms. The problem here is that critical *distance* was understood as *detachment*, the goal being an allegedly "objective" assessment of the text. Here a second suspicion arises, in recognition of the fact that it is neither possible nor desirable for an interpreter to suspend all preconception. Thus, we must also "interpret the interpreter," taking into account the biases and preunderstandings that inevitably shape the "meaning" he or she derives from the text. This suspicion may be applied not only to the ideas of the interpreter, but to their social class and political commitments in the real world as well.

This more complicated labyrinth of suspicion has been the domain of modern hermeneutics. Claims that the meaning of the text is "obvious," requiring no interpretation, or that someone interprets without bias, are no longer credible. Hermeneutics takes seriously the burden and responsibility of the interpreter as "translator," trying to bridge two vastly different worlds. Moreover, interpretation is a conversation between text and reader, requiring not detachment but involvement. This conversation is often called the "hermeneutic circle." Our life situation will necessarily determine the questions we bring to the text, and hence strongly influence what it says and means to us. At the same time, the text maintains its own integrity, and we owe it to ourselves and the text to try to enter into its world as much as possible. Then, if we are genuinely listening to the text, we will allow it to influence how we understand and what we do about our situation (it "interprets" us). Until the circle from context to text and back to context is completed, we cannot be said to have truly interpreted the text. I recommend W. Wink's clear discussion of this process for further consideration (1973:19ff.).

Hermeneutic theology, like so many other aspects of traditional theological discourse, has been challenged by liberation theology. The axiom that *practice* must predicate theological reflection, when applied to biblical interpretation, results in a somewhat different version of the hermeneutic circle. According to Juan Luis Segundo, the circle begins when our experiences of "committed Christian practice" bring us to critical awareness of the dominant ideologies and social structures that shape the world in which we live. This leads to suspicion about the prevailing modes of biblical exegesis, and raises "profound and enriching questions" that we bring to the text. From this interaction we emerge with a fresh interpretation of the Bible (1986:66).

The remainder of this chapter will briefly trace my own steps around Segundo's hermeneutic circle, beginning with an acknowledgment of my own historical context and commitments, or what I will refer to as my "reading site" (below, ii,iii). Key concerns arising from this site are not addressed in traditional biblical interpretation; what is required is a more expressly *political* "reading strategy" (below, B). I then briefly discuss the basis for such a reading strategy (below, C,D), and outline my alternative "socio-literary" method (below, E). Chapter 2 turns to investigate Mark's socio-historical "site," which prepares us for a reading of his text. In real life, of course, this circle is dynamic: our practice brings us to the text, our reading drives us to practice, and so on. This commentary is committed to fostering this process in all its parts.

ii. Locus Imperium

White North American Christians, especially those of us from the privileged strata of society, must come to terms with the fact that our reading site for the Gospel of Mark is empire, *locus imperium*. It may be true, as historian W. A.

Williams wrote, that "the words *empire* and *imperialism* enjoy no easy hospitality in the minds and hearts of most contemporary Americans" (1981:viii). But this only serves to confirm his contention that "we have only just begun our confrontation with our imperial history, our imperial ethic, and our imperial psychology" (ibid.:xi).

Facing this truth is exceedingly difficult for those of us who by race, sex, or class are the "rightful inheritors" of the imperial project—or who at the very least are promised a comfortable metropolitan existence in exchange for our political conformity. After all:

> Americans of the 20th century like empire for the same reasons their ancestors had favored it in the 18th and 19th centuries. It provides them with renewable opportunities, wealth, and other benefits and satisfactions including a psychological sense of well-being and power [ibid.:13].

But to fail to come to terms with empire is to have to cling more and more desperately to illusions about our culture (that is to say, ourselves). We are, of course, quite capable of self-deception, as demonstrated by the vigorous rehabilitation of imperial fantasies in the Reagan era. The human cost of our delusion, however, is staggering, for it renders the mechanisms that maintain American primacy abroad and "friendly fascism" at home all the more murderous (Gross, 1980).

It is not my intention to argue the fact of empire, but to state it clearly as an assumption. I agree with W. A. Williams that the "irreducible meaning" of empire is the geopolitical control of the periphery by the center:

> Adam Smith said it once and for all: the city enjoys and exploits a structural advantage over the country. . . . The essence of imperialism lies in the metropolitan domination of the weaker economy (and its political and social superstructure) to ensure the extraction of economic rewards [W. A. Williams, 1980:7f.].

"Metropolis" is indeed an appropriate image for the modern technocracy that is the United States today. Of course we must never forget that the line between center and periphery is not a strictly geographical one: there are many within the gates of the metropolis who are still on the peripheries, and a minority of those outside its gates who enjoy imperial privilege and power.

There is an important thing about this reading site that the reader of this commentary must keep in mind. The "center-periphery" model is in many respects germane also to the world, and hence the site, of Mark himself. The ancient Mediterranean world was dominated by the rule of imperial Rome. However, whereas I read from the center, Mark wrote from the Palestinian periphery (see below, 2,A,i). His primary audience were those whose daily lives bore the exploitative weight of colonialism, whereas mine are those who are in a position to enjoy the privileges of the colonizer. In this sense, Third World liberation theologians, who today also write from the perspective of the colonized periphery have the advantage of a certain "affinity of site" in their reading of the Gospels. As Jon Sobrino writes:

> There is clearly a noticeable resemblance between the situation here in Latin America and that in which Jesus lived . . . [but it] does not lie solely in the objective conditions of poverty and exploitation . . . [but also] in the cognizance that is taken of the situation [1978:12].

Although too much can be made of this affinity—the imperialism of Roman antiquity was very different from that of American modernity (see below, 2,A,iii)—the fact remains that those on the peripheries will have "eyes to see" many things that those of us at the center do not. This, however, does not relieve us of the responsibility to read the Gospel and respond to it. Indeed, to listen to the perspective of the periphery (both that of Mark and those of today) is fundamental to our awakening to the call to discipleship in the *locus imperium*.

iii. Radical Discipleship

Those doing theological reflection from a vantage point on the peripheries have properly focused upon the themes of liberation in the story of exodus (Gutiérrez, 1973:153ff.). We at the center, however, have no choice but to learn to "do theology in pharaoh's household" (Sölle, 1979)—that is, to take the side of the Hebrews even though citizens of Egypt. There is a significant minority of Christians in the U.S.A. and other First World countries who are struggling to find a lifestyle and politics that does just that. This movement also constitutes the site from which I read Mark.

The so-called Christian left, like so many other strains of dissent, arose amid imperial culture's crisis of credibility during the civil rights movement and the war in Indochina. This period brought disillusionment also with the churches—liberal and conservative, Catholic and Protestant—which, by their silence concerning the war, suggested that perhaps the gospel was irrelevant to history. Feeling betrayed, many sensitive persons left their church, pursuing the new and potent myths offered by secularization and the New Left. Others, though similarly disaffected, instead looked for the source of the betrayal by reexamining their roots (Latin *radix*, whence "radical"). For many there was a rediscovery of a nonimperial heritage within their own traditions: Lutherans found Bonhoeffer, Baptists remembered the Anabaptists, Methodists reread Wesley and the Abolitionists, Catholics found Francis and a host of martyrs and saints, and so on (Gish, 1973).

There have been many tributaries to this stream. One of the most important has been the witness of the church in the Third World and liberation theology, which began to be more broadly felt in North America in the mid-1970s. Challenges to dominant church ideologies also came from feminist, black,

Hispanic, Asian-Pacific, and Amerindian theologies. The 1980s saw the beginnings of real solidarity between churches of the center and periphery through
such popular efforts as the sanctuary movement, the free South Africa campaign, and movements against U.S. policies in Central America, Korea, and
the Philippines. Meanwhile, Christian participation in the domestic peace and
antinuclear movements steadily broadened, and the practice of nonviolent
resistance gradually deepened.

Above all, however, the source of renewal was the rediscovery of the gospel
story about the eminently nonmetropolitan Jesus, whose voice still reaches
across the ages in a call to discipleship. As Sobrino put it: "Access to the Christ
of faith comes only through our following of the historical Jesus" (1978:305).
Hence in my book and its companion volume I refer to this movement under
the rubric "radical discipleship." It is a label that some in the movement have
adopted and others avoid, more so now that the term "radical" is well out of
fashion in popular culture. But this seems all the more reason to embrace it, for
it is not vogue, but rootedness in the nonimperial gospel that will sustain the
movement.

It is not my purpose here to offer a portrait of contemporary radical
discipleship; this can be found elsewhere (e.g., Wallis, 1976; D. Brown, 1971),
and I will explore it at some depth in a forthcoming volume that carries out the
second part of this project. I will here simply introduce two key themes that I
believe should characterize our theological reflection and guide our practice in
the *locus imperium*. The first is *repentance*, which for us implies not only a
conversion of heart, but a concrete process of turning away from empire, its
distractions and seductions, its hubris and iniquity. The second is *resistance,*
which involves shaking off the powerful sedation of a society that rewards
ignorance and trivializes everything political, in order to discern and take
concrete stands in our historical moment, and to find meaningful ways to
"impede imperial progress." Both themes demand a commitment to nonviolence, as a personal and interpersonal way of life and as a militant and
revolutionary political practice. These themes will be in the background
throughout this reading of Mark, and I will return to them briefly again in my
Afterword (see also below, 2,A,iii).

Because we understand the present crisis of empire to have everything to do
with the ordering of power, the distribution of wealth, and the global plague of
militarism, radical discipleship necessarily approaches the Bible with social,
political, and economic questions in mind. What does Mark have to say
concerning our struggles to overcome racism? Or to find more proximate
forms of solidarity with the poor while we work for justice? Or to deepen our
use of nonviolent direct action? These questions explain why I have chosen to
entitle this commentary a "political reading," despite the fact that such an
idiom will inevitably arouse the suspicion of most North Americans. There
is another reason, however: I use it in order to distance myself at the outset
from the prevailing approaches to biblical interpretation in North Atlantic
circles.

1B. WHY MARK?

i. "Battle for the Bible"

To propose a political reading of scripture is immediately to pick an argument with a whole spectrum of exegetical schools. There are those, for example, who still believe that the crucial issues of biblical interpretation are the ones defined by the old fundamentalist-modernist debates of the late 19th and early 20th centuries; they are still trying to defend a doctrine of "biblical authority" against real and imagined secular and liberal opponents. But however much the theological right and left might diverge philosophically, their respective political practice shares more similarities than differences in allegiance to empire. From the perspective of radical discipleship, "biblical authority" is meaningful only insofar as it leads us to repentance and resistance!

A well-established rival is the tradition of theological hermeneutics, both scholastic and pietist. This tradition has exposited the Gospels in a way analogous to mining for precious metals: the "gold" of timeless and universal theological principle or churchly dogma is carefully extracted from the "ore" of historical or social particularities, which are sluiced away. Wrested away from history and practice, the *kerygma* thus becomes the domain of abstract thought or "spiritual" reflection—that is, the domain of the *theologians*! This "theological ideology which is ever-already at work in bourgeois exegesis" reads the text from the "idealist site of interiority" rather than the "bodily site of exteriority" (Belo, 1981:259). Such a suppression of the fully human, concretely socio-historical character of the Gospel is nothing less than a perpetuation of the docetic heresy.

More embedded in popular Christianity are the hermeneutics of privatism. Fundamentalists and modern existentialists may be philosophically antagonistic, but they share in an essential commitment to approaching the text with concerns about the individual's search for, respectively, "holiness" and "authentic existence." Conversion is a fundamentally individual affair. The "personal Savior" of American evangelicalism is domesticated, no longer Lord of the world but of our hearts, into which we invite him. Contemporary theology's preoccupation with the ravages of *Angst* and the search for personal wholeness is similarly caught up in the "labyrinth of intersubjectivity" (Hunter, 1982:40). Both reflect the modern tendency to flee from an increasingly uncertain conflict-ridden history to the refuge of self-absorption, or what Christopher Lasch has called the "culture of narcissism" (1979). Needless to say, the political powers have much to gain from the strict sequestering of the gospel to the private sphere; it was promoted by Nazi fascism, and still is today by military regimes in South Korea, Guatemala, Chile, and elsewhere.

Then there are the biblical scholars who tend to approach the texts as archeologists do ancient potsherds. I have affirmed the need to apprehend these ancient texts within their own narrative and socio-historical contexts, and scholarly rigor has made invaluable contributions, from the philological to the philosophical. The failure of the academic guild lies in its refusal to admit its own ideological commitments. There is no such thing as a "neutral" site from which to interpret the text, though it is widely feigned (Segundo, 1986:80f.). We need only look at the history of exegesis since the rise of historical criticism to see how studies thought to be "scientific" were revealed, by shifts in the intellectual climate, to be culture-bound and tendentious. I refer the reader again to W. Wink's brilliant tract on biblical interpretation for a systematic critique of the academic ideology of objectivism (1973). To make matters worse, professional exegetes have rarely been able or willing to address the text to their *own* historical situation. Because of this, the academic theological establishment has become deeply complicit, however unwittingly, in the ideological maintenance of the *locus imperium*.

The truth is, the "battle for the Bible" today has increasingly less to do with theological divisions and allegiances and more to do with political and economic allegiances. This is perhaps more evident in many Third World countries, where churches are becoming polarized along class and ideological lines. In Latin America, for example, we see the base communities empowering the poor masses through a more popular model of church. This predominantly Catholic movement has, with almost Protestant fervor, restored Bible study, along with grass-roots social analysis, to a central place in the life of the community. In stark contrast stand the words of Pope John Paul II in his opening address to the Puebla episcopal conference in 1979:

> We find "re-readings" of the Gospel that . . . purport to depict Jesus as a political activist, as a fighter against Roman domination and the authorities, and even as someone involved in the class struggle. This conception of Christ as a political figure, a revolutionary, as the subversive from Nazareth, does not tally with the Church's catechesis [Segundo, 1985:199].

While magisteriums continue to insist that the Jesus story has nothing to do with politics, peasants in Brazil, Paraguay, and El Salvador are thrown into jail on charges of subversive activity—for the crime of meeting to study the gospel. This is the true struggle over "biblical authority" today.

But here in the metropolis a shift is occurring as well. Until recently, for example, American fundamentalism insisted that religion had nothing to do with politics. However, the recent politicization of the Christian right in the U.S.A. under the banner of Reaganism has changed the landscape drastically. Behind the leadership of such figures as Jerry Falwell and Pat Robertson, Christian groups that were once staunch privatists now militantly insist that faith does indeed have everything to do with public life, and are busily organizing military aid to anticommunist guerillas, picketing abortion clinics, and stumping for increased military spending. It may well be that the new ideological synthesis they offer is protofascist, with disturbing parallels to the agenda of the religious right at the time of the rise of the Third Reich, as R. Pierard (1982) and R. Linder (1982) have argued. But the fact remains that the whole nature of the debate has changed: we need no longer belabor *whether* the Bible calls us to political practice—only *what kind* of practice. The churches, in my opinion, should welcome this renewed ideological struggle over how the Bible is politically interpreted and used.

This commentary enters that debate from an unabashedly partisan stance. But to speak of a partisan reading is not to endorse attempts to consciously manipulate and control the text through previously established assumptions, and a truly "critical" reading should ever be aware of this danger. The hermeneutic circle simply makes it incumbent upon interpreters to state preconceptions and concerns openly, where they can be seen and critiqued—not only by other interpreters, but by the Gospel itself. For it must be kept in mind that Mark's story overtly solicits commitment from the reader. We are bound therefore to use reading strategies appropriate to this text's intention; to suppress its profoundly partial character amounts to the worst betrayal of all.

ii. Mark as Manifesto

Mark's Gospel originally was written to help imperial subjects learn the hard truth about their world and themselves. He does not pretend to represent the word of God dispassionately or impartially, as if that word were innocuously universal in its appeal to rich and poor alike. His is a story by, about, and for those committed to God's work of justice, compassion, and liberation in the world. To modern theologians, like the Pharisees, Mark offers no "signs from heaven" (Mark 8:11f.). To scholars who, like the chief priests, refuse to ideologically commit themselves, he offers no answer (Mk 11:30–33). But to those willing to raise the wrath of the empire, Mark offers a way of discipleship (8:34ff.).

A reading of Mark's Gospel was fundamental to the genesis of the contemporary radical discipleship movement. Those of us who came from traditions of evangelical Protestantism that promised personal engagement but delivered social irrelevance thirsted for the "whole gospel for the whole person for the whole world." The discovery of the uncompromising call to commitment in Mark was the key, for many of us, to our "second conversion." We studied the Gospel with help from redaction critics such as E. Schweizer (1960), whose synopsis of Mark's thesis—"discipleship is the only form in which faith in Jesus can exist"—fired our nascent battle against acculturated Christianity. This compelled us to go on to recover the subversive discipleship traditions that have persisted throughout church history, from the old monks to the Confessing Church. But we have always returned to Mark—we have seen it as a kind of manifesto.

It is very much the contention of this commentary that Mark remains a manifesto for radical discipleship. Unfortunately, our movement has not been very successful in finding new reading strategies commensurate with the deepening politicization of our practice. Too much of our biblical study remains strictly devotionalistic and often frankly superficial. Rather than a hermeneutics of suspicion we persist in a suspicion of hermeneutics. For some reason, it is acceptable to appeal to political analysis, ideological criticism, or sociological method in discerning the meaning of contemporary history, but not the meaning of scripture. In a word, we "read" contemporary history better than we "read" the Bible.

This contradiction risks estranging our practice from our biblical foundations, and is reflected in the fact that more persons in our movement are less interested in reading the Bible. Some of them are still alienated because of having endured too much irrelevant preaching and teaching. For them I hope to offer a reading strategy that can overcome the betrayal of both pulpit and academy. Others still impatiently insist that the Bible be made directly relevant to their situation. I offer this book in the hope of challenging, encouraging, and perhaps inspiring them to take their Bible study more seriously. For like political discernment, Bible study is hard work, and yields more questions than answers.

There is another way in which our practice needs to be better buttressed by our reading. For example, we often claim that our practice of nonviolent direct action is grounded in the symbolic action of the Hebrew prophets and Jesus, but rarely does our biblical study demonstrate *how* exactly this is the case. Let us remember that if we can impose our views upon the text, so too can our ideological opponents. From what basis shall we then challenge them? These same concerns apply, I might add, to much of the exegesis offered by liberation theology. Although it often is exciting and suggestive, it is also highly selective and more impressionistic than systematic (see Sobrino, 1978). Is it not curious that contemporary radical Christian movements, which appeal so readily to the biblical narratives of liberation, have produced so few in-depth commentaries on these texts?

Nor are we immune from the danger of domesticating the Bible so that we no longer allow it to pose disturbing questions to us. We must not forget that our movement was *founded* (in good radical Protestant fashion) upon a fresh reading of the scriptures; it can be continually renewed only in the same way. We must not be reluctant to venture beyond the conceptual work of our mentors! Fortunately, in our search for more useful methods of interpreting scripture, Mark is the best proving ground.

iii. New Reading Strategies

Skeptics enjoy pointing out that the Bible has been used to justify all kinds of contradictory positions, as if the fact that a text can be *made* to say anything means therefore that it has nothing itself to say. They are only confirming what I quoted from Ricoeur at the outset of this chapter: it is of the nature of texts to be vulnerable to an interpreter. As F. Jameson puts it:

Interpretation is not an isolated act, but takes place within a Homeric battlefield, on which a host of interpretive options are either openly or implicitly in conflict. . . . As the Chinese proverb has it, you use one ax handle to hew another: in our context, only another, stronger interpretation can overthrow and practically refute an interpretation already in place [1981:13].

There is probably no part of scripture that has been more the subject of both popular commentary and scholarly investigation than the Gospel of Mark, and it has a long and fascinating history of interpretation (Kealy, 1982). As the earliest Gospel, it has usually stood at the center of critical efforts to reconstruct the life of Jesus (or, more modestly, the history of the primitive communities). Each new epoch of modern biblical criticism has used Mark as a crucible in which new reading strategies are tested, established, and overthrown.

The historico-critical methods of form and redaction analysis that have prevailed throughout this century cut their teeth on Mark (Telford, 1980; D. Harrington, 1985), and on the basis of work in Mark have more recently been dethroned (Perrin, 1976). So Mark "remains tantalizingly at the center of critical pursuits. . . . Like Cinderella, the Gospel has at last been discovered but not yet explained" (Bilezikian, 1977:11). Since the late 1970s, two major new trends have been established in synoptic scholarship: sociological exegesis and literary criticism. What better text than Mark to test my own attempt to synthesize these two new methods?

There have also been many efforts to read the Gospel(s) politically in the last quarter century, though few have attained much methodological or exegetical sophistication (see my overview in the Appendix). One work, however, stands out, not only because it is a commentary on Mark, but also because it was the first attempt to bring together the insights of sociological exegesis, narratology, and political hermeneutics. I am referring to the "materialist" criticism of the Portuguese Christian Marxist, Fernando Belo. His *Lecture mâterialiste de l' évangile de Marc: Récit-Practique-Idéologie* was published in 1975 (English translation, 1981). It remains one of the most programmatic political readings of a complete biblical text. Yet it must be said that this ground-breaking book (and M. Clevenot's subsequent popularization, 1985) has been something of a non-event in the Anglo-American world.

The reason for its "failure to communicate" lies partly in the problem of its jargon: Belo and his disciples rely heavily upon the New Literary Criticism's ideologies of structuralism and linguistic semiotics. However popular they may be among European intellectuals, they have not been widely accepted in the U.S.A. The weighty methodological apparatus involved in such reading strategies become overbearing; few American readers made it through Belo's jungle of literary and social "codes." Nevertheless, Belo threw down the gauntlet to traditional theological reading strategies, and he deserves a response. Though his approach contains serious exegetical, literary, and political errors that need correction (see Appendix), Belo's many insights need to be translated and his method simplified, for a wider audience. Such a dialogue has not been forthcoming from the academic biblical guide, because of its fear of political hermeneutics. Hence, it seems incumbent upon someone willing to risk, as Belo put it, "passion and naiveté," to advance the conversation (1982:1).

Does all this stress upon the "political" negate the "spiritual" or the "personal" dimensions of Bible reading? For me it does not; the "metasymbolic" (transcendent) aspects of Christian experience cannot be denied. Indeed, I give narrative, symbol, and myth primary place in my reading. Yet Mark himself insists that all such discourse be understood also in terms of the socio-political practices it justifies (see below, C). Neither would I wish to minimize the importance of devotional and liturgical uses of scripture in the life of the individual and community. The same goes for the insights of the presently popular "psychological approach" to the Bible. The disciplines of analytic psychology and psychotherapy can and do play crucial roles in our self-understanding and healing, and are in my view necessary to true political criticism. Without the "inward journey," political practice cannot possibly be liberative, for we internalize to some degree the demonic forces that characterize the social formation in which we live.

I can think of at least one very interesting attempt to read Mark's Gospel from a Jungian perspective (McGann, 1985), in which many of the symbols I interpret politically he construes archetypically. I may disagree with McGann exegetically at several points, but I think his project is in principle not only worthwhile but fully compatible with my own. The fact remains, however, that there is no shortage of personally oriented readings of scripture around today, whereas political ones are scarce. It is a matter of priority; in our time, I say again, the fundamental betrayal of the Gospel in the *locus imperium* is political. Altogether *too much* Bible study among Christians remains preoccupied with our strictly private anguish and matters "heavenly"—while our world hangs in the balance on an imperial cross of violence and oppression.

1C. POLITICAL DISCOURSE AND THE "WAR OF MYTHS"

i. Symbolics and Social Practice

To lay the foundation for a political reading strategy of Mark, let us return to the vignette with which I began this chapter. A key "text" in this little story was President Reagan's claim that "America is back and walking tall." Archeologists in the distant future, far removed from the culture and history that produced this text, might well dismiss this "master metaphor" as having no concrete socio-historical meaning, concluding that it is "merely" a figure of speech. They would of course be mistaken, which only proves that the concrete "referentiality" of this particular symbolic discourse cannot be discerned outside the "semantic field" (the systems of implied or explicit meanings in the language) and socio-historical context in which it was uttered. Having been acculturated in the social world assumed by Reagan's metaphor, I may exegete it without great difficulty.

I know that "America is back" does not literally mean that the whole country has been away on vacation, or that the national team was behind in a football game but is now mounting a late scoring drive. The image may indeed invoke sports heroics, but as political discourse it articulates an "implied narrative" based upon the New Right's triumphal myth of imperial restoration. The plot of this myth is necessarily simple: America (the "home team") was "down" in the wake of a series of foreign policy defeats (read: challenges to imperial hegemony from the peripheries, i.e., Indochina, Iran, and Nicaragua) and economic setbacks (read: inflation, lowered productivity, deteriorating balance of trade). Under Reagan, however, America is shaking off its "malaise" (read: domestic opposition to the imperial project) and "impotence" (read: restraint upon geopolitical adventurism).

The result: we are "walking tall." This second image is immediately intelligible to anyone who has seen a classic cowboy movie or Marine recruitment commercial. It is distinctly macho, and functions to bolster national confidence by reviving the myth of American omnipotence. The fact that the political project implied here involves the rehabilitation of the full apparatus of the imperial state—hardly conducive to "getting government off our backs," another key theme of Reaganesque narrative—is neatly obscured by the myth. The upbeat notion that Uncle Sam is again freely striding the globe may thus be "read" as evidence for concrete historical policies: the unleashing of domestic and foreign intelligence operations; the reanimation of overt (Grenada) and covert (Nicaragua) military intervention; and a massive buildup of conventional and strategic arms.

Popular political discourse is always embedded in cultural metaphors and symbols. An economic analyst, describing a day's trading on the New York Stock Exchange when several issues rose in value early and then declined, reports that "the bulls stampeded early on Wall Street, but were turned out to pasture by the end of the day." Nowhere in our culture are symbols and narratives more powerful than in the high fictions of the advertising industry. Mundane products take on magical powers and promise to shape new character, reinforcing the primal subtext of capitalism: one is what one owns/consumes.

The political discourse of myth also takes on more complex narrative form in social texts. These might be hortatory (a State Department release warning of the growing "Soviet threat"), or historical (the Gettysburg Address), or even liturgical ("Battle Hymn of the Republic"). Urban and McClure (1983) have shown how an official Soviet text analyzing economic trends reflects the narrative character of "state folklore." Nor is myth restricted to linguistic forms. It may be expressed in images (a newspaper photo of two smiling heads of state shaking hands, the solemn portrait of a university dean, or Chicano mural art) and icons (a tribal totem, the robes of a judge, or a clenched fist). Most importantly, the war of myths is expressed through symbolic *action*. Why are U.S. citizens supposed to put their hands over their hearts and talk to the flag? How is it that they believe that by casting a ballot they are participating in a democratic process? Why do socialist countries parade military hardware annually on May Day? And why do Jews stand, Christians kneel, and Muslims face Mecca when they pray?

Before going further, let me define some terms. Obviously, I am using "myth" not in the usual pejorative or ethnological sense of a "prerational idea-system" (Eliade, 1963:1). Instead I understand it in its broadest sense as a kind of meaningful symbolic discourse within a given cultural and political system (see Barthes, 1972:109ff.). I use "political" also in the inclusive sense: having to do with the whole range of concrete relationships (economic, governmental, military, cultural, etc.) in a given social formation. "Discourse" refers to the various symbolic/linguistic systems and narratives employed in human communication: paintings, film, stories, jokes, songs, speeches, newspaper articles, academic papers, and so forth.

My approach accepts the anthropological axiom that human beings do not apprehend social reality directly, but always through the "cognitive filters" of cultural meaning-systems, especially our "natural capacity to use (significant symbols), primarily language" (Sykes, 1980:170; cf. Lenski, 1978). Thus "cultural acts, the construction, apprehension, and utilization of symbolic forms, are social events like any other; they are as public as marriage and as observable as agriculture" (Geertz, 1973:91). F. Jameson, borrowing from the structural anthropology of Lévi-Strauss, argues that all cultures produce mythic discourse about social realities, discourse that expresses what he calls the "political unconscious" (1981:79).

Social and political struggle between groups is thus articulated in terms of what I have referred to as the "war of myths." Take, for example, the European conquest of the Americas. On one side were the stories of the indigenous peoples: their legends of creation, their clan genealogies, their gods, their welcoming rituals, all of which reflected a living, concrete, cultural fabric, social organization, a relationship to nature and technology, and so forth. On the other side were the Europeans: their myths of "discovery," ideologies of conquest, the flag they planted as symbol of "ownership." And what is the struggle between the "invisible hand" of Adam Smith's marketplace and the "dictatorship of the proletariat" of Marx's communist socialism but a war of myths? What is the division of the planet into the "free world" and "totalitarian sphere," separated by an "iron curtain," but the "cold war" of myths?

I borrow the phrase "wars of myths" from Amos Wilder, a pioneer in literary criticism of the New Testament. He advocated study "not of the symbolism, but of the *symbolics* of Jesus . . . meant to suggest the social-psychological dimension of the symbol and the whole domain of cultural dynamics" (1982:103). What is usually described as the "theology" of the New Testament writers Wilder referred to as their challenge to the dominant symbol systems of both imperial Rome and Palestinian Judaism, "liturgy against liturgy . . . understanding that liturgy involves a whole lifestyle, action and ethic as well as recital" (1982:37). Wilder helped show that the "demythologiz-ing" project popularized by Bultmann, which attempted to strip away the trappings of cultural discourse from the biblical texts, effectively rendered them abstract ideas, divorced from the social conflicts in which they were uttered. I agree that the demythologizing project was quite wrongheaded; we should instead be about understanding how myth functions as political discourse—in antiquity and today.

ii. Ideological Strategies of Legitimation and Subversion

Another term for symbolic discourse about social realities and conflicts is *ideology*. I am well aware that this is a problematic term, even a red herring. Although it is part of the technical vocabulary of most modern social scientists, its definition is hotly disputed, especially within Marxism. In North America ideology is popularly used as a pejorative description of the doctrines of one's political or philosophical opponents. Because of the central role it will play in this book, I will clarify how and why I employ the term "ideology."

I recommend D. Kellner's (1978) lucid and helpful sketch of the history of the term "ideology," which first appeared in the period of the French Revolu-tion. It was Karl Marx, however, who redefined it according to his philosophy of historical materialism: "Life is not determined by consciousness, but con-sciousness by life" (Kellner, 1978:40). "Ide-ology" thus came to mean the study of ideas as social products. Marx tended to define ideology as the discourse of "false consciousness"—that is, the illusions generated by dominant social groups to both obfuscate and reinforce their class privilege. Lenin argued that ideology is class-specific; the working class would develop a progressive, revolutionary ideology, and the ruling class a reactionary, conservative ideol-ogy. It was under Lenin's influence, according to Kellner, that the term became increasingly associated with a strict materialism that saw ideas solely as epiphenomena of the economic base (ibid.:47). Later Marxists such as Korsch, Gramsci, and Lukács took a more dialectical view, which allowed for a more "reciprocal interaction" between ideas and the material base.

This gave rise to the discipline known as "sociology of knowledge," popular-ized by K. Mannheim's *Ideology and Utopia* (1929). Sociology of knowledge studies "the interrelation between the structural and the cultural systems of society" (Carlton, 1977:19), and defines ideology as the highest level of ab-straction in the cognitive process of the "social construction of reality." B. Holzner refers to ideology as "master symbols" (1972:145). To Berger and Luckmann, this "symbolic universe is conceived of as the matrix of all socially objectivated and subjectively real meanings . . . social products with a history" (1967:95f.). Symbolic discourse about social reality is thus a universal cultural phenomenon (for further reading I recommend Geertz, 1973, and Schutz, 1967, besides the works just cited).

I stand with those who see the symbolic and the social as always interactive (Sykes, 1980), and am content to adopt definition 3a in *Webster's Third*

International Dictionary : ideology is "a systematic scheme or coordinated body of ideas or concepts about human life or culture." In opting for ideology, broadly understood, rather than "theology," I am following Gottwald (1979:65). However, if the reader still considers the term "ideology" to be a rhetorical obstacle, he or she is free to substitute terms such as "worldview," "frame of reference," "social strategy" or "concrete theoretics," all of which are approximate synonyms. What is important is to be ever mindful of the fact that, as Georges Casalis put it (following Mao), ideas do not "fall from the skies," but "come from social practice" (1984:vii)—a reminder particularly to those trained in theology and steeped in the idealist tradition. I also hasten to affirm, with the Marxist tradition, that the study of ideology is for purposes of determining not only how symbolic discourse functions socially, but also on *whose behalf.*

There is a consensus among both Marxist and non-Marxist scholars that ideological discourse functions in one of two basic ways. It either legitimates or subverts the dominant social order: Berger calls these the "world maintenance" and "world shaking" functions (1969). The *legitimizing* function seeks to lend plausibility to social reality, "giving normative dignity to its practical imperatives" (Berger and Luckmann, 1967:93). This is what Kellner, following Gramsci, calls "hegemonic ideology":

> It is widely accepted as describing "the way things are," inducing people to consent to their society and its way of life as natural, good, and just. In this way, hegemonic ideology is translated into everyday consciousness and serves as a means of "indirect rule" that is a powerful force for social cohesion and stability. . . . They provide theories about the economy, state, or education that legitimate certain dominant institutions and ideas, and prescribe conformist acceptance [1978:50].

Specifically theological discourse often casts what Berger calls a "sacred canopy" over the dominant order: "The fundamental 'recipe' of religious legitimation is the transformation of human products into supra- or non-human facticities" (1969:89). One can see this in the concept of the "organic state" in Latin Catholicism, in which class division was legitimated by a theology of divinely appointed stations, but also in more secular doctrines such as the appeal to the "historical imperatives" of class struggle, "manifest destiny" or Social Darwinism.

Ideology can also function to subvert the dominant order, pursuing one of two general discursive strategies. The *reformist* strategy will usually argue its case from reference points within the dominant order, trying to give new meaning to established symbols. These appeals may be for purposes of retrogressive change, as for example in the New Right's nostalgic call to return to the "traditions of the founding fathers of the U.S.A." Or the strategy may be progressive, in the sense that the system has yet to realize its own ideological commitments. An example would be Martin Luther King's appeals to the Bill of Rights in order to attack racial segregation in the U.S.A.

Alternatively, *revolutionary* strategies usually repudiate the dominant symbolic system altogether, either fundamentally redefining the old terms or appealing to entirely different ones. Such an ideological project must simultaneously introduce and legitimate the new symbols even as it is "delegitimating" the old ones. Sometimes there is no desire to transform or overthrow the dominant order, the strategy being one of withdrawal and establishment of a "counter-culture" (Carlton, 1977:35), as in the case of Jehovah's Witnesses or Hutterites. In an atmosphere of tolerance or pluralism, such efforts represent only an incidental threat to the dominant order. It is when the subversive ideology is vigorously battling for the "hearts and minds" of the populace that conflict erupts into a "war of myths." In this case, the "subversives" become the target of ideological counterattack, with the "custodians of the 'official' definitions of reality . . . setting in motion various conceptual machineries designed to maintain the 'official' universe against the heretical challenge" (Berger and Luckmann, 1967:107).

Needless to say, revolutionary ideologies, once their proponents attain political power, can quickly become hegemonic—and usually do. We see this in Christianity after Constantine, the successful bourgeois revolts against feudalism (the French and American revolutions), and most significantly in the modern era, Marxism, which became "a 'legitimation science,' serving the interests of the new socialist ruling elite by legitimating the institutions of emerging socialist societies" (Kellner, 1978:47). In such cases, however, the revolutionary-turned-hegemonic ideology usually preserves what liberation theologians have called a "subversive memory" (see Welch, 1985:32ff.), which can become the seed of renewal movement within the tradition. This can be seen in the ideological systems of Christianity, liberal capitalism, and Marxism and, of course, the case directly relevant to a reading of Mark, Judaism.

In sum, there is no simple formula for ideological discourse. Although in any given social and historical situation ideology will function either subversively or hegemonically, the very themes that were liberating in one context can in another become oppressive. The social function of a given ideology cannot be discerned apart from its concrete relationship to the political and economic ordering of power in a determinate formation. For example, in cases where a common symbolic universe is being debated, the war of myths can be difficult to discern, for what on the surface might appear to be agreement is in fact sharp divergency. Thus socio-political analysis is intrinsic to the study of ideology as symbolic discourse; without it the sociology of knowledge becomes what its critics fear: simply another, more subtle, exercise in the history of ideas. The task of "reading" subversive and legitimating ideological discourse to discern the concrete social strategies they represent constitutes the fundamental premise of my political approach to Mark.

iii. Theology as Ideological Literacy

The "reading" of ideological discourse is not new. It dates back to postwar critical theorists such as Walter Benjamin and Ernst Bloch (Lamb, 1930). The

Frankfurt school focused upon the tendency for hegemonic ideology to "smooth over the rough edges of reality and provide an idealized view . . . reducing complex social processes and practices to simple, natural and unchanging states of affairs" (Kellner, 1978:54). Orwellian "double-speak" is still very much with us in a U.S. administration that refers to one set of Third World guerillas (e.g., Angola or Nicaragua) as "freedom fighters" and another set in a neighboring country (e.g., Namibia or El Salvador) as "terrorists." Nowhere is language more mythologized than in the arena of strategic armaments, the realm of the "Minuteman," "peacekeeper," and "nuclear umbrella."

For all the pretensions to rationalism of modern secular life, Jameson rightly insists that "no society has ever been quite so mystified in quite so many ways as our own" (1981:60f.). We need to learn to "decode" the various cultural texts thrown at us in the politics of everyday life, for it is these that are the real "opiates." Behind police torture rooms, the trade in military hardware, the rape of women, IMF economic blackmail, death squads, elite world price-fixing, or ICBMs, stand ideological systems that justify, sanitize, and reproduce murder in the hearts of ordinary persons. Thus the very same tools for reading the ideological discourse of Mark must be vigorously employed if we wish to challenge the infrastructure of empire.

Can ideological discourse be read from a non-ideological site? This was the belief of a movement among North Atlantic theologians in the late 1960s and early 70s, which called itself "political theology" (Richardson, 1974). As one writer put it:

> Ideological distortion [must be] disclosed . . . by theology without theology's assuming any ideological stance itself. If that happens in theology's ideological criticism, then it would only be another quarrel between two ideologies [Obayashi, 1975:392].

This effort to stand "above," rather than entering into, the war of myths predictably drew the fire of liberation theologians (Segundo, 1986:80). For Segundo the *crux theologica* in the concrete situation of Latin America demanded an ideological choice between capitalism and socialism (1979:247; see Moltmann, 1975). What political theology did not see clearly was that hegemonic ideology can be combatted *only* with subversive ideology. Moreover, it failed to acknowledge that the gospel writers were not mere observers of the ideological struggles of their time, but deeply involved in the war of myths.

This war rages between non-Christian ideologies (the differing visions of Muslim social order in Iran and Iraq) as well as between the church and its opponents (the Confessing Church under Hitler). But Christian ideological literacy must *begin*, especially considering the historical legacy of Christendom, in its own house: "The real task of theology is to liberate the church from false theologies" (Comblin, 1979:63). The war of Christian myths takes place in liturgy and icon, preaching and politics, seminary and barrio. The more conflict-ridden the society, the more polarized the ideological struggles *within* the church.

This contest inevitably centers upon christology: "The prospect for the immediate future in Latin America is that we will continue to find 'Christs' on both sides of the fence, among the revolutionaries and among the reactionaries" (Assman, 1979:138f.; see Bussman, 1985; Bonino, 1984; Trinidad, 1984). In South Korea evangelists from the U.S.A. are subsidized by the military regime to sponsor revivals, preaching a middle-class, moralistic Christ, in favor of the socialization of the growing urban managerial class in the "capitalist miracle" of this Asian nation. Meanwhile, Christians ministering among exploited industrial workers speak of the "Christ of the *minjung*," or oppressed (Suh, 1983:155ff.). This christological war of myths is reflected in the writing of poet and playwright Kim Chi-Ha (ibid.: 60ff.).

We find the same struggle in our own country, past and present. During the mid-19th-century struggle over slavery we find the intensely introspective and disciplinarian Christ of the white slave holder (a study in repressive parternalism); the Jesus of white abolitionism ranged from the gentle prodder of inner conscience (Quakerism) to the aggressive herald of social sanctification (Methodism). The plantation owners promoted the passive and obedient Jesus of the pietist black missionary C.C. Jones, feared the vengeful and rebellious Christ in the preaching of Nat Turner, and probably never understood the socio-political symbolics of Negro spirituals (Witvliet, 1984:62). Today, as already mentioned (above, B,i), Christ is invoked on behalf of both U.S. mercenaries fighting in Nicaragua and their Sandinista opponents. There is of course always an element of sadness and pain when, prompted by concrete historical issues, theological battles result in ecclesial divisions, as so many found during the domestic turmoil around the Vietnam war. But what is the alternative? We may rightly be suspicious of theologies of reconciliation that promote Christian unity at the price of political silence.

In sum, the proper vocation of theology is the practice of "ideological literacy," the critical discipline of political hermeneutics. It calls for discernment when liberating ideologies, including Christian theologies, become oppressively hegemonic. This task is not conducted from a neutral site, but from the perspective of the gospel, which itself has an "absolutely subversive" character that resists domestication and warns us against absolutizing any other ideological system.

1D. GOSPEL AS IDEOLOGICAL NARRATIVE

In the church, the beginning point for sorting out conflicting claims over christology and politics has always been a rereading of the Jesus stories. But how do we read the ideological discourse of a Gospel, a narrative text deriving from a distant historical and semantic-cultural universe? This immediately raises the question of exegetical method. In the following brief discussion, I show how the two most current methods of biblical criticism are "necessary but not sufficient" for a political reading of the Markan Gospel. Those interested in pursuing these methodological issues further are encouraged to consult the references I cite.

i. "Windows": Historical Criticism and Sociological Exegesis

N. Petersen has written:

> Today, the map of biblical studies looks different from a map drawn a decade or so ago. The difference is that today's map has two new routes on it. Broadly conceived, one route is that of literary criticism and the other that of sociology [1985:1].

Though each of these new routes have proven fruitful, they are still considered divergent. To understand why, one must look at the crisis in the historical critical method.

A political reading looks for a distinct relationship between a Gospel and its concrete historical situation, but determining the exact nature of this relationship is not at all straightforward. Some liberation theologians have tended to ignore the myriad of problems associated with the old "quest for the historical Jesus," preferring to extrapolate evidence of socio-political practice directly from the face of the text. We cannot, however, overlook more than a century of historical criticism, which has discredited attempts to both historicize (interpret literally) and harmonize (create a synthetic unity among) the Gospels.

Historical criticism focused upon the problems associated with establishing a relationship between the text and the historical characters and events about which the text spoke. Comparative study of the Gospels revealed that each version was heavily influenced by the needs and attitudes of the early communities that circulated it. That is, the Gospels are as much "about" the life of the early church as "about" the life of Jesus. Once this was accepted, form criticism set about the task of trying to determine the various layers of primitive tradition embedded in the text. Using methods such as the "criterion of dissimiliarity" (Perrin, 1967), form critics believed they could separate the "authentic" strata of tradition (i.e., the words actually spoken by Jesus) from early church tradition.

Redaction criticism in turn studied how each evangelist arranged and edited these traditions (Marxsen, 1969). The goal of this analysis was more modest, settling for the "theology" of the evangelist rather than that of Jesus (J.M. Robinson, 1982). The "new" quest, however, could not escape:

> Kähler's convenient distinction between *Geschichte*, what the early church believed about Jesus, and *Historie*, what actually happened. Kerygmatic theology, stemming at least partly from Bultmann's skepticism, has since assumed that because one can't get through this *Geschichte* barrier, it doesn't really matter [Baird, 1969:154].

Historical criticism thus took refuge in the historical ambivalence of existentialist hermeneutics.

The new sociological approach is attempting to rescue the project of historical criticism by repudiating its idealist bias and turning to the social sciences (Scroggs, 1980; Kee, 1980). On the one hand this has stimulated renewed interest in what has traditionally been called "extrinsic criticism," which culls the comparative historical sources of the New Testament period for economic and political *realia* (data), which are organized into a *social history* (J. Smith, 1975:19ff.). On the other hand, *sociological exegesis* works at "intrinsic criticism," looking for social indicators and correlations within the texts and the "social world" they reflect (Elliott, 1981:1ff.).

Sociologically oriented historical criticism is a welcome development, but has two main drawbacks from the perspective of political hermeneutics. First, North Atlantic scholars tend to use Weberian and Durkheimian sociological models (especially modern structural-functionalism), which, unlike Marxist models, minimize the role of social conflict (Mosala, 1986; the best survey of the field is Elliott, 1986). Consequently the tendency has been to portray the early Christian movement as quietist and socially conservative (Theissen, 1978, and his critic Stegemann, 1984:148ff.; see Elliott, 1986:10ff.). Those who have used a sociology of knowledge (also known as "symbolic interactionist") approach to examine the social world of the text have been similarly restricted by disinterest in a political reading of mythic discourse, and reliance upon pejorative sociological caricatures of sectarian movements (Gager, 1975:2ff.; Remus, 1982; D. Peterson, 1977; see below 2,A,F; 14,A).

Secondly, most of the current sociological exegesis carries on with the tools and assumptions of the old historical criticism, using form and redaction analysis to isolate units of tradition in order to reconstruct its "life-setting," or *Sitz im Leben* (Buss, 1978). The crucial presupposition here is that it is possible to reach "behind" the development of tradition, which is sedimented in the text, to "actual history" (Freyne, 1985). As N. Peterson put it, historical critics "look *through* the text by focusing on the relations between it and its sources," as if the text were a "window" through which to view historical events, making the text a mere means to an end (1978:19). More evidential value is given to hypothetical preliterary traditions than to the text itself, an approach that is methodologically problematic (ibid.:1–20).

By viewing the text not as the primary focus of, but as obstacle to, historical knowledge, the historical critic severs any direct relationship between the reader and the text (Wink, 1973:29,35). Moreover, it refuses to affirm continuity in the hermeneutic process—that is, Jesus interprets prophetic tradition, early Christian oral tradition interprets Jesus, Mark interprets oral tradition, we interpret Mark, and so on:

> Texts come before us as the always-already-read; we apprehend them through sedimented layers of previous interpretation . . . through the sedimented reading habits and categories developed by those inherited interpretive traditions [Jameson, 1981:9].

In fact, the historical critics cannot stand "outside" the process; Weimann argues that the quest for "history without interpretation" is misguided and must return to affirming the role of tradition in the "aesthetics of reception" (1976:13).

ii. "Mirrors": Formalism and Literary Criticism

The problems of historical criticism have come under intense fire from literary criticism, which represents the other main "route." A literary perspective views a Gospel as a whole cloth of narrative fabric, not a patchwork of traditions sewn together with greater or lesser awareness or skill. Instead of looking behind the text, literary criticism looks "*at* the text, in order to see, for example, how the units in its linear sequence are related to one another to form the whole" (N. Peterson 1978:19). The text is no longer seen as a "window" but a "mirror," which reflects a complex and rich life of its own.

This approach has been increasingly influential in synoptic studies, and Mark in particular, as reflected in an important 1976 essay by the dean of North American Markan studies, N. Perrin. He concluded that redaction analysis was not "a critical method adequate to the interpretation of the Gospel of Mark because it defines the literary activity of the Evangelist too narrowly. . . . Less than justice is being done to the text of the Gospel as a coherent text with its own internal dynamics" (1976:120). The majority of books on Mark published since the mid-1980s reflect, to one degree or another, the ascendancy of narrative analysis.

Two non-technical studies are of immense value in helping to construct a new attitude and orientation to reading Mark as a full-fledged narrative. W. Kelber's concise *Mark's Story of Jesus* demonstrates the viability of reading Mark without becoming embroiled in "tradition and redaction" debates:

> If we wish to grasp Mark's story, we must in a sense lose sight of Matthew's, Luke's, and John's stories. The reading of Mark demands a single-minded concentration on the Marcan text [1979:12].

It also contains insights into the structure of the Gospel that I have found very persuasive.

D. Rhoads and D. Michie's *Mark as Story: An Introduction to the Narrative of a Gospel* (1982) is a good primer, synopsizing the main literary characteristics of Mark, and I recommend it to the reader who wants an introduction to the elements of literary analysis, or "narratology."

The literary critical approach, however, is not without problems. Anxious to overcome historicism, it has in many cases tried to liberate the text from all historical referentiality whatsoever. Instead, the sole focus is upon what is referred to as the "narrative world" of the text. Every story "contains a closed and self-sufficient world with its own integrity, its own past and future, its own sets of values, and its own universe of meanings" (Rhoads and Michie, 1982:4). The narrative world is thus "the sum of propositions a narrative implies or expresses about its actors and their actions in time and space" (N. Petersen, 1978:40). And because it is of the nature of the literary event to "fabulate" this world through manipulation of characters, settings, plots, and possibilities, to attempt to find correspondence to the real world is denounced as the "referential fallacy":

> It is fallacious literarily because it mistakenly posits a real world where there is only a narrative world, and it is fallacious historically because it assumes that the historian must demonstrate, namely the evidential value of the narrative world [ibid.:4].

Modern literary criticism has been profoundly influenced by formalism, a movement that has fought a pitched battle throughout the mid-twentieth century to win status for the literary text as "autonomous cultural object." This position within literary theory is called "aestheticism," and argues that literature is an enclosed system of signs and symbols (for a discussion of semiotic theory, see N. Petersen, ibid.). In literary structuralism, the text is not about the world but syntactic relationships or (following Lévi-Strauss) mythic antinomies (see the work of E. Malbon, 1982, a leading structuralist interpreter of Mark). Another proponent argues:

> There is a sense in which structural criticism is referential, but it does not derive the meaning of a text from its reference to something nonliterary, that is, something historical, sociological, or ideational. It discloses rather how the text "refers" to the reservoir of formal literary possibilities. . . . Historical and literary disciplines . . . must be kept distinct, separate, and unconfounded [Patte, 1976:iv].

The ideology of the so-called New Criticism has been so formidable and pervasive that "even historical-minded critics found it difficult to move beyond formalism" (Weimann, 1984:3).

If historical criticism betrays the narrative integrity of the text, literary criticism betrays its historical integrity. Obviously, aestheticist literary analysis subverts the possibility of a political reading altogether, and indeed, when we consider the mystification of our own social formation:

> The urgency of the issues raised by the antirepresentation direction of poststructuralist thought must not be underestimated, especially when so many forms of interpretation and representation (including their political correlatives) can be shown to constitute a "technique of power," a form of "reduction, repression, obliteration of fact" [Weimann, 1984:291f.].

Even Wilder acknowledged aestheticism to be a product of "the experience of personal alienation from the public arena of significant action . . . associated with the modern cultural crisis and its texts" (1982:18). Needless to say, this alienation was not shared by the culture that produced the biblical texts, which knew nothing of either historicism or estheticism, and in which the referentiality of both language and narrative was assumed! T. Eagleton goes further, tracing modern deconstructionism to the failure of radical politics in the late 1960s: "Unable to break the structures of state power, post-structuralism found it possible instead to subvert the structures of language" (1983:142). For further examination, I recommend the critiques of estheticism by Marxist critics R. Williams (1977:166ff.) and Eagleton (1976, 1983).

We must conclude that neither of the two contemporary "routes" in biblical criticism—literary and sociological analysis—are alone adequate for a political reading:

> The former leaves us with free-floating texts which move toward gratuity and fantasy. The latter evacuate the recitals of their full import in the quest for facts and thematics [Wilder, 1982:32].

Yet each offers crucial correctives. Can their insights be combined, in view of the fact that each sees the other as antagonistic? It has been this question that has resulted in a synthesis of historical and literary criticism into a discipline known as "literary sociology."

iii. All Narrative Is Political: Literary Sociology

The sociology of literature arose from Marxist cultural criticism and its concerns to find determinate social factors involved in the production of texts as well as social meanings within the text (Laurenson and Swingewood, 1972: 78ff.). Against aestheticism it holds that extrinsic factors cannot be ignored, and examines both material (i.e., the economics of patronage, publishing technologies, markets and consumption) and social (i.e., the class alignment of the author, the historical, economic and ideological conditions at the time of writing) influences upon production. The formalist challenge, however, has persuaded literary sociology to concentrate its efforts on intrinsic criticism, looking for genre, structure, and narrative content as an expression of ideological values and strategies, an effort pioneered by L. Goldmann (1980).

More recently we have seen the rise of what is called "materialist criticism," which studies the esthetic codes of the text for ways in which it "represents" economic, social, and political relationships in the real world. Essentially, the resolution of the referential fallacy lies in the fact that narrative systems are modes of symbolic discourse, and hence are also themselves ideological systems. Like language itself, narrative is a system of differentiated signs through which human beings both interpret and "represent" their world. In this sense, there is a direct correlation between the "narrative world" of a literary text and the "symbolic universe" or ideology of an author. As an *ideological* product, narrative systems express particular social worldviews and "encode" or "signify" concrete socio-historical strategies.

English Marxist critic Eagleton has offered the helpful analogy of the "production" of a dramatic script that I will here embellish (1976:64ff.). Let us take as an example a novel, William Styron's *Sophie's Choice*. The subject of this novel, what it alleges to "refer" to, is the (historical) drama of Nazi concentration camps and those who survived them. The novel, however, is obviously a transformation, indeed a fabulation, of that history through selective and creative interpretation, such as characterization, point of view, emplotment and the like. Now, let us say that this novel is adapted in a screenplay and made into a movie, as it indeed was in 1980. The narrative undergoes yet another transformation as it is interpreted through camera angles, the acting abilities of Meryl Streep, the sets and costumes, and so forth. The film we see is the "subject" twice transformed: it is a reproduction of the novel, which was a reproduction of the historical fact of concentration camps and the psychoses borne by those who survived them.

This "production of a production" is analogous, claims Eagleton, to the relationship between history, ideology, and literature. Ideology, like the novel or dramatic script, is a production of socio-historical realities; literature, like the dramatic movie performance, is a production of ideology (ibid.:68):

history/ideology → dramatic text → dramatic production
history → ideology → literary text

Because these relationships can be studied inversely we are able to read a text inductively to determine both its ideology and, with the aid of extrinsic correlations, the concrete socio-historical circumstances involved in its "production."

We can now see the correlation between this kind of analysis and the "reading" of ideological discourse discussed above (C,iii). Combining literary sociology with political hermeneutics gives a method that can, as Jameson puts it, "explore the multiple paths that lead to the unmasking of cultural artifacts as socially symbolic acts":

It conceives of the political perspective not as some supplementary method, not as an optional auxiliary to interpretive methods current today . . . but rather as the absolute horizon of all reading and all interpretation. . . . From this perspective the convenient working distinction between cultural texts that are social and political and those that are not becomes something worse than an error: namely, a symptom of the reification and privatization of contemporary life . . . which—the tendential law of social life under capitalism—maims our existence as individual subjects and paralyzes our thinking about time and change just as surely as it alienates us from our speech itself. . . . The only effective liberation from such constraint begins with the recognition that there is nothing that is not social and historical—indeed, that everything is "in the last analysis" political [1981:17,20].

In modern life we are bombarded with ideological narrative in many forms. The news media, for example, are always "reporting" the world to us in the shape of stories, stories that are the result of a highly ideological process of selection and editing, carefully shaped with an angle for the "news producer" and a catch for the "news consumer." The advertising media promote the product (or the consumer) as "hero" in carefully manipulated images or 30-second plots. And of course the great story-telling media of television and cinema play major roles in socialization and ideological formation. We must learn to discern hegemonic and subversive characteristics and functions of popular narrative discourse. Sylvester Stallone's heroic cop/boxer/soldier-of-fortune films, for example, clearly legitimate and indeed glorify the twin imperial ideologies of super individualism and chauvinistic nationalism. Yet the ubiquitous romance novel or television soap equally functions to legitimate the dominant social order simply by uncritically accepting and reproducing it as normative in their story-scapes.

Given the political economy of art and entertainment in the metropolis, subversive narrative is less widespread, but it can be found. The challenge to the status quo is not always direct; it might occur through ridicule, for example, as in the satire of Jonathan Swift, or the recent South African play "Woza Albert." There can be subversive power in simply fabulating a narrative world radically different in character from ours, as does Ursula Le Guin's feminist/egalitarian fiction. An early practitioner of the ideological criticism of socio-cultural discourse was R. Barthes, whose book *Mythologies* (1957) examines a variety of everyday practices and texts, from wrestling and soap commercials to magazine covers, toys, and food. And Eagleton insists that ideological criticism should, like the classic discipline of rhetoric, include "speaking or writing, poetry or philosophy, fiction or historiography: its horizon was nothing less than the field of discursive practices in society as a whole, and its particular interest lay in grasping such practices as forms of power and performance" (1983:205).

iv. Fiction, History, and Ideological Narrative

In order to bring us closer to our task of reading Mark, let me now briefly consider two differing literary texts as ideological reproductions: a fairy tale, and a realistic novel. There is no more fictive world than "once upon a time." In his brilliant study of the ideology of German folk and fairy tales, J. Zipes (1979) examines *Hansel and Gretel*. This story, based upon an oral tale that may date back as far as the eleventh century, was committed to a text at a particular stage of its development by the brothers Grimm, because of whose work the story is still today in circulation. Reading it against the class conflicts inherent in the precapitalist social conditions of late eighteenth-century Germany, Zipes concludes:

The struggle depicted in this tale is against poverty and against witches who have houses of food and hidden treasures. Here again the imaginative and magic elements of the tale had specific meanings for a peasant and lower-class audience at the end of the eighteenth century. The wars of this period often brought with them widespread famine and poverty which were also leading to the breakdown of the feudal patronage system. Consequently, peasants were often left to shift on their own and forced to go to extremes to survive. These extremes involved banditry, migration or abandonment of children. The witch (as parasite) could be interpreted here to symbolize the entire feudal system or the greed and brutality of the aristocracy, responsible for the difficult conditions. The killing of the witch is symbolically the realization of the hatred which the peasantry felt for the aristocracy as hoarders and oppressors [1979:32].

Even a fairy tale (perhaps *especially* a fairy tale) can "encode" social relationships, tensions, and strategies—even if in later transformations these dimensions are largely suppressed, as in the case of Disney reproductions of these stories!

Of course the text does not decipher itself for us; the fairy tale does not include footnotes explaining that the witch is a representation of the aristocracy. The interpreter must have socio-political questions in approaching the text, and understand that the symbolism of folktale narrative is open to more than one interpretation. It is precisely their suspicion of speculation and "allegorizing" that makes historico-critical exegetes reticent toward highly symbolic literature: "Drawing inferences from mythical symbols," complains Theissen, "must be considered the most problematic way to attain a sociological analysis" (1982:191).

This bias against myth is already an ideological expression of our alienated Western culture; more traditional cultures understand and are engaged by symbolic narrative far more deeply. But Zipes cannot be accused of historicism, for he is not contending that the events in the tale actually happened; rather, he is showing how elements intrinsic to the narrative (e.g., the plot conflict between abandoned peasants' children and a wealthy witch) represent the world extrinsic to the text (social conditions among late feudal peasants). Zipes's study shows that literary sociology can make a persuasive, if not absolutely definitive, case for ideological signification in fabulated narrative.

For our other example let us take a different kind of literary discourse: a modern novel, say Ignazio Silone's *Bread and Wine*. This novel represents a style referred to by some as "historical fiction," but which I prefer to call "realistic narrative." The story is about Pietro Spina, a socialist organizer who is forced from fascist Italy into exile, and who returns fifteen years later to carry on the struggle disguised as a priest. As he travels in clerical ruse, encountering compassion and wisdom among the poor Catholic peasantry and factionalism among his old compatriots, his perspective on religion and politics is slowly transformed.

As realistic narrative, this novel employs fictional characters and events, but its settings and plot are historically plausible, and indeed in some instances are barely cloaked autobiography (the author wrote in 1937, in exile as a result of his clandestine communist organizing). Its representations are therefore very tightly knit, and it is not difficult to see the ideological orientation of the literary text. Silone's plot and characterizations are a production of two aspects of the same historical situations. One is Mussolini's Italy on the eve of its declaration of war upon Ethiopia in 1935. The other is the widespread disillusionment among many European communists due to the Stalinist purges in the Soviet Union in the mid-1930s. Silone himself had broken with Catholic dogmatism, only to later feel forced to also break with communist dogmatism. *Bread and Wine* is a profound reflection on the contradictions of the human condition, intending to subvert the fascist ideology ascending to predominance in Italy, while appealing to Silone's antifascist colleagues to look more honestly at the ambiguous tendencies of communism on the one hand, and the redeeming qualities of peasant Catholicism on the other.

These examples raise the problem of the relationship between fictional representations and historical actualities in narrative discourse, particularly germane because I consider the literary genre of Mark also as a kind of realistic narrative (below, 3,B,iii). The preoccupation with "historicity" belongs of course peculiarly to nineteenth-century rationalism. Contemporary historians increasingly admit that "history in the strict sense is a story about events, not events themselves . . . .[it] is always constructed, never reconstructed" (N. Petersen, 1986:10). As Malina puts it:

> The historian no less than the gossip, ancient and modern, necessarily weaves a set of implicit meaning into an explicit story. As story tellers select among events from the historical field (chronicle) they necessarily and simultaneously have to make their selections with a view to how the elements from the historical field will fit along some time framework (story). This selection process inevitably follows along a course set by three implicit questions: why did things happen the way they did (mode of emplotment), what is the point of it all (mode of formal argument), and what should we—author and audience—do about it (mode of ideological implication) [1984].

Historical discourse is "narrativized," and thus an ideological production. My high school U.S. history textbook (I believe it was entitled *We The People*) was no less *ideological* because it endeavored to be *historical narrative*.

Hence it does not impugn the *historical* character of Mark's Gospel to consider it as *ideological narrative*. The reader should not be troubled by all this talk of "fiction":

> "Fiction" in this context merely refers to the construction, the making, of an order which these formal devices [point of view, plot, and closure] make possible. In this sense fiction orders facts which themselves lack order. . . . The facts *may* be factual, but the order *is* fictional because it is an imaginative construction [N. Petersen, 1986:10f.].

Is the Gospel "historically reliable"? I believe there is reliable continuity between Mark, his sources, and Jesus—but I do not think historical-critical reconstructions of those sources is the best way to acknowledge this continuity.

My lack of interest in form- and redaction-critical questioning in this commentary does not constitute a denial of Mark's use of these sources, as if I am contending that Mark "made the whole story up." Rather, I am content to trust that Mark believed he was reworking traditions about *real* (not make-believe) events, sayings, and personalities, and put each detail in his narrative for a reason (a position that I suppose is not unlike some versions of "canonical criticism" that have been proposed). I will go still further, and contend that Mark is an *authoritative*, and therefore fully reliable, interpreter of the original ideology of Jesus and his movement. In all these ways, to "read" Mark is to "read" Jesus. None of this, however, changes the fact that Mark is involved in a process of *reproducing* tradition. Hence one fundamental axiom of historical criticism stands: the text is a production first of the "historical reality" of *Mark's* time, and only very indirectly that of *Jesus'* time. But such is the nature of *all* our knowledge of the past.

Consequently, I will throughout this commentary speak about Mark and about Mark's Jesus rather than directly about Jesus of Nazareth. This is for purposes of modesty, not skepticism. It is true that the object of faith is finally not the text but the powerful person to whom it attests. Yet Mark's text means to both establish and limit what we can say about this person (I will return to this matter below, 3,B). Nevertheless, in my concluding comments I will venture a brief characterization of the practice of Jesus of Nazareth, using some historical imagination and traditional christological terms (below, 14,F).

1E. A SOCIO-LITERARY READING STRATEGY

This commentary will read Mark as an ideological narrative, the manifesto of an early Christian discipleship community in its war of myths with the dominant social order and its political adversaries. The Gospel was the product of a concrete social strategy and practice within a determinate historical setting. I conclude this introduction with a brief explication of how my reading strategy proceeds. The first step is one of extrinsic criticism, which examines the historical and ideological setting and prevailing social strategies of Mark's "world" (chapter 2). The rest of the commentary consists of intrinsic criticism, the inductive study of the text, employing a relatively uncomplicated form of literary analysis that should be readily understandable to the reader unfamiliar with the fine points of narratology (for an overview and helpful bibliography I again refer the reader to Rhoads and Michie's discussion of "rhetoric," 1982:35ff.). Before beginning my commentary on each major section of the Gospel I overview its narrative character, both structure and story; I end each section with a retrospective consideration of discourse and signification. These terms are defined in the following discussion.

Diagram 1
Basic Elements in Narrative Production

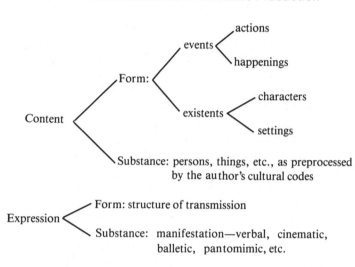

i Narrative Analysis: Structure and Story

A literary approach pays attention to both *what* Mark tells us and *how* he tells it. S. Chatman diagrams the basic elements involved in narrative production in Diagram 1 (1978:26). Let us take these elements one by one, from bottom to top.

The *substance of expression* in Mark is immediately obvious—the Gospel is a written transmission. But what *kind* of literary discourse it is will be essential as an expression of Mark's ideology. Why does he choose to invent a literary form rather than use a culturally familiar one? This will be discussed at the outset under "ideology of genre" (below, 3,B).

The *form of expression*, or composition of the text, is studied at three levels: the story as a whole, the individual elements and episodes as they stand in relationship to each other, and the internal composition of individual episodes (I prefer this term over the more academic "pericope").[1] The study of composition tries to engage these levels synoptically, and so is a continual process of examining the text up close, progressively backing away to put it in wider perspective, and moving in close again. The overall structure and composition of Mark is first overviewed (below, 3,C), in order to establish the main narrative sections and subsections and their interrelationship. Then, in order to keep the reader aware of the complex narrative fabric of the Gospel, I begin each major section of Markan text with an outline of its internal composition, under the heading of *Structure*.

Throughout my commentary I continually stress the importance of narrative structure for interpretation. A few examples will illustrate what I mean, beginning at the level of individual episode. In the first call to discipleship (Mk1:16–20), the form is a parallel doublet (below, 3,F,iii). The fact that Mark, whose overall style is quite spartan, chooses here (and a few other places) to tell a similar story twice draws attention to what is being repeated and why.

Locale and movement help to define narrative units, which Mark often arranges like "scenes." In the synagogue exorcism (1:21-29), the episode begins when Jesus comes "on stage" by entering the synagogue, and concludes with his exit (below, 4,B,i). This literary devise is called *inclusio*, or "framing."

Another Markan devise is anaphora, or the repeated use of a key word or theme around which an episode is constructed, as can be seen in the healing of the leper (Mk1:40–45), where the verb "to declare clean" occurs four times (below, 4,C,i). The "two step progression" is common (Rhoads and Michie, 1982:47f.), used as flourish (the poor widow gave "everything she had, even her whole livelihood," 12:45) and as antithetical parallelism (the Human One came "not to be served, but to serve," 10:45). It is masterfully employed to structure Jesus' second sermon, which begins with the disciples' double question ("When will this be, and what will be the sign when these things are all to be accomplished?" 13:4) and proceeds with a two part answer about the "times" (13:5–23) and "signs" (13:24-37).

When we examine a large section of narrative, we can observe the sequence and interrelationship of episodes. They are often linked, as has long been recognized by redaction criticism, by hook words or phrases, as in the case of Mark's composition of the "Galilee direct-action campaign" (1:40–3:6; below, 4,A,i). A well known linking device in Mark is "intercalation," or interrupting one story with another, as in the two healings of 5:22–43 (below, 6,D,ii). There Mark uses both this "sandwiching" device and repeated themes (the healing of female subjects each identified by "twelve years") to cross-reference the episodes. Mark also frames sections, as in his placement of a story about healing a blind man at the beginning and end of his "discipleship section" (8:22–10:52; below, 8,A,i).

Finally, broad structural patterns can be discerned if we examine the text "synchronically"—that is, abstracted from the time/space/plot considerations of the story. For example, I argue that the Galilee campaign narrative (1:40-3:6) exhibits a broadly concentric structure (A-B-C-B'-A'), which functions to draw our attention to the "center" (C) of the composition (below, 4,A,i). I will show that the Gospel overall consists of two "books," each with a prologue and epilogue and the same basic elements (below, 3,C,ii). Jesus' call to a discipleship of the cross lies in the structural middle of the story, as a kind of narrative—and ideological—"fulcrum" (3,C,iii).

The *substance of content* is the way in which the story represents a world coherent and intelligible to the reader. This includes the socio-cultural determinates of language, the "semantic fields" of reference, the literary traditions, and so forth. For example, Mark expected his readers to know that John's costume in 1:6 meant to invoke Elijah (below, 3,E,iii). Some of these aspects of content substance are discussed at the outset (below, 3,A), others along the way. The *form of content* is made up of what Chatman calls "existents," which constitute the narrative world (the "who and where"), and "events," constituting the plot (the "what"). At the beginning of each narrative section of the Gospel I summarize these under the heading of *Story* .

The "events" (or plot) include both what the characters do (actions) and what happens to them or around them (happenings). For example, in the Jerusalem campaign narrative and its aftermath there is a dialectical tension between Jesus' actions and the ongoing plotting of the authorities against him (11:18; 12:34b; 14:1f.,10f.). A major narrative transition occurs at the point where these two trajectories finally meet: when Jesus is arrested in Gethsemane (14:43–52), the disciples abandon him, and the discipleship narrative, begun in 1:16ff., collapses.

As we read closely each individual episode we must also remain attentive to linear plot development. For example, early in the story Jesus is involved in conflict with the authorities, but after 3:6 the plot takes on a new character, for it is hinted that this conflict may well cost him his life. The plot is often intensified or clarified by Mark's use of literary devices known as *prolepsis* and *analepsis*. Prolepsis is the introduction of something that refers "ahead" in the story, such as the mention in 1:14 that John was arrested (an event not narrated until 6:14ff., and then as a "flashback"). Conversely, analepsis is retrospection; when Jesus tells a parable of his struggle with a "strong man" in 3:27, we are meant to recall that John the Baptist has named Jesus the "stronger one" in the prologue (1:7). These devices send us back and forth through the text, and engender "the arousal and fulfillment of expectations and desires within the reader" (Robbins, 1984:7).

The analysis of existents involves the development and function of narrative setting and characterization. Mark uses geographical movement to effect transition between both individual episodes and major narrative sections. The story moves from the wilderness to Capernaum; it then zigzags across the Sea of Galilee in 4:35–8:21; thereafter it becomes a slow but sure march to Jerusalem beginning in the far north at Caesarea-Philippi in 8:27. We will also see that Mark uses narrative space in highly symbolic ways. We should take careful note of such things as the recurring use of the spatial theme "way," and the fact that the discipleship narrative begins in Galilee and ends by pointing back there.

As for the personalities who populate the story, we might justifiably summarize Mark in this way: his *characterization* usually takes on the form of *caricature* . His portrait of Jesus' opponents is almost wholly negative, whereas our impression of the disciples progresses from sympathetic to hostile. And who is Jesus? We are told at the very beginning who he is, but our certainty is undermined by the rest of the story, as we are increasingly caught up in the questions of characters (e.g.,1:27; 4:40f.) as well as Jesus' questions to them (e.g., 2:9; 3:23,33; 8:21,29). I will return to the matter of existents when considering Markan realistic narrative (below, 3,B,iii).

ii. Social Analysis: Discourse and Signification

Social analysis examines Mark's overall "narrative strategy" for its ideological signification—that is, the social strategy and stance it encodes: "every text intimates by its very conventions the way it is to be consumed, encodes within itself its own ideology of how, by whom and for whom it was produced" (Eagleton, 1976:48). B. Holzner (1972) identifies three tasks in analyzing symbolic/ideological discourse. The first focuses upon the "communicative dimension," that which renders the discourse intelligible within the shared semantic universe of the culture or the "epistemic community" (a subgroup with its own "language"). Here I examine the social function of what I called in my literary analysis the *substance of content*. For example, Mark's choice to write in Greek, and his assumption that his audience is familiar with Hebrew scriptures and cultural codes such as those dealing with purity and debt, tell us something about Mark's own situation and strategy. Much of the social function of the communicative dimension is discussed at the outset (below, 3,A).

Holzner's second task concerns the internal coherence of the discourse, or what we might call the "ideological syntax" of the narrative patterns. What is the social function of a narrative in which the promise of the kingdom begins and ends in Galilee? In other words, what are the ideological factors involved in the production of a text that has Galilee as its symbolic center (the "positive pole"of the story), when in the "real world" this center is in Jerusalem (which is the "negative pole" in the story!)? Other questions are raised in a similar fashion. What is the social function of Mark's fictions about feeding crowds with bread and traversing the sea in a boat, and why are there two cycles of ministry in the middle section of the Gospel? What does Mark mean by a triple cycle of death predictions and their relationship to Jesus' teaching in 8:27–10:44? Why does Jesus avoid the cities, and what is the meaning of his strategy of engagement and withdrawal? I summarize these kinds of findings at the conclusion of each section under *Discourse*.

The third task is to examine the "signification," or social meaning, of the discourse, by examining the correlations between the socio-political inferences within the narrative world and the socio-historical situation as we have determined it from extrinsic criticism. Mark gives us a portrait of first-century Palestine. How does it compare and contrast with other portraits, for example, that offered by the contemporaneous Jewish writer Josephus? There is nothing that prohibits us from assuming that when Mark's story mentions "Pharisees" he is referring to a historical party within Judaism—as long as we keep in mind that his account of them is overdetermined by his own ideological bias and narrative strategy. It is in fact precisely these distortions that signify Mark's social strategy. Mark's narrative settings of house, field, and synagogue, and his caricatures of poor crowds, rich landlords, and murderous kings, all have social signification as products of a real social environment. So too does his frequent reference to stories of social contact between an upright Jew (Jesus) and "sinners" and gentiles. Occasionally Mark will also make a direct "editorial insertion" into his story, which further provides a clue to its socio-historical setting (see 7:3; 13:14).

I pay close attention to stories of conflict in the Gospel, especially Jesus' protracted enmity with the scribes and the Pharisees. What was the social function of such stories in a world in which scribes and Pharisees still held political power? These stories must clearly articulate the war of myths: the symbolic discourse of Jesus (e.g., "the Human One is master even of the Sabbath," 2:28) is pitted against that of his opponents ("Why are your disciples doing something on the Sabbath day that is forbidden?" 2:24). And what is the social function of a story that has the hero repudiate the ideology of armed revolt, yet also has him arrested (14:48) and executed as rebel, between two rebels (15:27)? I reflect upon such evidence at the conclusion of each major section under *Signification*. I then provide an overall summary of my findings in chapter 14.

iii. Some Provisos

Before proceeding to the task at hand, a few qualifications are in order. N. Petersen has used a form of literary sociology very similar to my own in a reading of Paul, and I recommend his discussion of the methodological issues involved for a more thorough treatment than I have had room for here (1986:1ff.). Still, his work, like that of most North Atlantic scholars, lacks a commitment to political hermeneutics; I feel much greater kinship with the materialist school of criticism. For a method more strictly materialist than mine, see Eagleton's program (1976:44ff.).

I have already acknowledged my debt to the work of F. Belo (above, B,i), and discuss where I differ with him in the Appendix (D). It should be clear by now that I am firmly on the side of the Marxist tradition with regard to crucial elements of my approach, such as the theory of ideology, the task of ideological criticism, and a conflict model of society (see below, 2,A,ii). If this is annoying to North American readers it is in most cases because they are simply ignorant of the critical Marxist tradition. At the same time, I am aware that my use of Marxist theoretics (a field in which internecine debate is as furious as Protestant sectarianism once was) will seem simplistic and unqualified to the literate Marxist. For this I do not apologize; I have not wished to place unnecessary obstacles in the way of the reader, who I think will benefit more from a broad comprehension of some basic concepts without endless qualifications. Anyone interested in a more highly sophisticated argumentation of a similar thesis from a more strictly Marxist perspective can consult the work of F. Jameson (1981).

I am careful, however, not to claim my method as "materialist," because of where I demur from the Marxist tradition. Though contemporary Marxist cultural criticism repudiates the vulgar forms of economic determinism (see Jameson, 1981:45), historical materialism remains, as Jameson puts it, the "untranscendable horizon." According to him it alone "offers a philosophically coherent and ideologically compelling resolution" to the dilemmas of interpreting the "mystery of the cultural past . . . grasped as vital episodes in a single vast unfinished plot: 'the history of all hitherto existing society is the history of class struggles' " (ibid.:19f.). My disagreement with Jameson is that I identify the "single great collective story" of which he speaks not with historical materialism, but with the biblical narrative of liberation, from which Marxism is, at most, derivative.

Biblical faith insists that it is Yahweh who alone is the author of this story, who is the "untranscendable horizon." I am not anxious to enter into "meta-symbolic" debates in this book, and so have tended to avoid talk about God—but only because Mark himself does. Mark stands as part of this one narrative of liberation—as the Gospel puts it, the voice that "spoke" in the prophets "spoke" again in John the Baptist, and ultimately in Jesus of Nazareth. Moreover, the story continues where and when discipleship is practiced. I refer to this story throughout this commentary as the "script of biblical radicalism" (see below, 3,A,iii). It is a story that Yahweh generated and continues to regenerate, in which Yahweh may both intervene *and* remain silent, and in which the great law of materialism—entropy (that is to say, death)—does not have the last word.

A few provisos are also in order concerning the semantics of this commentary, issues that have everything to do with the exercise of social power and domination. First, I am committed to inclusive language, and have altered my sources where possible. Though I am not entirely sanguine about some of the inclusive alternatives to familiar biblical idioms in current use, I feel it is important to employ them anyway. I draw attention to one idiom in particular, the apocalyptic title "Son of Man," which is so important to Mark's Gospel. This thoroughly male epithet has been changed to "Human One" in the National Council of Churches' *Inclusive Language Lectionary* (1983), which suggestion I have adopted. I think it speaks not only to the meaning of the original Hebrew metaphor, but captures well Mark's own presentation of Jesus as the true human being.

On the other hand, I do not happen to agree with the inclusive lectionary's decision to alter the *political* semantics of the Bible, because of their allegedly hierarchical character (e.g., master, kingdom). To do this, at least where Mark is concerned, is to lose the edge of his political polemic, and often his sharp irony, for Mark's ideological strategy specifically expropriates these terms in order to invest them with new content. I have, for different reasons, used the traditional Hebrew "Yahweh" in place of the Hellenistic "God" or "Lord" whenever possible. Finally, I refer to the author of Mark's Gospel as a male. This is not to rule out the possibility that the writer was a woman; but in lieu of harder evidence to the contrary, I will allow tradition to prevail on this point.

This study portrays the structures and social groups that made up first-century Jewish culture in a very critical light, for the simple reason that Mark himself does. It is of the utmost importance that this not be construed by the reader as anti-Semitic in any way. Mark's social criticism, though necessarily historically specific, is addressed to *every* culture and political formation. To limit it to late second-temple Judaism is not only to miss his point badly; it is to perpetuate the murderous historical legacy of misunderstanding and oppression that has too often charactized the attitude of gentile Christians (and pseudo-Christians) toward the Jewish people. This commentary aims to be clear that the opponents of Mark's Jesus were, to use apocalyptic semantics, "powers," a rubric that embraces not only members of the Roman and Jewish ruling classes then, but also those in North America now.

This brief sketch cannot be expected to convince the reader of the socioliterary method; that is up to the commentary itself. In the long run, the methods change and the text remains the same; as the old Bible school saying goes, the scripture is the anvil upon which all our tools are shaped. But in the short run, in the midst of the political struggles of each interpreter's own time, the text remains vulnerable to misreadings that mute its power to animate us to discipleship. If there are parts of my reading of Mark that seem too polemical, it is because I recognize keenly the need to "overthrow and practically refute an interpretation already in place." Bible study is only one small but, I believe, indispensable, part of the wider ideological struggle going on in the church and the world today. We must "begin to listen to symbols," for indeed in our time we have "not finished doing away with idols."

NOTE

1. Obviously each episode consists of smaller units: individual sentences, clauses, and words. Linguistic analysis and philology is the domain of traditional exegesis, and any standard exegetical commentary (e.g., V. Taylor, 1963), will suffice. I will make reference to issues of syntax and textual detail only when it is relevant to socio-literary analysis.

CHAPTER TWO

The Socio-Historical Site of Mark's Story of Jesus

Antiquity . . . the golden panhandle of history, is an ideologically important era. Aryan heroes bestrode it, founding Western Civilization. It is variously remythicized by each generation of ancient historians. The voices that speak to us from antiquity are overwhelmingly those of the cultured few; the elites. The modern voices that carry on their tale are overwhelmingly those of white, middle-class, European and North American males. These men can, and do, laud imperialistic, authoritarian slave societies. The scholarship of antiquity is often removed from the real world, hygienically free of value judgments. Of the value judgments, that is, of the voiceless masses, the 95% who knew how "the other half" lived in antiquity.

—T. F. Carney, *The Shape of the Past* (1975:xiv)

Mark's story of Jesus stands virtually alone among the literary achievements of antiquity for one reason: it is a narrative for and about the common people. The Gospel reflects the daily realities of disease, poverty, and disenfranchisement that characterized the social existence of first-century Palestine's "other 95%."

In the very first scene of the story the crowds are there, flocking to John the Baptist and his subversive promise of a new order. Throughout the narrative of Jesus' ministry the crowds are there, continually pursuing, interrupting, and prevailing upon him. Jesus' compassion is always first directed toward the importunate masses and their overwhelming needs and demands. He responds to their desperate situation of hunger and hopelessness, and nurtures their dreams of liberation. And at the end of the story the crowds are there. Manipulated by the very Jerusalem politicians who enforce their subjugation and who fear their insurrectionary potential, the crowd clamors for the execution of the one who, as far as they were concerned, failed to deliver on his promises.

In all its heroic, comic, and tragic elements, Mark's drama of Jesus portrays the world of first-century Roman Palestine "from below." It breaks the "culture of silence" (Freire) of the poor by making them—fishers and farmers, the lame and leprous—the central subjects and protagonists of the gospel of the kingdom.

2A. THE GOSPEL IN POLITICAL TIME AND SPACE: FIRST-CENTURY ROMAN PALESTINE

This chapter seeks to provide a broad, analytical portrait of the cultural, social, economic, and political structures of the world in which Mark lived and about which he wrote. This background is essential to the inductive exegetical work that makes up the bulk of this book. I have tried to keep it general, nontechnical, and limited to that which is relevant for a socio-literary reading of Mark. In my conclusions in chapter 14 I will return to this portrait, within which I will situate the ideology and social strategy of Mark's community.

i. The World of Jesus and of Mark

At the very outset we are faced with a fundamental dilemma. Mark's text represents two worlds: the one he narrates and the one in which he lives. The former is an ideological product of the latter, and the "historicist fallacy" prevents us from assuming a perfect correspondence between the two. We know, for example, that the historical "time" of Mark is not the "time" of his story about Jesus; they are separated by at least two generations. Perhaps the historical "space" is different too: where (Rome? Egypt? Asia Minor?) and under what concrete social circumstances (persecution? prosperity?) was the Gospel produced?

How can we situate the Gospel within a concrete socio-historical setting when we have no fully reliable extrinsic testimony (evidence apart from Mark's own narrative) as to either its date or geographical provenance (origin)? This ambiguity presents us with what Markan scholar W. Marxsen called the necessarily "circular character" of the analysis of historical texts (1969:25f.). On the one hand, the socio-literary approach is mainly inductive: drawing inferences from the text as to its situation. On the other hand, one's presuppositions about provenance inevitably influence one's reading of the text.

A few examples will suffice to demonstrate the problem. Fundamental to my approach is the assumption that Mark is the first of our synoptic Gospels. The ways in which Luke and Matthew have reappropriated his story are therefore of only incidental interest to my reading. Obviously if one disputes the priority of Mark, as does a small but vocal scholarly minority, the synoptic relationships have to assume a central place in interpretation. Similarly, assumptions concerning the time and place of Mark's composition, about which there is longstanding debate, are crucial. Rather than recapitulating the major arguments here, which any good commentary can provide, I will show in two cases how divergent positions result in conflicting interpretations.

A major (though no longer dominant) school of thought believes that Mark was written in Rome by a Jewish author for a predominantly gentile audience. Those who assume this provenance interpret the presence of Latinisms in the text as confirming evidence—Mark would naturally use local idiom in writing to a Roman audience. If I concurred with this, my task would be to situate the production of the Gospel within the socio-economic context of a major Hellenistic city; the political context of the imperial capital under Nero (54–68 C.E.), the year of the four emperors (68–69), or Vespasian (69–79); and the ideological context of the second-third generation church in its interface with Roman society.

However, for reasons that will become clear in the course of my reading, I side with the growing number of scholars who place the production of Mark in or near northern Palestine; I refer the reader to H. Kee's discussion of this thesis for further reading (1977:176ff.). I therefore interpret the significance of the Latinisms differently; they indicate rather the expected linguistic penetration in the socio-economic and administrative spheres of the colonized culture of Palestine. My socio-political description obviously must focus upon conditions in agrarian Palestine—which, needless to say, were very different from urban Hellenism.

The matter of dating is still more difficult, but no less crucial. Whether or not one places Mark before or after 70 C.E., the date of the Roman destruction of the Jerusalem temple, has everything to do with how one interprets Mark's polemic against the temple. Those who date the Gospel after 70 C.E. typically argue that Mark was simply trying to justify the Christian community's theological rift with the Jewish cult. Those supporting Roman provenance also see an oblique endorsement of the Roman victory over the Jewish revolt that began in 66 C.E. In contrast, I hold that a date prior to 70 and during the revolt (thus after 66) is essential to the coherency of the political and economic ideology of Mark's narrative. Mark's vigorous criticism of the temple state and its political economy would obviously have been superfluous once the temple had been destroyed. I believe the general resistance to a pre-70 dating among scholars is an example of their (docetic) tendency to suppress the economic and political aspects of the text in favor of the theological.

It is necessary therefore to stipulate my own assumptions about provenance at the outset in order to explain the social description that follows, which in turn is to be used as background for reading the text. Because I believe there is some evidence for a more specific identification of Markan provenance with Galilee, I will focus the portrait below particularly on northern Palestine. Because of my pre-70 dating, I describe social, economic, and political conditions pertaining to Jewish society with the temple intact. In my conclusion I justify these assumptions in light of the evidence from the text, and attempt to sketch a more detailed historical portrait of Mark's community in its immediate social context.

To return to the original problematic, this does not yet solve how we can correlate the world of Mark's story with the world of Mark, but it simplifies it somewhat: both are situated in late second-temple Jewish Palestine under Roman occupation. The fact that the Gospel is a work of "realistic narrative" (defined below, 3,B,ii) further reduces the disparity: the social worlds intrinsic and extrinsic to the text do in fact *roughly* correspond. Jesus and Mark lived within the same historical "era," which can be marked off by significant alternations in the socio-political character of life in Palestine. This era began with the death of Herod the Great (4 B.C.E.). The division of his domain into three tetrarchies, and the subsequent transfer of Judea to direct Roman administration with the ouster of Archelaus (6 C.E.), were accompanied by major outbreaks of socio-political unrest by Jewish nationalists, which continued sporadically until the outbreak of the Jewish revolt (66 C.E.). The era closed with the defeat of the rebels and the destruction of the temple by the Roman general Titus in 70 C.E.

In saying this, I am not overlooking the fact that the cast of specific historical personalities who appear in the Jesus story, such as the Roman procurator Pilate (in office 26–36 C.E.) or the native Jewish king Herod Antipas (ruled northern Palestine 4 B.C.E.–39 C.E.), had changed by the time of Mark. Events had also changed the general political atmosphere; what was sporadic, predominantly rural resistance to Roman colonialism in Palestine at the time of Jesus had coalesced into a major, Jerusalem-centered insurrection at the time Mark wrote. Nevertheless, the basic social structures and dynamics that characterized this era did not alter significantly. Prophetic sects and social banditry plagued the colonial administrators throughout. No major land or tax reform altered the relationships of production, though local economic conditions naturally fluctuated, and generally deteriorated as the revolt drew closer. And the major social groups that the Gospel mentions, usually by way of caricature, were present both in the time of Jesus and Mark, with the notable exception of an organized national resistance, which did not exist in Jesus' time.

There is then a fundamental structural, if not exactly historical, symmetry between the world in which Mark sets his story of Jesus and his own world. This made it all the easier for Mark to insert into his story of Jesus issues that were pressing in Mark's time. It is upon these general structural characteristics, as well as the specific circumstances of the revolt, that this chapter will focus. It is thus a *synchronic* portrait, describing the function of institutions and social dynamics, rather than a *diachronic* one, which would be concerned with the chronological shifting of persons and events.

ii. *"Mapping" a Social World: Filters and Models*

It is necessary to begin by acknowledging a few key problems involved in any broad social description. A detailed portrait would be a huge undertaking, for which one chapter is hardly adequate. The following is thus limited to generalizations, though reliable ones, about the social character of Roman Palestine during this era, concentrating only upon those patterns most relevant to a reading of Mark. My portrait has been gleaned from the many comprehensive secondary sources dealing with this period, which I have cited; they give references to the primary sources for the reader who wishes to do further investigation.

All forms of narrative as we have seen are socially and ideologically conditioned, and historical discourse is no exception (above 1,D,iv). This presents two problems. The first has to do with the bias of our extrabiblical sources, particularly the major source of evidence for the era, the Jewish historian Josephus (Horsley and Hanson, 1985:xix–xx). His portrait of Palestinian social banditry or other elements involved in the revolt against Rome is no more or less caricatured than Mark's portrait of the Pharisees or high priests.

Modern historians have learned hermeneutic suspicion of these sources, but rarely turn the same critical light upon their *own* biases. This is the second problem: however scientific and dispassionate historians presume to be in their "reading and writing" of the past, they always employ "filters" by which they organize and interpret the great mass of diverse facts and events. Socio-scientific data are necessarily mediated by some kind of analytic framework, which, though only implicit, fundamentally determines the historical narrative (Elliott, 1986). T. Carney, in his important study of the historiography of antiquity, argues that the best way to control this factor is to employ models, which "bring values—in the subject matter and in its analyst—out into the open" (1975:xiv).

By model Carney means a general outline of characteristics, which outline (1) defines major components and their priority; (2) provides guidelines on their interrelationship; and (3) indicates a range of variance (ibid.:7). A model provides a kind of "map" to the foreign territory of a given historical era and social formation. My portrait will use models that are simple and thus perhaps relatively unsophisticated, but which have the advantage of being more intelligible to those uninitiated in the jargon of socio-scientific theoretics, especially the substructure-superstructure scheme of Marxist analysis.

My portrait makes use of a "matrix" model proposed by J. Elliott in his critique of G. Theissen's (1978) structural-functionalist sociology of first-century Palestine. Elliott's model is "designed to facilitate a more systematic comparison of the various interest groups . . . —not 'parties' or 'sects' but specifically *groups with distinctive interests*—which play key roles in the Palestinian social drama" (1986:20). He proposes the following four categories for analyzing these groups:

1. *socio-economic factors*: group constituency and size; geographic location; economic base and occupations; class, status; organization; roles, institutions;
2. *political-legal factors*: position and role vis-à-vis Jewish and Roman government; basis and exercise of authority; domestic and foreign relationships;

3. *culture, belief system*: pivotal values; accentuated beliefs and their symbolization; norms and sanctions; socialization and personality structure;

4. *strategy and ideology*: group interests, goals; tactics and foci of attention; oppositions; alliances, affinities; ideology (ibid.:18f.).

The weakness of this model is that it artificially categorizes social processes and groups, which are of course more organic—but this is unavoidable in descriptive sociological analysis. One can only caution against reification and overly positivistic use of categories, and then be explicit about why they have been chosen. For example, Elliott is self-consciously committed (and hence so am I) to a model that recognizes the "first importance [of] the material basis and economic relations of Palestinian life, then related social arrangements of collective activity, and then its modes of political control and symbol representation" (ibid.:17).

The greatest advantage of this model is that in comparing the social strategies of various groups, it affirms a conflict-based theory of sociology (from which the center-periphery metaphor is also derived). Rooted in the Marxist tradition, this approach stresses that social formations are defined by the competition among class, race, and gender interests. By contrast, the structural-functionalist school, dominant among Anglo-American scholars, presupposes:

Every society is a relatively persistent, stable . . . well integrated structure of elements. Every element in society has a function; it renders a contribution to maintaining society as a whole system. Every functioning social structure is based on a consensus of values among its members [Malina, 1981:19].

Such static models may be useful in characterizing the mechanisms of *dominant* institutions and ideological apparatus in a given social formation, but because they interpret social dynamics in terms of the maintenance of overall systemic equilibrium, they inevitably marginalize the role of dissenting groups. Social strategies of protest are explained by structural-functionalism as the adaptive response of less powerful groups, whose politics fill a cathartic function and pose little threat to the (basically sound) dominant social system. This approach has resulted in highly pejorative characterizations of the "sectarian" character of the primitive Christian communities (as in Theissen, 1978; see below, E,iv).

In keeping with my interest in strategies of social protest as expressions of ideological confrontation and struggle, my portrait will focus upon social *tensions* in each of Elliott's four spheres as they were manifested in active or latent conflict in the Roman Palestine of Mark's era. In the economic sphere I focus on the fundamental class disparities between the disenfranchised (often landless) peasantry and the (usually landowning) elite minorities (below, B,ii). In the geographical sphere I note the considerable tension between the encroaching patterns of Hellenistic urbanism and traditional agrarian society (B,iii). In the political sphere I portray the triangle of relationships between the uncommitted masses, the native ruling class, and the Roman imperial presence, against the backdrop of the Jewish revolt of 66–70 c.e. (below, C). I have drawn upon the excellent recent work of Horsley and Hanson on popular movements of social resistance and protest (1985). In considering the sphere of culture and belief systems, I turn to Belo's model of the "symbolic order" of Judaism (below, D,i). The tensions within this order have to do with the competition for access to or control over what K. Burridge calls "redemptive media" (1969). My analysis concludes with a brief examination of the various ideological strategies of social groups as they negotiated these tensions (below, E).

iii. History as a Cross-cultural Exercise

One of the most serious shortcomings of historico-critical study of biblical antiquity has been the tendency to ignore cross-cultural factors. Anthropologists speak of two perspectives on cultural systems and discourses: that of "insiders" (the "emic") and that of "outsiders" (the "etic"; Pilch, 1985:142). Too often biblical interpretation, for all its literacy in Greek and the philological arts, imposes its etic perspective upon the text, as we will see, for example, in the case of Mark's healing and exorcism narratives (below, 4,B,i,ii). B. Malina has argued that we must learn to see Bible-study as a cross-cultural proposition. It is like "eavesdropping" upon conversations of ancient Mediterranean "foreigners," and we cannot "presuppose that what they say embodies our modes of meaning as well" (1981:2).

This applies equally to socio-historical analysis. A good case in point are the modern competing analytical paradigms of Marxism and capitalism, both of which are etic:

> They tend to assume the same framework of reference, that of the maximization of profit ethic of industrial society. This reference set assumes (or repudiates) the marketization of thought (e.g., "time is money"), the monetization of relationships (most goods and services are for sale) and a rising ceiling of expectations (a consumer orientation) [Carney, 1975:137].

The assumptions of market-exchange models are inappropriate to preindustrial Roman Palestine, which had a pluralistic economy. This included the clan-based "reciprocity system" and the "redistributive system" of a central storehouse economy (below, B,i; see Malina, 1986b).

The same caution holds for modern assumptions about what constitutes "political" discourse and action. Our ideologies of participatory democracy or social mobility too often control our definitions of what qualifies as a socio-political "movement." We must take into account the fact that there was little popular access to political decision-making (as we would understand it) in oligarchic republican Rome (Carney, 1975:214), and still less in colonial Palestine. Dissent appears only in what social historians (somewhat paternalistically) refer to as "prepolitical" forms. Instead of high-level abstraction in political and economic discourse, therefore, we must look in Mark for forms *indigenous* to the rural poor of Roman Palestine. We will see that parables and stories of symbolic action are not at all "prepolitical" (though they are "prescientific"), but the very stuff of social criticism.

The single most important cross-cultural axiom to be kept in mind is that our modern differentiation between the "sacred" and the "secular" does not represent the world of first-century Palestine:

> In contrast to modern industrial society, there was no independent religious sector with its independent institutions, organizations, and social activities. In first-century Palestine, religion was instead embedded within all sectors of the system as a whole [Elliott, 1986:16].

It is difficult for us to lay aside our dichotomizing filters of church vs. state and faith vs. reason, but they wreak havoc upon any attempt to properly comprehend the socio-economic and political function of the symbolic order of late second-temple Judaism. No etic preconception has been more responsible for the failure of modern interpreters to recognize the political character of the Gospel, and no cross-cultural mistranslation has been more consequential for the life of the church (Maduro, 1979:54).

Another one of our unconscious etic assumptions is our post-Enlightenment preoccupation with the individual:

> Instead of individualism, what we find in the first-century Mediterranean world is what might be called "dyadism." . . . A dyadic personality . . . would conceive of himself as always interrelated to other persons while occupying a distinct social position both horizontally (with others sharing the same status, moving from center to periphery) and vertically (with others above and below in social rank) [Malina, 1981:55].

The dyadic personality will figure decisively in a correct interpretation of many of Mark's conflict and healing stories (see below, 6,D,i). Overcoming rigidly individualistic anthropology also enables us to see the symbolic action of Mark's Jesus as simultaneously a specific gesture as well as a dramatic representation of a social problem (below, 4,B).

Political hermeneutics has tended to be weak when it comes to cross-cultural analysis. In its enthusiasm, it too often repeats the mistakes of previous "historical quests" for Jesus, fashioning the biblical world into the image of modernity, what liberation theologian Hugo Echegaray calls "the easy temptation of concordism, which equates the social groups and forces of first-century

Palestine with those of our own time" (1984:xi). This is especially true with the notion of "class struggle." For all the indications of popular unrest and resistance mentioned below, any interpretive framework having to do with "proletarian consciousness" is hopelessly anachronistic. But the same warning must be applied to one of my central concerns in this commentary—namely, the "lens" of "revolutionary nonviolence" through which I propose to look at Mark's story of Jesus.

Horsley is basically correct in pointing out that in first-century Palestine "no one ever posed an issue in such abstract reflective terms as whether one should act violently or nonviolently" (1987:319). The whole debate about violence/nonviolence, and the conditions that have given rise to it, is distinctively modern—there is no getting around that. Thus my allusions to Gandhian *satyagraha* as a "hermeneutical key" for interpreting Jesus' practice are quite self-consciously heuristic. Heuristic refers to models or frameworks that are *consciously preconceived*, the intention being to see if they are confirmed by or useful for interpreting data being analyzed. I believe (and here I disagree with Horsley) that this framework is not inappropriate for Mark, for though he does not reflect abstractly upon the question, his narrative clearly presents the practice of Jesus as socio-politically revolutionary without recourse to an organized strategy of violence. Moreover, I am persuaded that this framework is both suggested by, and fruitful for exegeting, Mark's text.

In my treatment of this question, I have taken careful note of Horsley's objections against using the armed struggle of the "Zealots" as a convenient foil for presenting a nonviolent Jesus (ibid.:149ff.). At the same time, although Horsley is certainly correct that there was no organized military insurrection during the time of Jesus, there *was* one during the time of Mark, and so it is legitimate to assume that the evangelist's community took a stance vis-à-vis the revolt and its leaders, just as they did toward the other major social groups and practices (for further discussion of Horsley's theses, see Appendix, A). In sum, the most that can be concluded from this particular heuristic framework is that Markan ideology represents an *analogue* for our modern practice of revolutionary nonviolence; the hermeneutic imperative compels me to strongly assert that much. In any case, however we frame such questions, the Jesus story is always more radical when understood first in its own socio-historical terms.

2B. SOCIO-ECONOMIC TENSIONS

i. Political Economy

Carney, whose work I will draw upon heavily in the following sections, writes:

The economies of antiquity contain what the economic anthropologists term "plural societies." These are societies in which the value systems of different communities within the population share no common ground. . . . Society and economy are held together, in such cases, by the apparatus elite and the rigidly hierarchical social system. . . . Pluralism is produced by two things: regional subcultures and specific group lifestyles [1975:193].

The socio-economic valence of Roman Palestine was characterized by the complex interpenetration of the Hellenistic political economy of market-exchange and what Belo, following Marx, calls a "sub-Asiatic" agrarian formation. For Marx, the "Asiatic" mode of production was characterized by:

An opposition between the peasant class, which is organized into village communities (where relations of kinship play an important role in social organization), and the class-state, which directly appropriates the surplus for itself [Belo, 1981:60].

Belo calls Palestine "sub-Asiatic" because the state (Roman and Herodian) did not directly control agricultural production through infrastructure, such as irrigation systems, but instead appropriated surplus in advance through tribute, and controlled the exchange of goods.

Co-existing in the Asiatic sphere were two systems known by economic anthropology as "reciprocity" and "redistribution." Carney defines reciprocity as the clan-based system, which for Jews was rooted in tribal origins:

Among members of a family, goods and services were freely given (full reciprocity). Among members of a cadet line within a clan, gifts would be given; but an eye would be kept on the balanced return-flow of countergifts (weak reciprocity). Where distant tribal kin were involved, the element of watchful calculation grew greater, the time within which the countergift would have to be made grew less (balanced reciprocity). Outside the tribe mutuality ends . . . (negative reciprocity) [1975:167].

This "primitive" system, which characterized the tribal confederacy of Israel and is reflected in the law of Moses (Gottwald, 1979:293ff.), persisted in Palestinian village life in Mark's era. It determined that economic security and stability were bound up in the extended family household and kinship system.

Another, more developed nonmonetary system was that of redistribution. This was predicated upon the historical transition from tribalism to more stable and centralized communities, usually organized around a shrine or temple:

Initially a priestly group mobilized its labour force . . . to labour on the temple lands. The temple acted as central storehouse. Produce was stockpiled within that storehouse, and redistributed to feed the temple's nonagricultural work force (generally weaving women and artisans) as well as the agriculturalists who produced it. . . . As intensive settled agriculture now became possible, the little temple-centered communities grew in size and complexity [ibid.:173].

This in turn gave rise to walled cities, royalty, and military classes. We see this development in Israel with the rise of the monarchy (see 1 Sm 8).

Redistributive economies were controlled by the king or priestly aristocracy; they set "value equivalences," protected trade routes, and regulated volume and personnel. Business was conducted by "emissaries of the palace-centered economies," not entrepreneurs. As we can see in the construction of both the first and second temple in Israel, this system:

> Came to develop the logistical techniques for coordinating manpower, food, and material for huge building operations—always political be-cause of their massive social implications. Among these techniques were the direction of labour . . . taxation, bureaucracy, and controls on trans-portation [ibid.:174].

Within this regulated economy, the rise of large landed estates, whose internal operation was also based on the redistributive system, had to be controlled.

We see both the large house-estates and the central storehouse systems functioning in Roman Palestine. The latter of course was represented by the Jerusalem temple, originally the redistributive system for agricultural production through the tithing system. This production was dry-soil (nonirrigated) farming, predominantly cereal culture but including dried fruits, olives, wine, flax, with some forestry, fishing, and animal husbandry. Galilee was the most naturally fertile agricultural region in Palestine. There was certainly some degree of latifundialization (large estates under foreign ownership), though how much is uncertain. Rome often awarded land taken by conquest to native dynasties, and landownership was increasingly concentrated in the hands of royal estates during and after the reign of Herod the Great (37 B.C.E.–4 C.E.). In Galilee there is strong evidence of persistent family-based small holdings, but land alienation and resultant tenancy was ubiquitous among the poor.

Like all preindustrial societies, Palestine was economically stagnant due to low productivity and lack of capital formation and specialization, all of which inhibited development. Attitudes in the villages, based on reciprocation, deter-mined that cultivation was not for commercial purposes, but rather subsistence-oriented (see below). What trade surplus there was would have been controlled by foreign interests or state monopolies. Small producers had little or no access to export markets, which were in any case small due to high transportation costs and lack of technological means for preservation of goods. What little purchasing power there was, was dominated by the landed elites, and centered in the urban areas, with their small concentration of artisan class wage earners.

Indigenous social patterns in Palestine were already in the first century deeply transformed by the interface with the Hellenism, which began even before Alexander the Great (mid–fourth century B.C.E.) and was thus well advanced by the time of Jesus. Despite the fact that most of the scholarly literature concerns itself primarily with cultural and philosophical issues, Martin Hengel insists that Hellenism was first and foremost a secular force (1974:55–57). Military culture and technology made a particular impact, especially because of the large influx of veterans into Palestine, whose pay or pension was often in land grants in colonial territories.

Though a market-exchange system, the slave-based economy of Roman Hellenism differed radically from modern wage-labor economies:

> When the forces of production are based on slave labour, what we have is
> a political economy, in the sense that its relationships centre upon power
> and status rather than a maximization of profit [Carney, 1975:102].

More importance was attached to military affairs than to productivity; the availability of cheap labor predetermined the social milieu to be antitechnological. The business sector was characterized by "pariah capitalism," in which commerce was dominated by the state and its bureaucratic apparatus. This precluded the growth of a large business sector, and meant that the aristocracy consisted predominantly of "officialdom" (ibid.:103, 106).

Hellenistic administrative bureaucracies and their rigid hierarchies were widespread; the introduction of tax farming created local collaborative interests in colonized regions. In tax farming, rulers would lease out tax collecting rights in order to get the capital in advance from the lessee; "farmers" would then extract a profit in their collections. Under Roman rule, tax farming of tribute was abolished, but minor tolls and tariffs were still farmed out to local authorities. There is also evidence that Hellenism brought intensified economic exploitation of the land in order to develop some export trade. The subsequent romanization of Palestine planted a more commercialized and highly urban formation. In fact, David Rhoads points out that in the first century "the resettlement of new residents in these cities tipped the balance of population in Palestine in favor of non-Jewish residents" (1976:24f.), a situation that obviously portended trouble.

Reciprocity and redistribution are the systems most directly evident in Mark's narrative, though the Latinisms that pepper his semantic field indicate the impact of Hellenistic administration. Mark's economic criticism is directed more toward the "regional" than toward the imperial political economy, but the latter occasionally figures. It appears in the mention of absentee foreign landlords in a parable (12:1), the tribute dispute (12:14ff.), and of course allusions to the Roman military presence in Palestine (5:9f.).

ii. Class Relationships

Aside from the peasant majority, there was a very small independent artisan and bureaucratic class, and a tiny aristocracy, which of an estimated population of seven hundred fifty thousand in Palestine made up less than one-half of one percent. The local ruling class after Herod was increasingly urban-based, and tended to accommodate the colonial forces culturally and economically. The rural peasantry on the other hand experienced hellenization as further economic marginalization and cultural isolation, especially in Galilee, as Freyne has shown (1980). The main socio-economic conflict was the economic threat to the traditional agrarian way of life posed by the urban oligarchy due to the economic vulnerability of small landholders and tenant workers.

Horsley sums up the process of land alienation and the resulting class stratification in Palestine:

> There is considerable evidence, including the parables of Jesus of Nazareth, that by the time of Herod there had arisen many large landed estates. Simultaneous with the growth of these large estates there was a steady increase in population. Some peasant holdings were subdivided, but more often the younger brothers were left landless because of the inheritance laws. Moreover, large numbers of other peasants who had fallen into debt were forced into the ranks of the rural proletariat. Most of these became marginal day-laborers. Herod, and to a degree, his successors employed many of these in elaborate building projects. That these laborers, permanently uprooted from the land, formed a potential source of instability was a fact not lost on the ruling group. . . . Thus even without the factor of foreign rule there would have been intense hostility between the common people and the ruling gentry and chief priests [1981:416ff.].

The most prominent of the building projects referred to by Horsley was the reconstruction of the second temple, a project begun by Herod and still going on at the time of the revolt (Theissen, 1976).

Because the social location of the poor will be central to our reading of Mark, let us look at the portrait of peasant existence offered by Carney. Its "basic hallmarks" were "political powerlessness and straitened economic circumstances" (1975:198). Peasant families had three obligations for production. Above all they had to grow enough food to feed themselves and their animals, and to have seed for the following year's crop. Then there was the need for a surplus because of the demands of both the reciprocity and redistributive systems. At the village level, a little extra was needed:

> To obtain the occasional iron implement or utensil, to contribute to the local festivals, and to make a loan to a neighbor in need. Only by contributing to festivals and making such loans could he acquire the reciprocal rights to call on his neighbor when himself in adversity . . . —peasant social insurance [ibid.].

But it was the elite-dominated surplus extraction that cemented the peasant's cycle of poverty. A Galilean tenant farmer could have up to half his harvest extracted as rent. Small holders were subject to the land tax or tribute of Herodian kings or the *annona* of the Romans, either of which ranged from one-quarter to one-third of a harvest. Not included in this were the tithes to Jewish authorities, an obligation that (unlike the Sabbath) received no recognition from Rome. According to S. Oppenheimer (1977:23ff.) the tithing structure stipulated in rabbinic tradition was:

1. a tenth of the harvest as *terumah* for the priests;
2. a tenth of the remainder as a first tithe to the Levites;
3. a tenth of the remainder as a second tithe in the first, second, fourth, and fifth year, and the poor man's tithe in the third and sixth year of the sabbatical cycle.

In addition to all this were the various poll taxes and tariffs levied upon the small farmer when he took his produce to city markets.

These burdens were the principal cause of economic disenfranchisement among the peasantry. They also determined the distinctly stagnant aspects of the peasant way of life:

> To make ends meet . . . the peasant had to keep his desires and living standards to an absolute minimum. Hence "primitive wantlessness," the very reverse of modern sedulously titivated consumer demand ever yawping after more goods to spur the industrial economy on. Hence, too, the peasant idea of the "limited good." This holds that all good things—food, land, honour, standing—are in fixed quantities and short supply. As their quantities cannot be increased, if one peasant gains a greater share of any one of them than heretofore, he is deemed to have done so at the cost of all his fellows. This notion is the cause of unending, unrelenting disingenuousness, struggle, and suspicion in peasant communities. . . . If an unusually large surplus is somehow produced, it is spent upon a festival, to propitiate the group [Carney, 1975:198f.].

The notion of limited good and the struggle for surplus serves as a dramatic backdrop to Mark's symbols of the "eschatological harvest" in the sower parable (below, 5,B,ii) and the "economics of satisfaction" in the wilderness feedings (below, 6,E).

Clearly, the burdens of the redistributive system were not felt as intensely by the urban and small artisan classes. Such disparities inevitably produced extreme socio-economic tensions. Despite the traditional loyalty among the rural classes to the Jerusalem cult, they were understandably suspicious of the interests of the landholding aristocracy:

> The Galilean Jewish peasant found himself in the rather strange position that those very people to whom he felt bound by ties of national and religious loyalty, the priestly aristocracy, were in fact his social oppressors [Freyne, 1980:199].

Expressions of resistance among the poor varied, from noncooperation in tithing to organized brigandage and occasional local uprisings, as I shall discuss below (C).

iii. Geopolitical Conflicts

As noted, the center-periphery model also applied within Palestine itself. The more Hellenistic urbanism penetrated the colony, the deeper the contradictions grew between the different needs of city and village. The conflict was at once economic and cultural:

> Those with disposable income were the elites, masters of the great estates with their household economies. So it is that the cities, where the elites reside and consume conspicuously, are economically parasitic upon the countryside in antiquity. For the cities consume, relatively, far more in luxury goods, taxes, and impressed labor than their craftsmen produce in artifacts. . . . There was, then, a marked cultural gulf, not just a lag, between town and country. . . . Different sectors of the populations of such societies each hold completely different, and mutually unintelligible, pictures of their "world" and life space. . . . The thought world and the social world of the military-bureaucratic elite and the subelite of large landowners with which the former was linked were quite different from and manifestly superior to, those of the peasant [Carney, 1975:102,100].

This tension was especially acute in Galilee, where the "breadbasket" of the plains was literally surrounded by newer Hellenistic cities (see Freyne, 1980).

Whether Ptolemais on the coast, or Herodian-established Sepphoris in the interior and Tiberias on the Sea of Galilee, these cities were dependent upon the rural food supply in Galilee, and therefore determined to maintain geopolitical control. Josephus reports that village life in Galilee was densely populated, which gave rise to smaller cities (such as Caesarea-Philippi) as toparchies, or regional centers of government and administration (see *War*, III,iii,2; *Ant.*, XX,viii,4). As urban encroachment continued, the formal dividing line between city and village grew diffuse, forcing many to exchange clan identity for citizenship in the Hellenistic *polis*. The resentment among peasants as they watched the slow erosion of the social fabric of their agrarian way of life is reflected in Mark (below, 4,B,iii).

Also evident in Mark is the socio-cultural tension between Galilee and Judea. If for no other reasons than its geographical isolation and distance from Jerusalem and its greater level of intercourse with the gentile world, Galilee was regarded with general suspicion by the Jerusalem hierarchy (Freyne, 1980). To be sure, earlier historical portraits characterizing Galilee as wholly synonymous with the *'am ha' aretz* (the rural poor who were despised in the rabbinic writings), or as the sole haven for revolutionary activity and sentiment, have been overturned (Oppenheimer, 1977). Nevertheless, there remains a great deal of evidence in the literature of the period that demonstrates the generally second-class status of those who were from the north.

In sum, Galilee was doubly peripheral. It was increasingly controlled by the political and economic forces of Hellenistic urban penetration. Symbolically and socio-economically it was controlled by Jerusalem in the south. This makes it all the more remarkable that rural and village Galilee is placed at the narrative and ideological center of Mark's story, in explicit tension with both Jerusalem and the Hellenistic cities.

2C. SOCIO-POLITICAL TENSIONS AND THE JEWISH WAR

The political situation in Palestine during this era can be characterized by five major currents:
1. the waning fortunes of the native kingships;
2. direct and indirect Roman administration of the colony;
3. the power of the high priesthood and clerical aristocracy, including the Sadducean party;
4. the shifting political alignments of the Jewish renewal groups, especially the Pharisees and Essenes;
5. the various strands of popular resistance and dissent among the masses.
Each of these currents contributed to the rebellion of 66 C.E.

With renewed study of the social and political history of the period since the late 1960s, several issues have emerged around which there is considerable ongoing scholarly debate. Among those with a direct bearing upon a reading of Mark are questions concerning the definition and character of the Pharisaic movement and the origins of the main revolutionary parties. I refer the reader to the best recent discussions of these questions, J. Bowker's *Jesus and the Pharisees* (1973) and D. Rhoads's *Israel in Revolution, 6–74 C.E.* (1976). One current has been almost entirely neglected, however, which happens to be an important key to a political reading of Mark: grassroots nonelite forms of socio-political resistance to the dominant order. I will therefore give more attention to this current in my comments, and urge the interested reader to further consult Horsley and Hanson's important book, *Bandits, Prophets, and Messiahs: Popular Movements in the Time of Jesus* (1985).

i. Occupied Palestine

After almost a century of independence under the Hasmonean dynasty following the Maccabean revolt from Hellenistic rule in 167–142 B.C.E. Jewish Palestine became subject again in 63 B.C.E. to the ascendant empire of Rome. At that time, after a brief struggle, Emperor Pompey established Hyrcanus II as a native client king and instituted the tribute. The Parthian empire overtook Palestine briefly in 40 B.C.E., but Rome reestablished control in 37 B.C.E. and then began the long and brutal reign of another client king, Herod the Great. Rhoads summarizes Rome's colonial interests in Palestine:

Table 1
Palestine, 4 B.C.E. to 70 C.E.
(all years in Table, C.E.)

Period of the Tetrarchies

Emperor	Judea, Samaria, Idumea	Galilee and Perea	Northern Transjordan	Prominent High Priests
Augustus → 14	Archelaus, ethnarch → 6	Antipas, tetrarch → 39	Philip, tetrarch → 34	Annas 6–15
Tiberius 14–37	Pilate, procurator 26–36			Caiaphas 18–36
Caligula 37–41				Theophilus 37–41

Period of Direct Roman Rule

Emperor	Procurator	High Priests	Political Events
Claudius 41–54	Fadus 44–46		Theudas's movement, ca. 45? (see Acts 5:36)
	Alexander 46–48		Famine, ca. 46; two Jewish rebel leaders executed
	Cumanus 48–52	Ananias 48–58	Jews (& Christians?) expelled from Rome; several (armed?) clashes in Palestine
	Felix 52–60		Rise of social banditry, prophets, sicarii; revolt of the "Egyptian prophet"
Nero 54–68	Festus 60–62		Wilderness prophet executed; conflict between Jews and Syrians in Caesarea
	Albinus 62–64	six high priests, 59–66	Corruption and rural violence increase; feuding of revolutionary factions in Jerusalem
	Florus 64–66		General deterioration; riots in Caesarea and Jerusalem
			Sacrifices to emperor cease, 66; provisional government
Galba, year of 3 emperors, 68–69		Ananus	Zealot coalition rules, 68; revolt crushed, 70
Vespasian 69–79		Phineas	

Israel served as a buffer state between the Romans and the Parthian Empire to the east. The Parthian Empire was the only remaining formidable threat to the extensive dominance of the Roman Empire in the Mediterranean world. . . . For these reasons it was important for the Romans to maintain good relations or firm control . . . especially so in light of Israel's reputation for being an unruly territory [1976:27].

As already mentioned, the era we are concerned with was bracketed by popular uprisings at the time of Herod's death (4 B.C.E.) and the full-scale rebellion beginning in 66 C.E.

Herod's kingdom was divided into three native tetrarchies. Two of these survived until the brief reign of Agrippa I, under whom Palestine was again united from 41–44 C.E. The third tetrarchy (Judea, Samaria, and Idumea) came under Roman administration following the ouster of Archelaus during popular revolt in 6 C.E. After 44 C.E. all of Palestine came under direct Roman rule. We might thus legitimately distinguish two periods on either side of Agrippa: the tetrarchies (the "time of Jesus") and direct Roman rule (the "time of Mark"). The principal personalities and events are listed in Table 1.

Mark's narrative bridges these two periods. In 6:14 he refers to Herod Antipas, tetrarch of Galilee and Perea (a detached territory south of the Decapolis on the east side of the Jordan). J. Brown writes of Antipas:

> The original meaning of *tetrarches*, "ruler of the fourth part," had been lost, and it now marked its holder as ruling a Roman protectorate in a status inferior to that of a nominally independent king. . . . Through many shifts of Roman policy . . . Herod held his realm by favor of Augustus and Tiberius, and was removed by Caligula. . . . We can be sure that he paid the emperor tribute, but our sources give no figure. When first appointed . . . he was allowed by Augustus to keep only 200 talents annually from the taxes of Galilee and Perea; perhaps this was his private income, and the administrative budget, building program, and tribute were separate accounts [1983:360f.,363].

Antipas's contempt for Jewish dissidents is reflected in Mark's account of the execution of John the Baptist. The continuing colonial collaboration of the Galilean nobility after 44 C.E. is suggested in the Gospel's caricature of the "Herodians."

Mark also mentions Pilate, an Italian procurator of the equestrian order. As a general rule Roman administrators were less concerned with imposing Hellenistic values than with the tricky politics of colonial rule. Rome was relatively tolerant of the fierce exclusivism of the Jews; as long as the ultimate hegemony of Rome was recognized and the tribute paid, a modicum of local autonomy could continue. Rome remained, however, in firm control. The procurator had the power to appoint and depose the high priest, the symbolic leader of the Jewish polity, at will. He retained stewardship over the high priestly garments, thus effectively controlling its functioning. In classic colonial fashion, Rome maintained exclusive authority over matters of foreign policy and serious domestic dissent (e.g., capital punishment; see below, 12,D).

Through the ever-present legions, barracked adjacent to the temple in Jerusalem, the imperial state could—and did—brutally crush any signs of insurrection. Two dramatic examples from the beginning and middle of the era suffice to illustrate the savage retaliation that followed attempts at armed resistance:

> After Herod's death in 4 B.C.E. while the three sons were in Rome, the arsenal of Sepphoris was looted by Judas, son of the guerilla leader Ezekias who had been executed by Herod the Great. . . . The legate of Syria . . . marched south with auxiliaries from Beirut and Aretas IV retook and burned Sepphoris, and enslaved its people. . . . Antipas quickly rebuilt it and made it his capital until the founding of Tiberias; the *tektones* (carpenters and masons) of Nazareth must often have commuted [the four miles] there [J. Brown, 1983:362].

This incident has stirred the imagination of historians because of its close proximity in time and space to the birth of Jesus.

The second example, a series of violent clashes under the procurator Cumanus (48-52), dramatizes the cycle of revenge (Josephus, *Ant.*, XX,v,3-4). During the Passover feast in Jerusalem, provocation by a Roman soldier caused a riot of Jewish pilgrims. The restoration of order resulted in several Jewish deaths. Shortly afterward Jewish urban terrorists responded by murdering an imperial official traveling to the city. Cumanus's forces in turn pillaged several nearby villages and punished local officials. During these raids, a soldier desecrated a copy of Torah from a local synagogue, again infuriating the Jews and setting off a new round of protests. For failing to control these and other disturbances, Cumanus was eventually banished by Rome; Rhoads considers his tenure the turning point in colonial tensions (1976:70ff.).

For a political consideration of Mark's narrative it is important to point out that confrontations between Roman power and Jewish popular resistance almost always centered around "symbolic" actions, such as those mentioned above. Among other well-known incidents reported by Josephus are:

1. Pharisaic resistance to Herod involving the refusal of some to swear an oath to the emperor and the removal of the Roman golden eagle from the temple gate (*War*, I,xxxiii,1-3);
2. Pilate's allowal of Roman standards into Jerusalem in violation of the prohibition of images, provoking mass outcry (*Ant*, XVIII,iii,1-2);
3. the attempt by Emperor Gaius Caligula to erect a statue of himself in the Jerusalem temple, occasioning widespread protest, including an agricultural strike in Galilee (*Ant.*, XVIII,viii,3; see below).

No symbolic action was more consequential, however, than the cessation of sacrifices to the emperor in the Jerusalem temple in June of 66 C.E. This was tantamount to a declaration of insurrection, and it is this war that I will argue serves as the immediate historical context for the writing of Mark's Gospel.

ii. Popular Resistance

Horsley and Hanson (1985) criticize the fact that standard political histories of this era focus only upon the social groups who "left literary remains." They contend that the political problematic of Jewish Palestine cannot be characterized solely in terms of the conflicts between the so-called four philosophies (the priestly aristocracy, Pharisees, Essenes, and the Zealots). The standard "histories of the elite" ignore the fact that these groups represented only a small sector of the population, less than three percent, even if we include the entire aristocratic and upper artisan classes. Yet social historians routinely ignore evidence of popular social movements, including that attested to by Mark, or, if they are acknowledged, dismiss them as "apolitical" simply because they did not align themselves with the elite groups (Theissen, 1978). Rather than looking for prototypes of modern liberation ideologies (which we have no more chance of finding than prototypes of the internal combustion engine), we must learn to appreciate the forms of political expression available to the uneducated and poor majority who were structured out of the dominant mechanisms of social power.

The study of grassroots political culture was pioneered by sociologist E. Hobsbawm in his book *Primitive Rebels* (1959). Taking peasant movements of the nineteenth and early twentieth centuries, Hobsbawm looked at the various "primitive" or "archaic" forms of social agitation:

> Banditry of the Robin Hood type, rural secret societies, various peasant revolutionary movements of the millenarian sort, pre-industrial urban "mobs" and their riots, some labour religious sects and the use of ritual in early labour and revolutionary organizations [1959:1].

Many of Hobsbawm's insights are adapted to ancient Palestine in the work of Hanson and Horsley.

One form of popular resistance of particular importance to Mark's era is "social banditry":

> [It] arises in traditional agrarian societies where peasants are exploited by landowners and governments, especially in situations where many peasants are economically vulnerable and administration is inefficient. Times of economic crisis and social disruption (such as war) may produce banditry on an increasingly widespread scale. . . . Bandits usually enjoy the support of local peasants; far from aiding authorities in capturing the bandits, the people may actually protect them. Bandits share, and often symbolize, the peasant's basic sense of justice and religious loyalties . . . and at times social banditry accompanies or leads into peasant revolts [Horsley, 1981:412].

Evidence from Josephus indicates that social banditry was a persistent problem for the colonial authorities in Palestine from the time of Herod the Great. Horsley contends that it was a major tributary to the revolt in 66 c.e.: "The dramatic increase in banditry during the early 60s brought more and more of the population into open opposition to the established order. . . . In effect, it *became* a Jewish rebellion" (ibid.:427).

Horsley and Hanson further point out that Israelite popular kingship was itself predicated upon social banditry; David originally rose to power, they argue, as a brigand leader (1985:93; see 1 Sm 22:2). As discontent in the first century grew, social banditry continued to be fertile ground for the politicization of prophetic movements. On the eve of the revolt:

> Josephus claims that now "the majority of people" (*hoi polloi*) practiced banditry, and that whole towns were ruined. . . . The banditry evidently took its toll on the gentry, for many wealthy Jews left their estates in search of safer surroundings among the Gentiles. With little to lose from increasing disorder, a sizable portion of the population had become outlaws. . . . Large groups of brigands already held sway as a dominant force in Galilee when Josephus arrived to take charge of organizing the defenses in 66–67 [ibid.:69].

Horsley and Hanson go so far as to compare the most prominent Galilean social brigand chief, John, who went on to become a rebel leader in Jerusalem, to the legendary *bandido* Pancho Villa:

> The career of John of Gischala is strikingly parallel to that of Pancho Villa in the Mexican revolution of 1910. Both started as local brigands, but both were entrepreneurs of sorts, taking the opportunity of social turmoil to sell confiscated goods across the border and to exploit the wealthy for the sake of the common defense. They both rose to prominence as skillful leaders of popular insurrections [ibid.:84].

It is of utmost significance that the term used by Josephus as a technical reference to social bandits (Greek *lēstēs*) appears in Mark twice. In both cases the narrative context is one of implied subversive activity (14:48; 15:27; see below, 13,A,i).

Josephus mentions another form of armed resistance, the tactics of the sicarii or "dagger men" who specialized in urban political assassination. Horsley and Hanson compare the strategy of this group to that of modern Algerian or Palestinian anticolonial terrorists. The colonial situation had become so intolerable that secret societies took action against collaborators:

> In all cases mentioned by Josephus, the Sicarii were highly discriminate and always directed their attacks against fellow Jews, not against Roman soldiers or officials. They employed three tactics in particular: (a) selective, symbolic assassinations; (b) more general assassinations along with

plundering of the property of the wealthy and powerful; and (c) kidnapping for ransom [ibid.:205].

This strategy served to break down the social security and solidarity of the ruling classes, and was no doubt partly responsible for their increasing defection to the Romans just before and during the war. As we shall see (below, 12,F,ii), Mark appears to portray Barabbas as a sicarius terrorist (15:7).

Besides armed organizations there were numerous spontaneous popular uprisings, not unlike the slave rebellions we know of in Rome. Often these were nonviolent, as in the case of Pilate's provocative move to introduce Roman standards into Jerusalem, which was vigorously protested by Jewish leaders. When he ordered his troops to surround the protestors and threatened them with death, Josephus reports that they willingly bared their necks rather than give in (*Ant*, XVIII,viii,2–6). Petronius, Roman legate of Syria, was dispatched to Ptolemais with orders to enforce Caligula's wish to erect his own image in the Jerusalem temple, which would have certainly meant war. "Tens of thousands" of Jews came to Petronius in protest, vowing that the desecration of the temple would take place only over their dead bodies.

Petronius went to Tiberias in Galilee to consider the dilemma, and was again met by "tens of thousands" of Jews. Josephus reports the following exchange:

> Then Petronius said to them: "Will you then make war with Caesar, despite our advanced preparations for war and your own weakness?" They replied, "We will not by any means make war with him; but still we will die before we will see our laws transgressed." And they threw themselves down upon their faces and exposed their throats, announcing they were ready to be slain [*Ant.*, XVIII,viii,3].

This protest went on for forty days, but the action that elicited the greatest concern among Roman authorities was the simultaneous agricultural strike in the countryside by (Galilean?) peasants, who refused to sow the next year's crops. The Romans were well aware that not only would this endanger the food supply in coastal cities, but also would intensify the economic pressure posed by the tribute obligations, and hence cause an even greater number of peasants to turn to brigandage. Petronius finally agreed to petition Gaius to change his mind, though in the end it was only the emperor's death that resolved the crisis. John Yoder probably goes too far in describing this incident as "a concerted act of resistance which this time had all the marks of a Gandhian campaign" (1972:92), but it does indicate the presence and vitality of nonviolent kinds of popular protest during the era.

iii. Prophetic Movements

Besides armed resistance and spontaneous mass protest, Horsley and Hanson identify a third form of popular dissent, which is equally crucial to understanding Mark. These were movements whose primary expressions were prophetic and eschatological. The main literary groups (Pharisees, priestly class, Essenes) tended to focus upon canonical biblical prophecy. In contrast:

> There emerged during the first century c.e. among the Jewish common people several prophets of two distinctive types. The individual prophets of the oracular type appear to be a continuation of the classical biblical oracular prophets, while the action prophets and their movements appear to be heavily influenced by biblical traditions of the great historical acts of liberation led by Moses and Joshua [1985:186].

Josephus, as part of the educated aristocratic class, was hostile to these movements, but despite his pejorative descriptions, it is possible to discern their popular political character. When interpreted against the backdrop of traditional prophetic symbolism, they are revealed as subversive, which explains why they were invariably suppressed by the Romans.

The "action" prophets, or what P. Barnett calls "Sign Prophets" (1981), were leaders who performed or promised symbolic acts that heralded liberation. Josephus mentions three important examples. During Pilate's tenure, a Samaritan prophet led an armed group up to Mount Gerizim, the traditional Samaritan site of eschatological restoration; there he promised to unveil "holy vessels" buried by Moses (Horsley and Hanson, 1985:162f.). This action was a symbolic articulation of Samaritan secession from the Jerusalem temple-based order, into which Samaria had been unwillingly incorporated since the time of the Maccabees. This was understood by Pilate, who quickly sent troops to crush the prophet and his followers before they could ascend the mountain.

Two decades later, under the procurator Fadus, a prophet named Theudas (mentioned in Acts 5:36) began a movement, promising to part the waters of the Jordan. Though unarmed, this movement was also dealt with militarily by Roman forces (ibid.:164f.). Theudas's prophetic symbolism was, like that of Mark's Jesus as we shall see, multireferential. On the one hand his promise recalled the action of Elijah in the context of building a subversive prophetic movement (2 Kgs 2:6–8); on the other it alluded to a new exodus from slavery, in the expectation that enemy troops would again be swallowed by the parted waters. The movement was doubtlessly in reaction to the colonial reconsolidation of Palestine under Roman rule after the short reign of the native king, Agrippa.

A third example took place under the procurator Felix, probably around 56 c.e., for it is also mentioned by Luke (Acts 21:38). A Jewish prophet identified with Egypt built up a large following of the rural masses in the wilderness, preparing to lead an (unarmed) assault upon Jerusalem, and promising that from the Mount of Olives he would command the walls of the city to crumble (ibid.:167f.). There can be no doubt about the subversive nature of these allusions, on the one hand to the Jericho military tradition of Joshua (Jos 6:15ff.), and on the other to the apocalyptic tradition of Zechariah, in which

Yahweh would fight against the pagan nations from the Mount of Olives (Zec 14; see below, 10,B,i). Roman intelligence discovered the plan, and a heavily armed contingent intercepted the march and slaughtered hundreds of the prophet's followers.

From these examples we can see a "clear pattern of symbolic correspondence between the great historical acts of redemption and the new, eschatological acts anticipated by these prophetic movements" (ibid.:171). In other words, their ideological strategy was to draw upon and reenact traditions of liberation that fired the hopes of the oppressed Jewish classes. Mark will do the same, invoking the tradition of the wilderness and other exodus themes, and portraying Jesus' actions in light of the great prophetic signs of the past (see below, 6,E).

Turning to the "oracular" prophets, the most obvious example is John the Baptist, who figures decisively in Mark's narrative. John appears to have taken after Elijah, who withdrew to the wilderness to gain "both personal strength and a prophetic commission to return to his people as the agent of revolution against an oppressive regime (1 Kgs 19)" (ibid.:140). At the same time, he also followed in the tradition of the classic oracular prophets such as Amos and Hosea:

> Spokespersons for the peasantry and the covenantal social-economic policy that served to protect their interests. Because of the blatant exploitation of the peasantry, these prophets felt compelled to oppose the ruling class, which was failing to observe the covenant [ibid.:145].

Like the prophets before him, John was executed by the ruling classes (below, 7,B). Mark demonstrates a keen awareness of this prophetic legacy of opposition to the powerful and its consequences, using it as a kind of biblical "script" for interpreting the vocation of Jesus (below, 3,A,iii).

Immediately before and during the war there were many apocalyptic prophetic movements in and around Jerusalem. Josephus mentions a certain Jesus, son of Hananiah, a peasant who for some seven years publicly pronounced woe upon the city, in the tradition of Isaiah and Jeremiah (ibid.:173f.). The Jewish aristocracy tried to prosecute him, but the procurator Albinus only tortured and released him (in contrast to Jesus of Nazareth, who was executed!). Josephus notes the proliferation of prophetic oracles encouraging the war efforts once the revolt commenced, as well as the appearance of many wondrous portents, which were interpreted as either Yahweh's support of or opposition to the war effort, depending upon one's partisanship. In as much as there is ample literary evidence that the apocalyptic tradition was already widespread in this period (see below, 3,B,i), it is no surprise that there was an intense concentration of apocalyptic prophets at the time of the war. Mark vigorously engages these popular prophets in a war of myths over the proper interpretation of apocalyptic ideology and practice (below, 11,A).

iv. Ideologies of Popular Kingship

Closely associated with both armed resistance and popular prophetic move-ments was a fourth strand of dissent: the complex hopes surrounding the restoration of messianism and popular kingship. There is much confusion around this question because of the tendency of Christian scholarship to project the New Testament ideology of fulfilled messianic expectation back into the sources. In fact:

> Recent studies have made clear that in pre-Christian times there was no general expectation of "*The* Messiah." Far from being uniform, Jewish messianic expectations in the early Roman period were diverse and fluid. . . . The designation *messiah* is not an essential element in Jewish eschatological expectation [Horsley and Hanson, 1985:90f.].

This does not mean that messianic discourse was not intelligible in the mid-first century; only that there was no one dominant concept to which Mark could appeal. Instead, there was an ongoing struggle over royal ideology within Judaism, and this is reflected in Mark's cautious and polemical appropriation of the designation "Messiah" (below, 8,C).

The same applies to the rubric "Son of David," which Christian interpreters have assumed was an accepted messianic title based upon *genealogy*. On the contrary:

> [It]simply does not occur with any frequency in Jewish literature until after the fall of Jerusalem. . . . In contrast to the care and concern about legitimate descent and genealogy of the priestly and especially high priestly families in Jewish society at this time, it may be seriously doubted that there existed any families whose descent from the house of David could be confirmed. The point is that the imagery of a Davidic king symbolized substantively what this agent of God would do: liberate and restore the fortunes of Israel, as had the original David (ibid.:91).

Mark's own opposition to the temple-state explains his hostile treatment of the implied restorationist ideology of Davidic "sonship" (below, 10,B,ii,F,i).[1]

Conflict over messianic ideology had to do with what *kind* of kingship was being proposed. In the biblical tradition itself there was a tension between the popular, provisional, and covenantal kingship model of the early Israelite tribal confederacy, and the dynastic, centralized, and hegemonic royal ideol-ogy of Davidism (see 1 Sm 8). Prophetic criticism of Israelite royalty continu-ally raised the political question of legitimacy, arguing that the king's authority was based not upon a dynastic guarantee but rather his fidelity to "covenantal justice." In this sense the prophets were populist advocates:

When Jeremiah repeatedly delivered oracles of Yahweh that announced the punishment and end of the Davidic dynasty along with the destruction of Jerusalem and its temple, he appeared not only as a faithless heretic, but as an absolute traitor. . . . The fall of the Davidic monarchy could not have been as traumatic for the oppressed peasantry as it apparently was for the ruling elite, many of whom were taken into captivity along with the royal family [Horsley and Hanson, 1985:97f.].

Davidic/Messianic "restoration" thus meant different things to different classes. At the time of the Maccabean restoration of an Israelite monarchy, for example, "the fact that the Hasmonean high priests aggrandized their position by assuming the title of king provoked among their enemies, especially among the Pharisees and the Essenes, a revived expectation of the restoration of the true royal line, the House of David" (R. Brown, 1977:506).

In Mark's time the discourse of popular kingship from the perspective of the Roman colonizers obviously functioned subversively. The priestly aristocracy, if they were interested in it at all, saw native kingship in terms of the widening of their institutional power and privilege. To some of the leaders of the revolt, restored kingship may have articulated a vision of independence, perhaps even expansive regional hegemony, as under the Maccabees. But to the peasant masses it would have been the symbol for the establishing of justice and equality in Israel. It is this latter perspective that is adopted by Mark, who identifies the messianic vocation not with ruling class dynastic-royal ideology, but rather with apocalyptic resistance ideology and prophetic solidarity with the poor. Mark's Messianism thus repudiates the "son of David" designation in favor of Daniel's "Human One" (below, 8,C,ii, D,ii).

Mark's Gospel suggests a community influenced by each of these popular forms of resistance. Aspects of these movements and the environment that produced them are reflected throughout his text: from the murdered oracular prophet John to the sicarius assassin Barabbas; from the "false" sign-prophets to the true prophetic symbolics of Jesus; from the ideologically significant space of the wilderness to the politically charged atmosphere of Jerusalem at Passover. Above all we see it in the struggle over messianic discourse and practice that pervades the narrative.

2D. THE HISTORICAL MOMENT OF MARK: THE REVOLT OF 66–70 C.E.

In light of the above, we can see that the forces at play in Palestine on the eve of the revolt were much more diverse and complex than suggested by the standard portraits. Recent historical studies have made two things clear: (1) resistance to Roman domination took a wide variety of forms, and often was quite unconnected to the politics of the literate groups; (2) subversive activity was in most cases also directed at structures of class oppression within Jewish

Palestine. Nor can we any longer attribute every incident of sporadic resistance during this era to an alleged "Zealot party":

> A unified and decades-old liberation front . . . seen to be a modern fiction with no basis in historical evidence. . . . This view has served an important function in the concerns of many modern theologians and biblical scholars. As the supposed fanatical advocates of violent revolution against the Romans, the "Zealots" served as a convenient foil over against which to portray Jesus of Nazareth as a sober prophet of pacifist love [Horsley and Hanson, 1985:xv,xiv].

On the contrary, once we learn to read the discourse of popular movements of dissent in Palestine, it will reveal that Mark's Jesus had much in common with these currents of popular dissent, and can be historically interpreted only in light of them.

As already stipulated (above, A,i), it is one of my central theses that Mark was written during the period of the Jewish revolt. Because of the importance of this historical moment, both to an understanding of Mark and to the era itself, I will in this section depart from my synchronic account of this era to offer a brief portrait of the events of the war period. Drawing from the Rhoads narrative and the Horsley and Hanson narrative, both based upon the histories of Josephus, I divide the short four-year period of "liberated Judea" into two parts: the pre-Zealot provisional government and the rise of the Zealot coalition. This serves to emphasize the internal struggles of the insurrection, which will prevent us from taking a simplistic view of the dynamics of the revolt.

i. The First Two Years: The Provisional Governments

Several factors conspired to make the revolt inevitable: the poor economic and political performance of, and endemic corruption within, the Roman colonial administration; the equivocation and exploitation of the collaborating Jewish elite; and the diverse currents of resurgent Jewish nationalism and peasant disillusionment. Since the near debacle in 40 C.E. under Emperor Caligula, Jewish-Roman relationships had been increasingly volatile. They deteriorated under the procurator Cumanus (48–52 C.E.), fed by the fact that the Jews (probably including the Christians) had recently been expelled from Rome. Palestine now saw the first armed clashes between Roman regulars and Jewish brigands since the uprisings of 6 C.E. Josephus reports a sharp rise in social banditry throughout the countryside under the next three procurators. Finally, under Florus (64–66 C.E.), rural resistance reached epidemic proportions, especially in Galilee, where Roman military attempts at suppression only increased rebel sentiment.

In the spring of 66, fighting broke out between Jews and Greeks in the coastal city of Caesarea; pogroms followed in several cities in the region.

Florus, in May, under orders from Emperor Nero, attempted to expropriate funds from the temple treasury in Jerusalem. Mass demonstrations resulted, in which Jewish civilians were ruthlessly put down by Roman crack troops, who also tried to storm the temple. Clerical leadership was radicalized, and attempts to dissuade them from breaking with Rome by Agrippa II failed. Rhoads describes what happened in June:

> With the populace in a rebellious mood, the control of the city left in the hands of the high priests supported by a Roman garrison, and Agrippa banished from the city—the lower priests took action which was tantamount to a declaration of war. Led by the Temple captain, Eleazar, son of Ananias, and supported by the revolutionary leaders of the populace, they decided to refuse any further gifts or offerings from gentiles— including the sacrifices offered twice daily on behalf of the Roman empire and emperor [1976:74].

The revolt had begun.

It is true that the various tributaries to the Jewish insurgency were neither well organized nor coordinated: the rural social brigands, the urban terrorist groups, and their more moderate sympathizers among the aristocracy and literate groups, represented disparate interests. Still, the revolt would have been short-lived had it merely been a spontaneous uprising among various sectors. In fact, a provisional government was established in, and the war was prosecuted from, Jerusalem, and became a central point of reference for all Jewish social groups, within and outside Palestine, Mark's community included. The atmosphere of polarization made neutrality increasingly impossible between the Jewish liberation struggle and the forces of imperial law and order.

But almost from the beginning the provisional government in Jerusalem was racked by internal struggles for power, as the contradictions among the various rebel protagonists became political rifts. From this perspective, the drama of the revolt was as much centered around the warring factions in the city as around direct military engagement with the Romans. There were unquestionably elements of class conflict present in the insurrection.

According to Rhoads's reconstruction of events (1976:100 ff.), Eleazar's attempt to exclude the traditional high priestly aristocracy from the temple cult resulted in civil war. In August, sicarii from around Judea joined with Eleazar and successfully dislodged the clerics from control of the upper city, putting the Roman procurator and the royal collaborators to flight. The rebels promptly burned the public archives, where the records of debt were kept. This action again indicates the character of the insurrection also as a protest against socioeconomic oppression. A sicarius leader by the name of Menahem took over leadership and attacked Herod's palace, but then attempted to impose himself as king (below, 10,B,i). This bid was rejected and Menahem killed, his troops taking refuge in nearby Masada. Eleazar reassumed leadership and negotiated the surrender of the remaining Roman forces—and then massacred them.

In October 66 the first Roman attempt to quell the revolt by mounting a siege of Jerusalem failed, resulting in a route of the imperial forces (below, 11,A,ii). This unexpected victory brought some in the aristocracy over to the rebel side, and the traditional high priestly caste recaptured control of the government and cult. Another Eleazar, son of Simon, and a priest, now assumed an important role in the provisional government. The extent to which the aristocratic leadership was actually consolidating the revolt is questionable, however; it may well be that "by ostensibly assuming the leadership of the revolt (including preparation of defenses against the inevitable attack by Rome), they attempted to control and channel the rebellious energies of the people until they could negotiate with the Romans" (Horsley and Hanson, 1985:43).

Meanwhile, Josephus was dispatched by the provisional government to command rebel forces in Galilee. Josephus complains that he found it difficult to coordinate and win the trust of the various brigand bands, but this was probably due to the fact that his own loyalty to the revolt was suspect:

> Because of their own military strength, political leverage on the Galilean peasantry, and their alliances with other rebel forces, the brigand groups constituted the most important insurrectionary force in Galilee. Josephus' real strategy was to control the Galilean situation, with the assistance of its gentry, and to avoid direct military action against the Romans until negotiations with them were possible. . . . The result, of course, was a standoff between the brigands (who must have been aware of his double game) and Josephus himself with the Galilean notables, who were attempting to hold the lid on the rebellion. That standoff ended when the Romans reconquered Galilee the following summer (67), and Josephus was able to desert to the enemy and write his memoirs [Horsley and Hanson, 1985:80].

Sporadic brigandage continued in Galilee after repacification, but the main rebel forces fled south to take the last stand in liberated Jerusalem.

ii. The Second Two Years: The Zealot Coalition

The Romans relentlessly pursued a policy of scorched earth in their pacification of the rebel areas. They spared only those who offered full collaboration (usually the local aristocracy); those (usually peasants) unable to flee were slaughtered or enslaved. Not unlike the effects of the "strategic hamlet" tactics of modern U.S. counterinsurgency:

> The Romans in effect created the phenomenon of dispossessed fugitives forced to plunder their own former territories now in the hands of the pro-Roman factions. These brigands now had virtually no alternative but to fight against the Roman advance. . . . Once they had fled, it was

impossible for them to return to their villages and towns, which had either been destroyed or were now in the hands of their wealthy enemies who had deserted to the Romans. . . . The brigand groups formed and operated in areas which the Romans had not yet completely "pacified." But as the Roman forces advanced farther into Judea, the brigand bands were eventually forced to seek refuge in the fortress-city of Jerusalem itself [ibid.:222f.].

Horsley and Hanson contend that it is this influx of desperate and disillusioned rural rebels that accounts for the ascendancy of a Zealot coalition in Jerusalem.

Under the leadership of Eleazar ben Simon, the Zealots overthrew the provisional government in a coup in the winter of 67–68. They then began a systematic purge of the aristocratic elements remaining in Jerusalem, commencing what from the perspective of Josephus was a "reign of terror," resulting in the wholesale defection of those who had economic interests to protect:

Many people were inclined to desert to the Romans; some of them sold even their most valuable possessions for relatively little, and swallowed pieces of gold, that they might not be discovered by the rebels. Then when they had escaped to the Romans, they emptied their bowels, and thereby had abundant means with which to provide for themselves. And Titus allowed many of them to resettle wherever they wished around the country. . . . But the rebels and their leaders were more vigilant for these deserters that went with the Romans. If someone was at all suspected, his throat was immediately cut [*War*, V,x,i].

Josephus mentions that the particular focus of the Zealot purge was the Herodian nobility, with whom old scores were settled. "The Zealots, no matter how much their struggle was against the alien Roman oppressors, were first fighting a class war against their own Jewish nobility" (Horsley and Hanson, 1985:225f.).

The socio-economic dimensions of Zealot radicalism are also indicated by the direct challenge to the priestly elite by electing a commoner, by lot, to the position of high priest. Here was a move by rural dissidents to overthrow the control of the urban clergy over the temple state, and an attempt to establish a more democratic and popular administration of the temple state. This resulted in yet another civil war within the city, in which the priestly establishment mounted forces that drove the Zealots back into the temple precincts. The Zealots then called upon rural supporters from the southern province of Idumea, who responded by entering the city and reestablishing Zealot control. More purges followed, directed at the former leaders of the provisional government, who were (probably rightly) suspected of plotting to surrender the city to the Romans.

Internal power struggles, however, continued to plague the Zealots. A brigand chief from Galilee, John of Gischala, vied for sole leadership. Meanwhile, another Judean brigand, Simon bar Giora, was amassing formidable forces in the countryside, and surviving members of the local Jerusalem power structure conspired to persuade Simon to overthrow the Zealots. With the second Roman siege of the city imminent, in the spring of 69 Simon launched his counter-coup and successfully forced the Zealots back into the temple:

> For a time there was a three-way battle raging, with the main body of the Zealots in the inner court of the temple above, John of Gischala and his followers in the temple courtyard in between, and Simon bar Giora in control of most of the rest of the city [ibid.:219].

Throughout the rise and fall of provisional governments, the temple was the center of the struggle for political control.

Once the final siege began under the Roman General Titus, the factions were forced to cooperate. But lack of resources and slow starvation beleaguered those now trapped in the city, as the Romans cut off all avenues of escape and resupply. According to Josephus's unabashedly pro-Roman account, Titus took great pains to persuade the remaining rebels to give up and avoid the desecration of their city and temple (*War*, VI,ii–iii). After several unsuccessful attempts to storm the temple, the Romans burned it to the ground and looted it. The city was plundered, the rebel leaders executed, and a great part of the population enslaved. The revolt was crushed.

It is unhelpful to caricature the war either as the misguided fanaticism of a few malcontents, as did Josephus and later imperial scholars who relied upon his account, or on the other hand as a heroic and progressive insurgency of popular forces. This period of "liberation" was relatively brief, largely restricted to Judea, and riddled with contradictions. But all of Palestine, whether actively in solidarity with the revolt or not, was profoundly impacted by the war. The poor, as usual, suffered greatly, especially the peasantry of Galilee. Distant from the drama of power-broking and ideological struggle in Jerusalem, they were left defenseless before the avenging wrath of the Roman counterinsurgency program, betrayed on the one hand by their regional rebel commander Josephus who defected to the Romans, and on the other by brigand leaders such as John who abandoned Galilee to join the struggle in Jerusalem. It is not difficult to understand, therefore, that someone such as Mark, writing from the perspective of the Galilean poor, might well have brooked little hope in the insurrection.

2E. SOCIO-CULTURAL TENSIONS: THE SYMBOLIC ORDER

To return to my structural portrait of Roman Palestine, an essential aspect of the social formation, which is perhaps more important than any other for a political reading of Mark, is the dominant ideological system and its vehicles within Palestinian Judaism. Here I wish to nuance Elliott's matrix with yet another matrix model of Belo, whose analysis of the "symbolic order" is his most important contribution (1981:37ff). By symbolic order Belo means the values and norms—in the language of social semiotics, "cultural codes"—both implicit and explicit, which regulated and represented social life and meaning. In this section I will try to interpret Belo's basic insights, modifying and expanding his model. Throughout this discussion, it is necessary for the reader to keep in mind that in cross-cultural interpretation, the symbolic order is usually difficult to comprehend because its intelligibility relies entirely upon a semantic and social universe foreign to ours. For this reason, I begin with a brief hermeneutic discussion of "socio-symbolics" from an anthropological perspective, that extends and applies what I have discussed in chapter 1.

i. What Is a Symbolic Order?

As we have seen (above, 1,C), symbols as expressions of social order, anxiety, or meaning are everywhere used in modern society, but largely unacknowledged. Anthropologist M. Douglas is foremost among interpreters of the "concordance between symbolic and social experience," which according to her is usually articulated through the natural symbols of the human body and its parts (1973:16).

Though I find her "grid and group" sociological modeling overschematic, her general thesis is instructive—namely, that every society has symbolic systems that function in the following basic ways:

1. defining and reproducing social power through the symbolics of hierarchy and organization;

2. maintaining group boundaries through the symbolics of "danger" or taboo;

3. ordering and giving social meaning to the chaotic universe of material things through the symbolics of "contagion."

Ideological discourse then lends overall coherency and plausibility to the symbolic order, which is both a reproduction of, and shaping force in, concrete economic, political, and social relationships.

The symbolic order of capitalism is a complex network of assumptions about the relative value of material things (natural and fabricated) and persons, from the high abstractions of "cold war" political dualisms, to U.S. immigration law's floating definitions of "insiders" and "outsiders" (depending upon economic conditions), to the way in which an American middle-class kitchen is organized. Every national holiday and patriotic event, every ritual of pomp and parade, every liturgy of remembrance or election serves to remind us of this system. Its structures and discourses socialize individuals and groups to conceive of their vocation according to prescribed values and limits set by class, race, and gender.

Social anthropologist K. Burridge speaks of institutional vehicles of the symbolic order as "redemptive media," through which the discharge of obligations is facilitated (1969:6). The U.S. Constitution for example might be seen as a redemptive medium. It functions (ostensibly) to define and guarantee individual and collective "rights"—an invisible but socially efficacious symbolic notion. This "sacred" document is a representation of the ideology of "liberty and justice for all." It is not hard to understand how groups that take (or are given) the task of administrating and interpreting the redemptive media accrue considerable social power. Thus in our society the powerful groups include politicians and lawyers (not unlike Mark's Palestine, in which the redemptive medium of Torah was controlled by the scribal class; see below, iv).

In considering the symbolic order of ancient Palestinian Judaism we will encounter the discourse of "debt" and "purity." The cultural code of debt articulated social organization and hierarchy, and is not entirely alien to our modern social formations. Unlike the Israelite notion of debt, however, which was rooted in the practice of reciprocity and gift-exchange (below, iii), our modern debt code is based upon an ideology of social contract and a political economy of market-exchange. Thus we instinctively think of debt in economic terms. Whereas in ancient Palestine social power was exclusively determined by kinship and class, today it is usually based upon material accumulation. Thus the "captains of industry" gain prestige according to ability to control markets and labor, rather than traditional assets such as physical strength, family line, or even education (though all these things can help). Yet in fact debt does include notions of legal obligation and moral duty in our social world. There are the imperatives of "citizenship," expressed as what we "owe to the country," such as military or civic service, and in the name of social contract, we cede social or political power to qualified "authorities."

Modern persons have a much greater difficulty appreciating the concept of purity. Malina describes it as:

> Specifically about the general cultural map of social time and space, about arrangements within the space thus defined, and especially about the boundaries separating the inside from the outside. The unclean or impure is something that does not fit the space in which it is found, that belongs elsewhere, that causes confusion in the arrangement of the generally accepted social map because it overruns boundaries [1981: 125].

Purity first concerns ordering the material world around us. The Mosaic law, with its elaborate rituals concerning cleansing, appears odd to the modern worldview—few of us find Leviticus intelligible, much less inspiring. We think of "taboo" as relegated to archaic religion; yet if I come and dump a pile of dirt or manure on the living room carpet of a suburban home, there will certainly be a reaction of horror.

Douglas rejects the argument that this reaction is based not upon a symbolic system but concern for "hygiene and aesthetics":

Dirt is the by-product of a systemic ordering and classification of matter, in so far as ordering involves rejecting inappropriate elements. This idea of dirt takes us straight into the field of symbolism and promises a link-up with more obviously symbolic systems of purity. We can recognise in our own notions of dirt that we are using a kind of omnibus compendium which includes all the rejected elements of ordered systems. It is a relative idea. Shoes are not dirty in themselves, but it is dirty to place them on the dining room table; food is not dirty in itself, but it is dirty to leave cooking utensils in the bedroom, or food bespattered on clothing; similarly, bathroom equipment in the drawing room . . . out-door things indoors . . . under-clothing appearing where over-clothing should be, and so on. In short, our pollution behaviour is the reaction which condemns any object or idea likely to confuse or contradict cherished classifications [1966:35f.].

Douglas offers similar modern analogies to the segregation of the anomalous in the Levitical distinctions between certain cloven footed animals (ibid.:41ff.).

Notions of "clean and unclean" (or order and chaos) in the material world also apply to the body politic, functioning to establish and maintain group boundaries and communal identity. Our "advanced" social mores still tend to prefer segregation of the physically and mentally disabled. Expected modes of dress and behavior in certain places, which we call "etiquette," in fact function to enforce a bourgeois purity code of class separation. Today group boundaries are no less efficacious for being implicit. A white matron who roams freely on the wide avenues of the suburbs would walk furtively and anxiously on the sidewalks of a black urban ghetto—if she ventured there at all. Indeed, de facto racial segregation is the norm in most parts of the U.S.A. today despite the absence of state sanction. And, as in ancient Israel, modern purity codes function politically as well as socially. The very same myths of "chosenness" that shape patriotic ideologies in the U.S.A. also shape the dreams of neo-Nazi white supremacists and the social codes of Afrikaaner apartheid. And what about the socio-symbolic apparatus of our national security state, with its "priesthood" of the security-cleared and its "holy places" surrounded by barbed wire?

This brief discussion has been intended to make the notion of socio-symbolic codes, so crucial to a political understanding of the gospel, more meaningful to the reader. Obviously there are vast differences between our symbolic order and that of ancient Judaism. But we must learn to see the analogies; as Douglas puts it, when it comes to purity there "are no special distinctions between primitives and moderns: we are all subject to the same rules" (ibid.:40). Only by a critical consciousness of our own symbolic order (elaborating what is culturally invisible), she says, can we be true social critics:

The elaborated code provides a means of assessing the value of one kind of social process, the codes derived from it, and the values and principles that go with both. . . . The elaborated code challenges its users to turn round on themselves and inspect their values. . . . This would seem to be the only way to use our knowledge to free ourselves from the power of our own cosmology. No one would deliberately choose the elaborated code and the personal control system who is aware of the seeds of alienation it contains [1973:190].

Interestingly, Douglas is especially critical of the failure of contemporary theology to provide this critical function: "The theologians who should be providing for us more precise and meaningful categories of thought are busy demolishing meaningless rituals and employing the theological toolchest to meet the demands of anti-ritualists" (ibid.:188). This confirms my contention (above, 1,C,iii) that the proper vocation of theology is not demythologization, but critique, creation, and redemption of socio-symbolic discourse. This is exactly what Mark's Jesus was about in his context.

ii. The Symbolic Order of Ancient Judaism: A Matrix Model

I return now to a consideration of Belo's model of the dominant symbolic order of Palestinian Judaism. As noted, he builds it around the two interpenetrating and mutually reinforcing systems of debt and pollution (purity).

The debt code regulated social aggression and formed the basis of the covenant paradigm with Yahweh, including the Ten Commandments and other socio-ethical elements of the law. It was originally rooted in the primitive peasant political economy of reciprocity, and sought to promote justice and equity in the community. As Belo exposits it:

The earth which humans till and on which they live with their livestock can only *receive* the rain which is given to it to make it fruitful; thus a *gift* is the source of fruitful blessing. This basic fact explains the *principle of extension* that rests on the notion of giving; it says that what Yahweh has given to human beings, they must in turn give to their fellow humans who lack it. . . . The victims [sacrifices] and tithes given to Yahweh, the sabbath and feasts on which people stop working so that they may give the time to Yahweh—these simply make evident the gift that lies behind people's work and their abundance at table. . . . At the same time, the giving of people helps them avoid coveting the abundance of others— their property, their lives, their blessings. Giving thus forestalls violence against the neighbor, the brother, the equal. This equality between people and "houses" is the purpose of the principle of extension: "Let there be no poor among you" (Dt 15:4) [1981:50].

The pollution code had its ideological basis in Israel as a "holy" people, set apart from the surrounding cultures and their contrary (idolatrous) social practices. Thus the great variety of complex rituals essentially functioned for

the same purpose: to reinforce group boundaries. At the same time, as we have
seen, the socio-symbolic taboos functioned to maintain internal order in the
world. This will have specific importance when we examine Jesus' symbolic
action (below, 4,B).

Belo observes that these two systems operated in three basic social spheres or
"sites": the "table" (e.g., the production and consumption of goods), the
"house" (e.g., kinship and community relations), and the "sanctuary" (e.g.,
the temple cultus and the priesthood). I have expanded these sites into land/
table, village/house, and synagogue/sanctuary, in order to suggest correlation
to recurring narrative sites in Mark's Gospel (see below, 4,B,iii). By laying out
this matrix, one is able to locate within it virtually every element in the Levitical
code as in Diagram 2. It helps us see the function of the ideological system in all
spheres of social existence.

Diagram 2
Elements of the Levitical Code

	Pollution/purity	Debt/gift
Land/ table	dietary taboo (Lv 11,17)	tithe; Jubilee/Sabbath (Lv 23, 25, 27)
Village/ house	sexual/body relations (Lv 12–15)	socio-ethical statutes (Lv 18–20)
Synagogue/ sanctuary	idolatry/blasphemy; priests (Lv 21–22, 24, 26)	cultus; sacrifice (Lv 1–10)

The two main institutional "vehicles" in which the symbolic order was
objectified and in which its authority was invested were the law (Torah) and the
temple, which represented, respectively, the covenant and presence of Israel's
God. As the primary redemptive media, they defined (in the case of law) and
controlled (in the case of temple, through propitiatory sacrifice and other
symbolic actions) debt and impurity in the body politic. S. Isenberg (1973) has
shown how the various factions among the elite in Roman Palestine competed
for influence and control over the symbolic order in order to increase their
social and political standing. Other groups simply struggled for access to the
redemptive media, or disputed the authority of the elite over them. Occasionally a group would challenge the system as a whole as well as its stewards; Mark
is a case in point. Even Mark, however, is selective; he rejects the temple as an
institution, but not the Torah, instead challenging the elite in their interpretations of the sacred texts. Let us briefly look at some of these social tensions in
relation to the dominant ideological systems.

iii. Purity and Debt

J. Neyrey, similarly drawing from Douglas's anthropology, has provided an excellent sketch of specific Jewish "purity maps" as they relate to Mark (1986). He argues that from the rabbinic literature we can reconstruct several socio-symbolic systems: "Jews could be identified by special *times* (Sabbath), special *things* (diet) and special *bodily marks* (circumcision)" (ibid.:100). In *m. Kelim* (1:6–9) a hierarchy of places is given in order of ascending holiness: "The *Land of Israel* is holier than any other land," after which come the walled cities of Israel, space within the walls of Jerusalem, the temple mount, the rampart, the court of women, the court of the Israelites, the court of the priests, between the porch and the altar, the sanctuary, and the Holy of Holies (ibid.:95). We cannot miss here the center-periphery structure of this map, and its geopolitical implications for both Mark's world and his story-scape (above, B,iii).

The *t. Megillah* (2:7) ranks *persons* according to purity: (1) priests; (2) Levites; (3) Israelites; (4) converts; (5) freed slaves; (6) disqualified priests (illegitimate children of priests); (7) *netins* (temple slaves); (8) *mamzers* (bastards); (9) eunuchs; (10) those with damaged testicles; (11) those without a penis (ibid.). The place on this list of the physically impaired (not to mention the general exclusion of women) should be kept in mind when we examine Jesus' attitude toward such disenfranchised groups (below, 4,B,ii; C). In *m. Kelim* (1:3) there is a relativizing of pollution derived from contact with *things*: impurity contracted from a dead thing is exceeded by that from a menstruant, which is exceeded by bodily issues such as semen, urine, spittle, and so on. Finally, *times* are ordered in the Mishnah, with Sabbath considered most sacred, followed by Passover, Day of Atonement, Feast of Tabernacles, festival days, Rosh ha-Shana, and so forth (ibid.:99).

These various maps are all assumed in the world of the Gospel, in which almost every episode narrates Jesus' transgression or criticism of these boundaries and divisions. Oppenheimer, in his careful social history of the late second-temple period, draws the following important conclusion concerning the purity code:

> The great strictness characterizing matters of ritual purity and impurity, the difficulty of complying with it, the danger of transferring ritual impurity from one person or object to another, all this led to a situation whereby ritual impurity became the guiding principle in the division of Jewish society into classes [1977:18].

He points out that the sheer "profusion of these laws, and the difficulty of observing them" inevitably marginalized the masses. The major obstacles to rigorous conformity to the demands of the symbolic system for ordinary persons were economic. The daily circumstances of their lives and trades, especially for the peasantry, continually exposed them to contagion, and they simply could not afford the outlay of either time or money/goods involved in ritual cleansing processes.

Groups wishing to control the redemptive medium of purity recognized these practical difficulties, and responded in sharply divergent ways. The Pharisees attempted to extend the purity code to the masses by liberalizing it in order to facilitate observation, a program that relied upon the elaborate interpolations of their oral tradition and their distinctive rituals. This contrasted sharply with the strategy of the Sadducean elite, which assumed that only the priestly caste could, and therefore should, comply with the demands of purity. Predictably, the Sadducees refused to recognize the legitimacy of Pharisaic oral tradition, for it threatened their exclusive hegemony over the symbolic order.

The economic and political self-interest that lay behind this competition is neatly demonstrated in the following example offered by William Herzog:

> According to Leviticus 11:38 if water is poured upon seed it becomes unclean. The passage, however, does not distinguish between seed planted in the soil and seed detached from the soil. . . . In years of poor harvests, a frequent occurrence owing to poor soil, drought, warfare, locust plagues and poor methods of farming, this text was a source of dispute. Why? During such lean years, grain was imported from Egypt. But the Egyptians irrigated their fields (putting water on seed) so that their grain was suspect, perhaps even unclean. The Sadducees judged that such grain was unclean and anyone consuming it also became unclean. They were quite willing to pay skyrocketing prices commanded by scarce domestic grain because they could afford it. . . . One senses economic advantage being sanctioned, since the Sadducees were often large landowners whose crops increased in value during such times. By contrast, the Pharisees argued that the Pentateuchal ordinance applied only to seed detached from the soil; therefore . . . one could be observant and still purchase Egyptian grain [1982:13].

The elitism of the Sadducees' position is obvious; the Pharisaic position is more ambiguous.

The Pharisees were certainly committed to making piety possible for the masses as the above example indicates, and in that sense promoted greater access to the redemptive media. But this could be—and was—seen as a strategy of courting the artisan and lower classes in order to build a regional and popular base of socio-political power over against the Jerusalem elite. And in their alternative program, the Pharisees preserved not only their privilege but their indispensability as adjudicants of the system. Their actual social solidarity with the poor was minimal, as reflected in their own observance of strict purity regulations for table fellowship. It is this reproduction of the elitist system under the guise of popular piety that Mark objects to in his negative portrayal of the Pharisees in the Gospel.

The Essenes responded in yet a third fashion. For them the solution to dilemmas of purity lay not in a lower common denominator, or in elitism, but in a withdrawal from the social mainstream in order to preserve rigorous observance. They criticized the Pharisees for what they saw as "liberalism," and the Sadducees for their self-interested classism. All three responses, however, have one crucial thing in common: the purity code itself is upheld as central. None of these strategies seemed able to prevent the code, which was originally intended to promote the social solidarity and identity of the people of God, from engendering further social stratification. Mark realized that as long as the system remained intact, the ability of persons to meet their obligations would be determined by, and thus enforce, their class standing.

The debt system was the realm of the priestly class, not only because of their role in the sacrificial cult, but perhaps more importantly because of their oversight in the collecting of tithes. I have already mentioned (above, B,ii) the economic burden of the tithe structure fell upon the food producers, and this was cause for resentment among the peasantry. They could see that many of the clergy receiving tithes were no longer really dependent upon them, as in the primitive stages of the redistributive system at the time of Moses. In fact, in many cases they were landowners, making the tithes not only gratuitous but redistributive in the wrong direction!

Serious conflicts also arose over who should control the distribution of the various tithes. Most producers could not afford the annual journey to Jerusalem to take in the tithes, so the Jerusalem clergy tried to control local distribution, often to the disadvantage of local priests and Levites (who had been disenfranchised to a great degree by the Jerusalem power base). Josephus gives accounts of this conflict in action: in two separate instances during the reign of Agrippa II he tells of the slaves of the high priest coming and forcibly removing tithes from the threshing floor. This expropriation caused poorer local priests to starve (*Ant.,* XX,viii,8; ix,2).

Oppenheimer shows how the halakic tradition (early rabbinic writings and legislation based upon Pharisaic practice) insisted on the right of the producer to determine distribution of tithes. This indicates that the Pharisees were again in conflict with central clerical control. Again, however, their program cut both ways for the peasant, for there is also halakic evidence of peasant resistance to Pharisaic attempts to enforce Sabbath regulations that prohibited sowing or harvesting on the seventh day and in the seventh year. These restrictions presented obvious hardships for the subsistence economy of the peasant, who could expect no relief from the state in hard times.

Another example was the problem of the Sabbatical release of debts. Peasants needed to obtain loans to pay their tax and tithe obligations, but:

> Potential creditors were reluctant to make loans in the last few years prior to the sabbatical year. . . . This was the context and the purpose of the *prosbul* established by the Pharisaic sage Hillel, under Herod's reign. . . . Hillel designed a legal ruse by which the provisions of the law

of sabbatical release of debts could be bypassed. . . . The short-term effect of such a provision was surely relief for hungry and overtaxed peasants.The long-range effect was permanent debt [Horsley and Hanson, 1985:59f.]

The Pharisees in these ways put themselves in a position to wrest from the Jerusalem clergy some of the economic control over the rural classes.

iv. Torah and Temple

With the emergence of the synagogue system, Torah was increasingly central to the symbolic order. It was the domain of the scribal class, which Jeremias tells us consisted of both Pharisees and Sadducees, higher and lower clergy (1969: chap. 10). The scribes dominated the Sanhedrin, which held ultimate juridical authority in Israel. This "exclusive class of Sages enjoying special privileges by reason of their engaging in study" (of Torah) maintained considerable social power and prestige (Oppenheimer, 1977:1).

The struggle over Torah interpretation was a major source of social conflict among the social groups:

A fixed, written scripture requires interpretation. The authority to interpret was disputed by the various groups, and it is no wonder, for those who have the authority to interpret have the closest possible relation to the power of God, a position which may be and was translated into enormous political and economic power. . . . It is not surprising that the basic dispute between Pharisees and Sadducees was over authority to interpret revelation and that the Essenes also claimed such exclusive authority [Isenberg, 1973:31].

Of particular concern was the Pharisaic oral tradition, which represented a directly competing basis of ideological authority, for they claimed it to be parallel with Torah and traced its origins back to Moses. This confirms the social basis of the ongoing dispute between Sadducean "biblical conservatism" and Pharisaic tradition (see below, 7,C,ii). Meanwhile, apocalyptic movements, which felt excluded from the redemptive media altogether, fought back with "secret" revelations and esoteric interpretive schemes of scripture. It is of utmost significance that Mark affirms the Hebrew scriptures while rejecting the rest of the dominant symbolic order; in his Gospel we see him vying with scribes, Pharisees, and Sadducees over the issue of hermeneutic authority.

S. Safrai (1976) argues that even though synagogues began to decentralize the symbolic system, even synagogue liturgy focused on the temple. Cult was indisputably the center of the symbolic order, as was true of every major social formation in Middle East antiquity. The Jerusalem temple had an imposing stature, both literally as a building and as the heart of the Jewish nation:

It was firmly believed that the Temple was destined to exist eternally, just like heaven and earth. . . . With the destruction of the Temple the image of the universe was rendered defective, the established framework of the nation was undermined [Safrai and Stern, 1977:906].

It was where God dwelt, and in it the whole ideological order was anchored and legitimated. It was the one holy place universal to all Jews, toward which all pilgrimages and contributions were directed. Politically the temple served as a constant reminder of the tradition of Davidic kingship and an independent Israel, for which reason it naturally lay at the heart of dreams of liberation from Rome.

J. Lundquist has shown how temple construction and maintenance was quintessential to the process of "state formation" in the ancient Near East:

Only with the completion of the temple in Jerusalem is the process of imperial state formation completed, making Israel in the fullest sense "like the other nations." The ideology of kingship in the archaic state is indelibly and incontrovertibly connected with the temple building and with temple ideology [1982:272].

He then notes the four elements of the "primordial landscape" that are "reproduced architecturally and ritually in ancient Near Eastern temple traditions": (1) the cosmic mountain; (2) the primordial hillock that first emerged from the waters of creation; (3) the spring waters of life, symbolizing both chaos and salvation; (4) the tree of life (ibid.: 274). These aspects of symbolic discourse in Oriental antiquity were appropriated by Israel, and will be directly relevant to our reading of Mark (below, 10,C). Finally, Lundquist confirms that the Jerusalem temple stood as the center of the Israelite symbolic order, and thus eventually the spatial and geographical heart of the nation as well (ibid.: 284ff.).

Economically the temple dominated Jerusalem, and to a lesser extent all of Judea. Though originally intended as the "central storehouse" of the redistributive economy, it had come to represent massive capital accumulation:

From the tithes and other dues to the priesthood and temple, through repayment and interest on loans, and even through the contributions which Diaspora Jews from around the world sent to the Temple, surplus wealth flowed into, and piled up in, Jerusalem. There were no mechanisms, however, by which these resources could be channeled to the people most in need. . . . Rather, some of the surplus wealth was used on luxury goods or simply stored in the temple treasury, in the form of valuable metals or objects [Horsley and Hanson, 1985:61].

Temple trade undergirded the thriving commercial sphere in Jerusalem, and provided both revenue for and contributions to the welfare of the city. Its maintenance and renovation generated countless jobs upon which the urban population depended (Theissen, 1976).

Needless to say, as the primary domain of the native ruling and high priestly castes, the temple was the theater of constant political posturing. It is not hard to see why the first act of revolutionary defiance in 66 c.e. was the suspension of the daily sacrifices on behalf of Rome; why the rebel factions competed for control over the temple during the provisional government; and why the last part of Jerusalem to fall to the Roman siege in 70 was the temple mount. Obviously, every Jewish social group and strategy had to take an ideological stance in relation to the temple. The Essenes, who otherwise wholly rejected the authority of the Jerusalem clergy and its social order, remained committed to the eschatological purification of the temple. However much rebel groups may have been motivated by a desire to overthrow the temple aristocracy, there is no evidence that they fundamentally questioned the legitimacy of the temple-state itself.

But for Mark, the temple state and its political economy represented the heart of what was *wrong* with the dominant system. He had no wish for greater access to, or control over, the cultus—only its demise. In the same breath, he was at pains to reassure his Palestinian readers that God's existence was not tied to the temple.

2F. IDEOLOGICAL AND SOCIAL STRATEGIES

The final task of this portrait is to indicate the strategies of the main social groups within the Palestinian formation of this era. B. Holzner writes:

> Any dominant ideology, especially one maintained defensively by a group threatened by change or by hostile forces, tends to emphasize collective identities and group boundaries. . . . In the integrated social system every segment must somehow come to terms with the dominant ideology, and its projections of collective identity [1972:157].

Of particular interest will be attitudes toward the colonial arrangement that simultaneously demanded "membership" in the Roman empire and "membership" in the house of Israel. I will first look at the groups that accommodated and collaborated with the dominant order (legitimating strategies). Then, drawing upon Holzner's three types of subversive strategies (escapist, loyalistically radical, and confrontative/alienative), I will mention attempts to reform or resist that order.

i. Colonialism and Collaboration

The ideological strategy of Roman colonialism at the time of the high empire, according to a concise study by J. Fears, was "a notably successful attempt to bring a large number of different ethnic groups and their political units under a single government," accomplished largely through a "network of personal alliances with the ruling classes throughout the empire" (1980:98f.). Roman propaganda promoted the divine vocation of Rome to rule the world in peace, backed by military might, guaranteeing its citizens freedom:

> The ideological justification for empire rested firmly and unabashedly on a political theology of victory, or what we might call a clear sense of Manifest Destiny. . . . The Roman Republic and its empire thus rested upon ideological foundations similar to those twin pillars of the modern nation-state: democracy and nationalism [ibid.:99,101]

By the first century c.e., however, the original republican mythology of pre-Caesarian Rome had fully succumbed to the cult of the charismatic autocrat, the emperor. I recommend to the reader Klaus Wengst's recent study of the ideological legitimation of the "Pax Romana" for the best summary analysis of the military, political, economic, legal, and cultural dimensions of imperial Rome (1987:7ff.). He correctly argues that we cannot understand what I am calling the war of myths in the New Testament without an appreciation of the rhetoric of Roman apologists and propagandists, and the brutal realities they masked.

The imperial cult was the most important ideological vehicle in the provinces:

> Official Roman imperial propaganda was a highly sophisticated political tool. Public festivals of all sorts, local celebrations, religious feasts, and most particularly, imperial anniversaries and other imperial occasions provided a number of opportunities in each year for public ovations, proclamations, and pageants celebrating the virtues of the Emperor [Fears, 1980:102].

Because the emperor cultus could not formally operate in Jewish Palestine, Jewish feasts as times to affirm loyalty to Rome became all the more crucial. This helps explain why, as relationships between the Jewish state and the Roman colonizers grew increasingly strained, the annual high holy days were almost always occasions of political tension and potential violence.

Rome's strategy of allowing limited internal autonomy was based upon, as in so many neocolonial formations today, the cooperation of the native aristocracy. After the demise of the Hasmoneans, the Herodian royalty and the high priestly aristocracy depended utterly upon Rome's good favor for political survival. Indeed, "the high priestly families which Herod brought in and which monopolized the chief priestly offices right up to the Jewish revolt were, some of them, not even Palestinian Jewish families, but powerful families from the Diaspora" (Horsley and Hanson, 1985:62).

The ideological strategy of the ruling classes reflected their realism. On the one hand they were well aware of the power of Jewish nostalgia for the bygone days of the independent Hasmonean state, and were ever fearful of eruptions of Maccabean sentiment. They endeavored to appease nationalist sentiment by winning small concessions from Rome, and paid lip service to eschatological eulogies of Davidic rule. On the other hand the aristocracy appreciated the fact that the days of Israel's independence were over forever. They made every effort to assure the procurators that they could and would control their own people, knowing that the necessity of Roman intervention would mean further circumscription of their facade of power.

Thus, the collaborative ruling class promoted an ideological synthesis of "cooperative nationalism" in order to satisfy both patriotic longing and imperial overlords. This strategy was typified in many ways by the half-Jew Herod the Great; though he was responsible for the magnificent reconstruction of the Jewish temple in Jerusalem, "yet it was typical of him that he placed a golden eagle, symbol of the Roman Empire, above the entrance gate" (Rhoads, 1976:25).

But attempts at walking a middle road beween Hellenism and Judaism often backfired, as in this case: the eagle was torn down by patriotic Pharisees. Despite the many internecine conflicts among the Jewish elite, Rome recognized that those Jews had a common interest in maintaining stability; consequently their curious theological squabbles were of little concern to the procurators. Overall, the servility of the ruling factions became a powerful ideological asset to Rome, the basis for their political rationalization of the colonial status quo.

At the same time, Rome was vigilant against any and all forms of resistance, and the sight of captured insurgents being crucified was not uncommon throughout Palestine. Any Jewish dissident group that did not accept its fundamental subservience—however seemingly bizarre or harmless its alternative symbolic claims may have seemed to the Latin mind, as with the sign prophet movements—was brutally suppressed by Rome. This served as a sober reminder of the limits of imperial benevolence, and it was not lost upon the Jewish ruling classes. As polarization increased in the early 60s, and the strategy of accommodation became increasingly bankrupt in its tolerance of blatant Roman corruption and provocation, it was still the fear of Roman retaliation that made the elites the last to join, and the first to defect from, the revolt.

ii. Renewal Movements: Reform and Withdrawal

It is fair to say that among the literate Jewish elite of the era, there were two concerted reform movements: the Essenes and Pharisees. The latter first gained notoriety for their resistance to the oppressive policies of the Hasmonean dynasty, and later to Herod as well. It has been difficult for scholars to gain an accurate picture of the Pharisees of the first century. Modern Jewish scholars have rightly disputed the biased and almost wholly negative portrait of the Pharisees in the Christian Gospels, and hence traditional Christian interpretation. Yet these efforts have themselves been polemically apologetic, as S.

Sandmel points out, for "Judaism is in a sense a lineal descendant of Pharisaism" (1978:158).

Three things can be said with reasonable certainty. First, Pharisaism was a vigorous challenge to the elitist clerical classes that made attempts to be populist. Their strategy was not disinterested, however, but rather an effort to build an alternative political base. Their oral tradition was an elaborate legitimating ideology for this project. The triumph of the synagogue Judaism of the rabbis after the fall of the temple in 70 C.E. is testimony to the success of this strategy. Secondly, theirs was clearly a reformist strategy; they worked to extend the redemptive media of the dominant ideological order, not overturn them. Thirdly, the movement was diverse, and we find criticism of Pharisaic hypocrisy in the rabbinic tradition as well as the Gospels. J. Wilde, following Bowker, believes that it was only one strict wing of the Pharisees, the *perushim* table fellowship sect, that Mark attacks in the Gospel (1974:196ff.).

The attitude of the Pharisees toward the revolt is difficult to assess. They were certainly no strangers to political coalitions; a century earlier they had aligned themselves with the Romans against the excesses of the Hasmonean dynasty, and several Pharisees were executed by Herod for subversion. There is little doubt that many joined the insurrection, yet because their social power was not Jerusalem-based, the Pharisees survived the collapse of the revolt. As we will see, Mark's narrative reflects a particular concern to delegitimize the Pharisees, who no doubt were strong ideological competitors.

The renewal strategy of the Essenes falls somewhere between reformism and what Holzner calls escapism, in which a group resolves its conflicts with the dominant order through disengagement. Ideologies of withdrawal tend to focus first upon justifying the group's deviant behavior, and only secondarily upon criticism of the prevailing ethos; it reflects "no ostensible desire to change the existing social order" (Carlton, 1977:35). This stance characterized many of the mystery cults and secret philosophical guilds in Hellenism, as well as later gnosticism. Movements that were politically resigned but personally renovative proliferated throughout the empire in this era, from astrology to stoicism—not unlike many forms of religiosity in the West today.

The monastic vision of the Essenes criticized both Jewish collaborators and Roman colonialists, but did not include any real strategy of engagement. It is true, as has been argued, that the Qumran documents reflect certain elements that might be considered indicative of an alternative socio-political program, such as the communalism they lived as a conscious rejection of class distinctions in Israel (Flusser, 1973). But, like their activist rebel counterparts, their ideology called for purging—not overthrowing—the dominant symbolic order. Unlike the rebels, however, their militance appears to have been restricted to literary polemics such as their apocalyptic war scrolls.

iii. Loyalistic Radicalism: The Fourth Philosophy

Holzner labels his second subversive strategy "loyalistically radical," which seeks structural change for the purpose of restoring or purifying traditional values. As already pointed out (above, A,iii), we must remember that our concept of "revolution," assuming as it does the modern ideology of historical progress, does not really characterize antiquity. Insofar as we can speak of a classic "philosophy of history," it was based upon the concept of *stasis* in which minimal change was considered optimal. It was believed that time brought only deterioration, and the "Golden Age" was a past, not future, ideal: thus ideologies of "social change" were concerned with:

> The restoration of certain revitalized or resuscitated versions of a traditional or conservative system. Viewed in this way, the reactionary ideology is particularly characteristic of complex pre-industrial societies whose orientations were, by definition, archaic . . . retrospective rather than prospective [Carlton, 1977:45].

As Carney puts it, "political thinkers in antiquity, all of them members of their society's elite and schooled in its backward looking Great Tradition, proved incapable of changing their terms of reference" (1975:119).

This must be applied to advocates of the "fourth philosophy" and the other forces behind the Jewish revolt: they were essentially restorationist and retrogressive. We can be grateful that revisionist histories have emphasized the social and economic criticism implied by many aspects of the rebel program. As suggested above, the revolt was as much a reflection of class tensions as of anti-imperialist sentiment, and differences between moderates and radicals in the provisional government were largely based on class distinctions:

> The Zealot party was composed of dissident peasants from Judea and lower priests in Jerusalem who had been oppressed by the chief priests in the decade before the war. The early followers of Simon bar Giora were slaves and brigands who plundered the rich. Even the Idumeans who came to Jerusalem showed their distrust of the high priestly aristocracy by their readiness to support the Zealots. And the vengeance with which both the Zealots and the Idumeans treated the Jewish aristocracy can best be understood as the expression of accumulated frustration resulting from grievances against the wealthy and traditional authorities [Rhoads, 1976:178].

This does not mean, however, that we are free to understand the revolt as prototypical of modern proletarian insurrection.

In fact the aims of the rebels were relatively generic to other elite-directed movements of opposition to Hellenism in the first century. In a landmark but neglected study entitled *The King Is Dead* (1961), S. Eddy analyzed Hellenistic resistance literature from the time of Alexander to Herod, discovering that otherwise diverse movements shared three common ideological characteristics:
1. the reassertion of lost native kingships;
2. socio-economic discontent resulting from the supplanting of local aristocrats by Hellenistic colonialists;

3. the desire to regain local political control in order to preserve indigenous laws, social customs, and cultic life.

It is not hard to see each of these elements in the Jewish revolt. To whatever degree either apocalypticism or messianism shaped the political hopes of the insurgents, there is no evidence that the vision of a "liberated" future was not fundamentally restorationist.

Despite Horsley's contentions to the contrary (1987:54ff.), as far as I can see even the most radical Zealot faction never proposed more than supplanting the collaborationist priestly leadership, which had become thoroughly domesticated under the Romans, with a patriotic one. There is little indication of a rebel program for a systematic restructuring of wealth or power. Thus from Mark's perspective of the Galilean poor, the revolt promised no structural relief from a political economy of elitism.

iv. Alienated, Confrontative, Nonaligned: A Hypothesis

The third, and for purposes of reading Mark most important, strand of Holzner's trajectory of subversive social strategies is what he calls the "alienative/confrontative" stance. Immediately, however, we run into the bias of mainline modern historical sociology, which from Ernst Troeltsch to the present has almost without exception offered only pejorative caricatures of "sectarian" ideology. The problem has been correctly diagnosed as a hermeneutic one by S. Budd in her review of B. Wilson's "definitive" sociology of millennial sects: "The very alienness and separateness of the sect's cognitive world constitutes . . . the greatest pitfall on the road to a sympathetic and complete understanding of its members" by scholars (1974:156). This sociological bias has carried over into interpretations of the ideology of apocalyptic literature. Its mythic discourse is spurned as "otherworldly," its bitter social criticisms and violent imagery disdained as the vengeful rhetoric of disenfranchised social groups that have not only given up on the possibility of social reform but indeed abandoned historical "responsibility" altogether (below, 14, A, i).

According to the preconceived typologies of modern liberal sociology, an alienated group might well be critical of the dominant socio-political institutions, but if it refuses to pursue a reformist strategy, it *necessarily* becomes politically passive. It is portrayed as resolving social tensions through "introjected" or "symbolically transferred" aggression, and summarily dismissed as incidental to political culture. It seems to me that historian E. A. Judge is right in his criticism of the way in which historical sociology often is trapped in its own conceptual prisons (1980). But what if we at least posit the *possibility* of a group that is (1) radically alienated, *yet still* (2) politically engaged, *yet still* (3) nonreformist in its social strategy? I contend that the situation in Roman Palestine as portrayed above does not rule out such a possibility.

For the Galilean peasantry, the perennial burden of the imperial tribute, the social pressure of the nearby Hellenistic cities, and then the repeated experience of retribution at the hands of Roman legions would have been more than enough to sow deep-seated alienation. At the same time there would have been a natural class alienation from the native aristocracy, whom the peasant saw not as leader but collaborator and landlord. This double antipathy *could* have translated into solidarity with the local social bandits and subsequently the Zealots, and for many it did, but the evidence indicates that this was a minority. We know, for example, that in Galilee the organized insurrection collapsed early, and that Josephus complained bitterly of the difficulties of trying to organize rebel resistance there. The brigand leader John of Gischala appears to have been an exception in going to join in the defense of Jerusalem, and he is himself portrayed as an unscrupulous and opportunistic merchant and landowner.

Freyne believes that most rural Galileans, deeply attached to the land and therefore inherently parochial, were in fact politically ambivalent toward the revolt, but still loyal to the temple. He contends that the Pharisaic movement would have been more attractive to disaffected Galileans: an alternative to the urban ruling circles, a popularized form of piety, and most importantly a way of strengthening Jewish identity in pluralistic and pagan Galilee through an enforcement of the purity code. But Freyne's portrait is not without serious contradictions. The Pharisaic movement would not have been without its local opponents. If some Galileans were genuinely critical of the elitism of priest and landowner, they would not have been blind to the same privileges claimed by the Pharisees, nor to the conflicts regarding Sabbath restrictions upon agricultural production and the separation of tithes. Moreover, genuine Galilean commitment to the symbolic order would have generated more of a demonstrable patriotism toward the Jerusalem-based provisional government.

What if a prophet arose who advocated a strategy that disdained the collaborationist aristocracy *and* Romans equally, and who repudiated Qumranite withdrawal *and* Pharisaic activism on the grounds that neither addressed the roots of oppression in the dominant symbolic order? We know that uneducated peasants, largely unable to articulate their dissatisfactions, often looked to those able to express in popular discourse a populist vision. It is not difficult to imagine such a prophet invoking the Deuteronomic vision of a just redistributive system, and appealing to the subversive tradition of the great prophetic social critics of Israel. A pedagogy could have been developed to help the peasants unmask the oppressive economic self-interest of the Jerusalem hierarchy, their tithing structure, Sabbath regulations, and temple. There is no a priori reason why an alternative to the reformists and rebels could not have been proposed that addressed peasant grievances more concretely. And although it would have been remarkable, it cannot be ruled out that such a prophet might have taken the logic of solidarity among the poor so far as to challenge the artificial gulf that kept the oppressed Jew and gentile segregated.

There was ample social, economic, political, and cultural justification for a strategy that delegitimized both the Roman presence *and* the authority of the Jewish aristocracy as it was embedded in the debt and purity systems and reinforced in the temple cult and the dominant interpretation of Torah. We can only conclude, without further evidence, that the determinate social formation of Palestine in the 60s C.E. produced conditions that render such an "alienative, confrontative and nonaligned" ideology hypothetically *plausible*. Should such an outlook manifest itself in literature we know to have come from this period, this should be accepted as concrete evidence for a unique social movement that must be evaluated on its own terms, not according to the strictures of sociological typology.

I believe Mark's Gospel to be such a document, articulating a grassroots social discourse that is at once both subversive and constructive. This document was probably written during the Roman reoccupation of Galilee between the first and second Roman sieges of Jerusalem (see below, 11,A,ii). The immediate and specific issue occasioning the Gospel was the challenge of rebel recruiters in Galilee, who were trying to drum up support for the resistance around Palestine, and no doubt demanding that Mark's community "choose sides." Though sympathetic to the socio-economic and political grievances of the rebels, Mark was compelled to repudiate their call to a defense of Jerusalem. This was because, according to his understanding of the teaching and practice of a Nazarene prophet, executed by Rome some thirty-five years earlier, the means (military) and ends (restorationist) of the "liberation" struggle were fundamentally counterrevolutionary.

It is time therefore to begin an investigation of Mark's text in order to determine the socio-historical character of his movement, which identified itself with a murdered prophet from Nazareth in Galilee, about whom the elite sources say nothing.

NOTE

1. That the New Testament writers make messianic claims concerning Jesus' Davidic sonship is not at issue here. For a helpful discussion of this question in relationship to the genealogies of Matthew and Luke, see R. Brown (1977:505ff.).

Part Two

Reading the First Half of Mark

CHAPTER THREE

An Introduction to Mark's Literary Style and Strategy: The "First" Prologue and Call to Discipleship (Mark 1:1-20)

> Behold, I send you my messenger to prepare the way before me,
>   and the Lord whom you seek will suddenly come. . . .
> Behold, I will send you Elijah the prophet before the great and
>   terrible day of Yahweh comes.
>
> —Malachi 3:1; 4:5

The opening scenes of the Gospel of Mark remind one of minimalist theater, collapsing a world of meaning into a few concentrated images, or a chiaroscuro painting, with vivid profiles etched in a dark, obscure backdrop. Punctuated by divine voices offstage and human cries at center stage, the prologue narrates the story of an invasion, throwing existence-as-usual into sharp relief. Prophetic muses, long silent, suddenly sing again. A messenger is announced, and in turn heralds the advent, at long last, of one strong enough to wrestle the world away from the death-grip of the powers. This leader appears on the horizon of history, and in a dramatic symbolic action declares himself an outlaw. This immediately provokes a challenge from the prince of the powers himself, which takes the leader deep into the wilderness, where he disappears.

As the curtain falls upon act one, the leader reappears to take the place of his fallen predecessor. He boldly announces that the reign of God—with its dreams of justice and love, equality and abundance, wholeness and unity—is dawning. So begins act two, where, in a distant province, this leader begins gathering troops (oddly, common working folk, local residents), with whom he will mount his campaign to overturn the rule of the powers. In this prologue, Mark wields the scythe of apocalyptic symbolics, clearing narrative space from among the weeds so that the seeds of a radically new order—to borrow the author's own metaphor (4:7)—might be pressed into the weary soil of the world. This subversive story is what Mark entitles *good news*.

3A. "AS IT IS WRITTEN":
THE IDEOLOGY OF TEXTUALITY AND INTERTEXTUALITY

It was something of a convention in ancient literature to use the first lines of the narrative to establish the "credentials" of the story, not unlike the credits in the opening moments of a modern film. This was usually accomplished by appealing to recognizable literary, mythic, or political traditions that would lend instant legitimacy to the work. So, for example, does Matthew the scribe begin his story of Jesus with a Jewish genealogy (Mt 1), whereas Luke the Hellenistic historiographer prefaces his account by acknowledging his benefactor and purpose (Lk 1:1–4). Mark, however, offers only a title: "The beginning of the gospel" (1:1). In so doing he introduced a new literary form to antiquity.

I indicated in chapter 1 that I will be examining Mark's narrative as a "production" of his ideology. In this production, literary *form*, narrative structure and discourse, is as much a vehicle of signification as is *content*. Formal processes, as Jameson puts it, must be examined "as sedimented content in their own right, as carrying ideological messages of their own, distinct from the ostensible or manifest content of the works" (1981:99).

Thus the first task of a socio-literary reading is a consideration of Mark's literary convention and style. Why did he choose to communicate through the medium of written text, instead of, say, a psalmic chant, oral epic, or sculpture? Why the choice of this particular literary form over the more classic genres of poetry, letter, or comedy? What does Mark's linguistic idiom tell us, quite apart from the story itself? Such questions are part of the author's overall narrative strategy, and represent what materialist critics call the "literary mode of production." I will refer to this as the "ideology of genre." In other words: What exactly does this literary phenomenon that Mark terms "gospel" tell us about his situation and social strategy?

i. Mark and Oral Tradition: Undomesticating the Words of Jesus

We must begin at the most basic formal level: the written word, or "textuality." Mark's choice to write might seem unremarkable to us, but its significance becomes apparent once we recognize the predominance of oral tradition in antiquity. The spoken word was considered the standard discourse even in educated circles; Jewish pedagogy especially centered upon oral recitation. The technology and the economics of writing precluded a preponderantly "paper" culture such as our modern one. Prior to Wycliffe's press (fully thirteen centuries after Mark), textual communication was viable only for the elite: the commercial, governmental, bureaucratic, and scribal sectors.

Given this premium, it is not surprising that textuality was, to the Jewish mind, practically synonymous with sacred tradition itself. In the New Testament most of the verbs and nouns for writing are associated with "scripture."

(The same semantic values have survived in English: "scripture," that which is written, and "Bible," the book.) In Mark we almost immediately encounter "as it is written" (1:2, *kathōs gegraptai*); this was a common Jewish idiom signaling that the Hebrew Bible was about to be cited. Scripture was stewarded and interpreted by "scribes" (*grammateus*—that is, those who knew how to write). In light of this, Mark's choice to commit his account to writing could be seen as somewhat bold—especially when his text is at pains to present itself in continuity with the texts of Jewish salvation history.

That Mark is indeed making such a pretense to authority is demonstrated by his use of the term "gospel" in structuring his prologue. The title (1:1) identifies the gospel with "Jesus Messiah" ("Son of God" is probably a later addition). At the close of the prologue he asserts that this gospel is the one proclaimed by Jesus himself, and that it derives "from God" (the first mention of the divine name in the story, 1:14). Finally, it is presented as the object of faith; the invitation to "repent and believe the gospel" is directed toward the reader, bidding us to listen to *this* story (1:15). Mark has thus constructed the following narrative syllogism:

> Jesus gets the gospel from God
> Mark gets the gospel from Jesus
> readers get the gospel from Mark

Mark's story *about* Jesus and the ideology *of* Jesus are an inseparable authority, guaranteed by God.

Later we read that all sacrifices incumbent upon a life of discipleship are made for Jesus' sake "and the sake of the gospel" (8:35, 10:29, see also 13:9f.). This phrase is not used by the other evangelists, whereas Mark avoids the verbal form of the word *euangelizomai*, "to proclaim the gospel") found throughout Luke and Paul. It would appear, then, that Mark was particularly concerned to "nominalize" *his* Gospel: *this* story is the one passed on by Jesus' followers (13:10; 14:9). In other words, the Gospel's textuality represents an attempt to establish something *definitive* about Jesus. Why?

W. Kelber attributes this to Mark's skepticism about the oral traditions that stewarded the memories of Jesus among the primitive Christian communities:

> In the face of anxiety and destruction of faith, the gospel text reconstitutes stability and reliability . . . a degree of permanence wholly unattainable in the world of oral uncertainties. Furthermore, it is one of the essential functions of the gospel that it facilitates a return to the *archē tou euaggeliou Iēsou* (1:1). This return to the beginning treats the oral failure to assure the presence of Jesus by restoring the authority of Jesus as one essentially belonging to the past. The gospel text recaptures the past of Jesus as his authentic presence [1980:44f.].

Kelber is referring specifically to the practice of "Christian prophecy" common in the earliest church, in which words of Jesus were quoted in the context of worship or preaching. This practice lent the existential authority of the risen and present Christ to the speaker and the pronouncement.

Because the scattered network of Christian communities had little infrastructure and poor methods of communication, the oral traditions about Jesus were doubtless subject to manipulation. This was Mark's concern: it was one thing to invoke the words of Jesus in addressing a given community situation, but quite another to allow the tradition to suffer from gratuitous misappropriation. Then, as now, one could "quote" Jesus for purposes inimical to the kingdom; the many apocryphal and gnostic "gospels" from the second century testify to this tendency in the early church.

There was also a social dimension to the problem. There is strong evidence that circulating among the primitive communities was a class of itinerant preachers (discussed by Theissen, 1978). In the oral culture of the poor, these prophets could, and did, wield enormous social power, analogous to that of the scribe vis-à-vis sacred texts. Some early Christian documents suggest that advantage was taken. Paul, for example, refused to avail himself of the apostolic privileges to which he allegedly had a right, because of the record of abuse (see 2 Cor 11; Hock, 1980). A second-century catechism placed restrictions upon hospitality to itinerant preachers (Didache, 11).

By fixing the gospel in writing, Mark could begin to normalize the tradition, in order to circumscribe the tendency to domesticate the words of Jesus inherent in orality (Kelber, 1983:94f.). It may also be that in part his opposition to the social power of oral prophets was analogous to his antipathy toward the Pharisees, whom he criticizes for subverting the clear textual imperatives of Torah with their self-justifying oral tradition (7:5ff.; 10:2ff.). Yet on the other hand Mark's "politics of textuality" in no way intended to legitimize the rule of the literate elite. After all, in the story Jesus continually defends the (illiterate) poor against the scribal establishment. Nor did it imply an endorsement of codified legalism over against charismatic spontaneity, what Paul calls the "dispensation of the dead letter" (2 Cor 3:6ff.). Mark obviously affirmed the preacher's freedom to adapt the traditions to the context at hand—for he himself does this in creatively editing his sources into the gospel narrative. Mark is an *author*, with control over his material, not a mere compiler, slavishly handing on tradition.

Inherent in Markan textuality, then, is a tension, even perhaps a paradox: he is interpreting and shaping a tradition at the same time that he is endeavoring to fix it. This ideological strategy simultaneously existentializes and distances the presence of Jesus. On the one hand, the "historical" Jesus and his community are not to be embalmed for the sake of reverence; the vision they embodied demands reappropriation into the concrete situation of communities belonging to a different time and context. On the other hand, Jesus is not subject to however one might experience him; he is the Jesus of *this* story and its demands of discipleship upon the reader. Mark presents his Gospel in a text both "open" and "closed," affirming the dialectic between canonicity and charisma that is essential to every community committed to a "living tradition."

ii. Mark's Semantic Field: The Politics of Language

As basic as the Gospel's textuality is the language in which it was written. Because the system of signs we call "language" is the most fundamental structural element in a given cultural formation, it reveals a great deal about a writer's ideology and historical setting. Moreover, linguistic friction between cultures and subcultures is necessarily political. For example, pidgin in Melanesia was originally the product of contact between Western traders and indigenous cultures, but became a way in which the latter resisted wholesale assimilation after subsequent colonization. Another example would be the way in which European languages dominate the education, and hence intellectual life, of Third World peoples, something liberation proponents refer to as "colonization of the mind."

Mark is written in Greek, but a notoriously poor Greek peppered with Latin and Semitic syntactic and idiomatic intrusions. This indicates that Greek was Mark's second language (Pryke, 1978; Maloney, 1981). Assuming that Mark writes from Palestine, this is not surprising. His Greek is the result of the cultural (hence linguistic) colonization of his homeland by Hellenism since the time of Alexander the Great. Semitisms would be expected, the influence of his native idiom; they might also be attributable to the Semitic sources about Jesus upon which he drew.[1] The Latinisms in the Gospel, on the other hand, have traditionally been used by scholars as evidence that Mark was written in (or to) Rome. Kelber, however, has shown that every Latin term in Mark is associated with either military-juridical or economic spheres of life (1973:129). Again, precisely such linguistic penetration would be expected in Palestine under Roman colonial administration.

Although his Greek was far from highbrow, Mark clearly was literate in Hellenistic culture, for he is influenced by some of its literary conventions. Was this a concession to the colonialization of mind? Not necessarily; it might equally attest to an ideological strategy—transcending merely parochial concerns—intent on reaching a broader audience, for which Greek was the logical vehicle. A modern analogy would be the way in which many contemporary Latin American and African writers choose to write in English or French, or employ the thoroughly Western literary genre of the novel. This is done, on the one hand, to *challenge* the colonizing culture, and on the other, to communicate with other oppressed linguistic groups in the imperial sphere. In Mark's case, there may have been another reason: I will argue that his community was not only bilingual but probably multicultural as well, inclusive of Jew and gentile.

Language is made up of complex, socially determined meanings, full of idioms and images that make up what socio-linguists call the "semantic field" of a given discourse. In contemporary U.S. culture, for example, we daily encounter newspaper headlines like "White House Warns Reds Over Star Wars," or commercial jingles like "Coke is It." These are as immediately intelligible to those of us formed in this society as they are mysterious to a foreigner, who may understand the language but not the social meanings. Sensationalist journalism or consumer seduction, however insidious they may be, are fundamental to the semantic field of capitalist culture, as are ceremonial chants or totems to more traditional societies.

In Mark we encounter a semantic field that presumes the meaning -worlds of first-century Mediterranean culture. The subtleties of his idioms are bound to escape the modern reader (see the examples in Malina, 1981:1f.), yet they provide key clues to the social setting of the Gospel. We may further detect the boundaries of Mark's semantic field by noting what he regards as self-evident to his audience and what he feels he must explain. For example, Mark assumes the intelligibility of his references to the Palestinian Jewish symbolic order of purity (e.g., the social segregation of lepers in 1:40ff. or menstruating women in 5:25ff.) and debt (the social code of "sin" in 2:5 or temple tithing in 12:41). Other references, however, he clarifies with editorial explanation, such as certain Pharisaic practices (rules of table fellowship in 7:3 and *Korban* in 7:11) or particular Aramaisms (*ephphatha* in 7:34). Because of these explanations many scholars argue for a non-Palestinian provenance for Mark. But the text assumes far more than it clarifies, and makes no attempt to *systematically* explain the semantic field of Palestinian Judaism. Mark's occasional help to the reader can better be explained by the social mix of his intended audience. It is quite plausible that gentiles in or around his community, and even the uneducated Jewish peasantry, would have understood the broad social codes but have been unfamiliar with specific practices of sects such as the Pharisees.

Of equal importance is the way in which an author might manipulate or subvert a given semantic field so that a term or symbol is given radically different value from what would normally be assumed. Such semantic anomalies function to shock the reader into new awareness. The image of the president of the U.S.A. squatting by a heating grate on a Washington, D.C., street, offering comfort to one of the homeless poor, is not one we would think is "normal"; it would challenge our socialized expectations. We would not expect a group of mentally retarded adults to present scientific papers at an academic conference. A good example of subversion of semantic value is found in the popular discourse of jokes, especially in social or political satire. In this way the dominant order can be indirectly but powerfully criticized, and "great" personages cut down to size.

We see much of this in Mark's Gospel. The image of a messianic claimant residing at the house of a leper (14:3) or being bested in verbal debate by a gentile woman (7:29) would have been shocking to the first-century Jew. His repeated use of "antithetical aphorisms" in the discipleship catechism (below, 9,E,i) undermines orthodox notions about social power. And Mark is a master of parody. He makes a joke about the rich, declaring that it is as hard for them to be saved as for a "camel to go through the eye of a needle" (10:25)—and summarily turns the assumed relationship between piety, wealth, and blessing on its head! His indecorous vignettes of the ruling class vilify a Herodian king, a high priest, and a Roman procurator. I will try to point out ways in which

Mark assumes, clarifies, or intentionally subverts his semantic field as we read through the narrative, indicating how they give us further insight into his ideological strategy.

iii. Mark and Written Tradition: The "Script" of Biblical Radicalism

Another clue to the ideology of textual discourse is "intertextual" inference—that is, the citation, allusion to, or adaptation of other written traditions. Although this expression of shared culture is perhaps easier to discern than is idiomatic tradition, intertextuality is rarely as straightforward as, say, the footnoted quotations of modern academic writing. This is because references are most often implicit: the author assumes the audience is familiar with the tradition and will catch the allusion. A preacher, for example, might today incorporate into a sermon texts from Calvin or Wesley, Barth or Tillich, a Dostoevsky novel or a papal encyclical, without *citing* them formally. We see this also in popular culture; in one day I heard a radio commercial use the phrase "We the people," a politician allude to the Monroe Doctrine in defense of foreign policy, and a social critic invoke the film character "Rambo" in describing presidential character. Intertextuality is the stuff of both everyday speech and high rhetoric. We must therefore pay attention to which textual traditions are, or are not, being reproduced, and how.

Mark often alludes to the discourse of his opponents, such as the Pharisaic oral code (7:5ff.); certain doctrines attributed to the scribes (9:11) or Sadducees (12:18ff.); the "text" of Roman currency (the coin's inscription, 12:16). The implicit (oral) "texts" of folk traditions such as parables and miracle stories also appear. But not surprisingly, the Gospel's intertextuality centers around the Hebrew scriptures. From the very outset Mark acknowledges a fundamental relationship between the authority of his "new story" ("the beginning of the gospel," 1:1) and that of the "old story" ("as it is written in Isaiah," 1:2). Mark is clearly trying to legitimate his account by anchoring it in the scriptural tradition; this we would expect. But, as we will see, he is implicitly claiming much more: he boldly asserts that the salvation history narrated in the law and the prophets is continuous with, indeed being "regenerated" by, his story about Jesus of Nazareth (below, 3,E,i).

Mark's Jesus will repeatedly appeal to the Hebrew Bible to justify his practice. He deploys it offensively (11:17) and defensively (2:24ff.), and argues hermeneutics with the scribal theologians (12:24ff.) and Pharisees (10:2ff.). His challenge to the interpretive competence of his ideological rivals often has a bitter rhetorical edge: "Have you never read what David did . . . ?" (2:25); "Have you not read this scripture . . . ?" (12:10); "Have you not read in the book of Moses . . . ?" (12:26). This shows that Mark was very much engaged in the battle over the redemptive medium of scripture with the other literate social groups of his time. (For a detailed examination of intertextuality in the Jewish tradition from a different perspective, see Neusner, 1987.)

Several times Mark cites the scripture directly, preferring the popular Greek version known as the Septuagint (LXX), which suggests that this was the Bible used in his community (Kee, 1977:45ff.). More often he simply makes allusions, even in stage directions; for example, he invokes the Elijah story through his costuming of John the Baptist (1:6), and he invokes the exodus-Sinai tradition by a transitional reference to time and setting (9:2). Mark relies heavily upon the prophetic tradition:

> For example, in Mark 11–16 alone there are more than 57 quotations. Of these, only eight are from the Torah, and all but one of those appear in the context of the controversy stories in ch. 12. Two are from the historical writings, 12 from the Psalms, 12 from Daniel, and the remaining 21 are from the other prophetic writings. An analysis of the allusions to scripture and related sacred writings gives the same general picture: of 160 such allusions, half are from the prophets (excluding Daniel), and about an eighth each from Daniel, the Psalms, the Torah, and from non-canonical writings [Kee, 1977:45].

These ratios are generally accurate for the rest of Mark as well.

Ideological significance lies not only in *which* texts are cited, but also in *how* they appear. Whether explicit or implicit, Mark's intertextuality is always subversive, using scripture in unexpected ways to argue a point. Mark will conflate two texts (1:2f.), give a well-known story a twist (2:25f.), add a commandment to the Decalogue (10:19), or manipulate familiar symbols (11:1ff.). We would expect such subversive hermeneutics from Mark, because scripture is the only aspect of the dominant symbolic order of Palestinian Judaism he does *not* repudiate altogether. He must necessarily be combative in his interpretation, for his opponents use the same textual tradition to support a system he is trying to delegitimize.

The struggle over "how to read" scripture is most intense around questions of messianic ideology, in which Mark pits the militant but nonviolent Human One of Daniel (below, 8,C,ii; D,ii) over against the restorationism of his opponents (12:35–37). Here, Mark appeals to what I will refer to as the "script of biblical radicalism" (below, 8,E,ii). Mark appears to feel that the prophetic texts, upon which he relies heavily, also witness to a prophetic "script"—that is, a vocation with a destiny that does not change with time. The "true prophets" are not identified by "proof" of miraculous signs (13:22; cf. 8:11f.), but by their stand on the side of the poor, pressing a "covenantal suit" against the exploitive "shepherds" (see below, 6,E,ii) of Israel. From Elijah to Jeremiah the result is always the same: opposition from the ruling class and a threat to the prophet's life.

This "script" is most clearly articulated in Jesus' political parable of the vineyard tenants (12:1–11). It does not change just because the prophet has been named by the Sender as "beloved son" (12:6f.; cf. 1:11; 9:7). Just as John the Baptist "followed the script," so too must Jesus (9:11–13). Thus Jesus' three portents concerning his destiny (8:31f.; 9:31f.; 10:33f.) should be understood in terms of neither prediction nor predetermination, but as indications that the script is being fulfilled. Mark is at pains to reassure the reader of this throughout the tragedy of the passion narrative (14:21, 27, 49). The ideological function of this "script" is twofold. First, it lends meaning to the suffering and persecution of the prophets: Yahweh's purpose is not thereby denied but mysteriously confirmed and advanced. Secondly, it functions to exhort the disciples of Jesus, and the reader of the gospel, to themselves participate in this prophetic vocation, but with a sober realism with respect to the consequences (8:34ff.).

Finally, Mark also maintains a conspicuous intertextual silence. Especially tricky for modern Christian readers is his avoidance of accounts of the "risen Jesus." It is difficult to believe that Mark was unaware of apostolic resurrection traditions such as those cited by Paul (1 Cor 15:3ff.). Certainly the other evangelists were quick to fill in the "blank" left by Mark—as did those who tried to give Mark's story a more palatable ending! But we shall see that this implicit intertextual silence is an essential part of Mark's narrative strategy (below, 13,E).

3B. "GOOD NEWS": THE IDEOLOGY OF GENRE

i. Wisdom Sayings or Dramatic Narrative?

The danger of speaking of narrative as a production of ideology is that it can be misunderstood to mean that ideology is simply the *content* of the communication. But as Jameson notes:

> Ideology is not something which informs or invests symbolic production; rather the . . . production of aesthetic or narrative form is to be seen as an ideological act in its own right, with the function of inventing imaginary or formal "solutions" to unresolvable social contradictions [1981:79].

Thus our next step is to examine the ideological signification of Mark's literary form. In light of the above discussion of textuality, we must not overlook the most obvious literary aspect of the Gospel—namely, that it is a dramatic *narrative*.

The primary sources Mark relied on in composing his Gospel were obviously the primitive traditions about Jesus. But according to most form critics, these sources (written or oral) already had a form: they were collections of sayings, not narrative as such. This is the case with the hypothetical "Q" document (R. Edwards, 1976:1ff.), or the *Gospel of Thomas* (written ca. 140 C.E.). Merely lending fixed textuality to such free-floating sayings would not in itself solve the problems of orality that Mark was facing (above, A,i): without the definition provided by a narrative context, the sayings were still vulnerable to manipulation.

Perhaps more importantly, the ideology of the literary form of a sayings collection functioned to promote a kind of cognitive passivity toward the text. This can be seen, for example, in the earlier Hellenistic Jewish wisdom literature (e.g., Proverbs) as well as later gnostic collections (e.g., *Thomas*). Hellenistic intellectualism interpreted Jesus as a great sage in the Socratic or Cynic tradition, whose words invited sublime reflection but demanded nothing more concrete than perhaps the improvement of individual character. Indeed, the ideology of Neoplatonism became increasingly influential in the early church; by the fourth century there was a tendency to interpret the gospel in terms of an intellectual and ethical system rather than as a call to discipleship.

Mark understood that without a narrative of practice, there could be no ideology of practice. Thus, he chose the form of a full-fledged dramatic recital of the ministry of Jesus as his narrative vehicle. Of our four Gospels, Mark has the lowest ratio of sayings to narrative action; he clearly prefers symbolic performance to extended monologue. Indeed, the structure of Mark's story is built around mission, journey, and conflict; in contrast, Matthew is composed around five "sermons" (see Mt 7:28; 11:1; 13:53; 19:1; 26:1), and Luke-Acts and John emphasize long speeches. The power of the word in Mark is subordinate to that of deed: against the reflective/speculative traditions, Mark's discipleship narrative demands engagement and a response of praxis. He might well have agreed with Marx's famous dictum: "Philosophers seek to understand the world; the point, however, is to change it."

But if Mark chose the form of dramatic narrative, which of the contemporaneous genres did he adopt? Kee, in a careful examination of the question, finds no parallels among the many established Hellenistic literary models. He cites with approval the conclusions of E. Auerbach's classic study of ancient rhetoric, *Mimesis*:

> The gospel portrays something which neither the poets nor the historians of antiquity ever set out to portray; the birth of a spiritual movement from within the everyday occurrences of contemporary life, which thus assumes an importance it could never have assumed in antique literature. . . . [It is] too serious for comedy, too everyday for tragedy, politically too insignificant to history—and the form which was given it is one of such immediacy that its like does not exist in the literature of antiquity [Kee, 1980:65].

This is not to say that Mark did not borrow from the literary conventions available to him. G. Bilezikian has offered a compelling study of Mark's use of the conventions of Greek tragedy. He concludes:

> [Mark] animated the presentation of his themes with the discreet utilization of resources available in the most powerful dramatic artifice ever achieved in literary history . . . plundering the rich tradition of this noble art for elements uniquely suitable for the attainment of his objectives [1977:22,21].

Bilezikian's insights are important, and particularly helpful in understanding Mark's prologue (below, 3,F,iv).

Still, it must be conceded that Mark found no one literary genre in the surrounding culture that would fully suit his purposes, neither Hellenistic eulogy nor heroic epic. Because he was convinced that Jesus of Nazareth had inaugurated an ideology and practice that was wholly unprecedented, the Gospel had to be a literary *novum*. As V. Robbins points out, "Distinctiveness, however, . . . does not presuppose isolation from popular sociocultural influences" (1984:5). There was one literary tradition that influenced Mark more than any other, and apart from it his narrative strategy cannot be properly interpreted: Jewish apocalyptic.

ii. The Narrative Strategy of Apocalyptic

Since the time of Daniel, a Jewish resistance tract written just before the Maccabean revolt during brutal persecutions under the Hellenistic ruler Antiochus Epiphanes IV, apocalyptic literature had flourished (J. Collins, 1981:130ff.; below, 11,A,i). By Mark's era it was well established as a discourse of political protest. According to Horsley, the social function of apocalyptic was to fire the socio-political imagination of the oppressed. First, in renewing old symbols and reappropriating Hebrew narratives of liberation, it functioned as "remembering." Secondly, it promoted a "creative envisioning" of a future in which God restored justice and a full humanity to all. And thirdly, the dualistic combat myth functioned as a *"critical demystifying* of the pretensions and practices of the established order":

> Emperors were not divine, and high priests were not sacrosanct. . . . The apocalyptic imagination thus had a strengthening effect on the people's ability to endure, and even a motivating effect toward resistance or revolt [J. Collins, 1987:144].

Certainly one can see in Mark's Gospel all three: subversive memory, vision, and the war of myths with the powers. It is also highly likely that apocalyptic discourse was employed by some of the Jewish rebels (see 13:6ff.; below, 11,C). Here too, then, Mark struggled on the interpretive battlefield, claiming the apocalyptic tradition for his own purposes even while trying to wrest it away from his ideological competitors.

Mark's semantic and intertextual debt to apocalyptic includes popular folk traditions such as the exorcism stories, or protoliterary sources such as the apocalyptic "propaganda sheets" (below, 11,A,i). But Kee notes:

> A disproportionate interest in Daniel prevails throughout [Mark]. . . . Daniel alone among all the Old Testament books is quoted from every chapter; it is of the highest level of significance for the New Testament as a whole as a result of its overwhelming importance for Mark [1977:45].

Indeed, quite aside from Daniel, Mark's use of the prophets draws equally "disproportionately" from texts that modern scholars attribute to late prophetic "proto-apocalyptic," such as Isaiah 24–27, 34–35, and 56–66 ("Trito Isaiah"); Ezekiel 38–39; Joel 3–4; Zechariah 9, 12–14; and Malachi 3–4 (D. Peterson, 1977; see below, E,ii).

Kee argues that Mark essentially adopts the narrative strategy of Daniel, moving from a focus upon miracles in the first half of the Gospel to martyrdom in the second half, and including both personal and cosmic revelation. Whether or not one agrees with Kee, it is possible to identify in Mark at least six major apocalyptic characteristics. First and foremost is the basic "form of historical description, in which, by the use of both literal and symbolic modes, the meaning of crisis in which the writer finds himself and his community is represented as providing the clue to the whole course and the culmination of human history" (Kee, 1977:65). That is, like Daniel, Mark uses a story about events and personalities from the past for the purpose of dramatizing concrete choices and exhorting fidelity in the face of adversity in the author's present (see below, iii).

The second characteristic is radical apocalyptic dualism (see below, 11,D,i), in which Jesus' new order (narrated as the "kingdom of God") is fundamentally opposed to the old order stewarded by the scribes. Mark's story is a dramatic interpretation of the "new heaven and new earth" tradition of apocalyptic symbolics, what Wilder calls the "theatre of world-palingenesis" (1982:34). The Gospel is "directed toward the creation of new worlds: old symbols are given new meaning and new symbols come to life. . . . A new order of the sacred is brought into being and perceived by the community as the source of all power and meaning; new rituals emerge to remind the community of this sacred order" (Gager, 1975:11). This dualism is evident from Jesus' first public homily about "new wine" and "old wineskins" (2:19–22; below, 4,D,i). The old order—its definitions of sacred space, social status, and cultic/political authority—is confronted and subverted through the narrative vehicle of conflict and exorcism stories. The new order—its imperatives of inclusivity, equality, servanthood, and suffering patience—is mediated through stories of conversion, miracles and healing, symbolic action, and parenetic teaching. Jesus' two long sermons (Mk 4 and 13) especially reflect the apocalyptic "two ages."

Related to dualism is a third characteristic: the apocalyptic "combat myth." From the very first wilderness confrontation between Jesus and his angels and Satan and his wild beasts (1:12f.), it is clear that there is more to Jesus' struggle with the scribal order than "meets the eye." This is a showdown with the Satanic order, as is clearly articulated in the apocalyptic parable of the strong man's house (3:23–27), which I have chosen as the hallmark theme of my reading. The essential question is, Who is "lord" of the "house" (13:35)? Is it the "strong man," a.k.a. the powers, or Jesus, a.k.a. the Human One, the apocalyptic *persona* Mark borrows from Daniel (below, 8,D,ii)? I will return to the combat myth and apocalyptic semantics of "principalities and powers" in discussing Mark 13 (below, 11,D,ii).

A fourth characteristic lies in Mark's portrayal of Jesus' special attempts to teach his disciples, and their inability to understand his real identity, which is not unlike the apocalyptic device of secret revelation. S. Freyne (1982) goes so far as to claim that Mark's characterization of the disciples is meant to call to mind Daniel's *maskilim*, the "wise" who receive special instruction in order to understand the mystery of God's work in a time of historical crisis (see Dn 12:3ff.). This "mystery," however, is not to be identified with esoteric or secret knowledge, as we shall see in discussing Mark 4:10ff. (below, 5,A,ii). Though it contradicts conventional wisdom, it can be comprehended by any simple peasant: the kingdom penetrates history like the "smallest of seeds," which grows, independent of human cultivation, into the largest of plants (4:26–32).

Mark's central mystery/paradox represents the fifth and most ideologically important apocalyptic characteristic: the Danielic conviction that the suffering of the just is somehow in itself efficacious in bringing down the old order and creating the new (Dn 7:21ff.). Thus for Mark the sole eschatological "sign" is the cross, which represents the "end of the world" in the true apocalyptic sense. The powers will be pulled from the highest places (13:25f.) only when and where the power of nonviolence ("to save life, one must lose life") is practiced (below, 8,C,D).

Mark's concern is not only liberation from the specific structures of oppression embedded in the dominant social order of Roman Palestine; it also includes the spirit and practice of domination ultimately embedded in the human personality and corporately in human history as a whole. The struggle against the powers *and* the individual and collective will to dominate is articulated over and over again in different ways throughout the story. This strategy of repetition represents the sixth apocalyptic characteristic of the Gospel: the narrative device of "recapitulation." First in his miracle stories and again in a cycle of visions, Daniel dramatized a single point: the imperative and possibility of resistance to the Seleucid state. So too does Mark restate the discipleship of the cross in a variety of ways. Because recapitulation is so central to the composition and discourse of Mark, I will address it in more detail below in my consideration of the discursive character of Mark's overall structure (3,C,iii).

Despite Mark's appropriation of all these aspects of apocalyptic narrative, however, the Gospel cannot be considered as conforming to the literary form of an apocalypse per se, at least as it has been generically defined (J. Collins, 1977; idem, 1981:130ff.). The perspective of the "apocalyptic technique . . . is framed spatially by the supernatural world and temporally by the eschatological judgment. . . . This transcendent world may be expressed through mythological symbolism or celestial geography or both" (J. Collins, 1984:32). It is just as important to recognize the way in which Mark departs from this narrative strategy. Though he uses the spatial and temporal discourse of classic apocalyptic myth selectively in his story, overall he has replaced the "heavenly" fiction with an earthly one. The Gospel has no entranced seer receiving special instructions and visions, as in Daniel, Revelation, and indeed most intertestamental apocalyptic literature. Instead, Mark builds his dramatic framework around mundane events: sea and land journeys, conflicts with family, synagogue, and state, and stories of teaching and healings. The "war in heaven" is brought to the real political landscape of Mark's time. The only exceptions to this are the three narrative moments of Jesus' baptism, transfiguration, and death, points at which Mark inserts "heavenly" symbolics into his story. These episodes, however, are designed not to "rescue" the terrestrial story, but precisely to ensure a true apocalyptic interpretation of its meaning.

Mark's departures from the more classic form are no doubt due to his criticism of the twin errors by which he felt apocalyptic was misunderstood by his contemporaries. His focus upon the cross set him against those who used apocalyptic symbolics to legitimate a militant practice of "holy war" against their enemies. By anchoring the story of discipleship firmly in the lived world of his audience he stood against those who used heavenly visions to legitimate a withdrawal from political struggle into gnostic communities.

iii. Realistic Narrative

Mark created a narrative form that maintained the tension between a flexible and a fixed tradition about Jesus. The existential power of its dramatic structure precludes intellectualization, challenging readers of every generation to participate in the discipleship adventure as defined by the specific practice of Jesus as Mark narrates it. It is a literary *novum*: a genuinely popular story, with the life of common persons as its subject, speaking both to and for them; an apocalyptic drama set in the real world. Mark achieves these tensions through the use of what I will call "realistic narrative."

Realistic narrative claims simultaneously the autonomy of literature and the plausibility of historical writing; it is at once both contemporary and removed from the reader. By literary autonomy I mean the creative freedom of the author to make use of "poetic license" in narrating settings, characterization, and plot. The Gospel does not pretend to be a "journalistic" account of events; Mark freely interprets and editorializes upon the traditions from which he draws (see Tannehill, 1975:12). By historical plausibility I mean the realism that characterizes Markan narrative: its settings are largely referential (i.e., they can be correlated to the world of first-century Palestine), its main characters are not inherently make-believe, and its events are not, for the most part, fantastic. Some modern critics might refer to such a literary genre as "historical fiction," like the Silone novel discussed above (1,E,iii). I do not, however, believe that this term is appropriate to antiquity, which did not share our (admittedly ideological) distinctions between "fact" and "fiction," between "history" and "story."

It is of utmost significance that Mark chose realistic narrative over the more highly fabulated fictions of apocalyptic. Even at points where his scenes and events must be considered to some extent contrived, they maintain a high degree of historical, geographical, and social verisimilitude. A good example is the boat journeys across the Sea of Galilee in the first half of the Gospel. These episodes, however they may ultimately be rooted in historical tradition, clearly have a symbolic function at the level of the narrative—they represent an important Markan fiction. Yet Mark's sea scenes are without exception quite realistic, at least from the perspective of a Palestinian peasant. The Sea of Galilee did in fact serve as the major transportation route to the eastern Transjordan (5:1; 6:53), it was the locus for a vital fishing industry (1:16), and it did indeed have violent and sudden storms that endangered the lives of those who traversed it (4:35ff.; 6:45ff.). It is precisely the commonplace character of these boat journeys that gives them their extraordinary symbolic power.

Many of Mark's settings are either indeterminate ("Gerasa," 5:1) or obscure ("the wilderness"), yet the villages and cities Mark names (Capernaum, Caesarea Philippi, Jericho, etc.) would have been readily identifiable to the Palestinian reader. Though scenes are usually set up and deconstructed so quickly as to be almost incidental, Mark occasionally surprises us with revealing detail and "local color," as in his portrait of the poverty of a village dwelling in 2:1-4. On the whole, Mark is more interested in symbolic coordinates than logical movement through time and space (below, 4,B,iv). Yet the broad movement of narrative action and the plot conflicts in the Gospel are all exceedingly credible: Mark's audience was well acquainted with the rural itinerant preacher, pilgrimages to Jerusalem, prophetic resistance movements, and the political trials of dissidents.

When it comes to characterization, we have no reason to assume that any of Mark's personalities were fabricated. Few, however, are developed at any depth. Mark does not have to persuade his audience about the historical existence of the story's main character, Jesus of Nazareth. Yet Mark does not intend to be Jesus' biographer: he offers us nothing about his birth, childhood, or adult life before his abrupt appearance at the river Jordan (1:9). In fact Mark only narrates a very small portion of Jesus' life; we learn little about his family, and almost nothing about his inner consciousness or private struggles—in stark contrast to the dramatic psychological fictions of most modern narrative!

Similarly, John the Baptist, a historical figure of considerable stature in Mark's time, barely gets honorable mention in the story. Indeed, John is given more attention in the histories of Josephus (below, 7,B,i)! Yet despite the fact that the Baptist appears onstage only twice in the Gospel (one of those being a "flashback"), such that we have only the most impressionistic sense of him, he cannot be considered an insignificant character. In Mark's narrative strategy, John functions as the crucial counterpoint to the controversy surrounding the messianic vocation and identity of Jesus (7,B,ii). Mark's highly selective characterization is even more evident with the story's minor characters. Most have no depth at all; some get important bit parts but remain unnamed (e.g., the woman in 5:25-34), and others (such as Levi or Bartimaeus) move on and off stage for crucial episodes, never to appear again.

The ideological function of realistic narrative is particularly demonstrated in Mark's characterization of the disciples. "The twelve" were quite probably known to Mark's audience as leaders of the second-generation church. This has led W. Kelber to argue that Mark's ultimately negative portrait of them must imply that he was engaging in a polemic against the Jerusalem-based church, especially its veneration of Peter, James, and John (1979:88ff.). Kelber is right in seeking the ideological element in Mark's characterizations, but I believe his thesis is incorrect. The portrait of the "apostles" in Mark is indeed a tragic one. Peter is an eager, if somewhat dense, disciple of Jesus; he is protective (8:32), excitable (9:5), and believes himself obedient (10:28) and loyal (14:29) to the messianic way. At the same time he is stubborn and deluded (14:31), and ultimately he betrays those he loves. In other words, Peter is just like us.

This portrait may indeed subvert apostolic veneration, but it does so in order to reduce the distance between the reader and these characters. As R. Tannehill correctly explains:

> We are encouraged in this identification by the positive portrait of the disciples early in the gospel, so that the negative turn in the disciple's story would lead the readers to reexamine their own discipleship. Thus the purpose of the author of Mark was not merely to present certain ideas about Jesus or to warn his readers against some group distinct from themselves but to lead his readers through a particular story in which they could discover themselves and thereby change [1980:149f.].

Thus, the ideological function of the plausibility of realistic narrative is to encourage readers' engagement in the story. Discipleship is not an otherworldly journey, but a following of Jesus in the vicissitudes of history.

iv. Who Is the Gospel "About"? Narrative and Historical Time

If Mark's realistic narrative has a target, it is not Kelber's hypothetical Jerusalem hierarchy, but Mark's Christian audience as a whole: "The tension between Jesus and the disciples, internal to the story, mirrors an external tension between the church as the author perceives it and the discipleship to which it is called" (Tannehill, 1980:150).

Mark existentializes the presence of the living Jesus in this story, but more as critic than as pastor of the church, as a hedge against those in the church who would domesticate Jesus to their own ends. Jesus is not presented as "the answer" but the *question* to the church; thus in the dead middle of the gospel stands the query "Who do you say that I am?" (8:29), which issues in a confessional crisis (below, 8,C). Similarly, Mark rejects the ideology of a "happily ever after" ending, offering nothing more or less than the promise that discipleship can continue, despite our own contradictions—if we respond to its call to join the ongoing journey of liberation (below, 13,E).

Realistic narrative was also the ideal vehicle for Mark's socio-political concerns, because it reflected the world of both its subject, Jesus, and its object, Mark's Palestinian audience (above, 2,A,i). The conflicts he narrates between Jesus and the Jewish leaders were living ones to his first readers: scribes, Pharisees, and priests were real persons with real social power. M. Cook has objected that Mark's characterization of these groups reflects "simply general constructs, not technical terms or precise descriptions of authority groups actually functioning" (1978:81). This is true as far as it goes: Mark's ideological narrative does not correspond *exactly* to historical sociology. But this is to miss the point; for Mark does not *intend* a dispassionate description—he was, after all, writing not to future historians but to an audience already familiar with these groups. Mark *caricatures* the opponents of the kingdom; he is offering a political cartoon, which to be effective must at once be exaggerated and unmistakably recognizable (below, 12,D,ii).

Though ostensibly set in the "time" of Jesus, the story clearly addresses issues more specifically germane to Mark's own time (some 30–40 years later). The challenge of Pharisaic practice is a good case in point. The Pharisees were certainly an important social group in the time of Jesus, especially in Galilee, and he no doubt contended with them. By the time Mark wrote his Gospel, Pharisaic social power was increasingly influential, so much so that after the destruction of the temple they emerged as the dominant leadership group in Judaism. It is not therefore surprising that they are portrayed by Mark as antagonistic particularly where the practice of the discipleship community is at stake (Mk 2:15ff.; 7:1ff.; 10:2ff.). It is plausible that the deviant social practice of Mark's community came under fierce Pharisaic attack on matters such as its inclusive table fellowship (7:14–23) and its criticism of Sabbath legislation (2:23ff.).

Second- and third-generation Christian communities needed to be reminded that the justification for their social deviance, such as their new communal economics (10:28–31), lay in Jesus himself, who both spoke authoritatively from the past and was still living and present, defending them against their opponents in the conflicts of the gospel story. Thus the parenetic sections of the Gospel are primarily concerned with defending or promoting the practice of Mark's community against its critics. In this sense the story is as much "about" Mark's community as it is "about" Jesus.

Recognizing this, N. Petersen (1980b) distinguishes between what he calls "story-time" and "discourse-time" in the narrative. Story-time is the temporal horizon within which events are narrated by the author. It is quite normal for a narrator to refer to events beyond this horizon, either in the narrative "past" ("before" the story began) or "future" ("after" the story ends). Mark alludes to the "past," for example, in 6:3, where he mentions Jesus' family life in Nazareth. Sometimes Mark alludes to events that we *think* are beyond this horizon (such as the events surrounding the arrest of John, 1:14), only to later return to narrate them after all (6:14ff.). Jesus' portents of his impending death (8:31, etc.) speak in the "future" tense, but are narrated at the end of the story. I will argue that Jesus' promises of the advent of the Human One (8:38, etc.) are also resolved within the bounds of the narrative.

There are, however, two important future references in Mark's story that he does not narrate, which represent Petersen's "discourse-time." The first touches on the events alluded to in the first half of Jesus' apocalyptic sermon (13:3ff.). This is the clearest instance of the author's transposing his own circumstances onto the narrative: the "time" of the Roman siege of Jerusalem and the "time" of Jesus are compressed into the same "moment" (below, 11,A,ii). The second is the young man's promise of renewed discipleship at the very end of the Gospel (16:7f.). Readers are called upon to "resolve" the crisis of failed discipleship by responding with their own renewed discipleship, thereby "continuing" the story. To avoid confusion over terms, I will refer to Peterson's distinction as the "narrative moment" of the text and the "historical moment" of the reader.

In fact, there are three "times" implied in the production of Mark. Stating the matter differently, we have:

—"past" (the time of narration): Mark's story of Jesus and before (i.e., his prophetic predecessors);

—"present" (the time of writing): the story as addressed by Mark to his original audience;

—"future" (the time of reading): the story fixed in a text, and thus continually reread by subsequent generations.

The primary goal of Mark was to mediate the "past" into his "present," which—as we have seen—he did by encouraging his audience to identify with the disciples in the story. But this strategy also extends to all "future" readers, including ourselves: we too are called to judge our own historical existence by the story of Jesus as told by Mark in terms of his historical situation.

Both Jesus and Mark are "past" to us, but the very nature of the Gospel's historical "elasticity" removes that distance once we enter into the story as reader. When Jesus calls the disciples, he is calling the reader; when he argues with them or despairs over their disbelief, he is contending with the reader. For that reason, throughout this commentary I will refer to Jesus' audience as the "disciples/reader"—for according to the Gospel, it is not only Peter, James, and the other characters who must struggle to follow, but *whosoever* has "ears to hear." As Mark's Jesus puts it: "What I say to you I say to all" (13:37).

To summarize, Mark's creation of the gospel genre implies discontinuity with and possibly distrust of the proven literary models (see Kelber, 1980:45). His realistic narrative grounds the historical practice of Jesus in a textual tradition, while also engaging the reader with the existential power of prophetic pronouncement and action. Although the story takes narrative liberty, moving freely between the time of Jesus and the time of his first readers, it never entered the minds of that audience, nor should it enter ours, that this was the stuff of "fantasy." Quite the contrary: Mark's realistic narrative affirms both the "historicity" of Jesus and the "historicity" of discipleship in each new situation.

The Gospel strikes precisely the balance advocated by Salvadoran Jon Sobrino in his call for "historical christology." What Sobrino claims for liberation theology could equally apply to Mark's ideology:

> Because it arose out of the concrete experience and praxis of faith within a lived commitment to liberation, it soon realized that the universality of Christ amid those circumstances could only be grasped from the stand-

point of the concrete Christ of history. The historical Jesus would serve as a satisfactory midway point between those extremes: turning Christ into an abstraction on the one hand, or putting him to direct and immediate ideological uses on the other [1978:10].

In the continuous ideological struggle within the church over christology, Mark stands as the first attempt to assert a definitive "history" of Jesus. This story calls the reader back to the messianic practice that Jesus embodied, and which he enjoins upon his followers in every age. Above all, the Gospel asserts the primacy of practice over speculative, cognitive faith. In the symbolic discourse of Mark, Jesus refuses to give a heavenly sign to his critics (8:12). The "sign" will appear only in the world and in history: the concrete practice of discipleship and the way of the cross.

3C. NARRATIVE ABSTRACT: THE STRUCTURE OF MARK

Before we begin reading the text of Mark episode by episode, it will be helpful to acquaint ourselves with the general *structure* (composition) and *story line* (plot, settings, characters, etc.) of the narrative. This brief overview at the outset serves to put the parts into the perspective of the whole, thus helping to overcome the "pericopal" or piecemeal approach with which the Gospel is usually approached. My understanding of Markan structure is already reflected in how I have divided my reading into the chapters and subsections that follow. After this summary, I will begin my commentary on each major narrative section with a closer consideration of its internal composition (*structure*) and the way in which it advances the overall plot (*story*).

i. Structure and Function

I begin with a reminder of the two key assumptions behind a literary approach to the text. One is that the relationship between form and content is fundamental to interpretation. The other is that every narrative detail has its purpose. Though the narrative function of a particular structural characteristic, or a detail of setting or plot, may not be immediately obvious, we cannot simply dismiss them by attributing them to pre-Markan sources, as does form and redaction criticism. Every element in the story is there for a reason, which we will discover only by combing back and forth through the text until it yields its own narrative coherency.

There is endless debate about how to outline the Gospel of Mark (see the summary by Kee, 1977:60ff.). In fact Mark's literary sophistication defies any definitive structural model. On the one hand, Mark's literary techniques, such as repetition or concentric composition, encourage the quest for overall structural symmetry in the story. On the other hand, any neat pattern that may emerge is inevitably upset by the way in which Mark weaves together his different narrative strands. This is illustrated clearly in the following example. Most commentators agree that Mark's Gospel can be divided into two parts.

The conversation between Jesus and his disciples on the Sea of Galilee (8:14–21) functions analeptically, referring backward in the narrative to such symbols and settings as boat and bread. Thus it draws the first half of the story to a close. The second half of the story opens in a new, far-removed setting (Caesarea-Philippi, 8:27ff.), and the episode (another conversation between Jesus and his disciples) introduces proleptic (forward-referent) symbols such as the cross. Between these two "acts" of Markan theater is an episode concerning the healing of a blind man (8:22–26). This scene serves a transitional function, "bridging" the two halves. On the one hand, it is analeptic, completing an intention introduced in 6:45—the unfinished voyage to Bethsaida (6:53). On the other hand, it is proleptic, carrying over the theme of blindess (4:12; 8:17) into the second half by anticipating another symbolic healing of the blind later in 10:46–52.

Thus at the same time the Bethsaida episode functions as the first part of Mark's most well-known narrative "frame." The cycle of discipleship teachings (8:27–10:45), the first major narrative section of the second half, opens and closes with healings of blind men. These stories are meant to be interpreted in relation to one another (below, 8,B,ii; 9,D,iv). And seen from yet a third perspective, both blind-man stories are part of a series of four healings that address the "faculties of perception": ears (7:31–37; 9:14–29) and eyes (8:22ff.; 10:46ff.). The last of Jesus' healings, this series clearly symbolizes the disciples' struggle to understand the vocation of discipleship; it spans and hence helps link the two halves of the Gospel.

Diagram 3
Three Functions of the Bethsaida Episode (Mk 8:22-26)

a) a bridge/transition between first and second halves:

Book I ⟶ *Bethsaida healing* ⟶ Book II

b) front end of a frame defining a major section:

⌐*Bethsaida healing of blind*
   discipleship teaching cycle
⌐*Jericho healing of blind*

c) part of a healing series articulating a symbolic theme:

deaf in Decapolis   deaf/dumb in northern Galilee

blind in Bethsaida   blind in Jericho

In Diagram 3 the three functions of the Bethsaida episode are identified in terms of the overall narrative structure of the Gospel.

In structural model *a*, the episode stands outside the formal two-part composition altogether. In *b* it is one of the defining characteristics of the first major subsection in Book II, and is thus integral to the internal structure of Book II. And in *c* it is part of a series that cuts across each of the first two models! This demonstrates the complexity of Mark's narrative fabric, and shows why any structural model of the Gospel must be both flexible and pluriform.

Having made this qualification, let me offer what I feel to be the story's basic structural characteristics. First, the Gospel is, as noted, bipartite. Book I takes place in and around Galilee, with first Capernaum and then the Sea of Galilee representing the gravitational middle of the narrative. There is a dialectical movement between the symbolic "peripheries" ("wilderness") and "center" (synagogue); there is also an implied movement from Jerusalem to Galilee (1:5; 3:22; 7:1). Book II, though building upon the narrative world of Book I, has an almost entirely different setting and plot structure. It takes place as a steady journey from Galilee to Jerusalem, and once in the city moves dialectically between "periphery" (Bethany) and "center" (temple).

Yet at the end of the story, the narrative suddenly points back to Galilee (16:7). This ending leads directly back to the beginning, giving the story a circular character, and functioning to "reopen" the discipleship narrative that had "closed" in the tragic climax of Book II. Thus the two parts of the story are also cyclical; this structure compels the reader to keep rereading the story so as to "understand" ever more deeply its meaning (8:21). The next section will diagram and fill out this model in more detail.

ii. Symmetry in the Two "Books" of Mark: A Synchronic Model

We can "freeze" the gospel into a structural model just as I did in the synchronic portrait of Mark's social world (above, 2,A,ii). If one were to diagram the story, it might look something like an infinity symbol (see Figure 1). Figure 1 shows the two major narrative cycles, with *x* representing the beginning and *y* the end of the story; the arrows show the chronological flow of narrative.

Figure 1
Mark, Books I and II

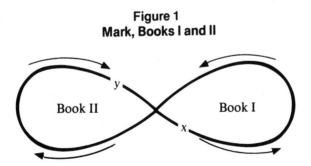

Unlike most commentators, I believe that a rough symmetry between the two halves or "books" of Mark is discernable, and I have organized my commentary to reflect that symmetry. I use the term "book" not to overemphasize the autonomy of the halves from one another, for they are interdependent, but rather to keep before us Mark's strategy of recapitulation (see next section). Each book exhibits the same set of constituent elements as seen in Table 2.

Table 2
Constitutive Elements in the Two Books of Mark

Narrative Theme	Book I	Book II
A) Prologue/call to discipleship	1:1–20	8:27–9:13
B) Campaign of direct action	1:21–3:35	11:1–13:3
C) Construction of new order	4:35–8:10	8:22–26; 9:14–10:52
D) Extended sermon	4:1–34	13:4–37
E) "Passion" tradition	6:14–29	14:1–15:38
F) Symbolic epilogue	8:11–21	15:39–16:8

Keep in mind that this is a synchronic prospectus; these elements do not necessarily appear in corresponding order in the linear flow of the narrative. I re-present the structural model, with the above elements visible, in Figure 2. Let me briefly justify this schema, with reference to the outline of my commentary.

Each *prologue* (**A** and **A′**) introduces the essential symbolic coordinates, characters, and plot complications of the respective books. The first (**A**), which I analyze in chapter 3, below, generates the narrative, and **A′**, occurring exactly at the story's midpoint, regenerates it in a new direction (below, chap. 8). The semantics and symbolics of the two prologues are parallel. Each takes place in the context of "the Way" (1:2f.; 8:27), and discusses the relationship between Jesus and John-as-Elijah (1:6; 8:28; 9:4,11–13). In both prologues, Jesus is confirmed as the anointed one by the divine voice (1:11; 9:7), in conjunction with intertextual symbolics drawn from both the Exodus tradition (1:2,13; 9:2) and apocalyptic combat-myth (1:12f.; 8:33). Each articulates a call to discipleship (1:16–20; 8:34–36) specifically in regard to the "inner circle" of the discipleship community, Peter, James, and John (1:16,19; 9:2).

The differences between the prologues reflect Mark's shift in narrative strategy from Book I to Book II. In **A**, Jesus inherits the powerful prophetic ministry of John the Baptist, and calls disciples to follow him in overturning the structures of the present social order. In **A′** the disciples are already "on the way," but their understanding of it is suspect. Thus Jesus must extend a "second" call to follow, in which he introduces the central symbol for the rest of the narrative: the cross. Jesus' relationship to John has moved from the "stronger one" (1:7) to co-sufferer (9:12f.).

I turn now to what I call the "*campaign of direct action*" narrative sections, which consist of a series of conflict stories (**B** and **B′**). **B**, set in Galilee in and around Capernaum, dramatizes Jesus' challenge to the Jewish symbolic order as it determines social life in the provinces (below, chap. 4). **B'**, set in Judea in and around Jerusalem narrates the actual confrontation with this symbolic order at the seat of its power: the temple and its political stewards (below, chap. 10). Both campaigns involve confrontative actions. In **B** these are predominantly healings and exorcisms, in **B'** they are verbal jousting and symbolic action. Each cycle centers around dramatic acts of "civil disobedience" (2:23ff.; 11:15ff.), which provoke the authorities to conspire to arrest Jesus (3:6; 12:12). Each culminates with an object lesson concerning the system's exploitation of the poor (3:1–5; 12:38–44) and closes with Jesus ideologically polarized from the scribal establishment (3:22ff.; 13:2f.). The main function of these campaigns is to delegitimate the dominant social order.

Figure 2
Mark, Books I and II, with Corresponding Themes

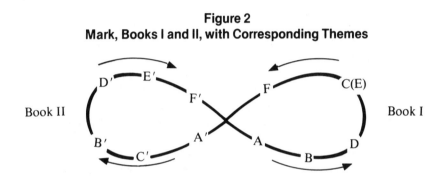

Each campaign is followed by a withdrawal from the sites of conflict, a narrative moment of reflection in which Jesus offers an *extended sermon* (**D** and **D'**). **D** (below, chap. 5) begins as an address to the crowd (4:1f.), but ends in a private explanation to the disciples (4:10f., 34). Conversely, **D'** (below, chap. 11) begins as strictly private revelation (13:3f.), and ends addressed to "all" (13:37). Both sermons rely heavily upon apocalyptic discourse, and include parables about seasons and trees (4:26ff.; 13:28ff.) and the command, "Watch!" (4:12,24; 13:5,9,23,33). The aim of both teachings is to exhort patience and discernment concerning the coming of the kingdom in history.

The two campaign narratives, which challenge the established order, are complemented by two sections that function primarily to legitimate the alternative social practice that is to characterize the discipleship community. I refer to these sections as Jesus' *construction of a new order* (**C** and **C'**). In both cases Mark relies heavily upon the narrative device of recapitulation in his internal structuring, and the narrative fiction of a journey. **C** (below, chap. 6) uses a broad double cycle (two sets of healings, feedings, etc.), which is correlated to trips back and forth between Jewish and gentile symbolic spaces. **C'** (below, chap. 9) employs a triple cycle of teaching, each of which is predicated by Jesus' three portents concerning his death at the hands of the Jerusalem authorities, which are correlated to a steady pilgrimage south to Jerusalem.

I refer to **C** as the "miracle cycle," because it narrates the construction of the new order primarily through a series of dramatic deeds, with some teaching (7:1ff.). It is structured around three kinds of symbolic action:

—journeys across the Sea of Galilee (representing the imperative to overcome the social structures of segregation between Jew and gentile; 4:35ff.; 6:45ff.)

—healings of social outcasts (representing the imperative to overcome the social structures of class division; 5:21–43; 7:24–37)

—feedings of poor masses in the wilderness (representing a practice of economic sharing; 6:33ff.; 8:1ff.)

In contrast, **C'** consists mainly of Jesus' instruction, with some healing (e.g., 9:14ff.); thus I call this the "teaching cycle." It is, however, similarly oriented around the problems of social, economic, and political status and power, but this time within the community. These include issues of group boundary (9:30ff.), nonviolence in the family (10:1ff.), a new economic order (10:17ff.), and leadership and domination (10:33ff.).

The main exception to the symmetry I have proposed is the *passion tradition*. There is nothing in Part I comparable to this extended narrative of Jesus' last days as a fugitive, his arrest, and political trial (**E'**). For this reason structural interpretations have always dealt with the "passion tradition" separately, and indeed my reading of these events (below, chap. 12) breaks the formal symmetry of my outline. A semblance of symmetry is nevertheless maintained by the account in Book I (**E**) of the last days of John the Baptist (below, first half of chap. 7), what we might call the "passion of John." Mark alludes to these events first in 1:14, then narrates them rather abruptly at 6:14ff., and alludes to them once more in Book II (9:13). Mark cites the fact of John's political execution at the hands of Herod first in 6:16, then in flashback fashion recounts John's incarceration as a result of his political criticisms (6:17f.). John's fate is determined not by a trial but by blackmail (6:19–29). Mark's parody of the court intrigues of the ruling class is in fact analogous to his account of the trial of Jesus, in which covert action and political railroading pass for "justice." And the account of John's execution, like Jesus', ends with the burial of his body in a tomb (6:29).

The general structural symmetry is completed in the respective *symbolic epilogues* (**F** and **F'**). Both represent Markan narrative symbolics at their most sophisticated, as the author attempts to interpret the meaning of the events he has recounted. In **F** (below, second half of chap. 7) Jesus poses questions to his disciples that force them to review his previous symbolic actions. Mark is implicitly turning to the reader and confronting us with the same challenge: "Do you not yet understand?" (8:21), instructing us to go back and reread. **F'** (below, chap. 13) is similarly built around analeptic symbolics, our understanding of which will determine whether or not we grasp the meaning of how the story has ended. Again, the final instructions to both the disciples and the reader is to "reread" the narrative, in this case pointing back to the symbol of the beginning of the discipleship adventure, Galilee (16:7). And as in 8:21, the response to the challenge is ambiguous and ultimately unsatisfactory (16:8). This functions both to subvert any possible triumphalistic conclusions the reader might be tempted to draw, on the one hand, and on the other, invites us to resolve the narrative crisis through a more appropriate response.

iii. The Discourse of Structure

This broadly symmetrical, bipartite and cyclical model is of course cross-hatched with many substructures, as we saw in the Bethsaida episode above. There is, for example, a discipleship call/ministry/rejection pattern in Book I, as pointed out by E. Schweizer (1978:388f.); I will refer to this pattern in terms of "generative seams" (below, 4,E; 7,A). Similarly, three times apocalyptic symbolics invade the narrative: near the beginning (1:9ff.), middle (9:2ff.), and end (15:37f.); I refer to these as "apocalyptic moments" (below, 3,F,i; 8,E,i; 13,B). Each major section also has its own internal structure, as does each particular episode or group of episodes (see the review of Markan compositional devices, above, 1,E,i). These will be explored as they come up, and I will occasionally illustrate the structure graphically. We must keep in mind that although a given substructure may reflect a rhythm different from the overall one I have proposed, it is not necessarily contradictory. As V. Robbins puts it, the "overarching rhetorical forms produced by the composition of the document have a powerful hold on the minor forms contained within it" (1984:7).

Before moving on to examining the general story line of the Gospel, let us consider the discursive characteristics of the structural model I have proposed. Remember that the "discourse" of the text (above, 1,E,ii) is the "message of form," the way in which the meaning and ideology of the text are already reflected in the structure of Markan rhetoric. I make two general observations here, and at the end of each major section of text I shall consider the specific internal discursive character of the narrative just read (*discourse*).

1. The broad two-part symmetry is an expression of the literary technique of "recapitulation." According to K. Burke, this discourse involves "the consistent maintaining of a principle in new guises . . . [a] restatement of the same thing in different ways" (Robbins, 1984:10). It particularly characterizes the narrative strategy of apocalyptic, as has been shown by A. Y. Collins in her analysis of the cyclic visions of the Book of Revelation (1976). There, seven overlapping visions (letters to churches, seals, bowls, etc.), which appear as a linear progression of events, are in fact a series of reiterations of John's central theme within a unified symbolic framework. Mark's appropriation of this discursive strategy is, as noted, an important indication of his ideological affinity with the apocalyptic tradition.

Mark articulates several key themes in the major sections of Book I, and then recapitulates each at least once in Book II. Referring to the model above, **A** aims to subvert the prevailing Jewish expectations regarding messianic intervention and salvation history by narrating the inbreaking of the "Day of Yahweh" at the margins, among the poor. **A′** recapitulates this theme by further defining the Messianic vocation as one of suffering rather than triumphalism. **B** articulates the incompatibility between the way of Jesus and the dominant social order of Roman Palestine. **B′** confirms and deepens this conflict, but in the setting of Jerusalem instead of Galilee. The other themes are all similarly recapitulated: the social character of the messianic community (**C,C′**), the need for patience and discernment (**D,D′**), and the inexorable consequences of kingdom practice (**E,E′**).

Mark also uses recapitulation in his internal composition of certain sections, as I have noted above in the case of the miracle (**C**) and teaching (**C′**) cycles. Similarly, the last four healing episodes in the story could be seen as reiterating the theme of overcoming deafness/blindness, and the double trial of Jesus as restating the theme of hostility between Messiah and the powers. In employing this narrative strategy of recapitulation, Mark appears to grasp the fact that repetition is the key to pedagogical success. The more ways he can find to articulate his radical ideology, the better chance the reader has of truly comprehending it—as opposed to the example of Peter, who misunderstands it (8:27ff.). Recapitulation also makes it more difficult for the reader to ignore or dismiss a particular theme as incidental.

2. The general structural "balance" of the story as a whole might lead us to suspect the existence of a "narrative fulcrum." The model I have proposed would seem to draw special attention to its midpoint as having particular significance (see Figure 3).

Figure 3
Mark, Books I and II Integrated

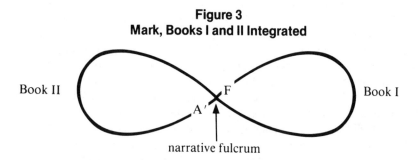

narrative fulcrum

This suspicion is confirmed by a look at this midpoint—that is, the first epilogue (**F**) and the second prologue (**A′**). As already noted, these two episodes are conversations between Jesus and the disciples/reader, in which he confronts us directly with a question. Thus at the heart of the Gospel are not propositions but challenges, which together put the reader on the "defensive": "Do you not yet understand?" (8:21); "Who do you say that I am?" (8:29).

We are further thrown off balance by the disciples' inability to answer these questions (in the first case they are silent, in the second they are plain wrong). This creates a crisis of reading, which prepares us for Jesus' second call to discipleship (8:34ff.). From here on, what has been implicit suddenly erupts onto center stage: Jesus now teaches "openly" (8:32a; see story-line summary below). The call to the cross is thus established as the ideological center of the narrative, the "fulcrum" upon which the whole story balances.

3D. NARRATIVE ABSTRACT: THE STORY OF MARK

i. Around Galilee: Book I

Rhoads and Michie have summarized the general tenor of Mark's storytelling style:

> The narrative moves along quickly, and is a lively representation of action, with little summary. The narrator "shows" the action directly, seldom talking about it indirectly. Episodes are usually brief, the scene changes often, and minor characters appear and then quickly disappear. . . . The reader is drawn quickly into the story by means of this fast-paced, dramatic movement. The brevity of style and rapidity of motion give the narrative a tone of urgency. . . . Whereas early in the narrative the action shifts rapidly from one location to another, the end of the journey slows to a day-by-day description of what happens in a single location, Jerusalem, and then an hour-by-hour depiction of the crucifixion [1982:45].

The first person on stage is John the Baptist, whose purpose is to introduce Jesus, after which he disappears (except for the flashback of 6:14ff.). After Jesus' baptism (the first apocalyptic moment) he announces his mission in Galilee (1:15), and his first act is to begin creating a community around him. Three key disciple characters (who will emerge as the inner circle of the community) are then briefly introduced (1:16ff.).

Mark next shifts to the first public scene in a Capernaum synagogue (1:21ff.), where the scribes, Jesus' arch-opponents, surface indirectly. A confrontation with a demon begins Jesus' first ministry cycle around the Sea of Galilee, a campaign of healing (1:32ff.; 2:1ff.) and exorcism. Jesus establishes a social practice of inclusivity, which defies established group boundaries (eating with sinners, 2:15), purity restrictions (contact with lepers, 1:41ff.), and sabbatic norms (2:23ff.). This in turn provokes conflict with the local civic leadership: first the scribal (1:22; 2:6) and priestly (1:43) sectors, then the Pharisees (a series of three episodes beginning in 2:15). In the course of the story virtually every identifiable ruling faction in Jewish society will oppose Jesus.

The first campaign has a double culmination. A public challenge in a synagogue ends with the formation of a political coalition of Pharisees and "Herodians" (representing the Galilean political elite), for the purpose of plotting Jesus' murder (3:1-6). Soon after, a shouting match with central government investigators ends in ideological polarization (3:22ff.). Between these episodes Jesus consolidates his new community (3:13ff.) even as he breaks with his own kin (3:31ff.). After each confrontation Jesus follows a practice of withdrawal (1:35; 3:7; 4:1). In a kind of narrative pause (4:2ff.), Jesus offers an extended reflection concerning the paradoxes of the kingdom's penetration into history.

Jesus next embarks on the first of several boat crossings of the Sea of Galilee (4:35ff.). Upon his arrival on the gentile side of the lake, Jesus for the second time inaugurates his ministry with a dramatic exorcism (5:1ff.). He then returns to Jewish territory for two interrelated healing episodes (5:21ff.). Traveling to his home town Jesus experiences more rejection (6:1ff.), and then sends his disciples on their first solo mission (6:7ff.). Inserted between the departure and arrival (6:30f.) of the disciples is the story (suspended since 1:14) of John's arrest and execution by Herod (6:14ff.).

The remainder of the first half is a continuation of symbolic actions, including more boat journeys (6:46ff.; 8:14ff.) and healings (7:24ff.), two wilderness feedings (6:34ff.; 8:1ff.), and a dispute episode with the Pharisees over the social boundaries of table fellowship. Throughout this middle section, the parallel cycles of ministry and the recurring debate concerning "the loaves" aim to dramatize the struggle to overcome the social enmity between Jew and gentile—the archetypical rift in the human family. The healings and brief parenetic section (7:14ff.) signify the repudiation of caste and class barriers. Book I closes with Jesus' attempt to tutor the disciples/reader concerning the real meaning of his symbolic action (8:14–21).

ii. Toward Jerusalem: Book II

As Book II opens, the narrative sites of boat and sea are abruptly abandoned, and a new journey begun. After the transitional Bethsaida healing (8:22ff.), the first scene opens in Caesarea Philippi, the northernmost reach of the narrative, from which it turns south in a slow march to Judea. From here on, the story is dominated by the proleptic force of the imminent showdown in Jerusalem, anticipated in Jesus' first portent (8:31f.). In the second prologue three major plot developments are suddenly brought into focus (see below, iii). First, the incipient conflict between Jesus and his own followers erupts into full-scale confrontation (8:29ff.), a complication that will continue to escalate until its tragic conclusion. Secondly the mystery surrounding the identity of Jesus deepens when he rejects Peter's "confession" (8:29). As readers we are now off balance, for we had been led from the beginning of the story to believe Jesus *was* in fact Messiah (1:1). Finally, the real consequences of Jesus' conflict with the authorities is revealed, and he demands that his followers be prepared to embrace the cross (8:34ff.). This new direction in the story is subsequently confirmed by the divine voice in the second apocalyptic moment of the transfiguration (9:2ff.).

The next section consists of a triple cycle I call the "discipleship catechism on nonviolence." Three times Jesus anticipates his execution at the hands of the Jerusalem powers; each time the disciples demonstrate an inability to understand or accept this destiny and each time Jesus responds by teaching them the social strategy of nonviolence and service. The tone of this section is clearly didactic, addressing the internal organization of the community, including marriage and family, group boundaries, leadership, and possessions. By the time it draws to a close with a final statement of the messianic ideology (10:45) and a second blind man story, the traveling band has arrived at the outskirts of Jerusalem (Jericho), now following Jesus with palpable trepidation (10:32).

The second campaign is a series of running debates, with Jesus moving in and out of Jerusalem. It commences with a theatrical procession (11:1ff.), a symbolic gesture (11:12–14, 20–26), and a dramatic direct action in the temple (11:15–20). With this assault Jesus throws down the gauntlet, declaring himself in full opposition to the temple state and its legitimating ideology of Davidic kingship. One by one he engages in rhetorical battle with the stewards of that state. He is challenged first by the representatives of the temple power structure (chief priests, scribes, and elders, 11:27ff.), then by provincial representatives of the colonial apparatus (Pharisees and Herodians, 12:13ff.). After locking horns with the archconservative elite (Sadducees, 12:18ff.), Jesus turns for a final offensive upon scribal authority (12:28ff.). In each of these debates, Jesus appears to prevail, finally silencing his antagonists (12:34).

Throughout most of this section the disciples are waiting offstage, reappearing only at the bitter culmination of the section, when Jesus decisively repudiates the temple-state (12:43ff.). Jesus' criticisms are aimed at the political economy of the temple and its exploitation of the poor, the ideology and hermeneutics of the scribal class, and the authority of the Jewish-Roman condominium. Sitting on the Mount of Olives, Jesus offers his second extended discourse (13:5ff.) on apocalyptic patience. He exhorts his followers to reject the eschatological claims of nationalist patriots in their commitment to a liberated temple-state, and to hold out for a more genuinely revolutionary transformation of the world.

Jesus withdraws for the last time to suburban Bethany, with the plot to arrest him now in full swing (14:3). At this point, the narrative takes on the sinister hues of covert machinations. The authorities infiltrate Jesus' community, collaborating with one of the disciples on an undercover operation (14:10f.). Meanwhile, the hard-pressed community has gone underground: Mark offers a tragic/pathetic portrait of the community celebrating the Passover feast in hiding, riddled by doubt and suspicion (14:17ff.). In counterpoint to their faintheartedness, Jesus emphasizes his solidarity with them (14:22ff.), insisting that, although their defection may be inevitable, the discipleship story will not end (14:26ff.). True to his prediction, the disciples collapse under pressure (14:32ff.), and flee when Jesus is seized by state security forces. At that point the discipleship narrative collapses, and the trial narrative begins.

The double trial and torture of Jesus serves to equate the Jewish ruling class and Roman imperialists in their common rejection of Jesus, who submits to the railroading in defiant silence. While the disciples hover in the shadows (14:66ff.; 15:40ff.), new characters come onto the stage: the high priest, the Roman procurator Pilate, a fellow prisoner Barabbas. The narrative builds a crescendo of irony, culminating in the crowd's insistence that the sicarius terrorist be spared in order that the nonviolent Jesus be executed. Amid the derision of his triumphant opponents, Jesus is summarily crucified, and the story appears to reach its tragic end.

Jesus' death, the third apocalyptic moment, brings to a climax Mark's symbolic representation of the Human One: as his opponents look on, he expires, and the world "ends." But this is revealed only to those with "eyes to see." Meanwhile, the mockery of Jesus continues in the postmortem responses of both a Jewish and a Roman representative. In the second epilogue the women, who have endured the ordeal of Jesus' crucifixion without abandoning him, attempt to give him the dignity of proper burial, and are shown to be true disciples. Their encounter with a "young man" at the tomb represents the third call to discipleship: the women are invited to follow Jesus to Galilee, with the promise that there the discipleship narrative will resume. The story ends with a new beginning, completing a narrative circle.

iii. The Three Major Plot Strands

Structuralist narratology speaks of the "deep structure" of a story as its "narrative syntax." A. J. Greimas has defined five elements essential to narrative syntax: (1) mandating; (2) acceptance or rejection of mandate; (3) confrontation; (4) success or failure; (5) consequence or attribution (Via, 1985:40ff.). If we consider Jesus as the subject of the main plot, it is not hard to see each of these elements in the story line as I have outlined it. Jesus is mandated at baptism, accepts the mandate to preach the kingdom, and confronts the opponents of the kingdom. Whether the cross is success or failure depends of course upon one's point of view; from Mark's point of view it is success, and guarantees that the attribution of Jesus as Messiah is indeed reliable.

In addition to this main plot, we can abstract three distinct "narrative strands" or subplots. Assuming Jesus as protagonist, each strand has a different subject, and can be read in terms of the above narrative syntax. The first subplot involves Jesus' attempts to create and consolidate a messianic community, the subject being of course his disciples. His mandate to them is to carry on the work of the kingdom (1:17; 3:14; 6:7), but this mandate is essentially rejected once it is revealed as the way of the cross. This leads to several confrontations (6:53; 8:17ff.; 8:33, etc.), and ultimately to the failure of the disciples to follow Jesus to the cross (14:50f.). This tragedy is, however, reversed by the promise that because Jesus lives, the discipleship adventure can continue (16:6f.).

The second subplot is Jesus' ministry of healing, exorcism, and proclamation of liberation, the subject being the poor and oppressed, who are embodied in the "crowd" in the Gospel. The mandate appears in the first synagogue exorcism, in which the crowd acknowledges that Jesus' authority exceeds that of their scribal overlords (1:22). By the time Jesus comes to Jerusalem, it seems that the crowd has accepted his mandate for a new social order, hailing him as popular king (11:9f.). There is an implicit confrontation with the masses in Jesus' repudiation of national insurrection, a warning he addresses to "all" (13:37). In the end, the crowd, like the disciples, rejects Jesus, calling for a pardon for the terrorist Barabbas and execution for Jesus (15:6ff.). The consequence is that the crowd remains under the control of those who dominate it (15:11).

The third subplot is Jesus' confrontation with the dominant socio-symbolic order, the subject being the stewards of that order: the scribes, Pharisees, Herodians, and ruling Jerusalem clergy. Jesus delivers his mandate to them several times in the first campaign of direct action, asserting his authority over the purity and debt system (2:10,28), and challenging the authorities to choose justice and compassion over domination (3:4). This is immediately rejected (3:6), and is continually rejected throughout the story (6:26; 11:27ff.; 12:13; 14:1f.). Jesus confronts each of the representative ruling groups during the second campaign narrative, conducts a direct action against their temple (11:15ff.), and appears to successfully silence them (12:34). But in the end the forces of Jewish and Roman state power join to vanquish Jesus. The consequence is that they behold the advent of the Human One, to their shame (15:29–39; cf. 8:29f.; 14:62); despite appearances, the cross event seals the doom of their domain (15:38).

It should be noted that all three subplots contribute to the climactic crisis of Jesus' arrest and execution, and are gathered together in the passion narrative. In the final scenes of the story we see the defecting disciples, the disillusioned crowd, and the hostile authorities, all juxtaposed to Jesus, who alone goes the way of the cross. These three narrative strands also represent the key aspects in Jesus' messianic program: confronting the old order, constructing an alternative order, and bringing liberation to the poor.

In order to appreciate the way Mark has interwoven this triple-stranded narrative fabric, it will sometimes be necessary in my commentary to "jump around" in the text. Although I strive to follow the chronological appearance of episodes in the story, I will occasionally cut across it, indeed across the logic of my own structural model. Sometimes it will be more fruitful to examine episodes in relation to one another (below, 5,D), or to investigate a particular theme by grouping episodes together (below, chap. 6). Although this makes for occasional digressions, I will make the reader aware of the moves I am making and the reasons for them throughout my analysis of the Gospel. We are now prepared to commence our reading of the Gospel, beginning with a look at the first prologue.

3E. A SUBVERSIVE STORY WORLD IS CREATED (1:1–8)

The prologue is defined by the opening (1:1) and closing references (1:14f.) to "gospel." This first "act" establishes Mark's ingenuous use of the theatrics of sight and sound as well as dramatic action. The first scenes are strung together in rapid succession, building a sense of expectation, as one prophecy after another is fulfilled in Mark's story time (below, F,ii). Most of the narrative action is indirect, with the exception of the baptism of Jesus, which is thus the focus of the section. The time of the prologue is indistinct ("beginning" in 1:1 and "fullness of the moment" in 1:15), tied only loosley to the historical ministry and arrest (1:14) of John. The settings are similarly vague, but loaded with symbolic meaning.

The rapid pace of these opening scenes allows Mark to capture the reader's attention while proceeding to the main story of Jesus' ministry as quickly as possible. The narrative of succession (Isaiah-John-Jesus-kingdom) culminates in the call of the disciples, which I have chosen to read together with the prologue. The horizons of the story world it sets in place function to subvert the symbolic universe of the reader, thus generating ideological and narrative space for the invasion of something radically new. It is the thesis of the prologue that the new order of the kingdom does not arise from within existing power relationships but quite independently of them, at the margins of society.

i. The Title: Subverting the Roman Cultural Code

Mark entitles his work simply "The beginning of the gospel of Jesus Messiah" (*archē tou euaggeliou Iēsou Christou, 1:1*).

> It can hardly be doubted that the *archē* of Mark 1:1 has a paradigmatic or metaphorical relationship to the *archē* (LXX) of Genesis 1:1, especially since Mark speaks of the *archē* of creation in 10:6. . . . There is another first time despite the fatigue of world-history [Via, 1985:45].

This echo of Genesis serves three functions. First, Mark is boldly suggesting that his story represents a fundamental regeneration of salvation history, as will soon be confirmed by his citation of the prophets. Secondly, it introduces at the outset the "palingenetic" thrust of Mark's apocalyptic discourse: this is a story about a new heaven and new earth. Thirdly, it has a specific meaning in light of the ending of the story (below, 13,E), where Mark will point back to the place where the discipleship narrative was originally generated—Galilee. A rereading of (reengagement with) the story offers a "new beginning" for the discipleship adventure.

Everywhere else in the story, "gospel" is construed as something independent of Jesus (1:14f.; 8:35; 10:29; 13:10; 14:9), but here it is bound to him: it is *about* Jesus Messiah. We must understand that here Mark is giving the reader privileged information, telling us what the characters in Book I are unable to grasp, perplexed as they are about Jesus' identity (4:41; 6:3). Then, as Book II opens, the term "Messiah" is finally introduced into the story world (8:29). To the reader's chagrin, however, Jesus immediately repudiates it, provoking what I call a "confessional crisis" (below, 8,C). From that point on, Messiah becomes an object of contention (12:35; 13:21; 15:32). Jesus never truly accepts the designation, deferring instead to a third-person epithet, the "Human One," an apocalyptic persona from Daniel (8:31; 14:61).

But if Mark has no intention of affirming this messianic designation in his story, why does he apply it to Jesus here in the story's masthead? As with so many elements of Mark's narrative strategy, this has to do with the story's circular character. The epithet is asserted at the "beginning," dropped by the end, and then reasserted in the new rereading—but now understood in new terms. Mark was not prepared to abandon messianic discourse altogether, which after all was the cornerstone of the early church's confession. At the same time, Messiah was a political title, a symbol of popular kingship, and thus easily misapprehended, especially by those who wished to put it at the service of "loyalistic" rebellion (below, 11,C,iv). By affirming the designation at the outset, Mark enters into the ideological struggle over how to properly understand it. This story aims to convince us what the messianic vocation is—and, just as vigorously, what it is not.

I have already noted the significance of "gospel" as an authoritative text (above, A,i) and a unique literary genre (above, B). But from what semantic field was the term drawn? So thoroughly religious to modern readers, what would "gospel" have connoted for Mark's first audience? A Hellenistic expression (literally "glad tidings"), it was, according to the *Theological Dictionary of the New Testament*, "a technical term for 'news of victory,' " especially in military battles. In the Roman empire it was especially associated with political propaganda. J. Fears describes the "imperial gospel" as a rhetorical tradition that wove together "allegory, contemporary reality, and historical archetypes" (1980). It promoted the paternal and benevolent colonial image of Rome throughout its far-flung provinces (see Wengst, 1987: 7–44).

Roman propaganda focused upon eulogizing Caesar as the "divine man." This ideological strategy is well documented in coins of the period, and of course in the later emperor cults of Asia Minor. The accession to power of a new ruler was cause for "glad tidings," and celebrations and sacrifices always followed (see Wengst, 1987: 46ff.):

> [Deification of the emperor] gives *euangelion* its significance and power.
> . . . Because the emperor is more than a common man, his ordinances are glad messages and his commands are sacred writings. . . . He proclaims *euangelia* through his appearance . . . the first *euangelium* is the news of his birth [*TDNT*, 2:724].

As one ancient inscription put it: "The birthday of the god was for the world the beginning of the joyful messages which have gone forth because of him" (ibid.; see above, 2,F,i).

From this there emerges yet another dimension of Mark's title. He is serving notice that he is challenging the apparatus of imperial propagation. His dramatic prologue (but not birth narrative proper, as in Luke and Matthew) heralds the advent of an "anointed" leader, who is confirmed by the Deity and who proclaims a "kingdom." In other words, Mark is taking dead aim at Caesar and his legitimating myths. From the very first line, Mark's literary strategy is revealed as subversive. Gospel is not an inappropriate title for this story, for Mark will indeed narrate a battle. But the "good news" of Mark does not herald yet another victory by Rome's armies; it is a declaration of war upon the political culture of the empire.

ii. "Isaiah": Subverting the Jewish Cultural Code

Before the curtain rises on the first act of the story, we hear a voice from offstage, reading from the Hebrew scriptures (1:2f.; above, A,iii). This citation from "Isaiah" is in fact a composite of several texts from the LXX, and Mark's redaction again reveals a subversive intent.[2] The first half of the prophecy (1:2) conflates two non-Isaian texts. The first is the heralding of a way for the Hebrew people in its journey toward liberation:

> Behold, I send an angel before you (LXX: *apostellō ton angelon mou pro prosōpou sou*) to guard you on the way (*en tē hodō*) and to bring you to the land I have prepared for you [Ex 23:20].

This way is identified with the way being cleared for Yahweh's advent as announced by the prophet "Malachi":[3]

> Behold I dispatch my messenger (LXX: *exapostellō ton angelon mou*) to make a way before me (*hodon pro prosōpou mou*) [Mal 3:1a].

Both texts function to introduce "the way" as the central discipleship motif in the gospel, though it is more predominant in Book II. A great deal has been written about this motif, which I will not belabor (see Best, 1981). Mark's citation, however, substitutes a verb not found in these texts: he speaks of the "construction" (*kataskeuasei*) of a way. This is the first indication that what is being forged is no mere path; a new way of life is being built in the shell of the old world.

H. Waetjen (1982) calls this a "remarkably ambiguous composite quotation," which in light of the rest of the prologue can be taken in three ways. Insofar as the messenger will be identified with John as an Elijah figure, whose role is to introduce Jesus, the passage would read:

"Behold, I (God) send my messenger (John/Elijah) before your face (Jesus) who will construct your way."

Yet is Jesus who later in the story will "go before" (*proagein*) the disciples "on the way" (10:32; 14:28), indeed who will "cry out in a great voice" (cf. 1:3) on the cross (15:34). The correspondence between the closing promise of Mark's ending ("He is going before you to Galilee," 16:7) and this opening prophecy further strenghtens the circular dynamic of the narrative. In this sense, the text could be interpreted:

"Behold, I (God) send my messenger (Jesus) before your face (the disciples) who will construct your way."

A third possibility, especially considering the strong claims being made by Mark in authoring this work (above, A,i), is:

"Behold, I (God) send my messenger (the evangelist) before your face (his addressees) who (by writing a gospel) will construct your way."

Waetjen concludes:

> This extraordinary verse, so full of possible meanings, which is attributed to Isaiah, is the result of the evangelist's midrashic (interpretative) reflection on Isaiah 40:3 *vis-à-vis* the good news of Jesus Christ and serves as a superscription of and key to the unusual literary composition of Mark [1982:11].

There is another, more compelling, dimension to 1:2. Its allusion to "Malachi," the last of the writing prophets in the Hebrew canon, is particularly poignant:

> From at least the first century C.E. onward, the ancient rabbis and scribes held that true prophecy had ended with Haggai, Zechariah, and Malachi . . . such a view prevailed in the emerging "canonical" thinking regarding which writings were to be recognized as authoritative scripture [Horsley and Hanson, 1985:146].

Mark would have been well aware of this, and of the fact that many of his Jewish contemporaries despaired that the prophetic voice in Israel had fallen silent forever. Here, by existentializing the prophetic voice, he boldly implies that the Word of Yahweh is now again being spoken. More than this, the "Malachi" oracle specifically announces that Yahweh is about to make a dramatic appearance in history.[3] The long-awaited eschatological judgment has drawn nigh at last!

This immediately introduces overwhelming tension: something wonderful must be about to happen. But what? Or, more importantly for Mark, where? "Malachi" envisioned the site of Yahweh's epiphany to be the Jerusalem temple: "The Lord whom you seek will suddenly come to his temple" (Mal 3:1b). Mark, however, conspicuously omits this part of the oracle, and in its place grafts on an almost literal quotation of Isaiah 40:3. The messenger will appear instead *in the wilderness* (1:3)—which is precisely where we find John the Baptist in the opening act (1:4).

"Wilderness" (or desert, *erēmos*) is a second crucial coordinate of Mark's narrative world, occurring nine times in Book I. Its semantic field for Mark's Palestinian readers was a complex one, each aspect of which is relevant to Mark. In literal terms, wilderness connoted an uninhabited and desolate place, marginal existence: John lives on locusts and honey (1:6), and persons hunger there (8:2f.). Symbolically, it was the site of a community in flight (as in the exodus tradition) or a refuge for the persecuted faithful who await deliverance (as in apocalyptic literature; see Rv 12:6,14). Jesus, like Israel, is "tested" there (1:12f.); there he also seeks solitude (1:35,45). In this, both Jesus and John follow the prophetic "script" of Elijah, who also withdrew to the wilderness when hunted by the political authorities (1 Kgs 19). And geopolitically, the wilderness would have been identified with the spawning of contemporary prophetic and revolutionary movements (see Acts 21:38; above, 2,C,iii). Indeed, it will be the site for Jesus' "mass organizing," in which he facilitates the feeding of the multitudes (6:31ff., 8:4; below, 6,E).

The principal narrative function of wilderness in the prologue, however, where it appears four times, is ideological: it represents the "peripheries." By inserting this coordinate in place of "Malachi's" temple (representative of the "center"; as the site of Yahweh's renewed action, Mark creates a spatial tension between two archetypically opposite symbolic spaces. This wilderness/temple polarity becomes explicit in Mark's wry report—a typical Semitic hyperbole—that "all the country of Judea and all the people of Jerusalem" seek John in the wilderness (1:5). According to the dominant nationalist ideology of salvation history, Jerusalem was considered the hub of the world to which all nations would one day come (see Ps 69:35f., Is 60:10–14). Mark turns this "circulation" on its head: far from embarking on triumphal pilgrimage to Zion, the crowds flee to the margins, for purposes of repentance.

Mark has herein set his sights upon the political culture of the Jewish ruling elite. The priestly/scribal establishment, whose social power derived from controlling the mechanisms of redemption in the Jerusalem temple, would necessarily take strong exception to this "wilderness revival." For a second time Mark has expropriated and subverted key elements in the prevailing cultural codes. And the story has barely begun!

iii. The Beginning of the End: John the Baptist as Elijah

The costuming of the first scene is as important as its setting. It opens with John the Baptizer preaching repentance at the Jordan (1:4), but Mark seems more interested in telling us what he is wearing (1:6). Why? Just as a gaunt, bearded face and a stovepipe hat would immediately conjure up the image of Abe Lincoln for those socialized into modern American mythology, so would John's garb have invoked the great prophet Elijah for Mark's readers (see 2 Kgs 1:8). The John-as-Elijah narrative linkage is well known to students of Mark, figuring at decisive intervals when the identity of Jesus is at issue (6:15, 8:28, 9:4,11–13, 15:35f.).

The political dimension of this representation is usually overlooked, however. Elijah and his prophetic disciples are portrayed in the Hebrew Bible as:

> Bringing the pronouncement of judgment on king and court and sentence for faithless violation of the covenant with Yahweh, often as a result of strong foreign cultural influence . . . the prophets also performed one of the traditional functions of the judge (*shophet*) in communicating Yahweh's redemptive action, his protection of his people against foreign invasion and domination. . . . Against the oppression . . . the prophets Elijah and Elisha and their followers, the "sons of proph-

ets," fomented a popular rebellion [against] the house of Ahab [Horsley and Hanson, 1985:139,141].

We know from Josephus that John was perceived by the Herodian court as such a subversive threat, and John's ideology of repentance, we will subsequently learn, earns him a prophet's reward (6:17ff.; below, 7,B). All this however, is only hinted at here (Mark notes John's arrest in 1:14a).

At the level of narrative, the introduction of "Elijah" here dramatically escalates the tension of expectation. What was the last cry before the prophetic voices died away? It was "Malachi's" promise/warning: "Behold I will send you Elijah before the great and terrible day of the Lord arrives" (Mal 4:5). The reader is thrown into turmoil: Is this the "beginning" (1:1) or "the end"? Yet the expectation is almost immediately short-circuited, for John's baptizing ministry, which Mark later acknowledges as one of considerable power and controversy (11:30), is not the subject of this Gospel. John is brought onstage only to introduce the double theme of the Gospel: the kingdom mission (the preaching of repentance and the forgiveness of sins) and the kingdom's envoy. Thus in Mark 1:7 John reveals that the "day of the Lord" is still only proximate; first must come "someone stronger" (1:7, *ho ischuroteros*).

What is meant by this? We will only later discover that the metaphor refers to Jesus' struggle with the "strong man" of 3:27 (below, 4,F,i). The one who is coming has "sandals" (*hupodeematōn*) that John cannot even loosen. This Semitic phrase (apparently strong in the tradition: it appears even in the fourth gospel, Jn 1:27) would seem to be a euphemism for subordination. The image may also have a symbolic connotation for Mark, for it appears again in 6:9, where Jesus instructs his disciples to be shod as they depart on the kingdom mission (below, 7,A,ii). In this case the footwear may represent Jesus' way of discipleship, to which John acquiesces.

But what happens next appears to contradict this, for it is Jesus who subjects himself to John in baptism (1:9). In order to make sure we do not misinterpret this, therefore, John's prophecy concludes by claiming that his baptism only predicates that of the coming one (1:8). We will come to understand baptism "by the holy spirit" in terms of confrontation with the powers (10:38f.), the political site of discipleship under divine guidance (13:11; see below, 8,D). John's anthem of anticipation has therefore synopsized the kingdom vocation as the subsequent story will narrate it: a mission ("sandals") to overthrow (the "stronger one") the powers ("baptism" by the holy spirit). But these symbolics can hardly be clear to us from this first reading. Thus we are left at the close of the first scene still wondering whether this "Elijah" will bring with him the "day of the Lord."

3F. A SUBVERSIVE MISSION INAUGURATED (1:9–20)

i. Jesus Baptized: First Apocalyptic Moment

The second scene of the first act is a good example of Markan narrative construction. It opens as Jesus appears *from* Galilee (1:9a), and closes when

Jesus reappears coming back *into* Galilee (1:14b). In between there is considerable movement across narrative time and space: a baptism and vision at the Jordan, scene change to the wilderness testing, and undefined passage of time until the first "historical" marker: John's arrest (1:14a).

If John/Elijah's prophecy delayed our expectation, the abrupt introduction of the story's main character further throws us off guard: "Having thus created a mood of dramatic expectancy, Mark described the entrance of Jesus in the most shockingly anticlimactic fashion conceivable" (Bilezikian, 1977:57). Jesus appears simply as one of the anonymous crowd coming to the baptist. The fact that he comes from "Nazareth in Galilee" (1:9) further intensifies the dislocation of symbolic space. One would expect the hero to be credentialed through miraculous origins or a solid genealogy (something Matthew and Luke cannot resist). Mark, however, stresses Jesus' obscure origins, "from Nazareth," tantamount to introducing him as "Jesus from Nowheresville." His entirely unremarkable home village is a place unattested in any ancient source. Moreover, throughout the story Mark insists upon reminding us of the humble Nazareth roots (1:24; 10:47; 14:67; 16:6).

Galilee, on the other hand, was notorious; the northern border of Palestine, it was regarded with contempt and suspicion by most southern Jews. As already pointed out (above, 2,B,iii), Galilee was surrounded by Hellenistic cities, populated heavily by gentiles, predominantly poor, and geopolitically cut off from Judea by Samaria. Mark has, in other words, confirmed the spatial tension between center and periphery implied in the Jerusalem/wilderness opposition of 1:5.

Yet it is precisely upon this figure, of these doubtful social origins, in this remote location, that the divine favor falls. In 1:10 the narrative, which to this point has been quite terrestrial, even mundane, is suddenly invaded by apocalyptic imagery. When Jesus rises from the waters of the Jordan, it is to a vision of the heavens being rent asunder and a voice speaking in election. Again, an intertextual image calls to mind the prophetic hope:

> Oh that you would tear the heavens open and come down
> to make known your name to your enemies,
> and make the nations tremble at your presence,
> working unexpected miracles
> such as no one has ever heard before [Is 64:1–2].

Could this unknown Nazarene villager be the fulfillment of Isaiah's ancient longing?

This is the first of three distinct "moments" in which Mark inserts explicitly apocalyptic symbolics into his narrative. Points of discourse between earth and "heaven," these moments function as structural pillars for the story, fundamental to both plot generation and ideological legitimation. Here the divine voice confirms the claim of 1:1, though this remains "privileged information," for Mark gives no indication that any of the bystanders at the Jordan saw or heard anything. As a dramatic device it reveals, as W. Bundy puts it:

the unseen forces actually operative in the destinies of the actors on the stage of history. It gives the reader a glimpse behind the scenes . . . a sort of dramatic aside which, at the very beginning, lets the reader in on the secret of the hero's true identity [in Bilezikian, 1977:122].

Jesus is identified as "beloved Son" (1:11; cf. 9:7; 12:6), the language calling to mind two key scriptural traditions. The first is the royal messianic psalm (Ps 2:7), in which the king is enthroned *over against* the "rulers of the earth" (Ps 2:2,10). Yet the triumphal tone of this Davidic tradition is qualified by the simultaneous allusion to the Suffering Servant of Isaiah:

> I will put my spirit upon him,
> he will bring forth justice to the nations,
> he will not cry or lift up his voice in the street,
> a bruised reed he will not break [Is 42:1].

Yet once again the scene ends anticlimactically: Jesus simply retreats deeper into the wilderness (1:12). Has Mark reduced the apocalyptic hope of a new heaven and earth to a hallucination?

The symbolics surrounding Jesus' baptism have a social function that indeed signals the creation of a new humanity. According to Waetjen, Jesus' baptism is genuine, not feigned; nevertheless, we should see him as distinct from those whom John baptized *in* the Jordan in 1:5:

> In contrast to his fellow Jews—and this is where the real difference lies—Jesus was baptized *into* the Jordan. . . . The implication is that the Jews from Judea and Jerusalem were not submerged in the river . . . they did not submit to the full depth of John's baptism; they did not abandon themselves to the radical way that John was offering them [1982:6].

Using K. Burridge's concept of redemption as the discharge of social obligation, Waetjen argues that the symbolic act of Jesus' baptism must be seen in specifically social terms:

> It is a genuine act of repentance. As such it ends his participation in the structures and values of society. It concludes his involvement in the moral order into which he was born. . . . The entire redemptive process of Jewish society as it is maintained by the institutions through which power is ordered . . . the totality of the Jewish-Roman social construction of reality, has been terminated. All the debts that have been incurred under this elitist ordering of power and its community life have been cancelled. The death experience of repentance has redeemed Jesus from his comprehensive indebtedness and the prescribed ways and means of discharging his obligations. He has become wholly unobliged [1982:6f.].

The new creation begins with a renunciation of the old order.

Thus what first appears anticlimactic is revealed through apocalyptic symbolics as truly subversive—but, as will be the case throughout the Gospel, we must have "eyes to see" the true political theater of Markan symbolic action. In baptism Jesus is declared an "outlaw," so to speak; his mission will be to challenge the oppressive structures of law and order around him. A modern analogy to baptism-as-declaration-of-resistance might be the public acts of draft card burning, which symbolized "induction" into the antiwar movement during the Indochina conflict. That we are justified in interpreting the baptism this way is born out by what happens next, for no sooner has Jesus declared himself "liberated" than he is confronted by the ruler of the world order (1:12f.). History is after all on the edge: the apocalyptic combat myth has commenced!

In keeping with his inverted notions of symbolic space, Mark resists the temptation to narrate a grand entrance of this "new human being." Instead, he drives Jesus off stage altogether. Somewhere in the heart of the wilderness another apocalyptic drama ensues: a struggle between Satan and the Spirit-led Jesus:

> He was in the wilderness forty days
> and Satan tried to tempt him there
> and he was among the wild beasts
> and the angels ministered to him[1:13].

The wilderness testing of course brings to mind Israel's liberation from the pharaoh's Egypt, but will gain a more specific meaning in Mark's narrative. At key points Jesus is "tempted" by his political opponents to compromise himself (8:11; 10:2; 12:15), and it is against this temptation that he will warn his disciples on the eve of his arrest (14:38).

Each side in this contest has its respective mythic "accomplices." Jesus receives help from the angels while surviving among "wild beasts." The latter (*thērion*) is a common apocalyptic euphemism, appearing in Daniel (7:3,7) and Revelation (11:7; 13:1ff., etc.). C. Cargounis's comments on Daniel are germane to Mark:

> The concept of wild beast in Daniel does not stand for any one king, but rather for the sum total of power as exercised by several earthly rulers who are inspired and directed by the invisible *archōn*. The wild beast . . . consists of the complex made up of the invisible guardian, the human delegate and the entire state mechanism that makes possible the execution of the *archōn*'s projects, in short, the genius of a nation [1977:159].

We will return to these political symbolics in reading Mark 13 (below, 11,D). In this episode the great apocalyptic struggle for history has commenced. Mark will develop this combat myth throughout the first campaign narrative, in Jesus' battle with the demons, the Human One's contest for authority with the scribes and Pharisees, and the climactic clash with the "strong man," in which Satan and the Spirit are again at odds (3:23–30).

ii. The Kairos Fulfilled: The Power of Plotted Time

The first two scenes of Mark's story, through their careful deployment of settings and symbols, establish Mark's first thesis: the great apocalyptic *novum*, which invades the world at Jesus' baptism and sets salvation history in motion again, does not occur at the center of the social order, but at its peripheries. The political edge of the narrative is sharpened by Mark's transitional closure of the prologue. Jesus commences his proclamation of the kingdom "after John had been arrested" (1:14), taking up the mantle of the fallen prophet. Jesus continues the proclamation of the kingdom and the demand for repentance—and all too soon he too will be targeted for arrest by the authorities (3:6).

N. Petersen (1978) has pointed out Mark's masterful literary use in the prologue of what he calls "story-time" and "plotted-time." The former is the "real time" between events, which may or may not be narrated. For example, the reader assumes that the events of the prologue—John's ministry, Jesus' baptism, John's arrest, Jesus' public preaching—take place over some specific period, although Mark chooses not to disclose when or how long a period. Plotted-time, on the other hand, represents the writer's freedom to manipulate chronological time in his narration of events. The author may draw out one particular moment (the baptism) or collapse days, months, or years into another (Jesus in the wilderness). Chronology may even be suspended, as in the use of "flashback" (Mark's account of John's death in 6:14ff.).

Plotted-time in the sequence of fulfilled predictions gives dramatic tension to Mark's prologue, generating a sense of the momentous. Mark announces a new "beginning," and immediately the prophetic voice awakens. "Isaiah" announces the arrival of a messenger, and John the Baptist straightaway appears in the wilderness. John in turn heralds the arrival of a "stronger one," and Jesus abruptly comes onstage to contest the rule of Satan—only to disappear offstage into the wilderness. Thus Mark keeps postponing the fulfillment of the expectations he generates. Just when it seems the new order will be unveiled, something anticlimactic takes place, and the scene changes.

Finally, in 1:15, Jesus announces the awaited moment of God's intervention: the "time is fulfilled" (*peplērōtai ho kairos*). The kingdom's arrival is "close at hand," an expression unique in the New Testament, connoting profound imminence, even liminality. Yet in 1:16, we are once again frustrated. Instead of a kingdom epiphany, the second act opens with Jesus wandering by the sea, bidding some common laborers to accompany him on a mission. The world appears still very much intact! Mark is obviously aware of the risk involved in his appeal to prophetic and apocalyptic traditions, for they also were being used to bolster the triumphalistic eschatological expectations of Jewish nationalism. For this reason, Mark pursues a narrative strategy that consistently frustrates the equation between epiphany and victorious holy war. And again, a more careful reading of his narrative symbolics confirms that Jesus is indeed commencing his assault upon the old order, as the next scene shows.

iii. The Call to Discipleship: Breaking with Business as Usual

There are three discipleship-call stories early in the narrative, unified by their common structure and setting "by the Sea of Galilee" (1:16f., 19f.; 2:14). The sea is a new and important symbolic location in Mark (below, 4,B,iv), and is here introduced as the domain of the discipleship community (3:7; 4:1f.). The first two call episodes (1:16–20) are structured as a parallel doublet, consisting of the following four-part action:

> 1) Jesus moves along the shore (1:16a,19a)
> 2) he apprehends a family fishing operation at work:
>   (a) Simon and brother Andrew casting nets (1:16b)
>   (b) James and brother John ordering nets (1:19b)
> 3) he calls them to follow (1:17,20a)
> 4) the fishermen abandon the workplace to follow:
>   (a) Simon/Andrew leave their nets (1:18)
>   (b) James/John leave their fellow workers in the boat (1:20b)

The call of Levi is roughly parallel with this form, sufficing to establish a paradigmatic substance to the call of discipleship.

There is perhaps no expression more traditionally misunderstood than Jesus' invitation to these workers to become "fishers of men" (1:17). This metaphor, despite the grand old tradition of missionary interpretation, does not refer to the "saving of souls," as if Jesus were conferring upon these men instant evangelist status. Rather, the image is carefully chosen from Jeremiah 16:16, where it is used as a symbol of Yahweh's censure of Israel. Elsewhere the "hooking of fish" is a euphemism for judgment upon the rich (Am 4:2) and powerful (Ez 29:4). Taking this mandate for his own, Jesus is inviting common folk to join him in his struggle to overturn the existing order of power and privilege.

However much the Jeremian image, as a double entendre, might confer a certain dignity upon their trade, the fishermen are called to abandon it. In fact, Mark pays exceptional attention to the social location of this episode. The fishing trade is accurately represented: we see an independent artisan class, distinct from day laborers, whom they could afford to hire (1:20). It is important to recognize that in antiquity, much more so than today, the social fabric of the rural extended family was bound to the workplace. Thus the break demanded by Jesus is not only with economic but social security as well, as will become explicit in 3:31ff. Some commentators have argued that this tradition reflects the "eschatological consciousness" of Jesus; in his expectation of the imminent end of the world, he bade others join him in abandoning all socio-economic responsibility. The implication, of course, is that such a paradigm for conversion is absurd in the "real world." This is another case of bourgeois hermeneutics trivializing apocalyptic narrative. The point here is that following Jesus requires not just assent of the heart, but a fundamental reordering of socio-economic relationships. The first step in dismantling the dominant social order is to overturn the "world" of the disciple: in the kingdom, the personal and the political are one. These concrete imperatives are precisely what the rich—Mark will later tell us—are unable or unwilling to respond to (10:17–30). In fact, Mark will have a great deal to say about concrete social and economic responsibility within the new order of the discipleship community (below, chapter 9). This is not a call "out" of the world, but into an alternative social practice.

The third and last call story concerns Levi, a customs official (2:13f.; below, 4,C,iii) who, though a social outcast, is nevertheless invited to follow. Levi, unlike the previous four, is never mentioned again after Jesus shares a meal with him and his professional associates (2:15), nor does he appear in the list of disciples in 3:17–19. This confirms that "the twelve" are not considered the only disciples in the Gospel.

Mark's call-paradigm contrasts sharply with the traditional method of rabbinic recruitment, as noted by E. Schweizer (1964). Normally the student sought the teacher and followed only for as long as it took to attain rabbinic status himself. The call of Jesus, however, is absolute, disrupting the lives of potential recruits, promising them only a "school" from which there is no graduation. This "first" call to discipleship in Mark is an urgent, uncompromising invitation to "break with business as usual." The world is coming to an end, for those who choose to follow. The kingdom has dawned, and it is identified with the discipleship adventure.

iv. The Gospel as Ideological Novum: Mark's Socio-Literary Strategy through 1:20

As I shall do at the end of each major section of the Gospel, I now step back to assess the socio-literary significance of what we have just read. This involves first a review of the ideology of form, or *discourse*, and the social function of the story line, or *signification*.

The *discourse* of the prologue constructs a narrative world in which the apocalyptic drama (the conflict between the kingdom and the old world order) will take place. The basic elements of this world are of course time and place, and Mark's realistic narrative establishes these at the outset as both historical and mythic/existential. For example, Mark is implicitly appealing to "historical time" by introducing the ministry of John the Baptist, which would have been well known to his readers. Mark's style of recital, in which most episodes begin with *kai*—"and"—is one Jeremias calls "an established characteristic of Palestinian historical writing" (Jeremias, 1966:174). Yet at the same time, the story commences, unlike, for example, Luke (Lk 1:5; 2:1f.), in the framework of an indeterminate, mythic story-time: "the beginning," "the fullness of *kairos*." This apparent contradiction is quite consistent with Mark's intention to narrate past events with existential power. I would not, however, go so far as Via (1985), who says that Mark intends to portray in this narrative world a symbolic return to primordial time (i.e., "before the fall"). Rather, the advent of Jesus represents the "moment" in which the world order is disrupted, a moment that reoccurs wherever the discipleship narrative is reproduced in the lives of real persons in real places. *This* disruption represents the realization of the apocalyptic "day of the Lord."

Similarly, the place of the story is both real-historical (the river Jordan) and mythic-archetypical. The Galilee/wilderness coordinate is introduced as the "positive axis" of the story: the place of the origin and ministry of Jesus, of the discipleship community (3:7; 14:70), and at the end of the Gospel the "resurrection" (14:28; 16:7). The Judea/Jerusalem/temple coordinate on the other hand emerges as the "negative axis": the origin of Jesus' scribal opponents (3:22; 7:1) and the goal of Jesus' final campaign of confrontation (10:32f.; 11:1,15).

B. Standaert (1978) has made a strong case for interpreting the discursive form of Mark's prologue in terms of Greco-Roman tragedy, in which an actor came out on stage to orient the audience to the play:

> This actor plays the role of a messenger (*aggelos*), often a messenger from a god, and his monologue introduces the spectators to the action. Often he does not take part in the main action but disappears once and for all at the end of the introduction. . . . He may communicate information that he alone knows . . . while . . . the characters in the drama continue in ignorance until the *recognition* [Stock, 1986:3].

It is evident that John plays such a specialized role in Mark's prologue. Similarly, the baptism of Jesus, or "first apocalyptic moment," might be seen in terms of the *deus ex machina* of Greek tragedy. In this theatrical device the god intervenes (often hoisted down by crane from offstage) in order to resolve the hopeless entanglements of characters or plot. As Mark's story progresses the disciples will prove themselves unable to discern the true identity of Jesus; it will be important later to recall this first apocalyptic moment—which is confirmed in the second "moment" of 9:3ff.—when we are faced with that crisis. Thus both John's "introduction" and the baptismal moment give the reader "privileged information," which functions to reassure us that the person and subversive work of Jesus are reliable despite the doubts of the characters. The third apocalyptic moment will also offer confirmation, but of a very different sort (below, 13,B).

We have also identified a discursive pattern of prediction and fulfillment in the prologue's rapid character introductions. Here we may identify an ideology of "succession": John/Elijah succeeds "Isaiah," and Jesus succeeds the arrested/murdered John. This narrative pattern suggests that when the time comes, the disciples will succeed the arrested/murdered Jesus. There is *solidarity* in this matrix of interrelationships as well. For example, later Jesus ties his own authority to that of John's baptism when challenging the Jerusalem elite (11:30). Again, precisely at the point at which the disciples are sent by Jesus on *their* kingdom mission, the story of the death of John is reinserted (6:7–31; below, 7,B,iii). This narrative linkage (John/Jesus/disciples) articulates Mark's conviction that the preaching of repentance will inevitably result in political detainment. This is the "script" of biblical radicalism (above, A,iii), made explicit in Jesus' last sermon (13:9–11) to the disciples.

Finally, Mark's discourse simultaneously creates and subverts expectation in the reader. Elijah has come, indeed *Messiah* is here—but the world does not end. Yet the world of the disciple characters is overturned in the call, and through Mark's manipulation of cultural codes so is the social world of the reader. By keeping the reader off balance, Mark subverts traditional notions about how Yahweh intervenes in the world. He also prepares us to wrestle more deeply with the ambiguities of discipleship, and ultimately for the surprising and disturbing ending to his story.

At the level of *signification*, Mark's story world reflects his deep alienation from the symbolic order of Roman Palestine. He wastes no time in challenging the hegemony of both Roman and scribal aristocracies by expropriating their respective ideological vehicles of legitimation for his own ends: his eminently nonimperial "good news," and his insistence that the prophetic voices ("Isaiah") speak again. His double portrait of John as Elijah and Jesus as the "Son" who does battle with Satan affirms the politics of a subversive prophetic movement of opposition to the oppressive ruling class.

Mark is as pointed in what he omits as what he includes. It appears that at least some in Mark's time believed that the liberation of the Jewish state relied upon the politico-military intervention of Messiah (a reflection of such sentiment may be reflected in the traditions that appear in Mt 4:6 and 26:53). Malachi 3:1 was understood to promise such intervention, and there is some evidence that the outnumbered rebels were counting on it during the Roman siege in the final days of the war. Mark's suppression of this temple epiphany in his Malachi citation, and his removal of the symbolic center from Jerusalem to the wilderness, thus represent his first foray into the ideological struggle over the meaning of liberative messianic action.

The spatial oppositions of north/south accurately express the socioecological tensions noted above (2,B,iii). But though Mark's Jesus appears at the margins, it is significant that he does not *remain* in the wilderness. It seems that the Essene community at Qumran also relied upon the text of Isaiah 40:3 to legitimate its withdrawal into the desert. Mark rejects this interpretation, for as the prologue closes the spatial direction has been reversed. Jesus comes *from* the wilderness *into* Galilee, and indeed shortly into the very heart of the provincial order: a synagogue in the city of Capernaum (1:21). This is a story of engagement with the world, not flight from it.

Mark's story of the call of the fishermen is not only a good example of how he weaves together symbol and verisimilitude in his realistic narrative, but an indication of social location as well. These family-fishermen are not on the bottom of the social scale, and indeed Jesus himself, we learn later, also belongs to a trade class (*tektōn*, 6:3). Levi and Peter can entertain Jesus in their

family homes, and the disciples can later point to the sacrifice of property they
have made (10:29f.). But these recruits are not from the privileged elite; their
socio-economic place is not so secure that they are unwilling to risk a change in
the status quo. This is emphatically not the case with the aristocracy; in Mark's
view its members had too much to lose to respond to the call of discipleship
(10:17ff.). This is not to argue (as does Nolan, 1978) that Mark reflects a
"middle-class" movement, for there was no such class in his social formation.
It is, however, to suggest a social location familiar with settled community life,
contrary to Theissen's portrait of "wandering charismatics" (1978).

The prologue narrates the dawn of the kingdom at the margins of the world.
In it Mark announces an offensive upon the strongholds of oppression and the
dawn of liberation, and launches the discipleship adventure. But from the very
outset, the tone of the story anticipates conflict. This erupts in Jesus' very first
public action in Capernaum, to which I now turn.

NOTES

1. Form critics usually consider traces of Aramaic to be an indication of "authentic"
strata of Jesus tradition; e.g., 11:9, 14:36, 15:34, and the many "Amen" sayings. For a
discussion of Semitic characteristics in the rhetoric of Mark, see Taylor, 1963:55ff.

2. Both Mt 3:3 and Lk 3:4–6 recognize the problem, and change the citation to reflect
only the Is 40:3 passage. The Mal-Ex conflation later reappears, however, in a Q
tradition about John the Baptist (Mt 11:10 = Lk 7:27).

3. I use "Malachi" in quotes because most scholars accept this little book as part of an
appendix to Zechariah:

> The superscription "Oracle, the word of Yahweh to Israel by Malachi" [Mal 1:1]
> is the same, as far as the first part is concerned, as those to be found in Zec 9:1 and
> 12:1. As far as the second part, "by Malachi," is concerned, *malāki* . . . is in
> reality not a proper name, but the noun with possessive suffix "(my) messenger"
> which appears in 3:1, and it is clear that this expression . . . has only as a result of
> misunderstanding come to be regarded as the supposed name of the prophet who
> stands behind the book. . . . The explanation would seem to be that the redactor
> of the Book of the Twelve appended to the last book which had the name of a
> known prophet—namely Zechariah—three anonymous collections—namely,
> Zec 9–11; 12–14; and Malachi. To each of these he gave the title "Oracle, Word of
> Yahweh" [Eissfeldt, 1965:441,440].

Significantly, Markan intertextuality draws heavily upon these three oracles, as noted
(above, A,iii).

CHAPTER FOUR

The First Direct Action Campaign: Jesus' Assault on the Jewish Social Order in Capernaum (Mark 1:21–3:35)

Thus says Yahweh: "Those captive to the mighty will be retaken; the prey of the strong will be rescued."

—Isaiah 49:25

From the moment he strides into a Capernaum synagogue, it becomes clear that Jesus' kingdom project is incompatible with the local public authorities and the social order they represent. A "demon" immediately demands that Jesus justify his attack upon the authority of the scribal establishment; Jesus vanquishes this challenge and commences his ministry of healing. He brings wholeness and liberation to the poor, and receives hospitality from the socially outcast, with whom his solidarity lies. The risk of provoking official hostility does not deter Jesus from pressing his criticism of every social code that serves to institutionalize alienation. Then, to dramatize his opposition, Jesus publicly breaks the law. It is at that point that the authorities determine that he must be neutralized.

Jesus will withdraw to the sea, and there reflect upon his mission in parables, drawing upon the wisdom of those who work the land in a plea for discernment and patience. But before retreating, he makes his intentions clear in a climactic debate with government investigators. Jesus spins a parable so shocking that it not only polarizes the political climate, but provokes a rift with family and friends. He compares himself to a thief struggling to break into the house of a "strong man," whom he intends to bind and whose captives he intends to liberate. And he claims that in this criminal venture, his accomplice is none other than the Holy Spirit!

137

4A. THE NARRATIVE CHARACTER OF THE CAPERNAUM CAMPAIGN

i. Structure

The next two chapters analyze Mark's story up to Jesus' exorcism of the Gerasene demoniac (5:1ff.), covering the first campaign narrative and Jesus' first sermon. The focus of the present chapter is Jesus' attack upon the legitimacy of the prevailing social order and his ministry of compassion and healing. Most of the action takes place in and around the city of Capernaum.

There are two possibilities in defining the structure of this first major narrative section in the Gospel. A common interpretation marks the beginning and end of the campaign by the two synagogue episodes (1:20–29; 3:1–6). After the latter confrontation, the authorities plot to kill Jesus, causing him to withdraw; after this rejection the narrative regenerates with the naming and commissioning of the disciples (3:6ff.). A new cycle of ministry then begins in 3:20ff., which culminates in the next rejection and the commissioning of the disciples (6:1ff.). Although there is much to be said for this schema, I do not believe it coheres with the overall structure of the Gospel as I have outlined it (above, 3,C).

A better model defines the parameters of the campaign as the shores of the Sea of Galilee, upon which it opens and closes (1:16; 4:1). This allows us to view 3:22–35 as a kind of "second climax" to the Capernaum campaign, followed by the "narrative rest" represented by the first sermon in 4:1ff. The transition to the next section is signaled at the conclusion of this sermon, when the site of the seashore is abandoned for a boat journey across the sea (4:35ff.). Thus between the inaugural, summary proclamation (1:15) and the first sermon (4:1ff.) we have Jesus' first campaign of direct action. This campaign exhibits a broadly concentric structure.

The first synagogue exorcism and the concluding controversy concerning exorcism are related by theme. In the synagogue in 1:21ff., Jesus casts out an "unclean spirit," which obliquely symbolizes the scribal class; in 3:22–30 Jesus is accused of himself embodying an "unclean spirit" by the same scribal authorities. Wrapped around these two key episodes are accounts of community consolidation and family/home scenes (1:16–31; 3:13–35):

A   disciples called (1:16–20)
          exorcism, indirect clash with scribes (1:21–28)
      at home with Peter's family (1:29–31)
A   disciples named (3:13–19)
          exorcism controversy, direct clash with scribes (3:22–30)
      at home, clash with Jesus' family (3:20f.,31–35)

This correspondence represents the outer frame of the concentric structure of this section.

The inner frame consists of two passages that synopsize Jesus' ministry (1:32–39; 3:7–12). Both summaries articulate the geographical expansion of his healing and exorcism mission (1:33f.; 3:10f.) to the masses:

> And he went throughout all of Galilee, preaching in their
>   synagogues and casting out demons (1:39);
> A great multitude from Galilee followed; also from Judea
>   and Jerusalem and Idumea and from beyond the Jordan and
>   from around Tyre and Sidon (3:7f.).

In each case Jesus has to convince his disciples of his need to withdraw from the press of the crowds (1:35f.; 3:9).

This leaves the main cycle of healing/conflict stories in the structural "middle," as shown in this diagram:

A exorcism clash/discipleship and family (1:16–31)
  B ministry of compassion to masses (1:32–39)
    C main "campaign" narrative (1:40–3:6)
  B' ministry of compassion to masses (3:7–12)
A' exorcism clash/discipleship and family (3:13–35)

The episodes in the main narrative are linked together by hook words or common themes. The series consists of a healing doublet (1:45–2:12), a transitional discipleship call story (2:13f.), a triplet of conflict stories with the Pharisees (2:15–28), and a culminating confrontation in the synagogue (3:1–5). It closes with the hatching of a death plot against Jesus (3:6).

I have presented my analysis below generally according to this structural model. Section 4B looks at the way Mark establishes the paradigmatic character of Jesus' ministry in 1:20–39, introducing all three of Mark's main plot strands (above, 3,D,iii): community building, healing and exorcism, and political conflict. Sections 4C and 4D examine the campaign narrative, in which Jesus struggles to overturn the social codes upon which an oppressive caste system is based. In 4E I read the first of the two campaign climaxes. There, however, I try also to bring out the "rejection/regeneration" pattern suggested by the alternative structural model mentioned above. I call this the first of two "generative seams," the other occurring in the next major section (below, 7,A). The second campaign climax is read in 4F. Chapter 5, below, analyzes Jesus' first sermon. The parables discourse (5A) is viewed as a critical reflection upon the "state" of the messianic mission (5B and 5C). Section 5D is the first major retrospective summary of the discourse and signification of the opening chapters of Mark's Gospel.

ii. Story

The settings of this section are all in and around the city of Capernaum. The narrative pattern consists of Jesus' forays into the city, followed by conflict, and ending in withdrawal to "safe" locations, either the "home" (1:29, 2:15, 3:20) or the sea (2:13, 3:7, 4:1). I will pay specific attention to the ideological significance of this movement and Mark's primary narrative sites below (B,iii). By the end of this section most of the key characters have been introduced: the twelve disciples (3:16ff.), the crowds (2:4), and Jesus' many opponents: scribes (2:6), Pharisees (2:16), Herodians (3:6), and Jerusalem authorities (3:22).

After the initial synagogue exorcism, the real work of the mission begins, with a general account of Jesus' ministry. The campaign proper commences with the healing of a leper and then a paralytic (1:40–2:12). These stories represent Jesus' subversion of the priestly control of the purity code and scribal control of the debt code. The call of Levi (2:13f.) serves as a transition to the next series in the campaign, in which Jesus' social practice is the target of criticism by the Pharisees in three successive episodes (2:15–28). The campaign achieves a carefully constructed narrative crescendo in a double climax of theatrical conflict (3:1–6) and ideological polarization (3:20–34).

The major plot dynamic in the section is the way in which Jesus' practice—specifically his healing, exorcism, and solidarity with the socially outcast—brings him into conflict with the authorities. At the outset of Jesus' ministry to the masses, Mark introduces an implied complication, though it is traditionally dismissed by form and redaction critics as arbitrary detail. We are told that Jesus commences public healing only at the close of his Sabbath day's (1:21) activity (1:32). Despite the fact that he has already healed Peter's mother-in-law privately in her home, Jesus waits for the Sabbath to end before going public. We are thus alerted that healing on the Sabbath is going to be controversial. This sets the tone for the following narrative: Jesus' healing again defies the debt code in 2:1ff., and in 2:24 the Pharisees mutter: "Why are they doing what is unlawful on the Sabbath?" The legal conflict finally becomes explicit in 3:2, where Jesus' opponents set a trap to see whether he will publicly heal on the Sabbath.

This issue results in Jesus' Deuteronomic ultimatum to his opponents concerning the meaning of Sabbath (3:4), and his fateful choice to provoke the issue by breaching the law in what we might call "theatrical civil disobedience." The resolution of this plot complication, however, only serves to provoke another: the secret plan to arrest Jesus (3:6). By introducing this development so early in the story (Jesus in fact is not arrested until 14:43!) Mark politicizes the entire subsequent narrative. The reader can thus hardly be surprised when the final episode in this section escalates the intensity of conflict, as authorities come all the way from Jerusalem to investigate the problem (3:21). Their counterattack provides Jesus with a pretext to make the political purpose of his mission explicit in his apocalyptic "strong man" parable. The true plot is articulated here: Jesus' struggle with the prince of powers (1:12f.) is being carried out across the political geography of Roman Palestine. After this parable, Mark retires the narrative to the sea one final time for an extended teaching in parables.

4B. THE MESSIANIC MISSION AND THE
MEANING OF JESUS' "SYMBOLIC ACTION" (1:21–39)

A new "way" has been announced, Jesus has begun forging it, and followers have been summoned to journey on it. The narrative now turns to the public inauguration of Jesus' ministry in Capernaum. In the following episodes Mark will establish the essential characteristics of the messianic mission. We encounter here for the first time Jesus' symbolic action of exorcism and healing.

These "miracle" stories raise important issues of interpretation. Is Jesus simply "curing" the physically sick and the mentally disturbed? If so, why would such a ministry of compassion raise the ire of the local authorities? Many commentators, anxious to portray Jesus as a politically innocuous miracle worker, have argued that the political opposition to him was based upon a tragic misunderstanding. This is social and historical nonsense: healers and magicians abounded and practiced freely in Hellenistic antiquity, but Jesus encounters official hostility almost from the outset. In the double-climax to this section, he is politically accused for both his healings (3:1–6) and his exorcisms (3:22–30). There must be more to these stories than is immediately obvious to the modern reader.

i. Challenging Authority: Jesus the Exorcist

I begin with the first of Jesus' "miracles," which is also his first public action: the episode in the Capernaum synagogue (1:21ff.). This provides a good example of how the *form* of a story serves as a key to understanding its *content*. As he will often do, Mark begins by constructing a setting: Jesus strides into a synagogue (*eiselthōn*, 1:21). The episode closes when the scene is "deconstructed" by his exit (*exelthontes*, 1:29). The prologue has made us attentive to the author's use of symbolic setting, and this narrative strategy continues here. In one sentence Mark moves Jesus from the symbolic margins to the heart of the provincial Jewish social order: synagogue (sacred space) on a Sabbath (sacred time).

The verbal repetition in the opening lines immediately establishes what is at issue in this episode: ". . . and he was teaching (*edidasken*) them. And they were amazed at his teaching (*didachē*), for he was teaching them . . . " (1:21f.).

Next the central conflict is revealed, articulated by the anonymous "they," presumably the synagogue audience; they distinguish Jesus' teaching "as (*hōs*) one having *authority*, not as (*kai ouch hōs*) the scribes" (1:22). This theme is then reiterated at the close of the episode: "They were all astonished such that they discussed it with one another saying: 'What is this? A new teaching (*didachē*)! With *authority* he orders . . .' " (1:27).

We observe, then, that this conflict "frames" the exorcism story proper (1:23–26), a structure suggesting that the exorcism has everything to do with the struggle between the authority of Jesus and that of the scribes.

The flow of dramatic action confirms this. Jesus has penetrated symbolic space acknowledged to be the domain of the scribes. No sooner has he stepped onto their turf than he encounters stiff opposition: "Immediately there was in the synagogue a man with an unclean spirit" (1:23). The demon's challenge to Jesus (1:24) is a curious phrase in Greek (*ti hēmin kai soi;*), translated by Taylor as "What do we have in common?" He suggests that the idiom is drawn from the Hebrew of Joshua 22:24, Judges 11:12, and 1 Kings 17:18, rendered there as "Why do you meddle with us?" (1963:174). It thus communicates defiance toward a hostile intruder, who here is adressed with the contemptuous "You from Nazareth!" But this defiance quickly turns to fear: "Have you come to destroy us?" Upon whose behalf is the demon pleading? It can only be the group already identified in the conflict theme—the scribal aristocracy whose space (social role and power) Jesus is threatening.

As we would expect of the first-century worldview, the demon attempts to gain control over Jesus by naming him. "Holy one of God" is a Semitic title that acknowledges Jesus' prophetic status to be the caliber of Elisha (2 Kg 4:9). But it earns the demon only a stern rebuke (as in 1:34; 3:11f.; 5:7), after which it is summarily subjugated by Jesus' command (1:25f.). The synagogue crowd nervously considers this new development (1:27). The terms at the start and finish of the episode that describe their reaction (*ekplēssō, thambeomai*) are strong, and are used by Mark almost always in relation to Jesus' teaching (6:2; 10:24, 26, 32; 11:18). They connote not just incredulity but a kind of panic associated with the disruption of the assumed order of things.

This is the first of many "miracle" stories in Mark's Gospel. How shall we interpret it? Do we demythologize it according to the discourse of modern medical anthropology, so that the exorcism becomes the cure of epilepsy or some other mental disorder? This is the typical modernist approach, preoccupied with concocting rational explanations for actions that appear to transgress natural laws. But it is also historicism at its crudest, and does nothing to address the socio-literary function of miracle stories. I will discuss in the next section the problems associated with interpretations based upon such "etic," or "cultural outsider" perspectives (see above, 2,A,ii). However we may view it, the possibility of manipulating the physical or spirit world was never questioned in antiquity. Nevertheless, the miracle stories of Mark go to great lengths to discourage the reader from drawing the conclusion from these stories that Jesus is a mere popular magician.

Instead, the meaning of the powerful act must be found by viewing it in terms of symbolic reproduction of social conflict. In a study of Mark's exorcism terminology, Kee argues that this first episode is paradigmatic:

> The details presented . . . are not concerned with the specifics of the cure, but with the manifestations of the struggle. . . . The word of the demon makes clear that the struggle is not a momentary one, but is part of a wider conflict of which this is but a single phase. . . . The narrative is

wholly compatible with the picture . . . emerging from apocalyptic Judaism of God's agent locked in effective struggle with the powers of evil, wresting power from them by his word of command (*epitimān*). . . . They were not intended, as was the case with the hellenistic wonderworker stories, to glorify the one who performed the act. They were told instead to identify his exorcism as an eschatological event which served to prepare God's creation for his coming rule [1968:243,244,255].

What Kee does not see, however, is that as symbolic action, this inaugural exorcism begins to specify the political geography of the apocalyptic contest begun in the wilderness (1:12f.). The demon in the synagogue becomes the representative of the scribal establishment, whose "authority" undergirds the dominant Jewish social order. Exorcism represents an act of confrontation in the war of myths in which Jesus asserts his alternative authority. Only this interpretation can explain why exorcism is at issue in the scribal counterattack upon Jesus later in 3:22ff. (below, 4,F,i).

Exorcism is one of the central characteristics of the messianic mission of Jesus (1:39; 3:11), and he will pass this vocation on to his followers (3:15; 6:7). It is the main vehicle for articulating the apocalyptic combat myth between the powers (and their earthly minions) and Jesus (as envoy of the kingdom). Although Jesus' identity is hidden to the protagonists (e.g., the disciples) in the story, the demons know exactly who he is. Clearly understanding the political threat he poses to the status quo, they struggle to "name" (that is, to control) him (1:34; 3:11f.). This apocalyptic drama will reach fever pitch in the debate over Beelzebub (3:22ff.), in which the scribal authorities launch a counterattack in the war of myths, and will climax when Jesus succeeds in turning the tables and extracting from a demon *his* name (5:9; below 6,B). Mark thus establishes the political character of exorcism as symbolic action. Though the later two exorcism stories (7:24ff.; 9:14ff.) take on a somewhat different tone, they too are concerned with the structures of power and alienation in the social world. In the first of them the true subject of the symbolic action is the deep rift between Jew and gentile (below, 6,D,iii); in the second, the agonizing struggle to believe in the new order of the kingdom (below 8,E,iii).

ii. Wholeness and the Symbolic Order: Jesus the Healer

On the heels of his inaugural exorcism, Jesus commences his healing ministry, another primary expression of his symbolic action (1:30ff.). We note that the first healing takes place in private, and that public healing begins only after Sabbath (indicated by the emphatic redundancy "that evening, *after* sunset," 1:32). Mark is hereby implicitly introducing a plot complication that concerns controversy over healing on the Sabbath, which will soon have dire consequences. Thus from the outset Jesus' mission of healing, like that of exorcism, is linked to his conflicts with the dominant symbolic order.

The brief account of Peter's mother-in-law (1:30f.) sets in place the paradigmatic scheme of action to which every subsequent healing episode will conform:

1. The subject is brought to Jesus' attention (often with the mediation of friends/relatives, as here).
2. Jesus encounters the subject (sometimes with dialogue first).
3. Jesus responds (with touch, as here, or word).
4. Healing is reported (often instructions are given).

This house-story is followed by the first of several Markan summaries of Jesus' healings and exorcisms (e.g., the "generative seams" in 3:7–13a and 6:5–7). These summaries function to articulate Jesus' compassion for the poor and ailing masses.

In order to understand the symbolic dimension of these stories, we must first acknowledge their socio-economic character. From the very beginning Jesus the healer experiences the incessant press of needy masses; in 1:33 Mark again employs the Semitic hyperbole, "the whole town was gathered at the door." The social setting of the paralytic's healing, for example, is one of bitter poverty (2:1ff.), as also in the story of the bleeding woman (5:25ff.). The way Jesus responds to these destitute subjects despite opposition dramatizes his preferential ministry to the poor.

These aspects of Mark's narrative world can be seen only as a direct reflection of his social reality. Economic and political deterioration, especially in the decade prior to the upheavals of the Roman-Jewish war, had dispossessed significant portions of the Palestinian population, especially in the densely populated rural areas of Galilee. Disease and physical disability were an inseparable part of the cycle of poverty (a phenomenon still true today despite the advent of modern medicine). For the day laborer, illness meant unemployment and instant impoverishment. The "crowds" (*ochlos*) form the background to the story and represent a major aspect of its social location. I will explore the character of this term when it arises in the narrative (2:4; below, C,iii).

Theissen goes so far as to say that there is a clear socio-economic bias in the gospel miracles tradition:

> Belief in miracles is concentrated here on specific situations of distress, on possession, disease, hunger, lack of success, and danger, in other words on situations which do not strike as hard in all social groups. . . . The popular character of these stories is that in them people whose social and economic position left them no other outlet articulate their hopes. . . . It seems to me that a degree of class correlation in the primitive Christian miracle stories can hardly be denied [1983:252].

Jesus' healing ministry is thus portrayed as an essential part of his struggle to bring concrete liberation to the oppressed and marginal of Palestinian society.

But liberation from what? The classical meaning of the Greek verb used in 1:34 (*therapeuō*, whence our term "therapy") is "to treat medically." Does this imply that Jesus cured the sick in a conventional sense? Before rushing to this conclusion, we must consider some cross-cultural issues. To begin with, J. Pilch has recently brought the insights of medical anthropology to these episodes, distinguishing between two approaches to the social meaning of sickness:

> Ethnomedicine places primacy on the culturally construed causes of illness. . . . In contrast, biomedicine places primary emphasis on biological symptoms and pathogens. . . . Disease derives from a biomedical perspective that sees abnormalities in the structure and/or function of organ systems. These are pathological states independent of whether or not they are culturally recognized. Disease affects individuals, and only individuals are treated. Illness is a sociocultural perspective that is concerned with personal perception and experience of certain socially disvalued states including, but not limited to, disease. Illness inevitably affects others: the significant other, the family, the neighborhood, the village. . . .
>
> The "sickness" described in the Old Testament as leprosy is simply not leprosy at all from a biomedical perspective. But from the sociocultural perspective—which is what the Bible always reports—this condition called leprosy threatens communal integrity and holiness and must be removed from the community [1985:142f.].

Pilch goes on to point out that the social processes of defining and treating sickness constitute the "health-care system" of a given culture. This system consists of the "professional healer" sector, the normal preventive and diagnostic measures taken by nonprofessionals, and the prevailing ideologies of illness.

In the context of the health-care system of rural Palestine, Pilch concludes:

> Jesus and all healers of that period could only perceive illnesses and not diseases. . . . Notice in each healing instance the almost total disregard of symptoms (something very essential to disease). Instead there is constant concern for meaning. . . . Jesus' activity is best described etically as healing, not as curing. He provides social meaning for the life problems resulting from the sickness [ibid.:149].

Every major healing episode in Mark, beginning with 1:41ff., demonstrates this thesis. In the symbolic order of Judaism, illness was associated with impurity or sin, a state that meant exclusion from full status in the body politic.

The reader might at this point refer to my earlier discussion of sociosymbolic systems (above, 2,E,i) to understand better the correlation between bodily and social wholeness. As Douglas reminds us:

> The physical body can have universal meaning only as a system which responds to the social system, expressing it as a system. What it symbol-

izes naturally is the relation of parts to the whole. Natural symbols can express the relation of an individual to his society at that general systemic level [1973:112].

The first two healing episodes we will encounter demonstrate the relationship between the purity and debt codes, on the one hand, and bodily integrity, on the other (below, C).

Mark's Jesus seeks always to restore the *social* wholeness denied to the sick/impure by this symbolic order. That is why his healing of the sick/impure is virtually interchangeable with his social intercourse with them. To one "leper" he offers a declaration of wholeness (1:41ff.), to another simply the solidarity of table fellowship (14:3). Both acts defy the symbolic order that segregates those lacking bodily integrity; both challenge the prevailing social boundaries and class barriers. This is why Jesus the healer was a threat to "civic order."

iii. Symbolic Action

The above cross-cultural and anthropological considerations caution us against equating "miracle" with "the supernatural." Such an equation is based upon a peculiarly modern mechanistic and technological worldview, which equates *power* with the ability to manipulate nature. We forget that the discourse of the "supernatural" was hardly extraordinary in antiquity. Even "historians" like Herodotus or Josephus regularly invoked cosmic signs and miraculous, super-human actions to explain or justify the events they narrated. So common were "magical" feats that Mark clearly wishes to discourage us from construing Jesus' work in such terms.

Throughout this commentary I will interpret the "miracles" of Jesus—exorcism and healing—as "symbolic action." This will undoubtedly trouble some readers, who will take me to be implying that these events did not really take place, that Jesus did not really heal or cast out demons. That is not what I mean by symbolic action. Similarly, in speaking of specific characters or narrative elements in these stories as socio-symbolic representations, as I have done in the case of the synagogue exorcism, I am not suggesting that Jesus did not in fact minister to or care about individual victims. By "symbolic action" I do not mean action that was merely metaphorical, devoid of concrete, historical character. Quite the contrary: I mean action whose fundamental significance, indeed *power*, lies relative to the symbolic order in which they occurred.

Let me illustrate what I mean with two examples. When Martin Luther tacked up his theses on the Wittenberg door, the *meaning* of his action extended far beyond the sum of its parts. Literally the act was that of a monk posting a note on a door; but it was not any note on any door, and history would prove this was not just any monk. Indeed, this powerful symbolic act of resistance came to take on bigger-than-life proportions, becoming an "etiological myth" of the later Lutheran Church. Yet its true historical significance can properly be understood only in terms of the socio-political configuration of forces within the dominant form of Catholicism that the dissident Luther was addressing.

Take now the monk's namesake, Martin Luther King, Jr. When King knelt and prayed in the face of police dogs and water cannons, or when his colleagues sat at lunch counters or at the front of city buses, they were engaging in symbolic actions. Their significance cannot be interpreted apart from factors of socio-symbolic "space" (segregation in the southern U.S.A.) and "codes" (discriminatory law and tradition). In these examples we can see actions whose historical character was not diminished for their being "symbolic." Nor are they any less "miraculous" for being nonsupernatural. Their "divine power" lay not in a manipulation of nature but in confrontation with the dominant order of oppression and in witness to different possibilities.

Many Christian interpreters, in their zeal to defend a "high christology," insist that Jesus' miracles may be understood only in terms of what we might call "divine thaumaturgy." From the point of view of biblical tradition, this is very skewed logic. To the Hebrew mind, Yahweh is revealed in, or may intervene in, the "natural" world as a matter of course—after all, Yahweh *created* that world. But this does not necessarily constitute "proof" of Yahweh's lordship. *That* is demonstrated by the way in which Yahweh presides over the rise and fall of nations and peoples—especially Israel. The "miracle" of the exodus story lies not in the nature epiphanies and plagues, but in the liberation of the Hebrew people from slavery in pharaoh's Egypt. To put it another way, the miracle is to be seen not so much in Yahweh's parting the Red Sea (which already "recognizes" the lordship of Yahweh), but in the vanquishing of the Egyptian military machine (which does *not* recognize it).

Even if we freely grant that Jesus acted with "supernatural" powers, social anthropologists will tell us that the meaning and potency of such capability is *still* socially determined:

> Magicality is an instrument of mutual coercion which only works when common consent upholds the system. It is useless for a witch doctor to invest a fetish with magic power by the sole authority of his charisma. Magic derives potency from the legitimacy of the system in which this kind of communication is being made. Like the notices which warn against contact with high-voltage wires, it protects the media of communication. As consent withdraws from the system of control, leaders lose their credibility, and so does their magic [Douglas, 1973:178f.].

We see these limitations in Jesus' ministry. Mark locates the agency of "power" in the *subjects* of Jesus' actions: a Jewish woman (5:34), a gentile woman (7:29), and a blind beggar (10:52) are all made whole on account of *their* initiative and action, or "faith." Conversely, in the presence of "unbelief" the power of both Jesus (6:5) and his disciples (9:18f.) to heal and exorcise is radically proscribed.

In sum, Jesus' symbolic acts were powerful not because they challenged the laws of nature, but because they challenged the very structures of social existence. To use Douglas's term, his healing and exorcism functioned to "elaborate" the dominant symbolic order, unmasking the way in which it functioned to legitimate concrete social relationships. Insofar as this order dehumanized life, Jesus challenged it and defied its strictures: *that* is why his "miracles" were not universally embraced. Depending upon one's status in the dominant order, one either perceived them as socially deviant (worse, heretical) or liberative.

There is another hermeneutical consideration to reading these stories as symbolic action; it concerns our own modern definitions of illness. Even in an overwhelmingly biomedical culture such as ours, what is "healthy" is still *socially* determined. The recent controversy surrounding AIDS demonstrates the persistence of popular myth and political epidemiology in our contemporary health care system. An even better example, which bears directly upon our reading of Mark, is the challenge being put to traditional definitions of physical and mental "disability" by the contemporary movements for independent living in developed societies. Wheelchair-bound persons, for example, insist on equal social access, decrying paternal and oppressive social policies that keep them dependent and segregated. Similarly, many in the deaf community insist that their unique culture, centered around sign language, should be given equal respect and treatment as any verbal sign system.

In other words, there are many today who simply do not believe that their liberation is dependent upon being able to talk or walk. They insist on their right to live fully human and "whole" lives in a society that continues to define them as "handicapped" only because they are different. Nonphysically disabled readers must be aware of the biases we unconsciously bring to biblical narratives of "healing." Obviously any interpretation that stresses the *biomedical* definition of "wholeness" excludes the physically disabled from the good news. If, however, we focus upon the broader socio-symbolic meaning of illness and healing, the stories address us all equally. After all, in Mark the true impediments to discipleship have nothing to do with physical impairment, but with spiritual and ideological disorders: "Having eyes can you not see? Having ears can you not hear?" (8:18).

All this is lost upon those who would demythologize Jesus' healing and exorcism. But it is also lost upon conservative interpreters who combat demythologizing by defending the literalism of miracles. The problem is that both sides of this debate "unquestioningly accept biomedicine as the only legitimate view of reality":

> From this starting point, such studies seek to examine Biblical events in biomedical terms, or explain why it is or is not possible on the basis of biomedical principles. Yet medical anthropology has discovered that the *materia medica* used in healing is often chosen because of the analogy to the situation or for other cultural symbolic reasons rather than because of the interaction between the chemical components and a microbe. But,

as anthropologists will point out, their efficacy is just as real [Pilch, 1985:149].

In sum, then, my socio-literary approach to Mark's healing and exorcism stories takes into account both the social and cultural dimension. It attends to the discursive function of the episode in the narrative strategy of the author: as symbolic action addressing a symbolic system that oppresses. This opens up and maintains access to the text for all. It also explains why Mark's Jesus is such a threat to the stewards of the status quo.

iv. Symbolic Space: Narrative Site and Social Sphere

In 1:21–38 Mark offers a portrait of Jesus' ministry in microcosm, using the fiction of a "typical" 24-hour span. It begins on the Sabbath (1:21), goes through sundown (1:32) and on into the early morning of the next day (1:35). Mark ends the section with a recapitulative summary statement (1:39). This synopsis tells us not only *what* Jesus does (healing, preaching, and exorcism), but also *where* he does it. And the fact is that prior to the passion narrative in 14:1ff., Mark is far more concerned with the socio-symbolism of narrative sites than with coherent movement through space or time.

I observed this in the prologue, and see it again here. For example, in this 24-hour period Jesus moves from a synagogue in Capernaum to a house (1:29) to an undetermined wilderness site (1:35). Similarly, later Jesus is portrayed as moving from synagogue (3:1) to sea (3:7) to mountain (3:13) to house and finally back to sea (4:1), an itinerary for which Mark gives us no sense of the passage of time. If this seems to be random movement, it is nevertheless a catalogue of key symbolic coordinates. It is these that Mark wishes us to appreciate.

The first observation we should make is that there is a public/private dialectic in Jesus' movement, with the former consistently exerting pressure on the latter. The synagogue exorcism concluded (1:28) with Jesus' sudden attainment of "fame" (the expression is literally "the hearing about him"—i.e., the reports and rumors, *he akoē autou*). Mark tells us of two attempts by Jesus to withdraw. He first seeks the privacy of his disciples' family home (1:29), but soon the crowd finds him there (1:32). Again he seeks solitude, this time in the wilderness; yet even there he is found (1:37). But in each case Jesus responds to the demand, as reflected in his announcement that he will itinerate the village circuit (1:38).

Thus the summary section begins with the establishment of Jesus' geographical sphere of influence, and ends with his ministry throughout this sphere:
—his fame spread through the whole of the surrounding region of Galilee
  (*eis holēn tēn perichōron tēs Galilaias*; 1:28);
—he went through "the whole of Galilee" (*eis holēn tēn Galilaian*) preaching
  (1:39).
This public/private dialectic also articulates Jesus' strategy of engagement

and withdrawal, which is reflected at several other points throughout the Capernaum campaign:

engagement	*withdrawal*
healing of leper	→ unable to enter a city, he is found "at home" (1:45–2:1)
healing of paralytic	→ sea → house (2:13–15)
synagogue conflict	→ sea (3:7) → [wilderness? 3:13] → house (3:20)
conflict [at home?]	→ sea (4:1)

This movement articulates another opposition: certain sites are assigned "positive" and "negative" value in the course of the story.

E. Malbon (1986) uses structuralist analysis to interpret these oppositions. Although I do not find her Lévi-Straussian mythic antinomies helpful, she has rightly identified three spheres of narrative space in the gospel: topographical, geopolitical, and architectural. Taking her lead, I would identify Mark's primary topographical sites as wilderness, river, sea, and mountain. These are all positive coordinates in the narrative, with the exception of the last two, which have negative counterparts. The mountain is a place of commissioning (3:13), solitude (6:46), and revelation (9:2,9) for the discipleship community. But once the narrative moves to Jerusalem, Mark draws an opposition between the Mount of Olives (positive, 11:1; 13:3,14; 14:26) and the temple "mount" (negative, 11:23). This, as we will see, is an ideological tension (below, 10,A,ii). Similarly, in Book I the sea (of Galilee) is a prime positive coordinate; by it the discipleship narrative commences (1:16; 2:13) and consolidates (3:7; 4:1). Yet it is also a symbol of opposition in the boat journeys (4:47; 6:48f.), and a symbol of destruction in 5:13, 9:42, and 11:23.

I have already argued that the main geopolitical opposition in Mark is between the social periphery (positive) and center (negative), which is of course itself a reversal of the dominant code. This opposition is articulated in the prologue as wilderness/Jerusalem and Galilee/Judea (above, 3,E). There is yet another expression of it in tension between urban and rural settings implied in these opening scenes. Capernaum was a "city" (*polis*, 1:33), "a reasonably well-known townlet . . . standing close to the highway which ran northeastwards from the lake into lower Syria" (Pearlman and Yannai, 1965). Yet after the synagogue conflict and Jesus' two attempts to retreat, Jesus tells his disciples that his mission is to preach not in the cities, but "in the neighboring country towns" (1:38, *kōmopoleis*). This term is unique in the New Testament. It probably refers to what Freyne describes as village "synoecisms," in which clans banded together in economic incorporation in order to survive. The major Hellenistic cities in Galilee formed a rough circle (Galilee itself meaning "circle"; Freyne, 1980:146). Yet again, despite the fact that Mark uses "circle" to describe Jesus' itineration (*kuklō*, 6:6b,36), it is in reference to villages (*kōmē*).

In fact, after Jesus is driven out of Capernaum in 3:6, he does not again enter a *polis* until his approach to Jerusalem (there is one exception in 6:56, a summary verse describing Jesus' ministry in gentile territory). Persons come to Jesus *from* the city (6:33), and tell of his mighty deeds *in* the city (5:14); but Jesus clearly prefers the village (8:23,27). Why this narrative "avoidance" of the city? Obviously it does not signify a social strategy of monastic withdrawal, for each of Mark's two "campaign" narratives take place in cities. We gain a clue from the first healing episode: due to the scandal associated with his social intercourse with a leper, Mark states that Jesus "could no longer enter a city openly" (1:45). This suggests that hostility to Jesus' radical social practice was centered in urban areas, where the symbolic order was concentrated, which may have been the experience of Mark's community. The narrative bias may also indicate that Mark shared the general rural suspicion of Hellenistic urbanization, which as we noted threatened Palestinian village life and culture, and dominated the economic environment (above, 2,B,iii).

Perhaps the most interesting sphere, however, is the architectural one, in which the central positive coordinate is the "household" (*oikia, oikos*, synonymous with livelihood, 10:29f.; 12:40). The house is portrayed as a "safe" site for the discipleship community (6:10). There Jesus dines with the outcast (2:15; 14:3) and attends to the crowds (1:32f.; 3:20); it is the locus for private instruction (7:17; 9:33; 10:10) and healing (1:29–31; 5:38; 7:24). Only once is the house a site of conflict (3:20ff.), and this is explained by the fact that this episode narrates the rejection of Jesus by his own family.

As more commentators recognize the significance of this narrative space in Mark, there have been attempts to make correlations with the social setting of the Markan church. E. Best ventures that "the three emphases on withdrawal, separation from the unconverted, and teaching represent in large part what the house-church would have provided for the early Christian" (1981:227). J. Donahue, citing the work of Elliott (1981), agrees: the *oikos*, the basic Hellenistic social unit, was adopted and modified by early Christians, becoming the alternative social site of resistance to the alienation of the dominant culture surrounding them (Donahue, 1983:31f.).

Malbon argues that the spatial tension in Mark between house and synagogue/temple might have specific signification:

With the destruction of the temple (13:2) and rejection in the synagogue (13:9), the Christian community must come together in "house churches." . . . Given . . . the archaeological observation that the "house church" became the ritual centre of early Christianity after its expulsion from the synagogue, intriguing historical questions concerning the basis of the Markan architectural schema arise. Could it be that in Mark's gospel . . . in its narrative manipulation of these architectural symbols, suggested a way of responding meaningfully to those historical realities? [1985:288,292].

Although these suggestions must necessarily remain at the level of intelligent speculation, their plausibility is bolstered by interesting archeological evidence attesting to primitive house-churches in Capernaum. I will return to this in my concluding discussion of the socio-historical situation of the production of the Gospel (below, 14,A).

We should also recall our working model of the symbolic order (above, 2,E,ii), which identifies the major spheres of agrarian Palestine as land/table (the economic), village/house (the social), and synagogue/sanctuary (the political). There is clear correlation between these spheres and the narrative throughout the Gospel. Besides the tension between the positive sphere of village/house and negative sphere of synagogue/temple, table fellowship will emerge as a primary site of conflict (e.g., 2:15f.; 7:1ff.). The "field" is also a site of confrontation (2:23ff.), whereas the land is both a potentially positive and negative sphere in Jesus' parables (4:1ff.). In sum, in his careful use of socio-symbolic space, Mark portrays Jesus as struggling against the dominant symbolic order as it manifests itself in each social sphere in his mission of liberation.

4C. CHALLENGING THE IDEOLOGICAL HEGEMONY OF PRIEST AND SCRIBE (1:40–2:15)

In 1:39 Mark closes his summary section with the programmatic statement that Jesus "went through Galilee, preaching in their synagogues and casting out devils" (1:39). This recapitulates the main theme of 1:20–28 and prepares the way for the first messianic campaign of "direct action." In the following series of stories, linked together by a variety of literary devices, Jesus launches his nonviolent assault upon the symbolic order of Jewish Palestine and the ideological hegemony of its stewards. Yet even as he challenges the social power and exclusivity of the ruling groups, Jesus is simultaneously introducing an alternative social practice based upon inclusivity.

i. Attack on the Purity Code: Healing a Leper

The first episode in the series (1:40–45) follows the healing paradigm noted above: approach, petition/response, and healing/instruction. This brief story functions to subvert the very purity regulations that at first glance it appears to respect. The essence of the extensive regulations regarding leprosy (see Lv 13:2–14:57) was (1) the disease is communicable and (2) a priest must preside over ritual cleansing. Both principles are challenged in this episode, as is indicated by the repetition of the theme verb (*katharizein*, used three times, and once in its nominal form *tou katharismou*). C.H. Cave, following J. Weiss, argues that this term meant not "to cleanse" but "to declare clean" in the Levitical sense. Hence, in responding to the leper's request, Jesus appears to be defying Torah and assuming the priestly prerogative (Cave, 1979:246). Not only that, but Mark makes a point of emphasizing that Jesus *touched* the leper. But, whereas according to the symbolic order Jesus should have contracted the contagion, instead Mark reports that the leper becomes clean (Belo, 1981:106). Through this symbolic action the power of the symbolic order has been overturned.

The aftermath of this healing (1:43–45) has been widely misunderstood by commentators. Even most English translations give the impression that Jesus instructed the leper to abide by the priestly ritual. In this case the above interpretation would be negated; as a simple healing miracle, the episode would be entirely uncontroversial. Taylor's comment is typical: "The instruction . . . illustrates the recognition by Jesus of the Mosaic Law (Lv 13:49) in cases where moral issues are not at stake" (1963:190). This, however, misses the point of the story, and its tone as well. The leper appears aware that his approach to Jesus, a nonpriest, was itself in violation of the symbolic system, which is why he gives Jesus a chance to refuse. It is almost as if he says, "You could declare me clean if only you would *dare*" (1:40). Jesus does indeed dare, but Mark tells us he is *angry* (*orgistheis*, 1:41). Then, after the declaration of wholeness has been delivered, Jesus, "snorting with indignation" (*embrimēsamenos*), dispatches the man *back* to the priests (the probable meaning of *exebalen*). How are we to makes sense of these strong emotions?[1]

They only make sense if the man had *already been to the priests*, who for some reason had rejected his petition. Deciding to make an issue out of it, Jesus sternly gives the leper these orders:

> See that you say nothing to anyone! Rather, go back and show yourself to the priest and make the offering prescribed by Moses for your cleansing as a witness against them [1:44].

The cleansed leper's task is not to publicize a miracle but to help confront an ideological system: the change in object (from "priest" to "them") suggests a protest against the entire purity apparatus, which the priests control. He is to make the offering for the purpose of "witnessing against them" (*eis marturion autois*). This is a technical phrase in the Gospel for testimony before hostile audiences (6:11; 13:9).

Jesus' anger, then, is directed against the symbolic order of purity of which this man is a victim. The system subjects the physically ailing to a double oppression: not only are they second-class citizens in Israel, but they must make special payment as well. This episode may well be a kind of midrash (commentary) on the "Malachi" oracle Mark has already cited in his prologue (1:2). That oracle goes on to promise that Yahweh will "cleanse" (LXX, *katharizōn*) the sons of Levi until they "bring their offerings in true justice" (LXX, *prosagontes thusian en kidaisunē*, Mal 3:3). It further promises that Yahweh will appear as a "witness" (LXX, *martus*) against those who use the cultic apparatus to oppress the poor and marginal (Mal 3:5). In this story, both cleansing and judgment have drawn nigh.

Yet Jesus' strategy backfires: the man aborts his mission, goes public, and Jesus is forced to go into hiding (1:45). Again, most commentators have wrongly attributed Jesus' retreat here to a desire to contain his popularity. Malina is correct in insisting upon the opposite: Jesus is now a marked man, considered unclean in the city due to his contact with the leper (1981:122). This first symbolic action of healing thus sets the tone for Jesus' campaign: liberation provokes conflict.

ii. Attack on the Debt System: Healing a Paralytic

After these ambiguous results, Mark tells us that Jesus does not return to Capernaum for several days, and then quietly. But word leaks out that he is back, and immediately he is beset upon, this time by both the sick and the suspicious (2:1f.). The conclusion to the leper story is linked to the beginning of the paralytic story by several "hook words," a Markan technique by which he chains episodes. In 1:45 the leper proclaims "the word" (*ton logon*); so does Jesus in 2:2. Also in these two verses we encounter the phrase "so that no longer" (*hōste mēketi*, occurring only here in Mark).

The narrative setting of this next healing contains several details that underline the poverty of the situation (2:4). The dwelling is typical, having an earthen roof, which explains why the carriers of the paralytic can dig through it (described by Mark as literally "unroofing the roof") in order to gain entrance to the crowded single room. The "stretcher" (*krabatton*) upon which the paralytic lies is a Latinism describing a poor man's bed or mattress (sometimes a bedroll used by soldiers). And here the "crowds" (*ochlos*) first appear in the Gospel, a term I will look at in the next section.

The internal structure of the episode is described by Dewey (1980) as a ring composition:

    2:1–5   introduction (crowd and paralytic)
    2:6–10a   controversy (scribes vs. Jesus)
    2:10b–12b   healing and conclusion (crowd and paralytic)

This form articulates Jesus' solidarity with the poor, from whom the scribes are insulated.

The repetition of key phrases again reveals the ideological discourse of the episode. As in 1:22, Mark posits an opposition between Jesus and the scribes: it is his "teaching" (*laleō*, 2:2,7) versus their "reasoning" (*dialogizomai*, 2:6,8). Mark then constructs a dialect equation between the phrases (a) "forgiveness of sins" and (b) "pick up your stretcher and walk":

    a   My child, your sins are forgiven (2:5).
    a   Who can forgive sins but God? (2:7).
         Which of these is easier: to say to the paralytic:
    a   "Your sins are forgiven" or to say,
    b   "Get up, pick up your stretcher, and walk"? (2:9).

But to prove to you that the Human One has

a   authority on earth to forgive sins. . . . I order you:

b   get up, pick up your stretcher, and go off home (2:10f.).

b   And the man got up, picked up his stretcher at once, and walked out in front of everyone (2:12).

By repeating this equation Mark is, as in the previous episode, emphasizing that Jesus' act of healing raises a deeper ideological issue.

It is Jesus who again forces the issue in 2:4, this time unilaterally pronouncing forgiveness of debt:

> *Aphientai* is here punctiliar . . . with the meaning "are this moment forgiven." The statement is an authoritative declaration . . . at a point where one expects the word of healing,[it] is abrupt (Taylor, 1963:195).

In choosing to introduce the language of the debt code, Jesus is elaborating the symbolics of hierarchy. The man's lack of bodily wholeness would have been attributed to either his own sin, or, if a birth defect, inherited sin; he was thus denied full status in the body politic of Israel (above, B,ii). Jesus summarily releases him from all debt—hence restoring his social wholeness and thus his personhood, which in turn is equated with the restoration of physical wholeness. The man walks, and the crowd glorifies God: the "body" (physical/social) has been restored (2:12). Once again, the crowd is amazed (cf.1:27) that Jesus has out-duelled the scribes.

The scribes are incensed, and for good reason. Their complaint that none but God can remit debt (2:7b) is not a defense of the sovereignty of Yahweh, but of their own social power. As Torah interpreters and co-stewards of the symbolic order, they control determinations of indebtedness. But as Jesus did with the priestly prerogative, he has also expropriated this function. Faced with this threat, the scribes accuse Jesus in the strongest possible language: "He blasphemes!" (2:7a). This will ultimately be the charge for which Jesus is condemned to death at the end of the story (14:64). Though here it is not yet pressed, it is no accident that the next time the scribal authorities appear it is in the person of government investigators from Jerusalem (3:22).

It is in this highly charged political atmosphere that Mark introduces the apocalyptic persona, the "Human One" (traditionally rendered the "Son of Man," 2:10). This figure is taken from Daniel's apocalyptic judgment myth (Dn 7:13), which will later figure centrally in the second call to discipleship; I will defer closer examination of it until then (below, 8,D). For now what is noteworthy is the fact that Mark has taken a recognized "heavenly" entity and claimed for it authority "on earth," specifically over the debt code. This further concretizes the combat myth begun in 1:12 and extended in Jesus' confrontation with the "demon" of scribal authority in 1:23. The political struggle has truly commenced: the Human One is wresting away from the scribal and priestly class their "authority on earth."

iii. The "Crowd": Jesus among Sinners and the Poor

The portrait now emerging is of a Jesus who is continually surrounded by the poor, who attends their importune cries for healing and wholeness, and who acts not just to bind up their wounds but to attack the structures that perpetuate their oppression. Mark has a specific narrative indicator of this social location among the poor: it is introduced in 2:4 as the "crowd" (*ho ochlos*). Korean liberation theologian Ahn Byung-mu has made an illuminating study of this term, which appears some thirty-eight times in Mark:

> We would normally expect the term *laos* rather than *ochlos* to be used for the people, since the term *laos* occurs far more frequently in the language of the biblical writers . . . used around 2,000 times in the Septuagint. . . . It is certain that in the New Testament, Mark is the first writer to introduce the term *ochlos*. . . . The term *ochlos* appears in Greek documents referring to a confused majority or to the ordinary soldiers in a combat unit but not to officers. It also refers to non-combat people who follow the army and perform menial duties. We must note that the anonymous people referred to as the *ochlos* are differentiated from the ruling class. . . . The Septuagint uses this Greek word with this general meaning of "the mass" [1981:139,149].

Byung-mu concludes that Mark understood this term as analogous to the rabbinic expression *'am ha'aretz* ("people of the land"). In preexilic times the term designated Jewish landowners, but during and after the exile it referred to the commoners left behind in Palestine who assumed ownership of the land. After the time of Ezra it came to mean specifically the lower class, poor, uneducated, and ignorant of the law.

Byung-mu abstracts the following characteristics of the *ochlos* as it appears in Mark's narrative:

1. They form the omnipresent background of Jesus' ministry.
2. They are identified as sinners and social outcasts.
3. Though differentiated from the disciples, they are accepted as part of Jesus' community (see 3:32ff.).
4. Unlike the disciples they are never directly criticized, or given special instructions or conditions.
5. They are alienated from the Jewish leadership, and thus largely supportive of Jesus in his struggle against that leadership.
6. They are feared by the ruling class, which in the end is able to manipulate them against Jesus.

If Byung-mu is correct in his identification of the *ochlos* with the *am ha'aretz* of Palestine, then it is of particular note that the rabbis taught that Jews should neither share meals nor travel together with the *'am ha'aretz*.[2] Yet Mark pictures Jesus as openly doing both with the *ochlos* (ibid.:150). This is well illustrated in the call of the toll collector Levi.

This call episode (2:13f.) serves a transitional function between the purity/debt doublet we have just read and the Pharisee conflict triplet we will look at next. It is linked to the paralytic episode by identifying the toll collectors as "sinners" (2:15), while Jesus' shared meal with them sets the stage for the following episode, the Pharisaic objection (2:16f.). Levi, a customs official, will have represented a socially outcast—though economically secure—class. Distinct from the so-called tax farmers, who oversaw collection of the major land taxes and tributes, toll collectors were usually Jews under the employ of Roman or Herodian administrators. They handled the myriad of local transportation taxes and tariffs, and such a customs station would be expected in a commercial center such as Capernaum, which was "the first town within Herod Antipas' territory after one crossed the border . . . from Herod Philip's territory, necessitating provision for import taxes and security" (Harrison, 1985:75f.). The toll collectors' widespread reputation for dishonesty, and the fact that they were bureaucratic representatives of the oppressive politico-economic order, meant they were a shunned caste in Judaism, even to the point of often being denied basic civil rights (Donahue, 1971).

As did the fishermen-disciples, the toll collector responds by leaving his vocation (2:14c). And as he did with Peter (1:29), Jesus joins his new disciple at his home (this makes better sense than do those who argue that Jesus is the host here, for Mark never makes mention of Jesus having a house). In describing the ensuing table fellowship, Mark leaves no room for doubt about Jesus' intimate social interaction with this outcast group: "And he was reclining at table in his house, and many toll collectors and sinners reclined with Jesus and his disciples, for there were many who followed him" (2:15).

"Reclining at table" is clarified by Taylor:

> *Katakeimai* . . . is here used, as in 14:3, of reclining at meals upon the left elbow. . . . This custom, due to Hellenistic influences, although ultimately eastern in origin, was universal in the time of Jesus. . . . Other verbs used in Mark with the same meaning are *anakeimai* (6:26; 14:18), *anaklinō* (6:39), *anapiptō* (6:40; 8:6) and *sunanakaimai* (here and 6:22) [1963:204].

It is of no small significance that Mark chooses this scene to introduce his term for "disciples" (*tois mathētais*). It seems he wants to stress here that Jesus' disciples may freely mix with "sinners," because Jesus' repudiation of the debt code has made everyone equal again before God. There are now only sinners on the road of discipleship, as Jesus will argue in 2:17. Although the community of discipleship is in one sense distinct, its group boundaries embrace the socially outcast (below, 9,A,iii)—in utter contrast to the Pharisaic program of identity through separation.

4D. CHALLENGING PHARISAIC PRIVILEGE AND POWER (2:16–28)

i. Holiness: Table Fellowship and Fasting

Jesus has challenged the ideological hegemony of the scribal and priestly classes by undermining their control of the redemptive media of purity and debt codes. This alone would be a programmatic statement, but Mark is not done. He now turns to the Pharisaic movement, which represented a different—though in Mark's view equally problematic—approach to the ideological maintenance of the people of God. I have noted above how the Pharisaic sect, which included both priests and scribes, pursued a program to extend the imperatives of the symbolic order to the masses while themselves following a rigorous practice of purity (2,E,iii, F,ii). Their attempts at building a popular base put them in direct competition with Mark's community. In the next three episodes Jesus' direct action campaign confronts the central tenets of the Pharisaic holiness code: their rules of table fellowship, public piety, and maintenance of the Sabbath.

The odd phrase "scribes of the Pharisees" (2:16) serves to introduce a new set of antagonists by linking them with a group that has already appeared. In such fashion Mark later introduces the Herodians (3:6) and chief priests and elders (8:31). This narrative device expresses Mark's conviction that all sectors of the ruling class are ultimately aligned in their opposition to the kingdom. J. Wilde notes:

[The Pharisees] before the destruction of the temple were primarily a society for teaching and table fellowship. The dietary, ritual, and legal orientation focused largely on this table fellowship, which was the high point of their life as a group. The Houses of Hillel, Shammai, and others disputed, sometimes bitterly, on the laws of table fellowship, and the relative leniency or strictness of various masters consumed much interest [1974:196].

The issue was not gratuitous: table fellowship was the central expression of social intercourse in antiquity:

For the oriental every table fellowship is a guarantee of peace, trust, or brotherhood. . . . The oriental, to whom symbolic action means more than it does to us, would immediately understand the acceptance of the outcasts into table fellowship with Jesus as an offer of salvation to guilty sinners and as the assurance of forgiveness. Hence the objections of the Pharisees . . . who held that the pious could only have table fellowship with the righteous [Jeremias, 1966:204].

Thus in the repetitive rhetoric of 2:16, Mark is "elaborating" the Pharisaic symbolics of the meal to reveal their real concern: not the welfare of the masses, but their own class status.

This brief episode only anticipates the more extended confrontation concerning table fellowship with the "unclean" in 7:1ff. (where we again encounter the scribe/Pharisee link). Jesus' concluding maxim in 2:17 unmasks the Pharisaic duplicity: for all their rhetoric about extending holiness to all of Israel, their practice betrays their commitment to rigid social boundaries between the "righteous" and the "sinner." This boundary Jesus flatly rejects, and his mission is specifically aimed at transgressing it. His identification of the "sick" with the "sinner" ties the issue back to his attack upon the debt code in the previous healing story. Yet there is a sharp edge to the saying in light of the wider narrative: the "strong" (*hoi ischuontes*, see 3:27) may not need the "physician"—but he intends to contest their claim to being "just" (*dikaious*).

The second episode in this series finds Jesus having to defend his followers against the charge that they are not keeping a recognized fast day (2:18–22). The link to the previous episode is provided by the focus on the practice of "disciples," those of the Pharisees and John versus those of Jesus. Fasting seems to have been an important element in the public profile of Pharisaic piety:

> The only fast enjoined by the Law was that of the Day of Atonement (Lv 16:29; cf. Acts 27:9), but additional fasts were observed by the Pharisees, twice in the week, on Mondays and Thursdays (cf. Lk 18:12 . . .). Traditional fasts, commemorative of historical events . . . were also observed [Taylor, 1963:209].

It is important that Mark portrays the antagonists not as the Pharisees themselves, but referring to the *example* of the Pharisees as a point of comparison. This strongly suggests that Mark's community was being compared, and was competing, with the Pharisaic sect (and perhaps also the remnant of John's followers).

In response to the challenge, Jesus launches into his longest discourse yet, which reasserts apocalyptic imagery. Fasting per se is not the issue, for Jesus concedes that there will be a time for fasting when the "bridegroom" departs "on that day" (2:19f.). Both images are drawn from apocalyptic stock (see Mt 15:1ff.), and no doubt are intended as a proleptic allusion to the central apocalyptic event in Mark's story, the death of Jesus. This is then followed by two metaphors that articulate the traditional apocalyptic dualism of "two ages" (below, 11,D,i):

1. a "new" patch on an "old" garment (2:21);
2. "young" wine meant not for "old" but "new" skins (2:22).

"New" (*kainos*) is a term usually identified with eschatological re-creation (see 1:27). Mark is here concerned to distinguish the radical social practice of the kingdom from the cosmetic social piety of the Pharisaic holiness code. The "young" discipleship movement must not conform to a practice that looks novel, even progressive, but in truth is "old," meaning fundamentally aligned with the dominant symbolic order. To do so would be to jeopardize the messianic project, represented by the images of "a worse tear" and "the wine and skins will both be lost." The "new" wine will later be revealed by Mark as the genuine social practice of nonviolent love (14:24f.).

ii. Sabbath: Civil Disobedience in a Grain Field

In the final episode of the series the practice of the disciples is again at issue (2:23–28). It appears they cut through a field, trampling grain in order to "make a way." They then stripped the fallen plants to eat the grain. The Pharisees accuse them of a legal violation of the Sabbath (2:23f.), probably referring to regulations concerning transit as well as sowing and reaping (Derrett, 1977:89ff.). This is a difficult story in which Mark takes on the most important aspect of the Pharisaic program: Sabbath observance.

Jesus' defense appeals to 1 Samuel 21:1-6. Mark's wry poke—"Have you never read?"—prepares us for an ingenuous bit of exposition on his part. Jesus claims the precedent of David's assertion of his kingly right to violate the law when he *and his followers* (the Greek is emphatic) were in need (*chreian eschen*). Now David, Derrett points out (ibid.), was in that instance on an important campaign, and essentially "commandeered" bread for his soldiers. Mark will use the same terminology in describing Jesus' "need" when he "commandeers" an ass during his march on Jerusalem (11:3f.). The point would seem to be that the disciples have a right to commandeer grain, because they too are on a campaign with Jesus, who will later be revealed as superior to David (12:35). As a clinching argument, Mark asserts that not only has the Human One expropriated authority over the debt code, but the Sabbath as well.

But to think the point of this story is Jesus' "christological prerogative," as do most commentators, is to miss the real issue. It has been argued that Jesus' defense does not conform to the rules of rabbinic argumentation from scripture, but that should come as no surprise (Cohn-Sherbok, 1979). Indeed, closer examination reveals that Mark has added something to his (already free) rendition of the Old Testament story: David and his men were *hungry*. L. Schottroff and W. Stegemann, in a recent redaction-critical study of this text, have pointed out that Matthew, Mark's first interpreter, clearly understood Mark's point to be the issue of "mercy, not sacrifice" (Mt 12:7; cf. Hos 6:6): "The hunger of the poor is explained in a symbolic way as setting Israel its central religious task, one taking precedence even over the duty of observing the Sabbath" (1984:125). It is surely significant also that Mark chooses this passage to introduce the term "bread" (*arton*, 2:26). This will figure decisively in the later narrative as a symbol of that which must be shared—not least in the stories of the feeding of hungry masses in the wilderness (6:33ff.;8:1ff.).

This reading is confirmed by the larger narrative context of Mark itself. In all three episodes in which the Pharisees figure, Mark has focused upon some aspect of food consumption. First Jesus defended his (and his disciples') right to break bread with the socially outcast. Then he asserts their freedom to ignore ritual noneating practices; such piety, after all, was a luxury for the affluent, not for the poor for whom hunger was an involuntary and bitter reality! Now Mark escalates his attack: he justifies the disciples' right to break the law by procuring grain on the Sabbath in a situation of hunger. Mark is doing more than simply deflating the Pharisaic holiness code. He is implicitly raising a political issue of criticism by identifying the Pharisees with issues of "land and table."

The Pharisees played an ambiguous role in matters of production, consumption, and distribution of produce in rural Palestine (above, 2,E,iii). On the one hand, since the time of the Hasmoneans they had been consistent critics of the centralized tithing structure, which dictated that agricultural tithes had to be brought to Jerusalem. The Pharisees advocated local distribution, to ensure that provincial priests received their due. But what the rural producers gained in terms of local control over the separation of tithes they lost in terms of both production and consumption. There is evidence in the *halachic* tradition of tension between Galilean peasants and the Pharisees over issues of marketing produce, for the latter determined what was and was not suitable for consumption according to strict purity rules. This is perhaps also implied in the disciples' plucking of grain: once produce was detached from the ground, it became subject to purity regulations (Safrai and Stern, 1977b:830). Another point of conflict was the prohibition against sowing a crop in the Sabbath year, something the subsistence economics of the peasant could scarcely afford.

The disciples' commandeering grain against Sabbath regulations must from this perspective be seen as a protest of "civil disobedience" over the politics of food in Palestine. Jesus is not only defending discipleship practice against the alternative holiness code of Pharisaism, he is going on the offensive, challenging the ideological control and the manipulation of the redistributive economy by a minority whose elite status is only aggrandized. Mark consistently argues that solidarity with the poor also means addressing oppressive structures. This may well mean breaking the law, but such action is legitimated by the Human One, who in overturning the authority of purity and debt codes is being revealed to the reader not only as "lord of the Sabbath" but lord of the entire "house" itself (13:35).

4E. REJECTION AND CONSOLIDATION: THE FIRST "GENERATIVE SEAM" (3:1-19)

We come to the first part of the double climax to Jesus' nonviolent campaign. As noted above (A,i), one of the subordinate narrative patterns in Book I is the recapitulation of "rejection and consolidation." After being spurned in the synagogue (3:6), Jesus will withdraw and commission his community (3:13-19). The same pattern recurs in 6:1-13 (below, 7,A; some commentators also see it in 8:14-26, but I do not believe the pattern holds there). I refer to these as "generative seams" in the narrative, in which a crisis in Jesus' mission is reached, requiring a retreat and regrouping of forces.

i. Civil Disobedience as Theater: Jesus' Deuteronomic Ultimatum

The disciples' violation of the Sabbath leads directly into another conflict story (3:1-6). At least one commentator has suggested:

> [2:24] may be the legal warning necessary before actual prosecution on a charge can be made. . . . In 2:28 Jesus asserts his authority over the sabbath, an answer not acceptable under Jewish Law. Then in 3:2, the opponents are watching Jesus in order to accuse him legally if he violates

the sabbath. . . . If he acts illegally on the sabbath in 3:1-6, he is liable to arrest. . . . The claim of Jesus in 2:28 prepares the reader for the higher level of hostility and the greater stakes involved in 3:1-6 [Dewey, 1980:100].

For this showdown, Mark returns us to the heart of the Jewish symbolic order (synagogue/Sabbath). This is the first of several episodes that Mark will construct as "summary" actions, integrating rhetorical aspects of preceding stories. In this case, there are echoes of the inaugural exorcism (synagogue setting), the leper's cleansing (role of the "hand"), the paralytic (structure of healing/conflict/healing) and the conflict series with the Pharisees (Sabbath, their mention, 3:6).

André Trocmé, in his provocative book *Jesus and the Nonviolent Revolution* (1964), argued that this episode, as the turning point of Jesus' public ministry, represents carefully staged political theater. Jesus could presumably heal the man with the withered hand in private without provoking a reaction (as in 1:29), but chooses yet again to force the issue. Under the glare of media lights, as it were, with the hostile officials hovering, waiting for Jesus to "cross the line," Mark finally resolves the lingering subplot concerning healing on the Sabbath (see 1:32). As in the modern practice of civil disobedience, which might break the law in order to raise deeper issues of its morality and purpose, so Jesus, just before "crossing the line," issues a challenge to his audience. Pitting his mission of compassion and justice to the poor against the imperatives of the dominant order, Jesus calls the entire ideological edifice of the law to account. He paraphrases the watershed question of Deuteronomic faith (Dt 30:15ff.): "Is it lawful on the Sabbath to do good, or to do evil?" (3:4). He then adds bitterly, "To save life, or to kill?," drawing a sharp contrast between his messianic intentions and those of his opponents (*apokteinai* is always used by Mark in reference to political execution; see 6:19; 8:31; 12:5; 14:1).

The authorities, predictably, refuse to respond, refuse to allow Jesus to make this into a "political trial." Mark's indictment is sharp: the strong language describing Jesus' rage is unparalleled in the New Testament (3:5). Mark then introduces another key narrative theme: obstinance—literally, "stubbornness of heart." But the reader cannot become smug, for this charge will eventually be leveled at the disciples as well (6:52, 8:17). The man's hand is healed, the line is crossed, and immediately the local officials "take counsel" (*sumboulion*) to plot Jesus' demise (3:6). Pharisees and "Herodians" are an unlikely coalition, but will appear again later in 12:13. The latter group is probably a Markan construct (Bennett, 1975b), meant to represent the native Galilean aristocracy, with its interest in maintaining order. Their mention here prepares us for another official death plot—the execution of John by Herod (6:14ff.). No sooner has one plot-conflict been resolved (will Jesus heal on the Sabbath?) than another one opens, which will be resolved only when this coalition's "counsel" is carried out at the end of the story, in the Sanhedrin's decision to execute Jesus (15:1).

ii. A New Sinai: Jesus Forms a "Confederacy"

Jesus is not unaware of these machinations, and "withdraws" (*anechōrēsen*, "takes refuge from peril") to the sea with his disciples (3:7). Yet the ministry continues, which Mark indicates by again relating it in summary form (3:8–12). I call this a "generative seam" because a plot complication has thrown the discipleship narrative into doubt. It needs to be regenerated, which Mark does by recapitulating key elements from the beginning: a sea setting (1:16) and a summary of mission (1:32ff.). This is a device Mark will use again at the end of his Gospel.

The summary indicates the growth of the mission: a "great crowd" comes to Jesus from Galilee, and now also from all over Palestine. The meaning of "Judea and Jerusalem and Idumea and the other side of the Jordan [e.g., Peraea] and from around Tyre and Sidon" (3:8) is effectively "from north, south, east, and west." Jesus' campaign has attracted persons who have "heard of his actions," a double-edged reference, for shortly we will see that it includes political opponents coming from Jerusalem to investigate Jesus (3:22).

In 3:9 Mark introduces a new narrative site: just as Jesus has previously tried to distance himself from the press of the crowd in a house, so here he gets into a boat. This sets the stage for his teaching of the masses (4:1), and anticipates the subsequent departure in the boat across the lake (4:35). From this new vantage point Jesus continues his ministry of healing and exorcism (3:10f.), vanquishing the unclean spirits who struggle to name him (3:12).

In Mosaic fashion (see 9:1), Jesus then ascends a mountain for his next symbolic action (3:13). As he has called disciples, so now he will forge an identity for them by "naming" them—a new solidarity that will be crucial, for shortly Jesus will repudiate the social fabric of the kinship system (3:35). And as he "commissions" the disciples to inherit the messianic mission of proclamation and confrontation (3:14) in this generative seam, so will he send them out on mission in the second seam (6:7f.). Jesus is preparing a community to carry on his vocation "after the bridegroom is taken away" (2:20), and from here on out he will tutor this group in his alternative social practice—for to it is entrusted "the secret of the kingdom of God" (4:11).

Simon, James, and John head up the list, and are given "new names" (an apocalyptic motif? See Rv 3:12; 22:4). They become, respectively, "Peter" ("the rock") and "Boanerges" (translated by Mark as "sons of thunder," 3:16f.). These three will emerge in the story as a kind of "inner circle" of the community, but the list is not intended to represent an exclusive cadre of disciples. Levi, who was also called to follow, is not named; seven others who are named (Philip through Simon) do not appear again. The naming functions rather as a literary fiction, connoting Jesus' consolidation of his alternative community. Indeed, Mark's characterization of the inner circle will be very critical. Mark also tempers this (potentially triumphalistic) founding moment with cold realism, extending the shadow cast by the introduction of the death plot: the last named is Judas, who, we are told in a dispassionate proleptic glimpse, will betray Jesus.

What is usually overlooked is the political dimension of this symbolic act. By reenacting a "new Sinai" covenant on the mountain, Jesus is attacking the ideological foundations of the dominant order. He chooses (*epoiēsen*) a new leadership, a word that is used in the LXX to refer to the *appointing* of priests (1 Kgs 12:31; 13:33; 2 Chr 2:18) and Moses and Aaron (1 Sm 12:6; Taylor, 1963:230). The choice of "twelve" obviously invokes the tradition of the twelve tribes of Israel; in other words, Jesus is forming a kind of confederacy.

Unfortunately we have been captive to a "religious" understanding of the primitive ecclesial metaphors of the church as "new priesthood" and "new Israel." But the political character of this discourse would not have been lost upon Mark's Palestinian audience: Jesus, having repudiated the authority of the priestly/scribal order, now forms a kind of vanguard "revolutionary committee," a "government in exile"! The community of resistance has been founded.

4F. CAMPAIGN CLIMAX: JESUS DECLARES IDEOLOGICAL WAR (3:20–35)

Jesus returns to the safety of "the house," only to find that he is no longer welcome. Again the importunate crowds invade, disrupting table fellowship (3:20), and this is the tense setting for the second climax, in which Jesus must face the consequences of his campaign. A new conflict surfaces, representing a quantum leap in Mark's narrative of hostility. His family believes he has gone too far and demands that he give up his mission (3:21). But their caution is too late; already government investigators from the capital have come ready to press charges (3:22).

This section is composed as an intercalation, or "sandwich," a favorite Markan technique of beginning one story, interrupting it with another, and then returning to the original story. The form functions to establish a fundamental relationship between the two elements, represented by the two consecutive charges:

1. And his family . . . said: "He is out of his mind."
2. And the scribes . . . said: "He is possessed by Beelzebub."

The Capernaum campaign ends with this double counterattack upon Jesus: to his extended family he is deluded, to his political opponents he is demonic.

i. Polarization: Jesus vs. the "Strong Man"

We begin with the inner part of the sandwich, in which we encounter for the first time "Jerusalem scribes." Jesus has formed his "confederacy," and the scribes are commencing their "counterinsurgency," leading with the charge that Jesus is himself possessed (3:22). I. Lewis's anthropological study of demon possession in traditional societies notes that it is common for those in power to impugn exorcists who assume "a positive, active, and above all, militant role":

Witchcraft accusations represent a distancing strategy which seeks to discredit, sever, and deny links. . . . These upstart controllers of spirits are, by their very power over the spirits, suspected of causing what they cure [Hollenbach, 1981:577].

To put it in terms of the political war of myths, when the ruling class feels its hegemony threatened, it tries to neutralize challengers by identifying them with the mythic cultural arch-demon. The logic of the scribes was simple: because they believed themselves to be God's representatives, Jesus' "secession" necessarily put him in allegiance to Satan. To borrow from the symbolic canon of our modern cold war dualism, Jesus is being labeled a "communist."

The scribes use a double euphemism for Satan. The first is "Beelzebul," an obscure name probably derived from a Hebrew idiom connoting " 'height,' 'abode,' 'dwelling' . . . the name means 'Lord of the dwelling,' with reference either to the air or to the possessed in whom he dwells" (Taylor, 1963:239; cf. Mt 10:25). The second is "prince of the demons" (*en tō archonti tōn daimoniōn*), echoing the "principalities and powers" language found throughout the New Testament (e.g., 1 Cor 2:6; Eph 2:2). The semantic field is obviously that of apocalyptic, and the discourse is therefore specifically political:

We may understand the kingdom of Satan as a symbolic accentuation of the negative experiences of earthly rule. According to the apocalypse of the shepherds in Ethiopic Enoch 85–90, when Israel lost its political independence, God relegated rule over it to the fallen angels, the subjects of Satan. The mythological events here reflect political ones [Theissen, 1977:76].

Here the apocalyptic combat myth deepens significantly. From the wilderness (1:12f.) the struggle has moved steadily into the heart of the political geography of Roman Palestine, first in the synagogue exorcism and then in the Human One's challenge to the symbolic order (2:10,28). Now Jesus goes nose to nose with his opponents in the war of myths.

By introducing the discourse of *parables* at this point (3:23), Mark is preparing us for the first sermon (4:3ff.), which must also be understood in an apocalyptic context. Conversely, the sermon's demand that we attend to parables with "ears to hear" (4:9) applies here: Jesus is about to articulate something that must not be missed, despite the fact that it is somewhat cryptic. Demonstrating a style of verbal riposte that he will pursue masterfully in his later temple debates (11:27ff.), Jesus' defense becomes offense by turning his antagonists' words back upon them as a question and a riddle:

How can Satan exorcise (*ekballein*) Satan?
Should a kingdom be divided against itself,
    that kingdom cannot stand;

    Should a house be divided against itself,
       that house cannot stand;
    Thus if Satan has revolted against himself and is divided,
       he cannot stand and is coming to an end [3:23–26].

The intricate parallelism and cross-referencing of images in this series of rhetorical statements is clear, but what does it mean?

The famous hermeneutics of Abraham Lincoln notwithstanding, these are not placative platitudes about civil war weakening the body politic, as if Jesus seeks to assure the scribes that he is really their ally against a common enemy, Satan. No, Jesus is short-circuiting their self-serving ideological dualism by unmasking its contradictions and collapsing it in upon itself:

> Encountering the [structure of] presuppositions of the opponents . . . requires the awakening of a counter-vision with sufficient imaginative force to crack the hard shell of this structure. This is what these words attempt through their surprising adoption of the perspective of the accusation. . . . It wishes to drive a wedge deeply into the foundations on which the opponents have built their world [Tannehill, 1975:179,184].

The carefully chosen images of the domain of "Satan" (3:23,26) bear remarkable correspondence to the ideological foundations of scribal Judaism: the centralized politics of the Davidic state ("kingdom," 3:24) and its symbolic center, the temple ("house," 3:25). That these foundations are in crisis and "cannot stand" will be articulated later in the story, when Jesus battles these scribal opponents on their home turf in Jerusalem.[3] There Jesus will refuse to identify his "kingdom" with David's (12:35ff.; below 10,B,ii; F,i). When he finally encounters the temple itself, he will "exorcise" (*ekballein*) those who have "divided" the purpose of the "house of prayer" (11:15-7). Then, in his second sermon, Jesus will prophesy that the temple-state will not be able to stand (13:2), and the true "Lord of the house" will come and reclaim his domain (13:35).

    This much of the riddle is solved: Satan cannot "clean out his own house" (3:23); it is up to Jesus to lead the "revolt" against the powers, to bring their rule to an end (3:26). It is Jesus' declaration of ideological war with the scribal establishment. Having laid his opponents bare, Jesus then drops his semantic jousting and spins a thinly veiled political parable in which he likens his mission to criminal breaking and entering:

> No one can enter a strong man's house and plunder his goods (*ta skeuē*) unless the strong man is first bound (*dēsē*); then indeed his house may be plundered [3:27].

This introduces two more important proleptic references. "Goods" refers to "utensils of various materials . . . which are employed for the most varied purposes in home and field, in war and peace, in the secular world and the sacred" (Maurer, *TDNT*, 8:360). The only other appearance of the term in Mark occurs in 11:16—in reference to the vessels of the temple cult on which Jesus puts a ban! "Binding" appears in another exorcism context—referring to a "demon" whom no one had the "strength" to bind (5:3f.)! It also describes the political imprisonment of John (6:17), Jesus (15:1), and Barabbas (15:7). In other words, the parable illumines the later narrative, and vice versa.

Mark has come clean: Jesus (a.k.a. the "stronger one" heralded by John, 1:8) intends to overthrow the reign of the strong man (a.k.a. the scribal establishment represented by the demon of 1:24). In this parable the oracle of Second Isaiah lives again: Yahweh is making good on the promise to liberate the "prey of the strong (LXX, *ischuontos*) and rescue the captives of the tyrants" (Is 49:24f.). Imperial hermeneutics, ever on the side of law and order, will of course find this interpretation of the strong man parable strained, offensive, shocking. Yet Mark drew the image of breaking and entering from the most enduring of the primitive Christian eschatological traditions: the Lord's advent as a thief in the night (Mt 24:43 par; 1 Thes 5:2,4; 2 Pt 3:10; Rv 3:3, 16:15).

As if to underscore the seriousness of what he has just said, Jesus concludes with a solemn "Amen" saying (3:28). He now deals the final blow to the debt code: blanket pardon. But there is one exception: mistaking the work of the Holy Spirit for that of Satan. As Juan Luis Segundo puts it:

> The blasphemy resulting from bad apologetics will always be pardonable. . . . What is not pardonable is using theology to turn real human liberation into something odious. The real sin against the Holy Spirit is refusing to recognize, with "theological" joy, some concrete liberation that is taking place before one's very eyes [1979:254].

This is what the scribal class cannot "see." Thus by the close of his defense, Jesus has turned the tables completely upon his opponents: it is they who are aligned against God's purposes. To be captive to the way things are, to resist criticism and change, to brutally suppress efforts at humanization—is to be bypassed by the grace of God.

ii. Rift: Repudiation of the Kinship System

Mark ends this section by returning to the brewing family crisis in the house (3:31). This crisis began when "those belonging to him" (*hoi par' autou*—i.e., relatives), believing him to be deranged, had tried to get Jesus to cease and desist (3:21). His family had attempted to "seize" him, a word used elsewhere in Mark for political detainment (6:17; 12:12; 14:1,44,46,49,51). In light of Jesus' militant declaration, they redouble their efforts: Mark reports in 1:31 that his mother and brothers are outside the house summoning him. We might well be sympathetic with their intent to silence Jesus; for surely to them it was lunacy for a marked man to continue to provoke the highest authorities in the land. He was courting disaster, and they wished to protect him—as well as their family reputation. Such is the real anxiety of those related to political dissidents.

I have mentioned that kinship was the axis of the social world in antiquity. The extended family structure determined personality and identity, controlled vocational prospects, and most importantly facilitated socialization. For Mark, then, kinship is the backbone of the very social order Jesus is struggling to overturn, which explains his utter disinterest in Jesus' family line (in contrast to the genealogies of Mt and Lk). The anomaly of the picture he draws speaks clearly to the impending rift: his family is "outside" the house (3:31), whereas the crowd sits around Jesus "inside" (3:32). This suggests a new dualism; not unlike the "war oracles" of Qumran and other apocalyptic narrative, polarization ends in a new definition of "insiders" and "outsiders."

The alienation between Jesus and his family is mutual, and he refuses to see them (3:33). If they cannot accept his vocation, he cannot recognize their kindredness. Mark then introduces a new kinship model, based upon obedience, not to the family or clan patriarch, but to God alone (3:35). Jesus' challenge to the traditional authority structures of Palestinian society is now complete. He has repudiated the "old fabric" (2:21), in order to make way for the new order. The fundamental unit of "resocialization" into the kingdom will be the new family, the community of discipleship. And with those words, Jesus retreats to the sea to reflect upon the fortunes and future of his messianic mission (4:1).

NOTES

1. This is one of the rare places in Mark where a variant reading has specific bearing upon my interpretation. There is strong manuscript evidence for an alternative reading that replaces *orgistheis* with *splangchnistheis*: Jesus was "moved with compassion". Metzger (1975:76) considers the latter reading more likely. Its acceptance would not damage my reading, however, for 1:43 clearly indicates Jesus' anger, which traditional interpretation still needs to explain.

2. Byung-mu finds in this portrait of the *ochlos* a correlation with the term used for the disenfranchised in Korean society: *minjung*. I will return to this important contribution from Korean liberation theology in my conclusion (below, 14,E,i).

3. It is possible that "house divided" could refer to the rejection of Jesus by his own household, which would fit in with the other theme of the sandwich. However, the political context here and the analeptic force of 11:17 and 13:35 convince me that the primary allusion is to the temple-state.

CHAPTER FIVE

"Listen!" The First Sermon on Revolutionary Patience (Mark 4:1-36)

All of the trees of the field shall know that I Yahweh bring low the high tree, and make high the low tree, dry up the green tree and make the dry tree flourish.

—Ezekiel 17:24

The first kingdom campaign has ended in polarization, and the messianic community has been forced to break with the social mainstream. It is not surprising therefore that Mark's Jesus should withdraw once again to reflect upon his mission. The famous parables chapter is the first of Jesus' two extended sermons in Mark's Gospel. Drawing upon images of the land and the hardened wisdom of peasant life, this sermon offers hope in the face of overwhelming odds, and introduces the discourse of revolutionary paradox into the story.

5A. A DISCOURSE IN PARABLES

i. Structure of the First Sermon

Exegetical work on both of Jesus' sermons in Mark (4:1-34; 13:1-37) has traditionally been dominated by the form critical approach, with its primary interest in determining the sources behind the text (see below, 11,A,i). The parables of Mark 4 have long tantalized scholars in their search for the "genuine voice" of the rural Nazarene prophet, typified in M. Black's efforts to translate the Greek verse back into Aramaic poetry (1967). Nevertheless, the price of historical criticism has been the isolation of the parable from its literary context. Thus, for example, the sower parable (4:3-9) is dissected to "recover the original meaning of . . . Jesus, to hear again his authentic voice" (Jeremias, 1972:22), whereas Mark's own exposition (4:14-20) is dismissed as the allegoristic (and thus less interesting) voice of the early church. Driving such a wedge into the text is not useful to the socio-literary approach, which is concerned with the narrative coherency and meaning of the parables sermon as a whole, its internal composition and relationship to the rest of the story.

Historical criticism has largely overlooked the significant symmetry between the two Sermons in Mark, and their narrative function within the Gospel. Following the conclusion of each of the two campaigns of direct action, Jesus withdraws from the site of conflict and sits down to offer an extended reflection (4:1f.; 13:3). The primary discursive characteristic of the first homily is parabolic, and the second apocalyptic, but each includes aspects of the other. We see apocalyptic motifs in the first sermon (e.g., special instruction to "insiders," 4:9–13; light/darkness dualism, 4:22; the image of "harvest," 4:29) and parables in the second (e.g., the fig tree, 13:28f.; the watchful householder 13:34–36). Indeed, the parable form was often employed as a fiction by the apocalyptic literary tradition (see Patten, 1983:246ff.).

The first sermon introduces two themes central to the narrative strategy of Mark: the commands to "listen" (*akouein*, 4:3) and to "watch" (*blepein*, 4:24). These metaphors will come to represent the struggle by the disciples/reader to understand and follow the practice of Jesus (7:14; 8:15–20; 9:7). Just as the structure of the first sermon is organized in two parts around the refrain of "listening," so is the second sermon a two-part composition structured around the refrain of "watching" (see below, 11,B,ii).

The parables sermon takes place by the sea, with Jesus addressing the crowd from a boat (4:1), and ends when Mark deconstructs this setting (4:36). It is framed with two summary statements concerning Jesus' "many parables" (4:2,33), and is composed in two parts. The first part weaves together three elements:

1. the sower parable (4:4–8) and its explanation (4:13–20);
2. Mark's reflection on the paradoxical nature of parable discourse: as mystery to be obscured (4:10–12), but also as secret to be revealed (4:21f.);
3. the thematic refrain of listening (4:3,9,23).

The second part begins with an exhortation to discern what one hears (4:24a), warning against the "conventional wisdom" (represented by the proverb of 4:24b–25), which asserts the futility of trying to alter the ordering of power and privilege in the world. Against this cynical realism Jesus offers two more seed similitudes, one calling for revolutionary patience (4:26–29), the other for revolutionary vision and hope despite the odds (4:30–32). The two parts are tightly knit together by the relationship of form and content between the parable of the lamp (4:21–23) and the proverb of 4:24f.:

a　And he said to them,
b　"Is a lamp brought in to be put under a bushel . . .
c　For there is nothing hid . . .
d　If anyone has ears to hear, let them hear."
a′　And he said to them,
d′　"Beware what you hear;
b′　The measure you give is the measure you get . . .
c′　For to the one who has . . . "

Not only is the structure of the sayings similar (a = introduction, b = statement, c = corollary), but also the catch themes of listening (d) and "measuring" (b; "bushel" is a unit of measurement).

ii. "Ears to Hear": The Kingdom as Mystery?

The parables have been the subject of a great deal of debate in synoptic studies. In the history of exegesis, allegoristic interpretation was already ubiquitous in rabbinic and Hellenistic hermeneutics, and so also predominated in the Christian tradition from the start until the advent of modern biblical criticism (Stein offers a helpful synopsis, 1978:45ff.). Jeremias is correct in claiming that form and redaction analysis helped to liberate the parables from this "process which for centuries concealed the meaning . . . under a thick layer of dust" (1972:13). Indeed, foremost among these efforts to restore their *socio-historical* character are Jeremias's own, which make invaluable contributions to our understanding of the "life setting" of the parables in agrarian Palestine. Unfortunately, in Jeremias's form-critical quest to trace the parables from the primitive church to the "historical Jesus," Mark's narrative context and *its* social function is ignored (see above, 1,D,i).

More recently, literary structuralism and existential hermeneutics have explored the parables as exercises in semantic play and paradox, which create a liminal situation for hearers, upsetting their rational or accepted meaning-constructs in order to create new possibilities. As Tannehill puts it, the "surprising twist" in parabolic discourse:

> invites the hearer to cross over and see what the speaker sees. Such a bridge cannot be built in the public world of literal meanings, the world reduced to what all accept for purposes of interpersonal commerce, for this public world is itself being challenged. The speaker must disclose truth by using words which, taken literally, are false, as happens in the case of metaphor. The words are successful insofar as they are able to induce an imaginative vision with sufficient power to undermine the obviousness of literal meanings [1975:183].

This holds true of most parables in Mark, as we shall see, for example, in the case of the image of the "eschatological harvest," though in some instances the parable has a specific parenetic function (e.g., 7:15ff.). Again, however, those who have focused upon the existential force of parables-discourse have done little to illuminate their socio-literary significance.

Whatever their foretextual shape and history, Mark's parables stand in fundamental relationship to the story as a whole and cannot be properly interpreted apart from it. I believe there are four main characteristics of Markan parabolic discourse.

1. They function primarily as a kind of mirror to help the disciple/reader

understand the narrative of Jesus' practice (Belo, 1981:121). Mark tells us (4:13b) that the parable of the sower and its interpretation is a *crux interpretum*: to grasp it is to comprehend not only all other parables but the story as a whole. Thus we are urged repeatedly to listen carefully, for this "allegory" of the fortunes of the messianic mission projects backward and forward in the story, recapitulating what we have read and preparing us for what is to come.

2. Jesus relies upon parables when faced with intense ideological conflict. Mark introduces them in the context of Jesus' attack upon his scribal opponents (3:23), where the divided house and strong man images simultaneously summarize and escalate his criticism of the dominant order and its stewards. Similarly, the riddle of 7:17ff. culminates Jesus' censure of Pharisaic piety; the parable of 12:1ff. his repudiation of the Jerusalem political hierarchy; and the image of 13:28 his rejection of the means and ends of the revolt.

Mark appears to have adopted parable-as-political-criticism from Ezekiel's use of the term (*mashal*):

a. "Son of Man, propound a riddle, and speak an allegory (LXX, *parabolēn*) to the house of Israel" (Ez 17:2).
b. "Is he not a maker of allegories?" (20:49).
c. Utter an allegory to the rebellious house" (24:3).

Mark's seed parables (and the parabolic action of the withered fig tree in 11:13f.) not only strongly echo Ezekiel's cypress tree parable and interpretation (Ez 17), but specifically adopt part of its conclusion for their own (Mk 4:32 = Ez 17:23).

3. The political character of this discourse goes a long way toward clarifying Mark's notion of "hearing but not understanding." His appeal to Isaiah's harsh dictum (Is 6:9f.) in 4:11f. has long troubled exegetes, with its implication that Jesus is willfully obscuring his message to "outsiders." Many have accepted Jeremias's solution that Mark (inappropriately) inserted this saying—which "originally" referred not to parables but Jesus' "preaching in general"—into the sermon based upon his "mistaken" understanding of the catchword *parabolē* (1972:18). Disparaging the redactional skills of Mark is not only unacceptable to the socio-literary approach, it fails to resolve the problem. For the "outsiders/insiders" theme is woven into this sermon from beginning to end, not just in 4:10–12.

It is puzzling why most commentators cannot recognize this dualism as a standard fiction within the apocalyptic tradition. Consider the closing lines of Daniel, in which the prophet is told that the revelations given to him are "sealed" (Dn 12:4,9):

a. "I heard but did not understand" (12:8; LXX, *ēkousa kai ou dienoēthēn*)
b. None of the wicked shall understand, but those who are wise [lit., those paying attention] will understand" (12:10b).

Daniel and Ezekiel also interpret the parable/vision given to the baffled seer, the explanation making explicit their veiled political message. Mark 4 simply follows in this tradition.

Commentators who try to soften or displace the Isaiah quote in 4:12 are therefore missing the point of its inclusion. The sower parable reflects frankly upon the obstacles encountered by the messianic mission. The disciples will inherit this mission (3:13ff.), and when they are later dispatched on it (6:7ff.), Jesus' words to them include instructions about what to do with the inevitable prospect of rejection (6:11). It is for this reason that Mark cites Isaiah 6, because this text is also concerned with "apostolicity" ("Whom shall I send?" Is 6:8). The "command" to obscure the truth is a prophetic fiction based upon the tradition that Yahweh "hardens the hearts" of political opponents, as Yahweh did with the pharaoh (Ex 7:14,22, etc.).

The apocalyptic tradition, Mark included, adopts this fiction, whose purpose is to explain political hostility toward the movement, and intensifies it into a dualism: the word of God polarizes. The way Mark has edited the Isaian pronouncement makes it clear that he is applying its judgment to Jesus' political antagonists. Jeremias (1972:15) notes that Mark agrees with the Targum version of Isaiah 6:10 in speaking of "forgiveness" instead of "healing" as in the LXX, but fails to recognize the narrative purpose for this change. Who is it that Jesus has just warned may be excluded from God's forgiveness? His scribal rivals, who contest his ministry of liberation (3:29). It is they who will listen and yet not hear, a "deafness" that is also a part of the prophetic "script" (11:1ff.).

Isaiah's "commission" ends with his cry of despair—"How long, O Lord?"—to which the divine voice responds by foretelling the overwhelming decimation to come (Is 6:11–13). This motif was also adopted by the apocalyptic movement (e.g., Dn 12:6ff.; Rv 6:9ff.), and by Mark in his second sermon (13:4ff.). Isaiah concludes his oracle with the promise of a "remnant stump" that will be the "holy seed" (Is 6:13), and several commentators have acknowledged that Mark's seed parables may well represent a midrash upon this very theme (Evans, 1985).

What is remarkable about Mark's use of Isaiah, then, is not the fact that he fashions the "listen but do not hear" motif into apocalyptic dualism, but the fact that he will shortly attribute this obduracy to "insiders" as well as "outsiders." No sooner have Jesus' disciples received the benefit of special tutelage than Mark begins to tell us how little they in fact understand (4:41). By the close of the first half of the Gospel, Jesus will turn Isaiah's dictum upon the disciple/reader (8:17f., though, as we will see, Mark here switches the language to conform to Dt 29:4). This narrative crisis issues in a new form of enacted parable, the healing of the deaf and blind (see below, 8,B,i).

4. There is one more important socio-literary aspect to Jesus' parables discourse. In the allegoristic tradition, parables are still popularly exposited in the churches today as "earthly stories with heavenly meanings." But this is exactly what they are *not*! The parables are perfectly consistent with Mark's overall strategy of realistic narrative, in which any and all apocalyptic symbolics are kept "grounded." Jesus insists upon articulating the "mystery of the kingdom of God" in utterly mundane, indeed agrarian terms: it is *like this*! In describing the frustrations and hopes of any peasant farmer, Mark's Jesus is

not exalting the terrestrial into the heavens, or shrouding the plain and common in arcane mysticism, but rather bringing "theology" to earth in a concrete discourse intelligible to the poor.

5B. THE SOWER: A REFLECTION ON THE KINGDOM MISSION
(4:1-23)

i. Remnant Seed in Hostile Soil

Mark has carefully prepared us for this sermon and its setting. He introduced Jesus' ministry to the crowds from a boat on the sea back in 3:7-9, and shortly after that, the parables discourse (3:23). The carefully staged scene in 4:1f., however, lends a certain spatial tension between Jesus and the crowds, which appears to echo the tension in the previous scene between Jesus' family "outside" and those around him inside the house (3:31f.). Given the sermon's attention to Jesus' explanations to his inner circle (4:13ff.,34), this setting at the very outset suggests the dualism between "insiders" (the boat "on the sea" is later a place of special teaching; see 8:13ff.) and "outsiders" (the crowd "next to the sea on the land").

The central parable is a story of sowing, to which Mark devotes a long but symmetrical explanation. At least two themes from the Hebrew Bible have been suggested as the object of Markan midrash in this parable (Evans, 1985):

    a. the Shema (Dt 6:5), in which the three types of soil represent the struggle to love Yahweh with all one's heart, soul, and might;

    b. Second Isaiah's assertion that Yahweh's word goes out and does not return void (Is 55:10f.).

There is no doubt an element of each in the sower, as well as Ezekiel 17, as I have already suggested. Nevertheless, Mark's main concern is to present this parable as a foil to his own narrative of Jesus' kingdom practice.

The parable proper is framed by the command: "Listen!" (4:3,9; *akouete*). This echoes not only the great command of Yahweh to the people ("Hear, O Israel," Dt 6:4, quoted in Mk 12:29), but also the heavenly voice to the disciples (Mk 9:7). After introducing the notion of "mystery" (4:11) and "obduracy" (4:12), Mark has Jesus "privately" explicate the parable. This allegorical interpretation exposits the sower as the proclamation of the kingdom, while the hostile soil is representative of three concrete obstacles to the acceptance of the call to discipleship. Each kind of fruitless seed represents a type of "nondisciple," and significantly Mark will return to dramatize each obstacle later in his discipleship catechism (Mk 8:27ff.).

The first two scatterings of seed represent those who fall away "immediately, as soon as they hear the word," those in whom the word never really "takes root," so that their discipleship is "temporary" (4:17; *proskairoi*):

    a) *Obstacle*: Satan, whose opposition ensures that potential disciples will remain "by the way" (4:15; *para tēn hodon*), in contrast to "on the way."

Example: the crowd that only listens but does not follow, and more specifically the social leaders, whose opposition is attributed to the reign of Satan. Jesus will struggle against Satan's attempt to subvert Peter in 8:32f. Bartimaeus will be presented as the archetype of those who meet Jesus blind "by the way" (10:46), are given "sight," and respond by following Jesus "on the way" (10:52; *en tē hodō*).

b) *Obstacle*: tribulation and persecution (*diōgmou*, lit., "the chase"), which cause disciples to defect (4:17).

Example: the disciples for whom suffering is a stumbling block. The fruits of the messianic community come only with persecutions (10:30), and they must stand firm through the great tribulation (13:19,24; *thlipseōs*). "Falling away" (*skandalizontai*) is a technical term for the inability to accept or sustain discipleship practice (see 9:42–47, 14:27,29).

"But it is different" (4:18 *kai alloi eisin*) with the next two. In contrast to the first two "types," these genuinely "hear the word." Only one, however, bears "fruit."

c) *Obstacle*: the "worries of this age, the lure of wealth, and all other passions" (4:19). This resembles the general exhortations in early Christian ethical tradition, but Mark underlines the specific corruption of affluence (*tou ploutou*).

Example: the one "discipleship rejection" story in Mark—the rich man who turns away from Jesus' call (10:17–22). The piety of the rich is suspect (12:41), and their prospects for the kingdom dim (10:25).

Only the last example speaks of those who "welcome" (*paradechontai*) the word (later the disciples are instructed to welcome the kingdom "as a child," 10:15). This "good soil" yields a phenomenal return (4:20).

It has been pointed out that the positive conclusion is almost an afterthought; the emphasis in the parable is clearly upon the barriers to discipleship. Belo is right in arguing that this parable suggests a kind of hermeneutical key to why so many reject the narrative of Jesus' practice: "people read the gospel in accordance with the space they occupy" in the dominant social order, and respond accordingly (1981:123). If we "listen but do not hear" it is not because of the obscurity of the word, but because of our loyalty to the prevailing ideology.

The "mystery" and private explanation are, as noted, literary fictions, for Mark is making it "public" in his narrative. But to ensure that this is clearly understood, he appends the lamp image (4:21f.). Coming after the sower parable, this pronouncement is meant to balance and clarify the interpretation that follows the sower parable (4:10–12).

Mark was aware that the term "mystery" was loaded with esoteric implications in his Hellenistic world, and so wishes to assert that in using this term he most emphatically does *not* mean that the parables enshrine arcane knowledge.[1] They should not be misconstrued as a "lamp" being concealed (4:21), but as teaching meant to illuminate and reveal. This is articulated in the repetitive wordplay of 4:22:

> nothing is hidden (*krupton*)
>   except to be made apparent (*phanerōthē*);
> nor is it "secreted" (*apokruphon*)
>   but to be made apparent (*elthē eis phaneron*).

It is precisely because this discourse *unveils* the true loyalties of the hearer that it is polarizing, as we will see in the case of the vineyard parable of 11:1–12. And with one last thematic refrain, the first half of the sermon draws to a close (4:23).

ii. The Eschatological Harvest: An Ideology of the Land

The power of Markan "realistic narrative" is perhaps nowhere more evident than in these folktales of rural Palestine. As do the other two seed parables in this sermon, the sower story illustrates vividly the struggle to make a living by dry farming the rocky soil of Galilee. Jeremias's well-known excursus bears reproducing here:

> In Palestine sowing precedes ploughing. Hence, in the parable the sower is depicted striding over the unploughed stubble. . . . He sows intentionally on the path which the villagers have trodden over the stubble, since he intends to plough the seed in when he ploughs up the path. He sows intentionally among the thorns standing withered in the fallow because they, too, will be ploughed up. Nor need it surprise us that some grains should fall upon rocky ground; the underlying limestone, thinly covered with soil, barely shows above the surface until the ploughshare jars against it [1972:11f.].

The parable's focus upon the majority of the seed, which went fruitless, would be bitterly familiar to the peasant, for whom the grain seed represented his only "cash flow"—with it he fed his family, paid the rent and tithes, and sowed the next year's crop. The fact that above all it is the greed of affluence that chokes the seed also held special significance for the tenant farmer, for it reflected the latifundial reality. Wealthy landlords always extracted enough of the harvest to ensure that the farmer remained indentured to the land, strangling any prospects he might have to achieve even a modicum of economic security.

Against this background the promise of an astounding harvest (to the sower, not the landowner) is poignant indeed:

> On the one hand we have a description of the manifold frustrations to which the sower's labor is liable. . . . Jesus could have gone on to depict weeds, drought, scorching wind (sirocco), locust, and other enemies of the seed among which the Gospel of Thomas even mentions the worm. A hopeless prospect! But now a miracle happens. From the dreary fallow

land grows a field of waving corn, with a yield that surpasses all prayer and understanding. . . . The abnormal tripling, presented in true oriental fashion, of the harvest's yield (thirty, sixty, a hundredfold) symbolizes the eschatological overflowing of the divine fullness, surpassing all human measure [Jeremias, 1972:150].

Belo calls this "metonymy": "in a social formation in which agriculture is the dominant production, blessing takes the form, first of all, of superabundant fruits and the satiety these bring" (1981:124f.). A similar vision is reflected in other apocalyptic texts:

And then the whole earth will be tilled in righteousness, and shall all be planted with trees and be full of blessing. . . . And they shall plant vines on it: and these vines shall yield in abundance, and as for all the seed which is sown, each measure shall bear a thousand, and each measure of olives shall yield ten presses of oil. Cleanse the earth from all oppression and injustice and sin. . . . In those days I will open the heavenly store chambers of blessing in order to shower them upon the earth over the work and labour of humanity [1 Enoch 10:18ff.].

This "agrarian eschatology" is, however, not simply wishful dreaming; it has a specifically subversive function.

Jeremias points out that the Palestinian farmer might typically expect a yield of around 7:1, with a tenfold yield considered a bumper crop. The parable's harvest thus symbolically represents a dramatic shattering of the vassal relationship between peasant and landlord. With such surplus, the farmer could not only eat and pay his rent, tithes, and debts, but indeed even purchase the land, and thus end his servitude forever. "The kingdom is like *this*," says Jesus: it envisions the abolition of the oppressive relationships of production that determined the horizons of the Palestinian farmer's social world. Such images strongly suggest that Mark is articulating an ideology of the land, and the revolutionary hopes of those who work it. All this is of course lost upon modern urban theological commentators, preoccupied as they are with romanticizing the "earthly stories" of rural Palestine on the one hand, and probing for "heavenly meanings" on the other.

5C. THE MYSTERY OF ENDS AND MEANS, I² (4:24–34)

i. Cynical Realism or Seeds of Hope?

After punctuating the first part of the sermon with exhortations to "Listen," Mark suddenly changes directions, beginning the second part by issuing a sharp warning: "Beware what you hear!" (4:24a). He then offers a proverb about measuring, with a corollary about giving and getting (4:24b). This pronouncement is structured similarly to the previous proverb concerning the absurdity of putting a lamp under a "peckmeasure" (4:21f., *ton modion*, a Latin dry measure of about two gallons). Mark's placement of two measuring themes back to back reflects the familiar catechetical device of "verbal chaining" (below, 9,A,i).

Verses 24f. are, by any criterion, difficult maxims, and it would be more convenient to slide past them with superficial comment, as do most interpreters. But they are here for a reason we must discover, and this means making a commitment to one of two possible meanings. Is the reference back to the apocalyptic dualism of the "mystery," according to which those who are "given" special insight (4:11a, *dedotai*) will be given more (4:25, *dothēsetai*), whereas those to whom parables are obscure will lose everything? This is the most common interpretation (indeed was so construed by Matthew, who inserts this saying in front of the Isaian dictum, Mt 13:12). In this case its "have/have not" (*echei*) motif would refer to the "having ears to hear" of the refrain in the first half (4:9,23). But such a reading is not without problems. If the purpose of the previous lamp saying was to correct possible misconstrual of "mystery," why would Mark double back here, intensifying the dualism to the point of implying that the distribution of insight will be exceedingly unequal and unfair?

There is another, in my opinion more compelling, possibility better in keeping with the ideology of the sermon as a whole. Jeremias calls 4:25 a pessimistic proverb, paraphrasing it: "That's what life is like, unjust" (1972:62). But what if both are popular adages that Mark is citing in order to repudiate? Two factors favor this view. First, the caution in 4:24a (*blepete*) is always used in Mark to warn the disciple/reader against the rival ideologies of their opponents. In 8:15 it is the "yeast" (another parable?) of the Pharisees and Herod, in 12:38 the pious mask of scribal profiteering, and in the second sermon it is a refrain denouncing the propaganda of the militant nationalists (13:5,9,23,33). Why should 4:24a be the only exception? Moreover, if Ezekiel 17 is in the background of this sermon, as I have suggested, then we have another parallel. For Ezekiel follows his parable discourse by also quoting—and then denouncing—a popular platitude that counsels resignation to injustice (Ez 18:1ff.).

The first saying is a play on words: "With the measure you measure, you will be measured." Keeping in mind the economic semantics of the sower parable and the previous mention of the *modion* (with which grain was measured), this proverb would appear to refer to what modern capitalist ideology calls the "determinism of the marketplace." In other words, the only way to survive in the system is to play the game by the rules. This is then followed by an insistence that the system will never change: the "haves" will get richer and the "have-nots" will get poorer.

Such images have everything to do with the struggle of the peasant to produce enough "measure" to survive; indeed the verb *didonai* is also used to describe the material yield of the seed in the parable (4:7f.). This "conventional wisdom" urges abdication to present arrangements of power, however unjust they may seem. "Socio-economic stratification is divinely sanctioned; it is futile to protest." It is precisely *against* such misanthropic "realism" that Jesus strenuously warns. As if saying, "Instead, listen again to the miracle of the seed and the harvest," Jesus turns to the last two parables of the sermon.

ii. Despite Appearances, the Kingdom Will Prevail

Against the cynicism of the economic "determinism" of the system, Jesus pits the revolutionary patience and hope of the kingdom (4:26). It can be compared to "a man scattering seed on the ground," by which Mark directs our attention back to the sower story and its promise of an eschatological harvest to eradicate the very inequalities legitimated by "realists." But the obvious and urgent response of the peasant to that promise is "How?" and "When?" (questions that eventually find articulation at the outset of the second sermon, 13:4). In response, Jesus modifies the sowing parable, concentrating this time upon the inscrutable process by which the seed matures to the harvest (4:29).

In an accurate reflection of the worldview of first-century dry-soil (nonirrigated) agriculture, Mark says that once the seed is in the ground, growth takes place "of itself" (4:28 *automatē*). He again uses the term "bears fruit" (*karpophorei*) with which he described the miraculous yield in 4:20. *How* this happens, however, the farmer "does not know" (4:27; *hōs ouk oiden autos*); it comes about quite apart from his efforts at cultivation. But when the fruit is ready for reaping, he acts, for it is harvesttime (4:29). The parable is politicized by Mark's citation of Joel 3:13: "Put in the sickle, for the harvest is ripe." This text invokes the prophetic-apocalyptic holy-war tradition (below, 11,E,ii); the "day of the Lord" (Jl 3:14) will see Yahweh challenging the nations to a final military contest (Jl 3:9–12; cf. Rv 14:14ff.).

By citing this tradition is Mark approving of Joel's taunt (parodying Isaiah) to "beat your plowshares into swords" (Jl 3:10)? Is the answer to the peasant's predicament the taking up of arms to establish "revolutionary justice" by force? We must answer no, for this would cut against the clear implication of the parable, which is that the growth of the kingdom will be neither obvious nor controllable. The vocation of the disciple/reader lies not in trying to provoke the harvest (for that happens "of itself"), but in tending to the "sowing." The point of the harvest image is to assure the listener that Yahweh's judgment upon the powers and their system will indeed come, and so give the lie to the counterassertion of "realists" that nothing will ever change. Nevertheless, this parable introduces the idea of "the moment," and it will be the task of the second sermon to reflect at more depth upon the relationship between "knowing the time" of the "harvest" (13:28–33) and taking "appropriate action" (Pauver, 1987).

In the famous parable of the mustard seed Mark one last time expands upon the theme of sowing in the earth (4:30–32). There can be no question that this similitude concerning the disproportion between the seed and the mature plant is meant to instill courage and hope in the small and fragile discipleship community for its struggle against the entrenched powers. As in 4:29, the appended scriptural citation places the parable firmly within a political context. Mark adopts the conclusion of Ezekiel's cypress tree parable for his own: the "small sprig" planted by Yahweh will bear fruit, and its branches will give shelter to birds (Ez 17:22f.). In late biblical literature the sheltering branch was a common metaphor for political hegemony. Daniel explains the image to Nebuchadnezzar:

> The tree you saw, which grew and became strong . . . in whose branches the birds of the air dwelt—it is you, O king . . . our greatness has grown and reaches to heaven, and your dominion to the ends of the earth [Dn 4:20,22].

The tree image is a two-edged sword, however, for it can be used to criticize imperial hubris, as in Ezekiel 31. This oracle, directed to the pharaoh's Egypt, is also intertextually present in the mustard seed parable:

> Whom do you compare to (LXX, *tini hōmoiōsas*) in
>   your greatness? [Ez 31:2].
> How shall we compare (*Pōs homoiōsōmen*) the kingdom of
>   God? [Mk 4:30].

Ezekiel's description of Egypt expands upon the tree/forest image as a metaphor for the geopolitics of empire:

> It sent forth its streams to all the trees of the forest. So it towered high above all the trees of the forest; its boughs grew large and its branches long. . . . All the birds of the air made their nests in its boughs [Ez 31:4c–6a].

But this flowery prose is satirical, for the purpose of emphasizing Egypt's demise. In a startling reversal of the image, Yahweh causes the imperial tree to be "cut down," and "upon its ruin will dwell all the birds of the air" (31:2f.).

In so invoking Ezekiel's caustic reflections Mark surely had the Roman empire in mind. Israel was merely one of the nations "dwelling under its shadow" (Ez 31:6c), one small client-state being fed by the streams sent forth from Caesar. What, then, of the minuscule remnant-seed within Israel, the little band of commoners whom Jesus had boldly set up as a kingdom confederacy? The idea of this smallest of sprigs surviving in the forest, much less overthrowing the mighty Rome, was absurd. Yet the concluding mustard seed image proposes exactly such a mismatch! Such was Mark's firm apocalyptic conviction that Yahweh would "bring low the high tree and make high the low tree" (Ez 17:24).

Mark draws the first sermon to a close by reiterating that Jesus spoke the "word" only in parables as the crowd "was able to hear," with the disciples receiving special tutelage (4:33f.). The "mystery" of which it speaks pertains to how the revolution of the kingdom will penetrate history-as-usual. The sermon counsels both patience and hope. *Patience,* so that the apocalyptic militance of Jesus' "declaration of war" in 3:37 is not misconstrued. Mark sobers any illusion that change will be quick and triumphal. It is rather a matter of finding the right soil and trusting that the seed will grow, maintaining faith that the small seed will be "raised up" (4:32 *anabainei*) and the mighty brought down. *Hope,* because, according to the story so far, the results of Jesus' kingdom practice have hardly been encouraging: he has been abandoned by his family, driven out of the cities, and is hunted by the authorities. Mark thus wants to reassure the reader/disciple that the seed is being sown, and the harvest will surely come.

In this sermon Mark has for the first time articulated the least/greatest paradox, which will accompany Jesus' second call to discipleship (8:34ff.). The "way of the sower" will subsequently be revealed as the way of nonviolence: servanthood become leadership, suffering become triumph, death become life. The lesson of the "unknowing farmer" is that the means of the kingdom must never be compromised by attempting to manipulate the ends.

In 4:35 Mark reports that Jesus invites his disciples to accompany him to cross "to the other side" of the Sea of Galilee. Mark then "deconstructs" the sermon scene (4:1): the disciples take Jesus away from the crowd in the boat in which he had been sitting (4:36). Mark is making a major narrative transition, for this boat trip represents—both literally and in terms of Mark's overall literary strategy—a new departure. The story now moves in a new direction, as it will again at 8:22, 11:1, 14:1, and 16:1.

5D. WORLD SUBVERSION: MARK'S SOCIO-LITERARY STRATEGY THROUGH 4:36

i. Discourse

In introducing the structure of the first major narrative section of the Gospel (above, 4,A,i), I noted its concentric composition. At the center lies the main campaign narrative (1:40–3:6), which, through a series of specific episodes, articulates the character of Jesus' messianic ministry. This campaign precludes any distinction between Jesus' mission to heal the sick and his mission to confront the powers, for the one always leads to the other. The main aim of this discourse is to subvert the social construction of reality by the dominant order, its legitimating ideologies and practices.

Jesus' direct action and teaching are set firmly within the context of Mark's controlling apocalyptic fiction: the struggle between Jesus and the powers, as introduced in the initial summary statement of 1:12f. At each end of the campaign the exorcist confronts the scribal authorities (1:20ff.; 3:21ff.). This struggle is then reiterated at two crucial points during the campaign where Mark appeals to the Danielic Human One:

1. he has authority on earth to forgive sins (2:10);
2. he is lord even over the Sabbath (2:28).

Mark has incarnated the combat myth in the concrete political geography of

Palestine, specifically referring to the redemptive mechanism of the debt system. Having established the subversive character of the Human One "on earth," Mark will leave this persona for the time being, to return to him in 8:31ff.

The discourse of healing and exorcism is central to this section. G. Theissen, in his study of the social function of primitive Christian miracle stories, points out that most contemporaneous Hellenistic miracle sources originated from the aristocracy, and through the highly institutionalized practice of divination and technique-magic were "concerned with the maintenance of the accepted order and way of life." Other pagan traditions of "sorcery and magic represent an individualistic reaction to growing social disintegration" (1983:264). In contrast, the gospel miracles assert the promise and possibility of radical socio-political change in behalf of the disenfranchised. They function to subvert, not legitimate, the dominant order.

The enthusiasm generated by the campaign is tempered by the shift to the reflective mood of the first sermon. In what sense is the parables discourse a "mystery" (4:11), and how is it that it provides the key to all parables and the story as a whole (4:13)? In 4:12f. "listening" is equated with "understanding" and "knowing." These are key concepts in the rest of the story. Mark uses several Greek terms more or less interchangeably. The following list shows the narrative interrelationship between this "perception" vocabulary and the parables:

sunienai

4:12: that they may listen and not *understand* . . .

6:52: they had not *understood* about the loaves . . .

7:14: Listen to me all of you and *understand* . . .

7:18: Do even you not *understand*? (*asunetos*)

8:17,21: Do you not yet perceive or *understand*?

noein

7:18: Do you not *perceive* that . . . ?

8:17: Do you not yet *perceive* or understand?

13:14: Let the one reading *perceive* . . .

ginōskein

4:13: If you do not know this parable, how will you *discern*
     all the other parables?

13:28f.: you *discern* summer is near . . . discern he is near . . .

eidenai

4:13: If you do not *know* this parable, how will you
     discern all the other parables?

4:27: the seed grows, though he does not *know* how . . .

13:32, 33, 35: About that day or hour no one *knows* . . . you do
     not *know* the time . . . you do not *know* when he comes. . . .

From this we can see that the parables are only part of the wider symbolic discourse of the Gospel, as is the metaphorical action of the next section. These "mysterious" symbolics have nothing at all to do with hidden teaching, but rather the paradox of smallness/greatness and power/powerlessness.

This paradox is first articulated through the seed parables. They explain to us the anticlimax of the prologue, in which the dramatic proclamation of the kingdom's imminence was followed not by cosmic upheaval but by the calling of some fishermen (1:15–20). The kingdom is *like that:* planting seeds of the new order in the midst of the old, in common persons called to the messianic vocation. The patience of the farmer (4:26f.) warns that the powers cannot be overthrown by seizing power. Indeed, the "Listen!" of the first sermon anticipates the "Listen to him!" of the heavenly voice, which confirms Jesus' call to the cross in the second apocalyptic moment (9:7). But let there be no mistake: the sermon's counsel to patience in no way mitigates the nonviolent militance of the first campaign. After all, the next narrative cycle is again launched with the Gerasene exorcism, a highly political symbolic confrontation with Roman imperialism.

It is true that Mark adopts a certain "insider/outsider" dualism in this sermon, and if unqualified it would present a serious contradiction in his ideology. How indeed is Jesus' practice of radical social inclusivism consistent with his exclusivist definition (3:13–19,35) of and private teaching to the discipleship community? First we must recognize that in any opposition movement the lines of social conflict are not eradicated but "redrawn." For example, the North American ruling classes insist that the essential struggle today in Central America or southern Africa is between the "free world" and the spectre of communist tyranny. Peace and justice forces do not deny that there is a conflict, but contend that it must be understood not in terms of East-West but North-South—that is, as the conflict between rich and poor.

Similarly, Jesus repudiates the social boundaries as dictated by the purity and debt codes, communing with the outcast, and rejects the self-serving Manichaeism of the scribes who accuse him of collaborating with Beelzebub. But as soon as he creates a countercommunity from among the common folk (1:16ff.), one with an alternative practice that will directly compete for the leadership of Israel (3:13ff.), new lines are drawn. Jesus understands that the crucible of political hostility and persecution facing his movement will demand a disciplined "vanguard," and it is these whom he seeks to instruct in the "mystery of the kingdom" (4:11). Still, Mark has no sooner acknowledged these new "lines" than he begins to diffuse them. Jesus disavows his teaching as secret gnosis (4:22f.), and throughout the next section of narrative the new dualism will begin to break down. By the end of the first half of the Gospel, "insiders" have become "outsiders" because of their lack of understanding (8:18f.)!

ii. Signification

The fact that the majority of sites in Mark's narrative world correspond to the main social spheres of Palestinian Judaism (land and table, house and village, synagogue) indicates his concern to apply the kingdom to the whole of public life. I have already discussed the social signification of these sites, as well as Mark's narrative alienation from Hellenistic urban culture and synagogue Judaism (above, 4,B,iv). The radical social practice of Mark's community had no doubt estranged it from the authority structures of both the extended family system and the synagogue. The narrative stresses therefore that the messianic community represents both an alternative kinship/family model (3:35) and a new political identity, the "confederacy" (3:13f.).

Mark constructs his story around a dialectic of public engagement and private withdrawal, a distinction that persists even in the first sermon. Though Jesus is often forced into temporary hiding, Mark does not endorse a strategy of permanent underground residence, emerging only for hit-and-run guerilla actions (below, 7,A). Rather, his portrait of Jesus' itinerant circulation is one of action and reflection. This is significant in light of the social strategies of other movements in Mark's time, which tended toward the extremes of either monastic withdrawal (the Essenes) or covert terrorism (the sicarii).

We may note that the disciples are not mentioned in the majority of Jesus' actions against the dominant order. They do figure directly, however, in all three controversies with Pharisaic practice (2:15–29). Though a few scholars have speculated that Mark was describing the practice of an extremist table fellowship sect within mainstream Pharisaism (the *perushim*; see Wilde, 1974:196; below, 7,C), I have argued that the series protests the degree to which the Pharisees exercised control over the Galilean economy. In any case the particular vitality of this conflict (reflected again in 7:1ff.) gives us a sense of the intense rivalry between Mark's community and the Pharisees, whose "holiness" program directly competed with Markan practice. Mark is realistic about how difficult it will be to promote solidarity and social equality with the dispossessed classes. He understands that the true barriers to justice are the legitimating ideologies, and these Jesus sets about undermining.

Having completed a reading of the first main cycle of Mark's narrative of Jesus, we may note the remarkable affinity between his portrait of the messianic socio-political strategy and Gandhi's satyagraha. Gandhi also repudiated the caste system, which segregated India's "untouchables" (*harijan*). He founded a disciplined community (*ashram*), which shared life with the poor. And he nonviolently assaulted the economic and political structures that undergirded an imperial system of privilege and exploitation. Because of his firm alignment with the poor and their interests, Gandhi too became a target, not only of the British but also the Indian aristocratic classes.

Mark's narrative, like satyagraha, legitimizes militant, direct action, yet at the same time severs any absolute relationship between such action and historical efficacy. It is up to the disciple/reader to sow the seed of the kingdom through nonviolent witness—but it is up to God to bring that seed to fruition. And by refusing to personify the enemy in the human face of the opposition, Mark affirms another cardinal characteristic of nonviolence, what Martin King called the "beloved community." The struggle for justice must always find a way to include its opponents in its vision of the future; just as no disciple is infallible, no adversary is "disposable."

With this in mind, the disciple/reader now joins Jesus on a new journey "to the other side" (4:35). This crossing will prove to be difficult, indeed one that almost takes our lives (4:38). And Jesus' calming of the storm is no mere nature-miracle; rather, it pivots the narrative into the beginning of a new campaign of symbolic action that will more deeply reveal the messianic way.

NOTES

1. Christian suspicion of this term is indicated by the fact that it appears only here (and par) in the synoptic tradition, and only elsewhere, outside the Pauline writings, in Revelation. Apropos, Paul calls the "hardening of Israel's heart" a mystery (Rom 11:25); a similar use of "revealed mystery" is used by the author of Ephesians (1:9; 3:3f.,9).

2. II = 11E

CHAPTER SIX

Jesus' Construction of a New Social Order, I: The Miracle Cycle (Mark 4:36–8:9)

Elisha said, "Give to the men, that they may eat." But his servant said, "How am I to set this before a hundred men?" So he repeated, "Give them to the men, that they may eat, for thus says the Lord, 'They shall eat and have some left.' "

—2 Kings 4:42c–43

In the second major narrative section of the Gospel, Mark's socio-literary strategy shifts from the symbolics of repudiation to the symbolics of reconstruction. Jesus' healing, feeding, and journeying articulate the forging of a new order in the very midst of the old one with which he broke in the Capernaum campaign. The disciple/reader has witnessed the Jesus who confronts the powers in militant nonviolence, and has been instructed about revolutionary patience by a withdrawn and reflective Jesus. Now we will receive one object lesson after another regarding the alternative kingdom practice of inclusivity and compassion from a Jesus who silences the storms and walks on water—that is, who breaks through the social and economic barriers to the realization of human solidarity. This progression in narrative discourse is precisely what we would expect if Mark is representing a dissenting socio-political movement.

The socio-literary function of the first section of Mark's Gospel was to tear down the "sacred canopy" that legitimizes what Mark perceived as oppressive social institutions. But he knew that the war of myths must at some point also offer a new and compelling symbolic world to warrant an alternative social practice if it hopes to attract and maintain converts. Thus in Mark's discourse in the second major section of the Gospel we witness what Amos Wilder called "the theater of world-palingenesis . . . the massive reality of cosmic transformation evoked by Jesus" (1982).

6A. THE NARRATIVE CHARACTER OF THE DOUBLE MIRACLE STORY CYCLE

i. Structure

This is the first of two "construction" sequences in the story, which together provide a balance to the two direct-action campaigns. The second, what I refer to as Mark's "discipleship catechism" (8:27–10:45), articulates a discourse of construction through the primary narrative vehicle of a triple cycle of teaching (below, 8, A; 9). Our present section, in contrast, employs a double cycle of miraculous symbolic action for the same purpose. Commentators have long puzzled over the so-called double miracle cycle in Mark 4:35–8:21. Outstanding are several parallel doublets: an exorcism that has close affinity to the first of Jesus' exorcisms (5:1ff.), two sea-rescue stories (4:36–41; 6:47–52), and two wilderness feedings (6:33–44; 8:1–10). Why would Mark, an author otherwise relatively spare in style, suddenly become repetitive here?

Some form critics argued that the repetition must have originated in Mark's sources (Achtemeier, 1978), only to have redaction criticism demonstrate that the parallel structure must be attributed to the hand of Mark (Fowler, 1981:30ff.). Recent literary approaches have asserted that Mark's discourse of repetition (or recapitulation; see above, 3,B,ii) serves a quite sophisticated narrative function:

> [It] represents a playful poetic and semantic interference of the more normal diachronic communication of content. Parallelism interrupts the merely sequential flow of content through a systematic repetition that requires readers and hearers to move forth and back through the text rather than simply straight through it. Once a parallel is discerned it becomes necessary to pause, however momentarily, and synthesize the relations between the parallels before moving forward through the text [N. Petersen, 1980a:204].

In other words, the form of the story, by its sustained reference to itself, challenges us to probe ever deeper into the symbolics of the narrative. That this is precisely what Mark intends is confirmed by the "review" in his "first epilogue," when he quizzes the disciple/reader directly (8:14ff.; see below, 7, C, iii).

Peterson's study of this section concludes that "a combination of topographical content and repeated content is an unambiguous key to the formal structure" (1980:193). This is also the view of Kelber, who goes still further in positing two distinct cycles of ministry around which the whole first half of the Gospel is narratively organized (1979:30ff.). He offers a scheme in which the two "sides" of the Sea of Galilee symbolize Jewish and gentile territory, and the two major boat journeys represent the crossing from one side to the other.

Kelber justifies this by pointing to Mark's apparently technical use of these phrases:

1. "to the other side" (*eis to peran*, 4:35; 5:1, 21; 6:45; 8:13);
2. "to embark" (*embainein*, 4:1; 5:18; 6:45; 8:10, 13);
3. "to cross over" (*diaperan*, 5:21; 6:53).

Thus the boat crossings are:

first voyage "to the other side"	→	4:35–5:1 (storm)
return	←	5:21 (no storm)
second voyage "to the other side"	→	6:45–53 (storm)
return	←	8:13, 22 (no storm)

Kelber's double-cycle scheme may be represented as follows:

Events	*Jewish side*	*Gentile side*
inaugural exorcism, fame	1:21–28	5:1–20
popular ministry	1:29–39	6:54–56
symbolic healings	5:22–43	7:24–37
wilderness feedings	6:32–44	8:1–10
noncomprehension of loaves	6:51f.	8:14–21

It is the parallels between the Capernaum and Gerasene exorcisms that first alert us to this wider scheme (below, 6,B). For Kelber, the two parallel sea-rescue stories and respective returns represent the crossing between "Jewish" and "gentile" sides of the sea (below, 6,C). Each cycle then consists of a pair of healing episodes (below, 6,D) and nearly identical conclusions: the feedings of the multitudes, followed by boat trips in which the disciples fail to understand the meaning of "bread" (below, 6,E).

Kelber's scheme has been disputed by Fowler, who otherwise affirms Mark's discourse of parallelism. Fowler argues that the alleged "crossings" (from the western "Jewish" side to the eastern "gentile" side of the sea) do not correspond with the actual geographical coordinates cited by Mark, and rightly points out that historically there was no such neat ethnic division between the sides of the sea. He concludes that Mark in more than one instance is simply geographically confused (1981:61ff.). E. Malbon, in an article that provides a helpful overview of this particular debate, agrees with Fowler's geographical objections, yet affirms Kelber's basic thesis about the symbolic connotations of the Jewish and gentile "sides" of the shore (1984:363ff.).[2]

But if Kelber's reliance upon rhetorical indicators has problems, so does Malbon's dependence upon literal, geographical ones. Throughout the Gospel Mark is far more interested in articulating geo-social "space" in terms of narrative symbolics than actual place-names. Indeed, it is not impossible that Mark may have intentionally dissociated the coordinate "other side" from a literal correspondence with eastern and western shores of the sea; straining the geographical credulity of the sea narrative would have forced his first readers to focus upon the journeys as *symbolic action* (which is their purpose) rather than upon details of marine transit around the Sea of Galilee (which is not). For this reason Kelber's symbolic-rhetorical reading remains the strongest; for however they are "mapped," the sea crossings function as a fiction dramatizing the struggle to "bridge" the deeply alienated worlds of Jew and gentile.

ii. Story

I divide my commentary on this section into two chapters. This chapter will concentrate upon the undisputed double cycle, generally following Kelber's scheme. In recognition of the author's parallelism, I will switch provisionally to reading episodes in their structural and thematic relationship to one another rather than chronologically. This will better aid the quest for the symbolics of the narrative, about which Mark will interrogate the disciple/reader at the close of this section.

In the next chapter, I will turn to the three main elements that lie outside the parallelism. The first element is the second "generative seam" (6:1-13, 30-32), which is represented as a land journey away from the narrative center of the sea (below, 7,A). The second is the flashback account of the execution of John the Baptist by Herod (6:14-29). This "interlude" is widely recognized as parenthetical, in which Mark interrupts his own story for purposes of keeping the political implications of the ministry of the kingdom in the foreground (see below, 7,B). The third element is the one direct conflict episode in this section, in which Jesus defends his community's practice of social inclusivity against the criticism of the Pharisees (6:53-7:20). This controversy is fundamental to the new social model being articulated in Jesus' symbolic action, for it addresses the main ideological barrier to the construction of an ecumenical community— purity/dietary regulations surrounding table fellowship (below, 7,C). I will then look at Mark's "interpretive epilogue" with which he closes the first half of the Gospel (8:10-21; below, 7,D).

As already indicated by the Kelber/Malbon debate, most of the narrative settings in this section are indeterminate; there is no overall coherent itinerary for Jesus' journeying, nor should one be sought. The primary narrative site is the boat upon the sea, and the section ends when this site is abandoned:

With the completion in 8:22 of a sea crossing begun in 8:13, both the boat and the sea cease to play a role in the narrative. Neither "motif" appears again in 8:27-16:8. Consequently, 4:1-8:26 is clearly distinguished from the preceding and following narratives by the roles the sea and the boat play in it [N. Petersen, 1980:194].

Despite the geographical ambiguities in the section, the verisimilitude of the sea journeys maintains the character of Mark's realistic narrative. Any Galilean could relate to the danger of being caught in a sudden, fierce storm upon the sea. Even so, the sea, like the boat, has fundamentally symbolic connotations. Malbon (1984:364) points out that Mark is the first writer to refer to the inland, freshwater lake (*limne*) as a "sea" (*thalassa*), in order to invoke images from the Hebrew scriptures, as we shall see.

There is one major plot development in the course of this section: the growing tension between Jesus and his disciples. The disciples figure in almost every episode in this section, with the exception of the three gentile healings/exorcisms. Tension is introduced when the disciples wonder out loud who Jesus might be, in the first boat story (4:41), and culminates in Jesus' exasperation in the last boat story (8:14ff.). Mark builds this drama around the theme of "blindness/deafness" introduced by Isaiah's dark warning in the first sermon (4:12): there is something crucial about the symbolics of Jesus that his disciples fail to understand. In closing the first half of his Gospel by posing an unanswered question to the disciples, Mark is of course actually addressing the reader. He is cautioning us not to proceed with the story until we have fully grasped the meaning of Jesus' actions.

Judging by the notoriously superficial treatment given this section of the Gospel by most Markan commentators, the author's warning has gone generally unheeded. Here perhaps more than in any other part of the Gospel a correct understanding depends upon a socio-literary reading, as Markan symbolics achieve a singular profundity and depth.

6B. THE SECOND INAUGURAL EXORCISM (5:1–21)

i. The Gerasene Demoniac

In 4:35ff. the disciples complete their first boat journey to "the other side" (I will examine this voyage in 6,C,i). Immediately upon his arrival on "the other side" Jesus is confronted by a demon. This confrontation contains more detail and embellishment than any other single episode in the Gospel prior to the trial narrative. In it Jesus inaugurates another round of powerful symbolic action in his ministry of liberation.

There are problems (which have resulted in textual variants) with Mark's identification of the setting as "the region of the Gerasenes" (see Taylor, 1963:278f.). The city of Gerasa was some thirty miles southeast of the seaside locale implied in the story. It may be that Mark's point was simply to establish "the other side of the sea" as gentile socio-symbolic space. Thus he identified the country around Gerasa broadly as the Decapolis (5:20), a Hellenistic region given a generic name (the "ten towns"): the loose confederation of territories that represented the eastern frontier of the Roman empire, beyond which lay the Arabian steppes. But there may be a more specifically ideological reason for Mark's identification of this episode with Gerasa, as I will point out below.

The elements of the setting contribute to its unmistakably gentile character. The demoniac's dwelling among the tombs and the presence and role of the pigs symbolize impurity according to the Jewish cultural code (tombs and swine are in fact connected in Is 65:4f.). It is perhaps relevant that Herod Antipas had built a major Hellenistic city that became his capital, Tiberias, on the shores of the sea not far from where Mark places this story. The king had to coerce Jews to populate the city, because it was considered unclean: it had been constructed on the site of a graveyard (G. A. Smith, 1931:289ff.). Even the demon's salutation to Jesus has a gentile flavor. In contrast to 1:24, Jesus is named "son of the Most High God" (5:7), a Hellenistic title we find elsewhere in the New Testament only in Hebrews 7:1 and Luke's writings (nine times—e.g., Acts 16:17).

In this, the most dramatic exorcism in the Gospel, Jesus puts an end to the efforts by the demons (a.k.a. the powers) to "name" him, by turning the tables. In 5:9 Jesus wrests from this powerful demonic horde its name: Legion. A Latinism, this term had only one meaning in Mark's social world: a division of Roman soldiers. Alerted by this clue, we discover that the rest of the story is filled with *military* imagery. The term used for "herd" (*agelē*, 5:11)— inappropriate for pigs, who do not travel in herds—often was used to refer to a band of military recruits (Derrett, 1979:5). Derrett also points out that the phrase "he dismissed them" (*epetrepsen*) connotes a military command, and the pigs' charge (*ōrmēsen*) into the lake suggests troops rushing into battle (5:13).

Enemy soldiers being swallowed by hostile waters of course brings to mind the narrative of Israel's liberation from Egypt (Ex 14), as Moses' victory hymn sings: "Pharaoh's chariots and his army Yahweh cast into the sea; his elite officers are sunk in the Red Sea" (Ex 15:4).

Perhaps Josephus' account (*Ant*, XIV,xv,10) of the seditious Galileans who drowned Herodian nobles in the lake during one of the many uprisings is relevant here. But *surely* germane is his account of Roman retaliation during Vespasian's reconquest of northern Palestine during the late years of the Jewish Revolt:

> Vespasian . . . sent Lucius Annius to Gerasa with a cavalry and a considerable number of foot soldiers. After taking the town by assault, he killed a thousand of the young men who had not escaped, took their families captive, and allowed his soldiers to plunder the property. Finally, he set fire to the houses and marched against the surrounding villages. Those who were able-bodied fled, the weak perished, and all that was left went up in flames. So did the war spread throughout the mountain and plain country [*War*, IV,ix,1].

In light of this, Mark's choice of "the region of the Gerasenes" as a site of symbolic confrontation with the "legions" takes on new and specifically political meaning.

The conclusion is irresistible that we are here encountering imagery meant to call to mind the Roman military occupation of Palestine. Having been confronted by the Jewish ruling class in the scribally controlled synagogue, Jesus here meets the "other half" of the colonial condominium: the demon now represents Roman military power. In the symbolic act of exorcism, the legion "begged him (*parekalei auton*) earnestly not to send them out of the country" (5:10)! Nor is it surprising that there would be worried opposition to such an "expulsion" from the residents of the Decapolis, given the concrete experience of the Roman scorched-earth campaign of reconquest. Thus, in direct contrast to the legion's petition, the locals "begged him (*parekalein auton*) to leave their district" (5:17). And in yet a third contrast, the "liberated man" begs permission (*parekalei auton*) to join Jesus "in the boat" (5:18). But it is not quite time for the ecumenical community, and Jesus dispatches the man back to the Decapolis to tell the good news that liberation has come, to the amazement of all (5:19f.).

ii. Exorcism as Political Repudiation

Nowhere else in the Gospel does Jesus converse directly with a demonic opponent except in the two "inaugural exorcisms" of 1:21ff. and 5:1ff. Closer examination reveals that the synagogue and Gerasene stories share rare Greek idioms found nowhere else in the New Testament. The list on page 193 details structural and semantic similarities.

Mark clearly intended these stories to be affiliated. In both cases, upon entering new symbolic territory Jesus encounters immediate resistance in the form of a demoniacally possessed man. Through verbal confrontation and powerful exorcism he overcomes this challenge, provoking amazement and publicity. This enables Jesus to commence his widespread ministry of healing to the poor: first to the Jews around Capernaum (1:32), and subsequently, on his next crossing back to the other side of the sea (6:53–56), to gentiles as well.

Given this parallelism, it is appropriate to expand upon my earlier comments concerning exorcism as symbolic action (above, 4,B,i). P. Hollenbach has done interesting work on the Gerasene demoniac, drawing upon the studies of Frantz Fanon and others in the social psychology of mental illness in situations of political repression. He notes that demon possession in traditional societies is often a reflection of "class antagonisms rooted in economic exploitation" or "a socially acceptable form of oblique protest against, or escape from, oppression" (1981:573). He concludes that the Gerasene demoniac typifies the cathartic response of the subjugated:

> The tension between his hatred for his oppressors and the necessity to repress this hatred in order to avoid dire recrimination drove him mad. . . . He retreated to an inner world where he could symbolically resist Roman domination. . . . Jesus' disruption of the prevailing accommodation . . . brought the man's and the neighborhood's hatred of the Romans out into the open, where the result could be disaster for the community [ibid.].

Though insightful, Hollenbach's approach demonstrates the combined weakness of the biomedical and modern psychologizing perspectives, in which political symbolics are confined to the sphere of strictly private neuroses.

Criteria	*Synagogue exorcism*	*Gerasene demoniac*
episode defined by:		
entrance	into synagogue (1:21)	sea crossing (5:1)
exit	from synagogue (1:29)	return crossing (5:21)
symbolic setting:	synagogue on Sabbath (Jewish)	Decapolis (gentile); tombs, swine (unclean)
demoniac's description:	a man possessed by an unclean spirit	a man with an unclean spirit
symbolic/implied representation:	scribes	Roman "legions"
conflict:	authority	colonial occupation
demoniac's challenge:	shouted:	shouted at the top of his voice:
	What do you want with us, Jesus of Nazareth? . . . Holy One of God . . . Have you come to destroy us?	What do you want with me, Jesus, Son of the Most High God? . . . swear you will not torture me . . . (they begged him not to expel them from the country)
Jesus' command:	said sharply, "Be quiet! Come out of him!"	saying to him, "Come out of the man, unclean spirit!"
demons' capitulation:	the unclean spirit . . . with a loud cry went out of him	the unclean spirits came out
crowd reaction:	the people were so astonished	they were afraid

Although not denying that oppression can generate mental illness, a socio-literary interpretation reads the exorcism more broadly as *public* symbolic action. The demoniac represents collective anxiety over Roman imperialism. What Fanon called the "colonization of the mind," in which the community's anguish over its subjugation is repressed and then turned in on itself, is perhaps implied by Mark's report that the man inflicts violence on himself (5:5). The formidable grip by which the powers hold the community is vividly portrayed in the opening lines (5:3–5). Mark carefully uses phrases that he has already loaded with political significance: no one was able to bind (*deō*) the man, for he had broken his shackles many times; "there was no one strong (*oudeis ischuen*) enough to master him" (5:3f.). This exorcism is thus another key episode in Jesus-the-stronger-one's struggle to "bind the strong man." In the synagogue exorcism he was identified with the scribal class, now with Caesar's armies.

Theissen agrees that " 'oppression' by a foreign ruling people sometimes appears in a code as 'possession' by a foreign spirit":

> Miracle stories involving exorcism can be understood as symbolic action which break the demonic spell of all-pervading dependence. . . . The fact that the charismatic miracle-workers of the first century A.D. were invariably from the east which was firmly under Roman domination invites the hypothesis that belief in charismatic miracle-workers can be treated as a reaction of subjugated Hellenistic and eastern cultures: the politically inferior proclaims and propagates his superiority on the level of miraculous activity [1983:256].

Indeed, Mark has just finished promising that the "mustard seed" of the kingdom community would overcome the "towering tree" of Rome. Now he narrates, much more explicitly, this very "miracle."

Given the odds against political liberation from the might of Rome, the disciple/reader was bound to be incredulous. Mark thus reassures the audience in no uncertain terms that the healed man was none other than "the very man who had been oppressed by the legion" (5:15). Mark will issue a similar reassurance when he speaks again of a symbol of the overwhelming power of the dominant order being "cast into the sea" (11:23f.; below, 10,C,iv). In Mark's narrative strategy, the synagogue and Gerasene exorcisms represent Jesus' inaugural challenge to the powers. Put in military terminology, they signal the decisive breach in the defenses of the symbolic fortress of Roman Palestine. The political and ideological authority of both the scribal establishment and the Roman military garrison—the two central elements within the colonial condominium—have been repudiated. The narrative space has been cleared for the kingdom ministry to commence in full, both to Jew and to gentile.

6C. THE KINGDOM AS RACIAL RECONCILIATION:
TWO PERILOUS CROSSINGS (4:35–41; 6:45–53)

i. A Discourse of Sea Journeys

The multiple boat journeys are structural devices for the organization of the narrative *and* important symbolic actions in and of themselves. Although Mark narrates six boat trips altogether, only two are narrated at any length, and these, like the inaugural exorcisms, are internally similar. It will be clear from the following comparison of texts that rhetorical repetition—not geographical exactitude—links the two crossings (phrases are listed according to the chronology of the first story):

1st trip: from ? to "Gerasa" (4:35–5:1)	2nd trip (unsuccessful): from ? to Bethsaida (6:45–53)
He said to them, "Let us go across."	He made his disciples . . . go before him
And leaving the crowd	while he dismissed the crowd. . . .
they took him with them.	after he had taken leave of them,
Just as he was	he went into the hills to pray
in the boat . . .	. . . get into the boat . . .
a great storm of wind arose.	. . . for the wind was against them.
The boat was already filling.	They were distressed in rowing.
[disciples plea for help]	[disciples cry out in fear]
[Jesus rebukes the storm]	[Jesus joins them in the boat]
And the wind ceased.	And the wind ceased.
"Why are you afraid? Have you no faith?"	"Take heart, it is I; have no fear."
And they were filled with awe.	And they were utterly astounded
They came to the other side.	when they had crossed over.

Both trips are also associated with the coming of evening (*opsias genomenes*, 4:35; 6:47), a temporal coordinate often used by Mark to signal important sequences (1:32; 11:11,19; 14:17; 15:42). Their common destination, "the other side," represents passage to gentile territory: symbolic transit to a symbolic locale, a journey to the unknown, the foreign, the "other side" of humanity.

Of the four remaining brief boat trips, two (5:21 and 8:13) explicate passage "to the other side," and two do not (6:32.f; 8:10). The former pair are seen by Kelber as the return voyages of the two longer crossings outlined above. All agree that 6:32f. is merely an aborted escape from the crowds, recalling similar instances earlier in which Jesus used the boat to distance himself from the crowds (3:9; 4:1), or unsuccessfully tried to withdraw for solitude (1:33–37). The boat trip to Dalmanutha (8:10)—geographical problems aside—is best explained in terms of an intercalation. Mark begins to narrate the return voyage of 8:13–21, and interrupts it with the inserted story of Pharisees looking for a sign (8:11f.). Thus, whether this sign-seeking episode is on the eastern (Kelber) or western (Malbon) shore of the sea, in terms of narrative composition it must be included as part of the "first epilogue" (see below, 7,D,i).

ii. The Drama of Difficult Passage

What is the meaning of the two main sea-crossings, each of which places the disciples in peril from the elements, only to be rescued by a miraculous act of

Jesus? The first trip is launched at the close of the first sermon, when Jesus invites his disciples to accompany him across the sea (4:35). Jesus is in the boat when the storm arises, unconcerned, and in a moment of high narrative pathos, the terrified disciples scream at their dozing leader, "Master, do you not care? We are dying!" (4:38, *apollumetha*). Unaware of the purpose of their journey, they betray their profound fear of abandonment, and Jesus silences this lack of faith as well as the storm itself (4:39f.).

Several Old Testament traditions have been suggested as background for this episode:

> Some went down into the sea in boats . . . then they cried to the Lord in their trouble, and he delivered them from their distress; he made the storm be still, and the waves were hushed [Ps 107:23, 29].

> The Lord hurled up a great wind upon the sea, and there was a mighty tempest on the sea, so that the ship threatened to break up. Then the mariners were afraid, and each cried to his god . . . but Jonah had gone down into the inner part of the ship and had lain down and was fast asleep. . . . Then the men were exceedingly afraid, and said to him, "What is this that you have done?!" [Jonah 1:4f., 10].

Jesus' rebuke of the winds (*epetimēsen ho anemos*) also echoes Psalm 104:7 ("at your rebuke [LXX, *epitimēseōs*] the waters fled"), and Psalm 106:9 ("He rebuked [LXX, *epetimēsen*] the Red Sea"). We now see that in choosing to refer to the lake as a sea, "Mark presupposes the connotation of the sea as chaos, threat, danger . . . from the Hebrew scriptures" (Malbon, 1984:376).

But it is clearly the nonunderstanding motif that lies at the center of the story, articulated by the back-to-back questions:

1. Jesus: "Do you not yet (*oupō*; cf. 8:17, 21) have faith?"
2. Disciples: "Who then is this that even the sea and the wind listen to him?" (4:40f.).

The disciples' wonder echoes that of the synagogue crowd back in 1:27, and as a double entendre it is poignant. For like the unclean spirit there, the elements are here "silenced" (*phimousthai*, 1:25; 4:39); they "listen" (*hupakouein*, 4:41) to Jesus; but will the disciples, who have also been so commanded, listen (4:3,9,20)?

The second crossing exhibits important differences by which Mark intensifies these same themes. If the first journey was made under the "protection" of the present Jesus, in the second the disciples are compelled to make the crossing on their own. In fact, the episode begins on a note of tension: Mark tells us that Jesus "forced (*ēnankasen*) his disciples to embark in the boat ahead of him to the other side" (6:45). The destination is Bethsaida, which they will not reach on this trip, but on a subsequent one (8:22; below, 8,B,ii). Veterans of one dangerous crossing, the disciples appear to be reluctant to repeat the journey. Thrice the text stresses the spatial opposition between Jesus and the disciples (6:45–47):

1. he forces them to go on ahead while he dismisses the crowd;
2. he leaves them to go pray in the hills;
3. the boat was far out to sea while he was alone on the land.

Finally, despite the fact that he observes the disciples far out to sea, straining hopelessly at the oars with a fierce wind against them, Jesus waits until the fourth watch of the night (i.e., early morning) to come to their aid (6:48).

The phrase "he was going to pass them by" (6:48c) should not, however, be misunderstood as a desire by Jesus to ignore his disciples' plight. Harry Fledderman (1983) points out that the phrase should be intertextually understood in terms of Yahweh's saving appearance (Ex 33:19,22; 34:6; 1 Kgs 19:11; Am 7:8; 8:2). This is confirmed by both the disciples' terror (the standard reaction in Old Testament epiphanies) and Jesus' reassurance: "It is I, fear not" (6:49f.; *egō eimi* corresponds to Yahweh's "I am" in the LXX, Ex 3:14). Once again Jesus quells the wind but not the disciples' apprehension. Jesus' verdict upon their failure to understand is harsh: their hearts had become hardened, like those of his opponents (6:52). The crossing is a failure, as they land back at Gennesaret (6:53).

This is a foreboding turn of events; according to the story so far, "hardening of the heart" represents the first stage of alienation, followed by total deafness/blindness (3:5→4:12). And indeed, this progression will be repeated in Jesus' next charge (6:52→8:17f.). I will have more to say about the theme of noncomprehension (below, 7,D,ii); but what about the symbol of a stormy passage itself?

These harrowing sea stories intend to dramatize the difficulties facing the kingdom community as it tries to overcome the institutionalized social divisions between Jew and gentile. Through this metaphorical action the community struggles to make the "passage" to integration (hence the difficulty is always en route to the gentile shore). The wind and sea as obstacles derive from the ancient Semitic mythic personification of cosmic forces of chaos and destruction (as in 5:13; 9:42; 11:23). It is no wonder the disciples demonstrate reluctance: all the power of the established "symbolic universe" of segregation oppose this journey. And no doubt the real-life social hostility to such a project of integration threatened to "drown" the community. But Mark insists that Jesus will rescue this project and silence the winds of opposition.

This is the meaning that the reader, unlike the disciples, must not miss. But perhaps such an interpretation seems at this point strained and speculative, even annoyingly allegorical. In order, therefore, to build the case fully, it is necessary to first examine the other elements within the cycle of symbolic action presented in this section.

6D. THE KINGDOM FIRST TO THE OUTCAST: THE TWO DOUBLE HEALINGS (5:21–43; 7:24–37)

I will first consider the two sets of double healings that take place in the Jewish and gentile cycles. These highly archetypical episodes extend and deepen the scope of the kingdom's social inclusivity, which was first introduced by Jesus' fellowship with tax collectors and sinners in 2:14ff. Specifically, the healing of Jairus's daughter (5:21–24, 35–43), framed around the healing of the woman with the blood flow (5:24–34), addresses *class* status within Judaism, dramatizing what today is referred to in liberation theology as the "preferential option for the poor." The successive healings in 7:24ff. articulate in turn that the poor of the gentile world *are* included in this bias of the kingdom mission.

i. Socio-Cultural Dynamics of Honor and Shame

In order to properly understand the social function of these stories, we will be aided by some brief cross-cultural background in the social dynamics of status. The structure and maintenance of social standing of persons and groups in Hellenistic antiquity differed radically from those of modern, Western societies. I highly recommend to the reader Bruce Malina's introduction to these issues in his *The New Testament World: Insights from Cultural Anthropology* (1981), upon which the following is based.

Judaism in first-century Palestine can be described as an "honor culture." Malina summarizes:

> From a symbolic point of view, honor stands for a person's rightful place in society, his social standing. This honor place is marked off by boundaries consisting of power, sexual status, and position on the social ladder. . . . Honor is a claim to worth along with the social acknowledgment of worth. The purpose of honor is to serve as a sort of social rating which entitles a person to interact in specific ways with his or her equals, superiors, and subordinates, according to the prescribed cultural cues of the society. . . . For honor has both individual and corporate or collective dimensions. Relations within the natural grouping are sacred, blood, or pure relationships that tie persons directly together. . . . Relationships within voluntary groupings are focused on posts and functions [1981:47f.].

One's status within this highly formal system determined to whom and how one could speak and interact, regulated social roles and transactions, and circumscribed mobility within the system. Malina highlights two dynamics of particular relevance to the stories we will examine, what he calls the "female" and "male" roles involved in the maintenance of this system.

The male role was concerned with the defense of status and entitlement; the female role preserved the consciousness of group boundaries, or "shame":

> Shame in this context refers to a person's sensitivity about what others think, say, and do with regard to his or her honor . . . natural groupings have collective honor and shame. But in the moral division of labor . . . honor and shame become sexually specific, sexually embedded. The male is to defend both corporate honor and any female

honor embedded in the corporate honor. The female, on the other hand, symbolizes the shame aspect of corporate honor, that positive sensitivity to the good repute of individuals and groups [ibid.].

Needless to say, this patriarchal system precluded women from assertiveness in public life, interpersonally and socially. This corresponded to women's general lack of what we today call "rights," as we will see later in the controversy over divorce law (below, 9,B,I) and levirate marriage (below, 10,E,i).

On the other hand, the male task determined the challenge-and-response nature of any interpersonal or social encounter, which became a contest in which the honor "ascribed" to an individual or group was defended or additional esteem acquired:

Ascribed honor befalls or happens to a person passively through birth, family connections, or endowment by notable persons of power. Acquired honor is honor actively sought and garnered most often at the expense of one's equals in the social contest of challenge and response. . . . Whenever the honor of another is bound up with an individual's own honor, that individual is required to defend and represent the honor of all bound up with him [ibid].

In the episodes we will look at, Jesus is portrayed in a way of social interaction that breaks the rules and expectations of the conduct that obtained in Palestinian honor culture, shocking those who heard the story and undermining their sense of social order and propriety. In the process of his symbolic construction of the new social order of the kingdom, Mark's Jesus was subverting the status quo in order to create new possibilities of human community.

The formalities of honor culture are difficult for modern North Americans to understand, not least those who assume certain cultural dynamics of egalitarianism. Unlike many of the issues that arise in reading biblical texts, however, this one can be illustrated through a contemporary cross-cultural example, for honor culture still predominates among many indigenous peoples today. I remember several awkward moments as part of a delegation to a political conference on liberation on a newly independent Pacific island nation in Melanesia. The traditional practices of hospitality and greeting were being extended to us by our hosts. A pig was slaughtered in front of us—a custom by which foreign visitors are given a grant of honor, or mana, in order that they may interact with their hosts. The next step in creating the environment for fellowship with the guest was the ceremonial drinking of kava—but this was restricted to the male representatives of each group. Finally came the "response" ritual, according to which the guests were to present gifts to the high chief, who symbolized the whole community. Needless to say, the younger, progressive urbanites from the Western delegations were nonplussed by all of this: queazy at the bloodletting, offended by the "sexism," and embarrassed because they had brought no gifts!

This is not to suggest that Western postindustrial urban culture is devoid of social roles and expectations, or of rituals in which there is a contest for honor! However, in capitalist societies status has largely become a function of the power accruing from wealth, education or media character. "Nobility" is no longer so much an inheritance (though this certainly persists) as it is a commodity; the symbols of status (expensive clothes, cars, and homes) are available to anyone who can afford them. Of course, access to material wealth continues to have everything to do with race and sex. Still, the formalities of traditional honor culture have waned.

The point of this observation is simply to remind the reader that much of what might seem to us unremarkable about the actions of Jesus in the Gospel—such as conceding a debate to a woman—would in fact have posed a radical challenge to the cultural sensibilities of Mark's original audience.

ii. Jewish Class Relationships: Healing Two "Daughters"

We pick up the story again upon Jesus' return to Jewish territory after the first voyage and exorcism in Gerasa. In 5:21 Mark re-creates the prevoyage setting (4:1,36): Jesus and the crowds are again "by the sea." This familiar narrative site should alert us that the following story will have particular didactic value for the disciple/reader.

Jesus is approached by a member of the Jewish ruling class, who begs Jesus to heal his daughter. Jesus complies, setting out with the man, but is interrupted en route by the advances of an impure woman from the crowd. Against the inclinations of his disciples, Jesus attends to the poverty-stricken woman, but as a result arrives too late to save the daughter. The story's tragic end is surprisingly reversed by Jesus' powerful deed of raising the young girl back to life. Mark again here uses the form of intercalation to interrelate these two episodes. They are also linked rhetorically by several elements, especially the number twelve: the woman has a flow of blood for twelve years, the daughter's age is twelve.

The socio-economic indicators in this narrative make it certain that the issue here is class status. The crowd, which as we have seen signifies the social location of the poor, appears at each of the first five stages of the first half of the story:

1. a great crowd gathers around Jesus by the shore (5:21);
2. it follows Jesus, pressing in on him (5:24);
3. the ailing woman reaches out from the crowd (5:27);
4. Jesus perceives it, turns around in the crowd (5:30);
5. his disciples discount his perception as due to the press of the crowd (5:31).

Mark also portrays the two main characters in this episode as archetypical opposites in terms of economic status and honor. On the one hand, the synagogue ruler, Jairus (one of the rare named characters in Mark's story), makes an assertive approach to Jesus, as befits male social equals. This man was both "head" of his family (thus appealing on behalf of his daughter) and "head" of his social group (leader of the synagogue, *archisunagōgoon*). The man falls down at Jesus' feet, a proper granting of honor prior to asking a favor.

On the other hand, the woman who reaches out from the cover of the crowd, an ashamed and covert attempt to gain healing, is anonymous. When Jesus tries to seek her out, the disciples discourage him: "You see how the crowd is pressing around you and yet you say, 'Who touched me?' " (5:31). The woman has no name, she belongs to the crowds—she is statusless, with no one to defend her (as Jairus defends his daughter). Mark spares no hyperbole for her destitution in four successive participial clauses:

1. having been with a flow of blood for twelve years,
2. having suffered much under the care of many physicians,
3. having spent all her means,
4. and having not benefited but instead grown worse (5:25f.).

This woman is doubly poor, doubly outcast. As a result of her physical condition of unarrestable hemorrhaging, she should—according to the Levitical purity code—be perpetually segregated. And she was a victim of exploitation as well. Taylor points out that the squandering of money upon inefficacious medical care was a perennial problem for the poor in antiquity (1963:290). Mark's parenthetical comment (dropped by both Matthew and Luke) is sharp and even cynical: not only did she suffer greatly under various physicians (*polla pathousa hupo pollōn iatrōn*), but she "spent all she had and profited nothing" (*mēden ōphelētheisa*; see 7:11; 8:36). In contrast, the true physician (2:17) will cure this woman without charge.

As we have come to expect, there are several levels to this healing story. The restoration of bodily wholeness is in the foreground, and indeed only here does Mark stress both the symptoms and the cure. This is dramatized in the double realization of physical sensation by both the woman and Jesus:

1. and immediately her issue of blood was dried up, and she perceived in her body that she was finally cured of the scourge (5:29, *tō sōmati hoti iastai*);
2. and immediately Jesus perceived that power had gone out from him (5:30a).

At the same time, as in the story of the cleansing of the leper (1:40–45), the purity code is very much at issue. Jesus again both violates and reverses the contagion by his "touching" (*haptomai*, four times in 5:27–31). The woman who was permanently outcast is restored to social as well as physical wholeness. M. Selvidge goes so far as to see this story as Mark's protest against the marginalization of menstruating women by the purity code (1984: 619ff.).

I would contend that the primary level of signification in this episode, however, lies in the fact that Jesus accepts the priority of the ("highly inappropriate") importunity of this woman over the ("correct") request of the synagogue leader. His mission to "lay his hands on" Jairus's daughter (5:23c) is interrupted by the "touch" of the doubly poor woman, and now she is the one who falls at the feet of Jesus (5:33). The most important symbolic reversal here is the status of the destitute woman. From the bottom of the honor scale she intrudes upon an important mission on behalf of the daughter of someone on the top of the honor scale—but by the story's conclusion, *she* herself has become the "daughter" at the center of the story! "My daughter," proclaims Jesus, "Your faith has saved you, go in peace and be in full health, free of your scourge" (5:34). Not only is her integrity restored, but she receives a grant of status superior to that of Jesus' own male disciples, who are "without faith" (4:40)! Such a profound reversal of dignity will occur only one other time in Mark: in the story of another destitute Jew, the blind beggar Bartimaeus (10:51).

But this delay results in the apparent failure of the original mission and violation of the agreement of honor that had been made: "As he was saying this" the synagogue ruler is informed that his daughter has died (5:35). But Jesus carries on as if nothing has been lost, exhorting Jairus to follow the example of the lowly woman: "Do not fear, only believe" (5:36). He takes only Peter, James, and John with him to Jairus's home; here Mark formally introduces the inner circle of the discipleship community, indicating that something important is about to occur. The scene at the family house is appropriate to the fact of death, connoted by the customary ritual of weeping and wailing (5:38f.). Jesus' announcement that "the child is not dead but asleep" suddenly transforms the remorse into derision—Mark's rather sarcastic indication of the lack of faith in this household (5:40).

Jesus, perhaps angered, "throws out" (*ekbalōn*; cf. 11:15) everyone but the child's parents and his disciples, and finally completes his mission: he takes the girl by the hand (5:41). The result of his command is the raising of the little girl—who, Mark interjects, was "twelve years old"—back to life. J. Moiser finds the symbolism of this story irresistible:

> The girl, who represents in her age the tribes of Israel, is laid low with a temporary illness (5:23). Some think her actually dead (5:35), excluded from life forever. Jesus does not intervene in that quarrel; he simply says that God will raise her up (5:39). He takes her by the hand, and she rises at once and walks about [1981:180].

I agree with Moiser that the details of this story make perfect sense as symbolic coordinates.

Mark shapes this story to intentionally juxtapose the two extremes of the Jewish social scale. The little girl had enjoyed twelve years of privilege as the daughter of a synagogue ruler, yet was now "near death" (5:23). The phrase used by Mark in 5:23 (*eschatōs echei*, lit., "near her last") faintly echoes the term he will later use in speaking of the reversal of the social order (first vs. *last*, *eschatos*, 9:35; 10:31). Indeed, as far as Mark's Jesus is concerned, the social order represented by the synagogue ruler's Judaism is on the verge of collapse. The statusless woman had suffered twelve years of destitution at the hands of the purity system and its "doctors"; yet she still took initiative in her struggle for liberation. The object lesson can only be that if Judaism wishes to "be saved and live" (5:23), it must embrace the "faith" of the kingdom: a new social order with equal status for all. This alone will liberate the lowly outcast and snatch the "noble" from death. Mark's narrative of symbolic action thus achieves the same effect as Matthew's blunt announcement to the Jewish leaders that "tax collectors and prostitutes are making their way into the kingdom of God before you" (Mt 21:31)—and with equal shock value!

Finally, at the level of narrative strategy, Mark has in this episode also prefigured what will emerge as the central theme in the second half of the Gospel. Through dramatic enactment he continues (as in the seed parables) to prepare the way for the "last shall be first" and "least/greatest" (10:31,43) discourse of the second "construction" section. And the resurrection symbolism of the raising of the little girl anticipates the "death/life" paradox (8:35f.) that Jesus teaches and embodies. For indeed upon the announcement that "your daughter is dead," the narrative of mission begun in 5:23 came to a grinding halt. However, Jesus "ignored this message" (5:36 *parakousas ton logon*) and exhorted faith. So too will the reader have to ignore the message of Jesus' death as the close of the narrative of the messianic mission, and demonstrate faith to continue on the journey. Indeed, the term here describing the observers' astonishment at the little girl's recovery (5:42b, *ekstasis*) appears again only once in Mark—when the women are told that Jesus too has risen from the dead (16:8).

iii. An Ecumenical Community: Healing Two Gentiles

We move now to a healing sequence in the gentile cycle (7:24–37). The setting this time is the faraway region around Tyre (*eis ta horia Turou*), representing the northernmost geographical penetration of Mark's narrative (see 3:8) and, socially speaking, quite beyond the horizons of the Palestinian Jew. According to the chronology of the story, Jesus has just engaged in a lengthy dispute with the Pharisees (7:1–23); the phrase "he entered a house and wanted no one to know it" (7:24) thus suggests that the intention of this trip across the Syrian border was to withdraw for reflection—not missionary work per se (Taylor, 1963:348). As each time before, however, the attempt at solitude fails; the interruption this time is by a gentile woman.

In an intentional parallel to Jairus's request, the woman falls at Jesus' feet to petition an exorcism in behalf of her daughter (7:25; cf. 5:22f.). The woman, Mark adds as if to make a point, is Greek, a Syro-Phoenician—in other words, a pagan. This is another Markan archetype, representative of the hellenized populations of the area. Unlike the approach of Jairus, her solicitation is an affront to the honor status of Jesus: no woman, and especially a gentile, unknown and unrelated to this Jew, would have dared invade his privacy at home to seek a favor. A rebuff by Jesus thus is not only understandable but expected; and indeed he appears to sharply thwart her advances by defending the collective honor of the Jews: "Let the children be satisfied first, for it is not right that the children's bread be thrown to the puppies" (7:27). Taylor comments:

> Gentiles are sometimes described as "dogs" by Jewish writers, generally with reference to their vices. . . . Rabbi Eliezer [said] "He who eats with an idolator is like unto one who eats with a dog" [1963:350].

Although Taylor does not believe this is implied in Jesus' use of the diminutive ("little dogs," i.e., household pets), I think rather that Mark is indeed citing this traditional insult as a way of dramatizing the encounter. Theissen agrees that the story both assumes and reflects the ethnic, cultural, and sociopolitical hostility between Jews and their gentile neighbors [1985:202ff.].

The fact that the woman wishes to argue the point deepens her affront to Jesus, yet it is precisely her verbal riposte that gives the twist to this story: she argues that puppies might at least be entitled to the crumbs (7:28). Suddenly it is she who seeks to defend the "rights" of her people to the liberating power of Jesus' exorcism ministry. Given the utterly shameful behavior and pagan character of the woman, it is shocking that Jesus concedes her the debate: "The demon has left your daughter" (7:29). Moreover, he grants her request, not because of her faith but because of her argument (*dia touton ton logon*); a remarkable turn of events, given Jesus' powerful verbal mastery over his opponents in the Gospel! This drama represents another example of status-equalization. Jesus allows himself to be "shamed" (becoming "least") in order to include this pagan woman in the new community of the kingdom; so too Judaism will have to suffer the indignity of redefining its group boundaries (collective honor) in order to realize that gentiles are now welcomed as equals.

The story of the Syrophoenician woman bears certain affinities with its counterparts in the Jewish cycle. She, like the hemorrhaging woman, demonstrates inappropriately assertive female behavior that is vindicated. The parallel with the Jairus story goes beyond the common petition on behalf of ailing daughters at home. Both these episodes articulate feeding-symbolics that are carefully correlated to Jesus' feedings of the masses in the wilderness. Jesus' somewhat anticlimactic instructions in the aftermath of his dramatic raising of Jairus's daughter were for those present to "give her something to eat" (5:43, *dothēnai autē phagein*). In like fashion, Jesus instructs his disciples in the first feeding to "give the crowd something to eat" (6:37, *dote autois humeis phagein*). Similarly, Jesus tells the gentile woman that "the children must first be satisfied" (7:27 *chortasthēnai*)—which satisfaction has indeed already been reported in 6:42 ("they all ate and were satisfied," *ephagon pantes kai echortasthēsan*)! This is how Mark prepares the way for the fulfillment of the Syrophoenician woman's request—the feeding and satisfaction of the gentiles—which will indeed shortly take place (same verb, 8:4,8).

If Jesus' exorcism of the Syrophoenician woman's daughter suggests that the kingdom has dawned among the gentiles, the following healing story confirms this beyond a doubt. Jesus' trip from "the region of Tyre" to "the region of the Decapolis" (7:31) recounts an itinerary that many commentators consider "improbable," though F. Lang (1978) notes that there was in fact a route from Sidon to Damascus to the eastern shore of the Sea of Galilee, one that may have been traveled by early Christian missionaries. In any case, the narrative purpose of the journey is to symbolically embrace the entire Hellenistic neighborhood surrounding Galilee.

Jesus encounters there a man unable to communicate verbally (7:32). He is brought by an unknown "they," who beg Jesus to lay his hands upon him. This healing too contains elements in common with the story of Jairus's daughter: the healing is done away from the crowds, and only here in Mark does Jesus utter a special Aramaic phrase in the process (7:34; cf. 5:41). Here, however, the purity code is again sideswiped, for Mark tells us that Jesus "spat" on his fingers to effect the healing. D. Smith (1985) points out that saliva was considered as pollutive as was bodily excrement (see Lev 15:8). But—as in the case of the Jewish leper in 1:40ff.—the contagion is reversed, and the gentile healed. And here too the anonymous group, despite Jesus' admonitions to the contrary, begins to "preach" (7:36, *ekērusson*), a technical term for gospel proclamation in Mark (see 3:14; 6:12; 13:9; 14:9).

The main point of the story is articulated in the crowd's great awe at its conclusion: "He makes even the deaf hear and the nonspeaking speak!" (7:37). Is this a reference to the gentile mission (see parallels to 5:20)? Perhaps; but its more compelling significance has to do with Mark's wider narrative strategy, within which it holds a strategic place. It is the final healing in the series of four in this section, and the last in the first half of the Gospel. At the same time, as we will see (below, 8,B,i), it is the first of another series of four that articulate the theme of "blindness/deafness." Finally, it anticipates the ambiguity of the first epilogue, with almost overbearing irony: Jesus can make the gentile deaf hear, but not, it will turn out, his own disciples (8:18)!

These two pairs of healings demonstrate Mark's mastery in using narrative action to illustrate the ideology of inclusion, which is the cornerstone to the new social order being constructed by Jesus. The social dynamics of status and honor, fundamental in the life of antiquity, have been turned upside down to make way for the outcast Jew and the alien gentile. We now turn to the culminating element in Mark's legitimation of the ecumenical community: the wilderness feedings.

6E. THE KINGDOM AS ECONOMIC SATISFACTION: TWO WILDERNESS FEEDINGS (6:33–44; 8:1–9)

Each cycle of ministry ends in a story about feeding the masses in the wilderness. Austin Farrer, in his 1951 classic protoliterary study of Mark, gave an especially symbolistic interpretation of these stories. Farrer may have gone too far in the direction of allegory, but he was not wrong in his basic intuition that here we encounter Markan "high symbolism." These stories also represent the flowering of Mark's socio-economic ideology.

i. Feeding the Jewish Masses: The Economics of Sharing

The first feeding story opens upon the return of the disciples from their mission (6:30). Jesus instructs his disciples to withdraw to the wilderness for reflection, as is his own practice (1:35), at which point Mark signals a transition with the pregnant comment that "many were coming and going and there was no time to eat" (6:31). The picture painted by Mark is full of pathos. Once again the community's escape from the continual press of ministry is frustrated by the crowds (6:32f.). Now even the wilderness is congested with those in need. Yet rather than responding in exasperation, Jesus demonstrates compassion (*splagchnizomai*, lit., having one's "guts" be torn apart), and he proceeds to teach them until the late hours (6:34).

The exchange between Jesus and his disciples in 6:36–38 is the crux of the story. Apparently concerned about the welfare of the crowd, the disciples suggest that the people be allowed to leave so they can go to the surrounding ("circle," cf. 6:6) farms and villages to buy themselves something to eat. Jesus responds bluntly and emphatically, "Give them something to eat yourselves" (*dote autois humeis phagein*). The disciples assume this means they are to spend their own money to buy food, a prospect that arouses their indignation. Taylor (1963:323) detects a "tone of astonishment, amounting to reproof" in their response (6:37), rendered by another translator the incredulous "Are we to buy bread to the tune of 200 denarius?" (Zerwick and Grosvenor, 1981:124). Jesus then urges them to go see how much bread they have (6:38). Fowler rightly reminds us not to miss the irony here. The disciples have just returned from a mission for which they were instructed to carry neither bread nor money (6:8, see below, 7,A,ii). But they turn up with both!

Twice the disciples suggest to Jesus that the solution to the hunger of the crowds is to "buy" food (6:36f.; the first appearance of *agorazein* in Mark). But Jesus' solution has nothing to do with participation in the dominant economic order. Instead he determines the available resources, organizes the consumers into groups (6:39f.), pronounces the blessing (cf. 14:22), and distributes what is at hand (6:41). We should be clear that there is nothing "supernatural" reported to have transpired in this feeding of some five thousand men; only that "they all ate and were satisfied" (6:42). The only "miracle" here is the triumph of the economics of sharing within a community of consumption over against the economics of autonomous consumption in the anonymous marketplace.

Mark is working with several images from the Hebrew scriptures here. The Exodus account of Yahweh's sustenance of Israel in the "wilderness" obviously comes to mind. But it is upon an episode in the Elisha miracle cycle that Mark's story is directly patterned (2 Kgs 4:42–44), in particular these lines:

And Elisha said, "Give to the men, that they may eat" (LXX, *dote tō laō kai esthietōsan*). And his servant said, "How am I to set this before a hundred men?" So he repeated, "Give them to the men, that they may eat, for thus says the Lord, 'They shall eat (LXX, *phagontai*) and have some left.' " So he set it before them. And they ate, and had some left, according to the word of the Lord.

This story is illuminating for two reasons. First, Elisha's successive food miracles take place in the context of "famine in the land" (2 Kgs 4:38), and thus are directly related to retarding the scourge of starvation. Secondly, the "bread" (LXX, *artous*) brought to Elisha represents firstfruits (2 Kgs 4:42). It may be that Mark invokes this tradition because of these factors, which would relate back to the conflicts over hunger, tithing, and the distribution of the fruit of the land articulated in 2:23–28 (see above, 4,D,ii).

The third Old Testament allusion is the phrase "sheep without a shepherd" (6:34), which would appear to insert a dimension of political criticism into this episode as well. This deserves more careful examination, especially because it has inspired some interesting political interpretations.

ii. Sheep without a Shepherd: A Political Polemic?

In the early 1960s, H. Montefiore argued that this implied allusion to Joshua had militaristic implications:

> The phrase "sheep without a shepherd" means, according to Old Testa-
> ment usage, not a congregation without a leader, but "an army without a
> general, a nation without a national leader." . . . Mark probably intends
> a reference to Numbers 27:16ff. . . . It may be noted that according to
> Numbers this incident took place in the wilderness, there is a reference to
> the coming and going of people, and the name of the man appointed was
> Joshua (Jesus) [1962:136].

Drawing off the (admittedly conspicuous) parallels in John 6:1–15, Monte-fiore conjectured that these scenes represent an oblique historical account of a political-messianic assembly, similar to the many movements that began in the desert during this period. This impromptu gathering was for the purpose of plotting strategy, and in the process the crowds tried to make Jesus their leader (ibid: 135ff.).

Montefiore's thesis has been dismissed by most scholars, and indeed most of the exegetical observations around which Montefiore builds his case are gratui-tous. These include his arguments from the way the crowd ran around, the allegedly military configuration of the seating arrangements, the time of year, and the contention that by "5,000 men" (6:45, *andres*) Mark means a fighting force! I would reject Montefiore's historicist presuppositions, but his thesis is wobbly on socio-literary grounds as well. For example, he is forced by Mark's text to immediately backpedal: Jesus had to talk to the crowd out of its plan to appoint him Messiah:

Under the pressure of the actual situation Jesus knew that he could not be the kind of military leader that Joshua had been in times past. "And he began to teach them many things" (Mk 6:34b). Jesus had to explain to the mob why he could not accede to their wish. Mark uses almost the same phrase with a similar meaning a little later in rather similar circumstances [ibid.: 136].

This last reference is to Jesus' rejection of Peter's messianic triumphalism in 8:31. Montefiore thus ends up unsure whether Mark is endorsing or repudiating militant messianism.

Montefiore also sees political significance in the fact that Mark places this story directly after the narrative of the execution of John: one leader had been murdered, and the crowd wanted to organize before Jesus became another victim. Indeed Jesus' hosting of the masses in the wilderness would bear provocative relationship to Josephus's assertion that it was Herod's fear of organized crowds under the spell of messianic preaching that led to his murder of John—except for the fact that Josephus's account cannot be read into Mark. Nor is Mark's narrative flow intended to reflect historical chronology. The John/Herod interlude is a "flashback" account (below, 7,A); Jesus' "succession" of John took place in story time back in 1:14f.! These are the problems that inevitably accompany attempts to reconstruct historical events from symbolic narrative. If there is a relationship between the John/Herod episode and this one, it lies in the fact that together they articulate the radical economic/class disparities in Galilee: John is murdered by the ruling classes he criticized, whereas Jesus calls for the hungry in the wilderness to be fed.

The most that can be salvaged from Montefiore's efforts is to affirm that Mark is decidedly presenting Jesus as an "organizer," but with the intention of feeding the needy, not plotting a military campaign on Jerusalem. This, however, hardly makes the narrative ideology less subversive! Indeed, there is an *implied* political criticism here, which we see if we do not limit the intertextuality to the Joshua tradition. The "sheep without a shepherd" motif is seized upon by the prophets to criticize the leadership of Israel. Ezekiel 34 spins a parable around it that specifically condemns class stratification: "I will judge between the fat sheep and the lean sheep" (Ez 34:20). The ruling class protects its privilege rather than the collective prosperity of the people, becoming predator instead of shepherd:

> Should not shepherds feed the sheep? You eat the fat, you clothe yourselves with the wool, you slaughter the fatlings, but you do not feed the sheep. . . . With force and harshness you have ruled them. So they were scattered . . . and they became food for all the wild beasts [Ez 34:2ff.].

The motif is reproduced again in the apocalyptic section of Zechariah 11–12, for similar reasons:

Woe to my worthless shepherd, who deserts his flock [11:17]. Those who buy them slay them and go unpunished; and those who sell them say, "Blessed be Yahweh, for I have become rich"; and their own shepherds have no pity on them [11:5].

Clearly, linking Jesus—as one who attends to the hunger of the crowds in the wilderness—with these prophetic traditions is meant as a criticism of the political economy of Palestine and the ruling class who profits from it. And, as we shall see, Mark will again draw upon the Zechariah parable at the end of the story (Mk 14:27; see below, 12,C,i).

iii. Feeding the Gentile Masses: Sustenance for the Way

When we turn to the second feeding at the end of the gentile cycle, the account is far briefer, as if the disciple/reader should by now readily grasp the symbolics of the narrative. Mark quickly sets up the scene in 8:1: a crowd gathers without food, and Jesus again turns to the disciples. And again his comment is significant for intertextual reasons:

I am moved with compassion for the crowd because already three days they have continued with me and they have nothing they might be able to eat; and if I should send them away to their homes fasting they will grow faint on the way for some of them are from far away [8:2f.].

Here Mark characterizes the gentiles in terms of the scattered poor of Yahweh, as narrated in Psalm 107 (LXX, 106):

Some wandered in desert wastes (LXX, *en tē erēmō*), finding no way (*hodon*) to a city to dwell in; hungry and thirsty, their soul faltered within them [LXX, Ps 106:4f.].

Here Jesus' concern is not about the betrayal of the shepherds (as with the Jews in 6:34) but the problem of sustenance for those "from afar" ("from east and west and north and south," Ps 107:3).

There is analepsis as well: Jesus will not send his hearers home "fasting" (*nēsteis*, 8:3), recalling the episode from the series of eating controversies in the first campaign (2:18–22). There the ritual fasting of the Pharisees was contrasted with the disciples' real hunger (2:25). Jesus' concern here is that the gentile crowd should not "faint on the way" (*en tē hodō*), the Markan metaphor for discipleship (cf. the "way" made by the commandeering of grain in 2:23). Among the masses, where hunger is a concrete reality, Jesus again rejects the piety of fasting in favor of the practice of meeting the real human needs.

The disciples' response (8:4) this time is not indignation but despair: in the wilderness (that is, outside the dominant social order and its markets) how can one possibly find the resources to feed the hungry? Jesus again determines what is available (8:5), organizes the crowd, and gives the food to the disciples to "pass on" (*paratithemi*; in Mark only in 6:41 and here twice in 8:6f.). And yet again "they ate and were satisfied" (8:8); only then does Jesus "send them away" (8:9b). In this feeding, as in the first, a superabundance results, and the remaining food is gathered up. For the second time Mark has presented the apex of his symbolic world-construction with a vision of the economic satisfaction of the masses and an ideology of sharing.

NOTES

1. II, "The Teaching Cycle" = chap. 9, below.

2. The crux of the problem lies in Kelber's second "crossing/return." The alleged trip over to gentile territory (to Bethsaida, 6:45) is in fact a zigzag. The boat departs from an unknown location on the western shore, arriving however not on the eastern shore but at Gennesaret, probably to be identified with the northwest shore below Capernaum. Similarly, Kelber's alleged "return" trip back to the Jewish side (8:13) is in fact a trip eastward. The voyage of 8:10 appears to be a crossing from east (the Decapolis?, 7:31) to somewhere on the western shore—Dalmanutha is an unknown location, but is probably either "Magdala" (as in variant readings, see Mt 15:39) or a corruption of an older name for Tiberias (see Taylor, 1963:360f.). This makes the trip in 8:13 a west-east journey to Bethsaida (8:22).

Malbon points out that in 6:53 the disciples are "turned back" (by the wind?) and return to the western shore. Thus this attempt to "cross" the sea eastward is unsuccessful; the goal of Bethsaida is achieved only later, in the second attempt of 8:13,22. Still, she argues, the essential parallelism of Kelber's double-ministry cycles is preserved by the "land journey" of 7:24,31, in which Jesus again (as in 5:1ff.) travels to unmistakably gentile turf. Malbon differs with Kelber therefore only in contending that 6:53–7:23 and 8:11–13 take place upon Jewish, not gentile, soil. This, she claims, explains why both episodes involve disputes with the Pharisees.

CHAPTER SEVEN

The Execution of John and the "First" Epilogue (Mark 6:1-32; 7:1-23; 8:10-21)

> Blind yourselves and be blind! . . . The vision of all this has become to you like the words of a book that is sealed.
>
> —Isaiah 29:9,11

In the epilogue of Book I, Mark's Jesus warns us against the "leaven of the Pharisees and the leaven of Herod" (8:15). This leads us to consider the remaining components of the construction cycle. The "interlude" (6:1-32) reminds us of the social and political opposition generated by the kingdom preaching of repentance with three interrelated stories of rejection: Jesus by his home town, the missionary apostles by inhospitable households, and above all the "leaven" of Herod, which results in the murder of John the Baptist. The "leaven" of the Pharisees is articulated in the dispute over purity and kosher requirements, concrete barriers to the social experiment of integration in the new community (7:1-23).

Finally, the epilogue directs us to review Jesus' symbolic action in the first construction cycle (8:10-21). It is not the purpose of this epilogue—nor of the second and final one—to provide a neat resolution to the plot crises Mark has introduced, but rather to deepen them. Thus Mark ends Book I by turning to interrogate the disciple/reader; here, like the final "ending" of the story, our ability to continue the narrative depends upon whether or not we have understood specific elements of Mark's narrative symbolics.

7A. A PROPHET WITHOUT HONOR, I: THE SECOND "GENERATIVE SEAM" (6:1-13,30-32)

i. Rejection in Nazareth: A Stranger at Home

On the heels of the "resurrection" symbolics of Jesus' raising of Jairus's daughter, Mark inserts the second generative seam (see above, 4,E). As before, this consists of Jesus' rejection in a synagogue, followed by his withdrawal and recommissioning of the disciples. The pattern of engagement and withdrawal was established in the opening sequence of the Gospel, where the discipleship mission was first generated; the two subsequent "seams" regenerate the discipleship narrative after it has been thrown into doubt by an experience of rejection:

Discipleship-consolidation story	Synagogue/Sabbath conflict/rejection	Withdrawal and ministry
1. 1:16–20 (calling)	1:21–28	1:29ff. → home
2. 3:13–19 (naming)	3:1–6	3:7ff. → sea
3. 6:7–13 (sending)	6:2–6	6:6b → villages

These "seams" function to remind the disciple/reader that despite apparent failure, the narrative (i.e., the messianic mission) can and must regroup and continue. This will of course become crucial at the end of the story, for there we will be faced with the apparent total collapse of the discipleship narrative—and a promise of "regeneration."

We pick up the story at 6:1, with Jesus' visit to his home region. There he makes what will be his last public appearance in the symbolic space of a synagogue on the Sabbath (6:2). His neighbors are suspicious at his renown, questioning his wisdom and the "mighty works wrought by his hands" (6:2c, *hai dunameis toiautai dia tōn cheirōn*). To them Jesus is "the carpenter (6:3, *tektōn*), the son of Mary," and from his hands more mundane things are expected. It may be that here the locals are accusing Jesus of economically abandoning his family (see 3:34f.), for if his mother is a widow, she would likely be dependent upon her oldest son. Only here do we learn anything of Jesus' immediate family: a mother and brothers who are named and sisters who are not. Though there is textual difficulty with the phrase "the carpenter, the son of Mary," it is possible that it is intended as a slur, for the identification of Jesus by his maternal side could have suggested illegitimacy (on this, see R. Brown, 1977:537ff.; see also Taylor, 1963:299).

The point of the episode is precisely the derogation of Jesus' honor from his own people—the ultimate put-down. The name that Jesus was making for himself scandalized the neighborhood, upset the status quo (6:4). Without their cooperative faith (6:6)—that is to say, their openness to a new order— Jesus can accomplish none of the "mighty works" (6:5, *oudemian dunamin*) that have aroused the hometown crowd's suspicion. Jesus' retort represents his programmatic break with the social structures of kinship: he understands now that his vocation will be rejected in his native region, by his relatives, and finally in his own household (*en tē patridi autou kai en tois sungeneusin autou kai en tē oikia autou*). He must concede that he is a "prophet without honor," stripped of status and robbed of clan identity. Disowned, Jesus withdraws and takes up again his itinerant mission to the village circuit (6:6b, *periēgen tas kōmas kuklō*).

ii. Mission and Hospitality: At Home among Strangers

As in 3:13, Jesus now "summons" his community to him (6:7, *proskaleitai*). Originally the community of "the twelve" was constituted for two reasons: "in order to be with him and in order that he might send them to preach and have authority to cast out demons" (3:14f.). Mark has narrated the first (companionship), and now turns to the second (mission, 6:7b). The community's apprenticeship in the messianic mission now appears to be complete, and its members are sent out on their own. We are told that they now fully practice the vocation of exorcism and healing (6:13).

In fact, however, Mark is beginning a shift in his narrative strategy. For into this third and final generative seam he has inserted the retrospect concerning John the Baptist (6:14–29). We will see that intercalation functions to create an essential narrative interrelationship between the mission and fate of Jesus, his disciples, and John (below, 7,B,ii). In fact, the community's apprenticeship is only beginning for it has yet to reckon with Jesus' "second call" to a discipleship of the cross (8:27ff.; below, 8,D), in which the inevitable clash between the kingdom and the powers is made clear. From now on, Mark will take us into the inner life and conflicts of this community, showing us its humanity, its tragedy, and its promise in its struggle to understand and truly embrace the mission with which it is *already* engaged.

This explains why Mark is not particularly interested in the apostles' mission itself, reporting it in bare summary form (6:12f.,30), and focusing instead upon Jesus' instructions. The missionary lifestyle Mark articulates (6:8–12) is used by Theissen as the centerpiece of his pioneering attempt to reconstruct the "sociology of early Palestinian Christianity" (1978). He believes this portrait of "wandering charismatics" has particular historical evidentiality because it could not have survived within the oral tradition unless it reflected an actual practice in primitive Christianity. Unfortunately, Theissen's work displays all the historicist problems of form criticism (see below, Appendix, C), and is not particularly useful in determining the socio-literary character of this text.

There is no indication that Jesus' "orders" (*parēngeilen autois*) are unique to this mission; they are for "the way" (*eis hodon*)—that is, paradigmatic of discipleship lifestyle (6:8). Their narrative significance lies not in some model of heroic asceticism (which would contradict Jesus' ambivalence toward, e.g., fasting), but in the emphasis upon the utter dependence of the disciples upon hospitality. The "apostles" (so designated for the only time in Mark upon their return from the mission in 6:30) are allowed the means of travel (staff, sandals) but not sustenance (bread, money bag and money, extra clothes). In other words, they, like Jesus who has just been renounced in his own "home," are to take on the status of a sojourner in the land. We might note that the "donning of sandals" as a Markan metaphor for discipleship (*hupodedemenous sandalia*; see above, 1:7) was missed by both Matthew (who forbids them, Mt 10:10) and Luke (who omits the reference, Lk 9:3).

The focal point of hospitality is the household (6:10, *eis oikian*) whose socio-literary importance as a narrative site I have already mentioned (above,

4,B,iv). The apostles are told to "remain there until you leave that district," perhaps indicating a strategy by which the missionary establishes a local base for ministry. Jesus, however, also reckons with the inevitable prospect that certain places will refuse to "receive or hear" the apostles (6:11, *mē dexētai humas mēde akousōsin humōn*). The symbolic gesture of shaking dust from the feet connotes "a witness against" these places, Mark's technical phrase for describing those whom the movement perceives as opponents. The vocation of hospitality is taken with deadly earnest by Mark; households that refuse it are thereafter shunned.

It could certainly be conjectured that these instructions reflect an actual social strategy by which the early movement procured a network of "safehouses" around the countryside for purposes of mission and travel. Whatever the de facto missionary practice may have been, it is interesting to reflect upon the similarities and differences between the marching orders for this nonviolent campaign and the traditional strategies of other subversive movements. Like modern guerillas, for example, Jesus' disciples are subject to the social and political perceptions of the local populace, which will determine whether or not they will be "received"—always a good test of one's "popular base." Unlike guerillas, however, who must "eat and run," the Christian missionaries make no effort to be covert; where they are offered accommodation, they stay and establish a profile. And whereas a military-based movement will usually seize by force what is needed, at least in situations of acute need, Jesus forbids retaliation in the event of rejection. This makes the missionaries completely vulnerable to, and dependent upon, the hospitality extended to them, and obviously precludes them from being able to impose their views by force.

7B. A PROPHET WITHOUT HONOR, II: THE "LEAVEN" OF HEROD (6:14-29)

i. Murder in High Places: John's Death as Political Parody

Few commentators have understood Mark's earnest admonition against the "leaven of Herod" (8:15), despite the fact that in this section Mark articulates exactly what the threat is. The intrusion of the account of John the Baptist's death at the hands of Herod is indeed abrupt. After a summary of the apostles' ministry (6:12f.), Mark offers a threadbare transition in which we are suddenly told that the Galilean king was aware of Jesus and his work (6:14a). This is followed by a summary of how Jesus is being publicly perceived in the "media," represented by the phrase "people were saying" (6:14f., *kai elegon . . . alloi de elegon . . .*), which leads into the story of John and Herod.

Let us look first at this narrative digression in its own terms. Many commentators have noted that Mark's version of why John was executed by Herod (that is, Herod Antipas, tetrarch of Galilee and Perea, 4 B.C.E.–39 C.E.) contrasts sharply with the account by the Jewish chronicler Josephus (see Rivkin, 1983).

Josephus contends that John had to be removed for specifically political reasons:

> Herod had John put to death, though he was a good man and had exhorted the Jews to live righteous lives, to practice justice towards their fellows and piety toward God, and so doing join in baptism. . . . When others too joined the crowds about him, because they were aroused to the highest degree by his words, Herod became alarmed. Eloquence that had so great an effect on the people might lead to some form of sedition, for it looked as if they would be guided by John in everything that they did. Herod decided, therefore, that it would be much better to strike first and be rid of him before his work led to an uprising, than to wait for an upheaval, get involved in a difficult situation, and see his mistake (*Ant.*, XVIII,v,2).

This leads many to dismiss Mark's account, with its interest in Herod's vacillations and his moral predicament with his brother's wife, as pious legend.

We must keep reminding ourselves that the point of the Markan narrative is ideological, not documentary. It is true that the exact historical character of the Baptist's charge against Herod is unclear from the narrative (6:17f.; Taylor outlines the problems, 1963:310f.). Yet even as it stands, John's charge would have been highly political on two counts. First, we must remember that intermarriage was a matter of politics among royalty, fundamental to the building and consolidation of dynasties. Horsley and Hanson explain the issues involved:

> Antipas' first marriage to the Arabian princess was in effect a diplomatic alliance with her father, Aretas IV, king of Nabatea, one of the strongest Near Eastern kingdoms of the time, which was quite capable of mounting an attack on Antipas' realm, a region then forming part of the eastern flank of the Roman Empire. In the potentially explosive international circumstances created by Antipas' second marriage and the flight of the Nabatean princess, condemnation by the popular prophet posed a special threat to Antipas. There was a definite possibility that John's preaching could provoke the Jewish inhabitants of Perea (Transjordan) into common action with his Arabic subjects, i.e., a popular insurrection parallel to, or perhaps in response to, invasion by Nabatean forces which might be sent by Aretas to avenge Antipas' abuse of his daughter [1985:180f.].

Ironically, Antipas was indeed subsequently defeated by Aretas, which many Jews interpreted as punishment for his execution of the popular prophet John.

Secondly, the issue of the relationship between political authority and the Jewish law within the neocolonial formation of Palestine at the time was also volatile. The part-Jewish native kings of the Herodian dynasty conformed to the requirements of Torah only when it was politically convenient or expedient.

John—like many in the Jewish nationalist resistance throughout the century—here represents the view that to claim to rule over the Jewish people is legitimate only if Jewish law is recognized. Conflicts such as this lay at the heart of the tension between Jewish exclusivity and the Hellenistic accommodationism of the Herodians, continually plaguing the colonial arrangement, and was one reason why Rome eventually assumed direct control of Palestine.

The portrayal of Herodian court intrigue gives an even sharper edge to the episode; the dinner party (6:21-28) becomes the occasion for the murderous whims of the ruling class of Galilee to be revealed. The guest list of his birthday banquet (6:21) reflects, in the words of Sherwin-White, "the court and establishment of a petty Jewish prince under strong Roman influence" (1963:137):

1. his court nobles (*tois megistasin*);
2. his army officers (*tois chiliarchois*);
3. leading Galileans (*tois prōtois tēs Galilaias*).

Mark accurately describes the inner circle of power as an incestuous relationship involving governmental, military, and commercial interests.

And yet among all these powerful men it is a dancing girl who determines the fate of the Baptist! At the center of the story is Herod's "oath" to Herodias's daughter, stated twice for comic emphasis (6:22f.). This fiction is no more an attempt to excuse Herod from culpability in the death of John than is the fiction of Barabbas or the crowd's demand an attempt to excuse Pilate for the death of Jesus (see below, 12,D,i,ii). The dilemma created by the oath is a parody on the shameless methods of decision-making among the elite, a world in which human life is bartered to save royal face: Herod trades the "head" (symbolizing his honor) of the prophet to rescue the integrity of his own drunken oath (6:24-28).

Mark's account of the death of John is scarcely apolitical! A more sarcastic social caricature could not have been spun by the bitterest Galilean peasant! Yet it stands well within the biblical tradition that pits arrogant kings against truth-telling prophets. The tale is a kind of hybrid between the story of Nathan and David and that of Esther and Ahasuerus. And above all, it paves the way for Mark's supreme political parody, the trial and execution of the Human One by the collaborative Jewish and Roman powers.

ii. Jesus as the Successor of John: The Political Destiny of the Kingdom Mission

It remains to discern the wider narrative function of the intercalation of this flashback into the account of the apostles on mission. The key is provided by the "transition" between the two, the discussion of the lingering question of Jesus' true identity in 6:14-16. This discussion is both analeptic and proleptic in regard to the framework of the story. On the one hand, the fact that Herod endorses the view that Jesus is John *redevivus* (6:16) neatly introduces the story of the Baptist's execution. This now resolves the earlier passing mention of John's arrest (1:14), and thus lends new and foreboding significance to Mark's (unresolved) allusion to the plot against Jesus (3:6). On the other hand, the same discussion will occur again at the crucial midpoint of the story (8:27f.) as a prolegomenon to Jesus' anticipation of his own execution.

In both discussions there are three prevailing opinions concerning the identity of Jesus, each of which articulates a different political interpretation of Jesus' vocation. The last of the three states that Jesus is a prophet "just like any other prophet" (*hōs eis tōn prophētōn*); this idiom appears to be taken from the LXX of Judges 16:7,11, in which Samson speaks of ways in which his remarkable powers might be neutralized, making him "just like any other man." If this is the case, Jesus is hardly a threat, for he has already been shown to be a "prophet without honor" (6:4). It is quite another matter if he is the eschatological Elijah, for then Yahweh's judgment is imminent. The worst case, however, as far as Herod is concerned, is if Jesus is "John whom I executed" (6:16); for if John (that is, John's mission) has been brought back to life, then Herod's power, symbolized by capital punishment, has been broken.

Mark is here intentionally blurring the lines of distinction in the Jesus/John/Elijah complex. On the one hand, we have known since 1:7f. that Jesus is not John but the "stronger" one, and we will soon discover that John is in fact the eschatological Elijah (9:11-13). So Herod is wrong about Jesus. But not entirely. For John was executed because he preached repentance (specifically to Herod!); and Jesus indeed took up John's mantle and message upon his arrest (1:14f.). Moreover, Mark's description of John's fate at the hands of the state is proleptic of Jesus': seizure and imprisonment (6:17), execution (6:27), burial in a tomb (6:29), and implied resurrection (6:14).

The point of the identification of Jesus and John is this: the political destiny of those who proclaim repentance and a new order is always the same. Now we can understand why the John story has been inserted into the narrative of the apostles' mission: insofar as they inherit this mission, they inherit its destiny. This is expressly articulated first in 8:34, then again in 13:9-11, but it is already here implied by the structure of intercalation in the last generative seam. We are not surprised, then, later when Jesus explicitly articulated what he here implies: the "script" of biblical radicalism (12:1ff.).

7C. THE STRUCTURES OF SEGREGATION:
THE "LEAVEN" OF THE PHARISEES (6:53-7:23)

Immediately after the first wilderness feeding (6:33-44) and the second major sea voyage (6:45-53), we are given a summary report of Jesus' widespread ministry in "Gennesaret" (6:54-56). Despite the fact that this location is probably on the western shore of Galilee, Kelber regards this as the gentile equivalent to the summary of 1:32ff. In any case, the synopsis suffices to show that Jesus' ministry of healing extends to every social sphere of that region: the marketplaces (*en tais agorais*) of villages, cities, and rural areas (6:56). Having already established the motif in 5:27-30, Mark now reports that those who suffer need only touch Jesus' garment for restoration. Following this précis is the one conflict section in this cycle. It makes little difference whether this controversy episode is located on Jewish (Malbon) or gentile (Kelber) turf (above, 6,A,i), for it has to do with the obstacles to an *integrated* community.

i. Attacking Exclusive Table Fellowship: Pharisaic Practice

A direct narration of official opposition to Jesus has been absent since the strong man parable of 3:22ff. It is not surprising, therefore, that when conflict finally again erupts, that episode is recalled. In 7:1 we again meet "scribes coming from Jerusalem," and as in 3:23, Mark uses setting and controversy as a pretext for a teaching of Jesus, once more in parable form (7:17).

This episode resumes Mark's polemic against the Pharisaic movement, begun in 2:15ff., over the issue of the purity code as it defines the propriety of table fellowship. At least two elements firmly link 2:15ff. and 7:1ff.: Pharisaic criticism of the community's inclusive eating habits (*esthiō*), and the joint opposition of Pharisees and scribes. The issue at hand is maintenance of strict group boundaries, represented here by practices of ritual purity and dietary restriction (above, 2,E,iii). The Pharisees defend the purity code as fundamental to the ethnic and national identity of the people; Jesus repudiates these exclusivist definitions by attacking their ideological foundations.

Once again, Mark's composition provides the key to interpretation. The debate unfolds in three layers:

1. the conflict is set up with a short excursus concerning Pharisaic practices of ritual washing (7:1–5);
2. Jesus begins by challenging not the purity code itself but Pharisaic oral tradition (7:6–13);
3. Jesus returns to the original question by renouncing the kosher regulations of the purity code (7:14–23).

The first and third parts are thus related, each defined by the repetition of their respective themes: in the first case the objection of the Pharisees; in the second, Jesus' counterthesis:

1. 7:2   "They noticed that some of his disciples were eating with unclean hands."

   7.5   "Why do your disciples . . . eat their food with unclean hands?"

3. 7:15c   "It is the things that come out of a person that make that person unclean."

   7:23   "All these things come from within and make a person unclean."

This compositional structure is didactic, stating the problem and the solution, while also isolating the middle section (2). There Jesus attacks "the tradition of the elders" (introduced in 7:3,5), which represents the deeper issue of legitimating ideology. Accordingly, I will read (1) and (3) together, and then look at (2) below.

The conflict is first set up (7:1f.) and then explained to the reader (7:3f.). Mark identifies three aspects of ritual cleansing in preparation for table, which he claims as universal Jewish practice (*kai pantes hoi Iodaioi*):

a. the washing of hands;

b. the purification of food bought in the marketplace;

c. the cleansing of utensils.

In reality such a strict practice of ritual purity was probably kept only by an extremist sect of the Pharisees, the *haverim*, and perhaps priests. Booth suggests that the *haverim* are here, as in 2:18ff., challenging Mark's community to match their "supererogatory" piety as befits the truly holy (1986:130ff.). Mark's generalization, however, may simply mean to imply that all Jews are captive to the elitist conception of purity.[1]

Of particular interest is Mark's mention of the marketplace (*agora*) in 6:56 and 7:4. This narrative site represents of course the economic sphere, and Mark later refers to it as the public site of scribal "piety" that oppresses the poor (12:38ff.). The practice of "sprinkling" (*hrantisōntai*) food would appear to refer to Pharisaic concern to guard against consuming produce that may have been rendered unclean at some stage of the production process (it had nothing to do with hygiene). Impurity could have been contracted in one of two ways: the farmer could have sown or harvested in violation of Sabbath or other regulations; or the fruits may have not undergone proper separation for tithes. We have already seen (above, 4,D,ii) that Pharisaic control over production and distribution were touchy issues for Galilean peasants.

It is also noteworthy that here (unlike in 2:16) Mark twice emphasizes that the disciples are eating bread (*tous artous*). This is now emerging as a central motif, especially in light of the wilderness feeding of the Jews (6:37f.) and the disciples' misunderstanding in 6:52. Mark here is making narrative preparation for the wilderness feeding of the gentiles, which continues, as we have seen, in the following story of the Syro-Phoenician woman (7:24ff.). The Pharisaic objection to "unwashed hands" may in this case be an allusion to the fact that the disciples are assumed to be contaminated *because they have already been eating with gentiles and sharing their unclean foods* (Booth, 1986:120ff.). This is confirmed by the fact that in 6:14ff. Mark returns to the specific issue of kosher. The parable teaching is introduced in a manner meant to call to mind the first sermon: Jesus summons (*proskalesamenos*) the crowd (7:14 = 3.23), exhorts it to "listen and understand!" (7:15 = 4:2f.,12), and finally explains the parable to the disciples in private, with a reproach (7:17f. = 4:10–13b).

The parable itself (7:15) is a word play on the "external/internal" antithesis: "nothing coming into a person from the outside can pollute; it is that which comes from a person that pollutes."

The explanation in turn is in the form of a loose doublet:

a. "nothing that enters from the outside can pollute a person, because it bypasses the heart . . ." (7:18);

b. " . . . for from within from the heart of a person designs of evil come . . . all these evils come from within and pollute a person" (7:21,23).

This doublet frames Mark's parenthetical comment in 7:19b and the so-called vice list of 7:22.

The "declaring clean" (*katharizōn*) of all foods emerges as the "interpretation of the interpretation." Here Mark climaxes his assault upon the purity code, which Jesus began by "declaring clean" the leper back in 1:41ff. Booth points out that the "medical" argument—that food cannot defile because it passes through as excrement—is "Hellenistic," not Palestinian, for purity was a symbolic, not physiological, matter. This can be explained if Mark intends this episode in particular to be intelligible to the gentile part of his audience. In effect, he grants the medical argument—precisely *because* he rejects the definition of purity given by the symbolic order.

His ideological alternative confirms this: Mark introduces in 7:19 the true "site" of purity/impurity: not the "body" but the "heart." In the place of external ritual is the far more rigorous scrutiny of internal disposition (the "heart" being the moral seat of the person in Jewish anthropology). The boundaries of collective identity, which the kosher diet and other aspects of the purity code were originally instituted to maintain, are now redrawn in essentially moral terms, as indicated by the vice list. This list is "formally based on the Ten Commandments" (Neyrey, 1986:120). It reflects traditional material from the primitive Christian catechisms, providing the form critic with interesting connections to Pauline (1 Cor 6:9–11; Gal 5:19–21; Rom 1:29–31) and other New Testament parenesis (Col 3:5, 8; see Taylor, 1963:345f.; Dodd, 1968:11ff.).

But in Mark the list takes on a political dimension as well. Three of the "vices" appear in Hosea's condemnation of Israel (theft, murder, and adultery; Hos 4:2, LXX). Moreover, the list targets the key crimes of power, which Mark elsewhere imputes to Jesus' antagonists:

a. murder = the crime of the terrorist Barabbas in 15:7;
b. stealth, deceit = the description of the planned covert action by the high priests and scribes in 14:1;
c. blasphemy = Jesus' charge against the scribes in 3:28, and the high priest's accusation against Jesus in 14:64.

These are the "reasonings of the heart" toward evil (7:21)—precisely the phrase used twice of the scribes in their first public clash with Jesus (2:6, 8)! In this teaching the purity code is ethicized and universalized, and the justification for social segregation is subverted.

ii. Attacking Oral Tradition: Pharisaic Ideology

Embedded in Mark's attack on the purity code is a vigorous counteroffensive that attempts to delegitimize Pharisaic authority altogether (7:6–13). At issue is the Pharisaic oral tradition, or halakah:

> The Pharisees, as other groups, engaged in interpretation of the written Torah . . . [but] distinguished themselves from other groups by a peculiar claim for the authority of their traditions and, by extension, for the authority of the Pharisaic tradents. They established their right to interpret authoritatively by placing themselves in a chain of tradition going back to the original revelation of Torah at Mt. Sinai and then by putting

the contents of their interpretive activities into that very revelation. This they did by telling a myth which reports that both Written and Oral Law were revealed on Mt. Sinai. . . . Such claims to authority put them implicitly in competition with the other groups that claimed and had legislative authority, the priests and their supporters, the Sadducees. . . . It is reasonable to assume that they clashed on the matter of the Oral Law, and there is reasonable evidence from Josephus and the rabbinic literature to support the assumption. Certainly the matter was worth disputing since the outcome of the argument established who had control over the redemptive media in Jewish Palestine [Isenberg, 1973:32].

Mark's charge that the halakah abrogates Mosaic law would not, therefore, have been unique to him, but the *reasons* for it were.

Jesus' attack is twofold. He begins with a citation (with only minor changes to the LXX) of Isaiah 29:13, which not only specifically repudiates "human precepts" but (in light of Jesus' teaching in 7:19) reiterates that the Pharisees are alienated from God's justice in their "hearts" (7:6f.; cf. 3:4). This carries Mark's use of the prophet in criticizing Jewish leaders to a new intensity, for the verse is part of an oracle in which Isaiah extends two themes upon which Mark has already drawn. The first is the blindness of the leaders (Is 29:9; cf. Mk 4:12). The second is their inability to "read" the word of God (Is 29:11f.; cf. Mk. 2:25; 12:10,26). Mark drives home his charge by repeatedly stating the antithesis between scripture and oral tradition:

1. 7:8: "You let go of the command of God (*tēn entolēn tou theou*) and hold fast to human traditions (*tēn paradosin tōn anthrōpōn*)."
2. 7:9: "Skillfully you negate the command of God in order to observe your tradition."
3. 7:10f.: "Moses said . . . but you say. . . ."

The second part of the attack lies in the example chosen by Jesus to illustrate his objection, which seems at first tangential, but serves a deliberate purpose (7:10–13). The *korban* vow concerned a practice of consecrating or "willing" one's property and resources to the temple. Once this vow was made, personal assets belonged to the temple treasury and, though still in the hands of the owner, could not be used (see Josephus, *War*, II,ix,4). But Jesus describes a situation in which the "vow" becomes a "curse": the traditional exercise of economic responsibility for one's parents according to the Torah (Ex 20:12; 21:17; Lv 20:9; Dt 5:16). The *korban* vow would preclude:

Not only support but all the other things a son might do for a father, e.g., help in the performance of religious duties, care in sickness, etc. Even commercial dealings are forbidden in such a case [Rengstorf, 1965:865].

Derrett comments:

The social aspect obviously lies at the roots of Jesus' comment. Ancient, like contemporary, oriental societies were built upon reciprocal bonds

between husband and wife, parent and child, brother and brother. . . .
The vow, impeding a claim by a dependent parent, rendered ineffective,
nullified *pro tanto*, the biblical obligation to maintain. "Honour" implies *inter alia* "maintain when he/she is indigent;" "curse" implies
"abuse," or any diminution of honour. The son has lost his balance, and
his vow, ostensibly religious, is unquestionably "abuse" of the parent
[1970:365f.].

Such financial ostracism and the resultant impoverishment of the elderly in
the community was in effect a nullification of the will of God. Mark's adden-
dum ("and many such things you practice," 7:13c) anticipates a later dispute
with the Pharisees, again over an issue of justice within the family system
(10:1ff.).

Again it has been objected that Mark unfairly represents the position of the
Pharisees on *korban*, a practice about which there is still a great deal of
historical unclarity. Some rabbinic sources indicate that the Pharisees in fact
may have sometimes released persons from binding vows in the case of conflict
of values, but this evidence dates from after the fall of the temple (and hence
the centralized financial institution). In any case, we are reminded again that
Mark's descriptions of his opponents are caricatures; fairness can hardly be
expected from a polemical narrative. But Mark has a specific ideological
purpose here.

The appeal to *korban* cements the link between Pharisees and scribes (7:1).
The temple treasury (which in some literature of this period is referred to as
korbanas) was to a significant degree dependent upon wills and vows for
revenue. Later in the story Jesus confronts this temple treasury (12:37-44), at
which time he lambastes the scribal class for hiding economic exploitation
behind public piety—with the elderly again as the victim. Thus, despite the fact
that the Pharisees actually differed with the scribal leaders on many points,
Mark insists that insofar as the former upholds the temple as the symbolic
center of Judaism, they are implicated with the latter in a political economy
that oppresses the poor. By insisting that the local Pharisees are merely an
extension of the long arm of the Jerusalem establishment, Mark undermines
their credibility to his Galilean audience.

The implied criticism of the scribal/clerical classes serves another purpose as
well, for it distances Mark from those who would have joined him in denouncing Pharisaic halakah, but for diametrically opposite reasons. The Sadducees,
for example, also took what Isenberg describes as a "strict constructionist"
approach to Torah, but did so in order to prevent other groups from sharing
their control over this redemptive medium (1973:34). That is, Mark's Torah
"conservatism" envisioned overthrowing the clerical establishment; the
Sadducees sought to maintain their privileges within it.

By conflating the issues of table fellowship and (implicitly in his criticism of
korban) the political economy of the temple, Mark demonstrates his consciousness of the central ideological underpinnings of oppression in the sym-

bolic system. This story serves not only to legitimize the community's practice of integration with gentiles, who otherwise would have been excluded by the rules of ritual purity, but also serves to persuade poorer Jews that the very purity system that purports to "protect" their ethnic/national identity is the system that exploits them. Against the dominant group boundaries Mark offers a countervision in which a new, morally defined community upholds the radical demands of scriptural tradition, which condemns profiteering and defends the welfare of the weakest members of society.

7D. JESUS' SYMBOLICS DECIPHERED: THE FIRST EPILOGUE
(8:10-21)

We come finally to the three brief exchanges constituting the epilogue with which Mark closes the first half of his Gospel. After completing the gentile cycle with the feeding of four thousand hungry persons in the wilderness (8:1-10), Jesus and his disciples depart for the final boat sequence. In the final conversation about "bread" Mark returns to deepening the lack of comprehension on the part of the disciples regarding the new order Jesus has been forging. The purpose of the epilogue is to give what Fowler calls "reliable commentary," offering the disciple/reader hermeneutical keys to the meaning of the preceding narrative of Jesus' symbolic action.

i. No Heavenly Sign and Bad Leaven: Political Commentary

The last boat voyage takes place in two stages, the first of which is the trip to "Dalmanutha" (8:10). According to Mark's rhetorical signals, this is not a crossing to the "other side" (so Kelber). However, if Dalmanutha is to be identified with the western shore near Tiberias (which is by no means certain), the trip would represent a quick foray back into Jewish territory from the Decapolis, whose purpose would be one last confrontation with the Pharisees (so Malbon). In either case, most commentators regard 8:11f. as an arbitrary and abrupt intrusion; but I believe Mark has intentionally inserted it into the final boat narrative in order that it be taken as part of the interpretive epilogue. If so, what clue does it offer?

Mark emphasizes that the Pharisees, who have since 2:16 been portrayed as the primary Galilean antagonists of Jesus, are "testing" (*peirazontes*) Jesus (8:11). This is a crucial ideological indicator, for Mark began his narrative of Jesus' apocalyptic struggle against the powers with Satan's "testing" in the wilderness in the prologue (1:11). Significantly, it is only the Pharisees who "test" Jesus in the Gospel (again in 10:2 and with the Herodians in 12:15). This confirms the thesis that they represent a particular historical challenge to the Markan community.

The Pharisees demand a "sign from heaven" (8:11, *sēmeion apo tou ouranou*). An incensed Jesus ("sighing deeply") steadfastly refuses to provide such signs to "this generation" (8:12, *hē genea autē*). This disavowal of miraculous spectacles will become absolutely crucial for a proper understanding of the "heavenly" portent that *will* be given to "this generation" in 8:38 (below, 8, D,ii). The notion of signs has positive value for the other evangelists, especially John. Luke considers "signs and wonders" as proof of divine anointing some nine times in Acts, and both he and Matthew produce the Q tradition of the "sign of Jonah" (Mt 12:39; 16:4; Lk 11:29). For Mark, however, signs are sought only by unbelievers, and are an unreliable indicator of the meaning of events (see 13:4,22). The only unhypocritical appeal to "heaven" (12:25) is to confirm the earthly practice of justice (6:41; 7:34; 10:21; 11:30f.).

Belo rightly interprets Jesus' rejection of the Pharisees' request for "theological proof" as Mark's clear assertion that the sole significance of messianic ministry lies in its concrete, historical commitment to justice and compassion:

> the powerful practice of Jesus has not invoked heaven. . . . This fact enables us to read Jesus' refusal . . . you have signs enough in my practice here on *earth*, signs which even the Crowd has often read. . . . Read *these* signs, therefore; be readers, semiologists, of my narrative . . . there will be no more signs from *heaven*, because there are signs on *earth* [1981:147].

Mark inserts this exchange hard on the heels of the second wilderness feeding as if to say that the "sign" of the kingdom is the very terrestrial vision of a new order where all can "eat and be satisfied."

As if to reiterate the point, Mark follows this exchange with another dispute about "bread" (8:14f.). The warning about "leaven" has also been labeled by commentators an "intrusion" into the boat story, which has begun with Jesus' departure in the boat to the "other side" in 8:13. And again closer scrutiny reveals it to be an essential part of Mark's reliable commentary. The final bread discussion is introduced in what appears to be an awkward manner (the curious comment of 8:14), only to be interrupted by Jesus' double warning ("Look out! Beware!" 8:15). As already mentioned in the discussion of 4:24, the caution (*blepete*) functions in Mark to identify the political opponents of the kingdom (see 12:38; 13:6ff.). Thus the "leaven of the Pharisees and the leaven of Herod" represents the second clue to the political discourse of the narrative.

The Pharisee/Herodian coalition first appeared in 3:6, and will strike again in 12:13–17 (the tribute question, a test of political cooperation with Rome). The term "leaven" (only here in Mark) obviously appears in relation to the metaphor of the "loaves," a symbolic discourse Mark is setting up here. Mark is reminding the disciple/reader of the two main political forces in Galilee hostile to the kingdom project of reconciliation between Jew and gentile. On the one hand the Pharisaic party opposes integration on grounds of social boundary and purity, as we have just seen. On the other, the Herodian-sponsored program of hellenization offers a style of "integration" based on cultural imperialism and collaboration with Rome. Those who resist such a program are disposed of, as in the case of John the Baptist (6:14ff.). Either "leaven" will destroy the delicate social experiment of the "one loaf."

ii. Only One Loaf: Social Commentary

The discussion about bread (8:14,16–21) is the third and final clue to Markan symbolics in this section. Despite this, this passage is one of the most underappreciated passages in the Gospel, as Norman Beck's survey has shown (1981). In an attempt to "reclaim" its central significance, Beck correctly points out that the exegetical key to this passage is the distinction between the plural "loaves" (*artous*) and the singular "loaf" (*arton*); this is obscured by most translations, which use the one term "bread." Literally the text reads:

> They had forgotten to bring loaves, and had none except for one loaf with them in the boat. . . . And they were discussing with one another the fact that they had no loaves. And Jesus perceived this, and said to them, "Why do you discuss the fact that you have no loaves?" [8:14, 16–17a].

It is the inability of the disciples (and the reader!) to understand the difference between loaf and loaves that triggers the tirade Jesus now delivers.

In 8:17b–18 Jesus unequivocally attributes to the disciples the stubbornness warned of by Isaiah in the parables sermon (4:12). By now Mark has woven a complex fabric of cross-referencing with motifs of blindness, and so forth (see above, 5,D,i). But here the form of the condemnation ("heart/eyes/ears") is an unmistakable allusion to Moses' interrogation of his people in Deuteronomy 29:2–4:

> You have seen all that the Lord did before your eyes in the land of Egypt, to Pharaoh and to all his servants and to all his land, the great testings (LXX, *peirasmous*) which your eyes saw and the signs (LXX, *ta sēmeia*) and those great wonders; but to this day the Lord has not given you a heart to know (LXX, *kardian eidenai*) or eyes to see or ears to hear (LXX, *ophthalmous blepein kai ōta akouein*).

Significantly, the Deuteronomic theme of "remembrance" (Dt 32:7, LXX, *mnēsthēte*) also appears here in 8:19: "Do you not remember . . . ? (*ou mnēmoneuete*).

Just as Moses expressed exasperation that Israel would not believe despite having been sustained by Yahweh in the wilderness after being liberated from the pharaoh (Dt 29:5f.), so too Jesus is confronted with disciples who have "forgotten" the loaves and their meaning (8:14). He too refers the disciples/reader back to his great works of liberation and sustenance in the wilderness. As Kelber puts it, Jesus in 8:19f. "makes them repeat the symbolic numbers which should have tipped them off: twelve and seven" (1979:41). Beck sums up the symbolism involved:

> The number 5 (5 loaves and 5,000 men), the number 12 (12 baskets) and the Hebrew name for basket (*kophinos*) belong to the Jewish circle; the number 7 (7 loaves and 7 baskets), the number 4 (4,000 men or people),

and the Greek name for basket (*sphyris*) belong more specifically to the Greek. . . . One loaf in the boat is all that is needed! Separate bread (eucharistic?) is not needed for Jewish . . . and non-Jewish followers of Jesus [1981:52, 54].

Having thus revealed the final hermeneutical key to his discourse of boat trips and feedings, Mark turns to the disciple/reader and, as if to break the "spell" of 4:12, asks, "Do you understand *yet*?" (8:21). With this challenge, the first half of the Gospel comes to an end.

In the first epilogue the three crucial elements of this section of the Gospel come together in one last scene, and then disappear from the stage: sea, boat, and bread. What have the sea journeys to "the other side," the two cycles of healings, the attack upon exclusive table fellowship, and the feedings added up to? They have each played a role in Mark's construction of the new social order of the kingdom, in which the two alienated social factions are brought into one, indivisible humanity. This is not Hellenistic idealism; it is the solidarity of hungry and oppressed persons. The task of forging this new community is like a harrowing voyage across deadly waters; there is enough bread for the journey, but there is only one loaf. Do the disciples in Mark's story see this? They do not. And on this troubling note, Mark opens the second half of his Gospel—with a story about Jesus' restoration of sight to the blind (8:22–26)!

7E. WORLD-CONSTRUCTION: MARK'S SOCIO-LITERARY STRATEGY THROUGH THE FIRST HALF OF THE STORY

i. Discourse

Having arrived at the end of the first half of the story, we would do well to review Mark's overall narrative strategy. The story so far has been shaped around two dominant socio-literary trajectories. The "subversive" trajectory has been articulated in the *militant* aspects of Jesus' ministry in Galilee: exorcism, argument, and confrontation. The "constructive" trajectory has found expression in the *redemptive* and *affirmative* dimensions of the mission: the creation and maintenance of the discipleship community, the healings, journeys, and teaching. The distinction is somewhat artificial, for Mark weaves these two strands tightly together throughout. Still, we have seen that the first major narrative section (1:16–4:35) concentrates primarily on the subversive trajectory, the second (4:36–8:21) on the constructive.

Each trajectory has its related plot crisis—hence the double plot-line of the story. The subversive narrative sees the conflict between the stewards of the dominant social order and Jesus with his kingdom program. We already know (3:6) that this crisis involves a conspiracy against the life of Jesus, and this tension is implicitly deepened in the second section by the interlude describing John's fate at the hands of Herod. The plot crisis of the constructive narrative is the disciples' failure to comprehend Jesus' program. We are (rightly) beginning to suspect that this will lead to some form of betrayal. The former—political—crisis has been established virtually from the outset of the story, whereas the latter—community—crisis has been revealed to the reader only gradually, but with increasing urgency.

Accordingly, it is this second plot-complication that dominates the section we have just read. It is indicative of Mark's masterful use of irony that throughout most of the section the community *appears* to be achieving a deepening intimacy with its leader. The inner circle is privy to the resurrection miracle of Jairus's daughter; the community is twice rescued from danger on the sea by Jesus; it receives more instruction (7:17–23); and most importantly, its members are sent out alone on their first mission. Nevertheless, conflict grows steadily between Jesus and his followers, and by the close of the section, as we have just seen, it is acute. N. Petersen concludes, "They, who were recipients of the mystery of the kingdom of God that was concealed from others, proved to understand no more than the others" (1980a:217).

Mark narrates this conflict through a discourse that plays metaphorically with the realm of the three "perceptive senses": eyes, ears, and heart. Initially, in the first sermon, the crisis of incomprehension is related to the leadership of Israel (3:6, 4:11f.); however, by the end of the second section there has been a major shift:

Accusation	*Directed at*
3:5 hardness of heart	synagogue opponents
4:11f. everything in parables:	those "outside"
see but not perceive;	
hear but not understand;	
6:52 hardness of heart/	disciples
nonunderstanding	
8:17f. nonunderstanding/	disciples
eyes not seeing	
ears not hearing	
not remembering	

In Book II, this conflict will be articulated with increasing sharpness. In the discipleship catechism (8:22–10:45) misunderstanding of the way becomes antagonism and, finally, in the passion narrative (14:12–16:8), defection.

What is the social function of such a discourse? The ethnically defined social boundaries of the dominant order have been subverted and replaced with new, morally defined ones: "the will of God" (3:35), "the unpolluted heart" (7:20f.). This is analogous to the insiders/outsiders motif introduced in the parables sermon (above, 5,A,ii). Mark is keenly aware of the contradiction of revolutionary practice. On the one hand, a genuinely subversive movement presupposes a disciplined "vanguard," or community of faith; on the other, the "revolution is always betrayed by her children." Mark knows how easily messianic "insiders" can become outsiders—and how "outsiders" can become scapegoats for the failures of insiders. To put it in modern terms, revolution too often becomes reaction, and the "new dualisms" (whether defined by class struggle and socialist internationalism or the "body of Christ" and denominational membership) too readily become justification for the recycling of old forms of human oppression. The practice of domination is always legitimated by the existence of an "enemy." Mark's discourse therefore forbids objectifying the "enemy" outside oneself: the enemy is blindness/deafness itself. So does he guard against a new elitism.

It is also necessary to say something about the role of the reader in Mark's discursive strategy. Since the very beginning of the story, Mark has given us the power of knowledge that the characters do not have: what we might call a "privileged" reading-context. But Q. Quesnell has described how the boat conversation at the close of the first half of the Gospel abruptly overturns this ostensible advantage:

> The reader is suddenly forced to ask himself whether he has really understood after all. . . . He suddenly feels his superiority to the ignorant first disciples slipping away. The smiling self-confidence engendered in him by the earlier preparatory development makes him all the more exposed and vulnerable to the particularly deep-cutting piece of Christian parenesis now directed at him. He must frankly ask himself whether he is not himself still caught in the same ignorance as were the first disciples [1969:171f.].

Jesus' interrogation of his disciples is in fact Mark's challenge to the reader. It functions to suddenly yank us directly into the story. We are being warned: to proceed with the story without having understood Jesus' symbolics is to remain captive ourselves to the "blindness" narrative.

At this point in the story, the object of the disciples/reader's incomprehension is the "loaves." When Mark has us "remember" the two feeding stories, he is reminding us of the two major ideological themes of his discourse in this section. The first, articulated in the discourse of parallel cycles and boat voyages across the sea, concerns the social project of integrating gentile and Jew. In the gentile cycle we observe a discourse of dramatic progression:

1. intention: sea-crossing as reconciliation ("loaves," 6:52);
2. conflict: objections to common "table" on the basis of the institutions of purity/kosher (7:1ff.);
3. ideological resolution: Jesus' new teaching (7:14ff.);
4. conflict: collective honor of Jews (7:24ff.);
5. ideological resolution: there is enough on the "table" (7:28);
6. intention realized: feeding of gentiles (8:1ff.).

Not only does this masterful fiction warrant the social experiment of integration, but it also realistically addresses the many barriers to this project: the sociocultural obstacles (the purity code and collective honor of the Jews), the key political opponents (the Pharisees and the Galilean ruling class), and not least the community's own resistance (unbelief when beset by storms on the sea).

The second theme is economic justice. Fowler is one of the few commentators to have noticed the "frequency with which references to food and eating are to be found in the gospel . . . eating, drinking, cups, loaves, foods, feasts, banquets, fasting, hunger, and leaven" (1981:132). There are at least nine references to "bread" and eating in the first half of the Gospel excluding the wilderness feedings. In the second half of the story this vocabulary disappears, with the exception of 11:14 and the story of the last supper (14:12–22). Let us turn to examine how this socio-economic discourse illuminates Mark's social situation.

ii. Signification

Fowler is correct in pointing out the metaphorical nature of many of Mark's meal references, as in the two proleptic indicators of the feedings (5:43; 7:28). Still, the persistence with which food/eating motifs shape Mark's semantic universe indicate that economic issues are integral to his ideological purpose in the Gospel. The world Mark portrays is one in which crowds often prevent the community from eating (3:20; 6:31), crowds that are themselves hungry (6:36; 8:2). The disciples are expected to respond to this reality (6:37), for Jesus recognizes that there must be sustenance "on the way" (8:3).

Mark offers three characteristics of a discipleship lifestyle in his narrative. The first is voluntary austerity:

1. the asceticism of John (1:6; sharply contrasted with the opulence of his executors in 6:21ff.),
2. the call to forego the economic security of the extended family (1:16ff.);
3. the missionaries' dependence upon hospitality (6:8f.).

The second is solidarity with the outcast, which centers around table fellowship (2:16f.; 7:2–5). The third is the politics of symbolic direct action used to protest against socio-economic inequities (2:26).

If the first sermon described the kingdom in terms of an eschatological harvest for impoverished sharecroppers, the wilderness feedings reenact this vision in terms of the Old Testament story of Yahweh's sustenance of the people in abundance. But unlike Malbon, I see more than intertextual symbolics here. In the feedings, "market" economics (6:36) are repudiated in favor of a practice of sharing available resources so that everyone has enough. This, together with Mark's negative portrayal of the city, correlates to the de facto socio-economic tensions in Mark's Galilee. The market was controlled by urban interests, and it was the rural sectors that suffered from the unjust production systems. That the community's own concrete economic practice will be patterned on the wilderness model of "multiplication through sharing" is made explicit later in 10:29f. There, it is contrasted with the nondiscipleship of the rich man, a class bias confirmed in the double healing of the two Jewish "daughters" (5:21ff.).

Mark was not unaware that hunger among masses was the result of structures of power and privilege. Hence he links purity issues to the political economy of the temple-based order in the *korban* debate (7:8–13). Jesus' refusal (8:3) to allow the gentile masses to be sent away "fasting" reiterates Mark's suspicion of religious asceticism (2:18ff.). He will repeatedly criticize the piety of the affluent when others hunger (10:17–22; 12:34,38ff.). Such attentiveness to concrete problems of deprivation adds weight to the argument that the Gospel was produced in an environment where the socio-economic disenfranchisement of the common people was a keenly felt problem. The narrative world of the text reflects a strong bias toward the rural poor, and a commitment to a redistribution of wealth.

In addition to economic justice Mark envisions social reconciliation. This includes not only a practice of inclusivity that overturns class and gender oppression within the Jewish social formation, but also the integration of Jew and gentile. The construction of an ecumenical community is narrated in two ways: boat journeys and parallel wilderness feedings. Although theologians love to read "eucharistic" meaning into the feedings, it is not legitimate to control the interpretation of all the eating references in Book I by a single episode in Book II. Instead, the last supper (below, 12,B,iii) must itself be understood in light of the fact that meal-sharing is for Mark a test of social reconciliation. Recent work by Theissen in the eucharistic ideology of the Apostle Paul has aided the recovery of these socio-economic dimensions of the ritual communal meal so central to primitive Christianity (1982:145ff.).

That the task of reconciliation was not only arduous but well-nigh inconceivable is articulated by the dangerous sea voyages, in which the disciples struggle to reach the "other side" against the cosmic elements. It was G. Bornkamm, in his classic study of the sea miracles in Matthew's Gospel (1963:55ff.), who first suggested that the boat in these stories was meant to represent the church itself (the ship on the sea was an ecclesial symbol in primitive Christianity, and is preserved today in the World Council of Churches logo). Modern readers cannot readily appreciate the boldness of the social proposition of integration. The enmity between Jew and gentile, which manifested itself at every level of politics and culture, was considered in Roman antiquity to be the "prototype of all human hostility" (D. Smith, 1973:35). It is part of the tragedy of modern theology that the social dimensions of the primitive Christian struggle to reconcile Jew and gentile has been so thoroughly suppressed—despite the fact that it is central to the writings of Paul and his disciples (see Rader, 1978; Barth, 1959).

Mark (like Paul) had to fashion new metaphors to articulate this kingdom ideology, and once again shows the strength of his realistic narrative. The wilderness feedings and boat journeys preserve the mundaneness of Markan symbolics and the verisimilitude of his fictions. By making the sea his narrative center of gravity in the first half of the story, Mark was indeed reflecting the fact that the lake in fact lay at the heart of life in eastern Galilee. It determined the attractive climate of the region, enabling agriculture, tourism, and urban growth around its shores, as well as the all-important fishing industry; its fierce and sudden storms were also well known. His Palestinian audience was all too familiar with the omnipresence of dispossessed crowds, and above all the structures of segregation between Jew and gentile. In constructing his alternative order, Mark offers not fantasy but transformed reality. The kingdom was the laborious project to be undertaken by human disciples in the real world.

Finally a word must be said about the "leaven" of the Pharisees and Herod, for although this section gives less attention to political conflict, it is never far off in the background. The Pharisees have emerged as the primary mouthpiece of Jewish officialdom in criticizing Jesus' practice; there is every probability that this was in fact the case for Galilean Christians. Similarly, the Herodian nobility, with its base in the royal court at Tiberias, also had reason to be resented and feared by Mark's community. Though Jesus had been murdered in Jerusalem, John was the local martyr; the juxtaposing of his story with the Galilean missionary effort of the disciples strongly suggests that martyrdom was a continuing reality for Markan Christians. However caricatured these antagonists may appear in the Gospel, it is certain that they did historically represent the paramount opposition to any attempt to build a community in Galilee committed to integration and the preaching of repentance to the powerful.

In the first half of his Gospel, Mark has firmly established the subversive and constructive aspects of his narrative, and sketched a social, political, and economic portrait of kingdom practice. In the next two sections of the story he sets about intensifying these two trajectories, as he begins to build toward his narrative climax. When the disciples arrive at Bethsaida in 8:22, the site of the boat is abandoned, and the second half of the story begins with a symbolic action of hope: the healing of a blind man. The community then embarks upon the boldest and most dangerous journey of all: the long march with Jesus to Jerusalem.

NOTE

1. Much of our uncertainty over the de facto practice of the Pharisees during Mark's era lies in the fact that the rabbinic traditions, both the halakah (legal rulings) and the haggadah (homilies on scriptural texts), were collected in the Mishnah at the end of the second century C.E. These traditions date back to 200 B.C.E, but because they are not dated, it is hard to tell which ones predate the fall of the temple. The same is true for the Tosephta, a still later compilation including even earlier traditions. Two other sources, the Talmuds, are yet later: the Palestinian Talmud ca. 400 C.E., the Babylonian Talmud ca. 550 C.E.

Part Three

Reading the Second Half of Mark

CHAPTER EIGHT

Midpoint of the Story:
The "Second" Prologue and Call
to Discipleship (Mark 8:22-9:30)

> But Moses said to Yahweh, "Who am I that I should go to Pharaoh, and
> bring the children of Israel out of Egypt?" Yahweh said, "I will be with
> you; and this shall be the sign for you . . . you shall serve me upon this
> mountain." Then Moses said, "If I come to the people of Israel and . . .
> they ask me, 'What is God's name?,' what shall I say to them?" Yahweh
> said, "I am who I am."
>
> —Exodus 3:9-14

We have arrived at the midpoint of the story. Once again, Mark's Jesus turns
to challenge the disciples/reader. "Who do you say that I am?" (8:29a). This
question is the fulcrum upon which the gospel narrative balances. Not only
that: upon our answer hangs the character of Christianity in the world. Do we
know who it is we are following, and what he is about? Mark began the story by
telling us who Jesus is (1:1); the reader, like the Christian church, "knows the
right answer" to this question. Thus we are shocked when Peter's answer,
which is "correct," is rejected by Jesus! With this "confessional crisis" Mark
opens the second half of his Gospel.

This is the "second prologue." Like the first prologue, it begins "on the way"
(8:27, cf. 1:2). The former articulated the "way through the wilderness"; now
this is redefined as "the way to Jerusalem." Thus this new journey is punctuated by a series of "portents" of Jesus' political fate at the hands of the
Jewish and Roman authorities. It is also the "way of the cross," a specific kind
of political and community practice that takes the disciples/reader into the
deepest paradoxes of power. We are told that we cannot save our lives by
preserving them, nor lose them by giving them up; that to be "last" is to be
"first," and to be "least" is to be "great."

This second prologue is knitted into the second "construction" cycle, a catechism of dialogue and instruction concerning nonviolence as a way of life. Yet as this way becomes clearer, the disciples' resistance to it increases, which Mark portrays with almost cartoonlike exaggeration. This is the drama of blindness and vision, deafness and hearing; in it we are compelled, like the man with the demon-ridden son, to come to terms with our belief and our unbelief (9:24).

8A. THE NARRATIVE CHARACTER OF THE DISCIPLESHIP CATECHISM

i. Structure

I should begin by justifying my choice of the term "second prologue." The rough symmetry between the opening of the story and this new introduction is demonstrated in the following list of common themes:

Theme	First Prologue	Second Prologue
The "way"	1:2f.	8:27
John as Elijah	1:6	9:11–13
Exodus symbolics	1:2,13	9:2
Divine voice	1:11	9:7
Call to discipleship	1:16–20	8:34–36
Peter, James and John	1:16,19	9:2
Struggle with Satan	1:12f.	8:33

The second prologue regenerates the narrative and the war of myths with a second call to discipleship, a second "apocalyptic moment" in which the new journey of Jesus receives divine confirmation, and another episode of direct confrontation with Satan.

The overall construction of 8:22–10:52 is widely agreed upon, being one of the very first discoveries of redaction criticism (Schweizer, 1978). The section is framed by stories of blind men receiving sight (8:22–26; 10:46–52). Peter's "confession" in Caesarea-Philippi (8:27–30) introduces a triple cycle. Each cycle consists of Jesus' prediction of his own political fate (portents), the disciples' inability to recognize the implications of the way ("blindness"), and Jesus' rejoining instructions concerning the practice of nonviolence and servanthood, each stated in the form of a paradox. The cycles also plot a journey in three stages. The section is outlined in Table 3. The struggle launched by Peter's answer to Jesus' question—the struggle over the meaning of messianic politics—is deepened in each of these cycles.

The first cycle is composed in fundamental relationship to the confessional crisis; it stands at the structural center of the Gospel. Peter's "confession" is "corrected" by the first portent, which is then followed by the second call to discipleship. The way of the cross is then underscored by the two dramatic-symbolic actions that follow. The transfiguration is the second of the Gospel's three "apocalyptic moments," and like the baptism is a legitimating device meant to resituate the story around the new theme. Here the heavenly voice again invades the narrative to lend divine credibility to the apparently incredible proposition that the only way to save one's life is to lose it. After a brief "interpretive sequel" to the transfiguration, in which its meaning is pondered, comes the second symbolic episode. The healing of the deaf-mute boy, Jesus' final exorcism, functions as a symbolic reproduction and resolution of the disciples' struggle to believe. In this present chapter I examine the text through the conclusion of this first cycle.

Table 3
Mark 8:22–10:52

1. Healing of the blind: first stage, 8:22–26
2. Peter's "confession," 8:27–30
3. Triple cycle:

Site	portents	"blindness"	teaching	paradox
Caesarea- Philippi	8:31	8:32f.	8:34–37	save life/ lose life
Galilee to Judea	9:31	9:33f.	9:35ff.	first/last
on the way to Jerusalem	10:32–34	10:35–39	10:40–45	great/least

4. Healing of the blind: second stage, 10:46-52

The second and third cycles, which will be examined in chapter 9, replace dramatic action with a series of teaching episodes dealing with issues of group boundary and social power within the community of faith. The lengthy teaching section in the second cycle exhibits clear rhetorical affinities with other catechetical/parenetic traditions in early Christian literature. The third cycle is the briefest, and addresses the problem of leadership and political power in the new order. Jesus' invitation to his followers to stand in solidarity with his "baptism" and "cup" reiterate the "second call to discipleship." They also represent midway narrative coordinates, designed to draw together the beginning (John's baptism) and end (the cup of suffering, 14:23,36) of the story of Jesus' ministry.

ii. Story

The second half of the Gospel abruptly abandons the narrative sites of sea, boat, and wilderness. The journey across the waters now becomes a journey from the margins of Palestine to its center. Beginning in the extreme north of Mark's "world" (Caesarea-Philippi), Jesus slowly winds his way south, back down through Galilee (making one last stop at the former narrative center of Capernaum, 9:33), and on into Judea (10:1). It is not until the third cycle, however, that Mark reveals to us the destination of this new way: Jerusalem (10:32). The section closes in narrative movement toward the great city, "as they were leaving Jericho" (10:45).

This section develops the double plot complication as it was established in the first half of the story. Actual face-to-face conflict between Jesus and the authorities, which since the ideological showdown in 3:22ff. has been relatively sporadic (7:1ff.; 8:11ff.), remains marginal in this section (Jesus' opponents appear only twice, 9:14; 10:2). But the conspiracy to murder Jesus, held in narrative suspension since 3:6, resurfaces in Jesus' three portents of his execution at their hands (8:31; 9:11; 10:33). Mark is rebuilding this plot tension in preparation for the showdown in Jerusalem.

It is the conflict between Jesus and his own community that receives the most direct development in this section. The disciples are almost always at center stage, and the problem of their incomprehension is intensified by ever more blatant incidences of misunderstanding:

1. 8:31–33 Peter refuses to accept Jesus' political fate;
2. 9:5–7 Peter misinterprets the transfiguration vision;
3. 9:33ff. the disciples discuss who is greatest among them;
4. 10:35ff. James and John petition Jesus for highest ranks.

Mark is caricaturing the disciples to the point of hyperbole; the leader Peter, the inner circle, and the whole community are all implicated. Yet, as I will point out momentarily, embedded in this embarrassing and depressing narrative is an opposing discourse of healings, which offer unmistakable signs of hope that the disciples' minds and hearts can be opened.

The confessional crisis brings into the foreground a third plot crisis, previously only implicit: the struggle over Jesus' identity. Peter identifies Jesus as "Messiah," but each of Jesus' three "death portents" argue that *this* Messiah—whom Mark renames the "Human One"—is not what the audience expects. Instead of coming to fight alongside the traditional political leadership to reestablish the *ancien régime* of David over against the Romans, the Human One will actually be murdered by a political coalition of Jewish and Roman authority. The *confessional* crisis ("Who do you say I am?") in other words is straightaway eclipsed by a crisis of *political practice* (What is genuinely revolutionary leadership?).

8B. A NEW SYMBOLIC DISCOURSE:
JESUS HEALS THE DEAF AND BLIND (8:22–26)

i. *The Healings as a Counter-Discourse of Hope*

By the end of the first half of the story we were compelled to conclude that the disciples, because of their lack of comprehension, had been demoted to a status previously reserved for "outsiders" and opponents of Jesus. With the reproach of 8:18, the blindness/deafness theme had captured center stage. I contended that this was a crisis not only of plot but also of reading: Are we also blind? The confessional debacle will further undermine our readerly confidence: the "correct" answer is repudiated. The story is beginning to seem locked in a downward spiral of contradiction and tragedy.

Against this discourse of incomprehension stands a counter-discourse, represented by four episodes in which Jesus heals blind or deaf persons:

healing of deaf and dumb man, 7:31–37
healing of blind man, 8:22–26
exorcism of deaf and dumb spirit, 9:14–29
healing of blind man, 10:45–52

This series, the final four healing episodes in Mark's Gospel, also narratively bridges the first and second half of the story. An unmistakable counterpoint of hope, this discourse culminates in the healing of Bartimaeus—a discipleship story (10:46–52).

As well as being interrelated, each healing has a specific narrative function. The first (see above, 6,D,iii) represents a transition in Mark's discursive use of healing "fictions." It closes a series of four symbolic healings in the construction cycle, in which the healings articulated the ideology of social inclusion. It also opens the series of four in this catechism section, whose focus switches to the struggle within the community for faith. The two blind men function to frame our present section, acting as "entry" (see next section) and "exit" ports (below, 9,D,iv) to the catechism. The third healing I will show represents a kind of summary conspectus of all Jesus' previous healings (below, E,iii). In each case, I will argue that it is the disciples/readers who are the true subjects of these symbolic actions.

Still, the healings do not *formally* resolve the plot crisis of incomprehension—the discipleship narrative will yet collapse altogether. Rather, they function to encourage the reader to continue; they represent a discourse of hope even as the story-scape grows more ominous. As such, they prepare narrative space for the other new theme introduced in this section along with the portents: the promise of resurrection (8:31b; 9:9, 31b; 10:34c). This is stated symbolically (as in 5:41) in the "raising to life" of the demon-oppressed boy who was "dead" in 9:26f. The disciples of course understand the meaning of neither cross (9:32) nor resurrection (9:10). Nevertheless, this counterdiscourse firmly extends hope to the reader: the blind and deaf *can* be healed. The "lifeline" of promise that keeps the narrative open when it threatens closure is an important aspect of Mark's literary strategy in the second half of the Gospel, and prepares us for its surprising and baffling conclusion.

At the ideological level, Mark adopts the theme of healing the deaf and blind from Isaiah, who uses it as a symbol of the messianic age. A sampling of this pervasive motif includes:

1. In that day, the deaf shall hear the words of a book, and out of their gloom and darkness the eyes of the blind shall see (Is 29:18);

2. Then the eyes of the blind shall be opened, and the ears of the deaf unstopped (35:5);

3. Bring forth those who are blind, yet have eyes; who are deaf, yet have ears! (43:8).

Thus this "fiction" also functions intertextually to confirm that the new order has dawned.

ii. Eyes That See; First Stage: Bethsaida

Immediately after Jesus and the disciples leave the narrative site of the sea and boat for the last time, they arrive at Bethsaida. This simple site change is the formal bridge between the first and second halves of the story. We remember that Bethsaida was the place toward which the community embarked on the second major sea journey (6:45). This trip had ended with Mark's first indictment of the disciples' blindness (6:52). We should also recall that the voyage was unsuccessful; the community *never actually arrived* at Bethsaida (above, 6,C,ii). That "journey" is now resolved: the "blind" community finally arrives at Bethsaida, where blindness is healed.

The ambiguity in the setting of this healing episode was pointed out by Bultmann (1963:64f.). On the one hand, the community arrives at Bethsaida; on the other hand, Mark says that Jesus led the blind man "outside the village" (8:23, *kōmē*). The problem is that Bethsaida should have been considered not a *kōmē* but a *polis*. Formerly a fishing village at the mouth of the Jordan (Taylor, 1963:328), it had been rebuilt and upgraded into a Hellenistic city renamed Bethsaida Julius by Herod the Great (see Josephus, *Ant.,* XVIII,ii,1). The confusion is removed if we remember Mark's ideological antipathy toward urban Hellenism. There are not two places being referred to here in this story (so Taylor, 1963:370). Bethsaida as a point of *arrival* is necessary for reasons of narrative analepsis, as just mentioned. Jesus takes the man *out* to heal him because of Mark's "narrative avoidance" of the city (see above, 4,B,iv). And Bethsaida is called a *village* because Mark refuses to recognize its new Hellenistic identity.

The Bethsaida healing echoes the cure of the deaf-mute in 7:31–37, the first of this series, through two common dramatic elements: the private setting, and Jesus' use of saliva on his fingers. As that story focused upon "hearing" ("he even makes the deaf hear!" 7:37), this centers around "seeing":

Jesus: Do you see anything?

Man: I see persons that look like trees walking (8:23f.).

The verb *blepein* was used four times by Mark in the first half of the story as warnings to the disciples about perception (4:12,24; 8:15,18), and will continue to be so used in the second half (12:38; 13:5,9,23,33). The "fuzzy vision" here is a symbol of "eyes that do not see."

When compared proleptically to its twin, the Bartimaeus episode (10:46ff.), we see that this healing represents a kind of "first stage" of Jesus' project of eradicating blindness. Jesus' healing touch is only partially successful, and the man requires a second in order to "see plainly" (8:25). E. S. Johnson has correctly related this ambiguity to the following confessional struggle; the disciples' blindness "will be turned to sight when they understand Jesus' *logos* about the meaning of Christian discipleship and his teaching about his own suffering, death and resurrection" (1978b:383). Peter's identification of Jesus may be in one sense "correct," but he does not "see" its meaning clearly; hence there is at Bethsaida no discipleship motif involved. That will come at the end of the catechism section, with the decisive—not tentative—healing of Bartimaeus the blind beggar. Still, though tentative, the narrative signal is one of encouragement to the reader. If the final boat conversation was a "red light" to the reader, a warning against reading "blindly," the healing in Bethsaida is a "green light" to continue in the quest for "understanding" (8:21).

8C. THE CONFESSIONAL CRISIS (8:27–33)

i. "Who Do You Say I Am?"

The community's journey now takes them from Bethsaida deeper into the territory of the tetrarchy of Philip (8:27). They arrive in the district of Caesarea-Philippi, a major Hellenistic city which, according to Sherwin-White, "controlled an extensive territory and even had the privilege of coining money" (1963:131):

[It was] so named to distinguish it from Caesarea, the seat of Roman government on the coast. . . . The town in ancient times was called Paneas, so named from a grotto sacred to Pan. Near the grotto Herod the Great had built a temple in honour of Augustus. Centuries earlier the place was associated with the worship of the Baalim. The city was rebuilt by Herod Philip and named by him Caesarea [Taylor, 1963:375].

It is here in this "alienated" narrative site—the far north of what could still be considered Palestine, in a region that reflected the Herodian sell-out to Hellenism—that the political narrative proper commences.

Against this site Mark reintroduces the true narrative site for discipleship: "on the way." This is the way that Isaiah through John announced in the wilderness; the kingdom lies *on*, not *beside* it (4:4,15; cf. 10:46). The disciples must take no sustenance for this way (6:8), for Jesus will sustain them upon it (8:3). In this section this metaphor figures centrally, occurring near the beginning of each of the three cycles (8:27; 9:33f.; 10:32). It is also the site of the section's two contrasting call stories: the nondiscipleship of the rich man (10:17) and the discipleship of the blind beggar (10:52). And it will shortly be revealed as the way that leads to Jerusalem (11:8).

The action begins with Jesus again suddenly turning and interrogating his disciples, a Markan device, as in the boat scene we have just left, by which he addresses us directly. Both questions have to do with how Jesus is perceived;

Mark is addressing the question both to the narrative ("Who do people say that I am?" 8:27b), and to the reader ("But who do you say that I am?" 8:29a). This query reintroduces the subplot concerning the crisis of Jesus' identity, which has been lingering in the doubt of his disciples (4:41) and his opponents (6:3). It also, like the Isaiah quote in the first prologue (1:2), reaches back to the "old story" of the Hebrew scriptures to reanchor the second half of the Gospel.

Though not cited directly, the "Who am I?" is clearly an allusion to the great dialogue between the founding prophet Moses and Yahweh at the burning bush (Ex 3). Why is this story invoked here? Certainly there could be an implied analogy: Jesus is ready to begin his long march to Jerusalem to confront the powers, as Moses was summoned to Egypt to liberate the people from the pharaoh. Mark's introduction of Moses into the narrative shortly (9:7) would seem to confirm the allusion. But if this is the case, Mark is again employing intertextuality with a bold twist. On one level, we might see Jesus' question as an echo of Moses' uncertainty, indeed his protest: "Who am I, that I should go to Pharaoh and bring the children of Israel out of Egypt?" (Ex 3:11). More likely, however, given Jesus' subsequent self-witness in 14:62, it is meant to render the great self-revelation of Yahweh ("I am," Ex 3:14) into a question: "Who am I?" This represents the very heart of Markan discourse-as-challenge.

The disciples' response to the first question is almost exactly parallel to Mark's editorial report back in 6:14f. (above, 7,B,ii), which introduces his interlude concerning the death of John the Baptist at the hands of Herod:

Mark's report	*Disciples' report*
1. they were saying that John the Baptist had risen from the dead . . .	John the Baptist,
2. but others said that it is Elijah;	and others Elijah,
3. and others said a prophet like any prophet;	and others one of the prophets.

Will the disciples draw the same conclusion as Herod: that Jesus is John *redivivus*? No, though Jesus will soon clarify that relationship (9:12f.). Peter's answer is far more momentous: it introduces into the story world for the first time the politically loaded term "Messiah" (*Christos*). Jesus is not simply a great prophet; he is a royal figure who will restore the political fortunes of Israel. The revolution, Peter is saying, is at hand.

ii. The First Portent

The reader (who knows the term from 1:1) approves of Peter's remarkable identification; not bad for one who is "blind"! But to our chagrin, Peter is immediately silenced by Jesus. Mark uses the same strong command (*epetimē-sen*) with which Jesus earlier silenced the demons (1:25; 3:12; and the wind, 4:39), preparing us for the somber accusation of 8:33. Then, as a direct repudiation of Peter's triumphalistic confession, he introduces the first of Jesus' three portents concerning his political fate. With the phrase "Then he began to teach them that it was necessary" (8:31), the entire story is set veering off in a new direction: the long march toward Jerusalem has begun.

This portent is carefully drawn from a semantic field that Mark's audience would clearly have identified as apocalyptic (see Kee, 1977:64ff., 129ff.). First, Jesus insists that his suffering is "necessary" (*deï*). According to Bennett:

> It is crucial to understand that this sort of deterministic statement is not made out of a generally fatalistic belief or hope. It belongs specifically to apocalypticism. . . . The theological emphasis of this assertion is to strengthen the faithful in times of frightful suffering. This is the way *deï* is used in Mark 13:7 and also in Revelation. . . . The reader is to understand that the sufferings of Jesus were a crucial part of the eschatological drama. So also were the sufferings of John before him and, as chap. 13 should make clear, so are the times of persecution and hardship through which Mark's community was passing [1975a:128f.].

Mark will tell us that it was "necessary" for John/Elijah (9:12f.) to challenge the highest powers and be executed by them; so too with Jesus, for that is the "script" Yahweh has given to the servant/prophets, as Mark will make clear through his parable of the tenants (12:1ff.).

Secondly, Jesus drops Peter's Messiah title and replaces it with "Human One." Mark has already established within his own story that the Human One is someone who challenges the authority of the scribes (2:10) and Pharisees (2:28). I mentioned at that time that this apocalyptic persona is taken from Daniel:

> I saw in the night visions: behold, with the clouds of heaven there came one like a Human One; and he came to the Ancient of Days and was presented before him. And to him was given dominion and glory and kingdoms, that all peoples, nations, and languages should serve him [Dn 7:13f.].

This figure, who also appears in the later apocalyptic tract of 4 Ezra (Kee, 1977:129), represents true "human" government as opposed to the brutality of the "beasts" in the visions. Mark is invoking Daniel, written under the pogroms of Antiochus Epiphanes IV two centuries earlier, as a manifesto of Jewish political resistance to imperial oppression by Hellenistic rulers. The "courtroom myth" of Daniel's Human One will figure decisively in Jesus' second call to discipleship (below, D,ii).

Thirdly, Jesus predicts his condemnation and execution at the hands of a new political coalition. As is his pattern (cf. 2:16a; 3:6), Mark introduces new opponents (the elders and high priests) by linking them with already established ones (scribes). This coalition, in Mark's story world, will represent the Jerusalem authority structure, which does in fact engineer Jesus' murder (10:33; 11:18,28; 14:1,15,43; 15:1,31). The word used for their "rejection" (*apodokimasthēnai*) denotes something "thrown out after a test" by an official court.

Mark will return to it when he cites Psalm 118:22, again in the context of Jesus' criticism of the Jerusalem establishment (Mk 12:10).

Each of these elements helps establish a new apocalyptic landscape to the story: the war of myths will now be played out in the docks of the powers. Why is this "necessary"? Is Mark betraying a "theological discourse of predestination," as Belo complains (1981:156f.)? No; but he is challenging the accepted bounds of political discourse in the war of myths. According to the understanding of Peter, "Messiah" *necessarily* means royal triumph and the restoration of Israel's collective honor. Against this, Jesus argues that "Human One" *necessarily* means suffering. This is so because, as the advocate of true justice, the Human One as critic of the debt code and the Sabbath *necessarily* comes into conflict with the "elders and chief priests and scribes" (8:31). In other words, this is not the discourse of fate or fatalism, but of political *inevitability*. It is in this sense that Jesus addresses his political vocation "openly" (8:32a), *parrēsia*, used only here in Mark; meaning frankly or boldly). Peter's fantasies of power must be censured by clear-eyed realism.

iii. The Triple Rebuke and Jesus' "Counter-Confession"

As if to prove Jesus' point about the predictability of opposition to his way, Mark has Peter harshly rebuke Jesus. But this only earns Peter (as representative of the whole community: "and turning and seeing his disciples, Jesus rebuked him," 8:33a) even sterner silencing. Note the dialectical interplay of this verbal struggle:

 Peter: Jesus is Messiah
 Jesus silences Peter (8:30)
 Jesus: the Human One must suffer (8:31)
 Peter silences Jesus (8:32)
 Jesus silences Peter (8:33)
 Jesus: Peter is Satan

The series begins with Peter's dramatic confession, but by the end this has been eclipsed by Jesus' still more remarkable double counter-confession: he is not "Messiah" but "Human One," and Peter is the mouthpiece of Satan. This shocking reference brings to mind the polarization in Jesus' war of words with the scribes in 3:22ff., and reminds us of the essential war of myths, begun with Satan in the wilderness (1:13). Such a discourse obviously attests to a fierce contest raging over messianic ideology in and around Mark's community.

This drama also recalls Jesus' interpretation of the parable of the sower:

The sower sows the word. And these are the ones beside the way where the word is sown; when they hear, Satan immediately comes and takes away the word sown in them [4:14f.].

We saw (above, 5,B,i) that Jesus' interpretation of the sower parable was a device whereby Mark reflected upon three concrete obstacles to "the word."

We are now witnessing the enactment of the parable, for throughout the discipleship catechism, Mark will make allusions to each of the three obstacles. Jesus here has explained "the word" plainly to those on the way (8:32a), and Satan is challenging him.

The bitter exchange with Peter ends with a sharp opposition posited between divine and human authority, echoing the earlier conflict with Pharisaic ideology in 7:8f. The phrase "you are not on the side of God, but of men" is difficult to translate. The verb *phroneis* (occurring only here in Mark, but more than twenty times in Paul's writings) must be understood in terms of making a commitment or holding a conviction. The radical dualism implies that there is no middle ground—a theme indigenous to the political perspective of apocalyptic. This verse, N. Petersen suggests, neatly expresses the two possible "points of view" for reading the narrative, only one of which is "reliable" (1980b:160f.). Mark is serving us notice that we have arrived at the heart of the ideological conflict.

8D. THE TRUE SITE OF CONFESSION: THE COURTROOM AND THE CROSS (8:34–9:1)

i. The Second Call to Discipleship: "Life/Death"

Jesus now proceeds to teach not just openly, but inclusively, as indicated by the way Mark has him turn from Peter to the disciples (8:33a) and from the disciples to the crowd (8:34a). What comes next is no private instruction, but a public call to discipleship, involving three imperatives:

$$\left\{ \begin{array}{l} \text{deny yourself} \\ \text{take up your cross} \\ \text{follow me} \end{array} \right.$$

The second call to discipleship uses the same vocabulary as the first (e.g., "follow," *akoloutheitō*; "after me," *opisō*). And here Mark's subversive narrative bursts into the open.

There can be no equivocation concerning the political semantics of this invitation. The "cross" had only one connotation in the Roman empire: upon it dissidents were executed:

Crucifixion was and remained a political and military punishment. . . . Among the Romans it was inflicted above all on the lower classes, i.e., slaves, violent criminals, and the unruly elements in rebellious provinces, not least Judea. . . . These were primarily people who on the whole had no rights, in other words, groups whose development had to be suppressed by all possible means to safeguard law and order in the state [Hengel, 1978:86f.; see also H. Reudi-Weber, 1975].

Precisely because of this singularly political connotation, some (e.g., Brandon, 1967:57) have argued that Mark may have been borrowing a recruiting phrase from the Jewish insurgents, who were regularly crucified for their guerilla activities.

Whether or not that is the case, the turn of phrase could have no other meaning except as an invitation to share the consequences facing those who dared challenge the ultimate hegemony of imperial Rome:

> "Taking up the cross" was a specific, though not invariable, part of the Roman custom. The person condemned to crucifixion was ordered to carry his own cross to the place of death [Griffiths, 1971:360,62].

The cross was also a symbol of the shame of the convicted:

> The chief reason for its use was its allegedly supreme efficacy as a deterrent; it was, of course, carried out publicly. As a rule the crucified man was regarded as a criminal who was receiving just and necessary punishment. . . . By the public display of a naked victim at a prominent place—at a crossroads, in the theatre, on high ground, at the place of his crime—crucifixion represented his uttermost humiliation. . . . With Deuteronomy 21:23 in the background, the Jew in particular was very aware of this [Hengel, 1978:87f.].

Mark's first readers could in no way have missed the terrible implications of such a saying—conveniently avoided by so many modern, privatizing interpretations!

The true antecedent to "taking up the cross" is "self-denial." Is this, as often argued by bourgeois exegesis, indication of a spiritualizing tendency already within the text, as if Mark defines the cross as personal asceticism? Emphatically not; as has been carefully argued by van Iersel, the semantic context is one of the courtroom:

> We are faced with an appeal to Christians who are taken to court in a situation of persecution similar to the one described in 13:9-13. They have to opt between either professing Jesus or denying him. The former requires self-denial, i.e., the risk of one's own life [1980:25f.].

To further illustrate the political meaning of "denying oneself," Jesus offers an apparent paradox (8:35): to "save" (*sōzō*) one's life is to "destroy" it (*apollumi*). The inverse is also true: life is saved by allowing it to be lost "for my sake and the gospel's." Interestingly, this latter phrase will appear again when Jesus speaks of political trials of Christians (13:9)!

Beardslee (1979:52ff.) has pointed out that almost identical rhetoric can be found in speeches by Hellenistic military officers on the eve of battle, anxious to exhort the faltering spirits of nervous soldiers. To prevent defection in combat the promise of immortality was given to those who might die nobly, whereas cowardly attempts to preserve life by fleeing would mean certain death at the hands of the enemy. But Mark is not goading the disciples to military heroism; he is introducing the central paradox of the Gospel. The threat to punish by death is the bottom line of the power of the state; fear of this threat keeps the dominant order intact. By resisting this fear and pursuing kingdom practice even at the cost of death, the disciple contributes to shattering the powers' reign of death in history. To concede the state's sovereignty in death is to refuse its authority in life (Mark will argue this again later in 12:27).

The rhetoric of 8:36f. switches from juridical to economic, in what seems to be a kind of pun about the temptation to "bail out" of the legal-confessional bind of a political trial:

1. To renounce Jesus in order to try to redeem one's life would be a "bad investment";
2. for even if it showed a "return" (*kerdēsai*, cf. Jas 4:13; Ti 1:11) of "the whole world," it would not represent a "profit" (*ōphelei*, cf. Mk 5:26; 7:11);
3. but rather a "dead loss" (*zēmiōthēnai*, always in the New Testament referring to economic privation, cf. 1 Cor 3:15; 2 Cor 7:9; Phil 3:8).

This is true "double-jeopardy"; fidelity to Jesus simply has no price. This ultimatum will be enacted in the discipleship narrative yet to come. There is Peter, who despite vowing "self-denial" (14:31), at the moment of truth will scurry to "save" his life (14:67ff.). There is the rich man, who will turn away from Jesus' call because of his wealth (10:21f.). There is Judas, who will betray Jesus for a small profit, arranged by the authorities (14:11). Everyone, it seems, has their price. Except Jesus. On Golgotha, he will be reviled by his enemies for his commitment to "save" others, but not his own life (15:32).

The argument of this second call to discipleship can be summarized as follows. Jesus has revealed that his messiahship means political confrontation with, not rehabilitation of, the imperial state. Those who wish to "come after him" will have to identify themselves with his subversive program. The stated risk is that the disciple will face the test of loyalty under interrogation by state authorities. If "self" is denied, the cross will be taken up, a metaphor for capital punishment on grounds of insurgency. Through *these* definitive choices (the grammatical force of the present durative imperative following two aorist imperatives in 8:34) the disciple will "follow Jesus."

ii. The Human One: Defendant or Prosecutor?

The much debated apocalyptic saying of 8:38–9:1 brings Jesus' homily to its conclusion by restating the choice in yet another way. To be "ashamed" of Jesus' "words" will bring reciprocal shame, as would be expected in Mediterranean honor culture (8:38; cf. Ps 25:1–3). The verb *epaischunomai* in the New Testament denotes identification with someone or something which, according to the prevailing social dynamics, would result in loss of status (cf. 2 Tm 1:8,12,16, where it specifically refers to the shame of Paul's imprisonment; see also 2 Tm 2:9–15). Given the juridical flavor already established in the previous verses, it is no surprise that Mark should again allude to Daniel's mythical courtroom scene. The "judgment" of the Human One is pitted against the "judgment" of earthly courts and the tyrants who enforce them. To be acquitted by one is to be found guilty in the other.

In 8:38 we have the first of three references in the second half of the Gospel to the epiphany or "advent" of the Human One (13:26; 14:62). Because of their longstanding failure to understand apocalyptic symbolics, most commentators have interpreted this "coming in glory" to refer to the tradition of the parousia. Few, however, can come up with a good reason *why* Mark should insert such a tradition at this point. But Mark is not attempting to solve the paradox of power he has just articulated by promising eschatological retribution. Such a view is merely a last-ditch attempt to resolve the scandal of the cross by an appeal to a hermeneutics of triumphalism: "Bear the cross and wear the crown!" Moreover, Mark has given us an unmistakable narrative clue to warn us against misconstruing these apocalyptic symbolics. Jesus addresses this warning ("whoever is ashamed") to "this unfaithful and sinful generation" (*genea*). But this is the very same "generation" to which Jesus earlier announced that no heavenly sign would be given (8:11f.; the connection is strengthened by the fact that both of these are solemn Amen sayings)! "This generation" will see "the kingdom come in power" (9:1) *and* receive no sign from heaven. This, then, rules out the possibility of the advent of the Human One as a heavenly spectacle. We shall discover that Mark identifies it instead with the event of the cross (below, 11,D,i; 13,B); *that* is what "some of those standing here" (9:1) will live to see.

The reference must be understood in terms of the apocalyptic courtroom myth here. In the Danielic vision, the "beast-rulers" wreak havoc upon the world, and in particular upon the people of God, until at last they are dragged before the divine court of the true judge (the "ancient of days," Dn 7:9), at which time true hegemony is handed over to the saints. Daniel 7, in typical apocalyptic fashion, recapitulates this drama three times:

elements of the vision	I	II	III
the struggle between beasts	vv. 2–8	19–20	23–24
persecution of the saints	—	21	25
judgment of beast	9–12	22a	26
dominion handed over to saints	14,18	22b	27

At the center of this vision is the "true court of justice," adjudicated by the Human One (Dn 7:13f.); through him, sovereignty passes to the people of God (Dn 7:18), leading J. Schaberg to conclude that the figure is really meant as a collective representation of Israel (1985).

In the story world of Mark, the "relations of power" in the myth appear to be reversed. It is the Human One in 8:31 who, in his *inevitable* conflict with the powers, becomes a defendant in their court, where he is tried, convicted, and sentenced to death. In this sense, Mark's Human One has more affinity with the persecuted saints of Daniel. But in the saying of 8:38f., the Human One again appears as true judge, who comes "with the angels" (the "saints of the Most High" in Daniel) to receive the kingdom. In all of this, Mark has reproduced the "bifurcation" of reality effected by Daniel's myth. In Daniel, the prophet "sees" (Dn 7:2) oppressive rulers who *appear* to be prevailing in the historical moment. But if the prophet looks *more deeply* ("as I looked again," Dn 7:9), he sees the Human One establishing justice. Thus in Mark, the Human One represents at once both defendant and prosecutor—depending upon which court, "earthly" or "heavenly," is being considered.

In this transformation we see the social function of mythic discourse clearly. In the original myth, the apparent triumph of the beast over the saints is subverted by asserting an entirely contradictory interpretation. So too with Mark's Human One; what appears to be his defeat and the triumph of both Rome and the Sanhedrin (narrated in his trial and execution) will *really* be his vindication and their judgment. This mythic discourse functions to help us interpret the outcome of the story; it gives us "eyes to see" the apocalyptic moment of the cross as the "glory of the Human One." But more important still is the way in which the myth instructs us in our real, historical choices between these two competing "authorities" and their respective "courtrooms." The disciples/reader must choose which "reality" we will trust: to be vindicated in the "Danielic" courtroom is to be condemned in the Jewish/Roman one, and vice versa. We either stand *with* Jesus, deny ourself and lose our lives "for his sake and the gospel's" (8:34f.), or we stand "ashamed" *before* him and the angels (those who have stood with him; 8:38f.). This bifocal reality accounts for Mark's discourse of paradox (death/life).

The discourse guarantees that this challenge is not limited to the past (Daniel) or the story (Jesus), but illuminates Christian existence at all times and places. Myth collapses time (past, present, future) and space ("heaven" and "earth") into the one "moment of truth" (more on this below, 11,D,F). This moment, understood by Daniel, impinges upon us once we accept the discipleship of the cross. It has already arrived in narrative time with the death of John, and will arrive again at Jesus' trial (he "confesses" the Human One, 14:62) and execution (he will not "save" himself, 15:30). And according to Jesus, it will *inevitably* arrive (13:10, *deï*) for the disciples/reader. In that historical "moment" the myth will instruct and empower us ("in that hour it is not you who speak but the Holy Spirit," 13:11) to choose to stand with the Human One, a choice that will in reality overthrow the highest and deepest powers (13:26f.).

8E. THE CROSS CONFIRMED: TWO SYMBOLIC SEQUELS (9:2–29)

i. *Jesus Transfigured: Second Apocalyptic Moment*

Just as Daniel confirmed his courtroom vision with a subsequent vision of a man in glorified clothing (Dn 10:5ff.), so too Mark, in an episode traditionally called the transfiguration. Daniel, in fear before this "man clothed in linen," receives the true interpretation of the combat myth pitting the angels against the beasts (Dn 10:13ff.). The disciples, equally petrified before Jesus in "radiant garments," receive only a confirmation that the word of the cross stands.

There is another intertextual allusion here, for the symbolics of Mark 9:2 clearly mean to call to mind Moses on Mount Sinai (Ex 24:15f.). The inner circle of disciples is taken up onto a mountain where they encounter a kind of salvation-history summit conference at which Moses and Elijah stand by Jesus, and where a cloud subsequently descends and the heavenly voice speaks. What is the meaning of the appearance of Moses and Elijah here? At the level of intertextuality, each of the two great prophets represent those who, like the disciples at this moment, beheld Yahweh's epiphany on a mountain at crucial periods of discouragement in their mission. In the story of Elijah, the great prophet has for his trouble become a man hunted by the authorities. He tries to flee, but is met by Yahweh who dispatches him back into the struggle (1 Kgs 19:11ff.). And in the case of Moses, he is Yahweh's envoy whose message has been once rejected by the people, and who must thus ascend the mountain a second time (Ex 33:18ff.). Both stories are clearly instructive at this point in Mark's narrative.

At the level of Mark's own story, the appearance of these two should not be surprising, since both Moses (alluded to in Jesus' "Who am I?") and Elijah (embodied in John the Baptist) have already been implicitly present. Finally, at the level of ideological legitimation, they lend credibility to the teaching Jesus has just delivered; the cross stands now with "the law and the prophets." This is meant as a dramatic confirmation of Mark's repeated claim that his story stands in continuity with the "old story" (1:2).

In 9:3 we are given a detailed description of the transformation of Jesus' garments (*himatia*). It almost seems as if this marks a kind of symbolic "transfer" of clothing, an enactment of the call to forsake the "old" garments (2:21). The "new" garments are described as extremely "white" (*leukos*).[1] Once again, this term recalls the Danielic courtroom (Dn 7:9; see also 10:8); more importantly, in apocalyptic intertextuality, white garments came to symbolize the clothing of martyrs (as in the Book of Revelation, 3:5,18; 4:4; 6:11; 7:9,13). And at the end of the story we will see, in "place" of Jesus, a "young man" who also, as we shall see, had cast away one garment (14:52) and now wears white (16:5). We must conclude that in the transfiguration, following as it does directly upon the first portent and teaching of the cross, Jesus' new garment is symbolic of the martyr's white robes.

In awe of this spectacle, once again Peter speaks for the group. But he has changed his tune: he addresses Jesus here not as "Messiah," but "Rabbi" (9:5). At the two later points in Mark's story in which "Rabbi" occurs, the disciples are standing with the dominant Jewish ideology over *against* Jesus: (1) their lament over Jesus' repudiation of the temple (11:21), and (2) Judas's greeting even as he betrays Jesus to the high priests (14:45). Is this also such a moment? It seems so, for again instead of understanding the way of the cross Peter proposes a cult of adulation. He offers to construct a memorial, "a temporary dwelling place like the 'booths' made of interlacing branches at the Feast of Tabernacles (Lv 23:4ff.)" (Taylor, 1963: 391). For the second time in as many episodes Peter has misconstrued the discourse of Jesus! And, for a second time, the lead disciple is rebuked. This time, however, it is not by Jesus but by the heavenly voice itself (9:7). But this voice does not condemn Peter; neither does it, the intertextual allusion notwithstanding, pronounce any new commandments (Moses), whisper in a still small voice (Elijah), or exposit the combat myth (Daniel). It simply reiterates the testimony of the baptism, and then adds, "Listen to him" (9:7). There is no need for new revelation; "the word" has already been delivered in Jesus' teaching of the cross.

As in 1:11, the heavenly voice invades the narrative to legitimate (on even higher authority than that of Moses and Elijah) this new phase in the discipleship narrative. This second apocalyptic moment exhibits strong parallels with Jesus' baptism, as has been recognized by several commentators (e.g., Standaert, 1978). In both cases the setting is a remote, marginal location, and the divine commendation ("This is my Son, beloved") almost identical. Van Iersel (1980:28f.) points to the presence of numerous common elements in the immediate supporting narrative environment of each episode:

Theme	First apocalyptic moment	Second apocalyptic moment
gospel	1:1,15	8:35
Jesus as Messiah	1:1	8:29
the way	1:2	8:27
Peter, James, John	1:16–18	9:2
the kingdom	1:15	9:1
as it is written	1:2	9:13
angels	1:13	8:38
John = Elijah	1:6	8:28; 9:12
call to follow	1:16	8:34
John's fate	1:14	9:13

Just as the mission of Jesus, "the stronger one," was confirmed at his baptism (1:10f.), so is the new mission of Jesus as the one to be executed here reconfirmed. In both cases the divine testimony stands directly opposite to Jesus' encounter with Satan (1:13 = 8:33), the core of the war of myths.

ii. Eschatological Vision or Script Confirmed?

The vision ends, and Mark quickly deconstructs the scene with a descent from the mountain (9:9a). As with Peter's confession, Jesus forbids the three to declare what they have seen "until the Human One should rise from the dead"

(9:9b). The disciples' reaction to this saying begins a conversation in which Mark considers the interpretation of the transfiguration vision.

Many commentators construe 9:10 to suggest that it represents a kind of "preview" of the risen Christ, who otherwise never actually appears in Mark's story. Indeed, form criticism has long felt that the "legend was originally a resurrection story" (Bultmann, 1963:259). Once again, imperial exegesis searches for a narrative of triumph, a crown to go with the cross.

This is exactly what the text instructs the disciples/reader *not* to do. What does 9:9f. really say?

1. he warned them (*diasteilato*) not to proclaim (*diēgēsōntai*) what they had seen;
2. until the Human One should rise from the dead;
3. and they held fast (*ekratēsan*) to the word
4. while they discussed among themselves what "to rise from the dead" meant.

Jesus' warning is strong, and—as in 5:43 and 7:36—it is meant to undermine an interpretation that exalts "miracle." This vision is not itself to be the subject of "proclamation" (cf. 5:16), for the disciples will not understand *its* meaning until they have understood the meaning of "resurrection." This is Mark's direct narrative pointer to the "young man" at the empty tomb at the end of the story, who also wears the martyr's clothes.

It is clear that the disciples do not comprehend the meaning of resurrection, either now or at the end of the story (16:7). What they *do* "hold fast" to (a verb in the New Testament often associated with ideological fidelity; see Mk 7:3f.; 2 Thes 2:15; Heb 4:14; Rv 2:1), is "the word" (*logos*). And what is that? As already established in this section, it is Jesus' teaching of the cross:

"He preached the word to them openly" (8:32).

"If anyone is ashamed of me and my words" (8:28). . . .

All of this is meant to ensure that we do not consider the transfiguration vision, or the subsequent promise of resurrection, as eschatological signs that "rescue" the narrative of the cross. At the perplexing and abrupt conclusion of this Gospel we will have to ponder "among ourselves" the "meaning" of the announcement that Jesus has "risen from the dead." Though we may not fully understand it, we must nevertheless hold fast to the "word" of the cross, the new way of discipleship.

The very same issue is at stake in the disciples' question to Jesus (9:11). Significantly, they are reluctant to ask him what he "means" by resurrection, but probably assume, like modern imperial hermeneutics, that it does indeed have to do with eschatological triumphalism (as later indicated by their response in 10:37). Hence they inquire about an alleged scribal assertion that, according to the "eschatological timetable," Elijah "must first come." The disciples are comparing notes with the dominant ideologists; they have missed the point again.

There is ongoing scholarly debate about the degree to which the Elijah-asforerunner myth characterized popular messianic expectation among Jews in the first century (see Horsley and Hanson, 1985:149).[2] Whatever the evidence from extrabiblical sources, this text suggests that the tradition of Malachi 4:5f. was in fact invoked by some as assurance that "restoration" (9:12; *apokatistanei*; see Oepke, *TDNT* I:388) would precede "judgment." It is this notion that Mark attributes to the scribes, consistent with his ideological portrait of them: they are sanguine about the "end time" because according to the promise of Malachi 4:5, Elijah "must come" (note the reoccurrence of the apocalyptic *deï*, 9:11) in order to "turn the hearts" of the people, and thus guarantee that Yahweh's "curse" will be forestalled (Mal 4:6).

Once again it is the war of myths: triumphalist eschatological "necessity" vs. Jesus' political "inevitability." What if, argues Mark's Jesus, Elijah *has* come, and the ruling classes not only ignored him but murdered him? This was precisely the meaning of Mark's appeal to Malachi 3:1 at the outset of his story: John the Baptist was Elijah, preaching repentance in order to "turn the hearts" of the people. The "necessity" of biblical radicalism ("as it is written") is that prophets are neither welcomed nor heeded, but killed. Hence the discourse of Mark's alternative interpretation in 9:12f.:

A   how is it written about the Human One
  B   that he will suffer many things and be repudiated
    C   but I say to you Elijah has come
  B'   and they did to him what they wished
A'   as it is written of him.

The concentric structure recapitulates the discourse of 6:14ff., which stated that Jesus is the "successor" to John in the political vocation of witness to the powers (above, 7,B,ii). This is now restated, this time using the "intertextual pseudonyms" of each: the Human One is the successor to Elijah.

Once again, then, a question of eschatology is referred back to the cross. The link with the Elijah myth also further confirms my thesis that the advent of the Human One will be identified with the execution of Jesus. For contrary to expectations, "Elijah's advent" occurred not as an eschatological spectacle, but as the political ministry of John, resulting in his trial and execution. Mark is telling us to expect the "advent" of the Human One in exactly the same fashion. This collapsing of identity also closes the circle of the argument that was reopened (from 6:14f.) in 8:27. Is Jesus John, or Elijah (8:28), or the Human One (8:31)? It is in one sense irrelevant: according to the "script" of biblical radicalism, all true prophets face the same political destiny. And it is this destiny to which the heavenly voice summons the disciples/reader to "listen." But do we have "ears to hear"?

iii. The Deaf-Mute Boy: The Struggle for Faith

The first cycle of the catechism closes with a second sequel, the third in the series of four symbolic healings, appropriately the exorcism of the "demon of mute deafness" (9:14–29). We can note at the outset that this story is a kind of conspectus; it alludes to at least one element of each of the previous healing/ exorcism episodes before Bethsaida:

1. synagogue exorcism (1:26f.) =	exorcism of "unclean spirit"; amazement of crowd (9:15,17)
2. healing of leper (1:41) =	verb for having compassion (*splagchnistheis*, 9:22)
3. healing of paralytic (2:1,6) =	presence of crowd and scribes (9:14)
4. healing of man's hand (3:5) =	took him by the hand (9:27)
5. Gerasene demoniac (5:3–6) =	details of how the demon has ravaged its victim (9:18,20,22)
6. synagogue ruler's daughter = (5:41f.)	raising back to life the son who was apparently dead (9:27)
7. hemorrhaging woman (5:34) =	issue of "faith" in healing (9:23f.)
8. exorcism of Syro-Phoenician = woman's daughter (7:25ff.)	parent with child of same gender (father/son, 9:17,24)
9. deaf and dumb man (7:31ff.) =	deaf and dumb (9:25)

These subtle elements of analepsis remind us that we have learned to "read" healing also as symbolic action.

The episode opens when Jesus finds his disciples arguing with the scribes, yet another suggestion of the way in which they feel threatened by the establishment. The crowd greets Jesus with "fearful amazement" (*exethambēethēsan*, 9:15), an intensified verb that appears otherwise only in 14:33 and 16:5f. as a reaction to the prospect of martyrdom. Jesus is *already* being dimly perceived as a martyr figure. Emerging from this crowd is the father of a demon-tortured boy. The man claims that he brought his son to Jesus, and apparently unable to find him, had requested his disciples to cast it out (9:17f.). They, however, were not "strong enough" (9:18, *ouk ischusan*). In the man's appeal to Jesus in 9:22, Taylor notes the "lifelike" qualities of the man's "doubt about the healer's power, his appeal for compassion and help, [and] his identification of himself, and perhaps his family also, with the lad, shown in his use of plural" (1963:399). The conversation concludes with the father's poignant cry: "I believe; help me in my unbelief!" (9:24).

After Jesus' dramatic exorcism (9:25–27), there is a discussion with the disciples, as before in the "safe" narrative site of the home. The disciples are exasperated by their inability to drive out *this* demon (9:28). Jesus simply refers them to prayer, Mark's first mention of prayer in relation to the disciples (9:29). In this seemingly anticlimactic manner, the episode abruptly concludes. The symbolics of this story are difficult to decipher, which explains why commentators so often pass over it. But there are two hints in its discourse that offer important clues to its interpretation. The first is its structure, another ring composition (cf. 2:1–12):

vv. 14–16   crowd arguing with disciples
vv. 17–27   Jesus' interaction with the father, exorcism of the boy
vv. 28f.   Jesus' discussion with his disciples

This instructs us that the matter of the disciples' impotence, the "frame," should interpret the actual exorcism.

Secondly, the episode is structured around the dialectic of faith and doubt/unfaith:

1. I told your disciples to drive it out, and they could not.
2. O unbelieving generation, how much longer must I be with you?
3. If you can do anything, help us and have compassion on us.
4. If I can! Everything is possible for the one who believes.
5. I believe! Help me in my unbelief!

This discourse reveals the central problem of the episode: the struggle for belief. The focus is not upon the miraculous healing of the boy, for no amazement is reported after 9:27; rather, the concern is "Why could we not drive it out?" (9:28).

To understand this episode as symbolic action let us begin by tracing the rhetorical connection between faith and power in Mark. The logic runs as follows. The disciples have been given the power to exorcise demons (6:12), but this seems here to have failed them. We know from Jesus' earlier experience in Nazareth that even his power fails *in the presence of disbelief* (*dia tēn apistian autōn*, 6:6a).

Whose unbelief is at issue here? The discourse noted above suggests that it is really the disciples who are impotent; the "fiction" of the father and his son dramatizes this crisis, just as the fiction of the synagogue ruler and his daughter dramatized Israel's crisis. The father is caught between belief and unbelief, which also characterizes the disciples' following of Jesus. Similarly, the boy's "demon" keeps him mute and deaf, just as the disciples seem to be "deaf" to Jesus' teaching about the cross, to which they have been instructed to "listen" by the voice from heaven (9:7). That teaching articulated a death/life paradox; this story similarly revolves around a life-threatening "demon," who when cast out appears to leave the boy dead (9:26). But Jesus intervenes to "raise up" (*anistēmi*, as in 9:9f.) the boy. What is the meaning of "resurrection," the disciples wondered? Is it not the exorcism of crippling unbelief, which renders us dead in life (9:22) rather than alive in our dying (8:35)?

I suggest this is the meaning of this symbolic exorcism. But how, then, will the disciples be able to cast out *this* demon (9:28)? Only, says Jesus, through prayer. And what is prayer? When Jesus next returns to this subject (11:23f.), he will explicitly connect prayer to "the power of belief." To pray is to learn to believe in a transformation of self and world, which seems, empirically, impossible—as in "moving mountains" (11:23). What is unbelief but the despair, dictated by the dominant powers, that nothing can *really* change, a despair that renders revolutionary vision and practice impotent. The disciples are instructed to battle this impotence, this temptation to resignation, through prayer. "Keep awake and pray, that you may not succumb to temptation!," Jesus later will urge them (14:38). The "strength" (or inability) to cast out demons is deeply connected to the "strength to stay awake" (14:37); tragically, the disciples will sleep while Jesus sweats in prayer in Gethsemane, and they will flee when he turns to face the powers.

By introducing prayer at this stage of the narrative, is not Mark trying to suggest that he understands it to be the practice of critical reflection upon the "demons within"? (The motifs of "fire" and "water," 9:22, will appear again in the next section in reference to apostasy.) Is not prayer the intensely personal struggle within each disciple, and among us collectively, to resist the despair and distractions that cause us to practice unbelief, to abandon or avoid the way of Jesus? And has not this demon, so embedded in our imperial culture, not kept us impotent, docile subjects of the status quo "since childhood" (9:21)? Yet just as the synagogue ruler's daughter, who was presumed lost (5:39ff.), is raised, signaling a "future" for Israel, so too this boy, giving us hope for the future of the deteriorating discipleship narrative. To acknowledge that we are impaled on the contradiction of our belief and our unbelief is to take the first step toward healing.

So does the first catechetical cycle close. Standing at the structural heart of Mark's story, it has redefined the meaning of the discipleship journey in decidedly concrete terms. Yet how many generations of interpreters have insisted on spiritualizing the cross, transforming it from a strictly political to a strictly religious symbol? And how many still read the negation, rather than affirmation, of martyrdom in the visions of the advent of the Human One and the transfiguration, despite the fact that Mark identifies both with the one moment of the cross? This is a longstanding conspiracy of hermeneutical suppression by those who have never stood in an earthly court charged with messianic subversion, those who are busy building booths to dead prophets rather than struggling with the demons that mute their own prophetic voice. But it cannot hide the truth of Mark's discourse: there is no discipleship to Jesus that does not take up the cross.

NOTES

1. Culpepper has correctly noted that "the chain of references to *himatia* in Mark suggests that it has symbolic value" (1982:132). Up to this point in the narrative, Jesus' garments have represented a positive narrative coordinate, healing those who touched them (5:27–30; 6:56). But from here on they signify a negative image: Bartimaeus will cast off his garment to follow Jesus (10:50); Jerusalemites will throw their garments onto the road to make way for Jesus entering their city (11:7f.); and disciples will be forbidden to salvage their garments in the critical time of war (13:16). As for Jesus' garments, they end up the booty of soldiers (14:20,24), while Jesus is crucified naked.

2. Jeremias contends that the scribes' social power of "knowledge" (below, 14,B,i) was based in part upon a body of esoteric tradition that included apocalyptic; he argues that some apocalyptic literature may have been authored by scribes. This might explain Mark's attribution of an Elijah timetable to the scribes (Jeremias 1969:238f.).

CHAPTER NINE

Jesus' Construction of a New Social Order, II: The Teaching Cycle (Mark 9:30-10:52)

By his knowledge shall the just one, my servant, make many to be accounted just.

—Isaiah 53:11b

If the "way of the cross" is not religious asceticism or a pious approach to human anguish, but a concrete political choice of resistance to the powers, is it then to be identified solely with the heroism of martyrdom? And does this not immediately suggest a new elitism? More importantly, how is it that the cross is the way to revolution and not mere tragic failure? The second "construction cycle" sets about clarifying these questions. A discipleship of the cross makes a far more difficult demand: the application of nonviolence to every sphere of life. As Gandhi put it, "If one does not practice nonviolence in one's personal relations with others and hopes to use it in bigger affairs, one is vastly mistaken" (1948: I,187). Genuine revolutionary transformation occurs "from the bottom up."

The first construction cycle (above, chap. 6) portrayed the vision of a new order based upon social reconciliation and economic justice through the symbolic action of miracle. The second cycle now turns to the vehicle of teaching to articulate more specifically the practice that will bring this new order about. The way of the cross is not only the *via negativa* of resistance to political oppression, but also the positive experimentation of a genuinely new way of social organization, called by Mark's Jesus the vocation of "servanthood." So deeply has the practice of domination infected human relationships that it must be eradicated from the roots: the radical way of nonviolence thus takes us into the deepest paradoxes of life and death. Accordingly, throughout this section Mark alludes to Jesus' discourse of "mystery" in the first sermon (above, chap. 5), which promised that, despite appearances, the "seeds" of a new order *will* grow into maturity.

9A. THE SECOND CYCLE: A CATECHISM ON NONVIOLENCE
(9:30–50)

i. Rhetoric and Structure in the Second Cycle

The first cycle of the "discipleship catechism" (above, 8,A,i) was internally structured around the second call to discipleship and its confirmation in two symbolic stories. The second cycle turns from a consideration of the "inevitable" political consequences of subversive messianic practice to the practical imperatives of its daily maintenance in the life of the community. It exhibits certain similarities with the parenetic discourse of the so-called house-tables found in late New Testament literature (the classic specimen is Colossians 3:12–4:6). We find here teaching concerning children (9:36f.; 10:13-16), parents (marriage and divorce, 10:2-12), group boundaries (9:38-41), and fidelity within the kingdom community (9:42-50). The section concludes with the only "discipleship rejection" story in Mark—a wealthy landowner who is unwilling to "follow" (10:17-22)—and teachings on possessions and communal identity.

The second cycle is internally organized around three narrative sites: the house, the progressive journeying southward, and the symbolic space of "the way." The section begins back in Galilee with the second portent (9:30-32). There follows a teaching section composed of two sections, defined by the double frame of "children" and the "first/last" theme (see Diagram 4). Each episode within this section is an illustration of the theme: first/last. The discursive pattern suggests, however, that *children* serve as the primary example, and hence below I will deal with both ends of this inner frame together.

Diagram 4
Mark 9:33–10:32

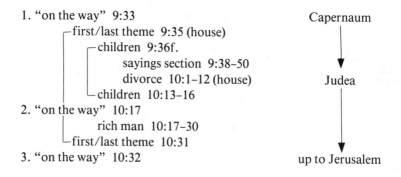

```
1. "on the way"  9:33                              Capernaum
     ┌─first/last theme  9:35 (house)                  │
     │   ┌─children  9:36f.                             │
     │   │   sayings section  9:38–50                   │
     │   │   divorce  10:1–12 (house)                   ▼
     │   └─children  10:13–16                        Judea
     │
2. "on the way"  10:17                                 │
     │   rich man  10:17–30                             │
     └─first/last theme  10:31                          │
3. "on the way"  10:32                                  ▼
                                                   up to Jerusalem
```

There is one other noteworthy rhetorical characteristic to the second cycle: the remarkable "word-stitching" composition of the "sayings section" (9:37-50). The theme saying is first represented in the example of a child. The "lesson" from this ("whosoever receives a child in my name") in turn issues into two trajectories: one set of sayings addressing the problem of "little ones" being "scandalized" and another set reflecting upon the problem of group boundaries ("in my name"). The verbal chaining can be seen in Diagram 5.

Diagram 5
Mark 9:35–50

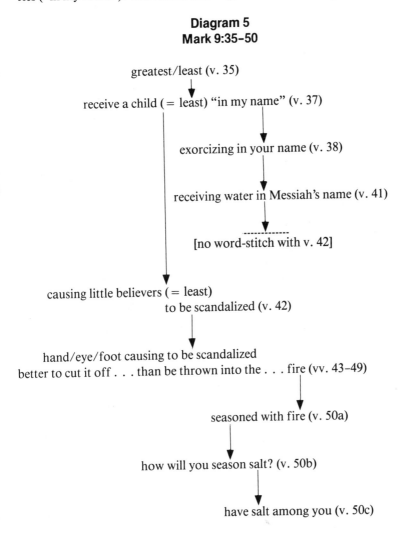

Form criticism has rightly attributed this rhetorical pattern to the influence of oral catechetical word-association techniques in Mark's sources (Taylor, 1963:408f; Dodd, 1968; McDonald, 1980). It wrongly argues, however, that this indicates the author's lack of literary sophistication. Fledderman (1981:57ff.) has demonstrated that Mark has thoroughly adapted these traditions (he identifies at least four Q sayings) to his own purposes. The teaching is in fact a careful and coherent exegesis of what it means to "receive the least."

ii. The Second Portent: First/Last

The discipleship community now begins to wind its way back through Galilee (9:30). There Jesus delivers the second portent (9:31), this time in a more generalized form. Mark reintroduces the juridico-political term "deliver into the custody of" (*paradidōmi*, cf. 1:14; 3:19), which will figure importantly in the arrest/trial/execution narrative. In case the reader is entertaining any doubts, Mark stresses twice that Jesus will be *killed* (*apokteinō*). Schaberg suggests that this portent in particular is linked with Daniel 7:25 and 12:2, which speak respectively of being delivered into the hands of rulers and the resurrection of the just (1985:210–13). The disciples again do not understand this "saying" (*rhēma*, 9:32). This word occurs only one other time in Mark (unlike the other Gospels, in which it is frequent): Peter's recollection of Jesus' prediction of his denial (14:72). Mark is thus fixing the relationship between the failure to comprehend and accept the political destiny of Jesus and its consequence: betrayal.

They next reach the home in Capernaum (9:33). That the community would stop in here on its way south, specifically for instruction on internal matters of power and discipline, is significant, for Capernaum was the center of gravity for the first part of the Gospel (1:21; 2:1; above, 4,B,iv). It is here that Jesus really begins to unmask his disciples' true aspirations to power. Not only do they not understand where Jesus is trying to lead them; they are headed full speed in the opposite direction. Mark contrives the episode for maximal irony: the disciples are caught debating who was greatest among them "on the way" (twice, 9:33b, 34a)! For Jesus' response, Mark sets a familiar stage: the twelve are called (cf. 3:14; 4:10; 6:7; 10:32; 14:17) and Jesus takes his seat (cf. 4:1; 12:41; 13:3). The narrative signals: Pay attention to the teaching that follows!

As he did in the first catechetical cycle, Mark employs the force of what Tannehill calls "antithetical aphorisms:"

> These are brief, pointed sayings which contain a sharp contrast. The saying tends to divide into two halves, with the same key words, in negative and positive form, or with antithetical terms. . . . As the saying develops, the speaker reverses the terms or ideas in a sort of word-play. . . . The saying also gains force by its absoluteness. The claim is sweeping; no qualifications are added [1975:89].

The introduction of the theme of servant leadership (9:35b) represents the "topic sentence of the discourse" (Fledderman). The way of nonviolence means being attentive to the actual dynamics of social power and privilege among family, friends, and neighbors. The follower of Jesus must expect the fate of a subversive, but the ultimate choice of the cross must also be daily reproduced in the concrete life of the messianic community.

Jesus sets about illustrating what "becoming least" means, beginning with an object lesson close at hand (9:36). Children represented the bottom of the social and economic scale in terms of status and rights in the ancient Mediterranean world:

> Age divisions, and commensurate power and responsibility, were hierarchical, sharply demarcated, and significant. Authority ran vertically downwards. Age and tradition were revered and powerful. . . . Early training was harshly disciplined. It was not until early adulthood that the young person began receiving serious consideration as a member of the family group [Carney, 1975:92].

It is remarkable enough that Jesus draws attention at all to children, for they were considered nonentities. It is quite shocking that he would advance them as models for his social program. Yet he does, not once but twice, returning to them in 10:13–16. Again throwing the hearer's social world into crisis with the radical status-reversal of the kingdom, Jesus launches his assault on the disciples' concern for power. I will return to the children theme in detail below (B,ii,iii).

iii. Social Boundaries: The "Good Outside"

Mark escalates the tone of the discourse in 9:38 by injecting another strong dose of sarcasm in the next scene. John (who comes off very badly in this section, relieving us of any illusions that Peter's faults might have been exceptional) complains of the activity of a maverick exorcist. It would appear that Mark is making an allusion to the story of Moses and the "unregistered prophets" recounted in Numbers 11:27–29. He frames Jesus' response in direct contrast to Joshua's request to Moses:

"Lord Moses, forbid them" (Nm 11:28, LXX, *kōluson autous*);

"Do not forbid him" (Mk 9:38, *mē kōluete auton*).

By intertextual implication Mark's episode is illuminated by Moses' retort: "Are you jealous . . . ?" (Nm 11:29). With Moses the issue was power sharing in the community ("Would that all Yahweh's people were prophets!"); here it is the problem of "exclusivity."

The arrogance in John's objection lies in its attempt to erect boundaries around the exercise of compassionate ministry "in Jesus' name." He equates exorcism with the accrual of status and power, and wishes to maintain a monopoly over it. This is especially ludicrous in light of the disciples' lack of exorcism power, which we have just witnessed (9:14–29). But more importantly, it cuts directly against the grain of "receiving" in 9:37, an exhortation to *inclusion*, not exclusivity. On top of all this, John's censure is based on the fact that the stranger "was not following *us*." The disciples want to be followed, not followers. Never was a "royal we" less appropriate!

Rather than attacking such utter incomprehension directly, however, Jesus simply gives three reasons why the disciples must not "hinder" (cf. 10:14) the exorcist (see Fledderman, 1981:65f.). The first reason seems practical enough:

anyone who engages in "powerful practice" (*poiēsei dunamin*, cf. 6:5) in Jesus' name cannot soon afterward speak ill of him (9:39). The second reason expands this into a general rule of thumb: "those who are not against us are for us" (9:40). There is a tone of irony here: for in fact Peter will at the end of the story indeed "speak ill" of Jesus, and even now he and the rest of the disciples, who are allegedly *for* Jesus, are progressively turning *against* him.

It is the third reason that is central (9:41), stressed by its solemn tone (the only *Amēn* saying in this subsection) and by the fact that only here (apart from 1:1) in Mark does the term "Messiah" appear outside the context of confessional struggle. Not only is Jesus willing to endorse the redemptive practice of "outsiders," but also the simplest act of hospitality ("a cup of water") shown to anyone "who bears the name of Messiah." John is worried about those with competing power, but Jesus is welcoming *all* those who do the works of mercy and justice. John is entertaining "holier than thou" delusions, but Jesus points out how his followers will often find themselves on the *receiving end* of compassion. In other words, disciples have no corner on the ministry of healing and liberation, and therefore should without prejudice work alongside those whose practice is redemptive. Conversely, those who minister in any way to Christians receive due recognition in the kingdom.

This would appear to affirm what Karl Rahner had once called "anonymous Christianity." Mark is extending the principle articulated in the "confessional crisis": it is practice, not "the right name," that is recognized in the kingdom. This teaching also forbids the erection of exclusive and rigid social boundaries around the community of faith. Jesus seems to understand the relationship between the power of monopoly and the monopoly of power; the quickest way to undermine aspirations to social control is to keep the definitions of "belonging" ultimately fluid and inclusive. As if to further secure this argument, Jesus now turns to show how, just as good can come from "outside," betrayal can come from "inside."

iv. Community Solidarity: The "Bad Inside"

Verse 9:42 alone in this subsection is not verbally linked to the verse that precedes it. "Little ones" (*mikrōn*) stands in contrast to "greatest" (9:34, *meizōn*), and signals a return to the original theme of least/child. "Whoever scandalizes one of these little ones who believes in me" suddenly inserts the theme of conflict within the community. To scandalize, usually translated "cause to stumble" (*skandalisē*), is a technical term in Mark for rejection of the kingdom message (6:3) or desertion of the way (14:27,29). This is now the second allusion to the sower parable: "when tribulation or persecution arises on account of the word they immediately fall away" (4:17, *skandalizontai*).

But can such stumbling blocks come from *within* the community? The story will assert that indeed they can and do. The "hard saying" that "it is better (*kalon estin*) to die" will be repeated by Jesus in reference to Judas's cooperation with the political authorities to betray him (14:21).

The next set of sayings thus addresses the problem of apostasy within the community (9:43–48). Having established the death/life paradox in 9:42, the meaning of save/lose is extended in a series of three parallel statements concerning hand, eye, and foot. Each saying is formulated thus:

If your (hand/eye/foot) scandalizes you, (remove) it . . .

. . . for it is better (*kalon estin*) to enter life (without) it . . .

. . . than be thrown (with it) into Gehenna.

The Gehenna saying may have been a colloquial reference to the Jerusalem trash pile that always smoldered (9:43c). However, the second mention of Gehenna (9:48) alludes to the eschatological judgment that closes the book of Isaiah (66:24). It is significant that the only time Mark alludes to "divine retribution" in any eschatological form apart from the Danielic courtroom myth is in reference to apostasy within the community of faith.[1]

The traditional interpretation that these sayings concern individual moral discipline—the hand, foot, and eye, considered by Jews to be the "site" of aggressive acts, "you got into trouble"—misses the point. Mark's community was facing the terrible reality of the breakdown of solidarity in the face of persecution, as I will argue below (11,A,ii; C,ii; 14,A,iii). The pressures of the war had caused some members not only to defect, but to betray other members ("little ones who believe"). How was this situation to be handled?

Derrett sees specific juridical significance here (1974:4ff.), arguing that in the first century (and still today in some Muslim societies) amputation of "the member that offended" was in fact a *liberalization* of punishment for capital offenses:

1. the hand: theft, fraud, and forgery (right hand symbolizing property transactions);
2. the foot: robbery, persistent theft, fugitive slaves;
3. the eye: adultery, sexual misconduct.

Derrett concludes that Mark, in drawing images from known secular administration of justice, was advocating leniency in the enforcement of discipline within his own community. According to my interpretation, this would mean that Mark rejected the kind of "revolutionary justice" that executes informers and defectors in the interests of internal security.[2]

These verses are, by any reading, difficult, especially if one does not believe Mark's "exhortation to amputation" should be taken literally. It may be that these images should be seen as analogous to some of Paul's instructions regarding discipline in the *ekklesia* (e.g., 1 Cor 5), or deference to the "weaker member" (e.g., Rom 14, especially the connection between "judgment" and "scandal" in v. 13). They also bring to mind Paul's metaphor of the community as "body" (1 Cor 12), which mentions hand, eye, and feet. This may be too much of an interpolation, but I have pointed out that this section reflects early catechetical patterns, and we cannot rule out the possibility that the "body" metaphor was in common circulation among the communities. Understood more metaphorically, Mark's exhortations call for the expulsion (but not execution) of the informer/apostate, for the sake of the "whole body."

This interpretation also makes better sense of the long-debated concluding statement, that everyone in the community must be "seasoned" with salt and fire (9:49f.). Derrett speaks of the use of salt and fire to close amputation wounds in the medicine of the time, and it may well be that the entire discourse is filled with such double entendres. But Fledderman's suggestion is most compelling:

> "Have salt" is parallel to "be at peace." In the Old Testament salt is a symbol of the covenant. One of the clearest texts is Leviticus 2:13b: "Do not let the salt of the covenant of your God be lacking from your cereal offering." In Numbers 18:19 an everlasting covenant is called a "covenant of salt" (see also 2 Chr 13:5). The background of this idea probably lies in the sharing of salt in a meal (Ezr 4:14). To share salt with someone is to share fellowship with him, to be in covenant with him. The discourse began with two situations of conflict and strife, the self-seeking arguing of the disciples about rank and the conflict with the strange exorcist. It went on to discuss the problem of scandal in the community. To all of this Mark opposes the peace of covenant fellowship [1981:73].

It is entirely appropriate to this nonviolence catechism that Mark's warnings against apostasy conclude with a reminder of the imperative to work for conflict resolution, the reestablishment of unity and peace within the messianic community. Throughout this subsection Mark has maintained a sophisticated dialectic between community solidarity (strong group boundaries) and nonexclusivity (weak group boundaries). The good from "outside" must be affirmed, and the bad "inside" cut out. But in the latter case, "receptivity" must finally include even the apostate: as we will see, forgiveness must stand at the center of the community's life (11:25).

9B. SOCIAL POWER AND THE FAMILY: THE ROOTS OF VIOLENCE (10:1–16)

i. *Marriage and Divorce: A Critique of Patriarchy*

In 10:1 there is a change of scenery, signaling that the sayings section has closed, and a new, though related, teaching begun. The growing tension of the journey should now dawn on the reader: for the first time in the story Jesus crosses the threshold across the Jordan into the district of Judea (see Taylor, 1963:416f. for textual and geographical problems with this passage). Mark is building the drama, coaxing the narrative slowly southward. Although it has been implied in the portents that Jerusalem is the goal of this long march, Mark will not explicitly reveal this destination until 10:32. The double use of "again" (*palin*) in 10:1, the reappearance of the crowds (only here in the plural in Mark), and the phrase "he taught them as he was accustomed" are stage directions meant to recall the first half of the story and prepare us for a conflict episode.

Jesus' debate with the Pharisees (10:2–12) is closely parallel to his earlier confrontation with them (7:1ff.). Here again is a dispute concerning proper interpretation of the law on a practical matter, a criticism of the way in which the Torah is undermined by Pharisaic hermeneutics, and a private explanation to the disciples. The issue, however, is quite different than before: it concerns the legal grounds for divorce (*andri gunaika apolusai*, 10:2). Because there was no recognition of reciprocal rights for women in Jewish family law at the time, this issue was limited among the rabbis to determining sufficient reason for a man to "dismiss" his wife. Jesus' position on this would have been particularly interesting in light of the fact that it was hotly debated between the two main rabbinic schools of the period, Hillel and Shammai.

Unlike the previous debate over *korban*, however, in which Jesus argued from Torah against the Pharisees' oral tradition, here he appears to set scripture against scripture, as if to suggest that the Genesis covenant (alluded to in 10:6) takes precedence over the Mosaic statute (Dt 24:1, cited in 10:4). This practice according to Bultmann would have been "unheard of among the Rabbis. They often enough constructed an *aporia* out of two apparently contradictory texts of scripture, but only in order to pass on to its solution" (1963:49f.). Matthew, apparently seeing this, rearranged the Markan argument to conform to more acceptable scribal reasoning (Mt 19:1–12). But this misses Mark's point.

Jesus *refuses* to enlist in the legal debate over the divorce statute itself (*tēn entolēn tautēn*, 10:5b). Instead he questions the way in which Pharisaic casuistry simply legitimates the already established social practice of divorce. The problem, as E. Schüssler Fiorenza sees it, is that the legal issue is "totally androcentric," and "presupposes patriarchal marriage as a given." Jesus argues:

> Divorce is necessary because of the male's *hardness of heart*, that is, because of men's patriarchal mind-set and reality. . . . However, Jesus insists, God did not intend patriarchy but created persons as male and female human beings. It is not woman who is given into the power of man in order to continue "his" house and family line, but it is man who shall sever connections with his own patriarchal family and "the two persons shall become one *sarx*". . . . The [Genesis] passage is best translated as "the two persons—man and woman—enter into a common human life and social relationship because they are created as equals" [1985:143].

Jesus' conclusion (10:9), then, is not meant as an absolute prohibition upon "divorce," which would both overturn the Mosaic statute and return to a legalistic solution. Indeed, it drops the term for divorce (*apoluse*) in favor of a different term (to "separate," *chōrizetō*). Rather it protests the way in which patriarchal practice drives a wedge into the unity and equality originally articulated in the marriage covenant.[3] Understood in the true sense, this famous phrase rightly belongs in the Christian marriage liturgy.

The principled critique of patriarchy having been stated "publicly," the internal understanding of the community on this issue is once again given in a private explanation to the disciples in the safe narrative site of the home (10:10; cf. 7:17ff.). Jesus here accepts the reality of divorce but prohibits remarriage—as does the similar catechetical tradition in 1 Corinthians 7:10 (though there, "separation," *chōrizō*). The reciprocal formulation of the prohibition in 10:11f., however, reveals that the principle of equality has been maintained. The first clause—a man cannot divorce a woman and marry another without committing adultery against her—already went beyond Jewish law, "in which a man can commit adultery against another married man but not against his own wife" (Taylor, 1963:419). But the second clause, in which the rights of the female partner are expanded to include her right to divorce (or "leave," see Taylor, 1963:420), directly *contradicted* Jewish law, which stipulated that only men could initiate and administer such proceedings (Kee, 1977:155).

This teaching recognizes the fact that divorce is a profound spiritual and social tragedy. No one who has undergone the fire of "one flesh" torn apart (as I myself have) can dispute the weight of Jesus' plea in 10:9:

> [In] the suffering perhaps more than in the happiness a man and a woman may discover how deeply involved they are. They may discover that they are no longer simply individuals, for in the poisoning of their marriage a part of them is dying [Tannehill, 1975:97].

The teaching also acknowledges, however, that divorce is a reality, within which the fundamental issue of justice must not be lost. *Both* parties must have the right to take initiative, and both must accept the responsibilities and limitations involved in the death of marriage. Again Mark refuses to overlook the *actual* relations of power, no matter how "sacred" the institution. The "least" in this concrete case is the woman, and Mark is making clear to his community that she can be protected only if she is no longer treated as object, but as equal subject, in situations of conflict resolution.

ii. "As a Child": Jesus' Solidarity with the "Least of the Least"

It may be under influence from the parenetic tradition of the "house-codes" that Mark moves naturally from "parents" to "children" (10:13–16). Or it may be due to the fact that children were then, as now, the special victims of divorce (there would have been few childless divorces in antiquity). In any case, he chooses to close this subsection on "first/last" in the same way he opened it: considering the children. The two child vignettes have almost identical stage directions: Jesus "takes them in his arms" (9:36; 10:16, *enagkalisamenos*, a verb unique in the New Testament). Let us return for a moment to look at the former incident.

In 9:37 Mark constructed a kind of syllogistic argument based upon the notion of "receiving" (*dechetai*): "Whoever receives one such as this in my name, receives me; whoever receives me receives not me but the one who sent me." In order to understand the earnestness of this equation, the reader is supposed to recall the disciples, who were themselves "sent" on mission (6:11). There they were vulnerable, dependent upon being "received" in hospitality— in a sense, they were "as children." The warning issued there was: "Whatever place does not receive you or hear you, shake off the dust . . . as a witness against them." Now the child threatens to become "a witness against" those disciples who refuse to accept the social transformation of which Jesus spoke in 9:35. Thus in 10:15, the circle of references closes and the syllogism is extended: "Whoever *does not receive* the kingdom *like a child*, will not enter into it at all!"

The structure of tension in this brief episode shows that Mark understood the difficulties his community faced in restructuring social power at the most intimate level: the household. Followers bring children to Jesus in order for him to touch them, but are rebuked by the disciples (10:13; again, the strong *epetimēsan*). This provokes yet another hostile exchange with Jesus, who responds with indignation (10:14, *ēganaktēsan*; a similar response is later attributed to the disciples, for opposite reasons, see 10:41; 14:4). The "war of myths" rages even at the heart of the community: Jesus is committed to inclusivity, his disciples to exclusivity. Jesus' solemn pronouncement thus turns this seemingly minor skirmish into nothing less than a watershed challenge about participation in the kingdom (10:15)! The episode ends with the pointed mention that Jesus carried through with his intention despite the disciples' opposition, gathering the children into his arms and "blessing them" (10:16, *kateulogeō*, only here in Mark).

This episode for the second time illustrates the way of nonviolence by reversing the normal socio-cultural assumptions about status, elevating the "last" to "first." And certainly the child represented the "least of the least." In a significant symbolic action, Jesus rescues children from the margins of the new community and places them at its *center* ("in their midst," 9:36), as a fundamental object lesson. Again, contrary to the resistance of his own disciples, Jesus *insists* that children "not be hindered" (10:14). Why this remarkable emphasis upon children?

Is not Jesus' call to "become a child" just a hyperbolic example of status reversal? Surely we are not meant to take him seriously; after all, the whole point of life is to "grow up." Mark must be speaking metaphorically here. According to such logic, most commentators do *not* take this text seriously. It is the occasion for passing tributes to the happy innocence of childhood, or appeals to the "child within," or homilies on "Jesus' love for the little children" (see Via's review, 1985:129). But what if Jesus means what he says?

D. Via sees the call of 10:15 as a demand to return to "primal origins," which would then extend the "original vision" argument of the previous one concerning divorce. He then tries to make sense of "child" here in terms of a Jungian archetype:

> In the archetype itself the child as potential for the future moves through the abandonment of a secure origin, through risk and danger toward adulthood. In the Gospel of Mark the adult is called on tacitly to become

a child. . . . The adult has become hardened in heart, so that the inner center of life is not open to a different future . . . one must move back to childhood and begin again. This entails renouncing the shape of one's present existence in order to recover an abandoned potential [1985:130].

Via is not wrong to look to psychology for clues, but this archetype is too mystifying.

Why should not the child represent an actual class of exploited *persons*, as does every other subject of Jesus' advocacy in Mark? The impure and the poor and the gentile are representations of real social marginalization; Why not also the child? This would certainly be more in keeping with the ideology of this catechism, which is concerned to unmask the realities of domination within community and even within kindred relationships. Indeed, from the narrative world of Mark we have cause to suspect that all is not well for the child in first-century Palestinian society. For where do we meet children in the Gospel? In every case, it is in situations of sickness or oppression: the synagogue ruler's daughter (5:21ff.), the Syrophoenician's daughter (7:24ff.), the deaf and dumb son (9:14ff.). Despite my own treatment of those episodes in a symbolic manner, I do not wish to be overly instrumental. The social signification of such a consistent narrative portrait suggests that Mark understands the child as victim.

Via cannot see this because, like every other commentator, he idealizes childhood, referring to it as the site of "secure origins." But what if this is a romantic illusion? What if the "site" of the child, vulnerable, credulous, and dependent, is in fact the very beginning point in the spiral of both exploitation and violence? Could it be that the discourse of Mark is arguing that if we are to forge a nonviolent way of life, we must weed out the structures and practices of violence at their roots? That the validity of nonviolence must pertain to the most basic building block of human social existence: the family? To explore this possibility, I will briefly digress to discuss a thesis advanced recently by philosopher and psychoanalyst Alice Miller.

iii. The Child, the Family System, and the Roots of Violence

One of the surest findings of the modern psychological disciplines is perhaps a recovery of an old truth, lost due to the break up of traditional kinship structures and overconcentration on the individual. That is, the family unit is a social system in its own right, and patterns must be examined structurally. The "family systems" approach to psychotherapy, combined with the basic insights of Freud, who located the origin of neurosis in early childhood, have begun to reveal a startling truth: the child is always the primary victim of practices of domination within the family.

Miller wonders "whether it will ever be possible for us to grasp the extent of the loneliness and desertion to which we were exposed as children, and hence intra-psychically, as adults" (1981:5). She portrays children as the ideal candidates for exploitation by virtue of their complete dependence (material and emotional) upon the adult: "The love a child has for his or her parents ensures that their conscious or unconscious acts of mental cruelty will go undetected. . . . Their tolerance for their parents knows no bounds" (1983:4). Children cannot have critical awareness of manipulation by adults, nor can they react to it:

> Adults are free to hurl reproaches at God, at fate, at the authorities or at society if they are deceived, ignored, punished unjustly, confronted with excessive demands, or lied to. Children are not allowed to reproach their gods—their parents and teachers. By no means are they allowed to express their frustrations. Instead, they must repress or deny their emotional reactions which build up inside until adulthood, when they are finally discharged, but not on the object that caused them [1983:254].

Thus adults who were themselves humiliated as children cannot but unconsciously reproduce that humiliation, argues Miller. The pedagogical tradition of corporal punishment is in fact a dramatic enactment of adults' struggles to regain power they once lost as a child to their own parents (1983:16). Yet this exercise of power by the adult over the child goes largely unchecked in the wider social system: the family is "private domain." The *subjection* of the child thus represents the basic building block of socialization into wider socio-political structures of domination.

According to Miller, the "silent drama" of children consists of the following stages:
1. to be hurt/dominated as a young child without anyone knowing;
2. to be unable to react to or process resultant anger;
3. to internalize the sense of betrayal by rationalizing or idealizing the parent's "good intentions";
4. finally, to so repress the painful memory as to forget;
5. to later, as an adult, discharge the unconscious store of anger onto either self or others.

The result is what she identifies as a "vicious circle of contempt for those who are smaller and weaker," patterns of domination that are maintained and psychically enforced intergenerationally (1981:67). The legacy of this drama is twofold, psychic and social, for the adult will both *introject* and *project* the deep pain and anger that is stored from childhood. The personal cost is manifested in *depression* and various forms of despair. The social cost is manifested through *oppression*, the concrete reproduction of intrapersonal violence. Both are tragic, but it is the latter that I wish to focus upon here in my political reading.

One social consequence is the adult's passive acceptance, or indeed active promotion of, ideologies and practices of oppression, "in whose service they allow their inmost selves to be completely dominated, as had been the case in their childhood" (1983:66). Miller cites as an example the "heroic willingness" of adolescents to fight the wars of older men, in which they are "able to avenge their earlier debasement" and "divert this hatred from their parents if they are given a clear-cut enemy whom they are permitted to hate freely and with impunity" (ibid.:170). Of particular interest to Miller, a Swiss of the generation that remembers Hitler, is how so many otherwise intelligent and critical persons can readily submit to authoritarianism:

> When a man comes along and talks like one's own father and acts like him, even adults will forget their democratic rights or will not make use of them. They will submit to this man, will acclaim him, allow themselves to be manipulated by him, and put their trust in him . . . without even being aware of their enslavement [ibid.:75].

It is difficult to resist drawing the analogy to the repressive paternalism of the Reagan cult of personality that has so thoroughly dominated mainstream American political culture for almost a decade.

Miller cites another consequence: the historical experience of colonialism, in which the classic eighteenth- and nineteenth-century pedagogies of domination in imperialist countries resulted in the need to dominate newly "discovered" cultures. She asks: "Who will bear the brunt of this humiliating treatment later when the colonies are no longer there to perform this function?" (ibid.:58). Finally, she wonders whether the compulsion does not find its ultimate expression today in the need "to build up a gigantic war industry in order to feel comfortable and safe in this world" (ibid.:280).

Miller believes that "our sensitization to the cruelty with which children are treated . . . and to the consequences of such treatment will as a matter of course bring to an end the perpetuation of violence from generation to generation" (ibid.:280). Her contention that child-rearing is the fountain of social domination and political violence is worth considering. It follows also that nonviolence, as a part of a radical practice that seeks to address structural injustice at its roots, must begin with the family system. It is then in *this* sense, I would argue, that we must comprehend the saying "Unless you receive the kingdom as a child, you cannot enter it." A new social order *cannot* be constructed unless and until we have dealt with the very foundations of oppression: "It is part of the tragic nature of the repetition compulsion that someone who hopes eventually to find a better world than the one he or she experienced as a child in fact keeps creating instead the same undesired state of affairs" (ibid.:241).

The vicious circle of contempt and violence can be broken not by idealizing childhood, as does Via, but only by understanding the unconscious dynamics of primal indignation; "intrapsychic, structural transformation" can be achieved only by moving from rage to mourning to reconciliation (ibid.:270). Moreover, if "what is unconscious cannot be abolished by proclamation or prohibition" (1981:90), then it is worth noting that Mark's discourse here is not a "command." The central syllogism of this section understands liberation as a matter of invitation:

Whoever receives the child receives me,
and whoever receives me receives . . . the one who sent me (9:37);
whoever does not receive the kingdom of God like a child
cannot enter it (10:15).

Here is the promise of a new family system based upon both *access* and *acceptance*.

Perhaps the reader thinks I am simply placing the words of a modern psychoanalyst into the mouth of Jesus. This hermeneutical digression must not be so misconstrued. Miller's observations are based upon the alienations of modernity, Mark's of antiquity. To draw direct correlations, the characteristics of family-system oppression would have to be examined historically and cross-culturally (though I suspect the rigid and hierarchical kinship structures of first-century Palestine would only confirm Miller's thesis). I am convinced, however, that Miller's thesis gives us "ears to hear" the radical teaching of Jesus at this point in a way that the traditional, idealizing exegesis does not. The child is not a mere symbol in Mark, but a *person*. To deal with this person is to deal with our own repressed past, the roots of violence, and the possibility of a transformed future, our own and our children's.

9C. ECONOMIC POWER AND COMMUNITY PRACTICE
(10:17–31)

i. The Rich Man as Nondisciple: On Class

Having concluded this dramatic teaching on social relations within community and family, Mark turns to give an equally special place to the last illustration of the "greatest/least" issue: the problem of economic class and privilege. The rich man episode is linked to the preceding two stories in two ways. Like the debate about divorce, a question of the law will be eclipsed by a consideration of actual practice, and there will be a private explanation to the disciples. Like the blessing of the children, there is a pronouncement concerning the kingdom of God (10:24b).

As already observed, the episode begins and ends with reference to "the way" (10:17,32a). The structure of action is meant to be didactic, unfolding in three parts, each of which includes the "gaze" of Jesus:

1. conversation with the rich man (10:17–22): "Jesus looked upon him" (*emblepsas*, v. 21):
2. teaching on kingdom of God and the rich (10:23–26) "And Jesus gazed around at his disciples and said . . . " (*periblepsamenos*, v. 23)
3. teaching on community and property (10:27–30): "Jesus looked at them . . . " (*emblepsas*, v. 27).

The unity of the episode is revealed in its discourse, which is composed concentrically:

A question about eternal life (v. 17)
B rich man cannot leave possessions and follow;
C Jesus' explanation, disciples' reaction (twice)
B' disciples have left possessions and followed;
A' answer to eternal-life question (v. 30).

The story concludes with a restatement of the section's theme: "first/last" (10:31).

One hardly need emphasize that this text, which is so crucial to the community ideology of Mark, has been notoriously mishandled by those whose self-interest lies in soft-peddling its criticism of wealth. Popularly known as the story of the "rich young ruler," Mark's character is in fact neither young (Mt), nor a ruler (Lk); what we are told, and only *after* he has turned away from the call to discipleship, is that he was a large landowner. At the start, however, he is simply described as someone who, as had the leper in 1:40, came to Jesus, kneeling, with a request. But from the first words we know this will be an extraordinary exchange.

Taylor says "the address *didaskale agathe* ['good teacher'] is very rare in Jewish literature" (1963:425), and is probably meant as flattery (10:17b):

> He tries to impress with a compliment and perhaps hopes to be greeted with a lofty title in return. In the Oriental world, one compliment requires a second. . . . This seems to be the tension of the text, because Jesus answers with no title at all [Bailey, 1980:162].

Theologians have agonized over the christological implications of Jesus' apparent self-effacement in 10:18. The problem disappears once we see that Jesus is repelling the man's hopes for return ingratiation. Instead comes a reproof: there is only "the One" who is good.

The man's question is singular in Mark for its use of the term "eternal life," which functions as the key to the story's discourse. Jesus responds in a fashion that at first glance seems uncharacteristic: he simply quotes the Decalogue with no apparent commentary. Is Mark, having just intimated that parts of Torah were given as concession to human "hardheartedness" (10:5b), trying to reaffirm here his commitment to the law? Perhaps; yet a closer reading reveals that there is once again a twist in his citation. For one of the statutes listed by Jesus does not in fact appear in the Decalogue! It is "do not defraud" (*mē aposterēsēs*), and is dropped by both Matthew and Luke. The reference in this addition is clearly to economic exploitation:

> In the Greek Bible the verb is appropriated to the act of *keeping back the wages* of a hireling, whereas in Classical Greek it is used of refusing to return goods or money deposited with another for safekeeping . . . cf. Ex 21:10, Dt 24:14 [Taylor, 1963:428].

This is our first indication that much more is being discussed in this story than the personal failure of this one man: judgment is being passed upon the wealthy class.

The man seems to have missed Jesus' point that "no one is good," for he claims in response to Jesus' challenge that he is blameless before the law (10:20). Bailey writes:

> In the Talmud, Abraham, Moses, and Aaron are reported to have kept the whole law. The rich ruler seems to calmly put himself in rather exalted company [1980:163].

Yet Mark tells us that Jesus looked at the man and "loved him." How do we account for the fact that this is the only place in Mark where Jesus is described as loving someone? I suggest there are two related points of narrative logic, either of which provides an explanation.

The first has to do with a later episode parallel to this one: the conversation with another class opponent, the scribe (12:28–34). The issue there also is with the key commandments of the law, and also involves a "hard" kingdom of God saying (12:34b). There, however, the central thrust is the imperative to love God and neighbor (the only other appearance of *agapaō*). Anticipating this teaching, Mark is careful in 10:21a to imply that while Jesus may be *reciting* the Decalogue, he is in fact *practicing* the "great commandment." Alternatively, it may have to do with the fact that Mark is about to offer his third and last midrash on the sower parable in this, his only discipleship-rejection story. The man will embody those for whom "the love of wealth (*apatē tou ploutou*) intervenes to strangle the word, rendering it fruitless" (4:18). In contrast to the love of wealth, a tragic illustration of the danger of possession by one's possessions, is Jesus' love for the man.

This man, however pious he may be, "lacks" (*husterī*) one thing. In Jesus' call to discipleship, the meaning of "self-denial" is further concretized in economic terms, articulated in four distinct imperatives:

1. Get up (*hupage*)
2. sell that which you have
3. give it to the poor (and you shall have treasure in heaven)
4. come (*deuro*), follow me.

The first command is usually used by Mark in healing stories (1:44; 2:11; 5:19,34; 7:29), and perhaps that is part of the invitation here: to be healed of the sickness of accumulation. The fourth command closely echoes the first call (cf. 1:16). Even the second can be seen as parallel, for we observed that Jesus' pattern was to call persons *from* the security of their vocation onto the way. The demand that this proprietor (10:22) divest his assets is not different from asking a fisherman to leave his nets (1:18).

It is the third imperative that is exceptional. Judging this man to be affluent, Jesus stipulates that his wealth must be distributed to the poor. The implied opposition between earth ("give to the poor") and heaven ("and there you shall have treasure") is yet another expression of apocalyptic status-reversal (see the Q tradition in Mt 6:19–21 par.).[4] It is "at this word" (*epi tō logō*) that the man slinks away. Mark's description that he departed gloomily (*stugnasas*) is an intertextual allusion to Ezekiel's judgment on the rich and powerful of Tyre (Ez 27:35). The man's "hurt" (*lupoumenos*) is proleptic of what the twelve will feel later on when accused of betrayal (14:19).

All this emotion becomes clear in light of the revelation that "he had much property" (*echōn ktēmata polla*):

> A possession is used to describe a piece of landed property of any kind . . .
> a farm or a field (Acts 5:1), and in the plural lands or estates [Taylor, 1963:430].

As we have seen in the discussion of the class structure of Mark's Palestine, landowners represented the most politically powerful social stratum. With this revelation, the story of the man abruptly finishes, as if the point is obvious. As far as Mark is concerned, the man's wealth has been gained by "defrauding" the poor—he was not "blameless" at all—for which he must make restitution. For Mark, the law is kept only through concrete acts of justice, not the façade of piety.

ii. The Eye of the Needle: Peasant Humor

Mark wishes to make sure the reader understands that this story means exactly what it says, and so, as he has with other controversial teachings crucial to the community's ethic, he devotes the rest of the episode to Jesus' explanation and the disciples' reaction. Jesus begins by reciprocating the man's rejection (not, as it turns out, the flattery!), saying that he is skeptical about the possibility of wealthy disciples. This dictum in turn provokes the amazement of the disciples, not once, but twice (10:23–26), indicating how important the point is to Mark:

    A And he said to his disciples "How hard it will be for those having riches to enter into the kingdom of God!"

    B And the disciples were amazed (*ethambounto*) at his words.

    A' And Jesus said again to them, "Children, how hard it is to enter into the kingdom of God!"

    B' They were exceedingly astonished (*exeplēssonto*), saying . . .

Noting the redundancy, Western exegesis has usually argued that the latter qualifies the former, as if Mark is hastily adding that the rich are merely a subset of humanity in general. But not only does the second statement (in the present indicative) not soften the first (in the future tense, indicating discourse time?), it actually hardens it.

Mark's wry joke about the camel and needle (10:25) in particular has received ingenuous "manipulation at the hands of bourgeois conscience-tranquilizing exegetes" (José Miranda). The famous medieval assertion that the "eye of the needle" referred to a certain small gate in ancient Jerusalem through which camels could enter only on their knees (!) is only one of the more obvious ways devised to rob this metaphor of its class-critical power. The proposition is plainly an impossible one. Bailey points out that the Babylonian Talmud records a similar hyperbole—an elephant going through the eye of a needle—and comments that "the elephant was the largest animal in Mesopotamia and the camel the largest in Palestine" (1980:166). Mark's stinging sarcasm is perhaps more recognizable in F. Beuchner's contemporary paraphrase: for wealthy North Americans it is harder to enter the kingdom "than for Nelson Rockefeller to get through the night deposit slot of the First National City Bank" (1977:63)!

Mark has again (as in 10:15) used a statement about "entering the kingdom of God" (*eis tēn basileian tou theou eiselthein*) to reinforce his alternative ideology; solidarity with "the least" is extended from the family system to the economic system. The disciples' incredulity (10:26) shows that it is not at all clear to them that anyone can be saved if not the pious at the top of the social ladder. This assumption would have been based upon the dominant ideology, which dictated that *wealth = blessing from God*. It is this that Jesus repudiates, contending instead that the *only* way to salvation for the rich is by the redistribution of their wealth—that is, the eradication of class oppression. The way in which this ideology legitimates the symbolic order will later (12:41–44) come under direct attack, in a temple episode that similarly juxtaposes the rich (*ē plousian*, 10:25) with the poor (*ptōchois*, 10:21).

Once again, the social world has been turned upside down in Markan narrative—but can this status reversal ever actually be realized? For the first time Jesus addresses this terrible question, which has loomed throughout the story. His answer: "What is humanly impossible is not for the God for whom all things are possible" (10:27). Again, this saying anticipates Jesus' direct confrontation with the political economy of the Jerusalem temple, which exploits the poor; for after calling for its overthrow, Jesus will once again remind his disciples of the "possible impossible" promised by this God (11:23).

iii. The Community of Goods: On Property

This last saying of hope would have made a perfect conclusion to the episode, but Mark is not yet finished. There is still the "unresolved" narrative of the rich man's nondiscipleship: What then *must* be done to inherit eternal life? The third part of the episode opens with Peter claiming that what the rich are unable to do, the disciples themselves have done (10:28). They have accepted the "economic condition" for discipleship (articulated in the aorist/perfect tense shift in "we have left everything and followed"). Jesus does not commit himself to affirming or denying Peter's claim, but he does offer a solemn *Amēn* saying that further illuminates the meaning of this condition (10:29).

Jesus' assurance (10:29f.) comes in two parts: the first concerning "this time" (*nun en tō kairō toutō*) and the second the "age to come" (*en tō aiōni tō erchomenō*), with the emphasis decidedly upon the former. Here the last part of the sower parable is being exegeted. The story so far has had occasion to dramatize the obstacles to the way: Satan, the fear of persecution, the deceit of wealth. Now it is time for the yield of good soil: forfeited homes, lands, and family (according to Bailey these represent the "unassailable loyalties that any Middle Easterner is almost required to consider more important than life itself," 1980:169) will be recovered "a hundredfold" (cf. 4:20). But the "eschatological harvest" occurs in *this time*! No signs from heaven, but the Kingdom *on earth*. The miracle of multiplication through sharing implied in the wilderness feedings is thus enacted in the new economic practice of the community.

The references to homes (in which the discipleship community has taken refuge throughout its journeys) and lands (that singularly priceless foundation of life in traditional societies) can only signify the gathered assets of the community of faith. In the family list, we see the influence of the teaching that has preceded this one; indeed it is a kind of summary. The "reconstituted" kinship structure (the old having been repudiated back in 3:35) is gender-equal ("brothers and sisters, mothers and fathers") and inclusive of children! It must be said: the social function of the text is to legitimate the practice of *communism*. I cannot resist citing in this context José Miranda's delightful polemic arguing that "Marxism is a mere episode in the history of the communist project" begun by Jesus:

> The doctrinal betrayal of later centuries . . . has sought to interpret this communism as a "way of perfection," not to be identified with the simple fact of being a Christian. But such an interpretation is dashed to smithereens when it impinges on the fact that Jesus made the renunciation of property a condition for simply "entering into the kingdom" [1982:18].

Mark characteristically adds a note of realism: this new social and economic order will be fiercely opposed, and will be realized only "with persecutions" (*diōgmōn*, cf. 4:17). He also inserts the persecution phrase "For my sake and the gospel's" (cf. 8:35 and 13:9). This suggests that "giving up" referred not only to voluntary status renunciation but forced privation as well. Only now comes the second assurance: "eternal life" (10:30c). Here at last we arrive at Jesus' answer to the original question, given not to the rich man, who was unable/unwilling to respond in costly discipleship, but to those struggling to put faith into practice. Mark then intones the section's "first/last" refrain, now imbued with economic as well as social and political significance (10:31). With this the second cycle closes.

9D. POLITICAL POWER AND COMMUNITY LEADERSHIP: THE THIRD CYCLE (10:32–52)

i. Toward Jerusalem: Third Portent

The first teaching cycle introduced the political vocation of the cross; the second applied it to the internal social and economic ethic of the community. The third now synthesizes the two in addressing the question of leadership. This last cycle, like the others, has its central theme stated as an antithetical aphorism ("great/servant," 10:43f.). Like the second cycle, this is framed by reference to "the way" (10:32,46), a way revealed at last as heading "up to Jerusalem."

Mark's description of the journeying group is filled with the pathos of this realization, a scene with three elements:

1. Jesus was ahead (*proagōn*) of them
2. they were astonished (*ethambounto*)
3. and those following were afraid (*ephobounto*).

The middle element of "astonishment" links this scene with the previous one (10:24). The first and third are proleptic narrative signals, pointing past the pending Jerusalem narrative to the end of the story. For after Jesus' execution some disciples who had "come up to Jerusalem" with him (15:41) will be told that he is not dead, but still "going ahead" (16:7, *proagōn*) of them to Galilee; they respond with "fear" (16:8, *ephobounto*). The point of inserting this signal here is to remind us, when we encounter it again at the end, that "fear" is a constitutive element of "following."

The third and final portent (10:33f.) is the most specific in its detailing of the political process of Jesus' trial and execution. Mark introduces each of the main elements that his "passion" narrative will detail:

1. the betrayal: "the Human One will be delivered to the chief priests and scribes . . ."
2. the double trial: "they will condemn him to death and deliver him to the gentiles . . ."
3. the torture: "they will mock him and spit upon him and scourge him . . ."
4. the execution: "and kill him . . ."
5. the resurrection: "and after three days he will rise."

Have the disciples understood the catechism so far? The episode that follows demonstrates that they have not, and does so in a manner so caustic in its caricature that it stretches the credibility of the narrative.

ii. Critique of Political Domination: Great/Servant

The petition by James and John (10:35–37) shows that the disciples are still "deaf" to Jesus' portents, continuing to understand his talk of the manifestation of the Human One's "glory" (*en tē doxē sou*, cf. 8:38) to mean some kind of messianic coup. Convinced their leader will prevail, they are already considering the administration of the new regime; they lobby for "first and second cabinet position." The image of "sitting on the right and left" could be an allusion to Psalm 110:1 (see below), or to places at the messianic victory banquet, or subordinate thrones (as elsewhere interpolated by the Q tradition; see Mt 19:28; Lk 18:28–30). In either case, it is an overtly political euphemism.

Having just completed teaching on the renunciation of social power, we can almost feel Jesus' weariness and exasperation as he listens to the request of the Zebedees. In characteristic style he throws the question back upon them (10:38), introducing two counter-euphemisms of his own. Narratively, these serve to unify the symbolics of the story as a whole: "baptism" reaches back to the beginning of the adventure (1:8ff.), whereas "cup" reaches ahead to the dramatic climax of the discipleship narrative, the last supper and Gethsemane (14:23, 36). Are they willing and able to undergo what Jesus is already undergoing (the force of the present indicatives in 10:38,39b)? The question is of course rhetorical, but Mark cannot resist sarcasm. Oh yes, say James and John; no problem.

The cup and baptism Jesus can "grant"—the disciples in time will indeed suffer before the powers (see 13:9ff.). As for the original petition for rank, however, it is deferred to "those for whom it is prepared" (*all' hois ētoimastai*, 10:40). The supreme irony is that the phrase "on the right and left" will appear again to describe those crucified with Jesus (15:27); it is the rebel Jews, not the disciples, who "take up the cross" (below, 13,A,ii). In any case, Jesus here does not repudiate the vocation of leadership, but rather insists that it is not transferred executively. Leadership belongs only to those who learn and follow the way of nonviolence—who are "prepared" not to dominate but to serve and to suffer at Jesus' side.

The episode escalates in 10:41; the other disciples are "indignant" not at the Zebedees' request itself, but rather that they are unfairly vying for advantage. Thus the whole community is indicted in the struggle for power, provoking an even more programmatic denunciation. Jesus' disgust in 10:42 faintly echoes Samuel, when the elders of Israel insisted upon having "a king to govern them like all the other nations" (1 Sm 8:4–20). We can capture the tone of Jesus' criticism of "politics as usual" in this free rendering:

> You know how it is:
> the "so-called" rulers of the nations dominate them,
> the "great ones" tyrannize them;
> but this is not so among you!

Here Jesus frontally attacks the same political powers (*tōn ethnōn*; the Roman colonial administrators, 10:34) who will in the end execute him. These "so-called" (*hoi dokountes*) rulers practice the very philosophy of leadership-as-domination that Jesus had laboriously taught against: they "lord over" (*katakurieuousin*) their subjects. Repeating himself for emphasis, Mark speaks of the "great ones" (*hoi megaloi*) who tyrannize (*katexousiazousin*) the people (searching for the strongest possible language, he may well have invented this intensive verbal form).

There is no little acerbity in this retort of Jesus. It is meant to provide sharp contrast to the original request of the Zebedees: they "did not know" what they were asking (10:38), but they "do know" how the ruling class operates (10:42). Similarly, Jesus also alludes to the messianic Psalm:

> Zebedees' allusion: "The lord said to my lord, 'Sit at
>   my right' " (Ps 110:1).
> Jesus' allusion: "Dominate (LXX, *katakurieue*) in the
>   midst of your foes" (Ps 110:2).

This is the opening round in what will become during the Jerusalem section a fierce ideological struggle over the meaning of Davidic messianism, and Mark will cite the Psalm twice more (12:36f.; 14:62). Jesus comes very close to repudiating the vision of this Psalm because of how it is popularly understood in the tradition of Davidic imperial restorationism. The concluding comment (10:43a) is usually interpreted as an imperative, but the present indicative (*ouch houtōs de estin*) suggests rather that it should be read as (yet again) dry sarcasm: "Oh, but this is not happening among *you!*"

Mark closes this programmatic rejection of "politics as usual" with one last recapitulation of power paradox: if the disciples wish to be "great" (*megas*), they must become servants (10:44b, *diakonos*). "Servant" appears only here and in 9:35 (bracketing the last two cycles), and as we shall see below it has a specific relationship to the leadership role of women in the community. Mark then restates the point for good measure: Whoever wishes to be first (echoing the second cycle) must become a slave (10:44, *doulos*). "Slave" is a euphemism for the political vocation of martyrdom, which Jesus will invoke later in his highly charged parable attacking the ruling leadership of Israel (12:2,4).

In conclusion, Mark identifies the Human One as the embodiment of the way of nonviolence about which the catechism is concerned (10:45). He has come to serve (now the verbal form, *diakoneō*) and also give his life, refusing to "save" it (see 8:35). The phrase "as a ransom (*lutron*) for many" appears to be an allusion back to "slave." The term referred to the price required to redeem captives or purchase freedom for indentured servants. Jesus promises then that the way of "servanthood" has been transformed by the Human One into the way of liberation.

Kee notes that the allusion to Isaiah 53 does not reflect a "developed doctrine of atonement"; rather, the main intent is to demonstrate that the death of Jesus was in accord with the scriptures (1977:135, but see below, 12,C,iii). Isaiah's suffering servant and the lowly Human One was not what Peter had in mind when he confessed "Messiah" at the beginning of this section. But it is the only Messiah Mark proclaims. The way of nonviolence, as Gandhi said, will not finally prevail on account of words or argument: "It shall be proved by persons living it in their lives with utter disregard of the consequences to themselves" (1948:1,122).

Having thus summed up the argument of the catechism as a whole, Mark brings this episode and the entire section to a close with a second story about being given "eyes to see" the way of discipleship.

iii. Patriarchy and Domination: Women as True Leaders

Before going on, it is worth looking back to notice a very important narrative inference in this catechism. Mark has offered critiques of three systems of power: political domination, patriarchy, and the family system. All three have everything to do with the subjugation of women by men. Against this, Mark has argued that women should have equal rights in the marriage contract; later he will again defend women against patriarchal ideology (12:18ff.). At this point we need to consider the fact that married couples are wholly absent from the stage of Mark's story, with only two minor exceptions (one is Jairus and his wife, 5:40, the other is the illegitimate union of Herod, 6:17f.!). More to the point, women otherwise always appear *without* husbands! Because the patriarchal system considered women as second-class citizens, and *unmarried* women as third-class citizens, this is truly a subversive narrative strategy. What could be its social signification?

To find out, we need to discern Mark's subtler argument about patriarchy and domination in this catechism. He goes out of his way to discredit the (male) disciples in this section, *especially* regarding their aspirations to leadership and power (9:34; 10:35ff.). In contrast, Jesus advocates and embodies a vocation of leadership predicated upon an ideology of "service." As I have pointed out, only women fulfill the vocation of *diakonia* in Mark, from the beginning of the story (1:31) to its end (15:41). The disparity between Mark's portrait of male and female disciples will be intensified in his conclusion: whereas the men desert Jesus at the very point at which their following becomes politically risky, the women stay with him to the cross and after. It is they, therefore, who will be witnesses to the resurrection (below, 13,C,iii, D).

There are four possible interpretations regarding the social function of such a narrative portrait. Kelber argues that Mark used it as a polemic against the actual Jerusalem-based church led by Peter, James, John, and Jesus' own family members (1979:90), a position I think overspeculative. Another option is that Mark simply wished to discredit any and all forms of leadership per se. This interpretation, too, I think is forced, for Mark does not dismiss but redefines the vocation of leadership; "leaderless groups" are, I think, a fantasy of modernism. More credible is a third possibility, that the story was meant to encourage critical accountability by those who "assume" leadership in the community. The negative portrait of the male disciples would certainly have helped to relativize and humanize their later leadership vocation, for it reminded the whole community that leaders can and do fail, and exhorted all to guard against the inevitable delusions of power that accrue in any social group. I think the narrative does encourage this, but this is not its primary function.

The fourth possibility is that in a thoroughly patriarchal socio-cultural order, women alone are fit to act as servant-leaders. Such a logical conclusion is fiercely resisted by Kee, who insists:

> It cannot be inferred from these passages that women occupied the leading offices in the community of Mark, but rather that the menial tasks they performed were regarded as praiseworthy and as fully compatible with God's purposes for his people [1977:91].

So much for male hermeneutics! In fact, there is no good socio-literary reason to reject this last interpretation (against Munro, 1982; see Selvidge, 1983). How else can a portrait that paints men as power-hungry and women as servants function, except to legitimate women as leaders?

This would help to explain the appearance of "independent" women in the Gospel. It is not that Mark rejects the vocation of marriage, just as he does not reject the vocation of leadership. However, he understands that the whole social system of patriarchy, which renders tyrants strong in the world and women subject in the home, must be overturned. The first concrete step in the "last as first" revolution is to bring women into leadership, and in order to do that the rigid definitions of their proper social roles (as wives and child-bearers only) must be itself undermined. This is what Mark's story does.

iv. Eyes That See; Second Stage: Bartimaeus

The community now approaches the suburbs of Jerusalem. Mark opens this second story of a blind man as he did the first: "And they came into" (*kai erchontai eis*; see 8:22) Jericho. Mark sets a scene for this episode, which was no doubt familiar to anyone who had gone to Jerusalem on pilgrimage. Jericho was the last stop en route to the city of David; the road out of town, representing the final, fifteen-mile leg of the pilgrim's journey, would have been the standard beat for much of that city's beggar population. The odds were good that pilgrims would have the mood and means to give alms. There Jesus, the disciples, and a great crowd meet Bartimaeus, the destitute blind man.

This is the last healing in the "blind/deaf" series and the Gospel as a whole. Unlike the Bethsaida episode, this symbolic statement is decisive; it is well known as a paradigmatic story of discipleship (Achtemeier, 1978). Often ignored, however, are its social and political dimensions. It is Bartimaeus who introduces the title "Jesus, son of David" (10:47), further preparing us for the imminent struggle over the ideology of popular kingship. There is also an implied class contrast between the discipleship of Bartimaeus and the nondiscipleship of the rich man, just as there was between the hemorraghing woman and the synagogue ruler in 5:21ff. These stories exhibit several common characteristics (Johnson, 1978a):

1. the hindering role of the crowd (cf. 10:48 with 5:31);
2. the commendation of faith, in both cases, *hēpistis sou sesōken se* (cf. 5:34 with 10:52);
3. ritual impurity; the bleeding woman and Bartimaeus, whose name in Hebrew could mean "son of the unclean."

Bartimaeus, like the rich man, encounters Jesus "on the way" (10:17 46). The rich man could not liquidate his fortune, but poor Bartimaeus throws away his garment, his sole element of livelihood (beggars spread out their cloaks to receive alms). The one at the top of the social scale rejected a direct call, but the one on the bottom does not even wait for a call, springing up and "following Jesus on the way" (10:52). The significance of the social, economic, and political fabric of the Bartimaeus story being placed on the eve of the Jerusalem campaign should be clear. The poor join in the final assault on the dominant ideological order, and the rich have walked downcast away. The first have become last, and the last first.

The structure of the episode emphasizes not the action or teaching of Jesus, but the struggle by Bartimaeus to regain his sight, which is complicated by the fickleness of the crowd:

1. Bartimaeus cries out; the crowd rebukes/silences him;
2. he cries out louder; Jesus instructs the crowd to call him;
3. the crowd calls him, saying, "Take courage, get up, he calls you."
4. Bartimaeus leaps up, casts away his garment, goes to Jesus.

As with the impure woman, the "least," against formidable odds, have been healed because they have taken the initiative of faith.

Mark draws a devastating contrast between this beggar's initiative and the aspirations of the disciples. Upon their approach, Jesus had asked James and John, "What do you want me to do for you?" (10:36). To the beggar's petition, Jesus responds with exactly the same words. But how different the requests! The disciples wished for status and privilege; the beggar simply for his "vision." The one Jesus cannot grant, the other he can. It is Bartimaeus who is told to "take courage" (*tharsei*), as the disciples were told earlier, during their dangerous crossing of the sea (6:50). And it is the beggar who follows. The narrative discourse of hope is now clear in this last discipleship/healing episode. Only if the disciples/reader struggles against the internal demons that render us deaf and mute, only if we renounce our thirst for power—in a word, only if we recognize our blindness and seek true vision—then can the discipleship adventure carry on.

9E. REVOLUTION FROM BELOW:
MARK'S SOCIO-LITERARY STRATEGY THROUGH 10:52

i. Discourse

The main discursive characteristics of this section are repetition and recapitulation. The latter is articulated through the four healings and the three cycles of revelation/misunderstanding/teaching. These address the central theme: the disciples' resistance to the messianic practice as defined by the Human One. Just as each teaching cycle broadens and deepens the meaning of servanthood/nonviolence in the life of the community, so each healing dramatizes the despair of the disciples' incomprehension and the hope for its healing.

I have noted the ways in which Mark draws upon the devices of apocalyptic narrative, especially Daniel. His use of parody in portraying the disciples is unparalleled. Although it is not uncommon in apocalyptic literature for the recipient(s) of the revelation to doubt or question it, Mark takes this to an extreme. The triple cycle is introduced by a pitched battle between Peter and Jesus, the earthly counterpart of the apocalyptic struggle between the Human One and Satan. It concludes with an equally severe conflict between Jesus and James and John, again with reference to the powers. In framing the section with these stories, Mark continues his strategy of discrediting the very discipleship community he has created, in this case particularly the "inner circle" (Peter, James, and John; see 5:37; 9:2; 14:33). This "anti-hero" motif has a specific ideological function, as we shall see.

The discourse of repetition has a more specifically didactic function, and is structured around two series of conditional relative clauses that directly challenge the reader. The first series consists of antithetical aphorisms, a subversive discourse that throws the listener's ordered worldview into turmoil. Two simple conditional/imperatival statements (*ei tis thelei*) establish the section's double theme as the political vocation of the cross and the social vocation of servanthood, the two essential elements of nonviolence:

8:34   All who wish to come after me must deny themselves, take
       up their cross . . .
9:35   If anyone wishes to be first, that person must become least of
       all and a servant of all.

Two subsequent restatements, in "future condition" ("if A happens, then B is sure to follow") increase their force:[5]

8:35   Whoever saves their life will lose it . . .
       Whoever loses their life saves it . .
10:43f. Whoever wishes to be great among you
       must become your slave
       Whoever wishes to be first among you
       must become your servant.

These antithetical statements, which represent the three "themes" of the respective cycles, function to challenge the primal congruities of the dominant order, such as wealth = blessing from God, or power = security. Inasmuch as "revolutionary consciousness" demands a new set of assumptions about social possibilities, the aphorisms promote a kind of liminality that undermines the ideological constraints of the reigning social orthodoxy.

The discourse of paradox is reinforced by the other implied or enacted antitheses in the section:

blindness/vision (8:22ff.; 10:45ff.)
belief/unbelief (9:24)
together/asunder (10:9)
poor/rich (10:21f.)
child/adult (10:13–15)

But paradox here has nothing to do with mere language games, as in modern deconstructionist theory; it is meant not to paralyze but to challenge the reader. The catechism insists that only a contradicting *practice* can subvert the dominant order and issue in a truly new one. This is confirmed by the second set of conditional relative clauses, interwoven as a kind of counterpoint. These are statements not of antithesis, nor of eschatological retribution, but simply of consequence-in-kind:

8:38   Whoever is ashamed of me . . . will be shamed . . .
9:37   Whoever receives one of these . . . receives me . . .
9:41   Whoever gives a cup of water . . . will be rewarded . . .
9:42   Whoever scandalizes one of these little ones . . . it is better that they (kill themselves)
10:11   Whoever divorces and remarries . . . commits adultery
10:15   Whoever does not receive the kingdom as a child . . . will not enter it at all.

The imperatives imply condition, yet the conditional relatives imply invitation: "whosoever will." Like the great didactic traditions of the Hebrew scripture, this catechism is founded upon a dialectic of challenge and promise.

Finally, as observed, this discourse is meant to recall the first sermon, and illustrates each of the four kinds of "seeds":

1. by the path, Satan intervenes (4:14 = 8:33)
2. rocky soil, tribulation causes scandal (4:16f. = 9:42)
3. thorns, wealth intervene (4:18 = 10:22)
4. good soil, hundredfold yield (4:20 = 10:30).

The way of nonviolent transformation is indeed a "mystery," and the heart of this mystery is Mark's conviction that by the "power" of the cross the powers will be overthrown.

ii. Signification

The catechism is organized around a journey toward confrontation with the authorities; it begins at one site of political alienation (Caesarea Philippi) and ends in another (Jerusalem). However "historical" the journey down through Galilee may have been (a question not important to this study, though I find little reason to doubt its essential accuracy), it is primarily a narrative fiction designed to maintain both plot and ideological tension. It is true that the emphasis is upon teaching, but the narrative vehicle of the journey stands in counterpoint to the two longer sermons of Jesus. Whereas these are delivered "sitting" to a passive audience, the catechism is a "school of the road" with a high degree of argumentation from the audience. Thus, like the Gospel as a whole, the catechism is not simply a body of wisdom sayings, but a drama, full of object lessons and symbolic action. In fact, its internal subplot actually recapitulates in outline form the narrative strategy of the Gospel as a whole:

Story-plot	*Section subplot*
first call to discipleship	first healing of blind
Jesus' powerful practice	Jesus' portents
disciples' failure	disciples' incomprehension
last call to discipleship	last healing of blind

To understand the dialectic between tragedy and hope in this part is to grasp it in the whole.

The "confessional struggle" at the outset brings to the surface the subplot concerning Jesus' true identity, which Mark has been suppressing (a narrative device long studied under the rubric "the messianic secret" (see Blevin, 1981). The voice from heaven identifying Jesus as Son was heard only by Jesus (1:11); the "confessions" of demons are silenced (1:34 and 3:12); and the disciples are mostly perplexed ("Who then is this . . . ?" 4:41). The matter of Jesus' public identity is not explicitly broached until 6:14–16, and then by Herod (just as the demons want to have power over Jesus by naming him, so too the political authorities). Jesus' direct solicitation in 8:27 appears, then, to be a sudden reversal in Mark's strategy—yet Peter's answer is straightaway again "silenced" in a disquieting confrontation. These conflicting narrative signals have a very clear purpose: to put the reader into a state of uncertainty, and hence ambivalence, about Peter's confession. The privileged information we as readers have possessed since the outset (1:1,11) about Jesus has been cast into doubt. Indeed, at no point in the story will any "confession" be unambiguous, including the centurion's cry as Jesus hangs dead on a Roman cross (15:39). The place of confession in Mark is usurped altogether by the call to discipleship, and this at the dead center of the story.

In doing this Mark is taking issue with the traditional ideological cornerstone of religious institutions: dogma. As far as he is concerned, theological orthodoxy ("Jesus is Messiah") has no meaning apart from political "orthopraxy" ("take up the cross"). Thus the fulcrum of the narrative is not a dogmatic assertion ("Jesus is . . .") but a question ("Who do you say I am?") addressed to every generation, moreover a question that can be answered only by embracing Jesus' political vocation. The choices of life and death spoken of by Jesus' invitation to the cross and self-denial are not high religious metaphor, but the most directly political and subversive discourse in the Gospel. Their concrete meaning will be dramatized in the narrative of Jesus' arrest, trial, and execution. Jesus "loses" his life by faithfully confessing the Human One before the powers (14:62); Peter tries to "save" his by denying Jesus (14:66ff.); Judas tries to "set a price on" his life in betraying Jesus to the political authorities (14:10f.).

The social function of the story is to undermine the legitimacy of "confession" apart from political circumstances. And although the disciples do not "take up their cross and follow" Jesus in *this* story, Mark assures the reader that they *will* have their own turn at costly confession (13:9-13). All this is lost upon First World Christians who still equate "self-denial" with pious gestures of "going without" at Lent. The meaning of the cross is surely better exegeted by sisters and brothers around the world today who work for justice and liberation under repressive regimes. Those who have suffered interrogation and torture by security forces seeking the names of their comrades know the intense psychological and spiritual trauma generated by the temptation to "save oneself."

It must also be said, however, that Mark's ideology of the cross has been betrayed not only by interpreters of the right but of the left as well. For in identifying his movement as a necessarily subversive one, the fact remains that he calls his followers to take up the cross, not the sword. The way of nonviolence reckons with execution, not dreams of Maccabean heroism and revolutionary conquest: in nonviolence, said Gandhi, "bravery consists in dying, not in killing" (1948:I, 265). But Mark's cross does not represent *only* the consequence of subversive practice, as liberation theology has contended. It is a deliberate revolutionary strategy, embraced in the conviction that only nonviolence can break the most primal structures of power and domination in the world, and create the possibility for a new order to dawn in the world. This proposition overturns all traditional notions of political efficacy, social power, and economic security. And truly it is the one that followers of Jesus (both in the story and throughout Christian history) have found most difficult to accept.

The second cycle applies nonviolence to the daily exercise of power; the fact that the catechism demonstrates as much concern for an "internal" ethic as for a public vocation is an indication of maturity. The same ones called to the heroic resistance of the cross are also enjoined to submit themselves to the least in the community (9:35-37). The messianic community must never be a personal power base or a closed group. Its boundaries are open, and it should acknowledge the others who also practice compassionate ministry (9:38-41). No doubt this "ecumenical spirit" was advanced by Mark with an eye toward the exclusivist ideology of both the Essenes and the Pharisees.

The primary site in which nonviolence must take hold is that of the family/household. The principle of equality obtains in marriage, and must be preserved even in tragic situations of family rupture. Children are recognized to be the primary victims, and the "circle of contempt" in the family system is radically challenged by Jesus' demand that the kingdom be "received as a child." It is not difficult to imagine the community's struggle to fully practice the nonpatriarchal, nonhierarchical social program of Jesus, given its utter cultural novelty. That they experienced external pressure, especially on family issues, is indicated by the challenges from the rival ideology of the Pharisees (10:1–12; cf. 7:9–13).

The contrast between the discipleship rejection story of the rich man (10:17–22) and the discipleship acceptance story of Bartimaeus—representing opposite ends of the social scale—would appear to be another indication of a clear "class bias" of Mark. The conclusion to that story in turn identifies the discipleship community with an alternative economic order based on sharing. The reader has been prepared for both the class-criticism and the communist solution in the first construction cycle, especially in the wilderness feeding stories, in which the little on hand is transformed into "enough" through the practice of sharing. This symbolic action becomes concretized in the new community of shared assets and extended family (10:28–31). Mark reflects an economic ideology of neither charity-dependent "wandering charismatic poverty," nor respectable middle-class autonomy (the ideology of the "ten-percent tithe"). It was a community of shared production and consumption.

Yet the disciples express amazement at Jesus' insistence that the dominant order of economic stratification is *not* ordained by God (10:23–27). This indicates the overwhelming legitimacy enjoyed by the prevailing political economy of privilege, symbolized by the rich man's claim to have kept the whole law! But this claim, and its masking of exploitive relations of production, is categorically rejected by Jesus, giving the community courage to continue the alternative economic practice it has begun (10:29). The function of the story is as pastoral as it is prophetic, and indicates that some form of communal arrangement was in place among Mark's people.

The third cycle makes a final synthesis of personal and political nonviolence, linking the vocation of community leadership to the political "apprenticeship" of the cross (10:42–45). A community cannot be resisting the powers' exercise of domination while reproducing their patterns in its own midst. The revolution must come from the ground up, beginning with the primary sites of social oppression: the family and economic existence. If practiced at the base, then conversely, Gandhi argued, nonviolence becomes the "weapon of the masses which enables a child, a woman, or a decrepit old man to resist the mightiest government" (1948:II,41).

It is clear that Mark's community was struggling in its efforts to embody this new order. This is articulated in the disciples' persistent inability to "see" (9:1) and "hear" (9:7). The way in which the disciples are plagued with self-doubt before the ideology of the scribes (9:11,14) suggests that the community was often intimidated by political authority. It is the vigorous *internal* criticism that sets Mark apart from the ethic of, for example, the Essenes. Mark refused to maintain community solidarity by projecting an external enemy; unlike Qumran, Mark acknowledges "children of light" outside the community and "children of darkness" inside. The historical experience of apostasy was raising difficult issues of communal integrity and discipline for Mark. Inclusivity could not afford to include those who were betraying other believers to the authorities. Yet even so, bodily "amputations" had to be healed; the messianic practice of peacemaking had to prevail within the community, as well as in the world.

This battle with the "demons within" is best represented in the only exorcism story in the second half of the Gospel. Like the "son" in the exorcism story, all who live in the imperial sphere are "struck dumb" by the powerful ideology of the dominant classes, which in fact has socialized us "since childhood"; unchallenged it will indeed destroy our movement (9:22). Like the father's cry, our faith is also tentative (9:24). We must learn that our deadliest enemies are within: they can be withstood only by self-reflection in prayer. Only in this way can we break the radical fluctuation between the twin pole of human brokenness: grandiosity ("We are able!" 10:39) and depression ("Why were we not able?" 9:29).

To summarize, this section gives us perhaps our most direct insight into the alternative ideology and practice of Mark's community. It is a catechism concerned not with *confessio* but *imitatio*. Jesus' way of nonviolence applies to real-life courtrooms and real-life community and family conflicts. The catechism's discourse of paradox (save/lose, first/last, great/slave) subverts the usual strategies of effecting social change by imposing it from the top. "A nonviolent revolution is not a program of seizure of power; it is a program of transformation of relationships" (Gandhi, 1948:II,8). This includes every form of relationship, from the systemic to the interpersonal, in order to address fundamental social and economic patterns of domination at their roots. This is a catechism for all those who labor in history "to build a new society within the shell of the old" (Dorothy Day), all those who work for a revolution from the grassroots up.

The journey to Jerusalem articulates an ever-deepening contrast between two kinds of social "power." There is the power of the "so-called leaders"—which the disciples are forever trying to reproduce among themselves. Pitted against this is Jesus' alternative power of *satyagraha,* which insists that the politics of the powers will not be broken until the discipleship community makes a fundamental break with power politics. Armed only with this vision, Jesus enters Jerusalem for the final battle in the war of myths.

NOTES

1. Note the similarities between the "punishments" of water (9:42b) and fire (9:44, etc.) and the demon's attempts to destroy the "son" in the previous exorcism story (9:22). In both cases there is a struggle for "belief" (9:24,42a). Do "water and fire" here symbolize the torments of unbelief, which leads to apostasy? But see Derrett, 1985.

2. Josephus writes of his attempts to persuade a certain Justus and another rebel leader to join him in defecting to Rome. In this context, he alludes to an incident in which some Galilean rebels had amputated the hand of Justus's brother sought for forgery—apparently an act of "revolutionary justice" (*Life*, 35). Elsewhere Herod reports of Galileans being burned alive for sedition (*Ant.*, XVII,vi,4).

3. D.O. Via makes a great deal of the citation of Genesis in terms of Mark's story time and his "beginning" (1:1) as a "tacit restitution of the primordial *archē* . . . the middle of the plot is also connected to the primordial beginning; therefore it is not surprising that at one point the Markan middle is itself seen by implication as a continuation of the unfallen creation situation. I have reference to the Markan teaching on marriage (10:2–9)" (Via, 1985:47). I think Via's preoccupation with a supposed relationship between Markan "time" and Markan "ethics," besides being a sophisticated literary-structuralist recycling of the old "interim ethic" theory, misses the point. Mark's argument here is no different from the earlier claim (7:6ff.) that the Pharisees' "human precepts" have overturned the true principle of justice in the "commands of God."

4. It is worth citing part of a second-century version of the same tradition which clearly understood the class criticism of the story: the well-known passage from *the Gospel according to the Hebrews*, cited by Origen (Taylor, 1963:429f.):

But the rich man began to scratch his head, for it did not please him. And the Lord said to him, "How can you say, I have fulfilled the law and the prophets, when it is written in the law: You shall love your neighbor as yourself; and lo, many of your brothers, sons of Abraham, are clothed in filth, dying of hunger, and your house is full of many good things, none of which goes out to them?"

5. The so-called future more vivid construction (*hos* + *an* + subjunctive + future indicative). We should probably also include in this series the antithetical construction of the conditional 10:29 ("no one who has left . . . will not in turn receive," *oudeis estin hos aphēken . . . ean mē labē*) together with the indicative 10:31 ("for many who are first will be last").

CHAPTER TEN

The Second Direct Action Campaign: Jesus' Showdown with the Powers in Jerusalem (Mark 11:1–13:3)

Because of the wickedness of their deeds I will drive them out of my house. I will love them no more; all their rulers are disobedient. Ephraim is stricken, their root is dried up, they shall bear no fruit.

—Hosea 9:15f.

Jesus comes to Jerusalem not as a pilgrim, in order to demonstrate his allegiance to its temple, but as a popular king ready to mount a nonviolent siege on the ruling classes. Mark now commences his second direct action campaign narrative. The long journey from the social and symbolic peripheries of Palestine (which began in the wilderness and the first direct action campaign in Capernaum) to its center is now complete. Jesus has arrived at the heart of the dominant order, and the time has come for a showdown in the war of myths. The Lord is now visiting his temple, as promised by Malachi since the beginning of the story (1:2b, cf. Mal 3:1f.), and in his actions we will witness the one whom Gandhi referred to as "the most active resister known to history—this is nonviolence par excellence" (1948:II,16).

10A. THE NARRATIVE CHARACTER OF THE JERUSALEM CONFLICT CYCLE

i. Structure

The remainder of the Gospel takes place in and around Jerusalem, and the narrative as a whole consists of three sections: (1) the conflict cycle (11:1–13:3), which will be the subject of this chapter; (2) Jesus' second sermon (13:3–37); chap. 11, below); and (3) what is usually referred to as the "passion narrative"

(14:1–16:8; chap. 12 and 13, below). The two action narratives (1 and 3) are each generated by a pair of symbolic episodes, which together function as narrative "bridges" between the major sections. This couplet consists of:

1. a "paradigmatic" disciple story (10:45–52 = 14:3–9)
2. carefully staged messianic theater (11:1–9 = 14:12–25).

Let me briefly describe the parallels between these bridges.

The couplet introducing the Jerusalem conflict cycle begins, as we have seen, with the Bartimaeus story, which functions as a bridge to the antecedent discipleship section. The blind man, over the objection of the disciples, solicits Jesus' healing and follows him to the city of David; it is *the* paradigmatic discipleship episode. Bartimaeus's faith contrasts sharply with the partially "blind" discipleship of the other followers. This story is followed by the inauguration of Jesus' nonviolent assault upon Jerusalem. The disciples follow instructions to prepare Jesus' kingly entry upon an ass; the procession then dramatizes powerful but paradoxical messianic symbolics. Jesus is hailed as bringer of the very Davidic kingdom he will in fact repudiate. This couplet of a poor, blind disciple and a lowly king prepares the reader for the intense political and class conflicts that will characterize the conflict cycle.

In direct correspondence, the couplet introducing the passion narrative opens with an episode in which a woman anoints Jesus' head with oil, again over the objections of the disciples. In doing this she recognizes and participates in his commitment to face death—an act that contrasts equally sharply with the other disciples who will abandon Jesus before the hour of his death. Mark draws the reader's special attention to the woman's act (14:9) in order to underline it as a (corresponding) discipleship paradigm. Then the disciples again are dispatched to prepare the Passover banquet in the hideaway of an attic. The Last Supper offers another kind of messianic theater, a banquet also riddled with paradox: the meal represents the most intimate moment of the discipleship community, yet at the same time introduces Mark's narrative of betrayal. This couplet prepares the reader for Jesus' final journey to the cross.

Having identified these two narrative "bridges," which frame the second campaign of direct action, let me turn to the structure of the Jerusalem campaign itself. Like the first campaign in Capernaum, it consists of a series of confrontations (11:11–13:3), followed by a withdrawal and extended sermon (13:4–37). The composition of the conflict cycle is as follows:

A. Symbolic action directed at temple state
    Jerusalem entry: Messiah's kingdom is David's kingdom?
    Temple entry: fig tree cursing/temple exorcism
    [11:27, Jesus walks around in temple]
B. Concentric triplet on political authority
    Whose baptism? the Jewish state
    Vineyard parable: leaders as tenants
    Whose coin? the Roman state

C. Doublet on ideological authority

You are wrong: Sadducees as interpreters of scripture

You are not far: scribes as interpreters of scripture

[12:35, Jesus is in the temple teaching]

D. Repudiation of temple state

Messiah's kingdom is *not* David's kingdom

Doublet on piety and profiteering: rich scribes and poor widows; exit from temple

The first and last elements (A and D, above) each articulate a criticism of both Davidic messianism and the political economy of the temple:

A. *Messiah and David*: acclamation of procession:

Is Jesus bringing the "kingdom of our Father David"? (11:10).

Temple: fig tree/temple cleansing sandwich (11:12–26):

Temple, not a house of prayer but a den of robbers!

D. *Messiah and David*: Messiah is not David's son (12:35–37):

Jesus is *not* heralding a restoration of Davidic rule.

Temple: rich scribes and poor widows (12:38–44):

Temple prayer is a facade for exploitation.

This frame articulates the main concern of the direct action campaign: Jesus' opposition to the Jewish temple state.

Within this frame are the remaining conflict stories in which Jesus engages his opponents both offensively and defensively. This series begins and ends with similar "stage directions" concerning Jesus' presence in the temple (11:27 = 12:35). I have grouped this series into two subsections (B and C in the outline). The first grouping is a concentric construction consisting of two debates about political authority on either end of a political parable (11:27–12:17). These three episodes together attack the credibility of both Jewish and Roman state power. The second grouping consists of solicitations by class opponents of Jesus, a Sadduccee and a scribe (12:18–34), both of whom he rejects. This doublet attacks the credibility of those who control the interpretation of Torah.

The second part of the Jerusalem conflict section is the extended discourse of Jesus' second sermon on revolutionary patience. It begins with the disciples' question (13:4) concerning signs that will herald the fulfillment of Jesus' prediction (13:3) that the temple-based world will come to an end. Jesus does not answer their question directly until the conclusion of the sermon (13:32–37). The internal structure of the sermon will be outlined in more detail below (11,B).

ii. Story

The disciples figure even less in this second direct action campaign than they did in the first. They come on stage only at the points where Jesus tries to explain his repudiation of the temple state (11:14,21,43; 13:1,3f.). These cameo appearances, however, manage to continue the "blindness" narrative. As they resisted Jesus' teaching about the cross and the way of nonviolence in the discipleship catechism, so they here find it difficult to believe in a political order apart from the temple. Their approbation of, and obvious awe before, the temple, right after Jesus has repudiated it (13:1), is similar in tragicomic character to their earlier rivalry for status (10:35ff.).

The character of Jesus on the other hand achieves virtual heroic proportions in this campaign. After three initial symbolic actions (entry, fig tree cursing, temple cleansing), he comes face to face for the first time with the actual political coalition that will soon engineer his imprisonment and execution: the chief priests, scribes, and elders (11:27). This launches a series of debates in which Jesus shows his mastery in answering challenges with counterchallenges (11:29, 12:16,24,34). Throughout the section Jesus exhibits little but contempt for all sectors of the ruling class; even the single overture from a sympathizer draws an ambivalent response (12:34). As a result of his militance, the latent plot to arrest Jesus is rehatched (11:18; 12:12; 14:1). The political mood of the pilgrim crowds in the city as a major factor in these maneuverings is also introduced (11:32).

In the Jerusalem section Mark begins to slow the story-time pace of his narrative, emphasizing the passage of the days, as he will again in the passion story. The opening of the Jerusalem campaign consists of three days and three visits to the temple:

1) 11:1–11   2) 11:12–19   3) 11:20ff.

Each temple visit is progressively longer and more significant: the first a mere reconnaissance, the second the cleansing, and the third commencing the long cycle of teaching/confrontation (on this scheme, see Telford, 1980:39ff.). During the second sermon, narrative temporality is suspended in favor of mythic time and space (below, 11,A,ii).

There are close parallels in the way in which the first and second campaigns are organized around particular narrative sites. The first is structured around the Sea of Galilee and the Capernaum synagogue; the second around two opposing mountains, the Mount of Olives and the Temple mount:

First Campaign

1:16	Jesus arrives at the sea (first of multiple visits)
1:20	Jesus enters the Capernaum synagogue first time for major confrontation/exorcism
	[*main cycle of conflict stories*]
3:7	Jesus leaves the Capernaum synagogue for the last time as a rejection, withdraws to sea
4:1	Jesus sits by the sea for a long sermon

Second Campaign

11:1	Jesus arrives at Bethany near the Mt. of Olives (first of multiple visits)

11:11	Jesus enters the temple the first time for major confrontation/ exorcism
	[*main cycle of conflict stories*]
13:1–3	Jesus leaves the temple for the last time as a rejection, withdraws to Mt. of Olives
13:3	Jesus sits upon the Mt. of Olives for a long sermon

Bethany is also used as a "safe" retreat from the hostility of the city—the section begins (11:1) and ends (14:3) there. These sites represent the "positive" and "negative" narrative coordinates for the discourse of the text.

10B. INTO THE HOLY CITY: SYMBOLIC PROCESSION (11:1–10)

The popular title usually given to this episode (the "triumphal entry") is a misnomer, for the procession is neither unambiguously "triumphal" nor does it actually enter Jerusalem (until the anticlimactic 11:11). The episode, resembling carefully choreographed street theater, is designed to give intentionally conflicting messianic signals.

i. Liberator on an Ass? Political Street Theater

Mark was well aware that the image of a march on the city amid Davidic acclaim would have connoted for his first readers the military procession of a triumphal nationalist hero. Indeed, he encourages this with his intertextual allusions. He puts the origin of the march "near the Mount of Olives," a place associated in early apocalyptic tradition with the final battle against the enemies of Israel in defense of Jerusalem:

> I will gather all the nations against Jerusalem to battle, and the city shall be taken and the houses plundered. . . . Then will Yahweh go forth and fight against those nations as when he fights on a day of battle. On that day his feet shall stand on the Mount of Olives [Zec 14:2–4].

Is Mark, then, implying that Jesus is "going forth to battle"?

The procession itself indeed recalls the military entry of the triumphant rebel leader Simon Maccabaeus into Jerusalem "with praise and palm branches . . . and with hymns and songs" (1 Mc 13:51). We must further consider Josephus's account of the Sicarius leader Menahem, who during the first months of the revolt, led a kingly procession into Jerusalem. Even as the insurgents were still fighting to capture the temple mount, Josephus writes:

> [Menahem] took some of the men of note with him, and retired to Masada, where he broke open king Herod's armory, and gave arms not only to his own people, but to other robbers also. These he made use of for a guard, and *returned in the state of a king to Jerusalem*, and became leader of the sedition, and gave orders for continuing the siege [*Wars*, II,xvii,8].

According to Horsley (1985), this was one of two episodes in which a clear pretension to popular kingship was asserted among the insurgents (for the other, see below, 13,A,i). He speculates that Menahem's procession may have been inspired by the intense optimism generated by the successful struggle to liberate Jerusalem from the Romans in the summer of 66 C.E.

Although Horsley warns against the tendency among modern scholars to make too much of rebel messianism as a foil for interpreting the political character of Jesus' ministry, he admits:

> Menahem's procession from Masada to Jerusalem "like a king" and his messianic posturing in the Temple appear as striking comparative material for interpretation of Jesus' "Triumphal Entry" and "Cleansing of the Temple." . . . The brief "messianic" episode among the Sicarii in 66 might legitimately be used in the interpretation of how the gospel writers shape certain traditions [1985:311].

In any case, Mark's narrative of Jesus' march on Jerusalem, composed only a few years after Menahem's procession, is all the more politically "loaded" for the striking parallel.

Yet for all these militant, indeed military, symbolics, other aspects of the narrative point in the opposite direction. Well over half of the episode concerns the instructions given by Jesus to "two disciples" in preparation for the procession (11:1–7). This gives the distinct impression that all is being deliberately planned and choreographed—hence the suspicion of "street theater." On the one hand, Jesus procures what he needs for his campaign (see "the need," *chreian echein*, of David on a military campaign referred to in 2:25). On the other hand, what he procures is a lowly ass. Obviously, Mark is making a big production out of the fact that this procession will meet the requirements of another, quite contrary part of the Zechariah tradition: the Messiah who comes to Zion "meek, riding upon an ass" (Zec 9:9f.).[1]

Although this text also belongs to the liberation-of-Jerusalem tradition, it is expressly antimilitary in its tone. Jesus does *not* intend to fight for the temple state, and the Mount of Olives will in fact be used for the purpose of judgment (13:3). This parade, then, is filled with conflicting signals, as if it intends to be a satire on military liberators.

Bilezikian has noted the interesting similarity between the narrative function of this procession and the "dramatic convention practiced especially by Sophocles," the *hyporcheme*:

> It consisted of a joyful scene that involves the chorus and sometimes other characters; takes the form of a dance, procession, or lyrics expressing confidence and happiness; and occurs just before the catastrophic climax of the play. The *hyporcheme* emphasizes, by way of contrast, the crushing impact of the tragic incident. It is a sudden outburst of joy, more or less ecstatic, not destined to be realized [1977:127].

From this perspective, the theatrics of the procession may have been meant by Mark as a kind of parody, contrasting Jesus' destiny of the cross with the popular messianic expectations of the disciples/crowds/readers.

ii. David's Kingdom? The Messianic Acclamation

Garments are thrown on the animal, then on the road (11:7f.). The strewing of cut straw "from the fields" (*ek tōn agrōn*) rarely draws notice from commentators. Given the antiurban bias we have already identified in the discourse of the text, it is not unreasonable to assume that Mark has included this detail in order to again contrast the rural crowds and the urban elite. It is the peasants, brandishing the only gifts (weapons?) they have, who usher Jesus into Jerusalem; it will be another peasant who will accompany Jesus out of the city at the end of the story (15:30). The crowd's rapturous chanting of anticipation stands in contrast on the one hand to the cold reception Jesus will shortly receive from the city fathers (11:27f.), and the disciples' fearful following of Jesus on the other. Mark uses the exact same stage direction ("those before him and following him") in 11:9a as he did to describe the community's approach to Jerusalem (10:32).

The acclaim of 11:9f. is framed by the traditional greeting of *Hosanna*. Taylor explains that this transliteration comes from:

> Psalm 118:25, where the cry to God means "Save now." In II Samuel 14:4 and II Kings 6:26 the word is used in addressing kings. . . . The psalm was used liturgically at the Feasts of Tabernacles and the Passover. "Hosanna" could therefore be used in addressing pilgrims or a famous Rabbi, but as a greeting or acclamation rather than a cry for help. At Tabernacles branches were waved and in popular speech were known as "hosannahs" [1963:456].

Here is more irony for Mark's story: the cry here is that God might "preserve" Jesus, who himself seems determined to go the way of the cross. The narrative interplay of the various cries (*ekrazon*) of the crowd in the story underscores this irony. Bartimaeus has just previously "cried out" (twice) to Jesus, addressing him as "Son of David" (10:47,49). In the procession this cry escalates into anticipation of "the coming kingdom of our Father David." In fact, Jesus will repudiate this ideology of restorationism. Consequently, after Jesus is arrested, a different cry will come from the crowd. They will clamor for the release of a "genuine" revolutionary—Barabbas—and demand the execution of the impostor, Jesus (15:13).

This procession is the opening round of the struggle over the character of messianic politics. The cries articulate the prevailing orthodoxy, which presumes the rehabilitation of the temple state in the "kingdom of our Father David." At this stage Mark does not directly repudiate this enthusiasm, but does so indirectly, as in the Prologue, through the vehicle of narrative anticlimax. Jesus does not actually enter the city until *after* the procession, and moreover his "epiphany" in the temple is not the dramatic intervention envisioned by popular messianic expectation. Jesus merely enters the temple, looks around, and withdraws back to Bethany (11:11). Many have puzzled over this verse, complaining that it adds nothing to the narrative; but this is precisely its power—*nothing happens*. Mark has drawn the reader into traditional messianic symbolics, only to suddenly abort them. This prepares us for the shock when Jesus *does* "intervene" in the temple—not to restore, but to disrupt, its operations.

10C. INTO THE HOLY PLACE: SYMBOLIC DIRECT ACTION (11:11–26)

The next three episodes represent perhaps the most famous Markan intercalation, the masterful fiction of the withered fig tree, which frames the temple action. Each element of this "sandwich" refers expressly to Jesus' criticism of the temple as symbolic center of the Jewish social order. The reader may wish to review some background on the temple (above, 2,E,iv); my discussion will draw heavily upon W. Telford's detailed study of the background of Mark's metaphorical imagery here (1980).

i. A Barren Fig Tree: "They Shall Bear No Fruit"

Jesus, returning to Jerusalem from Bethany for the start of his ministry of confrontation, curses a fig tree unable to relieve his hunger because it is not the "time" (*kairos*) for figs (11:13f.). The disciples "hear" this curse (11:14c), and find the next day that the tree has withered (11:20f.). Telford has demonstrated how the Hebrew Bible as well as contemporaneous Jewish and Christian literature clarify the semantic field of this odd magical tale. He points out that even if it were not narratively juxtaposed with the temple action, the fig tree image would have been recognized as a metaphor for the temple-based nation and its cultus.

Pointing out that the Old Testament literature "on the whole knows very little of nonsymbolical trees," Telford examines five primary (Jer 8:13; Is 28:3f.; Hos 9:10,16; Mi 7:1 Jl 1:7,12) and several supplementary texts. He concludes:

> The fig tree was an emblem of peace, security, and prosperity and is prominent when descriptions of the Golden Ages of Israel's history, past, present, and future, are given—the Garden of Eden, the Exodus, the Wilderness, the Promised Land, the reigns of Solomon and Simon Maccabaeus, and the coming Messianic Age. It figures predominantly in the prophetic books and very often in passages with an *eschatological* import. . . .
> The blossoming of the fig-tree and its *giving of its fruits* is a descriptive

element in passages which depict Yahweh's visiting his people with *bless-ing*, while the *withering of the fig-tree*, the destruction or withholding of its fruit, figures in imagery describing *Yahweh's judgement* upon his people or their enemies. The theme of judgement is, if anything, more pronounced in the prophetic books. Very often the reason given . . . is cultic aberration . . . a *corrupt Temple cultus and sacrificial system.* In some cases, indeed, the fig or fig-tree . . . can be used expressly as a symbol for *the nation itself.* . . . Who could doubt, then, the extraordi-nary impact that Jesus' cursing of the fig-tree would have produced upon the Markan reader, schooled to recognize symbolism wherever it oc-curred [1980:161f., emphasis in the original].

This intertextual evidence is further confirmed in later Jewish material, especially the halakah and haggadah. Again, Telford summarizes his find-ings:

We have seen how important the fig-tree was in the everyday life of Palestine, and the high esteem with which this, the most fruitful of all the trees, was regarded . . . its fruits being among the principal First-fruits to be brought to the sanctuary. . . . In Rabbinic imagery and symbolism . . . the good fig is the godly man, or collectively God's righteous people, and the search for figs a picture of Israel's God, seeking out those who are his own. . . .

In the Jewish Haggadah . . . we found a world of ideation within the context of which the Markan story has its rightful place. Features of the story that are problematic for the modern reader were found to be consonant with the haggadic view of nature and the affairs of men. In these stories, the world is endowed with human characteristics. The trees are sensitive to the moral dimension. They can be addressed. They can give or withhold their fruit in response to human need (whatever the season). Their blossoming or withering has moral and symbolic signifi-cance. In the world of the haggadah, the Rabbi's curse has incontrovert-ible efficacy. . . .

We took note, too, of the connection existing in the Jewish mind between the fruitfulness of the trees and the maintenance of the Temple service. According to Rabbis of the first and second centuries, the fruits had lost their savour when the Temple had been destroyed, a state of affairs that was, however, to be reversed in the Messianic Age. . . . By placing the story . . . in the context of Jesus' visit to the Temple, Mark has dramatically indicated that the expected fruitfulness associated with that institution is not to be true. Its destiny is rather to be withered, and that— *ek rhizōn* [to the roots]! [1980:193-96].

This same semantic field informs Mark at several points, notably the parables (especially the parable of the vineyard, 12:1ff.).

Indeed, the image of "withering to the roots" has already been introduced in the parable of the sower (4:6). Thus, the symbolic action of Jesus' cursing of the fig tree is Mark's own little haggadic tale, as well as a midrash on Hosea 9:16 (see below). Its narrative function is to begin Jesus' ideological project of subverting the temple-centered social order. The reappearance of the fig tree in the apocalyptic parable (13:28–32) at the conclusion to this section confirms this. In the second sermon, the leafy (i.e., fruitless) fig tree is offered as a sign of the "end time." The world that is coming to an end is the world of the temple-based state (see below, 11,E,ii).

ii. An Exorcised Temple: "I Will Drive Them out of My House"

We come to the text most often pressed into service by those engaged in political readings of the gospel: the so-called cleansing of the temple. Unfortunately, too much attention has been given to the futile pursuit of trying to reconstruct a historical event, which serves as a pretext for debates about whether such an action should be considered violent or not, or whether Jesus' protest was pro or anti "Zealotic." Instead, I will concentrate on the ideological aspects of Mark's narrative of the temple action, whatever historical tradition may lay behind it. From this perspective, the episode will be viewed as the centerpiece in Mark's unrelenting criticism of the political economy of the temple. Jesus attacks the temple institutions because of the way they exploit the poor.

As noted, Jesus' initial visit to the temple for "reconnaissance" (11:11) is anticlimactic: Mark reports that he simply "looked around" and left. This verb ("to assess," *periblepsamenos*; peculiar to Mark in the New Testament) Mark elsewhere uses to preface some important question or revelation (see 3:5,34; 5:32; 9:8; 10:23). Jesus then withdrew back to Bethany, "because the hour was late" (*opse*, see 11:19). We wonder what the hour was too late for? The suspense is soon resolved; immediately upon arriving in the temple the next day, Jesus responds to what he had "assessed" (11:15–17). His action takes four parts; he

1. began to drive out those buying and those selling;
2. overturned the tables of the moneychangers and the seats of those selling doves;
3. prevented anyone from carrying any vessel through the temple;
4. taught them.

Let us consider each in turn.

Jesus' first target is the temple marketplace, which was probably located in the outer Court of the Gentiles. Jesus "drives out" (*ekballein*) all who bought and sold (10:15a). Here now is the second Markan midrash on Hosea's judgment upon the ruling class of Israel (Hos 9:15, LXX):

I will drive them out of my house
   (*ek tou oikou mou ekbalō*)
. . . all their rulers are disobedient
   (*pantes hoi archontes auton apeithountes*).

This prophecy dovetails nicely also with the semantic field Mark has already constructed in his story. It recalls the exorcism in the Capernaum synagogue by which Jesus inaugurated his first campaign of confrontation with Jewish leaders (1:21ff.). More importantly, it draws the first of several crucial analeptic connections to the parable of the "strong man's house": "How can Satan drive out Satan?," Jesus had asked (3:24ff.).

Taylor writes:

> "Those who sold" are the people who traded in victims for the Temple sacrifices and in wine, oil, and salt, and "those who bought" are the pilgrims who required such things for the needs of the cultus [1963:462].

Christian commentators usually give the impression that Jesus was somehow surprised to find commerce in a place of prayer and worship. But this is to import into the text assumptions about the "secular" and "sacred" from our modern, highly differentiated social formation, which I have pointed out is foreign to the world of this text. In fact, commercial activity was an entirely *normal* aspect of any cult in antiquity. The Jerusalem temple, as Jeremias has shown (1969:25f.), was *fundamentally an economic institution,* and indeed dominated the city's commercial life. The daily operation of the cult was a matter of employment for curtain makers, barbers, incense manufacturers, goldsmiths, trench diggers, and countless others. Economic conflicts were to be expected: he cites the example of shewbread bakers who once went on strike for higher pay. Many rabbis were concerned with the fairness of temple-oriented commerce, and often worked to prevent the inevitable racketeering. Jesus' indignation could hardly be attributed to a discovery of the existence of temple trading per se.

What, then, upset him? We must remember that the Hosea prophecy is leveled against Israel's "princes." According to Jeremias, many of the commercial interests:

> Belonged to the high-priestly family. We may add here that the high priest Ananias (in office AD 47 to about 55) was called the "great procurer of money" by Josephus . . . and that the temple was said to be going to rack and ruin because of avarice and mutual hatred [1969:49].

It is the *ruling-class interests* in control of the commercial enterprises in the temple market that Jesus is attacking.

The second element in the action strengthens this view. Mark singles out two groups of temple entrepreneurs as specific targets of Jesus' disruptive tactics (10:15b). The money changers:

> Sat at their tables or "banks" for the purpose of changing the Greek or Roman money of the pilgrims into Jewish or Tyrian coinage in which alone the Temple dues could be paid [Taylor, 1963:462].

Jeremias adds that this group probably also dealt in general currency transactions. Given the fact that Jerusalem was extremely cosmopolitan, with revenues pouring in from the Jewish diaspora all over the Mediterranean world, we must see the money changers as streetlevel representatives of banking interests of considerable power. Mark considered these money changers suitable symbols of the oppressive financial institutions he so fiercely opposed.

"Those selling doves" refers to the staple temple commodity relied upon by the poor. Doves were used primarily "for the purification of women (Lv 12:6, Lk 2:22-24), the cleansing of lepers (Lv 14:22) and other purposes (Lv 15:14,29)" (Taylor, 1963:462). That there was an awareness of the fact that cultic obligations were especially hard on the poor is indicated by this interesting rabbinic case cited by Jeremias:

> We have evidence of an indirect attempt at maximum price fixing by Simeon, son of Gamaliel I (Paul's teacher, Acts 22:3), whom we meet as an influential member of the Sanhedrin at the time of the Jewish war.
>
> Once a pair of doves . . . was sold for two gold dinars. Then said Rabbi Simeon, son of Gamaliel, "By this dwelling [meaning the temple] I will not rest this night until I have made it so that they can be bought for one [silver] dinar." So he went into the court and taught thus: In certain cases only one offering need be brought instead of the five strictly necessary. [He was afraid that the high prices would prevent poor people from bringing any offering.] The same day the price of a pair of doves stood at half a silver dinar [M. Ker. i,7].
>
> Since the gold dinar is worth twenty-five silver dinars, this decree of the Sanhedrin had, according to the Mishnah, caused a reduction of 99 per cent, to 1 per cent of the original price [1969:34].

But Mark is not concerned with advocating lower prices for the poor or fair economic practices. For Jesus has already repudiated the purity and debt systems themselves—and its specific marginalization of lepers (1:41ff.) and women (5:25ff.).

Thus Jesus calls for an end to the entire cultic system—symbolized by his "overturning" (*katestrepsen*, which can also mean to "destroy") of the stations used by these two groups. They represented the concrete mechanisms of oppression within a political economy that doubly exploited the poor and unclean. Not only were they considered second-class citizens, but the cult obligated them to make reparation, through sacrifices, for their inferior status—from which the marketers profited. Jesus' action here is fully consistent with his first direct action campaign to discredit the socio-symbolic apparati that discriminated against the "weak" and the "sinners" (2:17).

The third and final action implies that the goal of these disruptive steps was a shutting down of temple operations altogether (10:16). He "forbade anyone to carry any goods [*skeuos*, here meaning any vessel or item needed for the cult] through the temple." Here is the second analeptic reference to the strong man parable: "No one can go into the strong man's house to plunder his goods (*ta skeuē autou* . . . ," 3:27). This action suggests some kind of barricade or "guerilla ban" on all further activities for that day. The point is not to try to speculate on *how* Jesus might have actually accomplished this so much as to understand the *legitimation* such a narrative lends to the practice of direct action (see further below, 11,F,ii). The boldness of this action obviously requires strong justification, and this is forthcoming in the last part of the temple action: Jesus' "teaching" (11:17).

iii. A Den of Thieves: "All Their Rulers Are Disobedient"

Jesus, as he will throughout the Jerusalem campaign, resorts to a defense/ offense based upon scripture. Instead of returning to the Hosea text, however, Mark cites the two great prophets, Isaiah and Jeremiah. His first audience would immediately have understood his intertextual argument; modern readers must return to the citations if we are to understand the point. The first quote is directly from the LXX text of Isaiah 56:7, the climax to an oracle that is perhaps the fullest Old Testament vision of an inclusive Israel. The opening hymn of a collection modern scholars call "Third Isaiah," Isaiah 56:1–8 narrates Yahweh's promise to the foreigner and the socially marginal (56:3,6). The "house of prayer" on the "holy mountain" (56:7) will be a place of joy for all who are dispossessed: "Thus says the Lord God, who gathers the outcasts of Israel: I will gather yet others to him besides those already gathered" (Is 56:8). By citing this tradition Mark has indicated what the temple is *supposed* to embody: inclusivity and community, especially accessible to "outsiders."

But to explain what it has *in fact become* ("but you have made it"), however, Mark draws upon another, quite different tradition. Many have argued that the reference here to "thieves" (*lēstōn*) is meant to suggest the social bandits (as it does in 14:48 and 15:27), and hence should be seen as Mark's veiled criticism of the revolutionary government that had taken power of Jerusalem and the temple cult. This could not be further from the truth, for as far as Mark is concerned, it is the temple itself that "robs" the poor. The prophecy of Malachi lies just beneath the surface here, with its criticism of the sacrificial system *as robbery*:

> The Lord whom you seek will suddenly come to his temple. . . . I will be a swift witness (LXX, *martus*) against . . . those who oppress the hireling in his wages, the widow and the orphan, against those who thrust aside the sojourner. . . . Will humans rob (LXX, *pterniei*) God? Yet you are robbing me; You say "How are we robbing you?" In your tithes and offerings. . . . Bring the full tithes into the storehouse, that there may be food in my house [Mal 3:5,8,10].

This tradition clearly condemns those who "cheated" in the older agrarian economic system of central-storehouse redistribution (see above, 2,B,i), which resulted in class oppression. This "subtext," in which the temple is portrayed as an apparatus of economic stratification rather than justice, runs throughout Mark's criticism of the cult.

Malachi may be in the background, but the metaphor "den of thieves" is taken directly from Jeremiah 7:11 (LXX). This tradition is—in contrast to the Isaiah text—one of the bitterest attacks upon the temple state in the Hebrew Bible. The oracle begins by a warning to Judah:

> Do not trust in these deceptive words:
> "This is the temple of the Lord . . ." [Jer 7:4].

Jeremiah insists that Yahweh's covenant grants Israel a dwelling only insofar as justice toward the alien, the fatherless, the widow, and the innocent is maintained (7:5–7). If idolatry and exploitation flourish, the temple will be destroyed, as was the first shrine at Shiloh (7:9–15).

It is significant that Mark has drawn upon *this* tradition to defend Jesus' action. We might perhaps have expected him, given his earlier allusions to Zechariah, to cite Zechariah 14:21: "There shall no longer be a trader in the house of the Lord of hosts on that day." The evangelist John on the other hand cites Psalm 69:9: "Zeal for thy house will consume me" (Jn 2:17). The problem for Mark is that these traditions, and for that matter even the Hosea and Malachi "subtexts," were essentially *reformist* in their attitude to the cult. Jeremiah, on the other hand, gives the more radical ultimatum that unless exploitation of the poor ceases, the temple will be destroyed. And according to Jesus' denunciation of the entrepreneurs, this exploitation is rampant. Later, in the last episode inside the temple, Mark will illustrate this explicitly: a widow is made destitute by her contribution to the temple treasury (12:41ff.). Witnessing this, Jesus will leave the temple and call for its destruction (13:1ff.).

Jesus' point is understood loud and clear by the high priests and scribes. Mark tells us they *hear* his teaching (11:18), just as Jesus' disciples *heard* his curse upon the fig tree (11:14). Having shown his hand, Jesus withdraws. Now the leaders, who know their scriptures and their interests, begin to show theirs. They "look for a way" (*ezētoun pōs*) to get rid of Jesus; this phrase throughout the Jerusalem narrative refers to their political maneuvering (12:12; 14:1,11,55). At this point in the story, however, their plot against Jesus will be repeatedly constrained by their fear of the unpredictable allegiances of the crowds.

The scriptural teaching has revealed the third and final analeptic reference to the strong man parable: Isaiah's metaphor for the temple as a "house" of prayer. By this time the reader can legitimately conclude that the obscure parable spun by Jesus, when he declared ideological war with the scribes from Jerusalem back in 3:24ff., is now being fulfilled. The "house" that is "divided" is the temple, its vocation betrayed by a political economy of exploitation; it "cannot stand." Jesus has "driven out Satan," and put a ban on the house's "goods." *This* is the apocalyptic struggle to bind the strong man and plunder his house.

iv. A Moved Mountain: Faith as Political Imagination

In 11:19–21, Jesus leaves the temple in the evening; back outside Jerusalem, Mark returns briefly to the fig tree story. Mark's own conflation of the temple action and the fig tree curse instructs us to use both the Malachi and Hosea traditions as the hermeneutical keys. The "whole nation" is implicated in "robbing" Yahweh through the corruption of the temple sacrifice and tithing system (Mal 3:9), which makes the "disobedient princes" rich (Hos 9:15). Israel is challenged to repent—that is, to restore economic justice—in order to receive "blessing" (Mal 3:10–12). If it does not, Yahweh will "send Elijah the prophet" to issue one last call to repentance, "lest I come and smite the land with a curse" (Mal 4:5f.). It is this curse that has been enacted; Ephraim has "borne no fruit," and "dried up to the roots" (Hos 9:16).

The curse/exorcism of the fig tree/temple is more than a political protest; Mark means for it to be a "proleptic" sign within his own narrative. When Jesus later speaks of the end of the temple state in his second sermon, Mark will point us back to this action, through the use of the expression "Look!" (*idē*):

11:21: "Rabbi, Look! The fig tree you cursed has withered!"
13:3: "Teacher, Look! What wonderful stones and buildings!"

The direct narrative connection between the disciples' encounter with the tree and the temple is a kind of inverse discourse, similar to the bifocal reality of the courtroom myth we saw earlier (above, 8,D,ii). The reader must choose which reality to believe in: the temple-as-withered-to-the-root (sign of a system that is coming to an end) or the temple-as-bigger-than-life (sign of a system that will never end; see below, F,iii). In other words, as in the second sermon, this narrative moment was meant to be instructive to Mark's original readers in their historical moment, in which they had to decide whether or not to join in the defense of the temple state during the revolt (below, 11,A,ii). This is the reason why in 11:21 Peter "remembers" (*anamnēstheis*, see 14:72) the symbolic action; Mark hopes his readers will also "remember" it in their historical discernment.

Jesus now has the task of convincing his disciples not only that the temple-based social order *can* be overturned, but that they should reconstruct their collective symbolic life apart from it. It is a most appropriate place to deliver a mini sermon on faith. "Believe in God!" is not the hortatory platitude it may at first glance seem (11:23). The modern reader must remember that in the social world of the first-century Middle East, a temple was closely identified with a deity's existence. This was supremely true for the Jew; one could not simply repudiate the temple without provoking the most fundamental crisis regarding Yahweh's presence in the world. Jesus directly challenges this identification, arguing that to abandon faith in the temple is *not* to abandon faith in God. The two following solemn sayings declare God's continued presence and activity to change the world through the powerful vehicle of *faith*.

The curious saying about the mountain may well have originally been an eschatological tradition, referring to Isaiah's promise that "every mountain will be made low" (Is 40:4; see Telford's discussion of the logion's interesting tradition-history, 1980:117). In its Markan narrative context, however, the "mountain" can only refer to the temple. Again, Telford provides necessary semantic background:

> In Jewish circles, the correlative mountain- and tree-uprooting images were found in legal, legendary, thaumaturgic, and eschatological contexts, and employed in connection with the Rabbi, the king, the hero, the thaumaturge or the Messianic follower. In a legal context, the term "uprooter of mountains" was found to have a *technical* meaning. Applied to the king (and to Herod in particular), it could be employed as a double entendre, bolstering a legal argument for the exceptional nature of Herod's pulling down of the Temple. . . . The function of [Mark's] redaction is therefore to announce, we believe, that "the moving of mountains" expected in the last days was now taking place. Indeed, about to be removed was the mountain par excellence, the Temple Mount. The Temple, known to the Jewish people as the "mountain of the house" or "this mountain" was not to be elevated, as expected, but cast down! [1980:118f.].

Faith in the God-who-is-not-in-the-temple, then, means that the disciples must also repudiate the temple state. The command to be thrown into the sea of course recalls the identical symbolic action narrated in the earlier story of the Gerasene demoniac. As impossible as it may seem, Mark insists that the overwhelming power and legitimacy of both the Roman "legion" and the Jewish "mountain" will meet their end—if the disciples truly believe in the possibility of a new order. That is to say, faith entails political imagination, the ability to envision a world that is not dominated by the powers.

The parallelism between 11:23 and 11:24 demands that they be interpreted together:

Amen I say to you	Therefore I tell you
whoever says . . .	all that for which you pray . . .
and believes . . .	believe that it is granted
it will happen for you	and it shall happen for you

The latter generalizes the former, as if to say "if this mountain can be moved, anything can happen!" The world *can* be remade. However, the second saying also functions to make sure the reader understands that this challenge to faith depends upon prayer—just as it did in 9:29!

The following saying on prayer (11:25) is textually problematic, and Telford

(1980:51ff.) in a careful analysis concludes it is a secondary addition, as is 11:26 without doubt (omitted in the RSV text). However, because most translations include 11:25, I will consider it part of the Markan narrative. The literary fabric is sound, since the theme of prayer was already introduced in the Isaiah citation of 11:17. The ideology is also appropriate to the context, for the connection between prayer and temple piety/profiteering is fundamental to Mark's criticism of the cult; he will return to it later in a biting satire on the practice of prayer by the ruling class (12:39f.). But most of all, the new practice of forgiveness is the necessary alternative to the temple cult.

The saying no doubt reflects the strong "Lord's prayer" tradition, which accounts for its uncharacteristic vocabulary (such as "your father in heaven"). It reflects that tradition's concern for forgiveness as the sole condition for prayer. Jesus' attack upon the temple thus appropriately concludes with a new "site" for prayer now that the "house of prayer" has been abandoned. This new site is neither geographical nor institutional but ethical: the difficult but imperative practice of mutual forgiveness within the community. As the discipleship catechism stressed, inequality can be prevented only by a living practice of reconciliation and the renunciation of power and privilege. The community's practice of forgiveness becomes the replacement of the redemptive/symbolic system of debt represented in the temple. The community becomes truly the "priesthood of all believers," the place of prayer "for all peoples."

10D. CONFRONTING THE POLITICAL AUTHORITY OF THE COLONIAL CONDOMINIUM (11:27–12:17)

Jesus now turns his attention to the very ruling class whose profitable control over the cult he has just challenged. He takes on two sets of opponents in episodes (11:27–33; 12:13–18) linked by their almost identical five-step narrative structure of challenge/riposte:

1. Jesus is approached by political opponents;
2. they challenge him with a question concerning authority;
3. Jesus poses a counterquestion, challenging his opponents to state their own loyalties;
4. opponents respond;
5. Jesus answers original question accordingly.

Inserted between these episodes is a parable that challenges the political leadership of the nation by attacking the ideological myth upon which it is popularly legitimated (12:1–11).

i. Whose Baptism? Jewish State Power

Jesus reenters Jerusalem and the temple and is immediately confronted by the high priests, scribes, and elders (11:27). This grouping signifies the authority of the Jerusalem Sanhedrin, which as far as historians can tell did consist of members from these three strata of the priestly aristocracy. The Sanhedrin, according to Jeremias:

> Was in origin and effect the first authority in the land, and so its competence extended throughout world Jewry. . . . After Judea became a Roman province in AD 6, the Sanhedrin was its chief political agency. A committee of the Sanhedrin was in charge of finance in the eleven Jewish toparchies into which the Romans had divided the land. Furthermore, the Sanhedrin was at that time the first communal court of justice in the province, and finally it was the highest Jewish court of law in all Judea [1969:74].

In Mark this coalition represents the archetype of the Jewish state, which as Jesus predicted (8:31) will engineer his execution (14:43,53; 15:1).

Their challenge to Jesus' temple action and the teaching they "heard" (11:28) is stated redundantly in order to underline their extreme anxiety:

> With what kind of authority do you do these things?
> Who gave you the authority to do the things you do?

The Sanhedrin, whose members see themselves as the authority "on earth" representing the temple, which is legitimated "from heaven," challenges Jesus to present his credentials. In his counterquestion, Jesus exposes this opposition (legitimation "from heaven"/"from men," 11:29f.) by taking the example of the baptizing ministry of John. According to Mark, John's was a ministry of considerable power, which Jesus inherited even more powerfully "after John was arrested" (1:7-15). Hence, what the leaders think of John will determine what they think of Jesus. Inasmuch as John was killed by political authorities who were threatened by his preaching of repentance, the question is a loaded one, and the answer moot. Jesus maintains that prophetic action is sanctioned either from "outside" or from "within" the present social order; inasmuch as the Sanhedrin has not granted Jesus authority, it must come from God. Realizing that Jesus has politically outflanked them, the leaders "equivocate" (*dielogizonto*, 11:31), a word Mark always uses to describe ideological confusion (2:6,8; 8:16f.; 9:33).

The mention again of the Sanhedrin's "fear of the crowd" reveals its members' vulnerability to the social power of prophetic movements. The discourse draws a parallel between their fear of Jesus the living prophet and John the dead prophet, equal political threats because of their popularity among the crowds (*hochlon*, cf. 11:18 and 11:32). Mark's purpose here is not to romanticize the "masses"—for they will in this story also betray Jesus—but to suggest that the Jewish leadership is politically isolated, fearful of the very people it purportedly serves. The episode ends in a draw: the leaders are unwilling to publicly commit themselves, and Jesus refuses their interrogation.

ii. Leaders as Tenants: The Central Political Parable

As in the first campaign, a clash over the issue of ideological authority (3:22–27) compels Jesus to resort to a discourse of parables (12:1 = 4:2). Like the earlier sower parable (4:3–20), the discourse of this vineyard parable (12:1–10) is clearly allegorical. Yet it is similarly set in the concrete life of Palestinian agricultural production, and again intends to subvert the social relationship between tenant farmer and landowner. For Jesus here tells a story in which the Jerusalem leadership, who were *in fact* the absentee landowning class, appear as *tenants* of an absentee landlord—that is, Yahweh.

Jeremias (1972:70ff.) marvels over the way in which Mark intertwines allegory and social realism in this parable. It is founded upon Isaiah's song of the vineyard (Is 5:1–7), with the description of the planting and fencing closely following the LXX text of Isaiah 5:1f. The "vineyard" was a well-known metaphor for Israel (fenced around by the law). The realistic note—"he leased it to tenants and went away"—is, however, Mark's. Noting the increased latifundialization of northern Palestine at this time, Jeremias sees in this addition a reflection of "the revolutionary attitude of the Galilean peasants towards the foreign landlords." Mark's listeners, well aware of the politics of land in Palestine, could revel in the role-reversal that demoted the ruling class to the lowly status of unruly tenants.

The allegory immediately reasserts itself in 12:2 in the symbolic discourse of phrases such as "at the right time" (*tō kairō*, cf. 1:15), "sent his servant" (*apesteilen . . . doulon*, cf. 10:44), "to get the fruits" (*tōn karpōn*, cf. 4:7f.; 11:14). The multiple missions by the owner's representatives are repelled with increasing violence by the tenants (12:2–5). This would seem to be an expression of the popular tradition that spoke of a line of persecuted prophets (cf., e.g., Mt 23:29–35). Finally the "beloved son" (*huion agapēton*), a designation already established in Mark as belonging to Jesus (1:11; 9:7), is dispatched.

The scheme of the tenants to seize the property switches back to realism (12:7). Jeremias thinks that this strategy can be explained on the basis of historical laws of assuming ownership:

> If [the landlord] is living in a distant foreign country we have, then, the simplest explanation of the otherwise incredibly foolish assumption of the tenants that, after the removal of the sole heir, they will be able to take unhindered possession of the property (Mark 12:7); they evidently have in mind the law that under specified circumstances an inheritance may be regarded as ownerless property, which may be claimed by anyone, with the proviso that the prior right belongs to the claimant who comes first. The arrival of the son allows them to assume that the owner is dead, and that the son has come to take up his inheritance. If they kill him, the vineyard becomes ownerless property which they can claim as being first on the spot [1972:70].

Mark is making a thinly veiled allusion to the greed of the ruling class—which Isaiah's vineyard song also condemns (Is 5:8)! Not only have they mismanaged the "vineyard" (i.e., the temple cult); they have connived to "own" it (i.e., turn it into a profitable commercial interest).

The son is killed and cast off (without proper burial, the ultimate insult; Jesus too will be cast "outside" the city of Jerusalem). For all this, the parable threatens, the tenants will be slaughtered, and the vineyard turned over to someone else (12:8f.). The violence and counterviolence of this climax are true to Isaiah's condemnation:

> For the vineyard of the Lord of hosts
> is the house of Israel
> And the people of Judah
> are his pleasant planting;
> and he looked for justice,
> but behold, bloodshed;
> for righteousness,
> but behold, a cry! [Is 5:7].

And however the vengeance of the owner may be interpreted allegorically, it certainly reflects a landowner's wrath, with which the landless Palestinian was all too familiar.

In conclusion to the parable Jesus again turns to scripture for legitimation, citing verbatim the LXX of Psalm 118:22 (12:10f.). Mark has now brought Psalm 118 into the center of the messianic war of myths. Most rabbinic literature interpreted David as the "rejected one" (*apedokimasan*) of the Psalm. But God restored David as king; thus the crowd acclaims Jesus as restorer of this promise (11:9f.). But Mark (with the rest of early Christian tradition, for this text is one of the most often quoted in the New Testament) expropriates this identification for Jesus. It is Jesus who will be "rejected" by the leaders of Judea (8:31), thus subverting the ideology of restoration of the independent temple state. The reference to "builders" and "cornerstones" here will take on still more significance later when Jesus predicts the destruction of the temple "stone by stone" (13:3), and in the subsequent charge against him that he was calling for the demolition and "rebuilding" of the "sanctuary" (14:58).

In case it was not perfectly obvious, Mark tells us that the Sanhedrin concluded the parable was aimed at it (11:12). Its subversive discourse has been understood, and there follows another attempt to seize Jesus. For a third time (see 11:18,32) the antagonists are foiled due to their fear of the crowd. If this was a *political* allegory, the question left in the reader's mind is this: If the Jewish state is bankrupt, who are the "others" (11:9) to whom the stewardship of the social experiment of Israel will pass? Christian commentators are quick to suggest that it is the "gentiles." If this were Mark's position, he would have to indicate so at this point by endorsing the hellenization of Palestine under the colonial rule of the Romans. Obviously, the interpretation of the next episode becomes crucial in understanding Mark's ideology.

iii. Whose Coin? Roman State Power

Mark, who clearly reserves his harshest criticism for the Jewish social order to which he belongs, now turns to directly confront the matter of Roman colonial rule. Collaboration was certainly an option, one chosen by many of Mark's contemporaries in the wake of the revolt of the year 66. Josephus is the most famous example of one who started in active support of the insurrection, became disillusioned, and finally chose to side with the Romans *in the conviction that this was best for the nation of Israel* (see above, 2,F,i). Does Mark do the same?

The episode opens with the Sanhedrin, again hindered by popular messianic sentiment from arresting Jesus, pursuing new tactics. Its members conspire with new allies: the Pharisees and Herodians. These are dispatched with a mission to try to "entrap" (*agreusōsin*) Jesus in his teaching (12:13). This verb appears only here in the New Testament, but in the LXX and secular Greek it means to catch by trapping or fishing. Jesus recognizes this as a "test" (*peirazete*, 12:15), recalling both his struggle with Satan (1:13) and Pharisaic harassment (8:11, 10:2). Mark is heightening the political drama: Jesus is a hunted man.

I will examine below (iv) exactly why the question of taxes was necessarily an *entrapping* one in the ideological environment of Mark. For now, we will simply recognize the obvious: it was a test of loyalty that divided collaborators from subversives against the backdrop of the revolt. Why is this challenge put on the lips of the Pharisaic-Herodian coalition? This coalition already exists on the Markan narrative map—we met it in 3:6, where the two groups held a "political consultation" to see about prospects for the murder of Jesus, on the heels of the summary confrontation in the Galilee synagogue. In Mark's world (both narrative and historical), the Pharisees are Jesus' most dogged Galilean opponents, and the "Herodians" represent the "royalists," whose murderousness was dramatized in the story of the execution of John the Baptist (6:17–29). We have already been warned against their "leaven" in 8:15, which threatened the "one loaf," or integrated community, advocated by Markan symbolics. Thus these antagonists were good candidates to "flush out" Jesus' position on the delicate tax question, because of their joint opposition to his messianic program.

Like the rich man (10:17), they use flattery in their approach (12:14). Commentators who claim that this functions only to establish their insincerity miss the trapping strategy. The sly compliment is a neatly structured concentric doublet:

> "Teacher, we know that you are forthright (*alethēs*), that you do not concern yourself with the opinion of others, for you pay attention to the position of no one; but teach the way of God forthrightly (*aletheias*)."

Jesus' "candor" is equated with an alleged scorn of equivocation; as Lightfoot paraphrases it, he is praised for his practice of "telling the truth regardless of the consequences." They are in fact daring Jesus to commit himself in this loaded political situation—*that* is why Mark calls them "hypocritical" (12:15). Yet at the same time embedded in their dare is the authentic discipleship concern of Mark's community. What indeed is "the way" in this crucial question facing them?

The tax referred to is the popularly despised poll tax (*kēnson*, Greek transliteration of the Latin *census*). Their first question—"Is it lawful (*exestin*) to give the tax to Caesar or not?"—recalls previous conflicts over the law in which Herod (6:18) and the Pharisees (2:24,26; 3:4; 10:2) have figured. The second question reveals that the dilemma is not academic: "Do we pay or don't we pay?" Is this "we" inclusive of Jesus? Jesus' demand that his challengers supply the denarius clarifies that it is not: he carries no denarius, his opponents do. (The denarius is mentioned by Jesus' disciples in 6:37 and 14:5, but in neither case does Jesus affirm the transaction). The question is theirs, not his, so they must "own up" to it. Mark is careful to distance Jesus from the coin and the collaborative politics it represents. This coin now becomes the dramatic center of the story.

Jesus (12:16) asks his opponents to consider the "discourse of the coin." He poses a double question: "Whose image and whose inscription is this?" As Mark's audience would have been well aware, the coin bore the head of the current Caesar, extolling him as "August and Divine Son." Such an "image" (*eikōn*) itself would have settled the matter for patriotic Jews, who regarded the mere circulation of Roman currency as an issue of idolatry. Brandon cites an ancient source that spoke of patriotic Jews who "never touch a coin on the ground that one should never carry, nor look upon, nor make an image" (1967:45). The more important reference for the Markan narrative, however, is the "inscription" (*epigraphē*). This word appears only one other time in the Gospel: the writ of conviction posted over Jesus' cross, which read "The King of the Jews" (15:26)! Obviously, a recognition of these conflicting "images" and "inscriptions" is indispensable for any interpretation of Jesus' final pronouncement.

Jesus' opponents began the discussion with reference to the way of "God" and the tax of "Caesar"; Jesus ends it by considering these two claims. The imperative commonly translated "render" (*apodote*) is widely used in the New Testament to speak of payment of debt or recompense, but occurs only here in Mark, and is best read as "repay." The sense of the dictum is: "Repay the one to whom you are indebted." Tannehill argues the case for 12:17 as an antithetical aphorism in form:

> Jesus' reply is a short, pointed saying consisting of two halves. The halves are linked with each other, for each speaks of the same relationship and expresses this in the same syntactic structure, the only important change being the insertion of the word "god" for "Caesar" in the second half.

. . . So the two halves of the saying are bound into a tight unity in which the parts interact with one another. Our attention is directed toward the two proper nouns which occur within the same pattern, and we are forced to think about their relation. Like most antithetical aphorisms, Jesus' reply is very concise . . . showing no concern for complications and qualifications [1975:173].

In other words, no Jew could have allowed for a valid *analogy* between the debt Israel owed to Yahweh and any other human claim.

There are simply no grounds for assuming (as so many bourgois exegetes do) that Jesus was exhorting his opponents to pay the tax. He is inviting them to act according to their allegiances, stated clearly as *opposites*. Again Jesus has turned the challenge back upon his antagonists: What position do *they* take on the issue? *This* is what provokes the strong reaction of incredulity (*exethaumazon*, only here in the New Testament) from his opponents—something no neat doctrine of "obedient citizenship" could possibly have done.

The parallels between this episode and the Sanhedrin's challenge concerning authority are manifest, especially the divine/human antithesis:

Was John's baptism from heaven or from men?
Pay back Caesar what is Caesar's, and God what is God's.

This is apocalyptic dualism, radically opposing the divine reign to the human one. Mark's own allegiance is made clear by the entire narrative of the last three episodes taken together. "What is God's" is stipulated in the vineyard parable—all leaders are only tenants. As Brandon argues, 12:17 is "indeed a saying of which any Zealot would have approved. . . . There was no doubt that God owned the land of Israel, not Caesar" (1967:347). Mark thus in no uncertain terms rejects the option of political cooperation with Rome, and repudiated the authority of Caesar and his "coin." This disposes of the notion that his political rejection of the Jewish leadership drove him into the hands of assimilationists and collaborators.

iv. Markan Nonalignment and the Political "Trap"

The reader will be well aware that 12:13–17 is one of the most abused texts in the Gospels. The fact that the episode is so unavoidably political catches most commentators off guard. *Here* (but not elsewhere) they admit that Mark's discourse is unintelligible without some nominal understanding of the historical situation of Roman colonialism and the revolt. Part of the problem is that this text is almost invariably treated in isolation from the rest of the narrative. When examined by itself, the *subtleties* of the story become *ambiguities*.

Jesus' pronouncement in 12:17, for example, taken out of context as an abstract general principle, is easy prey for manipulation. Its radical antithesis is presumed to be neat parallelism, and then exploited by those already committed to a Reformation "two realms" theory. This invariably occasions a homily on "church and state" or the responsibilities of the "Christian citizen"—pseudo exegesis, which is of course determined far more by the commentator's own ideological commitments than by those of the text. Exegetes who otherwise think the Gospel of Mark has little to do with political discourse feel free at this point to insert their own. Because a socio-literary approach reads the whole of Mark—not just this one text—politically, the problem of such ideological and literary "decontextualization" is avoided.

The three stories must be interpreted together in order to understand Mark's ideological position. In the question of John's baptism, Jesus rejects the Sanhedrin's right to judge his actions; in the vineyard parable he undermines any claims they might have to "authority." The Jewish leadership correctly understands Jesus to be repudiating its political legitimacy altogether. It then pursues an "entrapping strategy." Mark assumes his readers know *why* the tax question would be considered particularly dangerous and compromising. But we must review the socio-historical context of this controversy.

The weight of the imperial tribute had been felt since the time of Herod:

> [Who] bled the populace poor with taxes. . . . The tribute exacted by Rome was large in itself. Herod's revenues were huge, used primarily to maintain his own court and military troops as well as to support his extensive, luxurious building programs. Taxes were so high that twice Herod was able to remit sizable portions of the payment when he wished to ingratiate himself with the people. . . . Many popular outbursts occurred after Herod's death (4 B.C.E.). Masses in Jerusalem demanded reduction of taxes, abolition of duties, liberation of prisoners [Rhoads, 1976:24f.].

Taxation was a central issue in the brief rebellion at the time Judea first came under direct Roman administration in 6 C.E., as indicated in this passage from Josephus:

> The territory of Archelaus was now reduced to a province, and Coponius, a Roman of the equestrian order, was sent out as procurator, entrusted by Augustus with full powers, including the infliction of capital punishment. Under his administration, a Galilaean, named Judas, incited his countrymen to revolt, upbraiding them as cowards for consenting to pay tribute to the Romans and tolerating mortal masters, after having God for their Lord [*War*, II,viii,1].

Throughout the decades the burden of the tribute, born wholly by the peasantry, was a major cause of social banditry in the countryside; failure to meet the tribute demand often resulted in expropriation of the land of small holders (see Horsley and Hanson, 1985:52ff.).

There is reason to believe that as hostilities grew and polarization deepened in colonial Palestine, the degree of conscientization concerning the tax question as indicative of the political economy of colonial domination also increased. Things worsened immediately before the revolt, as imperial taxes were raised and economic corruption increased under the procuratorship of Albinus (c.e. 62–64; *War*, II,xiv,1). At the time of the breach with Rome in Jerusalem, there was apparently a backlog of imperial taxes to pay; the revolt solved this problem by stopping the tribute. During the revolt, we know that a series of coins for "liberated" Jerusalem were minted and circulated throughout Palestine. Thus Jeremias points out:

> During the siege of Jerusalem in AD 70 the refusal to pay taxes was considered to be the only cause of the war. . . . This was, of course, not strictly true, but it is significant as indicating the part which taxation played in the life of the people [1969:126].

The tribute question is an "entrapment" challenge therefore *because* of the crisis of political allegiance provoked by the Jewish liberation struggle. As noted, the fact that the challenge comes from the odd Pharisee-Herodian coalition, which appears only here in the Jerusalem narrative, indicates this was an extremely tricky question for Mark's Galilean community.

In terms of the narrative world, their strategy of pursuing the tax question is shrewd. Whichever side Jesus takes will facilitate his downfall: if he refuses to endorse tribute payment, the colonial government can move against him; if he cooperates, he stands to lose the very popular support that is protecting him from the Jewish leaders. This was exactly analogous to the dilemma facing Mark's community. From the standpoint of the political polarization of wartime, the tax question was one of the ways in which they were being pressured to declare their partisanship vis-à-vis the revolt. But the discourse of these three episodes strongly reasserts the ideology of "nonalignment," a rejection of both the Roman colonial presence and the revolt. Jesus deftly escapes the political trap by turning the political challenge back upon his opponents, refusing to commit himself unless and until they do. This skill reflected the political exigencies of a "hunted" community as well. Thus we may see in this section a specific historical insertion into the narrative, similar to the warnings in Jesus' apocalyptic sermon (below, 11,A,ii).

10E. CONFRONTING THE IDEOLOGICAL AUTHORITY
OF THE SCRIBAL CLASS (12:18–34)

i. Sadducean Casuistry: Eschatology vs. Patriarchy

The debating session continues but the rhetorical pace changes at 12:18. The next two conflict episodes switch to a fairly straightforward single challenge/response construction. The third constituent group of the ruling class to jump into the fray is a brand new opponent: the Sadducees. Not well understood by commentators, feminist hermeneutics has saved this story from trivialization. E. Schüssler Fiorenza has shown that the central issue is not an abstract theological doctrine (resurrection), as it may seem on the surface. Rather, Jesus demonstrates yet another way in which the kingdom subverts the dominant social order, in this case the patriarchal objectification of women.

The antagonists (Sadducees) and the term "resurrection" (*anastasis*) both appear only here in Mark (12:18). Jeremias tells us that the Sadducees were identified with the rich landowning patrician families, though at the time of the revolt their political influence was in decline. They were a distinct party, which included chief priests, elders, and priestly and lay nobility, and taught their own, very conservative ideology (1969:230). As Josephus puts it wryly: "The Sadducees have the confidence of the wealthy alone, but no following among the populace" (*Ant.*, XIII,x,6). Among the debates between their Torah conservatism and Pharisaic oral liberalism was the doctrine of resurrection (see Acts 23:6-8). It is not surprising therefore that Mark's narrative touches upon this issue, but his main interest lies in the oppressive ideology of the ruling class.

True to their reputation, the Sadducees pick a fight over the notion of resurrection, arguing that it is inconsistent with a Mosaic statute (12:19-23). After the manner of scribal argumentation, they cite the text:

> The quotation is a very free rendering of Deuteronomy 25:5f., excluding, in particular, the limiting clause ["if brothers dwell together"] and the reference to leaving seed, which shows that the main purpose is to maintain the possession of property within the family [Taylor, 1963:481].

They proceed to spin a typically rabbinic popular tale. By a *reductio ad absurdum* it insists that Moses would not have prescribed the practice of levirate marriage if it was going to cause moral chaos in the afterlife.

The "hidden" assumption of the Sadducees, however, as Schüssler Fiorenza correctly points out, is:

> Continuing the patriarchal family, by securing its wealth and the inheritance within it . . . the levirate law protecting and perpetuating the patriarchal structures of the "house" was of utmost importance [1985:144].

That is, moral chaos is not the issue; maintenance of socio-economic status through the posteriority of the seven sons is. They are certainly *not* concerned with the poor woman who did not bear offspring, barrenness being the deepest shame for her. They further objectify her by speculating who she would "belong to" in the afterlife.

Mark structures Jesus' response with a frame consisting of Jesus' answer to his own rhetorical question:

> Are you not in error . . . ? (*planasthe*; 12:24)
> You are greatly in error (12:27).

In their Torah literalism the Sadducees understand neither the text nor the power of the one to whom it attests. They are wrong, in other words, in theory and practice. Jesus conceives of the resurrection not as a static doctrine but a living hope for the transformation of the world, reflected in his switch from the Sadducees' *anastasis* to the more active notion of the *dead* "rising to life" (*anastōsin*) and "being raised" (*hoti egeirontai*). The Sadducees, on the other hand, have a vested interest in denying any other "world" except the present one, which they control.

Jesus begins his response by asserting what he knows very well his challengers reject: the eschatological vision of world transformation (12:25). His notion of "heaven without marriage," which has embarrassed so many commentators, does not claim:

> That sexual differentiation and sexuality do not exist in the "world" of God, but that "patriarchal marriage is no more," because its function in maintaining and continuing patriarchal economic and religious structures is no longer necessary [Schüssler Fiorenza, 1985:144].

The second argument (12:26f.) continues in this vein. It does not, as most commentators have thought, intend to prove a doctrine of the resurrection, for, as Kee points out, it would be poor argument indeed (1977:156f.). Rather:

> This reference replies directly to the question of the continuation of the patriarchal family: in the burning bush God is revealed to Moses as the God of promise and of the blessing given to the patriarchs and their posterity. The "house" of Israel is not guaranteed in and through patriarchal marriage structures, but through the promise and faithfulness of Israel's powerful, life-giving God. While the God of the patriarchal systems and its securities is the "God of the dead," the God of Israel is the "God of the living." In God's world women and men no longer relate to each other in terms of patriarchal dominance and dependence, but as persons who live in the presence of the living God. . . .The Sadducees have "erred much" in assuming that the structures of patriarchy are unquestionably a dimension of God's world as well. So, too, all subsequent Christians have erred in maintaining oppressive patriarchal structures [Schüssler Fiorenza, 1985:145].

This is very much the same ideological response to patriarchy we saw earlier in the question on divorce (above, 9,B,i; D,iii).

In this story, Mark has confronted the crude materialism of the powerful, who are concerned solely with class succession, with an eschatological hope that envisions a new world of equality and community in which both patriarchy and privilege will be eradicated. Moreover, it assails in the strongest possible terms the Sadducean ability to interpret scripture:

Do you understand neither the scriptures . . . ?
Have you never read in the book of Moses . . . ?

This is Mark's frontal attack upon the hermeneutical—which is to say ideological—authority of the ruling class.

ii. Scribal Piety: Orthodoxy Is Not Enough

The next episode is another example of a "conspectus," analeptic of key elements from previous stories. It is connected to the episodes immediately before and after it in that it is another rabbinic discussion of Torah. Its discussion of "commandments" recalls earlier clashes with the Pharisees (7:8f.; 10:5), and it exhibits close affinity with the story of Jesus' rejection of the rich man (10:17ff.). But this story is unique for three reasons:
  1. it is the climax to the series of debates with Jesus in the temple;
  2. it is the only place in which Jesus' interaction with a scribe is not wholly hostile;
  3. it deals with a central ideological issue: the "greatest commandment."
Indeed, it is Jesus' very last direct confrontation with his opponents until he is arrested and prosecuted by them—and in it he silences them once and for all.

Mark carefully constructs this encounter around ambiguity. On the one hand, we expect a conflict story, for the antagonist is one of the scribal archopponents. We assume—based on the previous stories—that his flattery of Jesus ("Well done, teacher, you have answered forthrightly!," 12:32, see 12:14) must be insincere. On the other hand, the scribe approaches Jesus, having "heard" him arguing and "seen" him answering well (12:28). These narrative signals suggest that this may be a prospective disciple, one who perhaps will not be deaf and blind. Moreover, he affirms Jesus' answer to his question, and Jesus is described as being impressed with him (12:34). Yet this sympathetic tone is elusive, for as we shall see, the subtleties of Jesus' answer in fact pave the way for an outright condemnation of the scribal class in 12:38ff. And Jesus' final comment falls far short of commendation, much less invitation to discipleship.

The man's question concerning the "first of all the commandments" is a common topic of rabbinic discussion, but could also be interpreted as yet another attempt to get Jesus to reveal his own political commitments. Jesus' answer (12:30f.) at first glance seems cautious in its orthodoxy: he quotes from the Shema (Dt 6:4f.), with minor changes to the LXX text. Suddenly, however, he adds a citation of Leviticus 19:18 about obligation to neighbor, and concludes that "No other command is greater than these." It is in fact quite a startling answer:

[It] brings together two widely separated commands. . . . While each is warmly commended by the Rabbis, so far as is known no one save Jesus has brought them together as the two regulative principles which sum up man's duty [Taylor, 1963:488].

The point Mark is trying to make by this bold conflation is consistent with his ideology: heaven must come to earth—there is no love of God except in love of neighbor.

The Leviticus tradition is of particular interest, for it defines love of neighbor in terms of nonexploitation. The verse Jesus cites is the culmination to a litany of commands prohibiting the *oppression and exploitation of Israel's weak and poor* (Lv 19:9-17), including:

1. leave your field for the sojourner to glean (vv. 9f.);
2. do not steal, deal falsely, or profane God (vv. 11f.);
3. do not oppress the neighbor, exploit employees, or discriminate against the disabled (vv. 13f.);
4. do no injustice or show partiality in judgment, or slander or witness against the neighbor (vv. 15f.).

But according to Mark's narrative, these are precisely the commands violated regularly by the dominant Jewish social groups, *especially* the scribes.

Surprisingly, the scribe not only appears to agree wholeheartedly with Jesus' assessment (12:32f.), but reinforces it with allusions to the scriptural tradition that gives priority to obedience over the temple cult (Hos 6:6; 1 Sm 15:22). This far the scribe is willing to go, and Jesus recognizes that he is "thoughtful" (*nounechōs*; only here in the Greek Bible). But this adjective (from the root *nous*, "mind") allows only that the scribe has *intellectually* grasped what Jesus has said. The story ends with Jesus' declaration that the scribe is "not far" from the kingdom of God (12:34); Jesus does not issue an invitation for him to follow (cf. 10:21). "Not far" once again implies that orthodoxy is not enough; it must be accompanied by the practice of justice to one's neighbor. Mark *appears* to reject the possibility of scribal discipleship. Why? Because however aware of biblical imperatives they might be, they are by definition committed to a *system* that oppresses. To repudiate that system would be to stop being a scribe within it.

The debating section of the Jerusalem narrative closes with a declaration of "victory" for Jesus: Mark tells us that no one had the courage to challenge Jesus thereafter (12:34c). He has thrown the commercial special interests out of the temple and in their place assumed a role as "teacher." He has met challenges and foiled plots with brilliant rhetorical skill. He has gone nose to nose with the political leaders and the intellectuals, questioning the legitimacy of their respective vocations insofar as they are based upon privilege and exploitation. And in the end he has silenced his social and political opponents, and done it on their own home ground: the temple. In other words, Jesus appears to have "bound the strong men," and ransacked their house.

10F. CAMPAIGN CLIMAX: JESUS DECLARES JUDGMENT ON THE TEMPLE (12:35–13:3a)

The drama of the Jerusalem conflict narrative reaches its climax, as did the first campaign, in a fierce ideological war of words. Then the dispute had ended in a rupture with the fundamental structure of social life—kinship (3:31–35). Now Jesus will make an even more dramatic break with the central structure of political and ideological life: the temple. This culminates Mark's delegitimization of the dominant ideology of scribal Judaism.

i. Jesus' Counteroffensive: Against Davidic Messianism

Verse 12:35 represents a narrative transition, as Jesus, still in the temple, goes on the offensive against the scribal class. His question ("Why do the scribes say . . . ?") echoes that of the disciples' back in 9:11. But theirs concerned the relationship of Messiah to Elijah whereas Jesus' concern here is the relationship of Messiah to David. Here Mark returns to the heart of the matter, which has been lingering since his messianic procession into the holy city: Jesus' messianic politics versus the restoration of the Davidic state (12:35–37).

"Sonship" here has nothing to do with whether or not the Messiah is a descendant of David (see above, 2,C,iv), but with the question of political ideology. Mark attacks the popular assumption that messianic politics necessarily affirms the myth of a restored Davidic kingdom, as was reflected in the triumphalist eschatology chanted by the crowds (11:9):

Blessed be the one coming in the name of the Lord;
Blessed be the coming kingdom of our father David.

He now serves notice that this ideology is to be wholly repudiated.

Jesus appeals to another key messianic Psalm, 110, in order to argue that the authority of Messiah "preexists" the authority of David. Mark has already alluded to Psalm 110 in 10:37 (above, 9,D,ii), and will again when Jesus stands before the Sanhedrin (14:62). Jesus is not disputing genealogy but ideology: to be "David's son" is to stand in solidarity with the restorationist vision—that is, the relegitimation of the temple state. Thus in his interpretation Jesus makes it clear that Messiah is *not* David's son (12:37), rejecting both of the earlier messianic acclamations, 10:47f. and 11:9f. He will not rehabilitate the old imperial vision; indeed, the Davidic tradition must submit to the authority of Messiah.[2]

The change to the imperfect tense in the next two phrases (12:37b,38a) indicates that Jesus continued to teach in the temple. The reader may wonder how Mark could characterize "the mass of people" (*ho polus ochlos*) as hearing Jesus "eagerly" (*hēdeōs*) if indeed he was undermining many of their expectations. But Mark used the same phrase to describe Herod's strong attraction to the troubling proclamation of John the Baptist (6:20). He captures the contradiction in the crowd's loyalty, as if to suggest that its delight in Jesus' attacks upon the ruling classes offset his messianic unorthodoxy. Jesus does not depend upon the support of the masses, but does sense their need to demystify the authority of the scribal class, instructing them in critical thinking: "Beware the scribes" (12:38b).

ii. Polarization: Rich Scribes vs. Poor Widows

Commentators have long recognized the rhetorical links between the next two "widow" episodes, the prayer of the scribes (12:38–40) and the "last mite" (12:41–44). However, bourgeois scholarship, oblivious to Mark's critique of the political economy of the temple, portrays the common theme as the contrast between the religious hypocrisy of the scribes and the genuine piety of the poor woman. Fortunately, recent work has overturned this exegetical tradition (Derrett, 1972; Wright, 1982; Fledderman, 1982).

Jesus warns the crowd (*blepete,* already applied to the Pharisees and Herodians in 8:15) against the pretense of scribal practice, articulated in four-part detail. They love:

> to walk about in long robes
> and greetings in the marketplace
> and the first bench in the synagogues
> and the first couch at dinners [12:38b–39].

Mark unsparingly caricatures the scribe as one who at every stage of social life wishes to be endowed with special privilege and status—the most important commodities in the attainment of social power in Mediterranean honor culture. These attitudes are of course antithetical to Jesus' instructions to his own community concerning being "last" and "servant." We now understand Jesus' ambivalence toward the scribe in 12:34; the entire class is being dismissed as unfit for discipleship.

These are hard words, but they get harder. Scribal affluence is a product of their "devouring the estates of widows under the pretext of saying long prayers" (12:40). There are two possibilities for interpreting this bitter euphemism. Derrett (1972) argues that Mark must be alluding to the practice of scribal trusteeship of the estates of widows (who as women could not be entrusted to manage their deceased husbands' affairs!). Through their public reputation for piety and trustworthiness (hence the "pretext of long prayers"), scribes would earn the legal right to administrate estates. As compensation they would usually get a percentage of the assets; the practice was notorious for embezzlement and abuse. In this case the issue here would be similar to the *korban* practice to which Jesus objected in Mark 7:9–13. The vocation of Torah Judaism is to "protect orphans and widows," yet in the name of piety these socially vulnerable classes are being exploited while the scribal class is further endowed.

Fledderman (1982) on the other hand believes that the explanation lies in Mark's narrative opposition between "prayer" and "robbery." The site of scribal prayer is the temple, and the costs of this temple devour the resources of the poor. Jesus, who fiercely opposed such exploitation in the temple action and demanded a new site for prayer, points to the tragic story of the "widow's mite" by way of illustration. Because of its narrative analysis this interpretation is probably the stronger one. In either case, however, the essential point is the same: scribal piety has been debunked as a thin veil for economic opportunism and exploitation. Mark charges them with full responsibility for these abuses, and in perhaps the harshest words in the gospel, announces that they will receive far heavier judgment (cf. 9:42).

The last episode in the temple is a story of a widow being impoverished by her obligations to the temple cultus (12:41-44). Long mishandled as a quaint vignette about the superior piety of the poor, Wright has shown that Jesus' words should be seen "as a downright disapproval and not as an approbation":

> The story does not provide a pious contrast to the conduct of the scribes in the preceding section (as is the customary view); rather it provides a further illustration of the ills of official devotion. Jesus' saying is not a penetrating insight on the measuring of gifts; it is a lament. . . . Jesus condemns the value system that motivates her action, and he condemns the people who conditioned her to do it [1982:262].

The episode begins with Jesus taking a position seated "facing" (*kateanti*) the temple treasury (12:41). This stage direction is proleptic of judgment, for Jesus will shortly "face" the temple mount in order to predict its demise (13:3). The setting would have been either that of:

> Thirteen trumpet-shaped chests placed round the walls of the Court of Women in which the people threw their offerings . . . [or] the treasury itself, [where] donors had to declare the amount of their gift and the purpose for which it was intended to the priest in charge, everything being visible and audible to the onlooker through the open door [Taylor, 1963:496].

This scene Jesus carefully "scrutinizes" (*etheōrei*).

Mark again reveals his class consciousness (cf. 10:21) through the use of extreme opposition in his description of what happens next:

> many rich persons put in from their abundance;
> one poor widow put in two little coins.

The contribution of the widow, *lepta*, was a term "used in late Greek for the smallest coin in circulation" (Taylor, 1963:497).[3] At this point Mark chooses to reintroduce the disciples (absent since 11:27). The phrase, "he called them to him" (cf. 3:13), and the Amen signal that we are about to receive an important teaching (12:43). For a second time Jesus poses the stark contrast:

> they all gave from their affluence . . .
> she in her destitution gave everything she had—her whole life.

The temple has robbed this woman of her very means of livelihood (12:44). Like the scribal class, it no longer protects widows, but exploits them. As if in disgust, Jesus "exits" the temple—for the final time (13:1a).

iii. Rift: Repudiation of the Temple

The narrative site of the temple has now been abandoned. As we have come to expect, the disciples have once more missed the point of Jesus' object lesson (but then again, so have most modern exegetes). One of them begins to marvel at the magnificence of the very temple Jesus has just criticized: "Look! Such stones, such buildings!" (13:1b). Indeed, the temple was an impressive structure, so much bigger than life in the socio-symbolism of Judaism. The disciples' amazement at the temple edifices undoubtedly captures the overwhelming impression it would have made on any rural pilgrim visitor to Jerusalem. At the time Mark wrote, the temple had just recently been completed and restored (a project begun almost a century earlier under Herod the Great).

Even as sophisticated a writer as Josephus had nothing but awe for the temple:

> Now the outward face of the temple in its front wanted nothing that was likely to surprise either men's minds or their eyes: for it was covered all over with plates of gold of great weight, and, at the first rising of the sun, reflected back a very fiery splendour, and made those who forced themselves to look upon it to turn their eyes away, just as they would have done at the sun's own rays. But this Temple appeared to strangers, when they were at a distance, like a mountain covered with snow; for, as to those parts of it that were not gilt, they were exceeding white. . . . Of its stones, some of them were forty-five cubits in length, five in height, and six in breadth [*War*, V,v,6].

Thus, rejecting its legitimacy was no small matter. How could one believe in a world apart from this household of God?

Jesus returns the rhetorical question to his disciples with an entirely opposite assessment: "Do you see these great buildings? There will not be one stone left upon another here that will not be toppled" (Mk 13:2). At the level of narrative, this announcement that the temple will be "thrown down" (*kataluthē*) will figure decisively in the Sanhedrin's prosecution of Jesus after his arrest (14:58), as well as their taunts as he hangs on the cross (15:29). At the level of ideological discourse, the fact that historically the temple was destroyed by fire (not torn down stone by stone) remains one of the strongest arguments in favor of my thesis that Mark's Gospel predates the Roman victory of 70 C.E.

Jesus then takes a seat "facing" the temple (13:3) in preparation for delivering his second great sermon. With this final dramatic action, Jesus utterly repudiates the temple state, which is to say the entire socio-symbolic order of Judaism. His objections have been consistently based upon one criterion: the system's exploitation of the poor. He now sets about warning his disciples against joining those who would wage a messianic war in defense of the temple (13:14). The "mountain" must be "moved," not restored. Jesus now offers a vision of the end of the temple-based world, and the dawn of a new one in which the powers of domination have been toppled.

NOTES

1. Taylor cites a third-century saying of Rabbi Joshua ben Levi indicating that the Zechariah tradition was interpreted later as representing judgment upon Israel: Behold, the Son of Man comes "on the clouds of heaven" and "lowly, and riding upon an ass." If they (Israel) are worthy, "with the clouds of heaven;" if they are not worthy, "lowly, and riding upon an ass" (1963:452).

2. As with Ps 118, Ps 110 was also crucial to the christology of the primitive church, cited well over a dozen times in the NT. Significantly, it was probably written during the Maccabaean period, with reference to the high priest Simon Maccabaeus (1 Mc 13:36; 14:41), "on whose name an acrostic is formed by the initial letters of the several lines in vv. 1-4" (Taylor, 1963:491). Whether such Maccabean overtones figure into Mark's choice of this psalm is difficult to say, for Davidic authorship of the Psalms was assumed in antiquity; Jesus says David spoke under the inspiration of the Holy Spirit (12:36).

3. Mark explains that the coin is a Roman *quadrans*. It has been a longstanding argument that this editorial insertion proves that Mark was written in Rome, for the *quadrans* allegedly was not in circulation in the East. But such semantic penetration would not be unexpected in a colonial formation as Taylor cautions:

> The credibility of the story is in no way affected by the fact that Greek and Roman coins are mentioned . . . [they] no more imply that the narrative was first composed far away from Jerusalem than *zwei Scherflein, das ist ein Heller* suggests composition in Germany [1963:497].

CHAPTER ELEVEN

The Second Sermon on Revolutionary Patience (Mark 13:4-37)

> The earth staggers like a drunken man, it sways like a hut. . . . On that day Yahweh will punish the host of heaven, in heaven, and the kings of the earth, on the earth.
>
> —Isaiah 24:20f.

At the conclusion to the first campaign of direct action in Capernaum, Jesus withdrew to the sea to reflect upon his ministry in a sermon consisting of parables (4:1). Here at the end of the second campaign in Jerusalem, he again withdraws, this time to the Mount of Olives. It is appropriate that his radical break with the temple state be followed by a consideration of the "end of the world," for this is precisely how any Jew would have interpreted Jesus' rejection of the symbolic center. In this second sermon, Jesus instructs his disciples on how to discern and endure this "end." Jesus has been revealed as a truly subversive proponent of messianic revolution. But how does his ideology and practice relate to the historical moment in which Mark writes? For there is already an insurrection underway in Palestine, which is promising to restore the fortunes of Israel by driving out the Romans with the sword. Should Mark's community join forces with the rebels?

To this moment Jesus speaks, warning against the temptation to seize power as a way of overthrowing the powers and, in the tradition of Jeremiah, exhorts the disciples/reader to abandon the defense of Jerusalem in its most critical hours. Instead, he says, we must look more deeply into history, in order to commence the revolutionary process at the roots. He thus closes his sermon with an apocalyptic meditation calling for historical vigilance.

11A. THE SERMON AS PARENETIC DISCOURSE

i. Apocalyptic Intertextuality in the Second Sermon

L. Gaston may well be right when he claims that "there is perhaps no one single chapter of the synoptic gospels which has been so much commented upon in modern times as Mark 13" (1970:8). Scholars have come to call this daunting sermon the "Little Apocalypse," even as debate goes on concerning the extent to which it can be considered formal apocalyptic literature (Laws, 1975). A socio-literary reading is not interested in reconstructing the traditions "behind" this text, but recognizing some of its sources helps us appreciate the complex fabric of intertextuality that characterizes this sermon. The three main opinions regarding the literary antecedents of Mark 13 are:

1. Mark has reworked a Jewish or Jewish-Christian source, often dubbed an "apocalyptic flyer," which allegedly would have been in circulation during any one of the several political crises in the mid-first century;
2. Mark is freely composing a midrash upon Daniel 7, 9, and 11, drawing from both other Hebrew Bible texts and Jesus tradition;
3. Mark is writing parenesis, using both apocalyptic and traditional primitive catechetical material.

There is something to be said for each of these hypotheses.

The "apocalyptic flyer" hypothesis (most recently argued by Wilde, 1974) focuses upon the many similarities between Mark's sermon and other apocalyptic literature, such as 1 Enoch, 4 Ezra, the *Assumption of Moses*, and the Qumran war scrolls. It is clear that in late second-temple Judaism the apocalyptic literary tradition was a freely intertextual one. The *Assumption of Moses* offers a good example of the generally accepted practice of rehabilitating older apocalyptic texts for a different historical context. The *Assumption* was originally written in response to the persecutions of Antiochus Epiphanes IV, the time of the Maccabees and roughly contemporary with Daniel (ca. 165–150 B.C.E.; see Nickelsburg, 1981:80f.). However, during the social and political upheaval at the time of Herod's death (4 B.C.E.) the *Assumption* was "updated." It clearly criticizes the Hasmonean dynasty as "kings usurping power, calling themselves priests of the Most High God; they shall assuredly work iniquity in the holy of holies" (*A.M.* 6:1).

The update goes on to describe the overthrow of the Hasmoneans by the Roman conquest of Palestine (63 B.C.E.), and the subsequent eradication of their influence after Herod's rise to power as the regional client-king of Rome (Herod executing some forty-five Sadducean nobles who were aligned with the Hasmoneans):

> An insolent king shall succeed them, who will not be of the race of the priests, a man bold and shameless . . . he shall cut off their chief men with the sword . . . then the fear of him shall be bitter unto them in their land [ibid.: 6:2,5].

Finally, the death of Herod and division of his kingdom among his children is reported, along with the popular rebellion among the Jews that accompanied the change, which was put down by the Roman legate Varus, whose soldiers burned part of the temple:

And he shall beget children who succeeding him will rule for shorter periods. Into their parts . . . a powerful king of the west shall come, who shall conquer them: and he shall take them captive and burn a part of their temple with fire, and crucify some around their colony [ibid.: 6: 7–9].

This "historical review" is inserted right into the apocalypse, and typifies the way in which apocalyptic literature was a popular vehicle for interpretation of current events during the Hellenistic era.

The view of Mark 13 as one such popular flyer is not, however, incompatible with the midrash theory articulated by Kee (1977:43f.) and Hartman (1966). This view recognizes Mark's concentrated use of Daniel, as well as other late prophetic, "proto-apocalyptic" traditions (D. Peterson, 1977; R. Miller, 1976). There are indeed examples that have been dated close in time to Mark in which we see a reworking of Daniel:

In IV Ezra we have a document preserved by an apocalyptically-oriented community which offers hope to a covenant people in the face of the destruction of Jerusalem by the Romans. The document's method and line of argument build on and modify the prophecies of Daniel, especially the visions of Daniel 7 (12:10–13). The present villain is not the Seleucids but the Romans, symbolized by the eagle (11:1ff.). The lion, who overcomes the eagle (11:37ff.), is declared to be the Messiah, descendant of David (12:31f.), who has been "kept until the end of days" [Kee, 1977:129].

There is no reason therefore to doubt that Mark has similarly reappropriated Daniel or other apocalyptic common stock. His more obvious allusions are:
  a. desolating sacrilege (13:14): Dn 9:27; 11:31; 12:11; 1 Mc 1:54
  b. great tribulation (13:19): Dn 12:1
  c. Human One (13:26): Dn 7:13 (see above, 8,C,ii)
  d. the apocalyptic query "How long?" (13:4): Dn 12:6
  e. cosmic upheaval (13:24f.): Am 8:9; Jl 2:10f.; Ez 32:17; Is 13:9–13; 24:18–23

We have already observed that Mark draws upon such apocalyptic traditions as Daniel's courtroom myth and Malachi's advent of Elijah. Now he expands his apocalyptic base.

There is no reason either to deny the influence of so-called eschatological parenesis, as argued by Marxsen (1969:164ff.) and Beasely-Murray (1983:414ff.). The "watch and pray" tradition (13:33–37), for example, is clearly a catechetical fragment, found in various forms throughout the New Testament (see below, E,iii). Attempts to form-critically isolate any of these preliterary traditions, on the other hand, are fruitless, for Mark thoroughly integrated them into his own narrative world. Lightfoot (1950) long ago pointed out the sermon's many narrative connections with the rest of the Gospel. I can cite as examples:

1. the persecution fragment (13:9-13) is part of the Jesus/John/disciples complex (see above, 7,B,ii);
2. the "watchful householder" parable (13:33-37) is proleptic of Gethsemane and Jesus' trial (below, E,iii);
3. the advent of the Human One and the cosmic darkness (13:26) is analeptic of 8:38f. and proleptic of the cross (cf. 14:62; 15:33; below, E,i).

The sermon, though it does have its own literary integrity as a unit, cannot be treated in isolation (the habit of most commentators) from the Markan narrative as a whole.

The power of the apocalyptic tradition was that it was both profoundly contextual and transferable. Its central myths could be reinterpolated into new circumstances. What is ideologically important about Mark's intertextuality here is the fact that he chooses to appeal directly to a literary corpus that was *already* recognized by his readers as the tradition of political resistance under Hellenism. But if Mark was "updating" the tradition, what was the situation he meant to address with apocalyptic discourse?

ii. The Narrative and Historical "Moment": Mark and the Revolt

Many commentators have been thrown by what they feel to be a switch in Mark's narrative style in the sermon. Grayston, in a study that otherwise quite perceptively analyzes the section's *internal* rhetorical structure, still considers the sermon to represent an "intrusion" into the Gospel (1974:371ff.). But as I have shown, quite aside from its proleptic and analeptic characteristics, the second sermon is strongly tied to the overall structure of the Gospel, balancing the reflective aftermath of the first campaign narrative.

Kelber takes an alternative position. He sees the sermon not as an intrusion but an intentional "narrative rupture," a historical insertion into the story for parenetic purposes:

> What surfaces in Jesus' speech, especially in its first part (13:5-23), is less the story of Jesus and more that of early Christians. The reason Jesus' biography ruptures, and ruptures at this moment, is that it has reached a point where it touches on problems in Mark's lifetime and that of his readers [1979:67].

This is a compelling thesis, especially in light of the sermon's direct addresses to the reader (13:14,37), but runs the risk of encouraging a retreat back into historicism. The temptation to identify a simple correlation between narrative world and historical events in apocalyptic has been the occasion for most of the abuse of the literature. I therefore do not agree with Kelber that Mark has abandoned his narrative world for *direct* parenesis in this section. Even those allusions considered to be most "referential" (e.g., "desolating sacrilege," "false prophets") are overdetermined by Mark's narrative symbolics. And the ideology of this sermon is unintelligible outside the wider discourse of the story as a whole.

Petersen improves upon Kelber's insight by distinguishing between what he calls "story-time" and "discourse-time" in the narrative (1980; see above, 3,B,iv), what I have chosen to call the "narrative moment" and the "historical moment." This distinction becomes particularly crucial here, for indeed in this sermon the two are almost joined in the collapsed moment of the myth (below, D,i). The critical narrative moment is the completion of the second direct action campaign of Jesus. As readers, we are balanced between the end of Jesus' public ministry (in 14:1ff. he goes "underground") and the beginning of his march to the cross (the passion narrative). This moment demands some clarification on the meaning of Jesus' nonviolent struggle to overthrow the powers. On the other hand, the historical moment, as we will see, demands similar clarification, for there is intense pressure being put upon Mark's community to declare its allegiance in the Roman-Jewish war. Mark believes that both "moments" are best served by a sermon, but one that he has integrated into the framework and fiction of his Gospel as a whole.

Thus when I speak of referential allusions in the text, they serve not as a door *out* of Mark's narrative world, but as a historical window "into" it. In other words, Mark is not suspending his story world, but using a particular narrative vehicle to show us as clearly as he can (or as he dares) the concrete sociopolitical situation to which his story world is addressed. What is this situation? It is almost universally agreed that the Jewish-Roman war forms the most immediate background for this text. Whether Jesus' prediction of the temple's destruction should be seen as genuine anticipation or *ex eventu* (after the fact) prophecy—that is, whether this text dates from before or after the tragic climax of the revolt, is a matter of debate (see below, 14,A,ii). As I have argued (above, 2,A,i), I believe the most compelling arguments have been advanced by Wilde, who places the production of the Gospel sometime around 69 c.e. (1974:281).

The reader may wish to review my summary of the main events during the period of the revolutionary Jewish provisional government (above, 2,D). The revolt was launched in Jerusalem in June of 66, and quickly spread to the nearby provinces of Idumea, Perea, and Galilee. In November of 66, Cestus Gallus, Roman legate of Syria, marched on Jerusalem in order to put down the insurrection. He occupied the northern part of the city, but was turned back in his siege of the temple mount. Stunned, he retreated in disarray, and sustained severe losses as Jewish guerillas pursued him to the coast. Gallus sent an emergency message to Rome, and there was euphoria in Jerusalem: Palestine was liberated! Against all odds, outnumbered and outarmored, the rebels had turned away the oppressors.

But the provisional government in Jerusalem was mired in internal power struggles, bordering on civil war. Indeed, the liberation was short-lived; Vespasian, probably the greatest general of the time and soon to become emperor, was dispatched to pacify Palestine. He gathered legions from Egypt and Syria, and with six thousand heavily armed troops, began a march down through Galilee toward Jerusalem. Despite heroic resistance by scattered guerilla forces, within a short time Galilee, Perea, and western Judea were retaken by Vespasian. By June of 68, he was ready to begin his siege of Jerusalem. Once again, however, the unexpected occurred: the anticipated siege was aborted. Slowly word filtered back to the Zealot coalition now in power in Jerusalem that Rome was locked in a fierce civil war; Nero was dead, four candidates were vying to succeed him as emperor, and Vespasian had been urgently summoned back to Rome. The Jewish resistance would get a reprieve of almost a year and a half to prepare for the inevitable confrontation. Only Yahweh could have worked not one but two miracles to save the holy city!

Still, everyone knew that the final hour would soon face Zion, as indeed it did. Vespasian would prevail in the power struggle back in Rome, and send Titus to finish off the Palestinian rebels. Titus would begin the siege in April of 70, and after five months of pitched battle, Jerusalem would fall, be sacked, and the temple burned to the ground. But in the grace period of 69, the Jewish resistance had reason to believe that Yahweh had intervened on its behalf. It does not take much historical imagination to assume that during this period rebel supporters were going throughout Palestine calling the faithful to the final battle. Calling upon the traditions of a hegemonic Israel, the myth of the Davidic restoration, they would have portrayed the war as a sure sign of the messianic age. All *true* Jews should come to the defense of Jerusalem.

11B. A PLEA FOR GUIDANCE (13:3f.)

i. The Double Question

Wilde argues that this historical scenario accounts for the atmosphere of urgency so clearly reflected in Mark 13, and although it can only ever be accepted as a hypothesis, it is in my opinion vindicated by the ideological discourse of the text. The political situation had put the community between a rock and a hard place:

> The Roman forces which were mobilizing for an entry into Judea intent on getting to . . . the Temple, on the one hand, and the Zealot resistance efforts, evidently recruiting troops from among the confused followers of Jesus in Judea itself and trying to convince them that staying around for the battle was important in view of the ancient messianic hopes and immediate prospects that the war effort was indeed divinely inspired, on the other. . . . Mark's concern with these movements and the political danger they brought to associates and members of his own community provided him with the immediate incentive to write things down for the benefit of the followers of Jesus who looked to him for support [Wilde, 1974:100f.].

The fact that the parties of the revolt are never mentioned by name in the Gospel may indicate that Mark felt deeply sympathetic to their protest against the social, political, and economic oppression of the Romans. On the other hand, the fact that Mark feels a need to reject the claims of the rebel recruiters suggests that members of Mark's community may well have already been drafted into the liberation war, or were sorely tempted to join. Who could resist the pull of patriotism, or the lure of the hope that here at last was the long-deferred prophetic promise of that final battle in which Yahweh would vindicate Israel? In such a moment, there was only one voice that could match the persuasive call of the rebel recruiters: Jesus the living teacher. So to this Jesus the disciples turn in a direct plea for clarity on the meaning of the historical moment.

The setting for the sermon is the Mount of Olives (13:3), which we recall was in the Ezekiel tradition the site of messianic intervention in the crucial hour of Jerusalem's need (above, 10,B,i). According to Josephus, the Jewish insurgents maintained until the bitter end of the revolt the strong conviction that they were defending the temple from desecration, for which reason Yahweh would come to their rescue. Josephus reports several natural spectacles that were interpreted by the rebels as divine signs, and numerous prophets who arose predicting Yahweh's imminent intervention (Horsley and Hanson, 1985:182ff.). Jesus speaks of war, but his vision is in utter conflict with the hopes of the rebels. Mark subverts the Zecharian symbolics by spatially opposing the Mount of Olives *over against (katenanti,* see 12:41) the temple; from that position Jesus will predict not intervention but complete destruction (13:3). The disciples, perplexed by Jesus' repudiation of the very temple before which they cower, approach Jesus "in private" (*kat' idian*), a stage direction used by Mark when Jesus explains a parable or problem (4:34; 6:31f.; 7:33; 9:2,28).

Their question is twofold: When will these things be? What will be the sign when all these things are accomplished?

"These things" (*tauta*), as in the authorities' challenge in 11:28, refer to Jesus' judgment on the temple. In turn, the rhetorical interplay of the disciples' "Do you see . . . ?" (*blepeis*, 13:2) and Jesus' "Watch!" (*blepete*, 13:5) links the temple to the war being waged in its name. The narrative moment suggests that the disciples are perhaps skeptical of Jesus' predictions that the temple, that overwhelmingly powerful and legitimate structure, will in fact meet its demise (a doubt identified in 11:23 as "lack of faith"). But in the historical moment, their anxious plea articulates the community's concern about the outcome of the imminent Roman siege of Jerusalem. Nevertheless, their request for a "sign" (*sēmeion*) aligns them with the Pharisees (8:11f.). And once again, Jesus will not give the promise of heavenly intervention but a sermon on how to read "signs on earth"—a sermon on political discernment directed at the historical moment.

ii. The Narrative Structure of the Second Sermon

In response to the double question, the sermon is divisible into two parts. The first half explains that the time of the war (the "when") is not the time of the "end"; the second half articulates what the "signs" of the end are. Mark constructs it around the repeated imperative to "watch" (*blepete*, vv. 5,9,23,33), a refrain that serves as the complement to the "listen" of the first sermon (above, 5,A,i).

The first half is neatly framed by the essential warning, consisting of (A) the *watch* command, (B) a caution against the deceptive recruiting slogans of the false prophets, and (C) a temporal clause (in concentric order):

A   *Watch* that no one (*tis*) *deceives* you;

  B   Many will come in my name, saying, "I am he!" and they will *deceive* many;

    C   But when you hear of wars . . . (13:5-7).

    C'   And then if anyone (*tis*) says to you, "Look, here is Messiah!" or "Look, there!" do not believe it.

  B'   False messiahs and false prophets will arise . . . to *deceive* even the elect if it were possible;

A'   *Watch*; I have told you beforehand . . . (13:21-23).

The discourse of this first half consists of two subsections; each begins with a temporal clause and ends with a reference to salvation and endurance:

1. *When you hear* of wars . . . (13:7)
   the one enduring to the end *will be saved* (13:13).
2. *When you see* the desecrating sacrilege . . . (13:14)
   unless the days were shortened, no one *would be saved* (13:20).

The first subsection is itself structured around the repetition of the "apocalyptic *deï*":

1. this *must* happen (13:7)
2. the gospel *must* first be preached . . . (13:10)
3. set up where it *ought* not be (13:14).

This discourse describes the atmosphere of the war, specifically the pending Roman siege of Jerusalem, and describes how Mark's community should respond to its pressures.

The second half of the sermon, beginning in 13:23, reverts to more traditionally "high apocalyptic" symbolics. It has three parts, similarly organized around the command to vigilance (*blepete, grēgoreite*):

1. Cosmic unraveling (vv. 23-27; *watch!*, 13:23);
2. Fig tree parable, the day and hour (13:28-33, *watch!*, 13:33);
3. Parable of the householder (13:34-37, *stay awake!*, 13:35,37).

Toward the end of the second half of the sermon, the disciples' original question is finally answered, but only with highly metaphorical signs and a flat statement that the times are not to be known. Moreover, what began as private solicitation for special revelation ends as a universal exhortation: "What I say to you I say to all" (13:37).

11C. THE REVOLT IS NOT THE KINGDOM (13:4-23)

i. "When You Hear": Mark vs. the Rebel Recruiters

The phrase "Beware that no one should deceive you" (13:5) calls to mind similar warnings against the Pharisees and the Herodians (8:15), the scribes

(12:38), and the deception of the Sadducees (12:24,27). It introduces yet another social group as an opponent of the Way, a group able to deceive many because its members present messianic credentials (13:6; cf. "in my name," 9:37–41). These royal pretenders brashly claim "I am the one!" (*egō eimi*), which stands in sharp contrast to Jesus' "Who do you say that I am?" (8:29). Mark's Jesus always speaks more modestly, in indirect terms of Messiah or as the Human One in the third person.

Many commentators have argued that these "false prophets" (as they are called later in 13:22) are some kind of competing miracle workers, but Mark is not worried about those who heal and exorcise in the messianic name (see 9:38–40). "When you hear" (13:7), the first of the four key temporal clauses in the first half of the sermon, in subtle but unmistakable fashion links these prophets to the Roman-Jewish war. They come speaking about their messianic authority—and the disciples *hear* "wars and rumors of war" (13:7). The discourse of the text thus supports Wilde's hypothesis that Mark is debating the rebel recruiters, engaging them in a fierce war of myths over popular kingship ideology (see further below, iv).

The images Mark uses in 13:7f.—wars, famines, earthquakes—are all virtually generic to apocalyptic literature. One need only consult contemporaneous apocalyptic literature such as John's Revelation, 4 Ezra, the *Assumption of Moses*, or the Qumran war scrolls. At the same time, these events *could* be correlated to contemporaneous history. "Rumors of war" aptly characterizes and describes the way in which news regarding the seesaw political events of 68–70 C.E. would have circulated around Palestine. Was the siege coming? Were the Romans withdrawing? "Kingdom rising against kingdom" might have referred to the wavering fortunes of Rome in 67, embroiled in a civil war and fearing a Parthian invasion. Major natural disasters were also part of contemporaneous history, such as the famine (which hit Palestine especially hard) of the early 50s C.E., or the earthquakes and volcanic eruptions that destroyed Laodicia and Pompei in 61–62 C.E. Both Mark and his opponents could—and did—appeal to the "plurivalent" (multi-referential) nature of apocalyptic symbolics in making their respective cases.

Where Mark differed with the rebels was the way in which they identified these cataclysmic political and natural events with the "end time." He implies that they are using this argument as a means to recruit support for their "messianic" war. The rhetorical structure of 13:7f. takes sharp issue, parodying the claim of the "end" by calling it "only the beginning":

A   When you hear of wars and rumors of wars . . .
B   . . . the end is not yet.
a   Nation will rise against nation . . .
b   . . . these are only the beginning of the birthpangs.

Against the rebel call to arms, Mark instructs the listener not to be alarmed (*mē throeisthe*), a rare word meaning to avoid precipitous action (cf. 2 Thes 2:2–4). These events, insists Mark, do *not* obligate the faithful Jew to join the revolt; indeed "it is necessary that they happen" (here again the apocalyptic *dei*). Mark is counter-recruiting, challenging the grounds upon which Jews are being conscripted into the "final battle."

What, then, *is* the meaning of the traumatic historical events around the war? Jesus calls them "the beginning of the sufferings" (*ōdiōn*), an image drawn from the prophets (Is 26:17; Jer 22:23; Hos 13:13; Mi 4:9f.), which can mean the pain of childbirth (1 Thes 5:3) or death (Acts 2:4). With this metaphor, Mark prepares the reader for a discourse not of revolutionary triumphalism, but of suffering and tribulation. Against rebel eschatology, Mark pits the death/life paradox of his own narrative symbolics and the politics of nonviolence.

ii. "You Will Be Delivered Up": The Political Destiny of Disciples

The next subsection (13:9–13) reintroduces the discourse of "courtroom discipleship," this time with specific reference to the political pressures that will result from a stance of noncooperation with the war. Again we see the "Watch!" warning, the temporal clause ("when they come for you," 13:11), and the apocalyptic *deï* (13:10). "Be on your guard" (the reflexive, *blepete de humeis heautous*, 13:9) warns the community of coming political persecution. In this historical moment, the time has arrived for the disciples to join the company of "slaves" (12:2ff.) in the political destiny of biblical radicalism. As John was (1:14) and Jesus will be (9:31, 10:33) "handed over" (*paradidōmi*) to the authorities, so too will the disciples/reader. Mark makes the point no less than three times:

1. they will hand you over (13:9)
2. when they take you and hand you over (13:11)
3. brother will hand over brother (13:13).

The disciples are told they will be pursued at every possible instance of legal jurisdiction in Palestine:

1. you will be beaten in the Sanhedrin and synagogues
2. you will stand before governors (*hēgemonōn*) and kings
3. for my sake as a witness against them.

The community's stand against the war will earn it the wrath of local and national Jewish authorities as well as that of the Roman procurator and even Caesar himself.

The second apocalyptic *deï* stands in tension with the previous one, as if each represents the logical conclusion of the two sides of the debate. The armed struggle of the rebels make the war (i.e., the siege of Jerusalem) *inevitable*; similarly, the nonviolent resistance of the disciples leads to the mission "to all nations." This missionary encouragement is usually interpreted as referring to the fact that the church will survive the persecutions to carry on its subsequent gentile mission, though for no particularly good reason, and probably due to the influence of Matthew 28:19f. (see Thompson, 1971). Not only does such an interpretation make no sense in the discourse of Mark, it represents precisely the reading that Mark is trying to challenge: namely, that because the disciples are in the service of Jesus, they will be spared. According to the logic of biblical radicalism ("as it is written," articulated in 9:11–13), the opposite is true. The clue lies in the temporal marker "first," which recalls this logic (9:11 is the only other point at which *prōton deï* appears). The importance (indeed, the *necessity*) of John/Elijah's mission did not prevent him from being "delivered up," nor will the Messiah's mission save him: thus *the disciples' mission will not "save" them.* This is the discursive function of Mark's placement of the affirmation of the *necessity* of the evangelistic mission between two statements on the *inevitability* of the disciples' being delivered up. Just as the war does not herald the end but the beginning of suffering (13:7), so political persecution signals not the end but beginning of the real discipleship mission.

As in the second call to discipleship (above, 8,D), the primary "site" of this proclamation is the courtroom: here the mission will be *accomplished* (13:10, force of the aorist passive form of *kēruchthēnai*). The temporal clause in 13:11 implies repeated arrests (*hotan agōsin* in the present subjunctive). Mark assures believers that "in this hour" they are not to be overanxious (*promerimnate*, a word Mark seems to have made up), for they will be instructed in their witness by the Holy Spirit. We remember that this spirit anointed Jesus' mission (1:8), but was rejected by the scribes (3:29). The earthly courtroom is the scene for the "war in heaven" between the powers and the spirit, as will be narrated when Jesus stands before the Sanhedrin (14:58; see below, D,ii).

It is the discipleship community that is now "hunted," but in 13:12 Mark emphasizes that the traps are laid also within the community itself. Family strife is an image that could be attributed to apocalyptic intertextuality (see Mi 7:6; 4 Ezra 6:24), and the conflict between children and parents brings yet another dark level of meaning to the "house divided and raised against itself" in the strong man parable (3:25f.). But I contend that there is referentiality here as well, for the polarized atmosphere and intense loyalties of the war period did indeed cause deep divisions among kin. Mark's mention here of "brothers, fathers, and children" (cf. his description of the new family in 10:30) indicates that his community was struggling not only with internal conflict but even betrayal. The pressures of the war resulted in the bitter experience of "brother delivering up brother to death," just as in the passion narrative Jesus is betrayed by his own "family" (see below, 14,A,iii).

During the war, suspected rebels were routinely executed by Rome, and suspected collaborators by the Zealots. Mark concludes this subsection by stating flatly that whoever stands in solidarity with the way of Jesus (*dia to onoma mou*, 13:13) will be universally despised. The fact that he anticipates political opposition from all sides is strong testimony to the difficulty and cost of the "nonaligned radicalism" that he was advocating in his debate with the rebels. As comfort Mark cites only the classic apocalyptic promise: "The one enduring to the end will be saved" (cf. 4 Ezra 5:9). This of course can be understood only in the context of Jesus' courtroom/cross discourse: to save life was to lose it "for my sake and the gospel's" (13:9f. = 8:35).

iii. "When You See": A Call to Abandon the Defense of Jerusalem

The next section begins (13:14) with another temporal clause: just as the disciples were warned about what they would *hear* from the rebel recruiters, so they are warned equally strenuously about what they will *see*: the "devastating sacrilege." This celebrated apocalyptic euphemism from Daniel 11:31, 12:11, and 1 Maccabees 11:54 was originally coined in reference to Antiochus Epiphanes IV's attempted desolation of the temple (168 B.C.E.). Why has Mark reappropriated this phrase, and why is he so cryptic about it ("Let the reader understand")? Mark occasionally uses editorial comment (e.g., 7:3,11,19; 14:9), but nowhere else does he address "the one reading" (*ho anaginōskōn*) so directly. This obviously concerns something crucial to the historical moment. D. Ford, in an exhaustive study (1979:158ff.), has surveyed the six major interpretations of the phrase "devastating sacrilege" (*bdelugma tēs erēmōseōs*) "standing where it ought not" (*hopou ou dei*; here the *dei* is in a negative form). He concludes that it refers not merely to one act of idolatrous desecration of the temple, but the devastation of the entire city by invading soldiers; it is "a comprehensive term applying first to the armies of Rome" (1979:163).

This part of the sermon specifically addresses the siege of Jerusalem. A word should be said concerning the common assertion that here, as in 13:2, we have an example of *ex eventu* (after the fact) prophecy, which characterizes so much apocalyptic literature. J. A. T. Robinson, in reviewing the arguments, points out that this allusion reflects neither precision nor accuracy; we need only compare the detail of Luke's redaction of this same tradition, written after the fall of the city (Lk 21:20f.). I agree with Robinson's conclusion that "lack of correlation between the initial question and Jesus' answer would suggest that the discourse is not written retrospectively out of the known events of 70" (1976:16; see also Reicke, 1972).

Mark's situation in Roman-controlled Galilee between 68 and 70 C.E. would better explain his parenthetical comment to the reader, which functioned:

> More like a dark hint, a clue to Christian eyes but an enigma to others, presumably the imperial authorities. . . . More precise language was politically dangerous [Taylor, 1963:512].

Here Mark comes closest to the secretive, "underground" political discourse so characteristic of classic apocalyptic literature written at a time of persecution, such as Daniel or Revelation. He simply cannot speak directly about Roman military operations, for to do so would be to betray his resistance community. Thus, when the siege begins Mark instructs Judeans to "*then* flee to the hills" (the *tote* functions as a temporal conditional). Wilde is correct in seeing this as specific counsel to Judean Christian associates (and perhaps Galilean readers as well) not to rally to the defense of Jerusalem. In the tradition of Jeremiah (Jer 21), defying the logic of patriotism, Mark abandons Jerusalem and the restorationist project as a lost cause.

Mark elaborates upon this urgent plea in 13:15–18. His description of persons on rooftops (*dōmatos*, the flat roof characteristic of village dwellings used for sleeping or keeping watch) and doing field labor (*ho eis ton agron*) is not meant to suggest that they will be surprised by sudden cosmic intervention (as in the dispensationalist doctrine of the "rapture"). It simply indicates that Mark writes "from the standpoint of the countryside" (Taylor, 1963:513). The notion of fleeing without time to pack possessions is a realistic assessment of the conditions of wartime refugees; this is further inferred in the difficulties anticipated for pregnant women and the prayer that the displacement not happen in winter (13:17f.).

On this last point speculation upon possible historical correlation becomes rampant among commentators. L. Gaston (1970) equates this "moment" with the winter crisis of Emperor Caligula's aborted threat to defile the Jerusalem temple in 40 C.E. S. Sowers sees here an allusion to the historical tradition (which we know from Eusibius) of a mass Christian migration from Jerusalem to Pella in 66 C.E., right after the outbreak of the revolt. This flight, argues Sowers, could not have taken place in winter because storms would have swollen the river Jordan, making the route to Pella impassible (1970:305ff.). Such efforts, however interesting, are overliteralist. Mark's plea was probably patterned after the tradition of sudden departure for the hills in 1 Maccabees 2:28. But again he subverts the original discourse; whereas the Maccabees were calling the people to hill-based guerilla resistance to the Hellenistic forces that were desecrating Jerusalem, Mark is calling for the abandonment of the city of David.

Even if we presume that the call to flight is strict apocalyptic metaphor, with no historical inference, the discourse of the text remains the same. As Belo put it:

> Judea, Jerusalem, and the temple are the center of the world for a Jew; their desolation is the worst of catastrophes according to the Jewish codes. Once the Jewish symbolic field has been destroyed, people must abandon it and flee from it, for it no longer guarantees blessing (that is why to be pregnant or to be nursing becomes a misfortune). In short, this desolation represents the disorganization of the current codes, their upheaval, and the collapse of the symbolic field and the codes that inscribe it [1981:198].

This has in fact been Mark's position throughout the Gospel; from its very beginning (1:5) he has been leading us "away" from Jerusalem.

iv. "Do Not Believe It": The Rebels and Messianic Kingship

The first half of the sermon draws to a close with another call to endurance (13:19f.), based upon the tribulation of Daniel 12:1 (cf. 1 Enoch 80:2,4; 4 Ezra 4:26). Whereas in 13:13 steadfastness could earn salvation, here the suffering is so great that even the most persevering can be saved only if the tribulation is shortened. With this Mark introduces two themes that will figure in the second half of the sermon: the days of universal suffering (*hai hēmerai ekainai thlipsis*; cf. 13:24) and the notion of the "elect" (a reference probably to his own community; *eklektous;* cf. 13:23, 27).

The last temporal clause ("if anyone should say to you") returns to the problem of the rebels' alleged messianic credentials, asserting unequivocally that they are not to be believed (13:21). "Signs and wonders" (*sēmeia kai terata*), Mark argues, are the tools of "pseudo prophets" (13:22), for Jesus has already scorned them (8:11). Here at the midpoint of the sermon, Mark serves notice how Jesus intends to handle the disciples' request for signs in 13:4—he will conclude the sermon *without* offering any unambiguous signs—for he is a *true* prophet. Still, Mark's concession that it may be possible "even for the elect to be deceived" (13:22b) no doubt indicates that members of his own community have been successfully persuaded by the war party.

Prophetic and protomessianic movements were sporadic throughout the first century in Palestine, an expression of popular resistance to both Hellenism and the native aristocracy (above, 2,C,iii). Horsley has argued, however, that formal messianism was only an occasional and exceptional characteristic of rebel ideologies (1985). Yet he also points out that the testimony of Josephus provides evidence of at least two incidents of rebel pretensions to popular kingship. One episode was with the Sicarius leader Menahem, which I have mentioned because of its parallels with Jesus' procession into Jerusalem (above, 10,B,i):

> The second and far more extensive messianic movement emerged among the Judean peasantry nearly two years after the revolt had started. This movement focused on Simon bar Giora, who eventually became the principal Jewish commander in Jerusalem. . . . In [Josephus'] account of Simon's rise from a leader of a local guerilla band, to one followed as *king* by a train of thousands in addition to a sizable army, one can detect a number of remarkable parallels with the rise of David, prototype of the ancient tradition of popular kingship [Horsley and Hanson, 1985:119,121].

That is, like David's rise to power, Simon's campaign involved first the capture of Hebron, then a march on Jerusalem.

When, in the third year of the war, Simon entered the city to overturn the rule of the Zealot coalition, Josephus says he was "greeted as a savior and guardian by the citizens," and proceeded to consolidate his power (ibid.:123). In the end, when the city was taken by Titus, Simon was taken to Rome, paraded, and executed, as was the Roman practice vis-à-vis defeated kings (ibid.:126f.; below, 13,A,i). Thus, although the exact nature of rebel messianism cannot be determined, these examples demonstrate that Mark's warning against "false messiahs" was not unfounded. This sermon concretely articulates the messianic war of myths between Mark's Jesus, who called his followers to the way of the cross, and the rebels, who called Jews to take up the sword against Rome.

The first half of the sermon closes with the third occurrence of the *watch* warning (11:23). The function of the editorial comment "I have told you beforehand" is to historicize Jesus' words—that is, to bind the narrative moment to the historical moment. The real issue is not the "time of the end time," but the imperative to discern the events of the war. The community is to take its stand against both the rebel restorationists and the Roman invaders. But if Mark will not forge either of these "historical alliances," if the revolt is not the kingdom, what *is* the concrete political shape of discipleship practices? Does nonalignment mean noninvolvement?

11D. THE SERMON AS MYTHIC DISCOURSE

Mark has just narrated a militant practice of resistance in Jesus' second direct action campaign, only to turn around to repudiate the rebel cause of the war. How is such a position coherent? In order to articulate how he can regard Jesus' messianic politics to be more genuinely revolutionary than rebel political messianism, Mark turns to what we might call "high apocalyptic." In the second half of the sermon the tenor of his literary symbolics attains more classically mythic character. But this new discourse presents us with a double problem. First, it *appears* to suggest a kind of eschatological timetable, beginning with a warning about what will transpire in "those days after that tribulation" (13:24). Secondly, Jesus' description of the coming cosmic catastrophe *appears* to invoke "heavenly signs." In other words, Mark seems to be doing precisely what the sermon strictly forbids (cf. 13:32)—namely, depending upon signs and speculating about the "end time"!

In fact, Mark's mythic discourse is designed not to encourage but discourage such speculation. To recognize this, however, we must look more closely at the temporal/spatial dimensions of apocalyptic myth. Failure to grasp this has of course been the the primary cause of the manipulation and abuse for which this literature is commonly known. I have alluded to these issues throughout my reading, and this is the best place to address them.

i. The "End of the World": Revolution

Mark's images of cosmic cataclysm are drawn from the traditional apocalyptic myth of "palingenesis," the surpassing of the "old" order by the "new heavens and new earth." This dualism between world orders is expressed temporally in terms of "two ages." Mythical time, however, is not conceived of chronologically (*chronos*) but archetypically (*kairos*). The two "ages" coexist in human history as "good" and "evil," each with their own respective "pasts" and "futures." The function of the myth is parenetic: the dualism compels listeners to clarify their allegiances in the historical struggle between fundamentally differing social visions. This is what I have called a "bifocal" perspective on reality (above, 8,D,ii), the collapsing of linear history into the political "moment" in which a choice is demanded between competing "histories" (e.g., that of domination and that of liberation). This moment is the same whether it involves John, Jesus, or the disciples; in it the Human One presides as either defendant or prosecutor. Obviously, the myth also diffuses the distinction between narrative and historical moment, which is why this sermon has more to say to the reader than to the plot of the story.

The collapsing of *chronos* into *kairos* is not, however, absolute in biblical faith: Yahweh's purposes will "in the end" prevail. Apocalyptic dualism is not static but dynamic, asserting that the corrupt age is already "passing away," the new one dawning. It is precisely the conviction that the new order is "here but not yet" that motivates the believer to join in the unfinished, genuine struggle for history. But as a radical dualism it represents, as theologian C. Braaten once pointed out, a political ideology of total revolution:

> The new world that is coming is mediated through a negation of the old, that is, *ex oppositione.* . . . God is the power of the future contradicting all history that wishes to build its future out of its present[1972:9,11].

This ideology opposes the loyalistic radicalism of the rebels, who wish to "reconstruct" the new order on the old model; it also rejects the reformism of the Jewish renewal movements. Both perspectives fail to see anything *fundamentally* wrong with the "system," analogous to modern theories of "development." But Mark's "radical criticism" (looking not for symptoms but root causes) has turned up serious structural problems, not only in the symbolic order and the dominant political economy, but indeed in the very ideology of domination that infects orthodox political culture. Thus he is committed to nothing less than the complete unraveling of the present order, resisting it with the practice of a new one that is "wholly other."

It is therefore a mistake to look for *chronological* meaning in the apocalyptic discourse of temporality. The sermon implies, for example, that the "moment of the end" (expressed by various euphemisms, e.g., day, hour, time, season, this generation) is identifiable; it will appear as the "great tribulation" (cf. "in that day/those days" 13:17,19,20,24). Yet Mark also states that the disciples *cannot* know "when the time is" (13:33), *nor even what to look for*, because the very character of the moment is a mystery: "concerning that day and the hour no one knows" (13:32). Is the "end of the world" an empirical, historical event? Mark's references to cosmic and political cataclysm suggest it is. Yet why, then, the exhortations to "watching"? After all, if the sun and moon stop shining, it will be obvious to all.

Mark's wider narrative world shows that references to "time" cannot always be taken literally. The crucial "moment" has been described in many different ways:

1. the *kairos* is breaking into the world in Jesus' proclamation of the kingdom (1:15);
2. "in that day" signals the point at which the "bridegroom's guests" will indeed have to fast (2:20);

3. it is the present *kairos* in which the discipleship community already practices its new way of life (10:30);
4. it is *not* the *kairos* in which the "fig tree" can be expected to bear fruit (11:13);
5. it is the *kairos* in which the master has sent his servants to check up on the tenants of the vineyard (12:2);
6. it is "the hour" when the Holy Spirit will instruct the disciples in their witness before the courts;
7. it is "the hour" of Jesus' struggle in Gethsemane (14:35,41).

There is similar ambiguity in Mark's narrative use of the temporal markers "when" (*hotan*) and "then" (*tote*). In the apocalyptic sermon they imply a specific unfolding of events, which disciples must discern and respond to accordingly (when: 13:4,7,11,14,28f.; then: 13:14,21,26f.). But throughout the rest of the story they represent a much broader "moment:"

1. *when* the bridegroom is taken away, *then* the guests will fast (2:20);
2. *when* the strong man has been bound, *then* his house will be plundered (3:27);
3. *when* persons hear the word of the gospel (4:15f.);
4. the "time" or season of kingdom harvest (4:29,31f.);
5. *when* the Human One comes in glory (8:38);
6. "*until*" the Human One should rise from the dead (9:9);
7. *when* the dead are raised (12:25);
8. *when* Jesus will celebrate supper in the kingdom (14:25).

This survey shows that the temporal character of the "end time" is not clear at all. Mark's terms are fluid, connoting the coming of the kingdom; the political conflict it provokes; the suffering of Jesus or the disciples; the tribulation of the whole world; and the "final" resurrection and "triumph" of the kingdom.

Time-as-metaphor functions precisely to subvert the notion of literal time—thus obviating "eschatological timetables." Which is to say that those who see apocalyptic discourse as *deterministic* have not understood it, for the very nature of the mythic struggle is to stress that history is open. As H. May has put it:

Apocalyptic has nothing to do with holding the carrot of eternity before the believer's nose. . . . The precise *raison d'être* for apocalyptic is to deny the imminence of easy victory, to force Jews and Christians alike to accept the agony of history, the birth-pangs of creation. . . . The total effect of the ever-retreating horizon of fulfillment is to support a mood of genuine hope amid frustration. . . . Mature faith accepts the enduring struggle that historical existence entails. . . . The apocalypse of all the New Testament literary forms expresses clear awareness of man's painful "fall into history". . . . They accept, and even yearn for, the end as fulfillment of a promise, God's promise of fidelity, but in the meantime turn their full attention to the ambiguous face of history. . . . Genuine apocalypse has always functioned as a warning against the presumption of man [1972:17–21,32].

As we saw above, Jesus' refusal to offer "signs" represents the rejection of just this presumption. Mark advocates neither fatalism nor escapism, but a revolutionary commitment to the transformation of history, which always demands political vigilance and discernment.

ii. "War in Heaven": Resistance

A consideration of the "spatial" dimensions of Mark's apocalyptic discourse will confirm its commitment to concrete history. The "vertical" imagery characteristic of apocalyptic, describing struggles between "heavenly powers," is based upon:

> The old idea that each nation has a corresponding angelic "prince" who rules over it. . . . We are dealing with a two-story universe, where events happen on one level on earth but also on another level in the heavens [J. Collins, 1974:32f.].

That this worldview was fundamental to the social construction of reality in the Hellenistic world was long ago established by the study of "principalities and powers" language in the New Testament (Morrison, 1960; Caird, 1956).[1]

More recently A.Y. Collins has done invaluable work on the function of the "combat myth" in apocalyptic literature. She argues, for example, that in Revelation the conflict between the beast and the lamb is a political parody of the Emperor Nero:

> The combat myth regularly involves a struggle for kingship. . . . At all stages ultimate power and the commensurate recognition are at stake. Thus when faced with such a struggle the people . . . must take sides. . . . The war on the saints is part of the threat, the act of rebellion of the chaos beast as it attempts to usurp power [1976:184].

Of particular relevance to the study of Mark is J. Collins's similar thesis regarding Daniel, from whom Mark's myth of the Human One is drawn. In Daniel 12:

> The reader is challenged to make a choice in the holy war between Michael and his angels and the armies of Antiochus. This is not an internal spiritual battle. Antiochus and his armies are very real factors in the political world. The reader of Daniel is challenged to resist Antiochus, and the apocalyptic visions of the outcome of the battle provide the basis for this decision [1977:213].

This two-level struggle is, I have suggested, exactly what is happening in Jesus' second call to discipleship (above, 8,D).

Apocalyptic euphemisms are often cryptic, as befits underground literature in a context of resistance and persecution; we have seen this with Mark's use of "desolating sacrilege." In the first-century Middle East, "war in heaven" referred to what modern political rhetoric calls the "struggle for hearts and minds," and what I described in chapter 1 as the "war of myths." Aside from the three apocalyptic moments, Mark makes several allusions to the combat myth in the course of his narrative:

1. Jesus (baptized by the spirit and aided by angels) tempted by Satan (aided by the "wild beasts"; 1:10—13);
2. Jesus vs. the scribes in the debate about Beelzebul, issuing in the strong man parable (3:22—30);
3. Jesus vs. Rome in the exorcism of the "legion" (5:1ff.);
4. Jesus vs. Satan in Peter's "confession" (8:32);
5. the courtroom myth and Human One as defendant/prosecutor (8:34–38);
6. Jesus vs. the Sanhedrin (14:62).

The combat myth is most explicit, however, in this sermon, where Mark juxtaposes the coming of the Human One and angelic hosts to the "falling of the stars" and "the shaking of the heavenly powers" *(hai dunameis hai en tois ouranois*, 13:25f.).

Wink cites a revealing passage from the first-century Jewish philosopher Philo concerning his understanding of the role of the powers in the structure of creation itself:

> The complete whole around us is held together by invisible powers *(aoratois dunamesin)*, which the Creator has made to reach from the ends of the earth to heaven's furthest bounds, taking forethought that what was well bound should not be loosened: for the powers of the Universe *(hai dunameis tou pantos)* are chains that cannot be broken [1984:160].

This captures Philo's conservative Hellenistic faith in the "highest and deepest" structures of cosmic "law and order." It was an ideology Mark the revolutionary did not share; what Philo believed "could not be broken," Mark insisted would be shattered.

Mark (like John the political prisoner of Patmos) looked to such prophetic radicalism as the so-called Isian apocalypse (R. Miller, 1976). This vision makes an interesting equation between two dualisms: heaven and earth (Is 24:18,21), and the "lofty" imperial city and the lowly agrarian poor (Is 25:2,4; 26:5f.). In the Isian apocalypse, when "the windows of heaven are opened, the foundations of the earth tremble" (24:19); when the celestial lights are "confounded," the "kings of the earth will be imprisoned" (24:22f.). Thus Mark is able to draw a direct connection between the fall of Jerusalem and the fall of the heavenly forces. The powers would be pulled from their high places, and the Human One would harvest a new world "from the end of earth to the end of heaven" (13:27).

In sum, the second half of the sermon employs apocalyptic myth in order to compel the disciples/reader to enter into the "historical moment," to choose between the old and new order, both of which stand at the edge of history. It is, to be sure, the moment of the war; but that very historical crisis drives Mark to look deeper still. Why not aid and abet the rebel cause? Because it was mere rebellion, the recycling of oppressive power into new hands. To journey deeply into history, to experiment with a political practice that will break, not perpetuate, the reign of domination in the world—that is the meaning of Mark's final call to "Watch!" (13:37). It is a call to nonviolent resistance to the powers.

11E. THE MYSTERY OF ENDS AND MEANS, II (13:24-37)

i. The Advent of the Human One and the Fall of the Powers

Cosmic portents symbolic of judgment are common in apocalyptic literature (1 En 80:4-7; 4 Ez 5:4; *A.M.* 5:50), and originated in the late prophetic tradition. Mark's mention of the three celestial lights (13:25) is based on Isaiah 13:10 (cf. Ez 32:7f.; Am 8:9; Jl 2:10). But whereas these traditions speak of the sun, moon, and stars darkening, Mark says the stars "fall," as in Isaiah 34:4 (see below). Wink points out that we should see the "stars" (*hoi asteres*, cf. Dn 8:9) as part and parcel of apocalyptic powers language:

> The equation "heavenly hosts = powers = angels = stars = gods" was already in place by the time of the LXX. There the stars were powers in their own right, considered as "conscious" beings. In the early sections of the Enoch literature, on the other hand, the sole sovereignty of God is buffered by the appointment of rulers *over* the stars, whose task is to regulate their movement through the heavens [1984:162].

The myth of Satan, ruler of the powers, "falling" from (or being cast out of) heaven is a tradition reflected elsewhere in the New Testament (Lk 10:18; Jn 12:31; Rv 12:9). Mark is alluding to the "fall" of the highest structures of power in history. How will this be accomplished? For the second time, Mark turns the apocalyptic myth of the Human One coming on the clouds (13:26f.).

Two things will accompany this advent, indicated by the parallel construction of "and then . . . and then" (*kai tote*). First, the fallen powers will "see his great power and glory." I have already indicated that I understand this event, within the narrative of Mark, to refer to the moment of Jesus' execution, the "third apocalyptic moment." There, as we shall see (below, 13,B), representatives of both Roman and Jewish powers are assembled, spectating—and the light of the sun fails (15:31-33,39). This is indeed the moment spoken of as "the coming of the kingdom in power" (9:1).

Secondly, the Human One will dispatch angels to "gather up" (*episunaxei*;

cf. 2 Thess 2:1) the elect—that is, those who have endured suffering (13:20) and resisted the powers (13:22). The phrase "from the four winds" and "from the ends of the earth to the ends of the heavens" is unique. It echoes intertextual traditions concerning the scattering of Yahweh's people (e.g., Zec 2:6) and the promise of their return:

> If your outcasts are in the uttermost parts of heaven (*ap akrou tou ouranou heōs akrou tou ouranou*), from there Yahweh will gather (*sunaxei*) you [Dt 30:4, LXX].

The scope of the ingathering is from one end of creation to another; Mark envisions the renewal of *everything* in the universe, the dawn of a new world now that the powers have been toppled.

If the advent of the Human One is narrated in the cross event, how is this vision of palingenesis related to his story world? I suggest that the implied regathering at the end of the story fulfills this function (below, 13,D). The "young man" (as we shall see, another apocalyptic motif) sends the disciples back to Galilee—that is, back to the "genesis" of the discipleship narrative. And how does Mark's story commence? "The beginning of the gospel" (1:1), the new creation! Like the "end," the "beginning" too is archetypal, representing the invitation to join anew in the journey of discipleship, that struggle for justice in the only world there is.

ii. The Fig Tree Parable: Climax to Mark's Political Symbolics

Are these heavenly "signs"? As if to discourage such an interpretation, Mark follows immediately with an exhortation to "learn from the parable" (13:28, *mathete tēn parabolēn*). This is the only appearance in Mark of the verb *manthanein*, from which the word *mathētēs*, "disciple" ("one who learns from practice") derives. Mark is moving toward the conclusion of Jesus' sermon, in a section that knits together several short sayings and finally returns to the question of the "end time." This is clearly an important parable, and it concerns an image we have already encountered: the fig tree.

The parallelism in 13:28f. is a comparative doublet:

A   learn from the parable of the fig tree:
     as soon as (*hotan ēdē*) its branch becomes soft and leafy you know
     (*genētai*) that summer is near (*engus*);
B   even so with you
     whensoever (*hotan*) you should see these things happening know
     (*ginōskete*) that it is near (*engus*), at the door.

Why does Mark reinsert the fig tree image at this point? And what is it that is "near the door"?

Intertextually, Mark's reference to a fig tree on the heels of the cataclysmic portents just examined is an allusion to another version of the combat myth in Isaiah (34:4, LXX):

> And the heavens (*ho ouranos*) will roll up like a scroll,
> and all the stars fall (*panta ta astra peseitai*)
> as leaves from a vine
> and as leaves fall from a fig tree (*hōs piptei phulla apo sukēs*).

But Mark has altered Isaiah to fit in with his narrative profile of the symbolic fig tree, whose leaves are not falling but blossoming. Mark has directed us back to his temple haggadah (11:13).

Telford suggests that the leafing of the tree in 13:28 is meant as a counterpoint to its withering in 11:20f. (1980:217)—against the curse of Jerusalem Mark implies a blessing for the Christian community. The narrative relationship, however, between the two "trees" does not in fact suggest contrast, but continuity. The tree that Jesus cursed in 11:13f. was also leafing; in fact, Mark stressed that it had "nothing but leaves" (*ouden heuren ei mē phulla*). Mark is now telling us to learn from this "parable." What did we learn from the first tree? Jesus' curse of the leafing fig tree was our first hint that he intended to repudiate the temple state. This was then made explicit through his temple action, and then in his departure from the temple and prediction of its destruction (13:1f.). As I have noted, from 13:20 this discourse has used the euphemism "these things" (*tauta*).

Hence when the second fig tree parable refers to "these things" we realize that Mark has led us in a circle of syllogistic reasoning in these narrative analogies:

If "leafy fig tree" = "temple to be cursed"
And "destruction of temple" = "the end time"
Then "leafy fig tree" = "end time to be fulfilled."

The "when you see" of the "desecrating sacrilege" is here correlated to the "when you see" of 13:29. The circle of inferences is complete: the reader must once and for all *learn* the lesson of the fig tree. Which was: the world of the temple-based social order must come to an end (11:20-26) in order for the new order to dawn. Which is precisely the opposite of what the rebel recruiters are saying.

Mark is offering a parable that summarizes his parables. The leafy fig tree symbolizes "not the *kairos* for fruit"; the "bad soil" (cf. the sower parable, 4:16f.) symbolizes the oppressive temple state, which causes fruit to "wither" (11:21). Similarly, the leafy fig tree means that "summer" (or "harvest," *to theros*, 13:28) is imminent. Mark may have in mind Amos's end-time judgment oracle about "summer fruit" (Am 8:1f.), or the apocalyptic motif of the judgment harvest (cf. Jl 3:13; Rv 14:14f.), which would be suggested by the ingathering of 13:27. This was already spelled out in the seed parable of 4:26-29: the kingdom seed grows unseen, but when it yields fruit the "sickle" is sent (*apostellei*) for "the harvest" (*ho therismos*). The war means that the "moment of truth" is "at the door" for the community (13:29).

This reading is strengthened by Jesus' solemn assurance in 13:30 that "this generation will not pass away until all these things have happened." The temporal condition "until" (*ou mē*) and reference to "this generation" yet again refers us back to Jesus' prediction of the advent of the Human One in 8:38–9:1. The "harvest" is the apocalyptic moment of the cross: "this generation" cannot pass away until the power of *satyagraha* is revealed. *Then* "these things" (the dominant order broken, the temple state dismantled, and the powers overthrown) will be fulfilled (13:4). The passing of this old order means the eclipse of the *fundamental* structures of the social universe (articulated as the "passing away of heaven and earth," in true apocalyptic fashion, 13:31). What *do not pass away* are "the words" of Jesus, which indicates that Mark indeed has offered us the parable *in place of* a sign. And Jesus' "words" (Mk 8:32,38; above, 8,D,i) offer only the way of the cross, which words the disciples/reader must remember (9:10).

To nail down this argument Mark reiterates one final time that the moment has nothing to do with speculative timetables:

> But concerning that day or hour no one knows (*oudeis oiden*),
> neither the angels in heaven nor the Son, only the Father;
> Watch, shake off sleep, for you do not know (*ouk oidate*)
> when the moment (*kairos*) is [13:32f.].

This is the last allusion to the seed parables: *how* the seed grows, "no one knows" (4:27). But of course the point of this sermon—of the Gospel as a whole—is that we will know the "moment" when it comes. That is, so that we will have "eyes to see" that the cross is not defeat, but the advent of the Human One and the toppling of the powers.

For this reason the final refrain of the sermon comes: "Watch!" (*blepete*). The disciples' question of 13:4 has received an answer: if they are looking for empirical data they are looking for the wrong thing. At every point this discourse is clear: the mythic "moment" is to be identified with the cross. It stands at the center of history, and is for Mark the focus of all true political discernment. Now, at the end of the sermon, he invites his readers to become truly discerning, offering a new metaphor: "Gethsemane."

iii. "Stay Awake!": The World as Gethsemane

Mark approaches the conclusion of the sermon by "deconstructing" his apocalyptic discourse. The "angels in heaven and the Son" (who will come "at the harvest," 13:26f.) share in the disciples' unknowing. But Jesus' ignorance will not prevent him from going the way of the cross, nor should it stop the disciples. The call to "Watch!" is now replaced with a synonym, the command to "shake off sleep" (*agrupneite*), indicating the introduction of a new, very terrestrial, theme: the struggle between "staying awake" and "falling asleep."

Jesus now spins one last parable, an unassuming little folktale that will be revealed as the heart of Mark's ideological discourse. In it we will hear proleptic echoes of the passion narrative and analeptic echoes of the story's two central political parables.

The story begins simply with the parabolic "It is like . . ." (13:34, *hōs*; cf. 4:31). The introduction unmistakably alludes to the "vineyard tenants" parable: the unknown "moment" (*kairos* = 12:2) is like a "man" (= 12:1) who went "away" (*apodēmos* = *apedēmēsin*, 12:1). The contrast with the vineyard parable, however, makes it clear that *this* parable is addressed not to Jesus' political opponents but to the discipleship community. Those in charge are not "tenants" but "slaves" (= servant-leaders, *doulois* = 12:2), and they are given "authority," not a "lease." Mark goes on to say that all servants are given their own "task." Preeminent among these is the command to the "doorkeeper" (*thurōros*), who must be vigilant about what "is at the door" (*thurais*, 13:29).

"Shake off sleep" is in turn replaced by yet another synonym, the command to "stay awake!" (*grēgorē*, 13:35,37). Mark reiterates that the servants will not know the time of the "coming" (*ouk oidate gar pote*). But the "man" who went away is now referred to as the "lord of the house" (cf. "lord of the vineyard," 12:1,9). The vineyard and strong man parables have here been fused: the one coming is not a Davidic king (11:9f.) but the Lord of David (12:36), and is also Lord of the strong man's house!

The disciples are told to vigil through the four Roman "watches" of the night. It was Lightfoot who first recognized that these watches correspond to moments in the passion:

1. evening (*opse*): the time (*opsia*) of the Last Supper (14:17), and the time after the crucifixion (15:42);
2. midnight (*mesonuktion*): night (*nux*) is the general time of Peter's denial (14:30);
3. the "cock crow" (*alektorophōnias*): specific time (*alektōr*) of Peter's denial (14:30,72);
4. dawn (*prōi*): when Jesus was handed over to the Romans (15:1).

No proleptic reference to the passion story is stronger, however, than the parable's warning not to be found "asleep." It is this very theme around which Mark will build the story of Jesus' final "hour": Gethsemane (14:35).

In Mark's story time, the tragedy is that the disciples in that episode will not "stay awake" with Jesus in Gethsemane; they will sleep. They will betray and finally abandon him at each "watch" of his final night because they do not understand his call to the cross. Yet this call to vigilance is primarily directed toward the historical existence of the reader. This mythic moment of watching, however eerie and uncorporeal it may seem to us, was a discourse widely understood by the early Christians. It was the cornerstone of the primitive church's understanding of eschatological existence on the edge of history, and perhaps the most strongly attested of all New Testament catechetical/parenetic traditions (cf. Mt 24:43–51; Lk 21:34–36; 1 Thes 5:2–8; Rom 13:11–13; Col 4:2; 1 Pt 5:8; Rv 3:2). For Mark, it is the culmination of Jesus' sermon on revolutionary patience. The discipleship community is exhorted to embrace the world as Gethsemane: to stay awake in the darkness of history, to refuse to compromise the politics of the cross. The revolution of means as well as ends, the nonviolent struggle against the historical lockstep of domination, will prevail because the strong man is not the true "Lord of the house." So can we join the struggle to bind him and liberate his domain.

11F. DO WE OBEY "HOUSE RULES" OR THE "LORD OF THE HOUSE"?: MARK'S SOCIO-LITERARY STRATEGY THROUGH 13:37

i. Discourse

Taken as a whole, the discourse of Mark 11–13 is first and foremost one of "action/reflection." The narrative moves from the supremely concrete political engagement in the temple to the supremely "mythic" apocalyptic sermon. For those to whom the action/reflection model is a familiar pedagogical and political tool this may seem unremarkable. But for most modern exegetes of apocalyptic literature, it will seem a novel solution to the "problem" of apocalyptic. For biblical scholarship has been telling us for years that apocalyptic literature advocates a generally passive, even escapist, attitude toward political reality. A typical expression of this view is that of P. Hanson, who claims that "prophetic eschatology is transformed into apocalyptic at the point where the task of translating the cosmic vision into the categories of mundane reality is abdicated" (1971:469). This bias has been carried into a reading of Mark 13. Its "war in heaven," and its counsel to abandon solidarity with the rebel cause in favor of the command to simply "watch," have been manipulated to mean that Mark advocates a noncommittal, passive attitude, waiting for God to intervene and resolve all political contradictions (so Wilde, 1974; more on this below, 14,A,i).

But the caution and patience of the apocalyptic sermon must be interpreted in direct relationship to the militance of the preceding series of temple conflicts. Otherwise the discourse of Mark is hopelessly incoherent. After all, Mark has constructed his entire narrative around the interplay of metaphor, action, and metaphoric action: the meaning of one is revealed and reproduced by another. This has been most evident in the two campaigns of direct action. These narratives build through a series of debates and confrontations within a recognizable political landscape, in the first case Capernaum, the second Jerusalem. They culminate with powerful expressions of mutual rejection, at which point Jesus literally "sits down" to reflect with his disciples about the meaning of the campaign.

The first campaign began on the keynote of Jesus' proclamation of the gospel of the kingdom (1:14f.). In 4:1ff., having "exited" the synagogue because of its lack of compassion upon the sick (3:6f.), and having broken ideologically with the scribal class (3:22–27), Jesus begins his reflection upon the concrete prospects of this mission. The first half of the sermon uses the protoapocalyptic device of parable (as mystery, 4:11) and commentary to metaphorically reproduce the kingdom mission: "it is like a sower." This parable addressed both Jesus' campaign in the story and the ongoing mission of Mark's community, articulating the many obstacles to discipleship as well as the promise of an "eschatological harvest." The second half of the sermon (4:24ff.) then introduces images that articulate the central ideological paradox of ends and means: despite the lack of visible signs of success, the kingdom would continue to grow and spread in the world.

In like fashion, the second campaign began on the keynote of messianic politics with the procession and assault upon the temple (11:1ff.). In 13:3ff., having exited the temple because of its exploitation of the poor (12:41ff.), and having broken with the ideology of the Davidic state (12:35f.), Jesus offers another sermon. The first half of this reflection draws upon the apocalyptic metaphor of "tribulation" in order to reproduce the struggle for a genuinely messianic politics. It transposes Jesus' struggle against the temple state with that of his disciples at the time of the Roman-Jewish war. The second half again takes a longer view, articulating through apocalyptic myth the overthrow of the temple-based social order. Again, despite the lack of visible success, the powers will be toppled through the nonviolent power of the cross.

In both campaigns, realistic action establishes the politics of the narrative, and the sermon serves as an interpretive foil. In each case, the sermon warns against equating Jesus' militant nonviolence with triumphalistic power politics. The same point made by parables of patient farmers and seeds growing secretly is made by parables of fig trees and doorkeepers. It has been clear that Jesus has parted company with the social strategies of reform; but now it becomes clear that he also dissociates from the militant but loyalistically radical strategy of the rebels. The new order of the kingdom as Jesus envisioned it could not be imposed upon history by seizing power. As Gandhi put it, *satyagraha* concentrated upon historical means; the historical "fruits" must be left in the hands of God.

There are other aspects to the discourse of this section, such as the narrative drama of "escaping entrapment." From Jesus' first appearance in the temple the authorities plot to destroy him, because they read his symbolic action and his parables perfectly. But Jesus escapes the traps set for him, and in every case is able to turn the tables on his opponents, exposing their hypocrisy and duplicity. This encourages Mark's community, which itself was caught in the pressures of the war.

There are only three narrative "sites" in this part of the story, a sharp contrast to the rapidly changing settings of the earlier journeys. The sites and their significations are:

Jerusalem/Temple = institutions of domination
Bethany = "safe" coordinate
Mount of Olives = conflicting messianic discourse.

At the outset, a spatial tension is established between all three (11:1). Afterward, Jesus comes and goes into Jerusalem from Bethany, almost as if he refuses to stay overnight in the city. He is not visiting the "heart of the world" as a devoted pilgrim, but mounting guerillalike raids on the heart of oppressive power from a base in a nearby village. The closing opposition between the Mount of Olives and the Temple Mount (13:3) recapitulates the theme of the section: messianic intervention has come, but in a totally unexpected way.

The messianic discourse is established at the outset by Bartimaeus' hailing of Jesus as Son of David and the crowd's acclaim for David's kingdom. This provokes the reader's expectations regarding what Jesus will do when he comes into the temple, the final place of messianic revelation. Jesus' temple action thus comes as a shock. Mark is aware that he is risking being misunderstood in his manipulation of popular and highly charged political symbolics such as Psalms 110 and 118. He does not appeal to them to prove that Jesus is Messiah (he stipulated that at the very beginning of the story) but to redefine the character of messianic politics by identifying them with Jesus' way of the cross, and wresting them away from both Davidic restorationism and the presupposition of a temple state.

The grounds for his rejection of the temple state and its leadership are its oppressive political economy. This is clear from Jesus' direct action against the entrepreneurial class, and again in the second part of the antitemple frame. Note the discourse of 12:38–13:7:

A   Beware (*blepete*) of scribes and their hypocrisy (12:38);
  B   they exploit widows and will be judged (12:40);
    C   the rich give from affluence, widows from poverty (12:44);
  B' the temple exploits widows and will be destroyed (13:2);
A' beware (*blepete*) of false messiahs and their wars (13:5–7).

This discourse links the entire political economy of the temple with those who call for a messianic war. It is no wonder Mark breaks with the rebels!

The second sermon shows that Mark understands that a politics that proposes to abandon the ideological site of the temple must necessarily speak in terms of the "end of the world." One cannot simply remove the symbolic center of a highly developed social world without having the whole collapse. This apocalyptic sermon is linked to Jesus' antitemple action through the two fig tree parables. This discourse can be deciphered by paying attention to the "trail" of narrative analogies and syllogisms proceeding from each:

leafy fig tree (11:13a)
not the *kairos* for fruit (11:13b)
  no fruit ever again (11:14)
    withered to the roots (11:21)
      mountain cast into the sea (11:23)
        when you pray, have faith (11:24)
leafy fig tree (13:28a)
summer (harvest) is near; is at the door (13:28b)
  when you see these things happening (13:29)
    this generation will not pass away before (13:30)
      earth and heaven will pass away (13:31a)
        my words will not pass away (13:31b)

In both cases, the leafy fig tree parable represents the imminent destruction of the temple ("mountain cast into the sea," "these things"). Is there life after the temple? The discourse is emphatically affirmative. The disciples can still pray, because God does not live in the temple but among those who "believe", they need not be anxious when the social world unravels, because Jesus' words do not pass away.

All of this symbolic inner referentiality is meant to contrast the rebels' thirst for signs and wonders. Mark parodies: the promise of signs is a "sign" of false prophets; the war is not the "end" but the "beginning"—of tribulation. The rebels cannot bring down the old order and inaugurate the new, they can only make the suffering worse, because they do not understand the parable of the fig tree. The old world, ruled by the powers, can be vanquished only by the apocalyptic moment of the coming Human One—that is, the politics of the cross. Through this weaving together of metaphor, myth, parable, and parenesis, Mark's "apocalyptic temporality" swings freely between the "hour" of the cross event (13:32; cf. 15:33f.), the climax of Jesus' struggle with the powers, and the "hour" of the war (13:11), at which point the disciples take up the same struggle themselves. The two "moments" are thus bound together: the way "through" the war is the way of the cross.

ii. Signification

I have noted that the role of the disciples in this narrative is relatively incidental. Although the discipleship community is portrayed as already practicing aspects of Jesus' socio-economic program (e.g., 10:29f.), it does not seem to have yet engaged the powers. It would be a mistake to conclude from this that the disciples are not meant to follow Jesus' political practice. This is the point of the mythic collapsing of the two "hours." But the suffering of the disciples is cast in the "future"; in the present, they appear to lack sufficient faith (11:22). This suggests that perhaps the community is either too cowed or too confused by the political options. Its members are still intimidated by the ideology of the scribes (11:35; cf. 9:11), yet are also hard pressed by the rebel recruiters. In order to "follow" Jesus in breaking with the temple state, they must repudiate both conservative-reformist and loyalistically radical ideologies. And to do that they must be able to envision an alternative social order beyond the temple-centered universe.

The modern reader must attempt some historical empathy to understand how difficult it was to "believe" in an end to the world of the temple. Mark was demanding a lot from his original audience, but he was unequivocal: they had to root out the "doubt in their hearts" (11:23) and "believe" (cf. 9:23,29). Not only was the ideological *novum* of messianic politics "radical but nonaligned," difficult for the community to grasp, it was also dangerous under war conditions. If the Gospel was produced in or around Galilee in the late war years, then Mark is writing in reoccupied—but probably not totally pacified—territory. To freely associate a historical analogy, the situation of the community is not unlike villagers today in El Salvador or Angola in areas that seesaw back and forth between guerilla and army control. Even if one has clear sympathies (as Mark did), a refusal to publicly align is regarded as apostasy by both sides.

We see this "trap" most clearly signified in the episode of the tax debate (above, 10,D,iv). The community might easily be "caught" by the very Pharisees and Herodians (their Galilean opponents) who are portrayed trying to catch Jesus. On the basis of his economic ideology, Mark would have certainly opposed the imperial tribute; yet to publicly advocate it would be to identify the community with a restorationist revolt it did not support. Hence, Jesus gives an answer that neither gives in to Rome nor falls into the trap! Indeed, throughout the Gospel Mark's criticisms of Rome are necessarily veiled; for Titus's armies are already in control of Galilee.

In contrast, Mark is open in his denunciation of the temple state. Jesus' direct action against the temple on the level of narrative signification must be understood as legitimating a politics of disruption. A word, however, must be said here about the historicist temptation to speculate on the actual shape of this action, to which many commentators succumb (see Brandon, 1967:9). They wonder how Jesus could have engineered such a barricade, and how he could have gotten away with it without some kind of military intervention from the temple guard. But such tantalizing speculation misses Mark's intention to narrate *symbolic* action. By portraying the sudden and dramatic shutdown of temple operations as part of the wider symbolic fabric of his curse/repudiation discourse, Mark is calling for the end of the temple-based order—for according to tradition the cult could not be interrupted, even for a day.

If I may venture an analogy, Jesus "shut down" the temple no more but no less than a nonviolent direct action at the Pentagon, which, say, blockades the entrances, "shuts down" the military industrial complex. The symbolic action signals the intention, which can be brought about as historical reality only by a protracted campaign of nonviolent resistance. The Jerusalem conflict section as a whole legitimizes this kind of militant, direct action against concrete manifestations of exploitation in the socio-economic system, even as the second sermon insists that such action must remain nonviolent if it is to be genuinely revolutionary. If the disciples/reader can "learn" (13:28) the parable of the fig tree, we will be empowered to practice our vocation of resistance. No longer must we abide by the "house rules" as dictated by the dominant classes, but we are free to follow the "Lord of the house" in both subversive and constructive messianic practice.

The fact that Mark devotes the entire first half of the second sermon to disputing the claims of the rebel recruiters signifies what a credible ideological competitor they were for his community. That is why the Jerusalem section is so intent upon expropriating and subverting the symbolic code of traditional popular kingship. Indeed, in drawing upon the tradition of apocalyptic resistance literature, Mark is engaging the rebels in a debate about the character of revolutionary politics.

The question has been raised as to whether Mark was historically fair in linking the rebels so closely to the clerical classes. After all, there is strong evidence that the rebels also were struggling against the class privilege of the Jerusalem hierarchy; I will look at this question below (14,B,iv). The fact remains that, however much common ground the two shared, as was certainly the case in their opposition to the Romans, they parted company over the issue of the temple; the rebels struggled for its "purification," Mark for its demise. Thus, Mark differed with them on ends as well as means. The "parable of the fig tree," including Jesus' temple action, was his litmus test of commitment to a genuinely new social order.

Mark knows that his "nonaligned radicalism," having rejected the scribal establishment, the Zealot opposition, and the Hellenistic collaborators, places him virtually alone in the historical moment: "you will be hated by all for the sake of my name" (13:13). So he chooses a metaphor of loneliness, of the trial brought on by the darkness of unknowing: "Gethsemane." Mark calls the discipleship community to live in history with open eyes, to look deep into present events, beyond the conflicting claims of those vying for power. They must search for and attack the very roots of violence and oppression that hold the human story hostage. The coming of the kingdom has nothing to do with triumphalism; it comes from below, in solidarity with the human family in its dark night of suffering. The world is Gethsemane, and we are called to "historical insomnia."

NOTE

1. Scholarly debate over "powers" language has produced quite a literature in the postwar period. The most up-to-date summary and analysis is W. Wink's *Naming the Powers: The Language of Power in the New Testament*, vol. 1 (Philadelphia: Fortress, 1984). I commend this volume wholeheartedly for its coverage of this crucial aspect of apocalyptic discourse.

CHAPTER TWELVE

Jesus' Arrest and Trial by the Powers (Mark 14:1-15:20)

I have been very jealous for Yahweh, for the people of Israel have forsaken your Covenant, thrown down your altars, and slain your prophets with the sword; and I, even I only, am left; and they seek my life, to take it away.

—1 Kings 19:10

There is a painting by a Guatemalan artist, in exile in Australia, that depicts the Last Supper against the political landscape of Latin America. Swirling around Jesus in the smoke-filled room is a vivid tableau; woven in and around the twelve disciples are military generals cavorting with high-class prostitutes, wealthy landowners making payoffs, guerillas whispering furtively, a peasant couple attending to their malnourished children, a priest saying Mass, land reform organizers being attacked by vigilantes, several mutilated bodies under the table. There is no religious aura around Jesus; instead, he seems hemmed in, caught in the middle of the wordly passions, intrigues, and suffering of life as it really is.

Never have I seen a painting that more accurately captured the tenor of Mark's story of Jesus' last days. It is an intensely political drama, filled with conspiratorial back-room deals and covert action, judicial manipulation and prisoner exchanges, torture and summary execution. These themes are characteristic of our modern political narratives, but they rarely emerge in the standard interpretations of "Holy Week." Conditioned by centuries of liturgical and theological reproductions, we think of the "Upper Room" as a lofty eucharistic moment, rather than as the conflict-ridden final hours of a fugitive community in hiding, whose solidarity is crumbling in the face of state power. We envision Gethsemane as Jesus' obedient submission to the preordained plan of salvation history, rather than the deep internal struggle of a leader coming to terms with the consequences of his subversive practice.

Mark's "passion play" is precisely such a political tableau, painted with hues of tragedy, realism, and parody. In it Mark dramatizes the final conflict between the nonviolent symbolic action of Jesus, the security apparatus of the authorities, and the revolutionary yearnings of the rebels, the "war in heaven" being played out in the real life theater of Jewish and Roman courts, jails, and docks. Here the irrepressibly political character of Jesus' call to discipleship at the center of the story (8:34f.) is articulated: "self-denial," "taking up the cross," and "losing one's life to save it" are finally enacted. And we would do well not to forget that this very narrative of arrest, trial, and torture is still lived out by countless political prisoners around the world today.

12A. THE NARRATIVE CHARACTER OF THE PASSION STORY

i. Structure

The passion narrative brings a greater degree of representation of historical tradition than elsewhere in the Gospel—this even the most skeptical form critics concede. But this does not mean that it is any less determined by Mark's narrative strategy and symbolic discourse, as has been demonstrated in recent redactional studies (see Juel, 1977; Matera, 1982). The narrative generally follows the "script" established in the third portent (10:33f.): Jesus will be "handed over" from his disciples to the chief priests and scribes, from the Sanhedrin to the gentiles, and from Pilate to the executioner. Time, setting, and action are all carefully plotted to heighten this drama toward the denouement and surprise ending of the Gospel.

This concluding part of the story can be divided into three main sections:
1. the last days of the community with Jesus (14:1–52);
2. the double trial narrative (14:53–15:20);
3. Jesus' execution and the "second" epilogue (15:21–16:8).

The first two will be treated in this chapter, the third in chapter 13. As already noted (above 10, A,i), the second half of the Jerusalem narrative is generated by the doublet consisting of the Bethany "anointing" and the preparations for the Passover meal, which parallel respectively the discipleship paradigm story of Bartimaeus and preparations for the messianic procession (10:45–11:10), the doublet that generated the conflict cycle.

The first two subsections (1 and 2) are tightly knit together by a series of frames, each of which introduces a major theme. The first is "conspiracy," the authorities' plot against Jesus, which frames the opening episode at Bethany:

a. leaders seek a way to arrest and kill Jesus (14:1);
b. leaders recruit Judas as an informer (14:10).

This plot leads to the second, which frames the Passover meal, a double prediction by Jesus that his community will abandon him:

a. Jesus predicts that one will betray him (14:18–21);
b. Jesus predicts that all will desert him (14:27–31).

The story of the community's last days together is thus defined by the twin themes of conspiracy and betrayal. It is linked to the trial by the episode of Peter's denial, which frames the first arraignment before the Sanhedrin:

    a. Peter follows Jesus to his interrogation (14:54);

    b. Peter denies Jesus (14:66–72).

From this we can see that the narrative is a pathetic litany of failed discipleship and intrigue.

The two trial episodes are structured in parallel, as will be articulated below (D,i). They are tied to the narrative of Jesus' execution by two devices. One is the temporal span of roughly twenty-four hours: Jesus' arrest and trial takes place at night, and by the evening of the next day he is dead and buried. The other device is the triple mockery:

    a. by Jewish security forces (14:65);

    b. by Roman security forces (15:16–20);

    c. by the gathered crowd at the cross (15:29–32).

As we will see, each mockery ironically confirms the vocation of Jesus as prophet, Messiah, and king.

The climax to the story is the third apocalyptic moment, defined by the two "cosmic portents" and the two great cries of Jesus (15:33–38). After Jesus expires on the cross, the aftermath or "second epilogue" commences. It is structured around three responses to Jesus' death: by a Roman soldier who presided over the execution, a member of the Jewish council that condemned Jesus, and the women disciples. The last act of the Gospel opens a few days later at the tomb, a scene consisting of a dialogue between some women and a "young man." This ending functions to reopen the narrative of Jesus—just as the stone with which the tomb was sealed is "rolled away"—and points the reader back to the beginning of the story.

Other repetitions emphasize the interrelationship between events in this narrative. Triads link Gethsemane (the disciples fall asleep three times) to Peter's triple denial of Jesus. Doublets pepper the trial/execution narrative. The arraignment procedure is collapsed into two accusations, only one of which Jesus answers. There are two mockeries at the cross, Jesus gives two great cries, and the bystanders twice exclaim that he is calling Elijah. Mark often relies upon temporal references to define action and scene changes (e.g., 14:1,12,17; 15:1; 16:1). His most formidable literary device, however, is the way in which the story ends, with its promise of a continued narrative (16:6f.) abruptly aborted by the flight of the women (16:8). In this Mark challenges readers to "complete" the reading through their own response to the "young man's" promise (below, 13,E).

ii. Story

As is appropriate to the denouement, in this section each major subplot reaches its conclusion. The twin themes outlined above correspond to the two main narrative trajectories: Jesus' relationship to the authorities (conspiracy) and Jesus' relationship to his disciples (betrayal). The former began in Galilee, with the very first synagogue confrontation (1:21ff.) leading to the seeds of a political conspiracy (3:6); now the official hostility to Jesus' life unfolds inexorably, culminating in an armed ambush in the dead of night. The latter crisis began with hints of the disciples' lack of understanding, and concludes with the complete unraveling of the community solidarity Jesus had so diligently labored to create. The two plots are of course joined at the point at which Judas assumes his undercover role, and simultaneously resolved at the point of Jesus' arrest and the disciples' desertion.

Mark articulates this tragedy through a series of somber predictions, each of which is fullfilled within the story:

1. prediction: one will betray (14:18f.);
2. fulfillment: Judas' kiss (14:44f.);
3. prediction: all will fall away (14:27);
4. fulfillment: disciples' flee at the arrest (14:50);
5. prediction: Peter will deny Jesus (14:30);
6. fulfillment: Peter denies Jesus (14:67–71).

At the same time, Mark articulates a narrative counter-discourse of hopeful "premonition," both overt and implied:

1. a promise that the stricken shepherd will again live to "go before" the community in Galilee (14:28);
2. the symbolic flight of a naked "young man" (14:51f.).

Both are "fulfilled" at the end of the story by the reappearance of a fully clothed "young man" who announces that Jesus indeed is continuing to "go before" the disciples in Galilee (16:5–7). Inserted into the dismal "resolution" of the subplots, these intimations promise that though the discipleship narrative collapses, it does not necessarily end, giving the reader hope and reason to continue reading.

After the arrest and flight of the disciples, the reader's attention is focused solely upon Jesus' stand before the powers. Yet the betrayal narrative persists through both trial episodes. The first hearing concludes with Peter's insistent denial of Jesus; at the culmination of the second hearing the crowd, with equal insistence, "denies" Jesus in its call for Barabbas's release and the Nazarene's crucifixion.

In the last "moments" of Jesus' life, Mark gathers together onto the stage all the characters in his political drama: Roman and Jewish authorities, the crowd, the disciples (in the background), and the rebels (represented by Barabbas and the two social bandits). These scenes represent in microcosm the polemic of the story as a whole, Mark's final plea to the reader to choose the ideology of the Human One over the other competing social strategies, all of which are hostile to, yet unwitting accomplices of, the way of the cross.

Time and space are carefully contrived by Mark to heighten the drama of the last days of Jesus. Mark closes the "mythic moment" created by the apocalyptic discourse of the second sermon by reentering the temporal dimensions of his story world: "It was two days before the Passover and the feast of Unleavened Bread" (14:1). In this sudden shift back to realistic time and space, Mark plunges the reader into the deepest heart of Jewish symbolic life: the high holy days in Jerusalem. We have seen that in Palestine under the Romans these feasts always occasioned messianic anticipation and political turmoil; it is not surprising therefore that Mark should in this context reintroduce the conspiracy against Jesus. The subsequent settings consist of brief vignettes: the house of a leper and a Jerusalem attic, the Mount of Olives and an open field, a courtroom and a courtyard, and of course "Golgotha" and the tomb. The tension increases through the covert movements of the discipleship community and its adversaries. The cat and mouse game of avoidance necessitates a strategy of infiltration by the authorities, which then becomes the central tragedy of the community's failing unity.

The final day of Jesus' life is organized around the "watches" of night and day. The arrest and trial narrative mentions each of the four night watches spoken of in the apocalyptic parable of the householder (see above, 11E,iii). The last of these ("daybreak," 15:1) also becomes the first of the day watches that Mark counts off during the execution narrative. Jesus is crucified at the third hour (15:25), darkness spreads at the sixth hour (15:33), he calls to Elijah and expires at the ninth hour (15:34), and is taken down and buried at evenfall (15:42). The final tomb scene takes place in the morning a few days later.

Like the first epilogue, the second means to decipher the narrative symbolics of the second half of the story. Key to its interpretation are the two proleptic hints inserted by Mark at crucial stages in the collapsing discipleship narrative to which I have just referred. It testifies to the genius of the author that the story has no "happy ending." Indeed, it concludes on a deeply ambiguous note as the women "flee" the message of the young man (16:8). Mark leaves the reader only with the promise of a new beginning in Galilee, which is also an invitation to begin the story again—that is, to follow anew in discipleship. The unique literary characteristics of this ending will be considered when we arrive there (below, 13,E).

12B. INTIMACY AND BETRAYAL: THE LAST DAYS OF THE COMMUNITY (14:1–25)

i. A Messianic "Anointing": "My Body To Be Buried"

The last chapter in the story of Jesus opens with another "discipleship paradigm" story, again just outside Jerusalem, in Bethany. The episode is curious in the details it gives us (the name of "Simon," the exact value of the oil) and withholds (the identity of the woman). The scene takes place at table in the house of a leper, a narrative reminder of the way in which Jesus' discipleship practice continues to challenge the social boundaries of the dominant order. This provides the first of many narrative links with the very beginning of the subversive narrative—his healing of the leper (1:41ff.).

The meal is interrupted by the (implicitly bold) approach of a woman, who proceeds to anoint Jesus' head with oil. Its structure is characteristic of a number of earlier conflict episodes (e.g., the paralytic in 2:1ff., the children in 10:13ff.) in which Jesus' attention shifts from subject to opponents and back again to subject. This "anointing" resumes Mark's subversion of messianic ideology (see 1 Sm 10,16):

> Since the prophet in the Old Testament anointed the head of the Jewish king, the anointing of Jesus' head must have been understood immediately as the prophetic recognition of Jesus. . . . [But] it was a woman who named Jesus by and through her prophetic sign-action. It was a politically dangerous story [Schüssler Fiorenza, 1985:xiv].

The story thus further strengthens the "feminist discourse" of Mark. It is not clear who it is that objects to the woman's act (14:4), but the "indignation" (*aganaktountes*) and Jesus' counter-rebuke ("Let her alone!," *aphete*, 14:6) recall the disciples' attempt to keep the children from Jesus (10:14). Here, as there, the action of the woman is taken as exemplary; this is yet another example of the politically "least" (women) assuming the position of "greatest" (prophetic anointment).

The "subtext" in this episode is economic: the action of this apparently wealthy woman (the perfume was "expensive," *poluteles*; see 1 Tm 2:9) is objected to as gratuitous in light of the need of the poor. In defending her, Jesus appears to be taking a contradictory position to the already established class bias of the narrative. Was not "giving to the poor" (*didōmi tois ptōchois*) Jesus' very command to the rich man (10:21), and was not the piety of the wealthy portrayed unfavorably in 12:42? It may be that here Jesus considers himself one of the poor—the guest of a leper, headed for death. In any case, he affirms that those raising the concern indeed have an ongoing responsibility toward the poor—though he carefully avoids endorsing their claim that almsgiving sufficiently fulfills this obligation. His argument distinguishes between the structural issue and the personal gesture (14:6–9). He maintains that the legitimacy of the woman's "task" (*ergon ērgasato*) lies in the fact that it was done *to him* (14:6). This recalls 2:19f.: just as the community was temporarily excused from fasting there, so can good gifts be reserved for the "bridegroom" here.

But why should we consider the woman's action a paradigmatic discipleship story, given the absence of any "following" motif? The justification lies in the fact that *this* messianic anointing is preparation not for the inauguration of a triumphal reign, but burial (14:8). The woman, unlike the disciples, is not avoiding but rather "anticipating" (*proelaben*) Jesus' "preparation for death" (*eis ton entaphiasmon*). In this she has done "all she could," and demonstrated her ideological solidarity with the way of the cross. This is why she is eulogized in 14:9: because she understands the "gospel," it will hereafter be identified with her. I suspect that herein may lie the reason she remains an unnamed "heroine": she represents the female paradigm, which in Mark embodies both "service" (above, 9,D,iii) and an ability to "endure" the cross (below, 13,C,iii). Finally, her care for Jesus' *body* narratively prepares us for the emergence of this body as the new symbolic center of the community in the corresponding "messianic banquet" (below, iii; see also 13,F,i).

ii. Fugitive Jesus: Authorities Undercover, Community Underground

The high holy days signal a return to the conspiracy narrative, begun back in 3:6, alluded to in Jesus' three portents, and reiterated in the Jerusalem narrative (11:18; 12:12). Again the authorities are "seeking" (ezētoun) to "seize" (kratēsantes) Jesus (14:2), but now they have decided to resort to covert means (en dolō). The reason is once more the unpredictable crowd factor (as in 11:32 and 12:12), specifically the possibility of riots due to the volatile political atmosphere of the high feast days.

This covert strategy is intelligible only if the community has gone underground, an implication suppressed by commentators, but confirmed by virtually every element in the ensuing narrative. There is no reason why the authorities would have needed "inside help" to achieve their goal, except to monitor the movements of the community. In 14:10, just such a collaborator is recruited. Judas is to help them arrest Jesus and take him away from the possibility of public protection or response, at the "right moment" (eukairos)—when the community can be caught unawares. Gethsemane in the dead of night, as we shall see, will meet all these requirements—an ironic contrast to the "moment" of vigilance enjoined by Jesus in the apocalyptic sermon.

Judas's switch of loyalties should come as no surprise to the reader; we were warned back in 3:19 about him. But Mark does not invoke a theory of "satanic inspiration" to explain it, as do Luke and John; the transaction is stated matter of factly in monetary terms. Perhaps now we understand why Jesus was so unimpressed by the economic argument in the anointing episode we have just looked at. At the point in the mission of the community where the deepest personal trust and loyalty are required, the woman's solidarity with Jesus and his way has no price, whereas Judas "sells out" for silver. The tragedy above all, repeated again and again, is that Judas was one of the twelve (three times: 14:10,20,43); it is from within the community that "betrayal" (paradidōmi, seven times) comes.

With the festival drawing near, the community prepares to celebrate the Passover meal in Jerusalem, as dictated by tradition, for the sacrificial lambs were prepared at the temple (14:12). There are several elements here that cause us wonder. First, if Jesus has repudiated the temple, why does he participate in this central feast of the cult? The answer to this will come when we look at how he celebrates the meal. Secondly, why do Jesus' instructions to the two disciples infer the need to be discreet in reentering the city? There are two explanations. The first is intertextual. I have noted the parallel to the earlier "instructions" of the two disciples in 11:1-6 (see the comparative chart in Taylor, 1963:536). There the allusion was to the Zecharian ass; here it faintly echoes the directions given by Samuel to Saul after the latter's anointing as a sign of its authenticity (1 Sm 10:1ff.).

The second reason I have just mentioned: Mark is shifting our attention from the undercover operation of the authorities to the underground movements of the community. An anonymous network coordinates prearrangements to facilitate the fugitive community's movement in the city. The man carrying a pitcher of water (14:13f.) connotes a "signal," just conspicuous enough (carrying water pitchers was the work of women) in a crowded city to draw only the attention of those watching for it. This "runner" leads the disciples to a "safehouse," in which they find the attic room already prepared. There the community will celebrate the meal after the manner of the original Passover: eating "as those in flight" (Ex 12:11).[1]

iii. A Messianic "Banquet": "My Blood To Be Spilled"

Jesus and *all twelve* disciples (that is, including Judas) come to the house under cover of night (14:17). Where we would expect a description of the meal itself (the "preparation" of which was emphasized three times in 14:12-16), we find instead a description of the conversation. The so-called Last Supper narrative is divided into two sections, each beginning with "they were eating" (*kai esthiontōn*, 14:18, 22). These two contrasting vignettes portray the lack of, and reassertion of, solidarity between Jesus and his followers.

In the first part, the "undercover" and "underground" subplots converge with Jesus' revelation that he is aware of the infiltration. His announcement (14:18) emphasizes the seriousness of the breach by citing the lament of Psalm 41:9:

> Even my bosom friend in whom I trusted
> who ate of my bread has lifted his heel against me.

If the common meal represents the most intimate form of fellowship (underlined by the euphemism "the one dipping in the same dish," 14:20), then to participate as an "agent" represents the deepest violation.

The community's faltering solidarity is indicated by the disciples' response to Jesus' charge. First they are dejected (*lupeisthai*, the response of the rich man as he turned away from Jesus!, 10:22), then self-incriminating (14:19). Jesus' concluding double pronouncement about the destiny of the Human One (14:21) is a statement of neither resignation nor predetermination, but simply of consequence for one's choices. For Jesus, the cost of fidelity to the scriptural tradition of biblical radicalism ("as it is written") is the official conspiracy against him. For Judas, under a lucrative contract to betray Jesus, the cost is truly staggering. "It would have been better not to have been born" (14:21b) recapitulates Jesus' earlier warning: "What profit is there in a return of the whole world if one forfeits one's soul? And at what price will one buy back one's soul?" (8:33f.).

The meal episode moves from profound betrayal to profound intimacy in the second part, the "eucharistic" tradition. J. Jeremias's classic study of this tradition explains the more formal tone of 14:22-25:

> When Mark's plain narrative style gives place to a solemn, stylized language which piles up participles and finite verbs; when words and constructions which Mark never uses elsewhere occur frequently—all

this is to be explained quite simply by the fact that any account of the Last Supper had to revert at this point to the liturgical formula, the wording of which had long been fixed and everywhere established by its use in the cult [1966:97].

However institutionalized this formula may have been, Mark fully integrated it into his own narrative symbolics.

Both Jesus' gestures and words are important. The double blessing is roughly parallel in form:

took bread / blessed / gave / said
took cup / gave thanks / gave / (they drank) / said

This act of blessing and sharing was not *in itself* extraordinary, being the normal symbolism of table fellowship at mealtime:

When at the daily meal the *paterfamilias* recites the blessing over the bread . . . and breaks it and hands a piece to each member to eat, the meaning of the action is that each of the members *is made a recipient of the blessing by this eating*; the common "Amen" and the common eating of the bread of benediction unite the members into a table fellowship. The same is true of the "cup of blessing," which is the cup of wine over which grace has been spoken, when it is in circulation among the members: *drinking from it mediates a share in the blessing* [Jeremias, 1966:232].

In the narrative world of Mark this breaking and blessing of bread is strongly analeptic, recalling the earlier feedings in the wilderness (6:41; 8:6). But here there is a conspicuous difference. The disciples are not commanded to "pass on" this bread to the crowds as before: this is a meal for *them*.

The cup, too, is for them. We remember that Jesus had promised a cup to his disciples (10:39), which he identified with a "baptism" (the "baptism" promised by John, 1:8). Mark will soon make it clear (14:36) that this "cup" refers to the witness of suffering at the hands of the powers. This "one cup" becomes the center of the community's new symbolic life. Baptism and eucharist both have the same meaning: solidarity with and participation in the way of the cross, embodied in Jesus. Mark says they *all* drank it (14:23)—ironic in that none of the disciples will share Jesus' suffering in story time. Yet as we have seen the story promises that they *will* share it in their own historical practice (13:9–13).

The extraordinary meaning to this meal comes out rather in Jesus' interpretation of it. Jewish readers would have expected in Jesus' words following his blessing some kind of traditional Passover homily:

The kernel of which was the interpretation of the special elements of the meal in terms of the events of the exodus from Egypt: the unleavened bread was usually explained as a symbol of the misery that was endured, the bitter herbs as representing the slavery, the fruit-purée which resembled clay as recalling the forced labor, the passover lamb as a remembrance of God's merciful "passing over" Israel. At the same time there were other interpretations, especially eschatological interpretations, of these elements [Jeremias, 1966:219; see also 84ff.; 206f.].

But Jesus' homily is quite different. He boldly interprets the symbols in terms of himself and his vocation. The bread that sustained the hungry masses "on the way" (8:2f.) has now become Jesus' "body"—which body has just been "prepared" for death. The cup symbolizes a new "covenant" (*diathēkē*, only here in Mark) to be ratified in the shedding of Jesus' blood (14:24).

Intertextually, the allusions are to Isaiah 53:12 and the "blood of the covenant" in Exodus 24:8 (see Zec 9:11). Within the story we think of the "ransom" of the Human One (10:45). Both make the conclusion unavoidable that Mark is portraying Jesus as the "eschatological paschal lamb":

> His death is the vicarious death of the suffering servant which atones for the sins of the "many," the people of the world, which ushers in the beginning of the final salvation and which effects the new covenant with God [Jeremias, 1966:231f.]

Belo complains that in this new metaphor the political narrative is being compromised here by "postpaschal theological discourse" (1981:210). He has missed the fact that this is Mark's final assault upon the Jewish symbolic field.

For suddenly we realize that Jesus is *not* after all participating in the temple-centered feast of Passover (note that Mark never mentions the eating of lamb). Instead he is expropriating its symbolic discourse (the ritual meal) in order to narrate his new myth, that of the Human One who gives his life for the people. Moreover, he is delivering yet another blow to the purity system:

> His blood is atonement blood which is "poured out for many" (14:24); it takes away uncleanness. The final irony is that death, the ultimate pollution, serves as the very source of purity for Jesus' followers [Neyrey, 1986:115].

We will see this reversal of the symbolic field in Mark's account of Jesus' dead body at the end of the story (below, 13, C,D).

This subversive purpose is confirmed by the *amen* saying of 14:25: Jesus turns the feast into a fast. He solemnly forswears the "fruit of the vine" (a common Jewish euphemism for wine) "until that day" (*heōs tēs hēmeras ekeinēs*) when he would drink the "new" (*kainon*) in the kingdom of God. This recalls the earlier saying on new cloth/wine (2:21f.): the "day for fasting" that accompanies the departure of the "bridegroom" appears now to have come— and the bridegroom himself is inaugurating the fast. Jeremias argues that Jesus' vow stands within a tradition of Jewish dissent, which consisted of abstinence and intercession on behalf of those who are in error (he finds such a prayer in Gethsemane). He cites as evidence the fact that the primitive church fasted on Passover, in order to pray for the Jews; hence the command of the early catechism, the Didache: "Fast for those who persecute you" (Jeremias, 1966:218). Whether or not this hypothesis is correct, it indicates the protest nature of Jesus' vow. On the occasion of the great Jewish feast day remembering emancipation from Egypt, Jesus calls for abstinence. The struggle for liberation is not a past memory, but a task that ever binds us to the future.

It is important for Christian readers to recognize that in Mark this "eucharist" is not described as a "memorial"; it is not backward-looking but forward-looking. Through the symbolic action of table fellowship, Jesus invites the disciples/reader to solidarity with his impending arrest, torture, and execution. In this episode, Mark articulates his new symbolic center, and overturns the last stronghold of symbolic authority in the dominant order, the high holy feast of Passover. In place of the temple liturgy Jesus offers his "body"—that is, his messianic practice in life and death. It is this very "sanctuary/body" opposition that will shape Mark's narrative of Jesus' execution.

12C. "THE HOUR HAS ARRIVED":
THE DISCIPLESHIP NARRATIVE COLLAPSES (14:26-52)

The betrayal narrative now reaches its climax, in a rapidly escalating series of defections. Jesus has already twice reinterpreted traditional Jewish symbolic actions in light of his impending death at the hands of the authorities (the anointing and the meal). He has predicted that one of his community will betray him (14:18). Now the "one" becomes "all," as he predicts that the whole community will abandon him, over their strenuous assertions to the contrary (14:27-31). True to form, the disciples sleep through Jesus' agonizing moments of self-doubt (14:32-41), and flee for their lives when an armed contingent comes to seize Jesus (14:43-49). In the face of such massive desertion, such complete unraveling, Mark sustains the reader's hope by inserting new portents and subplots that promise a future for the story. These occur at the beginning and end of this subsection: Jesus' promise concerning Galilee (14:28), and the parenthetical episode of a "young man" (14:50f.).

i. Jesus' Final Portent: The Scattering and Regathering

To assure the reader that this is not meaningless tragedy, Mark weaves in a refrain that these events are *expected* in the "script" of biblical radicalism. The "fulfillment of scripture" theme is stated no less than three times here, each coming at the point of Jesus' realization of his community's defection: Judas' betrayal (14:21), the disciples' defection (14:29), and the arrest and desertion (14:49). This discourse confirms that the messianic vocation is intact despite human failure (see my comments below in the Afterword).

After the hymnic close to the meal, Jesus leaves the city for the Mount of

Olives (14:26), as he did in 13:3. Here is Mark's final subversion of triumphalist Messianism, which he began when Jesus first entered Jerusalem (11:1; above, 10,B,i). The Mount of Olives, far from being the site of military victory, as implied in Zechariah 14, became the site where Jesus predicted the demise of the temple state (13:3), and now also of his own community as well. Jesus says simply, "You will *all* fall away" (14:27a). This is the last of his portents, now directed not toward the authorities but the disciples. As an interpretive text, Mark cites Zechariah 13:7, turning its imperative into a prediction: "I will strike the shepherd, and the sheep will scatter" (14:27b). Mark here offers a midrash upon the shepherd parable he has already alluded to in 6:34 (above, 6,E,ii). This time, however, Mark appeals to another part of the parable. The prophet, in despair over Israel's corrupt leadership, himself becomes "the shepherd of the flock doomed to be slain for those who trafficked in the sheep" (Zec 11:7); then in a symbolic action he dramatizes Israel's breach of the covenant (11:10f.).[2] It is in light of this tradition that Mark understands Jesus: the covenant is indeed broken, but will be renewed in Jesus' blood; thus the "sacrificial lamb" becomes the "stricken shepherd."

Ezekiel's shepherd parable also speaks of scattering, but promises a re-gathering as well (Ez 34:11–16,23ff.). So too Mark: after Jesus is raised to life he will resume going before his "flock" of disciples (14:28). This first augury of the end of the story is arguably the single most important narrative signal in the second half of the Gospel, a kind of "literary lifeline" that Mark throws to the reader. This promise will later be verified by a "young man" at the empty tomb (16:7), directing the reader back to the place where the discipleship journey began: Galilee. There, by implication, the reconstituted community will effect the "new covenant of peace" (Ez 34:25). In other words, the defection of the disciples will *not* mean the end of the discipleship story.

As we have come to expect, Jesus' portent is immediately refuted by Peter (14:29). And as surely as the lead disciple sets himself apart as the *exception* (14:29), Jesus counters that he *above all* will characterize the desertion (14:30). Peter's vehement protest of his loyalty (14:31) exegetes perfectly the meaning of Jesus' call to discipleship (8:34): to stand with Jesus indeed would require that he deny himself, and consequently share Jesus' death (*ean deē me sunapotha-nein soi*). But this is exactly the opposite of what he will in fact do in the story (14:66–72). "They all said the same"—and all will fail just as Peter did. Mark's discourse stresses the complicity of each and every disciple—not just Peter or Judas—in the collapse of the community's loyalty to the way of Jesus.

ii. Gethsemane: The Disciples Sleep

But the worst is yet to come. The scene changes to a "field" (*chōrion*) called Gethsemane, signaling a new episode (14:32). Here Jesus goes to pray, only the third time Mark has portrayed him at prayer. These vignettes correspond roughly with the beginning (1:35), middle (6:46), and end of Jesus' ministry, and always take place in an isolated environment at a late hour. If the two previous times suggested that Jesus was withdrawing from sheer weariness, this episode clearly indicates it is due to profound inner turmoil. The language of 14:33 is very strong: he "shudders in distress" (*ekthambeisthai*) and "anguishes" (*adēmonein*). Taylor calls it "one of the most important statements in Mark," and his survey of the varying attempts to translate its force is instructive enough to reproduce (1963:552):

> Lohmeyer: "The Greek words depict the utmost degree of unbounded horror and suffering";
>
> Rawlinson: "Suggestive of shuddering awe";
>
> Swete: "His first feeling was one of terrified surprise . . . the distress which follows a great shock";
>
> Moffat: "Appalled . . . agitated";
>
> Lightfoot: "It describes the confused, restless, half-distracted state which is produced by physical derangement, or by mental distress, as grief, shame, disappointment, etc."

Jesus is facing his "destiny" not with contemplative detachment, but with genuine human terror. There is no romance in martyrdom, only in martyrologies.

Citing the Psalmist's depressed lament (Ps 42:6), Jesus admits to his disciples that he is shaken to the core; as the *New English Bible* translation has it: "My heart is ready to break with grief." It is remarkable, in light of what has just transpired, and in such a state, that Jesus would call one more time for solidarity from the inner circle (Peter, James, and John; cf. 5:37; 9:2). Requesting them to remain and "stay awake," he goes off to sweat it out before the "Father" (14:34, the only occurrence of *Abba* in Mark). His petition is stated redundantly, indirectly and directly, using different forms of *parerchomai* to tie together two important symbolic coordinates:

14:35 if it were possible the *hour* might pass from him

14:36 all is possible to you; turn aside *this cup* from me

We now understand that the "hour" (*hōra*) spoken of in the second sermon (13:32) is drawing near in story time, and will be identified with the cross. The mythic moment of struggle between "staying awake" (*grēgoreite*) and "sleeping" (*katheudeis*; 13:35–37) is now being enacted. Can the disciples be with Jesus while he prays in the heart of darkness for the strength to face the journey into the heart of power?

They cannot; Mark underscores it three times. Even at this delicate point in the narrative he does not relinquish his unrelenting criticism of the three "leaders"! The first time Jesus returns to find them asleep, and his response is full of both pathos and symbolism:

> Simon, do you sleep? Did you not have the strength to stay awake one hour? Stay awake and pray that you might not enter into temptation; the spirit is indeed willing, but the flesh is weak [14:37f.].

Here Jesus reverts to the name used for Peter before the discipleship commissioning (3:16); what a caricature of the one who just a moment ago was boasting of his courage and steadfastness (14:31)! He does not have the "strength" (*ischusas*; echoing the accusation of 9:18) to participate in this apocalyptic battle with "temptation" (*peirasmon*)—that is, with the forces that would subvert or compromise the way (cf, 1:13; 8:11; 10:2; 12:15). And, as in that last exorcism (9:29), Jesus exhorts prayer. The difference here between Jesus and Peter is not that Peter's spirit is unwilling, or that Jesus' flesh is not frail (for he too feels the terror of death): it is that Jesus faces up to the struggle of the "demons within" through prayer.

A second time (14:40) the disciples are caught napping; "their eyes were heavy" (eyes that still do not see! 8:18). Mark adds that "they did not know what to answer him"—the same phrase earlier describing their confusion before the transfiguration (9:6). The story climaxes after the third time with Jesus' exasperated cry, which is difficult to translate (14:41f.). Taylor captures its incredulity:

Still asleep? Still resting? The End is far away? The Hour has struck! Behold, the Son of Man is being delivered into the hands of sinners! Arise, let us be going. Behold, he who delivers me up is near [1963:557].

The discipleship narrative is truly on the verge of collapse. But Jesus turns to face the music that has played in the background since the beginning of his ministry.

iii. The Arrest: The Disciples Scatter

Judas, who we may presume slipped out after the meal to plan the ambush, strikes suddenly (14:43). The next scene, it must be said, reeks of the overkill so typical of covert state action against civilian dissidents. The secret signal, the surprise attack at night, and of course the heavily armed contingent all imply that the authorities expected armed resistance. Their instructions to the security forces are to take the utmost security measures (*asphalōs*) in the seizure of the suspect (14:44). There is obviously concern to avoid the popular outcry they so fear. More bitter Markan irony can be seen in the signal by which Jesus is identified: an intimate embrace (14:45). The operation goes according to plan, and the security forces "lay their hands" upon Jesus, whose own hands have done nothing but the works of healing and exorcism throughout the story.

However, a certain "bystander" skirmishes, wounding one of the high priest's slaves (14:46f.). Interestingly, Mark does not condemn this spontaneous violence (as both Matthew 26:52f. and Luke 22:51 feel compelled to do). The defender is not necessarily a disciple; Taylor speculates that the designation *heis de tis* means "a certain one (known to us)" (1963:559). In any case, Mark uses the event as an occasion for Jesus to point out the sordid character of the entire operation. What he condemns is the ambush itself; he holds the attackers responsible for any violent reaction that has occurred. Eyeing their weaponry, he states dryly:

> So you have come to arrest me with swords and clubs,
>   as against a robber?
> Each day I was among you in the temple,
>   yet you did not seize me!
> But let the scriptures be fulfilled! [14:48f.].

He is accusing the authorities of trying to justify their armed response in terms of an "antiterrorist" action.

This is our first encounter with the term "robber" (*hōs epi lēstēn*), which we know from Josephus was used to describe social bandits (above, 2,C,ii). It is significant that here Jesus is taken as such a representative of the rural resistance, just as he will be crucified as one ("between two robbers," 15:27; see below, 13,A,ii). Jesus may reject armed resistance, but he understands it; his disdain is reserved for state violence, which forever passes its provocation off as "prevention." Only here does Mark substitute the verb *sullambanō* for his usual word for "arrest" (*krateō*, eight times), probably an oblique allusion to the arrest of Jeremiah (see Jer 36:26; 37:13 [LXX = 43:26; 44:13]). Jesus then taunts the authorities with the fact that their ambush only unmasks their political impotence: what they could not do in public they do covertly (14:49).[3]

Finally, Jesus throws back in the teeth of his opponents the higher and deeper authority: the "scriptures." Mark cites no specific text, as if he is alluding to the entire "script" of biblical radicalism. This script is now "fulfilled" (*plērōthō-sin;* only here and 1:15): just as the beginning of Jesus' ministry signaled the fulfillment of the *kairos* (1:15), so does the arrest signal that the "hour" (14:41) is fulfilled. It is this script that the leaders cannot understand (cf. 12:10,24), and that the disciples cannot follow. When the latter realize that he does not intend to turn away from his fidelity to this script, they flee for their lives (14:50). The sheep have scattered; the discipleship narrative has collapsed.

iv. The "Young Man": A Hint of Regathering

It is here that we are given a second augury of the end, but one that will not become evident to us until we arrive there. It takes the form not of promise/prediction but symbolic action: the curious flight of a "young man" who leaves behind a "cloth" (14:51f.). Some commentators have argued that this is a disconnected episode in which the author's "signature" upon his work can be detected; others attribute it to vivid eye-witness detail in the tradition. Such casual suggestions insult the literary integrity of the gospel. Mark has obviously inserted this cameo here, at the dramatic nadir of the story, for a purpose; it is up to narrative analysis to recover that purpose. For the very obscurity of this subplot engenders our expectation that it will be resolved, and prevents us from abandoning our reading as the disciples have abandoned Jesus.

This little episode sees the introduction of two new terms: "young man" (*neaniskos*) and "linen cloth" (*sindon*). These terms appear again only in the "second" epilogue: Joseph of the council wraps the dead body of Jesus in a *sindon* (15:46), and the *neaniskos* appears at the tomb of Jesus. We must wait until the end of the story to fully articulate these complex symbolics (below, 13,D), but this much can be intimated. The young man, who flees (*ephugen*) after the authorities try to seize him along with Jesus, is a symbol of the discipleship community as a whole, which has just itself fled (14:50). He escapes naked (*gumnos*), indicative of shame, leaving behind a cloth that becomes the "burial garment" for Jesus.

The end of the story will reintroduce the young man, but there he will be "sitting at the right" and fully clothed in a white robe—symbols of the martyrs who have overcome the world through death (cf. 9:3). This "exchange" of clothes between the first and second appearances of the "young man" represents (as in the earlier transfiguration of Jesus' garments) an implicit promise and challenge. The discipleship community can be rehabilitated, even after such a betrayal. The first "young man" symbolizes "saving life and losing it," the second "losing life to save it." At this stage in the story, however, without knowing the end, the episode of the young man represents a mystery. All we know is that everything has gone sour. The discipleship community, as has happened so often throughout history, has buckled under the boot of security forces, its dreams of a new order shattered by the brute reality of state power. Jesus, now alone, goes to stand in a kangaroo court with no hope of justice. There his final conflict with the powers will be played out.

12D. THE DOUBLE TRIAL OF JESUS: HISTORY AND PARODY

i. The Parallel Trials: A Markan Apologia?

Few scholars are prepared to dispute that Mark's narrative of the arrest, trial, and execution of Jesus is not based upon a core of relatively reliable historical tradition. Nevertheless, it is clear that the author has freely shaped this tradition according to his literary and ideological purposes. What those purposes were, however, is a matter of debate. Perhaps the most influential thesis must be considered before proceeding with our socio-literary reading. It is the contention that Mark endeavored to minimize Roman culpability for Jesus' condemnation while maximizing the role of the Jewish authorities.

This position was argued most forcefully by S. Brandon (1967:221ff.), who alleged that the entire Gospel is an apologia to the Romans. According to this thesis, Mark portrays Pilate as concerned to acquit Jesus, but pressured by the Jewish leadership to convict him on trumped up charges. Brandon assumed that Mark was written for the Roman church, which he claimed would have wished to dissociate itself from the notion that Jesus died at the hands of the Romans as a rebel. Brandon contended that the historical Jesus *was* such a dissident, which fact Mark attempted to cover up. Other scholars accepted the apologia thesis, but maintained that Mark was not covering over anything, because Jesus was in fact innocent of subversive activity.

Obviously, if Mark's intention was to portray an "apolitical" Jesus who was mistakenly condemned by a reluctant procurator, it would overturn my entire reading. But as a general hypothesis, despite widespread acceptance, it cannot stand on grounds of literary analysis or historical plausibility. The ideological strategy of "blaming the Jews" may not be in the text, but it is traditionally found within Western Christianity, which historically has legitimated not only anti-Semitism but a wholly benign view of imperial authority—to the benefit of more modern formations of empire.

Let us begin by considering the double trial that lies at the heart of this entire section. That it is Mark's narrative construction is demonstrated by the close parallel between the respective interrogations before the Sanhedrin and Pilate:

14:60–62	*15:4f.,2*

. . . the high priest
    questioned Jesus saying,
"Have you no answer to make?
What about the things
    charged against you?"
But he was silent
    and made no answer.
And again the high priest
    questioned him and
    said to him,
"*You* are Messiah,
    son of the Blessed One?"
And Jesus said,
    "Am I!"
	And again Pilate
	    questioned him saying,
	"Have you no answer to make?
	See what they
	    are charging you!"
	But Jesus answered nothing
	    further at all. . . .
	And Pilate
	    questioned him,
	
	"*You* are the king
	    of the Jews?"
	And Jesus answered him and said,
	    "You said!"

Aside from the fact that the second trial reverses the order of question/response, the two are almost exactly parallel. Both hearings are then followed by a kind of "consultation," in the first case between the high priest and the Sanhedrin, in the second between Pilate and the "crowds." Each ends with a verdict followed by a mockery-torture scene. This discourse of parallelism, far from suggesting favoritism, strongly implicates *both* parties of the colonial apparatus as equally culpable—indeed collaborative—in the political railroading of Jesus. Brandon and others misconstrue Mark's narrative strategy because they fail to appreciate the central role of both parody and irony: his caricature resembles a political cartoon.

The highest Jewish court in the land throws due process out the window in favor of a rigged hearing; their desperate attempts to unsuccessfully coordinate the testimony of hired perjurers, not to mention their frantic lobbying of the very masses they so deeply mistrust, is grimly comic. Yet there is also irony: the charge that Jesus pitted himself against the sanctuary is in fact true, as is the accusation of his Messiahship. In the end, Jesus convicts himself by his subversive confession of the Human One. Similarly, it is the Roman procurator who correctly defines the issue at the second hearing as one of native kingship. The parody here lies in his "consultation" with the Jewish crowds for a verdict and sentence. Yet his questions to them are as contemptuous and taunting as his phrase "king of the Jews." The fickle masses, too, are caricatured, switching in a matter of days from "hearing Jesus gladly" (11:38) to screaming for his head. These literary hyperboles work together to indict the entire politico-legal process of the colonial condominium, not just the Jewish leadership. The reader should not be surprised by this: *Jesus has already ideologically repudiated the system* that condemns him. The sharp edge of realism in the political cartoon recognizes the converse: the powers railroad Jesus because they know he is committed to their overthrow; in political trials, justice is subordinate to the need for conviction.

But political cartoons are effective only if the likeness is as recognizable as it is exaggerated. This raises the other objection to the apologia thesis: it assumes that Mark portrayed the proceedings in a way he knew would be patently unbelievable. In other words, he radically departs from his commitment to realistic narrative at this point. Anyone in the imperial sphere would have scoffed at the idea of a local judiciary dictating a legal or political course of action to a Roman procurator who was weak and undecided. This would be regarded as fantasy to those knowing the true relationships of power in Palestine, where the procurator installed and deposed the high priest at will. It would have been particularly inconceivable in the case of Pilate, whose tenure was infamous (and well-attested) for its stubbornness, provocation, and violence. It is a statement about the bankruptcy of his own theory that Brandon must conclude that "the way in which the author of Mark sought to explain . . . how Jesus came to be crucified as a Jewish revolutionary . . . is incredible both on historical grounds and because of its intrinsic impossibility" (1967:262).

Brandon's justification for Mark's lack of credibility is equally ridiculous:

> The story provided great relief; for it constituted a seemingly convincing explanation of a very embarrassing fact, namely that the founder of their faith had been executed as a Jewish revolutionary. The story, it is important to remember, was written for humble and poorly educated people, living in Rome, who would have had very little knowledge of Roman administration in Judaea some forty years before and no incentive to question the truth of so dramatic an episode that solved what had been a very awkward problem for them [1967:258].

Brandon would leave us with an implausible narrative entrusted to a wholly credulous audience. This flies in the face of the sophistication we have discovered thus far in Mark's narrative and ideological strategy! We must therefore pursue a reading that is both more historically plausible *and* attuned to the literary character of parody.

ii. Historical Plausibility in the Trial Narrative

The reliability of the trial proceedings has been a matter of long-standing debate for modern historical criticism. In raising this question, which elsewhere I have shunned, at this point, I am acknowledging that it impinges upon the undisputed historical fact—namely, that Jesus was crucified—that is, executed as a rebel. But I am considering Mark's narrative only in terms of historical *plausibility*—not *documented* detail of events ("reliability").

The first question that must be raised is why Mark reports that Jesus was found guilty by a Jewish court of heresy—a "domestic" offense in the socio-political formation of Roman Palestine—only to report that Jesus was handed over to the Roman authorities. And how do we account for the switch in charges, from *heresy* before the Sanhedrin to *sedition* before Pilate? At the center of this controversy is the historical issue of the actual legal jurisdiction of the Sanhedrin in the case of domestic capital crimes.

Did the Jewish high court need to secure the prior approval of the procurator before carrying out its own capital punishment? This is suggested in Josephus's account of the stoning of James (*Ant.*, XX,ix,1; cf. the stoning of Stephen, Acts 6:8ff.). Or did colonial law dictate that *all* capital cases had to be turned over to Roman jurisdiction? It must be conceded with Brandon (1967:253ff.) that the extrabiblical evidence concerning this question remains inconclusive. But in *either* case, Mark's double trial must still be explained. If the Jews did *not* need Roman approval to execute heretics, then the fact that Mark narrates a second trial means that he wished his readers to understand that Jesus was *also* wanted by the Romans on charges of sedition. If Roman approval *was* mandatory, we still have to explain why Jesus is crucified by the Romans instead of receiving a Jewish form of capital punishment. For one thing is historically certain: crucifixion was the form of capital punishment reserved in the provinces for enemies of the imperial state (cf. above, 8,D,i). Thus, the procurator's office had its own reasons for condemning Jesus. However we interpret the double trial in terms of historical plausibility, we arrive at the same conclusion: Mark's narrative means to portray Jesus as convicted on charges of sedition by a Roman politico-legal process.

Are the hearings themselves plausible? The historical problems surrounding Mark's account of the arraignment before the Sanhedrin are well-known (see Taylor, 1963:644ff.). Most problematic is the fact that the narrative context suggests that the hearing and verdict take place at night, which as far as we know would have been in violation of rabbinic law. Mark may be indicating awareness of this problem when he narrates a repeat convening of the Sanhedrin and formal indictment of Jesus in the early morning (15:1; but can *prōi* mean after daybreak?). In any case the nighttime hearing can be explained in terms of Mark's ideological caricature: doctored proceedings were part and parcel of the covert strategy to neutralize Jesus. Mark *means* to portray this as a political trial in which legal constraints are jettisoned.

Turning to the second hearing, we must consider the apologia theory's claim that Mark portrays a passive Roman procurator. Pontius Pilate, a member of the Roman equestrian class and provincial procurator in Judea from 25 to 36 C.E., had a well-known reputation for his tumultuous administration. He is described by a contemporary as "inflexible, merciless, and obstinate" (Taylor, 1963:578). Yet Mark identifies this formidable figure simply as "Pilate," with no further elaboration. In other words, it is safe to assume that Mark expects the reader to recognize the name, and hence the reputation. Mark's characterization of him fits with the profile of a procurator quite willing to cooperate in political machinations that will benefit Rome. The narrative makes perfect sense if we assume the opposite of the apologia theory—namely, that Mark's Pilate fully understands the political character of Jesus' practice as a threat, approves of his elimination, and is willing to exchange a known political terrorist (Barabbas) in order to secure it.

To explore this alternative reading, we should first recall the historical "triangle of power relationships" among the Roman administrators, native Jewish aristocracy, and shifting popular allegiances (above, 10,D,iv). That the clerical ruling class collaborated fully with the Romans is clear historically (above, 2,F,i). Next we must keep in mind that Rome was forever vigilant about the threat of latent native kingship movements in client territories throughout the empire. And Rome endeavored to exploit the opportunity presented by local seasonal festivals to both test and promote allegiance to Caesar, as well as to identify and prosecute dissident elements. In Palestine in particular, the combustibility of popular political sentiment during feast periods was the foremost security concern for the colonial establishment.

Against this background, let us test the plausibility of the Markan narrative, beginning with the context Mark sets in 14:1f. The colonial condominium wishes to eliminate a particular dissident, but is hindered by the political delicacy of the high holy days and perceived popular support for the person or his cause. In such a case, two strategies must be pursued. First, efforts to bring the person into custody must be covert, in order to circumvent the possibility of an escalated conflict and public interference. Indeed, "irregular" legal proceedings might well be demanded by this strategy. We have already identified these aspects of Mark's arrest/trial narrative. Secondly, popular support for the dissident must be neutralized or undermined; otherwise, once legal mechanisms are brought into play, the defendant might assume the profile of a "political prisoner." This might well be achieved by a propaganda ploy—such as the release of a figure of equal stature in the public eye. An analogy might be the present-day cold war "spy swap"; the state must discern the relative political trade-offs of short- and long-term security. Such a strategy is reflected in the Barabbas exchange, based upon a pragmatic policy that wished to minimize the possibilities for public disaffection to materialize.

A specific policy of selected amnesty during the Jewish feast time (as Mk 15:6 suggests) is historically unverifiable, though R. Merrit (1985) has argued that, given similar customs in Hellenistic antiquity, it is highly credible. There is evidence, however, of politically motivated prisoner deals struck by procurators in the years just prior to the revolt. Josephus tells us that Albinus (62–64 C.E.) was blackmailed into releasing political prisoners by the "sicarii" (*Ant.*, XX,xix,3), and was later regularly bribed to release social bandits (*lēstai*) who were apprehended in periodic sweeps:

> At this time it was that the enterprises of the seditious at Jerusalem were very formidable; the principal men among them purchasing leave of Albinus to go on with their seditious practices; while that part of the people who delighted in disturbances joined themselves to such as had fellowship with Albinus; and every one of these wicked wretches were encompassed with his band of robbers [*War*, II,xiv,1].

We can conclude from this that the release of one popular dissident in order to defuse public protest over the execution of another, in the context of a politically charged atmosphere, is not only plausible but probable.

Mark's narrative of the trial before Pilate, including the Barabbas deal, is quite intelligible as a portrait of procuratorial pragmatism at work. Pilate's banter with the crowd might easily be interpreted as a kind of ingenuous manipulation of the masses, which plays their Jewish patriotism off against itself. The high priests' lobbying of the crowds (15:11), though undoubtedly a narrative fiction of Mark's, suggests that the procurator and priestly establishment were working together to engineer the public relations ploy of the prisoner exchange. Such cooperation is probable, given their shared interest in the threat (real or imagined) represented by the dissident to their respective political stability. What is *least* plausible is that a Jewish crowd would have advocated that *any* Jew be crucified by the Romans. But here again Mark's caricature comes into play: the "cries" of the crowd, as we shall see, echo the cries of the demonic and the desperate, indicating that they have become in this sinister moment "possessed" by the powers.

This reading of the trial narrative is both more plausible historically and consistent with what we have already discovered about the author's ideological perspective on Palestinian politics. It is sensitive to the combination of caricature and realism in Mark's portrait of each of the major political forces, unlike theories that see a political apologia. We may conclude that Mark's literary structure and ideological discourse determine that *both* parties in the colonial condominium perceived Mark's Jesus as a supremely subversive and dangerous threat. He had to be railroaded, and they cooperated in doing so.

12E. BEFORE JEWISH POWERS: "*YOU ARE MESSIAH?*" (14:53–15:1)

i. Arraignment before the Sanhedrin

We return to the text with the above considerations in mind. The first trial narrative is sandwiched between the story of Peter's denial (14:54,66–72), establishing a spatial tension between Peter (outside in the courtyard) and

Jesus (in the dock). The hearing is structured in four parts. It begins (14:55) with the Sanhedrin members continuing to "seek" (even in their partisan court) evidence against Jesus. Their goal is not justice but "putting him to death" (*eis to thanatōsai*; cf. 13:12). The presentation of manufactured evidence follows (14:56–59). The climax is the interaction between the high priest and the defendant (14:60–64). In conclusion the desired verdict is successfully attained (14:64b), after which there is a brief torture scene.

Mark states (twice for emphasis) that the witnesses gave "false testimony" (*epseudomarturoun*), which did not agree (*isai ouk ēsan*, 14:56f.,59). In contrast to the true testimony that the disciples are exhorted to give in their moment in court (13:11), there are false witnesses, just as there are false prophets and false messiahs (13:22). Their central piece of evidence is an allegation that Jesus pledged to destroy and rebuild "within three days" the "sanctuary" (*ton naon*, referring to the entire cultic apparatus; 14:58). This sarcastic conflation of Jesus' public repudiation of the temple state and his portents of death and resurrection is advanced by Mark as the main charge for two reasons. First, it indicates that in the social consciousness of Jesus' opponents, to attack the temple was to attack the very heart of their way of life. Theissen (1976) has pointed out that a platform based upon rejecting the role of the temple would not have been popular among those economically dependent upon it—which was the better part of the Jerusalem populace! Certainly Jesus' talk of being "rejected by the builders" (12:10), and destruction "stone by stone" (13:2) would have incensed the thousands of laborers employed in the massive construction/restoration project (see above, 2,E,iv). Small wonder, then, that this allegation is repeated by the crowd at the scene of Jesus' crucifixion (15:29).

Secondly, the charge in 14:58 posits a fundamental opposition between that "made with hands" and that "not made with hands." In this Jesus' opponents have unwittingly articulated the central ideological struggle between him and the temple state. Mark uses this accusation to narratively prepare the way for Jesus' body to replace the temple as the new symbolic center. This has already been intimated by the symbols of the last meal, and will be made explicit in the "third apocalyptic moment." There Mark dramatically juxtaposes the "destruction" of Jesus' body to the "destruction" of the sanctuary curtain.

The stage direction of 14:60 brings the hearing to a climax, in another analeptic reference to the first direct action narrative. In the climactic synagogue confrontation at the end of the Capernaum campaign Jesus had called a crippled man "into the center" (*eis to meson*), and his opponents had been "silent" (*esiōpōn*) before his challenge (3:3–5). Here, the roles are reversed; the high priest gets up and moves "into the center," and Jesus is "silent" before his questioning (14:60f.). Mark emphasizes Jesus' noncooperation redundantly:

"Have you no answer to make?"

Jesus made no answer.

This formula will be repeated in the hearing before Pilate, and points to Jesus' refusal to recognize the legal charges. He understands perfectly that this is a *political* trial in which juridical arguments are gratuitous.

Jesus breaks his silence only when interrogated concerning his vocation—"character witness," as it were. "*You* are Messiah, son of the Blessed?" asks the high priest contemptuously, using the traditional indirect reference to Yahweh (14:61f.). Jesus' answer ("I am," *egō eimi*) is uncharacteristic in its directness. There is, however, a textual consideration:

> For *egō eimi* Mt 26:64 has *su eipas* and Lk 22:70 *humeis legete hoti egō eimi*. Cf. Mk 15:2 = Mt 27:11 = Lk 23:3, *su legeis* (in reply to Pilate). There is good reason to think that in 14:62 Mark wrote *su eipas hoti egō eimi*, for not only is this reading well attested . . . but it would also account for the text of Mt and Lk, and it illustrates the note of reserve regarding Messiahship so frequently found in Mk. . . . The reply is affirmative (cf. 14:64), but it registers a difference of interpretation: "The word is yours" [Taylor, 1963:568].

In light of this, the alternative translation is more appropriate; Jesus returns the high priest's mockery: "Am I?"

Here is, according to the courtroom myth of 8:38f., the proper "site" for confession of the Human One. Standing before the supreme representative of the temple state, Jesus is "not ashamed" of the Human One, setting an example for his disciples (cf. 8:38). This is the third and final prophecy of the "advent," and in it Mark fuses two of his main intertextual images into one: the psalmic (110:2) vision of Messiah at Yahweh's right hand (Mk 12:36) with the Danielic (7:13) vision of the Human One (Mk 8:38; 13:26). Jesus claims the Jewish leaders will "see" this spectacle, which indeed they will at the foot of the cross (15:31).

It is this confession that gives the high priest the pretext he is seeking. According to the narrative world, he cannot abide by the Human One having dominion, for he has defied the symbolic order, both the debt code (2:10) and the Sabbath (2:28). Furious, the high priest rends his coat:

> Originally a sign of passionate grief (Gn 37:29 . . .), the rending of clothes became, in the case of the high priest, a formal judicial act minutely regulated in the Talmud [Taylor, 1963:569].

This, he asserts, is blasphemy. He dismisses the need for witnesses (who were not working out anyway) and turns to the rest of the Sanhedrin for their consensus (14:64).

Jesus is judged to be "guilty" of the crime deserving death (14:64, *katekrinan auton enochon einai thanatou*). We recall that Jesus warned the Jerusalem scribes at the culmination of his first campaign that "whosoever blasphemes against the holy spirit . . . is guilty (*enochos*) of unending sin" (3:29). Later on he claimed that this holy spirit speaks on behalf of the defendant before the courts (13:11). By implication, then, in accusing the defendant Jesus of blasphemy, the Sanhedrin has accused the holy spirit. The war of myths, in other words, has ended in mutual anathema.

As Jesus has expected, the Jewish court has condemned him; all that remains now is to turn him over to the gentiles (10:33). First, however, for purposes of parallelism, Mark wishes to include an episode of abuse and torture, however brief, while Jesus is still in Jewish hands. Some on the council spit upon Jesus and slap him around; the "Human One coming in power" is now powerless. They ridicule him, commanding him to "play the prophet." This is the first instance of mockery that ironically utters the truth, for Jesus' words are being fulfilled even as his opponents speak; indeed his prediction of Peter's threefold denial comes to pass in the very next episode. But the real prophetic vocation lies not in predicting events, but in fidelity to the script of biblical radicalism. Thus, Jesus is "pommeled" by the attendants—an allusion to Isaiah's Suffering Servant (*rhapismasin*, cf. Is 50:6, LXX). Truly Jesus *is* a prophet, for he is being dishonored by his own people (cf. 6:4).

ii. Peter's Denial: The Betrayal Narrative Concludes

The story of Peter's denial begins in 14:54, where we glimpse the lead disciple warming himself by the fire together with those same "attendants" (*tōn hupēretōn*). Did Peter sneak into the high priest's "courtyard" (*aulēn*) undercover? We are not told; the point is that Peter is making a belated attempt to "follow" to the end as he had vowed—even if "at a distance" (*apo makrothen*; cf. the women in 15:40). This effort will of course collapse as soon as his identity is discovered.

Mark resumes the Peter story after the Sanhedrin hearing by re-creating the same scene. The attendants have just finished slapping Jesus around (14:65b), and we find Peter still in the courtyard warming himself (14:66). The episode unfolds in a three-step progression:

1. at fire; servant: "You were with the Nazarene, Jesus";
2. at gate; servant to bystanders: "This one is with them";
3. later; bystanders: "Truly you were with them, for you are a Galilean"

Standing just outside where his master is being interrogated and tortured, we can empathize with Peter's fear of being recognized and identified with the accused. He tries to beat a hasty but inconspicuous retreat from this dangerous situation, but his accent betrays him. The contempt of his accusers—that his master is a Nazarene, and he a Galilean—is colorful detail with a purpose. It is another narrative indicator of the movement's identification with the rural north—which is cause for antipathy and suspicion by urban Jerusalemites.

Denying Jesus twice, Peter has both violated the injunction of 8:34 and broken his own vow (14:31). Yet the language of his third denial is surprisingly strong (14:71): he calls down an anathema, even takes an oath (cf. Herod's oath, 6:23), in insisting that he does not "know" (*ouk oida*) Jesus. Here is another irony that speaks the truth: for all his following, Peter truly does not "know" who Jesus is (which even the demons knew, 1:24,34). The rooster then sings, and Peter "remembers" (*anemnēsthē*; cf. 11:21) Jesus' "word" (*rēma*; cf. 9:32). Peter breaks down, and the betrayal narrative ends in the bitter weeping of the one Jesus had first called, in a time and place that now seem worlds away.

The summary verse of 15:1, which recapitulates the judgment of the Sanhedrin, bridges the two trial narratives. The temporal marker—"early morning" (*prōi*)—is itself a transition. Analeptically it represents the last "watch" of the apocalyptic parable of the householder (13:36), and proleptically the first watch of Jesus' final day, which Mark divides into regular "watches": daybreak, third hour (e.g., 9A.M., 15:25), sixth hour (15:33), ninth hour (15:34), and evening (15:42). The Sanhedrin's "consultation" (*sumboulion*) brings to a close the subplot of the conspiracy, which opened with a similar "consultation" (3:6). In the last reversal of Mark's earlier symbolics, Jesus is "bound" (*dēsantes*) and led away to the Roman authorities. The strong man he had vowed to bind (3:27) remains, after all, firmly in control, his "house" intact.

12F. BEFORE ROMAN POWERS: "*YOU* ARE KING?" (15:2–20)

i. Arraignment before Pilate

The prisoner is turned over to Roman jurisdiction. Presumably the second arraignment takes place at Herod's palace, the procurator's temporary residence during the feast; Mark only later mentions the "praetorium" (15:16). Bracketed by the term "handed over" (15:1,15), this second hearing is patterned after the first. It begins with the remarkable accusation put on the lips of Pilate (15:2), which he later claims to have picked up from the crowds (15:12). Repeated no less than five times in Mark 15, the charge emerges as the crowning ironic "confession." It is the emperor's representative who accords Jesus his rightful political status, yet he does so in order to execute him on grounds of sedition (15:26). But to Pilate the sardonic title "king of the Jews" (as opposed to "king of Israel," cf. 15:32) is an expression of contempt. The title of the client King Herod (R. Brown, 1977:170), it is the procurator's reminder that the Jewish people does not have sovereignty in its own land (15:18).

Jesus, as before, answers only because he has been "named." His response returns the mock incredulity (15:2):

Pilate: "*You* are king of the Jews?"
Jesus: "*You* said it."

Although the chief priests continue to press their case (15:3), it is only the kingship charge which Pilate is interested in prosecuting. He asks whether Jesus understands the indictment, and as before (14:61), Jesus ignores it (15:4). His silence would appear to be an allusion to Isaiah's Suffering Servant, and thus an extension of the Zechariah shepherd parable:

like a lamb that is led to the slaughter,
and like a sheep that before its shearers is dumb,
so he opened not his mouth [Is 53:7].

Jesus' disdain for the legal game, his refusal to pleabargain or argue a defense, and his defiance of the power of Rome, are what cause Pilate to "wonder" (15:5; cf. 12:17). The procurator cannot understand how anyone can face the state's threat of capital punishment with such determination, and will puzzle over it again in 15:44, after the defendant is dead.

The narrative then switches to the Barrabas incident (15:6–15), which I will skip over and return to shortly. After the verdict is reached in 15:15, there is (as in the first trial) a "courtyard" aftermath (15:16 = 14:66). Jesus again undergoes torture and ridicule, this time at the hands of a Roman "battalion." The Human One has now been spit upon by Jew and gentile alike (15:19 = 14:65). Belo's commentary is poignant:

> Throughout this scene (in which the body of Jesus is dressed and undressed at the whim of the soldiers, thus calling attention to its powerlessness in this space that is dominated by the force of arms) we have a parody, a carnival. . . . This scene shows people being unleashed who have been subject to a constricting military discipline, and who now take advantage of a conquered adversary who might have forced them to fight and possibly even be killed. This sort of thing is often shown in the ferocity lower-rank police officials demonstrate when dealing with political prisoners [1981:224,330–31.]

Needless to say, if Mark was endeavoring to cast the Roman authorities in a sympathetic light, this was hardly the way to do it!

The soldiers commence their mockery, which again becomes the ironic statement of the truth. They ridicule Jesus by dressing him in purple (15:17; for parallel traditions concerning mock-emperors in antiquity, see Taylor, 1963:646ff.). Mark may mean here one of their own Roman cloaks—symbol of everything their prisoner rejects: the military option and imperial power. Alternatively, it may connote a royal cape, such as the rebel leader Simon bar Giora donned when he surrendered to the Romans as a defeated king (Horsley and Hanson, 1985:126). When they are done with their game, they will take off the purple and put Jesus' own clothes back on him (15:20)—clothes they will soon remove again and divide up among themselves (15:24). Thus, the parodying is framed by two disrobings of Jesus, emphasizing his shaming.

The mockery itself consists of a parallel doublet, each branch of which describes a painful insult to the head (symbol of dignity) and a play-acted parody of kingship:

they put on him a crown of thorns
and began to salute him saying,
"Hail! King of the Jews!"

and they struck him on the head with a stick
and spat on him
and knelt and did him homage [15:18-19.]

The thinly veiled references to the imperial cult pile up: the thorny "laurel wreath," the hailing befitting an emperor (*chaire*), and the prostration of homage indigenous to emperor worship. Mark is at pains to demonstrate the irreconcilable hostility between Jesus and the Roman *imperium*.

ii. Who Is the Real Revolutionary? Jesus and Barabbas

Returning to 15:6, Mark indicates that it was Pilate's practice at the time of the festival to release a prisoner to "them"—that is, the crowds (15:8,10f.). The introduction of Barabbas describes him, like Jesus, as "bound" (15:1,7 *deō*, meaning "in custody"). His name translates "Son of the Father." Is he therefore to be seen purely as a narrative fiction, a kind of counterpart, even imposter, to the political prisoner Jesus? Even if this is the case, Mark describes Barabbas in a manner that had concrete historical signification: as a Sicarius terrorist. Mark states matter of factly that he belonged to a cadre of imprisoned rebels "who had committed murder in the insurrection" (15:7, *meta tōn stasiastōn . . . hoitines en tē stasei phonon pepoiēkeisan*). This is the only time Mark uses the explicit language of revolution (*stasis* appears seven times in Luke-Acts), and it may be that Mark is again appealing to reader-recognition of a specific person or event, for there was constant insurrectionary activity in Jerusalem during this period. What Mark calls "murder" (cf. *phonos*, 7:22) would have been characteristic of the modus operandi of the Sicarii (above, 2,C,ii), or "dagger men," who were infamous for their stealth in political assassination. Thus Mark's narrative concern here is to dramatize the choice. Jesus and Barabbas each represent fundamentally different kinds of revolutionary practice, violent and nonviolent, both of which have led to a common fate: prison and impending execution.

With the reintroduction of the crowd (15:8), it dawns on us that Mark has assembled every major force in the spectrum of Palestinian politics onto the stage for a final showdown. The Roman and Jewish authorities are there; so is the rebel leader; the "crowds" represent the popular masses. Jesus is there too, alone, abandoned by his community. It is a masterfully composed scene, representing a microcosmic arena of competing interests. Upon its outcome hangs not only the "life and death" of Jesus, but as in the staged climax to the first campaign narrative (3:1-6), the future of the entire social project of the Jewish nation. Hence the echo of the Deuteronomic ultimatum, ironically stated by the procurator in his final challenge to the frenzied crowd: "What evil has he done?" (15:14, *Ti gar epoiēsen kakon*; cf. *kakopoiēsai*, 3:4). At the same time, this choice is no longer in the symbolic space of Judaism (i.e., the synagogue or temple), but the *Roman* sphere (the praetorium, 15:16). Accordingly, Mark portrays the scene in faint parody of a pagan "intertextual" tradition: the gladiator games of the Colosseum, in which combatants often included prisoners of war and criminals condemned to death. After the fight, the crowd was given "the choice to determine whether a wounded gladiator would be killed or allowed to live" (Merrit, 1985:68).

The crowd—the "sheep without a shepherd" (6:34)—is caught between conflicting revolutionary claims: the "kingdom" vision heralded by Jesus and the restorationist vision represented by Barabbas the guerilla. But it is only an *apparent* choice, for those *mediating* the contest are in fact the ones who presently hold social power with no intention of giving it up—after all, both candidates are *prisoners*. Between Pilate's taunts (and this is how we must read the procurator's "consultations" with the crowd) and the chief priests' frantic behind-the-scenes lobbying, Mark is indicating that the crowd is being manipulated to play into the hands of the status quo. As long as the masses succumb to the wily machinations of the ruling classes, their continued domination is guaranteed.

The narrative unfolds in controlled tension in two parts within the topical frame:

The crowd entreats Pilate to do according to the practice (15:8).

1. A   Pilate answered them saying: "Do you want me to release to you the King of the Jews?" (15:9)
   B   He knew the high priests had delivered him out of envy: the high priests stirred up the crowd . . . (15:10f.)
   A   Pilate answered them saying: "What then should I do with him whom you call the King of the Jews?" (15:12).
2. B   And they cried: "Crucify him!" (15:13)
   A   Pilate said to them: "What wrong has he done?" (15:14a)
   B   And they cried louder: "Crucify him!" (15:14b).

Pilate satisfies the crowd, releases Barabbas (15:15).

The crowd's "entreaty" to Pilate (*aiteisthai*, the word used for Salome's request to Herod for the head of John the Baptist in 6:24!) for the release of a prisoner sets the drama in motion. The first part reveals that Pilate continues to identify the issue as one of native kingship ("the man *you* call King. . . ."). Mark describes the "incitement" (*anaseiō*) by the chief priests, which he attributes to their "envy" (15:10f.). Mark's contempt for them is clear: the priestly class will build opportunistic coalitions with anyone—Sicarii, the crowds, the procurator—in order to eliminate Jesus, who alone poses a real threat to its social power.

In the second frame we witness the sudden and violent switch in the loyalty of the crowds, which had so recently (12:38) backed Jesus in his attack upon the scribal class! Their double "cry" (*krazō*) foreshadows Jesus' double shout as he hangs dying on the cross to which they condemn him (15:39). Their shrill call for blood echoes, on the one hand, the howls of the demons Jesus earlier confronted (1:23; 3:11; 5:5,7; 9:26), and on the other, the cries of those oppressed by the powers and their ideologies (9:24; 10:47f.; 11:9). It is a cry that is at once both demonic and despairing—the crowd is "possessed." Pilate in the end gives this crowd "satisfaction" (*to hikanon poiēsai*, a transliterated Latin legalism), releasing the lesser revolutionary and handing the true dissident over to the customary postverdict flagellation (*phragellōsas*, another Latinism). The trial narrative so concludes.

The powers and the people have considered the subversive claims of Jesus, and summarily condemned him to death. He is led out of the city for the last time (15:20). Jesus has denied himself, and he has not been ashamed of the Human One. The time has now arrived for him to take up his cross.

NOTES

1. The conflict between Mark's description and the actual historical practice of the Passover meal has been long debated. Those (e.g., Taylor, 1963:664ff.) who try to resolve the contradictions by contending that Mark did not intend for this meal to be a Passover celebration not only contradict the text, but miss the ideological point of why Mark has altered it (see Jeremias, 1966:15ff.).

2. Judas' betrayal in 14:10 may also allude to Zechariah 11:13f.; so Matthew, who attributes the prophecy to Jeremiah (Mt 27:9f.).

3. D. Senior (1987) agrees that this episode articulates Mark's critique of abusive Roman power; but he believes this was done from a Roman provenance.

CHAPTER THIRTEEN

The Execution of Jesus and the "Second" Epilogue (Mark 15:21-16:8)

> All who see me mock at me, they make mouths at me, they wag their heads, saying: "He committed his cause to Yahweh; let Yahweh rescue him, if Yahweh delights in him!"
>
> —Psalm 22:7f.

A story that began heralding a way through the wilderness now ends on the way of the cross—the cross, not a religious icon, but the ultimate deterrent to those who would challenge the sovereignty of Rome. Execution by crucifixion: so chilling and inhumane that Cicero, writing in 63 B.C.E., argued that it should be outlawed (Weber, 1975:1):

> If we are to be threatened with death, then we want to die in freedom; let the executioner, the shrouding of the head, and the very name of the cross be banished from the body and life of Roman citizens, from their thoughts, eyes, and ears!

The cross: according to humanists of antiquity, an intolerably cruel form of capital punishment; according to Jesus' call to discipleship, the concrete consequence of the liberating practice of the kingdom; according to the apocalyptic symbolics of Mark's story, the mythic moment when the sun retreats, the powers are overthrown, and the world comes to an end.

What a scene Mark paints, fraught with tragedy! In the foreground, beneath this Roman stake, all of Jesus' opponents have gathered to ridicule him. In the background, a few women disciples look on with horror. And what of us? Where do *we* stand in this pitiful finale, this consummate moment of desolation? Is there not a part of us lurking in each of the characters? A part that is, like the male disciples, altogether absent to this spectacle, having long ago abandoned Jesus at the first whiff of confrontation? A part that holds vigil with the women, incredulous and numb with sorrow? And also a part that,

383

from the safety of the crowd, joins in the ridicule of this "king" become Suffering Servant? "Who indeed can believe" (Is 53:1) that it has really turned out this way?

Let us give the "bystander" within us the benefit of the doubt. Is it not that part of us (however small) of genuine, uncorrupted longing for an end to oppression that here turns to rage, directed at the one who promised but could not deliver a new order? Is it not the bitterness of repeatedly crushed hopes that makes us look desperately for the last-minute intervention of Elijah, which is to say for *whatever* will make the story come out right? Insofar as we might truly thirst for the justice of Yahweh "with all our heart, soul, mind and strength" (12:33), as we might truly yearn for the imperial hammerlock upon history to be broken—we may legitimately come to this cross with all the others (the living, the dying, and the martyred, whose cries of "How long?" [Rv 6:9f.] echo down the corridors of history) and *demand* an explanation. For if *this* story ends in the triumph of the powers, then it is no new story at all, and a mockery of "glad tidings."

If only Jesus would come down from the cross so we might believe (15:32)! Who of us is really prepared to accept that by remaining there he shows the way to liberation, to acknowledge that in *this* moment the powers are overthrown and the kingdom is come in power and glory? And even if we should be able, with the women, to at least apprehend this spectacle "from a distance," who of us can embrace its implication for our own lives? If we, like those women, should receive an invitation from a martyr-messenger to follow anew *this* way, would we not also flee, struck dumb from trepidation?

13A. THE WAY OF THE CROSS (15:21–32)

i. The Triumphal Gloat of Rome

When the Roman security forces have completed the deeds of the torture-room, Jesus is marched out of the city to the place of crucifixion (15:20). The drama of the *via dolorosa*, like so many other aspects of the gospel narrative, has become in churchly tradition a pious exercise in personal anguish, replete with self-flagellation. Gone is its true signification: the political theater of imperial triumph. The Roman practice of putting its defeated military foes on parade is well documented (alluded to in the Pauline war of myths, Col 2:15). Josephus describes how Simon bar Giora, the general and self-proclaimed king of the rebel resistance at the time of the fall of Jerusalem (Horsley and Hanson, 1985:118ff.), was transported to Rome and underwent this political humiliation before being executed:

> The triumphal procession concluded at the temple of Jupiter Capitolinus, where . . . Simon bar Giora, who had just taken part in the procession among the prisoners, and, with a noose put over him, was dragged by force to the proper spot at the forum, all the while being

tortured by those who led him. It was at that spot where Roman law required those sentenced to death for villainy to be slain. When his death was announced, it was greeted with universal acclamation, and the sacrifices were begun [*Wars*, VII,v,6].

In the provinces, with lesser "kings," a local public march to the executioner's stake sufficed for the same lesson in imperial omnipotence.

The normal Roman custom was to subject the condemned to the ignominy of carrying their own death stake. Why, then, the story of "Simon the Cyrenian" (yet another named character given an important bit-part), who is forcibly recruited (*aggareuousin*) to carry Jesus' cross (15:21)? It may be that we can assume that Jesus was too weak from torture; after all, he later dies sooner than expected (15:44f.). But the more important meaning of this episode is the narrative irony it lends, once again showing there is no "incidental" detail in the literary construction of Mark.

The first ironic overtone lies in the fact that Simon is described as having "come from the fields" (i.e., rural areas, *erchomenon ap' agrou*). We recall that Jesus was accompanied (willingly) on his messianic procession into Jerusalem by rural crowds (they who cut straw "from the fields" to line his way, 11:8). Now Mark reproduces the scene in a negative image: Jesus exits Jerusalem in a Roman procession, accompanied (under duress) by a single rural dweller. This functions in two ways. It provides ironic narrative closure to the Jerusalem narrative. And it reminds us once more of the spatial (geopolitical) tension between city/country and center/periphery, which Mark exploits to the end.

Secondly, the episode has strong discipleship overtones. Simon the Cyrenian was "passing along" (*paragōnta*) when he was pressed into service. This verb has occurred only two other times in Mark—in both cases describing Jesus' movement in the discipleship call stories (1:16; 2:13). Was not the name of the first man called by Jesus also "Simon"? And has not this former Simon, who along with the others was exhorted to "take up his cross" (*aratō ton stauron autou*, 8:34), deserted this calling? So does Markan irony have a different Simon "take up his cross" (*hina arē ton stauron autou*). Yet again it is an outsider (Simon was father to Alexander and Rufus, names from which we must infer that he was a gentile) who, however unwittingly, answers the call to discipleship, while the twelve are nowhere to be seen.

Mark has now switched his narration to the historic present tense, in order to draw the reader in, making us eyewitnesses to these terrible events as they unfold (Taylor, 1963:588). Jesus is taken to the place of skulls ("Golgotha"), a suitably grim scene for the execution (15:22f.). H. R. Weber gives us a portrait of the practice of crucifixion drawn from ancient sources:

Sometimes the condemned had a tablet, stating the *causa poena*, the reason for his conviction, hung around his neck. He then had himself to carry the transverse bar of the cross (the *patibulum*) to the place of execution. There he was undressed and scourged, if this had not already been done. According to ancient custom, the executioners were allowed to distribute the condemned man's clothing among themselves. At the place of execution there usually already stood a pole (*stipes* or *palu*). . . . The convict was then laid on the ground, both forearms or wrists were tied or nailed to the transverse bar, and he was then raised by the *patibulum*. . . . If the condemned man was intended to be visible from afar, the high cross was chosen. Usually, though, the pole measured no more than about seven feet. This meant that wild animals could tear the crucified man apart. The feet of the victims were not supported by a footrest as Christian art has depicted it since the seventh century, but were tied or nailed to the pole. Usually, the condemned man "sat" on a peg (*sedile* or *cornu*) which was fixed to the middle of the pole. . . . Generally, the crucified one died of gradual asphyxiation [1975:6].

This may help modern readers appreciate the vivid and terrible image that Mark's simple "and they crucified him" (15:24) would have conjured up for his original audience.

Two symbolic gestures give an Old Testament coloring to the executioner's act. Jesus is offered drugged wine to ease his pain, after the admonition of Proverbs 31:6. Consistent with his vow of abstinence (14:25), however, Jesus refuses. The soldiers then draw lots for his garments, which once healed people (5:27f.; 6:56) but now, like their owner, are impotent. Here is the first of three allusions in the execution narrative to the great Psalm of lament, Psalm 22 (22:18).

ii. The Derision of the Jews

Jesus is nailed to the stake at the "third hour" (about nine in the morning)—the first of Mark's three "watches of the cross" (15:25). Mark now moves the reader's eye from the ground to the air as the cross is raised. First we are shown the inscription (*hē epiggraphē*), which represents the formal charges upon which Jesus was convicted: "King of the Jews" (15:26; the last of the five occurrences of this title). Pilate seems to have prevailed: Jesus is being executed for presuming to challenge the authority of Rome. With this the war of myths between Yahwism and imperialism, implied in the tribute episode (12:16), is definitively articulated. Those who would collaborate with the empire will "render" according to Caesar's inscription; those who would collaborate with the kingdom must "render" according to the inscription on the cross.

In the following scene Mark reproduces the triangle of Palestinian politics one more time (see above, 12,F,ii). There is unequivocal opposition between the kingdom and Caesar; what of the Jewish state? The mockery episode (15:27–32) is carefully structured in a framed doublet (see Matera, 1982:57f.):

Two bandits crucified with him.
Passersby blaspheme him
   "You who would destroy the sanctuary and rebuild it . . .
    Come down from the cross and save yourself."

Chief priests ridicule him to one another with scribes
"Others he saved; himself he cannot save;
Let Messiah King of Israel come down from the cross
that we may see and believe."
And those crucified with him abused him (15:27c–32).

As in the hearing before Pilate, Mark gathers representatives from the whole Jewish political spectrum—rebels, collaborators, and the everpresent crowds—for this final consideration of the way of Jesus. Let us consider each in turn.

Mark tells us that Jesus is crucified between two "bandits" (15:27; *duo lēstas*; see above, 2,C,ii). This is now Mark's second reference to the fact that Jesus is *perceived* by the authorities in terms equal to that of social bandits. When the Jewish security forces had seized Jesus in Gethsemane, their modus operandi had suggested to him that they understood him to be dangerous and armed "as a bandit" (14:48). Here Jesus is executed by Roman security forces along with two other bandits. It is not surprising that these bandits show up beside Jesus, for only political subversives were executed by Rome in this way. But what is the *social* function of Mark's insistence, from the point of his arrest to the point of his execution, that Jesus is being mistaken for a social bandit?

Mark distinguishes the bandits from the "revolutionary" Barabbas, who apparently represented the Sicarius faction of urban political terrorists. Social bandits on the other hand operated in the countryside; bandit leaders whose private armies came to defend Jerusalem—John of Gischala and Simon bar Giora—played a key role in the provisional government (Horsley and Hanson, 1985:77ff.; see above, 2,C,ii). So too Jesus, who also operated in the rural areas and who came to Jerusalem, like Simon bar Giora, with messianic pretensions. However historical the tradition may be, Mark is making a very important ideological statement here. Mark has in the second sermon clearly dissociated Jesus from the means and ends of the rebel cause. Yet he shares their fate, as a common opponent to both Rome and the socio-economic status quo. Jesus is traded for a Sicarius, taken for a social bandit; of all the factions in Palestine, Mark situates Jesus alongside *these*.

As if to underline the point, Mark tells us that the bandits were crucified "one on his right and one on his left" (15:27)—the very positions of "honor" for which the disciples had earlier competed (10:37). The implication is unmistakable: Jesus' call to messianic nonviolence asks no more, but certainly no less, of the recruit than do the rebels. The irony is that it is the armed insurgents, not his own disciples, who demonstrate the courage to undergo the "baptism" of death at the hands of the state (cf. 10:39f.). It is because of this very fact that Mark's Jesus can be said to stand in solidarity with the rebels he disagrees with, indeed the rebels who join the others in mocking his way. It seems to me that the lesson for disciples of messianic nonviolence still holds: only when our resistance *becomes* serious enough to be "reckoned with the transgressors" (to intone Is 53:12) will it be *taken* seriously by them as an alternative. Let it be recognized, says Mark, that those who have chosen armed struggle have taken up the cross, that place of honor, far more often than have practitioners of *satyagraha*.

We turn next to the bystanders, representing the uncommitted crowds. They "wag their heads," an allusion to the derision of fallen Israel in Lamentations 2:15. It is also the second citation of Psalm 22:

> All who see me mock at me
> they make mouths at me, they wag their heads;
> He committed his cause to Yahweh;
> let him deliver him [Ps 22:7f.].

The crowd repeats the charge of 14:58, which serves as Mark's reminder to the reader to prepare for the final conflict between the "sanctuary" and Jesus' "body," that will be dramatized in the third apocalyptic moment. Their taunt concludes with the challenge, or plea, for Jesus to "come down" from the cross and "save himself" (15:30).

Both themes are taken up and intensified by the last group, the chief priests and scribes, representing the collaborating ruling elite (15:31). Just as did the Roman soldiers (15:20), they "deride" (*empaizontes*) Jesus' failed political aspirations, maintaining the parallelism. Not only do they ridicule Jesus as "Messiah," the charge upon which the Sanhedrin convicted him of blasphemy (14:61), but add Pilate's charge of "king" as well (15:32). This only confirms their collaboration with Rome, though they correct Pilate's insult of 15:18. With yet more irony, in their taunt—"others he saved, himself he cannot save" (15:31b)—Jesus' opponents have once again exegeted the central messianic truth. Jesus was indeed committed to "saving" life (3:4), and he did indeed warn his disciples against trying to save their own life (8:36). The tragedy of the story is that no one has understood this paradox; his enemies ridicule it, his disciples have abandoned it.

As I suggested in the opening lines of this chapter, there is a touch of desperation in their final challenge:

> come down from the cross
> that we may see and believe (15:32b).

Jesus' opponents are imploring him to repudiate the cross. If there is what the structuralists call a "subtext" here, it is the secret desire by Jesus' critics for a better end to this tragedy. They are prepared to believe, *if* (but only if) Jesus can salvage a narrative of triumphalism. Indeed so strong is this desire for a last-minute intervention that in the end one is conjured up:

> *See*! He calls for Elijah! [15:35].
> Let us *see* whether Elijah comes to take him down [15:36].

This is the pitiful culmination to the struggle for belief that has characterized Mark's story (cf. 9:24). How can Jesus be the King of Israel, hanging on a

Roman cross? As the bandits join in the chorus (15:32c), it is as if the whole of Palestinian political culture has issued a rejection of the way of Jesus. Things have hardly changed today.

13B. JESUS CRUCIFIED: THIRD APOCALYPTIC MOMENT (15:33–38)

i. The End of the World

Mark shapes the final scene of Jesus' life concentrically:

      first judgment: darkness for three hours
         first cry in a great voice: Ps 22:1
            bystanders: "See he calls Elijah"
            man giving sour wine: "Let us see if Elijah comes"
         second cry in a loud voice; Jesus dies
      second judgment: rending of the sanctuary curtain

Here Mark's war of myths reaches its culmination in two great judgment motifs. The first is a sudden darkness over the land for three hours (from the sixth to ninth hour, the second and third watches of the cross). This is taken from Exodus 10:22, when Yahweh, in the war of myths with the pharaoh, blotted out the sun in Egypt for three days—the repudiation of the imperial order legitimized by the worship of the sun god Ra. Here, the motif represents the first indication that the apocalyptic "moment" spoken of in 13:24 is being realized: the fall of the dominant world order symbolized in the unraveling of the cosmic forces or order in the universe (see above, 11,D,i).

This is followed, at the ninth hour, by the first of two dramatic utterances, indeed "death rattles." This "great shout" is the third and final allusion to Psalm 22; Mark translates the hebraized Aramaic citation of Psalm 22:1 (15:34). In portraying Jesus as the suffering righteous man speaking in the Psalm, the emphasis is upon an unmitigated bitterness of abandonment:

> Jesus' cry is an allusion to the entire psalm, since in Old Testament and rabbinical usage the quotation of the first words of a book or a prayer indicated the entire book or prayer. . . . It is, however, remarkable, that in the crucifixion narrative only the first words, as well as the beginning and the end of the description (vv. 7,18) are quoted, but not the expressions of trust nor the concluding song of praise [Weber, 1975:38f.].

There is no reply to this agonized protest directed at heaven. Unlike the previous two apocalyptic moments, the voice from above is silent.

The bystanders take Jesus to be calling Elijah (13:35), and Taylor cites a popular belief "that Elijah would come to the rescue of the godly in time of need" (1963:594). The man offering Jesus the sour wine mash (the soldier's standard fare) extends the suspense (15:36): Will Elijah come to snatch Jesus from the jaws of death? With these appeals to the great prophet, the Elijah narrative closes. Jesus' great shout (*eboēsen phōnē megalē*) recalls the Isaian shout in the wilderness at the very beginning of the story (1:3; *phōnē boōntos*), a voice embodied by John, the embodiment of Elijah (1:6). But where is John/Elijah now? "Elijah has indeed come, and they did to him whatever they pleased" (9:13). There can be, in other words, no eleventh-hour rescue, for every servant of the vineyard owner shares the same fate at the hands of the tenants (12:1ff.).

The crowd wanted to "see" a miracle; what they "see" instead is the revelation of the Human One. For their speculation is abruptly cut short as Jesus expires with a "great gasp" (15:37, *phōnēn megalēn*). It is this very gasp that characterized the last gasps of the demon(s) as they were vanquished by Jesus in each of his two inaugural exorcisms (1:27; 5:7). The reader might at this point shudder. Is this the darkest reversal of all, inferring that the powers have "exorcised" Jesus? Has Mark's alternative symbolic field finally collapsed, the last victim of the steadily deteriorating narrative of betrayal and defeat? The evidence seems overwhelming. Elijah did not come, and heaven has remained silent. It was not the strong man who was bound, but Jesus; not the temple that was destroyed, but Jesus. Now he is dead; the story appears to have come to a grinding halt.

Then, just as we are forced to capitulate to this irresistible narrative logic, Mark dramatically overturns it. At that moment the "sanctuary curtain (*to katapetasma tou naou*) was rent in two from top to bottom" (15:38). Taylor points out that "in the LXX *to katapetasma* . . . is the curtain between the Holy place and the Holy of Holies (Ex 26:31–37), but the word is sometimes used of the veil which covered the entrance to the Holy Place" (1963:596). Mark's narrative of subversion regarding the efficacy and authority of the temple cult now is given closure. Jesus' death has unmasked the fact that the "tear" (*schisman*) in the "old garment" is irreparable (2:21); the symbolic order as it is centrally embedded in the sanctuary has been overthrown. Here then is the second great symbol of the "end of the world." The strong man has *not* prevailed, his "house" *has* been ransacked. But how can this be so?

ii. The Advent of the Human One

To understand how Mark can make such a claim, we must first consider the three "apocalyptic moments" synoptically. These moments have been placed like structural pillars at the beginning (Jesus' baptism), midpoint (Jesus' transfiguration), and end of the story. At the level of narrative, each moment is fundamental to the regeneration of plot: the baptism opened the subversive mission of the kingdom, the transfiguration deepened it by confirming the second call to discipleship. Golgotha becomes the "practice" of the first two moments: "baptism" (which according to 10:38 is a metaphor for political execution) and "cross" (8:34).

All three moments share four constitutive elements: (a) some kind of heavenly portent (which is otherwise eschewed by Mark); (b) a "voice"; (c) an identification of Jesus as "Son of God"; and (d) relationship to "Elijah":

Baptism	Transfiguration	Crucifixion
a) heavens rent	garments turn white	sanctuary veil rent
dove descends	cloud descends	darkness spreads
b) voice from heaven	voice from cloud	Jesus' great voice
c) "You are my son,	"This is my son,	truly this man
beloved."	beloved"	was son of God.
d) John the Baptist	Jesus appears	"Is he calling
as Elijah	with Elijah	Elijah?"

With this narrative identification between the three moments in mind, we can see how, at the level of ideological signification, the meaning of the third moment is to be understood in terms of the advent of the Human One.

Throughout the story Jesus has resisted the titles "Messiah" and "Son of God" (3:11; 5:7; 8:29), preferring instead an oblique (third person) reference to the "Human One." This Human One, Jesus has insisted, is a servant and will suffer and die; he will also come to vanquish the powers. This character, as I have noted, is drawn from Daniel 7:9–14, and this oracle brings immediate clarity to the war of myths taking place at Golgotha. For in Daniel's dream, it is precisely at the point at which the "beast" appears triumphant (Dn 7:3–8) that a counter-vision suddenly turns the tables. The beast is brought before a heavenly courtroom and, along with the other nations, is judged and forced to cede its sovereignty:

> With the clouds of heaven there came one like a son of man, and he came to the Ancient of Days and was presented before him. And to him was given dominion and glory and kingdom [Dn 7:13–14].

Mark's apocalyptic intertextuality is specifically political here, as it was in 13:14; he again freely substitutes the Roman-Jewish condominium for Antiochus Epiphanes IV as the new beast. The myth of the Human One overthrowing the rulers of the age is a revolutionary one that legitimizes resistance to the dominant order, and promises its demise.

Traditional theology grants the allusion to Daniel in the case of the second apocalyptic moment, but not this third one. Ever anxious to salvage an imperial ideology of triumph, it draws a distinction between Jesus on the cross and the Jesus of the transfiguration, usually by dichotomizing a "first" and a "second" messianic advent. Mark, however, has given us narrative clues that identify all the apocalyptic moments with the one event of the cross. We recall that three times Jesus has predicted that his audience would "see" the advent of the Human One: once to his disciples (9:1), once referring to the powers themselves (13:25), and once addressing the Sanhedrin (14:62). We now realize that the narrative of Jesus' execution does indeed fulfill his word: at the cross "some of" the disciples (represented by the women "watching" in 15:40) and the whole political spectrum of powers (including members of the Sanhedrin) are all present. They are "seeing" the advent of the Human One on the cross. That this is the moment spoken of in 8:29f. and 13:24f. is further confirmed by the two representative "apocalyptic portents." The sun darkens (the cosmic symbol), and the sanctuary curtain is rent in two (the political symbol). The world order has been overthrown, the powers have fallen (13:24f.).

The judgment and "enthronement" myth of Daniel is renarrated in Mark's third apocalyptic moment of the cross. It represents the conclusion to the "war in heaven," which, in the struggle between Jesus and temptation/Satan (1:13 = 8:33 = 14:38), is being enacted on earth. The Human One, who is given dominion over the powers in the mythic moment of "glory," is the very same Human One who "gives his life as a ransom for many" in the mythic moment of death. Here the war of myths between the two opposing ideological systems reaches its zenith: just as it was Yahweh vs. pharaoh's sun god Ra, as it was the archangel Michael vs. the prince of Persia (Dn 10:12f.), so now it is Jesus' "body" vs. the "sanctuary." Once we see this we can understand the correlation between Jesus' prophecy of his death and resurrection "after three days" (8:31) and his opponents' allegation that he would destroy the sanctuary and construct a new one "within three days" (14:58). The first part of both have been fulfilled: Jesus has been "handed over and killed," and the "sanctuary made with hands" has been symbolically "destroyed" (the renting of the curtain). It now only remains to be seen how the narrative will raise up the new sanctuary "not made with hands."

13C. AFTERMATH: THREE RESPONSES TO JESUS' DEATH (15:39–47)

We have arrived at the second "epilogue." Here, as with the first epilogue, the symbolics of the second half of Mark's story will reach their resolution. The Human One, coming in the "power and glory" of the cross, has been "seen" by both those who conspired with Jesus and those who conspired against him. Now Mark narrates brief stories of three such "witnesses": a centurion, a member of the Sanhedrin, and the women disciples. Each vignette occurs in two parts, such that all three are tightly woven together; in chronological order:

  centurion as witness of Jesus' death (15:39)
      women disciples "watch" the death (vv. 40f.)
          Joseph appeals for the body of Jesus (vv. 42f.)
  centurion as witness of Jesus' death (vv. 44f.)
          Joseph buries Jesus (v. 46)
      women disciples "watch" the burial (v. 47)

The function of this "aftermath" is to provide a narrative bridge to the final encounter at the tomb, at which point the discipleship story is regenerated. Throughout this epilogue, the "body" of Jesus lingers as the narrative center, hinting that death has not had the last word.

i. The Centurion: Rome Has Defeated Jesus

The first reaction by any character to the death of Jesus is the famous "confession" of the Roman centurion in 15:39. This utterance is widely regarded in traditional exegesis as the "climax" of the Gospel, providing narrative (and theological) resolution to the "messianic secret." It is argued that Mark's christology stipulates that only "at the foot of the cross" can Jesus' "sonship" legitimately be extolled; so Schweizer:

> It is the crucified one, not the miracle-worker, who elicits the first confession from one who really understands God's mighty deeds in Jesus. Not even an extraordinary experience of God's healing or saving power leads to genuine faith, but rather the spiritual poverty of a Gentile who realizes that Jesus had to go to this length to open for him a way of life [1978:396].

There is a certain truth to this conventional view, insofar as it recognizes the necessity of the cross for a genuine profession of Jesus. But this was already clear back at the first confessional crisis of 8:27ff. (see above, 8,C), and is not the point here. To put such a realization on the lips of a Roman soldier ("centurion" is a Latinism)—moreover the very one presiding at Jesus' execution—not only gives the man more credit than he deserves, it clearly betrays an imperial bias. It is yet another attempt to suppress political discourse in favor of theology.

In theory, given Mark's penchant for radical narrative reversals, the traditional view of the centurion's "conversion" would not be out of the question. But a closer reading makes such an interpretation impossible. There are a few narrative clues. First, Mark sets up the scene with the centurion "standing over against" Jesus on the cross (*ho paretēkōs ex enantias autou*); such spatial tension usually in Mark connotes opposition (*enantios* in 6:48), not solidarity. Secondly, this centurion will momentarily reappear to confirm to Pilate that Jesus has indeed died (15:44f.). The fact that the man did not defect from his role as a Roman soldier loyal to Pilate erases the possibility that this is meant by Mark as a *discipleship* story. What is remarkable is that a scholar such as Schweizer, who is otherwise so insistent upon discipleship as requisite to confession, fails to acknowledge its absence here.

Thirdly, is the matter of the "confession" itself. Many have pointed out that the centurion's words could just as easily be interpreted as a general Hellenistic statement of respect: "This man was a son of God." Nor does his solemnity ("Truly . . . ", *alēthōs*) carry particular weight, for Mark twice previously has put this exclamation on the lips of the discipleship community's opponents (12:14; 14:70). Yet even if we do accept this as a confession, we have no guarantee of, and the theologians offer no good reason why we should assume, its legitimacy. After all, Jesus as "Son of God" has previously been uttered "legitimately" only by Mark (1:1) at the beginning, and by the heavenly voice in the first two apocalyptic moments (1:11; 9:7). Every other occurrence of the designation "son" in reference to Jesus has been attributed to either demons or political opponents (3:11; 5:7; 6:3; 14:61). In other words, the title does not necessarily represent a "confession" at all, but more often the hostile response of those struggling to gain power over Jesus by "naming" him. And is not *this* view more appropriate to the political discourse of Mark to this point? Rome has triumphed over the Nazarene, he has been "named" by the executioner who pronounces him "dead" (15:44f.).

The only difference between the exclamation of the centurion and that of demon or high priest is that Jesus cannot silence or repudiate it, for he is dead. It is therefore up to the reader to discern. Our best clue lies in the third apocalyptic moment's contrariety to the first two. Whereas Elijah was "present" at both baptism (in the person of John) and the transfiguration (in the vision), at the cross it is those who deride Jesus who invoke Elijah. The heavenly (positive narrative coordinate) portents have been replaced with an earthly one: the rent sanctuary curtain (negative coordinate). And the "reliable testimony" from the clouds is here silent. Against all this, are we to see the centurion's words as trustworthy? If so, we will have failed to learn one of the most salient lessons of the whole story, which is that those in power indeed "know who Jesus is," and are out to destroy him, whereas those who follow him are often unsure who he is, but struggle to trust him nevertheless. In the end, the only reliable postexecution "witness" to Jesus will be a "young man," who tells the women that Jesus is alive and that the discipleship adventure may continue.

ii. Joseph: The Sanhedrin Has Defeated Jesus

Skipping for a moment the cameo of the women (15:40), we come to another story of an "oppressor's response" to Jesus' death: that of Joseph of Arimathea, the last of the named bit-characters. This episode is similarly ambiguous—and similarly misunderstood by most commentators. It begins with the penultimate temporal marker in the story: evening (*opsias genomenēs*). The long day of Jesus' condemnation and death is drawing to a close—there remains only for his body to be removed from the cross. Mark is careful to mention that we are on the eve of the Sabbath, for two reasons. First, it provides a narrative balance to the story of Jesus' ministry: it had commenced in relation to the Sabbath (1:21), and his vocation of public healing ministry had started "when evening had come" (*opsias de genomenēs*, 1:32); so too it ends on the Sabbath eve. Secondly, the issue of the Sabbath, a point of conflict throughout the story, will come into play one last time.

Most commentators have praised Joseph's act as an act of mercy by a repentant Jewish leader—a kind of "Nicodemus motif." But once again such a view withers under closer scrutiny. Joseph is described as "affluent" (*euschēmōn*; "the papyri make it clear that this means a wealthy landowner,"

Jeremias, 1969:96). He is also a member of the council (*bouleutēs*), presumably the Sanhedrin (15:43). In other words, Joseph, like the centurion, is one who has been deeply complicit in the process by which Jesus was executed. Mark distinguishes him (the emphatic *hos kai autos* is almost as if to say "but he unlike the others") by telling us that he was "expecting the kingdom of God." The verb (*prosdechomenos*) is derived from the hospitality verb *dechesthai* so important to Mark's ideology of "kingdom receptivity" (6:11; 9:37; 10:15). But given that in Mark the closest scribes may get is "not far from the kingdom of God" (12:34), we are unsure what to make of this description.

The fact that a member of the Sanhedrin had to "make bold" to petition Pilate for the body shows, somewhat sarcastically, how firmly in control of events the Roman procurator in fact was. But it also suggests that the Jewish leadership was anxious to hastily dispose of the whole matter before any protest could be made. Some see Joseph's action as a dignifying one: rather than leaving Jesus' corpse (*ptōma*, twice, 15:43, 45) at the mercy of the elements and wild animals, as was often the case with victims of crucifixion, he placed it in a proper tomb (15:46). But Mark makes no mention that Joseph tended to any of the traditional offices or rites of burial stipulated in Jewish law. Thus it is equally possible to interpret this as a hurried burial, the final indignity. Taylor points out that even the verb describing Joseph's wrapping of the body (15:46, *eneilēsen*) is "unseemly," used of fettering prisoners . . . holding people fast in a net . . . and generally in a bad sense" (1963:601).

This interpretation is confirmed by the fact that later the women disciples in 16:1f. take spices to the tomb—that is, they attempt to give proper last services. So R. Fuller:

> It must have been a scandal to the disciples that none of them had been present to pay the last honors to their Master. . . . There is no reason why, if the body of Jesus had been cast into the grave by his enemies without proper burial, the women should not have gone to the tomb with the intention of giving Jesus a proper burial if they could [1971:55f.].

Fuller further points out that this explains why Mark links Joseph's action to the approaching Sabbath; because "the Sanhedrin was the agent of Jesus' burial," they effected a "hasty burial lest the hanging of the dead body on the cross should profane the Sabbath" (ibid.). Joseph, in other words, is simply attending to a matter of ritual purity. In the end, the Sanhedrin has successfully repelled Jesus' challenge to the symbolic order; the one who claimed to be "Lord over the Sabbath" (2:28) is subjected to the ultimate insult—improper entombment—for the sake of the Sabbath order.

There is, finally, also an element of tragic pathos in this story. Joseph puts Jesus in a tomb (*ethēken auton en mnēmati*), recalling the identical action of John's disciples upon the Baptist's execution (6:29, *ēran to ptōma autou kai ethēkan auto en mnēmeiō*). He has wrapped the corpse in a "linencloth" (*sindona*), a symbol that alludes to the community's desertion of Jesus in

Gethsemane (14:50–52; the young man fled, leaving only a linen cloth). Jesus' disciples cannot even be as faithful in death as were John's; they were not there to "take up his cross," and they are not there to "take his body" (cf. 14:22). The episode ends with Joseph rolling the stone against the tomb (15:46). This act symbolically closes the narrative of Jesus, the debacle complete.

This aftermath does not present a new narrative landscape full of hope and triumph, as maintained by those who would have us marvel at the "confession" of a "repentant centurion" and the "merciful action" of a "secret Sanhedrin disciple." Rather, these stories are ambiguous in the extreme, suggesting if anything that Jesus' enemies have had, literally, the last word. His executioner has named him, in stark contrast to Jesus' lead disciple who denied his name (14:66ff.). It was not "Elijah" (15:36) who "took down" Jesus (*kathaireō*, "the technical term for the removal of a crucified person," Taylor, 1963:595), but a member of the council (15:46). Jesus is sealed away in a tomb, and the collaborative powers that joined to put him there have taken over the narrative. The discipleship community has disappeared. Except for the women.

iii. The Women: True Disciples

At the end of each stage of this twofold death/burial drama Mark makes reference to some "watching" women (15:40, 47). Of itself, this vigil would not necessarily be significant, for it was customary for charitable Jerusalem women to attend to the crucified. But Mark is quick to tell us that these women were not Jerusalemites, but Galilean disciples of Jesus (15:41). Nor does he stop there; in one sweeping phrase, he describes the group in a manner that virtually epitomizes them as model disciples. Not only did they "follow" (*ēkolouthoun*), but they "served" Jesus throughout the Galilee ministry. Here at the end, as at the very beginning of the story (1:31), Mark tells us that it is women who serve (*diakonein*), as if to say that they alone understand the true vocation of leadership (*diakonia*, 9:35; 10:43). Secondly, these women came up (*sunanabasai autō*) with Jesus to Jerusalem, and have stayed with him to death. In other words, not *all* deserted Jesus at Gethsemane. The women now become the "lifeline" of the discipleship narrative.

The women have done the two things that the males in the community found impossible: they have been servants, and they continued to follow Jesus even *after* he was arrested and executed. Who are these women? Three are named, of which one appears to be Jesus' mother—if the "mother of James and Joses" can be identified with the "mother of James, Joses, Judas, and Simon" in 6:3. This suggests an unnarrated reversal of the position of Jesus' mother as it was portrayed in 3:31. But there is no reason to rule this out; moreover, she is here described not as "mother" but as disciple (cf. 3:34). In any case, whoever the three women are, Mark presents them as an alternative to the three men of the former inner circle (Peter, James, and John): they are the true disciples.

This is the last—and, given the highly structured gender roles of the time, surely the most radical—example of Mark's narrative subversion of the canons of social orthodoxy. The world order is being overturned, from the highest political power to the deepest cultural patterns, and it begins within the new community. It will be these women, the "last" become "first," who will be entrusted with the resurrection message. Yet even if the narrative inference is that the women emerge as the true community leaders, even here Mark's portrait of them remains profoundly unromanticized and finally ambiguous, as we will now see as we turn to examine the last act of the drama.

13D. THE DISCIPLESHIP NARRATIVE RESUMES (16:1-7)

The final scene of the epilogue, which even as historicist an interpreter as Taylor admits to be a "dramatization," is a carefully crafted apotheosis, full of narrative symbolics that leave not answers but questions. In these few verses, however, the story is rescued from tragic irresolution. It is not a "happy ending" in which all is resolved; rather, the discipleship narrative is given a new lease to continue.

i. The Women and the "Young Man"

The genuine mission of mercy by the women (16:1-3) is portrayed in direct contrast to the actions of Joseph. Before the Sabbath, the council member:

1. bought (*agorazein*) linen;
2. wrapped Jesus' body in (improper) burial;
3. put Jesus in a tomb;
4. rolled a stone against the entrance.

The narrative was closed. Now after the Sabbath, the women:

1. buy (*ēgorasan*) spices;
2. go to the tomb;
3. in order to "anoint" Jesus' body for proper burial
4. discuss how to roll the stone away from the entrance

The women ask rhetorically how the closed tomb will be reopened (16:3); the reader wonders the same about the story itself. They discover that the seal to the "closure" has been removed (we are not told how); this ignites the reader's hope that there is life yet in the narrative.

The women "go into" the tomb, defying the "closure," and there meet not Jesus but a "young man" (16:5, *neaniskon*). At this point Mark's narrative symbolics begin to proliferate. First, the *neaniskos* is "sitting at the right." This is the position for which the former inner circle of male disciples competed (10:37), which the Psalmist attributed to Messiah (12:36) and Jesus to the Human One (14:62), and which was attributed to the bandits (15:27). It is the symbol of the true power of solidarity. Secondly, he is "wrapped in a white robe." The first *neaniskos* was similarly "wrapped" (*peribeblēmenos*) in a linen cloth (14:51)—which cloth cloaked Jesus in the tomb, the Jesus who is no longer in the tomb! But this *neaniskos* is now wrapped in a white (*leukēn*) robe, the same color as Jesus' garments in his transfiguration (9:3; see above, 8,E, i), and the identical phrase used to describe the apparel of the martyrs of Revelation 7:9, 13. Finally, the women are "deeply troubled" (16:6, *exethambēthēsan*), a verb that appears only twice elsewhere in Mark. In 9:15 it described the reaction of the crowd upon beholding Jesus *after* his transfiguration and public teaching of the way of the cross; in 14:33 it describes Jesus' struggle to come to terms with his own execution. Each of these apocalyptic symbolics compels us to conclude that the women realize they are in the presence of a "glorified" martyr figure.[1]

Mark now begins his reversal of the narrative inertia of the story. The women are reproved by the young man, who knows they "seek" (*zēteite*) Jesus. Throughout the story (1:24; 10:47; 14:67) he was "sought" by those who in the end betrayed him: the crowds (1:37), his own family and community (3:32; 14:11), and of course the authorities (11:18; 12:12; 14:1). But Jesus is no longer just "the Nazarene," or even the "beloved son"; the young man identifies him as "the crucified"—*this* is the proper confession of the "transformed disciple." Finally, this Jesus is *not* where Joseph laid him: the authorities have *not* had the last word after all! Jesus is "risen" (*ēgerthē*, 16:6), a word that recalls earlier healing episodes (*egeirein*, six times in healings).

ii. The Third Call to Discipleship: The Story Begins Again

The reversals continue in the young man's instructions. He commands the women to "get up and tell his disciples *and Peter* that he is going before you to Galilee; there you will see him, just as he told you" (16:7). Fuller suggests that this is an allusion to the "apostolic resurrection tradition" reproduced in 1 Corinthians 15:5 ("he appeared to Cephas, then to the twelve"). Such a historicist view misses the narrative function of the message as a reopening of the "closed" discipleship story. The community "destructed" in two stages: the flight of the disciples, then Peter's denial. So now Mark reconstructs it in two stages: tell the disciples, and Peter. With the reinstated community comes the reinstated journey of following: he is going before you. A fulfillment of Jesus' prophecy in 14:28, this new journey reverses the direction of the narrative. As they followed him "up to Jerusalem" (10:32), they must follow him "back to Galilee."

There, they "will see him." As commentators such as Lohmeyer, Lightfoot, and Marxsen long ago pointed out, this future verbal form (*opsesthe*) appears in only two other places: Jesus' portents of the advent of the Human One (13:26; 14:62). Commentators assumed therefore that Mark was indicating Galilee as the site of the Parousia of the Human One (Marxsen, 1969:75ff., 111ff.). Others (e.g., Taylor and Fuller) argued that the reference was to the resurrection appearances. But the advent of the Human One has already occurred at the cross, and Mark does not narrate the appearance of the risen Christ. I would contend that Mark is not pointing "beyond" his narrative world at all. This "future" point of reference is the same as the "past" one: Galilee. And where is that? It is where "the disciples and Peter" were first called, named, sent on mission, and taught by Jesus. In other words, the disciple/reader is being told that that narrative, which appeared to have ended, is beginning again. The story is circular!

The full revelation of the Human One has resulted in neither triumphal victory for the community (as the disciples had hoped), nor the restored Davidic kingdom (as the rebels had hoped), nor tragic failure and defeat (as the reader had feared). It has resulted in nothing more and nothing less than the regeneration of the messianic mission. If we have eyes to "see" the advent of the Human One we will be able to "see" Jesus still going before us. The "invitation" by Jesus, via the young man, to follow him to Galilee, is the third and last call to discipleship. He evokes both hope and terror. Hope, in that he who once joined in the naked shame of abandonment (14:51f.) now stands in new attire; terror, in that his new clothes are that of a martyr figure.

Is the disciple/reader also willing to undergo such a transformation? Here both the realism and genius of Mark are fully revealed, for the final narrative signal is fraught with ambiguity. As quickly as they had "entered" the tomb, the women exit, fleeing (*ephugon*). They are traumatized (*tromos*) and "ecstatic" (*ekstasis*); as befits an encounter with that which was thought dead, cf. 5:42). Then, abruptly, Mark terminates the narrative with the report that out of fear the women "said nothing to anyone" (16:8). If this scene is meant to recall a kind of "healing" (the command "arise" to the women was Jesus' word of healing, *hupagein*; 1:44; 2:11; 5:19, 34; 7:29; 10:52), then the discourse has been reversed. Whereas before the subjects had been commanded to silence but spoke nonetheless (1:44f.; 7:36), here the women are commanded to speak but remain silent! We suddenly freeze in our readerly tracks. After the promise of a new beginning, is this the final betrayal?

13E. "WHAT IS THE MEANING OF RESURRECTION"? (16:8)

i. Silence and Fear: How Will We Respond?

This sudden ending to Mark has spawned much consternation. Indeed, many (including Taylor) have hypothesized that the true ending was lost (the theories are summarized by Fuller, 1971:64f.). Such speculation can now be considered obsolete, along with the grammatico-literary objection that a book could not end in a *gar* clause. Bilezikian points out, for example, that it was not unknown for tragedies in antiquity to conclude upon a note of departure:

> Even on a hasty exit of the kind described in the last verse of the Gospel. A stage suddenly left vacant by the sometimes precipitate dismissal of the characters seems to have been an acceptable convention for ending tragedies. . . . If Mark was inspired by tragedy in structuring the Gospel, the dramatic effectiveness of graphic action in the form of rapid departure to bring a composition to an expressive end could hardly have escaped his notice [1977:135f.].

Petersen therefore is correct in asserting that problems with 16:8 cannot be attributed to the author but arise as a "result of readerly responses to that literary ending" (1980b:152).

But how does the author wish us to respond? Petersen has provided a useful analysis of the "narrative closure" problem posed by such an ending:

> The juxtaposition of the expectation introduced in 16:7 with the terminal frustration of it in 16:8 requires the reader to review what he has read in order to comprehend this apparent incongruity and its meaning for the narrator's message. . . . The end of a text is not the end of the work when the narrator leaves unfinished business for the reader to complete, thoughtfully and imaginatively. . . . The narrator creates an expectation and then cancels it, leading the reader to wonder why he raised the expectation in the first place. . . . For this reason the reader is forced to follow one or both of two lines of reflective inquiry—either to view everything before 16:8 in light of it or to view 16:8 in light of everything before it [1980:153f.].

Petersen refers to the first option as the "literal," and the second as the "ironic," reading of the text.

T. Weeden (1971) represents the former approach, claiming that since the women did not tell anyone (ever) about the risen Jesus and the rendezvous in Galilee, we cannot presume that the story did indeed begin again. Although this may fit with the unreliability of the disciples as Mark has portrayed them, N. Petersen points to its "contagious effect" that "contaminates the reliability of both Jesus and the narrator," until by a "domino effect" the entire preceding narrative is robbed of credibility (1980:161). In this case, the triumph of what I have called the "betrayal" narrative is indeed complete, such that finally even the reader is betrayed. The story is thus a bitter and even cynical tragedy—hardly "good news"!

Petersen rejects such a reading for the second alternative—namely, that Mark "does not mean what he says":

> He ceases his narration in the middle of an off-stage action and before another one which will be imaginatively on-stage. Mark 16:6–7 thus directs the reader's imagination to provide the proper closure to the narrator's story by supplying the satisfaction of the expectation generated in the prediction of a meeting between Jesus and the eleven in Galilee. Literarily, because the narrator knows about this meeting—*he* predicted it through the mouths of his actors—*he* could have described its consequences. But the irony of 16:8 . . . constitutes an artful substitute for the obvious [1980b:163].

Petersen's insights are valuable, but I believe Mark is doing more than inviting the reader to finish the last stroke of the painting; the openness/

ambiguity of 16:8 cannot be resolved "aesthetically," but only by practice.

We should not be surprised that the women are overcome with "fear." The disciples have in fact been described as "fearful" (*phobeisthai*) at several important "passages" in their journey with Jesus: both stormy boat crossings (4:41; 6:50), his transfiguration (9:6), the portents of his execution (9:32), and the journey up to Jerusalem (10:32). And does not this closing scene represent the most difficult passage of all? For in it the martyr-figure beckons the disciple to take up the journey afresh, to return to the beginning of the story for a new reading-enactment. The young man's invitation *ought* to provoke trepidation in us, if we take it seriously. As Bonhoeffer paraphrased Mark 8:34 in *Cost of Discipleship* (1953), "When Christ calls a person, He bids them to come and die."

The second epilogue, like the first (8:21), ends with a challenge to the reader in the form of an unresolved question. Will we "flee" or will we "follow"? This cannot be resolved in the narrative moment, only in the historical moment of the reader. Whether or not we actually "see" Jesus again depends upon whether the disciple/readers renew their commitment to the journey. It is at this point that we should recall the mysterious words of 9:10: "And they held fast to his word, but discussed among themselves 'What is the meaning of resurrection from the dead?' " Here at the end of the story we find ourselves in exactly the same position. We do not entirely understand what "resurrection" means, but if we have understood the story, we should be "holding fast" to what we *do* know: that Jesus still goes before us, summoning us to the way of the cross. And that is the hardest ending of all: not tragedy, not victory, but an unending challenge to follow anew. Because that means we must respond.

ii. The Apocryphal Endings: A Reflection on "Imperial Rewrites"

There have been, from the earliest days of the church, many who could not abide Mark's story of Jesus. There are to be sure many disturbing things about it. Its singularly unromantic portrait of the first apostles. Its demanding, raw edge. But above all, what sticks in our throats, what we find unacceptable, is the fact that Mark does not leave us with a happy ending. Two attempts to append to the Gospel a more palatable ending occur in the manuscript tradition; both are attached in the end notes of most RSV versions. I do not deem them worthy of exegesis (for that, see Taylor, 1963:610ff.). It is important, however, to reflect upon them as the first of a long theological tradition, which continues today, to betray the gospel by "rewriting" it.

The pseudepigraphy of the longer endings is revealed in their bald presumption to "rescue" Mark from his own deepest narrative and ideological commitments. The "dilemma" of the ending is precisely what Mark refuses to resolve for us; he *means* to leave us to wrestle with whether or not the women at the tomb (that is to say, we ourselves) overcame their fear in order to proclaim the new beginning in Galilee (16:8). To provide a "neat closure" to the narrative would allow the reader to finally remain passive; the story would be self-contained, in no need of a readerly response. As it stands, the discipleship narrative can truly resume only if the reader takes up the practice of the messianic vocation, which response is made possible by the fact that Jesus continues to "go before us." By such a "conditional ending," Mark ensures that the story can make no final sense to the "theological" reading strategy, in its search for doctrinal unity or abstract meaning, or to the "academic" reading strategy, which refuses commitment (see above, 1, B, i).

The longer endings, on the other hand, represent the work of those who cannot see the meaning of 16:8 as an invitation to which to respond, but only as a scandal that must properly be resolved. Instead of disturbing questions that reflect the human struggle and ambiguity of practice, we have pat answers. I began this commentary with a reminder about the "vulnerability" of texts (1, A, i); here we see power of interpretation as theft rather than restoration of meaning.

We might, for the sake of argument, even refer to these longer endings as "imperial rewritings" of Mark, which symbolize our unending efforts to domesticate the Gospel. Life in the imperial sphere depends upon triumphal narrative: the eleventh-hour Hollywood rescues, the arrival of the cavalry, the "happily ever after." Such endings allow us to avoid confronting ourselves, our mistakes, our frailty. Why else would the story of the Vietnam war need a heavily cosmetic face-lift before appearing in high-school history texts?

The so-called shorter ending salvages a "happy ending" by reporting unequivocally that Peter was restored as head of the community, that Jesus met the community again, and that he dispatched it upon the universal apostolic mission. What a "neat" closure: male dominance and triumphal aspirations are restored. But it is the "longer ending" that is the boldest imperial rewrite, one whose aim is far more than just an insertion of themes obtained from the other evangelists' resurrection accounts (endings, I might add, that differ fundamentally from Mark but have an integrity of their own when understood in their own narrative and ideological contexts). It represents three different attempts to subvert the ideology of "radical discipleship" ("orthopraxy," as the liberation theologians call it) with the ideology of "orthodoxy" and hegemonic Christianity.

The first betrayal lies in the concern of this apocryphal ending to suppress the central contradiction of Mark's story: the genuine struggle of the disciples to "believe." Thus "unbelief," a notion that appears only three times in the whole of Mark (6:6; 9:19, 24) is sharply upbraided no less than three times in the eleven verses of the longer ending (16:11, 14, 16). To be sure, in Mark, Jesus struggles against the "unbelief" of the world (6:6; 9:19). Yet Mark is profoundly sympathetic with how difficult it is for the human heart to break away from the old order when presented with the new. Thus the true "confession" of his Gospel is a "dialectical" one: "I believe; help me in my unbelief!" (9:24). This is the very point of his failure-riddled portrait of the disciples. Not so with the imperial rewrite. The one who "believes" (and is baptized!) will be saved, the one who "unbelieves" (the verb *apistein* does not appear in Mark, only the nominal and adjectival forms) will be condemned (16:14). This ideology not only sharply contradicts Mark's insistence that "they who are not against us are for us" (9:40), but finds historical expression in the redivision of humanity into "Christendom" and paganism. Needless to say, the imperial church's appropriation of "judgment" has turned the cross into a sword, the profoundest historical betrayal of the Gospel.

The second betrayal is its restoration of thaumaturgy (miracle-working) as the guarantee of belief: "These signs will accompany those who believe" (16:17). Such "theological proof" is of course exactly what Mark's Jesus repudiates in his debate with the Pharisees in 8:11f. (above, 7, D, i). It is easy to criticize the many efforts at "Christian magic" inspired by this text, right down to present-day snake handling and faith healing. But the betrayal lies not there but in the more widely accepted assumption that to be a Christian means to demonstrate visible power. This notion has been virtually essential to the success of the gospel in North America, from schools of "positive thinking" and "success" to the utter denial that the vocation of "chosen peoplehood" might mean servanthood and rejection rather than empire. The only "sign" in Mark is the suffering Human One; nothing could be further from the quest after "visible signs of power" that dominates imperial Christianity.

Finally, the third betrayal is the removal of Jesus from "earth" to "heaven" (16:19). Even Luke, who also narrates an ascension, is far more restrained (Lk 24:50; Acts 1:6-11). Mark had no intention of shifting the geography of presence; Jesus was left going before the disciples to Galilee, the site of discipleship practice (16:7). Perhaps Mark somehow anticipated the historical mayhem that would result from Christ as a heavenly monarch (the "gold-crowned Jesus") lording over an imperial church. The history of much of Western christology has consisted of rewrites similar to this one; we are still not prepared to accept the crucified Jesus, whose presence we discover not by "standing gazing up into heaven" (Acts 1:11) but by discipleship practice in the world.

The power of Mark's Gospel ultimately lies not in what it tells the disciples/readers, but what it asks of them. The discipleship narrative commences with an invitation: "Follow me" (1:17). In the "first" epilogue, Mark closes the first half of his story by interrogating us whether we have grasped the meaning of Jesus' symbolic action: "Do you not yet understand?" (8:21). Dead in its center, Mark dares to turn the great self-revelatory tradition of Yahweh from a declaration—"I am" (Ex 3:14)—into a question: "Who am I?" (Mk 8:29). And at its end, it invites us to once again follow: "He is going before you to Galilee" (16:7).

The Jesus of Mark provides very few answers, especially if we are asking the wrong questions. But as questioner himself, he compels us to reveal where we stand. If we wish to respond, he offers us only a cross and companionship on the way. If we cannot respond, neither can he. In this case, the story as a whole—just like the episode with the chief priests (11:33)—truly ends in a draw of noncommitment.

Much critical ink has been spilled by Christian apologists who have sought to defend the Christian doctrine of the resurrection of Jesus against its critics. Doubtless, such apologetic concern was also the desire of those who provided Mark with a more "orthodox" ending. Of course, nothing can stop "believers" from rewriting the story, betraying it by dulling its questions. Similarly, no one can convince "nonbelievers" of the resurrection as an abstract proposition. Mark, at least, offers no "proof"; did Jesus in fact appear to the disciples? We are not told. For Mark, the resurrection is not an answer, but the final question. There is only one genuine "witness" to the risen Jesus: to follow in discipleship. Only in this way will the truth of the resurrection be preserved.

13F. LOSING LIFE TO SAVE IT:
MARK'S SOCIO-LITERARY STRATEGY THROUGH 16:8

i. Discourse

There are four discursive patterns in Mark's narrative strategy that I want to examine here in terms of social function. The first narrates the steady erosion of solidarity between Jesus and his own community. There is a dialectical tension between intimacy and betrayal in the last days. A shared meal in which Jesus bids his followers to stand in solidarity with his life and death (14:22–25) is bracketed by predictions of their desertion (14:18–21, 27–31). Jesus calls his disciples to "watch and pray" with him in his moment of trepidation; but they fall asleep (14:32–42). And Judas betrays Jesus with a kiss, as the disciples flee (14:43–52).

If we look closely at this discourse, we see community solidarity unraveling; each member becomes concerned only for himself, which makes their collective desertion inevitable:

14:18	one of you will betray me
14:19	one by one they each asked: "Is it I?"
14:20	it is one of the twelve
14:27	you will *all* fall away
14:29	even if *all* fall away, not I
14:30	you will deny me three times
14:31a	I will never deny you
14:31b	*all* said the same

We should also note in this discourse the escalation from "betrayal" (*paradidōmi*) to "falling away" (*skandalizō*) to "denial" (*aparneomai*), each of which relates distinctively to the wider narrative of Mark. "Betrayal" or ("handing over") refers to the political fate of John (1:14), Jesus (thirteen times), and those who carry on the mission (13:9–12). "Falling away," the result of the threat of persecution, was foreseen in the sower parable (4:17), and sternly warned against in the discipleship catechism (9:42–47). The nadir is reached with "denial" of the Human One in the attempt to save one's life; for this was the central warning in the second call to discipleship (8:34). The social function of this discourse reminds the community of its own humanity and failures, thus guarding against presumption, and it warns against the ever-present temptation to apostasy.

The second discursive pattern is Mark's use of triads to refer to the cross event. Aside from Jesus' three predictions of his death in the "discipleship catechism" (8:31f.; 9:31f.; 10:33f.), we see in the execution narrative itself three citations of Psalm 22 and three "watches" of the period of Jesus' dying (third, sixth, ninth hours). In addition, I have uncovered several overarching triadic patterns in the story, all of which refer to the cross: three "calls to discipleship," three "apocalyptic moments," and three predictions of the "advent of the Human One." This is the strategy of recapitulation, in which Mark attempts to repeat over and over again his difficult thesis that the *crucified* Human One is the fulfillment, rather than negation, of the vocation of messianic kingship.

We see this discourse again in the three predictions of the advent of the Human One. Each comes in the context of the political struggle over Jesus' identity, as shown here:

I	II	III
Who do you say I am? (*tina me legete einai*), 8:29a	many will come saying "I am" (*legontes hoti egō eimi*), 13:6	I am (*egō eimi*), 14:62a
Peter . . . said to him You are Messiah, 8:29b	if anyone says . . . Look! Here is Messiah, 13:21	high priest . . . said Are you Messiah?, 14:61
Human One . . . when he comes in the glory of the Father with the holy angels . . . some of you will live to see . . . coming in power, 8:38f.	Then they will see Human One coming on the clouds with great power and glory and . . . the angels . . . . . . of heaven, 13:26f.	You will all see the Human One seated at the right hand of power and coming with the clouds of heaven, 14:62b

These are the three major confrontations over the meaning of messianic kingship in the Gospel, and each time the discourse replaces "Messiah" with "Human One." This new definition of Messiah is resisted by the disciples (I), ridiculed by the Jewish authorities (III), and rejected out of hand by the rebel recruiters, who assert an eschatological triumphalism in their understanding of kingship (II).

It is the radical novelty of Jesus' political understanding of the messianic vocation, so divergent from the prevailing views, that accounts for the need for

Mark's discourse of recapitulation. The triad also functions to make a kind of "christological equation": Jesus = Son of God = Messiah = Human One. When this unity has been broken, by the bifurcation of Jesus' character into two (earthly Jesus and risen Christ) or even three (first coming, resurrection, and parousia), the results have been disastrous for both christology and ethics. There is for Mark only one Jesus, and he is still on the road calling us to discipleship.

A third discursive characteristic is the focus in this last section of the Gospel upon Jesus' body, beginning with an anointing (14:8) and ending with the body buried (15:45f.). In between lie several key elements. In the eucharistic moment Jesus offers his body—that is to say, his practice of justice and acceptance of death—as a new symbolic center, in place of the temple cult, which the Passover meal was used to legitimate (see above, 12,B,iii). During his torture, the body that gave life to others is rendered powerless and abused. And at the climax of the section, Jesus' dead body on the cross again is juxtaposed against the rent sanctuary curtain (15:37f.). In the aftermath Jesus' body "lingers" in the narrative, presumably out of sight in the tomb, but then is suddenly absent (16:6).

What is the social function of this "bodily discourse"? I believe Belo is essentially correct in arguing that on the one hand the temple as the center of the Jewish symbolic order is replaced by Jesus' body; and that on the other, Jesus' body, which becomes absent at his death, is replaced by discipleship practice (1981:211). In other words, the old cult is not replaced with a new cult, but with practice alone. The focus upon the body confirms Mark's commitment to a discourse firmly fixed upon the historical world. This is further articulated through the contrariety between the third apocalyptic moment and the first two. The baptism and transfiguration alone in the Gospel feature a discourse of "heaven to earth." In the third and final moment all the celestial coordinates fall silent, replaced by terrestrial counterparts. There is no voice from the clouds, only Jesus' voice protesting his abandonment by God; it is not the heavens that are rent (*schizō*), but the veil of the earthly sanctuary; Jesus is not with Moses and Elijah, but between two bandits; it is not the heavenly voice that attests to Jesus as "Son of God," but an enemy, the centurion. When the story is regenerated, it is done so in bodily form: he is risen. The "resurrection" motif is situated not in heaven but in Galilee, the site of earthly practice.

Finally, we should note again the circular discursive pattern that reaches its completion. The story opened with a "voice" crying in the wilderness (1:2), extolling a stronger one who later promised to bind the strong man. It threatened to close when this stronger one was himself bound and led away, whose "voice" expired on the cross (15:37). However, with the announcement of the young man at the tomb again, the story begins again in Galilee. But what guarantee do we have that *anyone* will obey this new command to follow the way of the cross? The "voices" of both John and Jesus both assure us that some will:

1. he will baptize you with the Holy Spirit (1:8).
2. with the baptism with which I am baptized, you will be baptized (10:39).

These are reliable voices in the narrative. Jesus confidently envisions the day when the vocation of biblical radicalism, which has passed from the prophets to John, and from John to Jesus, will pass to the disciples. They too will be dragged before kings and governors; the gospel *will* be preached to the whole world (13:9f.). Jesus' cross has overthrown the powers, and the new beginning to be found in Galilee is truly a new creation.

ii. Signification

What do we learn of Mark's community practice? I wish to return to the implications of the role given to the women in this section, which begins and ends with them at the center of the narrative. If the portrait of the inner discipleship circle was negative in the nonviolence catechism (see above, 9,E,ii), here the contrast between the abandonment of the men and the fidelity of the women is surely polemical. Far from being "invisible" in Mark, as asserted by M. Munro (1982), women emerge as the true disciples. In this way Mark attempted to legitimate the leadership role of women in the new community. There is a very provocative affinity between women and angels in Mark. Consider:

1. the servant role assumed by women toward Jesus (1:31; 15:41) was only elsewhere ascribed to angels (1:13);
2. the eschatological life of women is compared to that of the angels (12:25);
3. Jesus said that "angels" would accompany the advent of the Human One (8:38)—women are present at the cross;
4. Jesus spoke of angels sent by the Human One to gather the elect (cf. 13:27)—the "young man" at the tomb sends the women to gather the other disciples (16:6f.).

Male scholars have yet to comment on this phenomenon in Mark. Perhaps too much can be made of it; after all, at the very end the women too appear to fail in their mission; they too are human. But I believe it is not too much to speculate that here Mark is engaging in a war of myths with patriarchy, structures of male domination and presumption in both the dominant order *and* within his own community.

The passion narrative says a great deal about Mark's political ideology. The story of the last days in Jerusalem suggests that the community knows something about living an underground life; it is likely that "safehouses" and clandestine movement was very much a part of the Christian movement at this time. No doubt the same can be said about the reality of infiltration (the Judas story) by the authorities into the community's life, one that threatens not only its integrity but its intimacy as well. The trial and execution narrative, meanwhile, clearly articulates an awareness of the political triangle between the Jewish elite, the Roman rulers, and the rebels. I have pointed out (above, 12,D) the fact that Mark constructs the narrative of Jesus' trial and execution in a way to emphasize the cooperation of the two colonial authorities. Both Jew and Roman have trials, "consultations," torture sessions, mockeries, and post-death affirmations of triumph. Inherent in this discourse is Mark's clear repudiation of the colonial condominium.

When it comes to the forces of the Jewish rebellion, however, Mark is much more subtle and nuanced. What is the social function of the fact that Jesus is exchanged for a Sicarius? As the political strategy of terrorism comes face to face with that of revolutionary nonviolence in Pilate's courtroom, Mark poses some sharp questions to Jewish rebels. What does the procurator know that they have missed, as he acknowledges Barabbas as the "lesser" threat, and affirms Jesus as "king of the Jews"? And how politically reliable are the Jerusalem masses, who in this episode demonstrate their vulnerability to manipulation by the forces of reaction? One might wonder whether the fickle crowds here are not meant to suggest a criticism of the civil warring and political upheaval that characterized the city under the provisional government. In any case, in Mark's view, by supporting the chief priests' lobbying for Barabbas, the crowds have unwittingly become like their scribal overlords, choosing death (a murderer) over life (a healer, cf. 3:4). Though Jesus is "for" the crowds throughout the Gospel, in the end they are not "for" him; this may indicate Mark's suspicion of the true intentions of mass movements.

And what of Jesus' arrest and crucifixion as a social bandit? Mark may criticize the strategy of the rebels as counterrevolutionary, but he does not shy from the fact, no doubt common to his experience, that subversive Christians will be "taken for" armed rebels. Mark is not aloof from the political realities of revolutionary Palestine, nor is he advocating a so-called third way of noninvolvement. The trial and execution narrative make it clear that he is *not* equally distanced from all factions. On the one hand, his discourse of parallelism articulates an unrelenting criticism of Rome and the Jewish establishment. On the other, not only do the rebels stand outside this indictment, but indeed they appear with Jesus as fellow prisoners, companions in the gallows. Mark was not politically nonpartisan; nonaligned, but by no means neutral.

The "implied resurrection" at the end of Mark functions to legitimate the ongoing messianic practice of the community. At the same time, because it demands a readerly resolution, it subverts the possibility of a glorified christology, which might render the community passive. The empty tomb means the story of biblical radicalism can continue in the living and dying of disciples in all ages (below, Afterword, A). The resurrection represents the apocalyptic hope that the blood of the martyrs will be vindicated and the pain of the world healed, and confirms the call to historical insomnia. This hope is articulated in the following lines taken from a poem by Guatemalan exile Julia Esquivel entitled "They Have Threatened Us with Resurrection":

> There is something here within us
> which doesn't let us sleep, which doesn't let us rest,
> which doesn't stop pounding deep inside,
> it is the silent, warm weeping
> of Indian women without their husbands,

it is the sad gaze of the children
fixed there beyond memory,
in the very pupil of our eyes
which during sleep, though closed, keep watch
with each contraction of the heart
in every awakening. . . .

What keeps us from sleeping
is that they have threatened us with resurrection!
Because at each nightfall,
though exhausted from the endless inventory
of killings since 1954,
yet we continue to love life,
and do not accept their death!

. . . Because in this marathon of Hope,
there are always others to relieve us
in bearing the courage necessary
to arrive at the goal which lies beyond death. . . .

Accompany us then on this vigil
and you will know what it is to dream!
You will then know how marvelous it is
to live threatened with resurrection!
To dream awake,
to keep watch asleep
to live while dying
and to already know oneself resurrected!
[1982:59ff.]

NOTE

1. Taylor argues that this term is found in intertestamental literature to describe angelophanies, but quickly retreats to saying that "Mark's description is imaginative" (1963:606f.). But *neaniskos* is dropped by all the other gospel writers in favor of the more conventional angelic vocabulary (see esp. Mt 28:2; Jn 20:12). Mark's choice of the term is all the more conspicuous, playing an important narrative role.

Part Four

Mark and Radical Discipleship

CHAPTER FOURTEEN

Summary: The Ideology and Social Strategy of Mark's Community

For you have made the city a heap
    the fortified city a ruin;
the palace of the insolent is no more,
    it will never be rebuilt.
Thus the mighty will honor you,
    ruthless nations will fear you.
For you are a refuge to the poor,
    to the needy in distress. . . .
On this mountain Yahweh will destroy the net that is cast over all peoples,
the veil that is spread over all nations. Yahweh will destroy death forever,
and will wipe away the tears from all the faces.
                                —Isaiah 25:2–4, 7f.

The present generation of North Americans has been weaned from some of their imperial illusions by apocalyptic images. Since Hiroshima, the dominant subliminal shadow over our lives has been that terrible icon of the nuclear age, the mushroom cloud. Despite severe repression, the nightmare has ruptured to the surface of our historical consciousness repeatedly, from the Cuban missile crisis to the Six-day war to the Persian Gulf war. But just as compelling have been other, less ultimate images of the "end of the world."

Take, for example, the spectacle associated with the fall of Saigon in 1975. Who can forget the newsreels of the frantic eleventh-hour evacuation on the rooftop of the U.S. embassy, even as Viet Cong tanks rolled into the city, with grim-faced Marines, diplomats and bureaucrats racing against time to pack up or destroy the apparatus of years of neocolonial and military administration? Their screaming, terrified South Vietnamese cohorts, begging to be spared a fate at the hands of the communists, desperately clinging to helicopter runners even as they wheeled away into the fire-darkened sky? And the ignominious finale to that tragicomical drama, as the multi-million-dollar choppers, having unloaded their refugee cargo onto U.S. aircraft carriers offshore, were pushed off the deck into the sea? Truly this was for the imperial mind the stuff of "Apocalypse Now."

But the dialectical nature of apocalyptic images is that they can in fact be "read" as either debacle or delivery—depending upon one's historical perspective and site. Hence the very same events and images that shocked patriotic North Americans, who were unaccustomed to defeat in the holy war against international communism, elated those who read them as the "liberation" of Saigon. Even as U.S. helicopter blades cut the waters of the South China sea and sank, Viet Cong regulars were parading through the city, hailed in almost messianic fashion. The long war was over! The strained and dour faces in Washington were contrasted by a celebration march in the streets of Berkeley. Whether apocalypse is perceived as the "end" or the "new beginning" of the world has everything to do with what side one is on in the war of myths.

Imagine the spectacle confronting the author of the Gospel of Mark in 69 C.E. What he saw could not have been further from the vision of the prophet Isaiah: instead of the destruction of the imperial "net over all peoples," he witnessed the pillaging and looting of Roman storm troopers as they marched south through Galilee, leaving in their wake the devastation of burned villages and fields—and a trail of crosses, upon which hanged captured Jewish rebels. Mark knew where the legions were headed: the city of David, the heart of the world, Zion in which the hopes and dreams of his people lay. In the face of such an apocalyptic moment, with the world of Palestinian Judaism on the scales, it hardly seemed the time to write a story about a Jewish prophet who, decades earlier, had himself been hanged on a Roman cross. Or to call it "good news."

Mark saw his own historical situation clearly, knew its suffering, took his stand. To him the apocalyptic moment represented *both* liberation and debacle, beginning *and* end. But his understanding was radically different from that of the Roman collaborators or the Jewish rebels of his time. The year 69 C.E. was indeed one of difficult and costly choices—which is to say, it was *precisely* the right time to write his good news about Jesus of Nazareth.

14A. THE HISTORICAL SITUATION OF THE PRODUCTION OF MARK

The purpose of this chapter is to summarize the socio-literary evidence that has been yielded by my reading of the gospel text, and to organize it into a brief portrait of Mark's community. I begin with a reconsideration of the historical "moment" in which Mark wrote, and then return to the hypothesis articulated at the outset of this commentary (above, 2,F). There I postulated that the determinate social formation of Roman Palestine in Mark's era allows the possibility of a social group that was alienated from the dominant order, which advocated a radical alternative practice, and remained politically engaged yet nonaligned with the major socio-political groups. Before reconsidering this hypothesis, however, a word needs to be said about hermeneutical barriers to achieving an accurate and sympathetic portrait of Mark's community.

i. Apocalyptic Discourse and the Bias of Sect-Sociology

It has become a commonplace recently among biblical scholars to understand apocalyptic literature in terms of the conceptual frameworks established by the socio-anthropological study of "millennial" communities (see the work of Kee, 1977, and Gager, 1975). There is much to be said for this approach; for example, K. Burridge's *New Heaven, New Earth* concludes that such movements closely resemble what we have seen in Mark:

> [They] involve the adoption of new assumptions, a new redemptive process, a new politico-economic framework, a new mode of measuring [humanity], a new integrity, a new community. . . . A prophet is he or she who organizes the new assumptions and articulates them; who is listened to and found acceptable; whose revelation is accorded authority [1969:13f.].

Burridge, however, also warned against the tendency of modern interpreters to caricature these new assumptions, ideals, and redemptive processes as social fantasy: "Whether or not they are bizarre is entirely subjective" (ibid.:8).

Yet the prevailing attitude of historical sociology toward the social and ideological strategies of so-called sects, which dates back to Troeltsch's classic sociology of religion, continues to be pejorative. Similarly, in the biblical field, W. Beardslee wrote that scholars have been "able to clarify apocalyptic only by distancing themselves from its inner spirit" (1971:421). But such objectification, at least according to the model of the hermeneutic circle advocated in this book (above, 1,A), is itself the biggest barrier to a true political appreciation of the text.

There is a kind of circular logic to correlating sect-sociology and the study of biblical apocalyptic. For example, I have shown that late Jewish prophecy ("proto-apocalyptic") figures decisively in Markan intertextuality. But listen to how Hebrew Bible scholar P. Hanson characterizes these traditions:

> The sociological setting of Daniel . . . like the communities behind Third Isaiah, the Isaiah Apocalypse, and Second Zechariah [is] a visionary minority living under oppression in a world seemingly fallen into the hands of enemies of Yahweh, convincing them that fulfillment of Yahweh's promises could no longer be anticipated within the existing order. Clinging to their vision, the community of Daniel passively awaits Yahweh's intervention. . . . The dialectic [between vision and reality] has dissolved. . . . Connections with politico-historical realities have been lost: neither the human community, nor any other human agent, takes part in the conflict which would be won "by no human hand" (Dn 8:25); nor does the kingdom given to the saints betray any connections with the mundane; they are saved by being lifted out of this order into the cosmic sphere of the vision [1971:473,476].

This illustrates the way in which apocalyptic symbolics are dismissed by a mainline liberal scholar as "pessimistic" and escapist. So caricatured, it is no wonder that apocalyptic seems uninteresting to both Marxist and liberal-reformist interpreters.

This bias is inevitably carried over into the study of Mark. So Kee, who rightly defends the Danielic character of Mark, concludes: "In keeping with the passivist tradition of the Hasidim, Mark portrays Jesus as refusing to take any initiative against the political authority" (1977:146). The same attitude characterizes J. Wilde's more detailed study of Mark as a millennial community. Wilde equates the Gospel's "nonaligned" discourse with a stance entailing socio-political ambivalence. Drawing upon the (notoriously slippery) method of "ideal typologizing," Wilde argues that Mark articulates the "revolutionist" type as defined in B. Wilson's influential sect-sociology:

> [It] looks for the destruction and re-creation (transformation) of the basically alien social world by supernatural agency (not human) on a cosmic level (not local or individual) very soon (not yet present); and therefore sees men (by themselves) as basically powerless and weak in the face of the oppression of the present world, but finds access to power and hope solely in the salvation brought by divine agency in the approaching cataclysm [1974:61f.].

Admitting that this "pure" type occurs rarely because it is so absolutist, Wilde nevertheless insists that it is the lens through which Markan radicalism should be interpreted.

It is not hard to see in Wilde's sociological caricature the mirror image of Hanson's theological one. Moreover, we can see in it an updated version of Albert Schweitzer's old "thoroughgoing eschatology" thesis, which held that because Jesus expected the literal and immediate end of the world, he abdicated all political and historical responsibilities, offering at best an impractical "interim ethic." In my view, such conceptual straitjackets are no closer to the truth of apocalyptic symbolics than the crude literalizing of a Hal Lindsey or the existentialist psychologizing of a Thomas Altizer (1971). Sectarian stereotypes fail utterly to explain the militance of Mark's Jesus, his persistent political engagement with—and death at the hands of—the powers. They do not begin to do justice to the activist ideology of discipleship that lies at the heart of the story. Mark looks for the end of the old world and the inauguration of the new, but it is discipleship—which he equates with a specific social practice and costly political engagement—that will inaugurate this transformation.

Mark could not have been ideologically further from groups such as the Essenes, who, as we *know* from historical records, pursued a social strategy of withdrawal in order to wait upon Yahweh's intervention. My reading has shown that Mark's Jesus is anything but "passive" toward political authority, his ideology anything but socially introverted. The problem with sect-sociology and the interpretation of apocalyptic literature is therefore hermeneutic: modern rationalists are unable to understand narrative symbolics in socio-political terms. Fortunately, there is a growing minority of scholars who have begun to interpret the documents of biblical apocalyptic, such as Daniel and Revelation, as political manifestoes of nonviolent movements of resistance to tyranny (J. Collins, 1977; A. Y. Collins, 1977). My commentary demonstrates that the same must be said of Mark.

ii. Is Mark an Apologia for the Destruction of the Temple?

In order to test my hypothesis about the Gospel as a document of "non-aligned radicalism" we must first return to the question of provenance. In chapter 2, I proposed that Mark was written in Galilee during the last years of the Jewish revolt. Let me address the question of time first. Brandon (1967) and Kelber (1973), despite their entirely different approach and conclusions regarding Mark, agree on one thing: the literary novelty of Mark could be attributed only to the world-shattering destruction of the temple by the Romans in 70 C.E. Yet Kelber asks himself:

> But is the gospel nothing but a retrospective legitimization of a new Christian situation in the wake of the Roman victory? Does Mark merely sanction the facts after the Fall? [But] the gospel is not an exercise in confirming the obvious, but a creative reconsideration on the past so as to be of immediate service to the present of Mark [1973:131].

Kelber has put his finger on one of the central problems of a post-70 dating. Simply put: If the destruction of the temple state was a *fait accompli,* why did Mark need to launch his polemic against it?

The answer usually given, as Kelber notes, is that Mark was providing a theological justification of its demise. It is argued that Mark was using *ex eventu* (after the fact) prophecy in Jesus' prediction of the temple's destruction in 13:2 to "sanction" this world-shaking debacle. Now Mark is quite capable of making use of *ex eventu* prophecy, for it was a common apocalyptic literary device. But if this is the case with 13:2, why does Mark not use a more accurate description of events, as does Luke (see Reicke, 1972)? J. Collins's assessment of Daniel's use of *ex eventu* historical review is relevant here. He points out that the events recorded in Daniel 11:1–39 are verifiable based upon a history of the Hellenistic wars—that is, up until 11:40ff., at which point Daniel turns to the career of his own contemporary, Antiochus Epiphanes:

> We can tell at what point the book of Daniel was written, since beyond a certain point the "predictions" are no longer fulfilled. . . . Antiochus, like Gog, is a king from the north, who will invade the land of Israel and fall there. This is not how Antiochus met his death, so we know that this prophecy was composed before he actually died late in 164 B.C.E. [J. Collins, 1981:105,107].

In other words, *ex eventu* prophecy freely mixes historical reviews, contemporaneous commentary, and anticipation of imminent events. If we then apply the same logic to Mark, it follows that Jesus' "prediction" that the temple will be razed "stone by stone" must have been written before the destruction of the temple—by fire.

It is true that Mark wishes to assure Christians that a symbolic life can and must be reconstructed apart from the temple-based order (above 10, C, iv; below, E,ii). But it does not necessarily follow that he could only have advocated this after the temple was already destroyed. In fact his narrative indicates the opposite. The disciples' question in 13:1 suggests that the temple was very much a living and imposing edifice. This is further confirmed by Mark's symbolic discourse of "destruction," specifically the correlation between 11:23 and 5:13. The "legion" that "no one had the strength to bind" (5:3f.) is symbolically driven out of Palestine "into the sea" (5:9–13); similarly, after "exorcising" the commercial interests in the temple, Jesus promises that only through the power of faith can the "mountain" be overcome and ordered "into the sea" (11:23). The historical power represented by Roman legions and the temple mount was, in both cases, intact; that is precisely what makes the two "exorcisms" so remarkable as an anticipation of the "impossible," provoking amazement (5:15–20; 11:24).

Mark's criticism of the temple is in fact not based upon "theological" considerations, but rather the exploitive political economy of the temple-based redistributive system (above, 10,C,F). This would hardly have been necessary once this system was overturned by the Romans. The same can be said of Mark's vigorous attacks upon the scribal and clerical aristocracy, which rapidly disappeared after 70 C.E. (reflected in Matthew's redaction of Mark, which shifts the criticism to the Pharisees, who were the dominant post-70 social group). And, needless to say, Mark's criticism of the rebels (above, 11,C) would have been moot once the revolt had been crushed. Conversely, the first half of the second sermon (13:5–23) makes perfect sense when interpreted against the backdrop of the late war years, just before or during the siege of Jerusalem.

Many of those who argue that Mark was theologically sanctioning the fall of the temple further assume that this is part of an overall pro-Roman apologia (above, 12,D,i). This is not an implausible hypothesis; we know that some Jews did repudiate the nationalist revolt, and later justified the Roman victory. Moreover, we have an example of just such an ideological stance in the writings of Josephus. But the contrasts between Mark and Josephus are striking, all the more so given the fact that they had faced the same historical situation (Josephus was a rebel commander in Galilee before defecting to the Romans in the middle of the war). Mark may have shared Josephus's belief that the Jewish insurgency would sooner or later collapse in the face of overwhelming Roman military power, but that was the extent of their common ground. Josephus, as a Jewish aristocrat, was vociferous in his criticism of the rebels, and sympathetic to the clerical elite. Although Mark does not agree with the rebels, he nevertheless refuses to criticize them directly, whereas he is strident in his attack upon the Jewish ruling classes. Similarly, Josephus, though openly pro-Roman, bemoans the temple's destruction; Mark celebrates the apocalyptic demise of both temple and legion.

If Mark wished to portray himself, like Josephus, as pro-Roman, he could scarcely have done a poorer job of it. His use of the anti-Hellenistic motifs of apocalyptic narrative, his veiled repudiation of imperial power (above, 6,B; 10,D,iii; 11,C,iii), and his parody of the procurator Pilate (above, 12,D,F) could hardly have curried Roman favor. These aspects of his narrative strategy did suit a different purpose, however: the need for a coded discourse of resistance that could elude Roman censors and military intelligence. We must conclude that Mark criticized the temple and the clerical aristocracy precisely because they were still operative, and was circumspect in his attacks on Rome because he was in occupied territory. In other words, his struggle to overturn the dominant social order and its legitimating ideologies was a real battle in the war of myths, not a rhetorical "exercise in confirming the obvious."

iii. "Brother Will Deliver Up Brother": Mark and the War

Another objection to a postwar dating of the Gospel arises from a consideration of Mark's discourse on suffering and martyrdom. At the most obvious level, it would have made no sense for Mark to anchor his discipleship ideology in the call to "take up the cross" if he agreed with Josephus's antirebel, pro-Roman stance. This image makes perfect sense, however, if his community was in fact subject to persecution on grounds of subversion. As B. van Iersel has demonstrated on purely literary grounds, "the significance of the book is most pregnant in an actual situation of persecution, when the reader or listener may be arrested at any moment" (1980:15). Once the war was over, the crisis of temple-destruction may have continued to be a "theological" one, but it would not have been an existentially political one. During the war, on the other hand, a Christian community that refused to defect to the Romans but also refused to fight alongside the rebels would have been liable to persecution from both sides—which is precisely the situation the text reflects (above, 10,D,iv; 11,C).

There is evidence in the discourse of Mark that the pressure of this persecution had made deep inroads into his Galilean community. The longer the war dragged on, the more polarized the political environment would have become. The double pressure of the Roman reconquest of Galilee and aggressive rebel recruitment may well have driven the community underground. And, like any minority group experiencing persecution, Mark's community would surely have been wrestling with faltering solidarity within its ranks: the suspicion of informers, the inevitability that some would break under interrogation, outright defection, and worst of all, the betrayal of some members by others to the authorities.

Virtually from the outset of Mark's portrait of the discipleship community, these kinds of tensions find articulation. At the commissioning of the "confederacy," the shadow of the betrayer is present (3:19). In the catechism, the problem of apostasy is specifically addressed (above, 9,A,iv). The plot-theme of the disciples' "blindness" anticipates the defection (above, 12,C,iii). Indeed, the last days of Jesus are filled with undercover intrigue, and the community is riddled with self-doubt (above, 12,B). But nowhere is the pressure of the historical moment more poignantly reflected than in Jesus' second sermon:

> Brother will deliver brother to death, and the father his child, and children will rise against parents and have them put to death; and you will be hated by all for my name's sake [13:12f.].

Not only must disciples stand political trial; they must also face the bitter prospect of betrayal from within the "family"—meaning both kin (for we know the war did divide relatives) and community. The seriousness of this prospect is reflected in the fact that the threat of eschatological judgment appears in Mark only in reference to such betrayal (9:42; 14:21).

That Mark builds his Gospel as a whole around an essentially tragic narrative—the disciples' failure—is explicable in terms of the historical reality of a community under persecution. Yet though "betrayal" is not lightly viewed, there is an equally strong counter-discourse of "pardon." Even as the solidarity of the community unravels in the story, Jesus assures his solidarity (14:22ff.). Mark asserts that even in the "fire" of persecution and apostasy, the "salt" of reconciliation must prevail (9:49f.). And this can happen only when the practice of forgiveness (11:25) is at the center of the community's life. And as the end of the story makes clear, even the most egregious "denial" of Jesus, the most blatant defection from the way, cannot bring the discipleship adventure to an end. Because Jesus "goes before" us (16:7), a new start can always be made on the discipleship adventure.

In sum, then, it was the crisis of the Jewish temple state engendered by the revolt against Rome, and the persecution of Mark's community for its "non-aligned" stance, that was the immediate context of the production of the Gospel (this is also the conclusion of Kee, 1977:100f.). We have both prewar and postwar texts from groups that responded differently to the same historical situation. Josephus, as noted, wrote a historical account that justified his defection and narrated the war from the victors' perspective. Later rabbinic writings obliquely reflect the strategy of many Pharisees, who responded to the defeat by reconceiving Jewish identity and practice in a way that maintained Jewish distinctiveness without a nationalist element. Qumran produced texts of monastic withdrawal, though its members, in the final hour, may have gone to fight in the defense of the temple. The rebels, for their part, left only the "texts" of coins minted during the period of liberated Judea—and the haunting witness of the ruins at Masada. And perhaps just as significant a testimony is the mute voice of those who were simply victims of the war, never its subjects. For many the collapse of the revolt would have crushed any hopes of liberation or a better life, merely confirming their cynicism about history: "the powers always win in the end; it will never be otherwise." Such persons left no text, oral or written, because there was nothing new to say. Who knows how many poor peasants resigned themselves, yet again, to historical silence?

Mark, a follower of Jesus, struggling and suffering through the apocalyptic moment of the late war years, responded with a story about a Nazarene and his followers. It legitimated neither defection, nor withdrawal, nor reform-minded moderation, nor Maccabean triumphalism, nor despairing acceptance of a world dominated by the powers. It called for resistance to the rule of the "strong man," and the creation of a new world: a practice of radical discipleship. This story heralded a way through the wilderness—and the war. But this way was the way of the cross: to the Romans a symbol of imperial hegemony, to Mark the sign of the kingdom come.

iv. Was Mark's Community Based Near Capernaum?

The place, like the time, of Mark's production, is something a socio-literary analysis can establish only plausibly, not conclusively. Kee's summary of the case against Roman provenance (still the majority thesis) confirms what I have found in reading the text:

> The preservation in Mark of cultural and linguistic features of the Eastern Mediterranean rural village culture—features which Luke, in writing for a Gentile audience, eliminates or alters—speaks against Rome. Marxsen, following the lines of reasoning developed by Lohmeyer and Lightfoot, proposes Galilee. The archaeological evidence from excavations there in recent years confirms the wide use of Greek in public inscriptions, including synagogues, so that for Mark to have written a Christian document there in the 60s as Marxsen suggests is not inconceivable. And the accurate reflection of practices having to do with agriculture, housing, employment, and land-ownership and taxation, that are characteristic of the whole of Syria-Palestine in the period do indeed speak for that larger area as the place of origin [Kee, 1977:102].

The strong "narrative bias" in the gospel toward Galilee, as Lightfoot and Marxsen argued, further confirms this area as the location for Mark's community. Because of alleged geographical ambiguities in the story, which he attributes to Mark's unfamiliarity, Kee opts for Syria over Galilee proper; I have argued that these ambiguities can be explained in socio-literary terms. I see no compelling reason not to place the production of the Gospel at the site of its own narrative center: Galilee. This is not historicism, but an argument from the ideology of the text.

More than this general conclusion is perhaps ill-advised, but I think it is worthwhile to at least mention a more specific possibility. If Galilee is the narrative center of gravity for the story as a whole, Capernaum is the narrative center of the Galilee narrative in Book I (see also 9:33). Capernaum is described by Harrison as a relatively bustling seaside village:

A very rough estimate might put the size of the first-century town at 150,000 square yards with a population of between five thousand and sixty-five hundred people. Capernaum's population is thought to have been mostly or exclusively Jewish. . . . The town was laid out in fairly regular blocks divided by east-west and north-south streets, each block consisting of three or four houses sharing common walls . . . houses were black and were relatively poorly and simply built [1985:74,76].

Many of Mark's most detailed descriptions of social location are in or around Capernaum: the fisherman's workplace (1:16–20), a humble village dwelling (2:1–4), the agrarian parables (4:1ff.), storms on the Sea of Galilee (4:35ff.), and specific conflicts over social practice with the Pharisees (2:16ff.).

To extend the logic still further, we have seen that the household is the narrative center in Capernaum (1:29; 2:1,15; 3:20; 5:38; 9:33) as well as in other areas (7:17,24; 9:28; 10:10; 14:3). Did Mark emphasize these aspects of life to color his realistic narrative because they were both familiar and important to the real life of his original audience? More specifically, were the households of the Markan community located in the vicinity of Capernaum? Speculation (and it can finally be no more than that) is fueled by recent archaeology at the site today known by the Arabic name of Tell Hum. Excavation has uncovered two important sites: a fifth-century synagogue and, a block away, a contemporaneous Byzantine church. The church was built carefully around another dwelling, which appears to have been venerated:

Beneath this fine church have been found the ruins of a simpler, rectangular building, interpreted as a church, from the fourth century, which in turn was built around the largest room of one of the houses of the block. . . . Why was this one room of a private dwelling singled out to become the center of a church? The excavators are satisfied that the lowest level was Peter's house in which Jesus lived, and that the large room was used as a public place of worship by the local Jewish-Christian community already from the second half of the first century, until with the coming of the Byzantine Empire Christians were wealthy and powerful enough to construct buildings in the fourth and fifth centuries. If this is true, then Capernaum preserves perhaps the oldest Christian sanctuary yet discovered, already from a few decades after Jesus' stay in the town. . . . [There are] reports of pilgrims beginning late in the fourth century that they visited the "house church" of Peter [Harrison, 1985:79].

The dig turned up coins dating from Agrippa's rule, Herodian lamps, and even fishhooks, as well as Christian graffiti and prayers referring to Jesus and Peter on plaster remnants, in Greek, Syriac, and Hebrew (Corbo, 1969). The oldest strata of the excavation revealed indications of a dwelling with the characteristics of humble class. There is no paste or mortar between the unhewn rocks, suggesting that the structure was unable to support a masonry ceiling. Thus the roof would have been beams, branches, and earth/straw mixture—precisely what is recorded in Mark 2:4 (Corbo, 1969).

There must be some significance to Mark's grasp of local architectural detail, which comes up again in 13:15 with the mention of "housetop" (*doma*), the flat roof used in Palestine for sleeping or keeping watch in village structures. These details should not be abstracted from their narrative function in Mark's story, but they can yet serve as indicators of the social setting involved in the production of the Gospel. They do not *prove* that Mark's community was located in Galilee, much less Capernaum itself; but they certainly lend credence to my hypothesis that the Gospel was produced in a generally, if not specifically, Palestinian village setting.

14B. THE GOSPEL AS SOCIO-POLITICAL CRITICISM

The rest of this chapter will summarize the ideology of Mark's narrative in the context of the socio-historical setting described in chapter 2. When discussing Mark's characterization of social structures, groups, and personalities, we must keep in mind that it was not his purpose to offer a dispassionate historical account of his world. He was involved in a fierce ideological struggle with his opponents in a world he assumed his audience knew; thus he employs shorthand, parody and caricature.

i. "An End to the Tenants": The Jewish Ruling Class

The Jewish ruling classes in the Gospel are represented by three groups: the Herodian nobility, the scribes, and the Jerusalem clerical aristocracy (chief priests, elders, Sadducees). These groups are unequivocally opposed to Jesus throughout the story. The Herodians represent the old nobility of the half-Jewish house of Herod, whose political power, but not wealth or privilege, had largely dissipated under direct Roman administration of the colony. Jeremias notes three outstanding characteristics of the Jerusalem court during the rule of Herod the Great: the significant presence of Greeks and other aristocratic foreigners; its great affluence; and its strong security apparatus. The influential gentile contingent reflected the fact that though Herod's domain was Jewish, he looked to the Hellenistic world for his power, identity, and political style. Herod's state wealth was demonstrated in public building projects; his personal riches were manifested in palace opulence. The rabbinic writings tell of a widow in his court who complained when the scribes limited her daily expense account to 400 gold denarii (Jeremias, 1969:95)! Finally, the king maintained a large personal police force, with a known and feared reputation for torture, used not only on dissidents but also on those within the court who fell into disfavor (see Josephus, *War*, I,xxiv, 7–8).

In Mark's time the royal aristocracy was more concentrated in Galilee, south of Capernaum in the Hellenistic city of Tiberius on the Sea of Galilee. The mere mention of "Herodians" would have conjured up in the minds of Mark's

readers all the abuses of this dynasty, singularly responsible for the hellenization of Palestine and well known for its long record of brutal oppression. But it
is the flashback account of the execution of John the Baptist by Herod Antipas
that gives specific content to Mark's criticism of the Herodian class. That
episode (above, 7,B,i) is a bitter parody of the whims of the royal aristocracy,
whose marital-dynastic alliances are forged in defiance of Jewish Law, and
whose political decisions are made at drunken parties. Yet Mark's vignette of
Herod Antipas is far more plausible than Matthew's censorious parody (in Mt
2), which casts Herod (the Great) as the new murderous pharaoh of Exodus 1–
2.

Both stories indicate class antagonism toward the house of Herod. But
Mark's specifically reflects the popular outrage that lingered in the historical
memory of Galileans regarding Antipas's martyrdom of the popular prophet
John. His account of the party at the royal court with all the "leading men" of
Galilee is highly realistic, including the custom of young Jewish maidens
dancing for the nobility (Jeremias, ibid.:362). The scene reflects the practice of
royal concubinage, and the fact that women were one of the prominent signs of
wealth in the patriarchal oriental court (ibid.:93). We can infer from Mark's
direct warning against the Herodians (8:15), and his portrait of their conspiratorial relationships with the Pharisees (3:6) that the royal house represented a
continuing threat to Mark's radical community in Galilee, especially as the
major collaborative force during the war (12:13f.).

The scribes are the archenemies of Jesus in the story and, as government
investigators from Jerusalem (3:22; 7:1), they provide the link for the political
machinations against Jesus in Books I and II. Jeremias portrays the scribes as a
rising class that was neither exclusively priestly nor aristocratic, though including both elements. It had by the first century usurped a great deal of the social
power traditionally controlled by the hereditary priestly aristocracy, building
an alternative power base founded upon academic/legal expertise:

> To such a student, such an "academic," as the bearer of this knowledge
> and authority, there were opened key positions in the administration of
> justice, in government and in education. . . . Apart from the chief priests
> and members of patrician families, the scribe was the only person who
> could enter the supreme court, the Sanhedrin. . . . When a community
> was faced with a choice between a layman and a scribe for nomination to
> the office of elder to a community, of "ruler of the synagogue," or of
> judge, it invariably preferred the scribe. This means that a large number
> of important posts hitherto held by priests and laymen of high rank had,
> in the first century A.D., passed entirely, or predominantly, into the hands
> of the scribes. The title ["Rabbi"], at the beginning of the first century
> A.D., was undergoing a transition from its former status as a general title
> of honour to one reserved exclusively for scribes [Jeremias, 1969:236f.].

Mark thus accurately speaks of "scribal Pharisees" (2:16), their connection
to the Sanhedrin (14:1; 15:1), and the tremendous social prestige they enjoyed

(11:38-40). His criticism is twofold. He correctly perceives the scribes as the architects of the dominant ideology, whose respectability and authority must be refuted (see 9:12; 12:35). Therefore from the outset of the Gospel he pits Jesus' teaching directly against theirs (1:22; 2:6; 12:35). Mark also sharply attacks the way in which their social status becomes the pretext for economic exploitation and aggrandizement (above, 10,F,ii). So alienated is Mark from this class that he is skeptical of the possibility of scribal discipleship (above, 10,E,ii).

Finally, Mark repudiates the entire traditional Jerusalem power structure. The "elders" Jeremias characterizes as the lay nobility, whose power derived from the period of the exile, during and after which they acted as the political representatives of the people. The wealth and power of these leading patrician families was incestuous, and derived primarily from landownership. The Romans acknowledged this power, and appointed them to positions of authority in the colonial structures (ibid.:228). As for the Sadducees, Mark mentions them but once, and only in order to show how their conservative ideology legitimizes patriarchal rule (above, 10,E,i). The fact that Mark is more concerned with scribal and Pharisaic social power is an accurate reflection of the situation of his time, in which the influence of the Sadducees was waning, and restricted largely to the Sanhedrin.

In considering the priestly aristocracy, Mark gives no indication of having the slightest interest in the disputes over the legitimacy of a non-Zadokite priesthood, a serious political conflict among the ruling classes, which dated from the period of the Hasmonean dynasty. To Mark priestly power was a function of economic class, not lineage, resulting from control over the temple cultus. Jeremias notes that the high priesthood "through family influence obtained possession of the administration of Temple," and that nepotism was regularly used to control the offices of the temple treasury (ibid.:198). This situation is directly reflected in Mark's report of their outrage over Jesus' attack upon the temple marketplace (11:27; above, 10,C,ii,iii; D,i).

Mark's trial and execution narrative gives us a clear idea of his political estimation of the members of the Jerusalem hierarchy. On the one hand he portrays it as disdainful, yet fearful, of the discontentment of the masses (11:32; 14:2), whom they manipulate for their own ends (15:11). On the other hand he considers the Sanhedrin fully collaborative with Roman administration of Palestine. In the double trial (above, 12,D,E), they ape the imperial mechanisms of "justice," and even attempt to deny Jesus a proper burial after his execution (above, 13,C,ii). Their self-interest in maintaining the colonial arrangement predictably results in their rejection of any hint of popular kingship articulated in messianic terms (14:61; 15:32). They are prepared to recognize only a Davidic state in which their power is maintained, a proposition Mark flatly rejects (above, 10,E,ii).

Mark summarizes his opposition to the ruling classes in his parable of the vineyard (above, 10,D,ii). In the classic prophetic tradition Jesus attacks the leaders of Israel. Although they should be servants (Lv 25:55), they make a pretense of "owning" the "vineyard." Such corruption is, in Mark's view, the *inevitable* result of economic and political power, which makes the ruling class "deaf and blind" to the message of the prophets, whom they murder—hence the "prophetic script." The subversive discourse of Jesus' parable, however, reverses the tables. The rulers are described as mere tenants who will be brutally punished for their insubordination by the true owner—for the landlord class, a taste of its own medicine! Mark roundly condemns this class (12:40), and in his mind there is no question of its compatibility with the new social order: "What will the owner of the vineyard do? He will come and destroy the tenants and give the vineyard to others" (12:9). These are the hardest, and most revolutionary, words in the Gospel.

ii. "My Name Is Legion": Roman Imperialism

Mark takes the same hard-line stance toward Roman colonialism. Given his political circumstances in reoccupied Galilee late in the war, Mark obviously cannot speak directly about Rome. Thus he relies upon two forms of more veiled discourse: the Jewish resistance tradition of apocalyptic and the literary device of parody. Though there are only six instances in which Mark alludes to the reality of foreign imperialism, each articulates his decidedly anti-Roman socio-political stance.

The first instance is his subversive expropriation of "gospel" as title for his story (above, 3,E,i). This term suggests that this story will extol yet another Roman military victory in the provinces, and at the surface of the narrative this indeed appears to be the case. The Romans, through the agency of the collaborative native aristocracy, successfully capture and execute a subversive prophet and aspirant to popular kingship. Yet Jesus throughout the trial remains uncowed by the imperial power of Rome, causing the procurator to "wonder" (*thaumazein*; 15:5,44). And in the discourse of Mark, the very moment of Roman triumph—the cross—is revealed by apocalyptic symbolics to be in fact the moment of Rome's defeat.

The true battle being narrated by the "gospel" is between Jesus the Human One and the domain of Satan, administrated by "strong men" such as Caesar. Just as Jesus first clashes with the Jewish ruling class through the symbolic action of the synagogue exorcism (above, 4,B,i), so too he serves notice to the Roman imperialists in the story of the Gerasene demoniac (above, 5,D,ii). Mark is nowhere politically bolder than in 5:9f., the only place where Jesus wrestles from a demon his "identity":

> Jesus asked him, "What is your name?" He replied, "My name is 'Legion,' for we are many." And he begged him earnestly not to expel them from the country [5:9f.].

Mark appears to acknowledge the reality that "no one had the strength to subdue" the demon of Roman military occupation (5:4)—including the Jewish rebels. Yet he makes his revolutionary stance clear by symbolically reenacting the exodus story through a "herd" of pigs. With the divine command, the imperial forces are drowned in the sea. It is no accident that in the aftermath of this action the crowd, like Pilate, responds with "wonder" (*thaumazein*; 5:20).

To invoke the great exodus liberation story was, as it has been subsequently throughout Western history, to fan the flames of revolutionary hope (Walzer, 1986). Yet Mark realized that the problem was much deeper than throwing off the yoke of yet another colonizer. After all, biblical history itself attested to the fact that Israel had always been squeezed, courted, or threatened by the great empires that surrounded it. And the Maccabean revolt against the Seleucids had only resulted in recycling oppressive power into the hands of a native dynasty, one that in turn became an early victim of a newly ascendent imperial power, Rome. Thus the meaning of Jesus' struggle against the strong man is not reducible solely to his desire for the liberation of Palestine from colonial rule, though it certainly includes that. It is a struggle against the root "spirit" and politics of domination—which, Mark acknowledges matter of factly, is most clearly represented by the "great men" of the Hellenistic imperial sphere (10:42).

Mark believes that both parties of the colonial condominium are "possessed" by this spirit, and so assesses each in exactly the same terms. The discourse of "equation" is reflected at the outset in the parallelism between the two inaugural exorcisms, and again at the story's end in the double trial of Jesus. There Pilate is indicted along with the high priest for engineering the railroading of Jesus. The ruthless procurator, infamous for his defiance of Jewish political opinion, is parodied as "consulting" the Jewish crowd (above, 12,F,i), yet nevertheless shrewd enough to release a convicted Sicarius terrorist instead of Jesus.

We can see the same discourse in Jesus' second campaign. On either side of the central political parable of 12:1–12 are conflict stories in which Jesus' opponents challenge him to reveal his ideological commitments, only to have their own duplicity revealed. They are unwilling to state their loyalty to the biblical vision of justice (represented by the prophet John, 11:27ff.) while implicitly advocating loyalty to Rome (represented by the coin, 12:13ff.). The political "trap" set for Jesus in the tax question indicates that Mark feels keenly the pressures of the war (above, 10,D,iii,iv). It provided him with a good opportunity to unambiguously instruct his readers to collaborate with Rome, if he was so inclined. But in 12:17, as in 11:33, Jesus refuses to be caught. He appeals, as he does throughout the Gospel, to the sovereignty of Yahweh, who is true "lord of the house" (13:35) despite the counterclaims of Caesar.

But is Yahweh truly sovereign? This claim must stand the test of Caesar's ultimate claim over life, articulated not by the coin but the cross: Caesar's power of capital punishment, the threat that renders his subjects docile. And so, in his second call to discipleship, Jesus faces Caesar's "lordship" head on (above, 8,D). Mark could not have chosen an image that indicated more unequivocally his opposition to the empire than the Roman executioner's stake. And Jesus *means* what he says about taking up this cross: Mark fully expects members of his community to "follow" Jesus in political trials not only before Jewish courts but Roman ones as well. "You will stand before governors (*hēgemonōn*) and kings" (13:9a), referring to procurator and Caesar.

By redefining the cross as the way to liberation rather than symbol of defeat and shame, Mark radically subverts the authority of the empire. The accepted meanings of "saving life" and "losing life," of being "convicted" and "acquitted," of what "belongs to Caesar" and what "belongs to God," are all turned upside down when the power of death, by which the powers rule, is broken. But to understand this takes "eyes to see" that the cross is the power of God, which alone can reanimate the exodus liberation story. It alone can drive the oppressive temple state and the repressive legions "into the sea."

iii. "Negating the Commands of God": The Reform Movements

I pointed out in chapter 2 that reform efforts among literate Jewish groups took two trajectories in Mark's era. The first strategy advocated withdrawal from the social mainstream in order to more rigorously attend to the demands of the symbolic order of debt and purity; it is represented by the Essene movement. The fact that Mark never addresses this movement directly may indicate he felt it less of an ideological competitor. His portrayal of John in the wilderness, and later his equation of the practice of John's followers with that of the Pharisees (2:18), may suggest that some of the Baptist's followers were drawn toward Qumran. It is noteworthy that Mark cites Isaiah 40:3, for this text appears to have been used by the Essene community to justify its monastic life in the desert. But the narrative movement of the Gospel, although it *begins* in the wilderness, does not *remain* there, proceeding inexorably from the periphery toward the center—that is, toward engagement.

Mark would not only have disagreed with the Essenes over their social strategy of elitism based upon intensification of the demands of the symbolic order, but their political eschatology as well, reflected in the so-called War Scrolls, which narrate the final battle between the "Sons of Light and Sons of Darkness." Archeological evidence indicates that the community site at Qumran was abandoned late in the war years, and Qumranite writings have been found at Masada (Sandmel, 1978:163ff.). It appears therefore that once the siege of Jerusalem began, the Essenes joined the rebels in their defense of Jerusalem. This would strengthen my hypothesis that rebel recruiters operated abroad in Palestine in 69 C.E., and did in fact successfully draft many.

The other trajectory of reform and renewal pursued a strategy of extending the symbolic order to a greater number of persons. This was represented by the Pharisaic movement, a far more formidable competitor in Galilee. Mark's portrait strongly suggests protracted Pharisaic antagonism toward his community; Pharisees are always pictured on the offensive against Jesus. Conflicts erupt over issues of practice that were hallmarks of Pharisaic piety: strictly segregated table fellowship (2:16ff.), asceticism (2:18ff.), Sabbath observance (2:23ff.), and ritual purity with respect to meals (7:1ff.). In each case, Jesus eclipses the Pharisaic objection by raising a deeper issue concerning the place of the poor in the symbolic order. It is as if Mark is trying to convince those impressed by the Pharisaic social strategy practice that it is not the populist alternative it seems, but merely a cosmetic alternative to the oppressive clerical hierarchy.

At every point Mark's criticism of the Pharisees concerns social relationships within Judaism, with one important exception. That is the dispute over handwashing in 7:1ff. (above, 7,C,i). It is clear that at issue here are the purity barriers to common table fellowship between Jew and gentile. The disciples' hands are unclean because they have eaten unclean food, confirmed by the fact that the episode ends with Jesus' pronouncement declaring all food "clean." Jesus again subverts the purity code, just as he did when he declared the leper "clean" in 1:43. But Mark does not stop with simply repudiating Pharisaic practices of ritual purity. By sandwiching the debate over *korban* into this consideration of kosher, Mark attacks the very heart of Pharisaic ideology: the halakah (7:6ff.).

The halakah allegedly make the demands of the symbolic order more accessible for the common people. But Mark contends that this legislation is in fact quite elitist. It is this very commitment to the symbolic order (i.e., the temple treasury) that allows the "commands of God" regarding the weak *within* the community (in this case the elderly) to be ignored or overridden (above, 7,C,ii). The same issue is at stake in Mark's other reference to the halakah, the question of divorce legislation (10:2ff.). Again, the Pharisees are revealed to be wholly unconcerned with the weaker member (here the woman), not to mention the original scriptural vision of equality in marriage (see above, 9,D,iii). Thus, Pharisaic halakah functions to guard the status quo, whether the political economy of the temple or patriarchy.

Mark's inclusive community, like Paul's, came under severe Pharisaic criticism, but his counterattack was just as vigorous. For Mark, Pharisaic concern for purity, allegedly in order to protect the social boundaries of Judaism, cannot possibly reflect a populist commitment if their own legislation is unconcerned with social equality *within* those boundaries. Segregation from gentiles, the poor, and the unclean did nothing to ensure that the "commands of God," which concern true justice for all, would be promoted. Mark concludes that the symbolic order and any group that supported it would never be able to fulfill Yahweh's vision of a humanity free of class and racial alienation. So does he reject the reform groups, withdrawn or engaged.

iv. Crucified between Two Bandits: The Rebels

Inasmuch as the Gospel was composed during the Jewish revolt, it is of utmost significance that Mark never *directly* addresses the rebels. His allusions, however, make it clear that Mark wishes to distance Jesus from the revolt. Jesus is portrayed as entering the city as a specifically nonmilitary, popular king (above, 10,B); he is contrasted with a Sicarius terrorist, Barabbas (above, 12,F,ii); and he repudiates all rebel claims to be fighting a messianic war (above, 11,C,iv). Most telling, Mark urges his Judean colleagues to abandon the defense of Jerusalem (above, 11,C,iii).

We must also acknowledge, however, the distinct tone of solidarity that Mark weaves into his passion narrative. Jesus is first arrested (14:48) and then crucified (15:27) "as a social bandit." Mark appreciated the fact that the very conditions he protests against, the systematic oppression of the peasantry by both the Romans and the Jerusalem hierarchy, had led many of his Galilean compatriots to engage in social banditry, and subsequently to offer guerilla support to the revolt. I have already noted that at least some factions of the rebellion took the opportunity to settle class scores (above, 2,D). Upon entering and gaining control of the city, certain rebels launched a series of attacks upon the houses of the royalists and high priests (see Rhoads, 1976:94ff.). The burning of the public archives building housing records of debt was certainly an action on behalf of those who had lost their land and become impoverished due to an inability to meet tax and tithe obligations. Noteworthy too were efforts to democratize the high priesthood and overturn the aristocracy's control of the temple during the civil war in 66-67. These actions against the institutions of autocracy suggest that there were many points of ideological affinity between Mark and the social bandits turned rebels.

Yet for all of this, and despite his unequivocal opposition to Roman colonialism, Mark refused to align himself with the revolt. Why? According to the latter half of Jesus' second sermon (above, 11,E), it had to do with his insistence that the real revolution must take place at a deeper level of both ends and means. Regarding means, Mark was convinced that only the way of the cross, not the sword, could truly overthrow the historical reign of the powers: "How can Satan cast out Satan?" (3:23). The same is true of ends; the rebellion was, in the last analysis, a struggle for the control, purification, and defense of the temple, which Mark could in no way support. Any attempt to restore a Davidic state meant a return to the politics of domination, and was thus counterrevolutionary (10:42f.). Mark therefore considered the prospect of the temple state's collapse a "sign" of liberation (13:28-31), whereas the rebels saw it as indicative of cataclysm and defeat, "the end" (13:7).

It is difficult to know exactly how much Mark, from his vantage point of repacified Galilee around 69 C.E., could have been aware of the power struggles raging within the provisional government in Jerusalem. In any case his first concern was not events down south but rebel recruiters challenging his community. His response was to counter-recruit; while the rebels were calling persons to Jerusalem, the Gospel points them back to Galilee (16:7). Mark then expropriates the great symbol of resistance to Rome, the cross. Jesus' call to a discipleship of the cross was directed not only to his disciples but to the "crowd" as well (8:34), and presumably Mark means this to include the rebels. When read against the backdrop of the siege of Jerusalem, it is significant that Jesus does not call for surrender, as did, for example, the prophet Jeremiah during the Babylonian siege of Jerusalem (Jer 21). He does, however, question the rebels' efforts to militarily defeat the Roman "strong man."

Yes, says Mark to the rebels, our movement stands with you in your resistance to Rome; after all, our leader was crucified between two of your compatriots (15:27). Our nonviolent resistance demands no less of us than does your guerilla war ask of you—to reckon with death. But we ask something more: a heroism of the cross, not the sword. We cannot beat the strong man at his own game. We must attack his very foundations: we must render his presumed lordship over our lives impotent. You consider the cross a sign of defeat. We take it up "as a witness against them," a witness to the revolutionary power of nonviolent resistance (13:9b). Join us therefore in our struggle to put an end to the spiral of violence and oppression, that Yahweh's reign may truly dawn (9:1).

14C. THE GOSPEL AS SOCIO-ECONOMIC CRITICISM

i. "Against the Law To Do Good?": The Symbolic Order

In Book I of the Gospel, Mark addresses the dominant ideological order as it manifested itself in the provinces. He wastes no time in repudiating the purity and debt codes in Jesus' first campaign around Capernaum. This campaign includes conflict at each of the three social sites of daily life (above, 2, E,ii):

1. house/table: conflict with paralytic at home (2:1ff.); table fellowship with "sinners" (2:16ff.);
2. village/land: civil disobedience in grainfield (2:23ff.);
3. synagogue/temple: clash in synagogue (3:1ff.).

The three great dictums of the campaign—the two Human One sayings (2:10,28) and the Deuteronomic ultimatum (3:4)—all make the same point: cultural systems must enhance and liberate human life, not marginalize it—or to put it in modern parlance, they must function "for people, not for profit." In the tradition of classical prophecy, Mark contends that the original intention of the symbolic order had been betrayed, and thus calls for justice and compassion over cultic obligation.

As mentioned above, Mark's concern has to do, on the one hand, with the way in which the institutions of purity and debt have created socio-economic stratification within the Jewish community and, on the other, the way in which they reinforce social segregation between Jew and gentile. Defying them, Jesus freely interacts with the sick/unclean and the foreigner, and instructs his disciples to do likewise. Included in Mark's criticisms are the dominant cultural codes of honor and status, which also function to promote social divisions. In the first construction section, Mark subverts cultural assumptions about propriety and what constitutes "first" and "least" in the hierarchy of status. For example, Jesus attends to the needs of an impure and destitute woman before the requests of a synagogue ruler, and concedes a debate to a gentile woman (above, 6,D). In the second construction cycle, Mark continues turning the social order upside down, this time through Jesus' teaching. Jesus gives priority to children and women over the rich and the "great"; a blind beggar is portrayed as a model of discipleship.

In the second campaign narrative Jesus confronts the symbolic order at its heart, the temple. There he delivers yet another prophetic dictum concerning the purpose of the house of God (above, 10,C,iii). The decisive break with the debt code comes with his advocacy of a practice of communal forgiveness (11:25). When Jesus dies on the cross, not only are the powers pulled from their thrones (the sun darkens), but the symbolic order itself is overthrown (temple curtain is rent). The curtained Holy of Holies symbolizes the ideological justification for priestly elitism: in this order, Yahweh is exclusive (reclusive?), dwelling "apart from and above" the people, mediated by the priests. That which divides the people from Yahweh also divides them from each other: the priest also lives "apart and above." Thus the destruction of this curtain symbolizes the end of such an order (below, E,ii). It is true that the symbolic order appears to prevail in the story, as Jesus' corpse (of the first order of impurity) is removed from the cross by a Sanhedrin representative so it will not profane the Sabbath. But the "absence" of that body from the tomb is the last word; the corpse does not need to be properly buried according to the demands of honor and purity, because the new order has now dawned. Moreover, that "body" becomes the center of the new order in the eucharistic feast— those who partake of it are "contaminated" with the subversive memory of Jesus.

The geopolitics of the narrative reinforces Mark's contention that the messianic community must now live outside the bounds of the dominant order. From its genesis in the wilderness peripheries, the kingdom movement is put in spatial tension with the "center," whether that is conceived of as Judea/Jerusalem or the Hellenistic *polis*. Mark's Jesus itinerates throughout northern Palestine, which may well be an indication of the missionary scope of Mark's own community. In Book II, the narrative slowly moves south toward the negative pole of Jerusalem for the final confrontation. But as soon as this mission is completed, Mark points immediately back to Galilee (16:7). This is the culmination to an ideology totally opposed to the dominant Jewish symbolic order, its institutions and its sites.

ii. "Swallowing the Property of Widows": Political Economy

I stated above that Mark criticized the temple cult not as a theological rationalization of its demise but because it anchored an essentially oppressive political economy. To begin with, Mark portrays a world in which hunger and disenfranchisement among the masses is widespread—a situation that corresponds to the reality he knew in wartime Palestine. I have noted (above, 7,E,ii) the way in which Book I is particularly preoccupied with eating and not-eating motifs. We might further consider the various expressions of economic deprivation, or "not enough," that we encounter throughout the story:

1. John's wilderness diet, 1:6
2. should we fast? 2:18ff.
3. disciples commandeer grain, 2:26
4. Jesus unable to eat due to press of crowd, 3:20, 6:31

5. Jesus' command to feed Jairus's daughter, 5:43
6. Jesus' command to go on mission without bread or money, 6:8
7. Syrophoenician woman's plea for crumbs, 7:24
8. Jesus hungers, 11:12
9. widow's impoverishment, 12:40, 44
10. famines, 13:8

For Mark, the experience of economic marginality, land alienation, and social disruption was proof positive enough of the corruption of the temple-based redistributive economy, which was originally envisioned to ensure "enough" for all those in Israel, as well as those sojourning in the land (see Lv 25:35ff.). He envisions the restoration of a system that will be committed to communal sufficiency (below, E, ii).

Mark does more than criticize the economic disparity of class divisions within the Jewish community; he also recognizes the mechanisms by which those divisions are maintained. The Herodian class, for example, is portrayed as deeply complicit in the colonial system by which its wealth and power are maintained. It is the Herodians who, again in cooperation with the Pharisees, try to extract from Jesus a position on the imperial tribute (12:13ff.). The Pharisees in turn are attacked where they are most vulnerable, from the peasant's perspective: their attempts to control the production and distribution of agricultural produce. Mark alludes, directly and indirectly, to each aspect of this control: their administration of purity regulations (2:16f.; 7:1ff.), which determined acceptable tithes, their jurisdiction over debt obligations (i.e., *korban*, 7:6ff.), and their enforcement of Sabbath law, which affected the peasant's ability to produce enough to survive (2:23ff.).

Patterns of landownership are reflected in Mark's frequent allusions to tenant farmers and absentee landlords. But it is the temple, as the central mechanism of this political economy, that is the focus of Mark's criticism. Jesus' attack upon the temple market, and the scriptural justifications that accompany this direct action, articulate a clear repudiation of this system (above, 10,C). The poor are directly oppressed by cultic obligations they cannot meet, as illustrated in Jesus' lament over the improverished widow in 12:41ff. (above, 10,F,ii). The redistributive system has failed to live up to its purpose, which was the maintenance of socio-economic justice and equality within the community of Israel. Instead, capital accumulates in the temple building and treasury, and landownership concentrates in the hands of those already privileged by the system—all of which is "robbery" of the poor. To claim that the temple is the domain of "thieves" (11:17) is the same as asserting that the rich are rich by "defrauding" the poor (10:18–21).

Throughout the Gospel there is a consistent narrative opposition between those representing the symbolic order on the one hand and the poor and marginal on the other:

1. priests (purity) vs. the leprous (1:41ff.);
2. scribes (debt) vs. the physically disabled (2:1ff.);
3. Pharisees (debt) vs. the dependent elderly (7:6ff.);
4. scribes (debt) vs. disenfranchised widows (12:40).

Although all the major social groups are indicted, it is the scribes, as ideological apologists for and economic beneficiaries of this exploitive political economy, who are singled out as the worst offenders. Mark's Jesus is unimpressed by their rhetorical affirmations of the prophetic insistence that "love of neighbor is more than burnt offerings and sacrifices" (12:34). The fact is that the system itself, which the scribes uphold, enforces the class stratification of Israel (above, 10,E,ii).

Mark, in other words, understands the nature of *structural* injustice, and for this reason refuses to consider strategies of reform. The disciples do not see this clearly, at least twice entertaining the idea that Jesus' concern for the poor might be satisfied by their making better use of their purchasing power in the market (see 6:37; 14:5). Their blindness is a result of a failure to see that the system cannot be redirected toward the purposes of justice. Instead, Jesus calls for its complete collapse (13:2), and in its place he advocates a genuine practice of equitable redistribution (above, 9,C,iii).

14D. A NEW POLITICAL PRACTICE

i. "This Is Not So among You": Constructive Politics

Mark believed that the kingdom would not dawn by divine cataclysm, but rather would grow slowly, a small seed in hostile soil. Advocating a "revolution from below" (above, 9,E), the discourse of the Gospel includes both subversive and constructive elements. Mark does not simply criticize the present order; he offers instructions for the building of a new order, which will center around the community of discipleship. The Gospel functions to legitimate this community as a political "confederacy" (3:13ff.; above, 4,E,ii), which represents a concrete alternative to the politics of domination.

How was this community organized? How was power exercised? The narrative undermines any absolute ideology of leadership: the leaders of the community are portrayed as failures. I would not characterize Mark's treatment of the male disciples as a "political polemic" against a Jerusalem-based Christian leadership, as does W. Kelber (1979:88ff.). However, its sarcastic tone does suggest that pretensions to authoritarianism were not unknown in the experience of Mark's people. Jesus' taunt—"Oh, but this is not so among you!"—referring to the practices of domination so bitterly familiar from Roman colonialism, functions as a sharp warning against aspirations to power (above, 9,D,ii). And "discipleship" as a permanent state of following Jesus the true leader, in contrast to rabbinic schools in which the student became himself a master, further guarded against the reproduction of hierarchy in the community.

Still, Mark's alternative is not leaderlessness, but leadership accountable to the "least" in the community. What concretely did the "politics of servanthood" mean? Our reading has identified a radical break with the traditional Palestinian patriarchal structures of clan, kinship, and marriage. The new "family" is egalitarian, both in its marital and community forms, and the traditionally weakest members of the system, women and children, are given central place. Mark does not have a lot to say about marriage except where he considers the problem of divorce (above, 9,B,i). The profile of women characters in the Gospel indicates that women were considered full persons outside their traditional roles as helpmeets. I have also argued that there is evidence that Mark's critique of patriarchy strongly implies that women are considered more suited to the vocation of servant-leadership than are men (above, 9,D,iii).

The unprecedented nature of such an ideology and practice in the context of Mediterranean antiquity cannot be overestimated:

> At this period Jewish, Hellenistic, and Roman perceptions of family life are quite conservative. Strong family bonds were supported not only by social pressure but by a host of laws governing marriage, inheritance, and the relation of different members of the natural and extended family. The power of the head of the family (*patria potestas*) was a virtual law unto itself. A Christian community which evokes a saying of Jesus to claim that doing the will of God is more important than loyalty to the natural family and which actually counsels leaving the family to form a new family without the governing power of the father and which rejects those structures of interrelationship which govern normal family life would naturally evoke suspicion and persecution [Donahue, 1983:45f.].

Donahue goes on to note that many of the earliest attacks upon the Christians by Roman writers centered upon their socially aberrant community lifestyle.

Against Theissen's theory of "wandering charismatics," I believe Mark reflects a settled community in which the extended household model is maintained. The household, however, is now understood as the primary site not of reproducing dominant socio-cultural patterns, but resisting them; perhaps it is also the haven for underground activity. Under persecution, the community appears to be struggling with the question of internal discipline (above, 9,A,iv), but the Gospel clearly comes down on the side of leniency and understanding for those who have fallen to apostasy. The practice of reconciliation and forgiveness is crucial to the community's life. Importantly, Mark advocates an "open" community—that is, one whose boundaries are not rigidly defined. Not only must the door always be open to the poor and outcast, but non-Christians who do the works of justice and compassion must also be accepted (above, 9,A,iii).

ii. "Lord of the Sabbath and the House": Subversive Politics

On the whole, the Gospel concentrates more upon subversive than constructive politics, probably because the pressure from both Jewish and Roman authorities demanded clarity on these matters. Jesus is presented from the outset as a rival authority, challenging the hegemony of the powers who hold sway over the dominant political order. After being declared an "outlaw" (1:10f.; above, 3,F,i) toward this order, Jesus proceeds to expropriate priestly authority over the purity apparatus (1:43), scribal authority over the debt system (2:10), and Pharisaic authority over Sabbath legislation (2:28). Later the conflict escalates as Jesus assaults the highest authority structure of his time: the temple. In each case he asserts that the original purpose of these institutions has been betrayed. Mark subsequently identifies Jesus as "Lord" not only of the "Sabbath," but of the "house" as well (13:35). As Malachi had warned (Mal 3:1ff.; cf. Mk 1:2), he has indeed come to judge the temple-community according to the proper exercise of justice. All of this functions to justify the community's practice of resistance.

The ideology of resistance is clearly articulated in Jesus' "strong man" speech: the goal is to bring down the old order and liberate those captive to it (above, 4,F,i). The practice of resistance consists of three elements, as we have seen: kingdom proclamation, healing and exorcism, and nonviolent confrontation. Jesus commissions and instructs his community in each aspect of this messianic vocation (3:13; 6:7).

The political strategy of the community, like so many modern revolutionary movements, begins with attempts to persuade the "base," or popular sectors, of the double imperative: the old order must be overturned and the new order welcomed. The community's proselytizing appears to consist of founding other cells of resistance, which become "safehouses" (6:7ff.; above, 7,A,ii). But the disciples cannot force the kingdom on the people, as some of the social bandit groups may have done—for example by extracting "revolutionary taxes." Instead, the mission is wholly contingent upon popular reception; thus the emphasis upon going without sustenance and the role of hospitality. It is anticipated that this preaching mission alone is enough to bring the disciples into conflict with the authorities, which is why it is juxtaposed to the story of John and Herod (above, 7,B). Despite the danger, the "good news" of liberation must be spread abroad, not only to oppressed Jews but to "all peoples" (13:9f.).

The proclamation must be accompanied by concrete expressions of the new order. These are not thaumaturgical "signs and wonders" (8:11f.), but the works of justice and mercy: feeding the hungry (6:37), healing the sick (6:13), promoting fellowship with the socially outcast (2:16) and the gentile (7:1ff.), and above all, exorcism. Jesus' ministry of exorcism, portrayed as the most threatening aspect of his practice to the political authorities (3:22ff.), is a discourse by which Mark articulates his ideology of opposition to both Jewish and Roman politico-military hegemony. The new order means the end of scribal domination *and* liberation from the colonial boot of the imperial legions. But exorcism is not merely the symbolic declaration of intent: it takes on a decidedly concrete character when Jesus "casts out" the temple entrepreneurs (above, 10,C). This episode links exorcism to the politics of symbolic direct action.

In both his first and second campaigns, Jesus employs the tactics of what we would today call "civil disobedience." The very first public action of his disciples is to break the law (2:23ff.)! Jesus then debates the true intention of the law in the ensuing "trial" (3:4). The same pattern of legal violation and defense occurs again in 7:1ff. The climax to Jesus' practice of symbolic direct action, however, is the parade from the Mount of Olives and the ensuing temple action. The procession, curse, and "cleansing" are, to be sure, painstakingly choreographed exercises in political theater; but we must not lose sight of the fact that they are also portrayed as specifically *disruptive*. Thus Mark legitimizes not only "classic" civil disobedience—in which the law is broken because it is unjust, as in the case of the Sabbath—but militant direct action as well.

The powerful practice of exorcism/direct action must not be exploited by the disciples in order to build their own power base (9:38ff.). Indeed, the power is linked to "faith," which means the ability not only to "name" the demons within and without, but to envision a new personhood and a new world free of the structures and patterns of domination (9:14ff.; above, 8,E,iii). Only by such faith can the "mountains" of the present order be overthrown (11:23f.). The disciples' struggle for faith-as-political-imagination is one of the central themes of the Gospel, narrated in counterpoint to Jesus' powerful practice. This indicates that Mark's community wrestled with self-doubt about the viability of its messianic vocation, and given the historical situation, it is not difficult to sympathize with its members. After all, their visible impact was small, and they were probably hard pressed by the rival claims of the Pharisees on the one hand and the rebels on the other. Yet Mark stuck by his belief that true subversive politics was to be found in neither reform nor rebellion.

iii. "Take up Your Cross": Revolutionary Nonviolence

In speaking of the political process, Mark offers his readers two key images: the "miracle" of a mustard seed and the "paradox" of the cross. The seed reminds us that a revolution from the bottom up is a slow process whereby the root causes of domination are exposed and transformed. It demands both patience and faith, for historical change will not be as evident as if the new order were imposed from the top. To believe in the "true" court of justice of the Human One is to believe that the smallest of seeds can grow into the tree in which all "the birds of the air" can nest. The cross reminds us that the powers cannot be overthrown by military means. But how was it that Mark (and all the early Christians) understood the cross to represent *victory* over, not defeat by, the powers?

I have shown how Mark weaves a sophisticated fabric of apocalyptic symbolics throughout the story. The combat myth in the wilderness is rearticulated in the parable of "binding the strong man and ransacking his house" (3:27). It is enacted in Jesus' direct action in the Jerusalem temple, and reaches its climax in Jesus' final confrontation with the authorities in his trial (14:62) and death. At this moment the apocalyptic signs of the "end of the world" occur (15:33–39): the Human One pulls the heavenly potentates down from their thrones (13:26f.). The "strong man," it turns out, is not identifiable *simply* with the scribal class or its political coalitions, or the temple, or even the "desolating sacrilege" of imperial Rome. Mark's apocalyptic discourse reveals the heart of the matter: Jesus is taking on the politics of domination itself.

W. Wink, in his study of "powers" discourse in the New Testament, has in my opinion correctly captured the meaning of this apocalyptic euphemism. His argument that we should interpret "the spiritual powers not as separate heavenly or ethereal entities but as *the inner aspect of material or tangible manifestations of power*" is worth citing at length:

> We encounter them primarily in reference to the material or "earthly" reality *of which they are the innermost essence.* . . . The expression "the Powers" should no longer be reserved for the special category of spiritual forces, but should rather be used generically for all manifestations of power, seen under the dual aspect of their physical or institutional concretion on the one hand, and their inner essence or spirituality on the other. Popular speech, often more accurate in unconscious matters than it is given credit for being, has quite properly referred to the whole range of phenomena as "The Powers That Be." . . . In all these cases, the simultaneity of heavenly and earthly events witnesses to the perception, mythically couched, that there is more to events than what appears. The physical actors and institutions are only the outer manifestation of a whole field of powers contending for influence [1984: 104,105,107).

For Mark, then, the practice of domination is so deeply embedded in human history that no mere rebellion will do.

Genuine revolution demands a radical break with all the accepted canons of power politics, with every expression of violence, exploitation, and dehumanization:

> "For we are contending . . ." against the spirituality of institutions, against the ideologies and metaphors and legitimations that prop them up, against the greed and covetousness that give them life, against the individual egocentricities that the Powers so easily hook, against the idolatry that pits short-term gain against the long-term good of the whole [ibid.: 140].

The means of the old order cannot bring about the ends of the new. Anything less than a politics of militant, nonviolent resistance is counterrevolutionary, a recycling of the old world. Mark's Jesus calls for a more radical (driving-to-the-roots) social transformation, a unity between means and ends. I have suggested at several points throughout this commentary that the cross is not only a reminder of the political "cost of discipleship," but can also be seen as a symbol of what Gandhi called *satyagraha*. I will return to this briefly in my concluding comments (Afterword, C).

14E. A NEW SOCIO-ECONOMIC PRACTICE

i. "One Loaf": Solidarity with the Poor and the Gentiles

Mark's Gospel legitimates the transgression of established social and economic boundaries for the sake of the re-creation of human unity. The subjects of this practice of inclusivity are first the poor and outcast. This is articulated both generally, in terms of Jesus' ministry to the "crowd," and specifically, in terms of episodes involving the disabled (2:1ff.; 10:45ff.), the ritually unclean (1:45ff.; 5:25ff.), the socially marginalized (2:15ff.; 7:24ff.); and women and children (10:1ff.). This solidarity is perhaps best represented in the first episode of the passion narrative (above, 12,B,i), in which Jesus is pictured residing at the house of a leper, and there teaches that one woman's act of compassion outweighs all the pretensions to faithfulness of his own disciples (14:3–9).

Because it is often raised in political readings of the Gospel, the question must be addressed: Does Mark's story portray Jesus as the author of a "mass movement?" This might be suggested not only by his clear "preferential option" for the poor of Palestine, but the evident class bias in the narrative. There are those who would see some of Jesus' "popular" actions, such as the wilderness feedings (above, 6,D,ii) or the procession on Jerusalem, as indicative of mass organizing. But we must keep in mind that Mark's discipleship narrative articulates a definite strategy of minority *political vocation*. That is, Jesus creates a community that is expected to embrace the messianic way regardless of how the masses respond to the "objective conditions for revolution."

In what sense, then, do we understand Jesus' solidarity with the poor? Liberation theologians working in South Korea have illumined the question with a term drawn from their cultural and historical experience: *minjung*. Kim Yong-bok defines *minjung*:

> Kingdoms, dynasties, and states rise and fall; but the minjung remain as a concrete reality in history, experiencing the comings and goings of political powers. . . . Power has its basis in the minjung. But power as it expresses itself in political powers does not belong to the minjung. These powers seek to maintain themselves; and they rule the minjung [1981:183].

Kim calls them "protagonists in the historical drama," but distinguishes the politico-cultural definition of *minjung* from Marx's strictly socio-economic understanding of the proletariat:

> The former is a dynamic, changing concept. Woman belongs to minjung when she is politically dominated by man. An ethnic group is a minjung group when it is politically dominated by another group. A race is

minjung when it is dominated by another powerful ruling race. When intellectuals are suppressed by the military power elite, they belong to minjung. Of course, the same applies to the workers and farmers [ibid.:185].

Another Korean, Ahn Byung-mu, sees *minjung* as analogous to Mark's "crowd" (*ochlos*; see above, 4,C,iii).

In Mark, argues Ahn, the *minjung* are outside the sphere of the dominant Jewish groups; it includes the poor, the tax collector, the impure [1981:150f.]. But he concludes:

> The *ochlos* are feared by the unjust and powerful, but they are not organized into a power group. Therefore, we cannot regard them as a political power bloc; rather, they should be regarded existentially as a crowd. They are minjung not because they have a common destiny, but simply because they are alienated, dispossessed, and powerless. . . . Jesus does not give the impression that he intends to organize the *ochlos* into a force. He does not provide a program for their movement, nor does he make them an object of his movement. He does not forcibly demand anything from them. He does not ask to be their ruler or head. He "passively" stands with them. A relationship between Jesus and the minjung takes place and then is broken. They follow him without condition. They welcome him. They also betray him [ibid.:151].

Mark clearly portrays Jesus as an advocate for the poor and outcast in his healing and symbolic direct action. Ahn means "passive" solidarity in the sense that Jesus does not objectify the Palestinian *minjung* in terms of its role in a revolutionary process "so that its name may be used to justify any kind of political dictatorship" (Kim, 1981:185).

Instead, Mark advances an ideology of "receptivity": the leper, the sinner, the woman, the child are all to be received unconditionally as subjects of the kingdom. Jesus teaches his disciples to live among them and look at life from their perspective. This receptivity is not based upon any inherent goodness on the part of the poor, but as a sign of Yahweh's unconditional acceptance of them as *minjung*. For Mark, the ideology of receptivity would appear to be rooted in the old Hebrew notion of reciprocity. The land belongs to Yahweh, and *all* who dwell upon it do so by grace, with equal status: "To me the people of Israel are servants, they are my servants whom I brought from the land of Egypt" (Lv 25:55).

The second subject of the messianic re-creation of human unity are the gentiles. Extending reciprocity and receptivity beyond the Jewish people was surely Mark's most radical proposition. That Mark is advocating not an abstract ideal but a concrete practice of integration is evident from the fact that he deals head on with the main obstacle to its realization: the purity and dietary restrictions, which precluded social intercourse with gentiles. There is ample testimony in the New Testament to the fact that this was a thorny issue for the early church, especially in the writings of Paul and Luke (above, 7,E,ii).

The discourse of Mark's gentile cycle (7:1–8:10) in fact closely resembles that of Luke in Acts 10. Both writers use the vehicle of narrative fiction for purposes of legitimating integration. In the case of Mark 7, it is the fiction of "bread," symbolizing common table fellowship:

1. dispute with Pharisees over eating bread in violation of purity regulations;
2. Jesus delegitimizes Pharisaic practice;
3. Jesus pronounces all foods clean;
4. Jesus concedes an argument to a gentile woman who asks for "crumbs" from the "children's bread";
5. Jesus feeds the gentile masses.

Table solidarity with gentiles, which was in jeopardy at the beginning of the cycle because of kosher regulations, is overcome first through teaching, then through symbolic action (exorcism). The original purpose is finally effected abundantly in the wilderness feedings, in which Mark re-presents Israel's wilderness experience of sustenance among gentile crowds.

In Acts 10 the fiction is a double vision:

1. gentile Cornelius is instructed to rendezvous with Peter in a vision (10:1–8);
2. Peter, hungry, has a vision in which he is told that he may hunt all animals for food (10:9–13);
3. Peter protests on grounds of purity; vision pronounces all foods clean (10:14–16);
4. Peter and Cornelius rendezvous (10:17–33);
5. gentiles receive the word, spirit, and baptism (10:34–48).

Again, the promise of integration is indicated, then jeopardized, but overcome through pronouncement and teaching. The vision is finally effected abundantly, as Luke represents the story of Pentecost among the gentile gathering.

Thus Mark, like the other early Christian writers, struggled to legitimate the radical social experiment of integration. Was his community itself integrated? I believe the narrative suggests that it was; Mark insists there is only "one loaf" (8:14,17). That the community was under considerable pressure because of this experiment is articulated in terms of the dramatic fiction of the boat struggling against the cosmic forces of wind and waves in its quest to get to "the other side" of the sea. Jesus cannot make this voyage for his followers, but promises to rescue them when the project threatens to founder. Just as Jesus silences the "demons" of scribal and Roman domination, he silences the overwhelming forces that oppose the re-creation of one humanity (4:39–41); it is this that makes this improbable social experiment possible.

ii. "All Ate and Were Satisfied": Community and the New Economic and Symbolic Order

In counterpoint to the portrait of economic deprivation that Mark paints of Palestine he asserts the vision of abundance. The images of "enough" are:

1. eschatological harvest, 4:8
2. Jewish crowds satisfied in wilderness, 6:44
3. all food declared clean, 7:19
4. gentile crowds satisfied in wilderness, 8:8
5. abundant leftovers, 8:19f.
6. communal abundance, 10:30.

These images imply a new practice over against the temple-based system of economic redistribution, which has failed. This is the practice of cooperative sharing, a return to the original Israelite vision of a community of production and consumption.

The old system will persist, of course, and the disciples on mission will be vulnerable to it (6:8); they are justified in commandeering food for sustenance (2:23ff.). Mark appears to reject asceticism (i.e., fasting) as a privilege of the affluent, offensive to those who genuinely hunger. But the central focus of Mark's ideology can be seen in Jesus' interaction with his disciples in the first feeding story. Note the dialectical play of Mark's discourse (6:36–38):

Disciples: "Send the crowds away into the villages so they can buy themselves something to eat."
Jesus: "You feed them."
Disciples: "Shall we go and buy two hundred denarii worth of bread and give it to them to eat?"
Jesus: "How many loaves do you have? Go and see."

The disciples can imagine only market scarcity in the dominant economy. Against this, Jesus keeps referring them to their own resources, challenging them to forge an alternative economics. The "abundance" envisioned in Mark's vision of the kingdom can be realized when the disciples learn to organize and share available resources. This is the "miracle" narrated in the wilderness feedings; by it no one need "faint on the way" (8:3).

The community model of economic sharing is articulated in 10:29–31 (above, 9,C,iii), there standing in tension with the dominant order represented by the rich landowner whose wealth "defrauds" the poor (10:19–22). The community re-creates the redistributive system: private ownership of land and houses is abandoned in favor of cooperative economics. This model is not intended to engender corporate affluence, but to provide surplus on behalf of the poor. The narrative strongly suggests that Mark's community is in fact practicing some kind of communal model (10:28), and experiencing social opposition because of it. It was one thing for Qumran monks to practice a style of communal economics in isolation in the wilderness; it was quite another to attempt it while residing in the midst of a hostile economic system.

There may be, however, a more specific dimension to the "persecutions" alluded to in 10:30. Did Jewish members of Mark's community refuse to cooperate with their tithing or other obligations to the temple-state? There is no direct evidence of this, but certainly such a position could be extrapolated on the basis of several episodes: the civil disobedience in the grain field, Jesus' attack on the temple (11:15ff.), his criticism of contributions to the treasury (12:41ff.), and his prediction of the temple's destruction (13:2). Moreover, the tribute question suggests that some form of economic resistance was a live issue for the community (12:13ff.). Mark's narrative bias against the city further suggests that the community stood in solidarity with the plight of rural producers in the dominant system, and may have been promoting alternative models of distribution that were considered subversive by authorities such as the Pharisees.

At the heart of Mark's political, social, and economic alternatives to the dominant order lies a radical new symbolic system based upon the primacy of human need (3:4). In place of the purity code Jesus exhorts moral imperatives concerning exploitation (7:21f.; above, 7,C,i). In place of the debt code he enjoins a community practice of forgiveness (11:25). Jesus' teaching functions to both ethicize and democratize the traditional symbolic order, undermining the legitimacy of those who mediate it—that is, priests, scribes, and Pharisees. Mark presses the bold claim that the temple is not necessary in order for Yahweh to dwell among the people. There is no sacred institutional site from which Yahweh must be addressed in prayer: that site is faith (11:24). This point is made dramatically in the rending of the temple curtain at the moment of Jesus' death. The messianic "sacrifice" of Jesus has reconciled the people to Yahweh and each other, thus rendering void the priestly apparatus. Yahweh is no longer a recluse in the Holy of Holies, but present among the community.

Given the importance of table fellowship to Mark's social and economic experiment, it is not surprising that Jesus chooses this site as the new symbolic center of the community. In place of the temple is a simple meal, which represents participation in Jesus' "body" (14:22–25; above, 12,B,iii). Yet it is the meal, not the body, that is "holy," for the latter is absent at the end of the story. We are left, then, not with a ritual but the social event of table fellowship. This meal, which itself was an expropriation of the great liberation symbols of Passover, is meant to bring to mind the entire messianic program of justice and the cost of fidelity to it. But it is a meal for a community in flight, or more accurately, a community that follows its true center, Jesus, who cannot be institutionalized because he is always ahead of us on the road (16:7).

There is one more aspect to Mark's reconstruction of a symbolic life within the community: that is the primacy of the word. Jesus' teachings remain not only after he is gone, but stand at the center of history: "heaven and earth may pass away but my words shall not pass away" (13:31). And how is this word mediated? Through Mark's story, of course! The Gospel is an integral part of the symbolic center of the community, inseparable from Jesus himself (above, 3,A,i). For the sake of Jesus and the Gospel, disciples give up the old order for the new (10:29) and pay the attendant price (8:35). And because the new story is linked to the old story, the community continues to read the Hebrew scriptures with "eyes to see" and "ears to hear."

To conclude, the literary *novum* called the Gospel of Mark was produced in response to a historical and ideological crisis engendered by the Jewish war. In this apocalyptic moment, a community struggled to maintain its nonviolent resistance to the Roman armies, the Jewish ruling class, and rebel recruiters, while sowing the seeds of a new revolutionary order through practice and proselytism. To be sure, 69 C.E. was not the best of times for a radical social experiment. Perhaps this would explain the urgency of the story, its expectation of suffering, and its ideology of failure and starting over. The profile of Mark's community does not fit in the strictures designed by sect-sociology, nor does it fit the caricatures of millennial groups. It must be taken seriously on its own terms, as a distinct socio-political strategy in a determinate formation, and indeed as an ideology of practice that begs to be heard in our own time.

14F. WHO WAS JESUS OF NAZARETH?
NOTES FOR A POLITICAL CHRISTOLOGY

The reader will note that throughout this commentary I have been circumspect in attributing the ideology of the text to Mark, rather than to the "historical Jesus." The reasons for that have nothing to do with any judgment concerning how much or little of Mark can be attributed to Jesus; that is the concern of historical criticism, not socio-literary commentary. The text is direct evidence for Mark's social strategy, only indirectly for that of Jesus. I am not particularly concerned to speculate about Jesus of Nazareth, not because I doubt that Mark portrayed him accurately, but precisely because I believe Mark was a faithful interpreter of Jesus' practice and vision. As I said at the outset, to "read" Mark is to "read" Jesus.

Still, historical modesty does not diminish the attraction exerted by the figure from Nazareth, whom Mark portrays not only as a past prophet but as a living leader, the symbolic center of the new order. Obviously, Mark could scarcely have advocated such a profoundly concrete and historical ideology of discipleship unless this "way" had actually been lived by the one who announced it. It is worthwhile then appending a few reflections concerning this Nazarene as a Jewish radical, based upon Mark's story. The following is not an attempt at historical reconstruction, but some imaginative extrapolations based upon the continuity of the very tradition of biblical radicalism to which Mark himself appeals. The classic christological categories of prophet, priest, and king, will do nicely for these notes.

i. Prophet, Priest, and King in the Tradition of Biblical Radicalism

It does not require a great deal of historical imagination to think that the young Jesus might have been stirred to the core of his being by reading prophetic texts such as the one from Isaiah cited at the beginning of this chapter. The world of this rural Nazarene would have been one of poverty and oppression. His elders could tell him tales of the ruthless King Herod. Perhaps some of them had participated in the uprisings at the time of Herod's death, when a Galilean social bandit named Judas had attacked and plundered the royal arsenal and sparked a short-lived rebellion. In retaliation, the Roman legions had razed the city, Sepphoris—a mere four miles from Nazareth.

What Jesus heard in the prophet Isaiah was the opposite of what he saw in Galilee: the fortified cities of aliens surrounded him, refuges not for the poor but for the rich. Rome had cast its net over all peoples, and the needy had no advocate. And tears—he had seen the tears flow from the death around him. Death by hunger, death by the cross. Yet Isaiah's vision might have haunted him nevertheless. It insisted that Yahweh took the side of the poor. It foresaw liberation not only for the Jewish people, but for all peoples. And it seemed that it promised more than the demise of Rome: it spoke of the defeat of the powers, indeed of an assault on death itself.

There may have been another word of Isaiah's that fired the imagination of the Nazarene: Yahweh's call for someone to proclaim the vision afresh (Is 6:8). It was not an attractive task, if indeed everyone was already "deaf" and "blind" (Is 6:9f.).But something had to be done, so the vision would not die. So did Jesus fall into a long line of prophets who lived and died in an effort to make the Word flesh.

Jesus thus became first a "prophet," in the tradition of Israelite radicalism. Like the popular prophets Elijah and Elisha, he pressed Yahweh's covenantal lawsuit against the wayward leaders of the people. The plaintiffs of this suit were the poor, whose full membership in the community had been denied. Reasserting the populist roots of the Israelite polity, he withdrew his consent-to-be-ruled from the usurpers of power, and counseled others to do the same; loyalty belonged to Yahweh alone. Like the classic oracular prophets, Jesus relentlessly unmasked the way in which the structures and stewards of the dominant order oppressed the poor. In the footsteps of Amos he delivered sharp oracles to the powerful; in the footsteps of Jeremiah he dramatized his message with symbolic action. And in the footsteps of "Second Isaiah" he understood the cost of telling the truth and of calling the people to account before the vision; he was prepared to be "despised and rejected, a man of sorrows" (Is 53:3).

Jesus of Nazareth was also a "priest," in that he took it upon himself to mediate Yahweh's healing to the poor and outcast. He unilaterally declared a Jubilee for those doubly oppressed by the symbolic order: the unclean were pronounced whole, the debt-ridden forgiven. And then he liberated Yahweh's presence from its controlled reclusion in the Holy of Holies, announcing that it dwelt among the people. The people could now eradicate debt by cooperating in a new community of sharing and forgiving; the people could welcome the impure and anoint the sick and cast out demons. Jesus' role as priest was to do away with priests, to radically democratize the body of Israel. The "blood of atonement" would no longer be a vicarious offering controlled by the temple stewards. The only acceptable sacrifice was that of one's own lifeblood, shed in service to the people and in resistance to oppressors. So Jesus embraced this priestly vocation: not to rule over, but to be "reckoned with the sinners," and in the end to "pour out his soul to death" (Is 53:12).

And Jesus was "king," but in the tradition of popular and revolutionary Israelite kingship. He was not a royal pretender to David's throne, for he repudiated the politics of imperial domination. Rather he was a "true shepherd," anointed to lead a new tribal confederacy into a new promised land. The Davidic tradition of kingship had resulted only in the realization of Samuel's worst fears: militarism, economic control, and slavery (1 Sm 8:10–18). In the end, it had rotted from within and collapsed: "A house divided cannot stand." The Maccabean restoration had fared no better. Thus Jesus identified with Zechariah's vision (Zec 9:9f.), which "evokes an image of the leader of tribal Israel prior to the time it even possessed the more advanced military technology of horses and war chariots: 'Lo, your king comes to you, triumphant and riding on an ass' " (Horsley and Hanson, 1985:100). He would die a rebel king.

ii. Human One: The Way to a New Heaven and New Earth

The prophetic-apocalyptic tradition promised a new creation in which the vision would find its time; but Jesus' own historical experience gave no indication that this was anywhere in sight. But could it not have been in his study of this resistance literature of his people, specifically Daniel, that Jesus came to his most revolutionary insight: namely, that the powers could only be defeated by the power of what we today call "nonviolence"? Domination would remain the law of the world order unless and until a people took upon itself to embrace the radical paradox: to lose life is to save life.

Daniel did not say *how* this paradox worked, only that through it alone would Yahweh's reign dawn (Dn 7:14). So Jesus founded an apocalyptic community committed to the overthrow of the powers. It was not a secret society, but a way of life and death, and a hope of resurrection—the apocalyptic promise of vindication (Dn 12:2f.). Drawing from the patriarchal, covenantal, and prophetic streams of discourse in his scriptures, Jesus fashioned a practice of liberation and instructed others in it. In Galilee he began to proclaim that the moment had arrived to realize the vision of Yahweh's reign. As a rabbi he gathered a small band of followers, and laboriously instructed them in the paradox, applying it to every area of life. He tried debating with other rabbis, only to get kicked out of several synagogues. He kept on, itinerating around the Galilean villages, a healer, exorcist, and friend of the poor. He could not be sure his own disciples understood the paradox, and in the end he could only demonstrate it in his own flesh. So he marched to Jerusalem; the final showdown was surely terrifying, but Jesus carried his vision through—and his followers fled. Alone, Jesus faced down the highest and mightiest powers of his world—and was duly defeated by them. He became an imperial statistic, another thorn extracted from the flesh of procurator and high priest.

What became of his disciples? It seems they experienced something that convinced them death could not hold the executed Nazarene. Was Jesus raised from the dead? I happen to agree with those who contend that nothing else can explain the genesis of the Christian movement. But with the empty tomb came a terrifying realization—for it meant that Jesus' radical paradox had been vindicated. The disciples were now haunted by the vision that had haunted the Nazarene. They began reflecting on his words, his actions, and upon the very texts Jesus had exposited to them; they came to identify the vision of biblical radicalism with the living Jesus. It was up to them to explain and above all to live the paradox of the kingdom. They probably returned to Galilee and founded the first community there, though some undoubtedly remained in Jerusalem.

By the time Mark wrote, the movement was still small and, by any account, unimpressive. The net had been drawn more tightly over the nations, death was still on the throne. But the seed of the kingdom had been scattered on the earth, and Mark composed a story about it and called it good news (Mk 4:3ff.).

Since then the weary world, like the farmer in the parable, has risen and slept, risen and slept, and it is, by any account, difficult to tell if or how the seed has sprouted and grown (Mk 4:27). History is not kind to paradox and mystery.

Today the net has become a noose, and death ridicules the vision by threatening to swallow the whole of creation in a moment. The poor remain distressed outside the palaces of the mighty. The "master" has gone away and not returned, and his servants, for the most part, are asleep (13:34–36). But he has left us the key to the door into a new heaven and earth.

AFTERWORD

On Continuing the Narrative of Biblical Radicalism

> I have lived inside the monster and know its entrails—and my weapon is
> only the slingshot of David.
>
> —José Martí (1975:3)

Recently I have become familiar with the wood sculpture of a Salvadoran refugee living in Los Angeles. A gentle, unassuming, serious catechist, Edgar knows the truth about life on the peripheries: his wife, children, and several relatives were all victims of right wing death squads while he was a student in San Salvador. Probably nothing less would have forced him to flee his home for *el norte*. Since arriving in the metropolis and getting work in a furniture factory, Edgar has found a voice for his pain in wood sculpture. Art of such intensity and power that it is beginning to gain national attention, his "folk realism" presents figures that blend Latin Catholic iconography with the strong, long-suffering countenance of the Salvadoran peasant. One piece in particular has stayed with me, perhaps because it expresses the question that lies behind this book. A young boy sits on a rough-hewn wooden bench, as if the young Jesus on Mary's lap. His right hand is raised, but he is pointing not to heaven but to earth. Our attention is drawn to his feet, where a lone flower grows next to a bomb (markings: USAF), half buried in the earth. We look back at his face, at once serene and anguished, his eyes fixed upon us in a riveting, searching glare.

As if asking, "Do you not yet understand?"

A. EMPTY TOMB, NEVER-ENDING STORY

We have completed a reading of Mark, and have articulated how his narrative strategy reflects an apocalyptic ideology and social strategy that his community struggled to live out in the historical moment of the Jewish war in first-century Palestine. But that is a world far removed from our own. Does this story have anything to say to our world, and if so, do we have "ears to hear" it?

The empty tomb at the end of Mark's Gospel symbolizes that his story, like its subject Jesus, has not ended but lives on. Just as Mark reached back across the centuries to bring the "old story" of Hebrew prophetic radicalism to life again in a new story about Jesus of Nazareth, so does he reach forward across the ages to us, challenging us to continue the story by "returning to Galilee" (16:7). But how is it that an invitation to "reread" this story is politically subversive? Does not the circle of narrative actually lead the reader *away* from practice, shutting out the real world and seducing us with one that exists only in our imagination? This is certainly what those who dismiss the fictions of apocalyptic narrative as the wish-dreams of the alienated would have us believe.

The question of whether the act of reading can animate the reader is nowhere better addressed than in contemporary German novelist Michael Ende's *The Neverending Story* (1983). High fiction in the tradition of Tolkien or C. S. Lewis, Ende's story within a story centers around Bastian, a boy alienated from his own world who tries to escape by immersing himself into the narrative world of a book about "Fantastica." He identifies closely with the book's protagonists, but becomes terrified when it begins to seem that the characters are soliciting *his* help in resolving *their* crisis. As the drama in "Fantastica" reaches its denouement, Bastian realizes that the story he is reading is doomed unless he responds to its cries for his active involvement. As he hesitates, frozen by fear, the story begins to turn back upon itself, unresolved, except that now Bastian is named in the text. So he finally "jumps into" the narrative, giving it a new beginning. After many adventures in which he learns more deeply about his true self, Bastian returns to his own real world, a transformed person.

In similar fashion, Mark's narrative of discipleship, which so tragically collapses because of "blindness," can continue only if we realize, like Bastian, that we are in fact characters in the very story we thought we were reading. Mark, like Ende's novel, puts the "future" of the narrative in the hands of the reader. And he can do so precisely because he believes that the story and its subject are not "dead past" but "living present." But how do we "jump into" the Gospel and make it our own? Mark's readerly crisis cannot be resolved through a mere leap of imagination, but only by "taking up the cross" and following. The new story is one in which we are no longer only readers but also actants.

Our "script" thus becomes that of biblical radicalism. But did Mark mean this script to be a *practical* guide to real, revolutionary transformation of the world? And even if it was a concrete socio-political strategy in the context of first-century Palestine, can it be so in ours? Are not Mark's criticisms too categorical, his apocalyptic dualism too Manichean, for our age of sophisticated ambiguities? Are not his constructive solutions overdemanding, indeed hopelessly idealistic? Above all, how is it that the "way of the cross" represents a realistic, positive practice in light of the complexities and the overwhelming violence of modern politics? Is it not simply an exercise in negation or, worse, an abandonment of the difficult and "dirty" tasks of long-term revolutionary struggle? These question are real, and many will surely find it easier to dismiss Mark's script of biblical radicalism in precisely the terms I have argued against: as the expression of alienated sectarianism or utopian dreaming.

Ours is not a hospitable world for visionaries—and not without good reason, for charlatans abound. Gospel radicalism is still dismissed in the metropolises of the West by the dominant ideologies of Christian realism. Yet many are reconsidering, for "realism" has demonstrably failed us. In its name the four apocalyptic horsemen of empire, militarism, economic exploitation, and environmental revolt (Rv 6:2–8) ride freely over the earth. Is it not true, as social critic C. W. Mills once put it in his "Pagan Sermon to a Christian Clergy," that "in our world 'necessity' and 'realism' have become ways to hide lack of moral imagination" (1960:165)? Perhaps, then, Mark offers a way whose *kairos* has truly come. I wish therefore to close with a word concerning the twin themes of radical discipleship introduced in chapter 1, repentance and resistance. These thoughts only anticipate the fuller discussion of radical discipleship today in the forthcoming sequel to this project (above, Preface).

B. REPENTANCE

Can Mark's story be ours? I stated at the outset that my most fundamental presumption in writing this commentary is that the Gospel of Mark has something very important to say to those of us in the *locus imperium* (above, 1,A,ii). I also acknowledged there that because Mark's story was and is first about and for the poor, we of the privileged metropolitan classes are only secondarily its subjects. Thus if we would identify with any of the characters in Mark's story, it can legitimately be only that of the rich man (10:17–22) and the scribe (12:32–34). Like the former, we North Americans are preoccupied with the religious prospects of "eternal life"—and are summoned instead to discipleship. Jesus' call comes to us too as a specific challenge to turn from our privilege and restore justice to the poor. And we should take careful note that this is precisely what the rich man found *too hard* to do. Or perhaps, like the scribe, we are more ethically concerned, ever inquiring after the character of the "greatest commandment." But when we think we know the answer, we are still only "not far from the kingdom"; for with the privileged class, it is easy to know and not do. For us the way toward liberating practice is riddled with seductive and compelling detours.

We North Americans must begin where Mark begins: with the call to repentance (*metanoia*, 1:4,15). Everything else in the discipleship narrative is predicated upon our response to that call, which, of course, presupposes a consciousness of sin. This must be understood not in our modern sense, as strictly personal angst or guilt, but in the Hebrew sense, as the admission of our solidarity with historical injustice. In the metropolis, the facade of imperial virtue—what M. Harrington called the "cruel innocence which prevents us from even seeing the wrongs we perpetrate" (1977:13)—must be stripped away. Only by repudiating the "American dream," and encountering the real world "outside the gates"—Edgar's world—will we see the dark side of this dream, which is a nightmare for the poor. The life horizons of two-thirds of the world are determined not by the promise of upward mobility and rising expectations, but by a bitter cycle of violence and poverty that is the necessary result of superpower economic and military control.

Against a political culture of triumphalism we must try to recover the "gospel experience of negation" and develop an "indigenous theology of the cross" (Hall, 1976). This means adopting a structural analysis that explains how we benefit from a system that routinely inflicts crosses upon the world's disinherited. The present arrangement of world power is not a reward for hard work, or a happy accident, or the white man's burden, or a divine vocation. The first awakening is that our prosperity is based upon a system of robbery and domination. If *metanoia* means a radical break with "business as usual" (above, 3,F,iii), its meaning for us is, as W. A. Williams puts it, to simply say no to empire. But he asks:

Do we have either the imagination or the courage to say "no" to empire?
It is now *our* responsibility. It has to do with how we live and how we die.
We as a culture have run out of imperial games to play [1980:213].

From my experience in the radical discipleship movement (above, 1,A,iii), I have found, and Mark would seem to confirm, that in order to facilitate a concrete process of repentance we need intentional communities and lifestyles that experiment with more just and compassionate patterns of social and economic relating (Kavanaugh, 1983; Finnerty, 1977; Herzog, 1980). But we must do more than turn away from capitalist culture, with its crippling consumption and affluence. We must also turn *toward* those who have been robbed and dominated, at home and abroad. It is they who, to paraphrase Hebrews 13:10–13, are forced "outside the city gates" by the metropolitan cult of modernity. But there Jesus lives and dies with them, and there we too must journey if we are to meet Jesus.

We do not encounter Jesus in the "abstract poor." The grip our illusions have upon us, reinforced by the fictions of bourgeois culture, is loosened only when we confront the human faces and voices of real victims, for whom the imperial truth is clear. But the North American middle class is structurally insulated from the poor: that is the meaning of the suburbs that ring our urban areas, and the Western hotels that rise like islands of affluence in Calcutta, Nairobi, or Santiago. Moreover, the historical presence of the poor is systematically repressed, distorted, or objectified through the imperial media: that is the meaning of Hollywood, the six-o'clock television news, and the self-censoring press. Repentance will also mean therefore that the struggle to breach the walls that segregate residents of the metropolis from those whose historical experience has been one of oppression (Neal, 1977). And if we do see and hear their testimony, we must be prepared to be implicated. For genuine solidarity with the oppressed leads not to vicarious satisfaction, but to a painful encounter with our imperial selves (Nolan, 1985).

C. RESISTANCE

To become "fishers" with Jesus (1:17) is to join him in his struggle to "bind the strong man" (3:27). If Jesus contested the powers through the subversive practice of symbolic direct action, then we must in our context find meaningful and clear ways to do the same. Challenging the symbolic order today surely means unmasking and resisting the institutionalized lies and hidden crimes of imperial domination and violence. The second awakening is this: the policies and ideologies meant to sustain and justify our system of robbery have resulted in a "fortress America." The cornerstones of this fortress are, on the one hand, triage economics and, on the other hand, nuclear militarism. Together they represent a Damoclean sword held over humanity, giving our era a decidedly apocalyptic character. The historical ultimatum they pose faces us with the bare truth of the biblical dictum: without prophecy, the people—indeed, now creation itself—will surely perish (Prv 29:18).

But how do we speak of hope that is not contaminated with either the notoriously naive optimism of the mainstream or the equally bankrupt eschatological romanticism of the left? How do we remain open-eyed to the various forms of technological proto-omnipotence and their seemingly inexorable inertia without succumbing to the despair that social psychologists call "psychic numbing"? In a word, is it even credible to speak of "impeding the progress" of the most entrenched system of domination the world has ever known? In such a situation, "response-ability" depends upon a Christian faith that refuses, as Thomas Merton wrote in the grimmest days of the Cuban missile crisis, to "stand frozen stiff in the face of the Unspeakable." A practice of resistance begins with a recovery of moral and political imagination—a formidable task in the *locus imperium*.

The metropolis indeed represents a social formation in which political discourse is almost wholly bankrupt. The managerial rationalism of realpolitik is only a secular restatement of the old myth of divine right, which in the American empire is articulated by the national theology of manifest destiny and cold war. Whether it is the scholarly articles of foreign policy journals, the commentaries of network news, or the high metaphors of campaign rhetoric, the aim of mainstream political discourse is the same: to justify geopolitical domination abroad and insular privilege at home.

Given this crisis of political imagination, the radical discipleship movement has looked to the discourse of nonviolent direct action with the intention of provoking a "moral crisis" commensurate to the hour (Douglass, 1980). Drawing upon the political traditions of Mohandas Gandhi and Martin Luther King, Jr., and inspired by the symbolic action of Jesus, nonviolent resisters have tried to confront the national security state's idols with biblical symbols in an ever-escalating war of myths. This movement is perhaps most clearly (though by no means exclusively) represented by the "Plowshares" actions, which symbolically commence the disarmament process in the utter absence of state intention to do so. At numerous sites Christians have penetrated high-security areas and brought carpenter's hammers ringing down upon the weapons of omnicide: Titan missiles, Trident submarines, and other demigods in the nuclear pantheon (Berrigan, 1984).

These and many other forms of noncooperation and resistance are seen as nothing more or less than "public liturgy." In the metropolitan context, the state is not threatened by churchly worship, unlike, say, El Salvador, where Archbishop Romero was cut down while saying Mass, or South Korea, where Presbyterian minister Hyung Kyu Park is regularly dragged from his pulpit by security forces. Direct action therefore attempts to move the site of worship to the sanctuaries of the "gods of metal," the barbed-wired sacred sites of weapons factories and missile silos. Although our practice of symbolic action rarely carries the cost borne by other dissidents and revolutionaries around the world, there are at this writing Christian resisters serving sentences of up to twenty years in U.S. prisons.

These efforts at nonviolent resistance, though preliminary and timid, are predicated upon a deeper concern: the historical imperative to arrest what Archbishop Helder Camara (1971) called the "spiral of violence." There has of course been a great deal of debate in ecumenical circles over the last three decades about the ethics of violence and nonviolence in modern revolutionary politics (Swomley, 1972). Unfortunately this conversation has, from the First World side, been all too academic; and from both sides it is riddled with platitudes and caricature. I can only indicate the position of our movement, and leave discussion of these difficult issues to the companion volume on radical discipleship. Our analysis of the structural characteristics of the global metropolitan-sponsored system of militarism persuades us that armed revolutionary struggle, although it may in the short term liberate political space, in the long term only strengthens the dominant system as a whole, and hence those who control it. To use an economic analogy from liberation theology, it is like trying to solve the problem of Third World dependence through redirected capitalist "development." This is a reformist strategy, attacking symptoms rather than causes, and in the long run serves only to strengthen the international capitalist system. Similarly, recent history suggests that liberation movements that are fundamentally military in character can never fully eradicate the infrastructures of an oppressive system that was itself founded and perpetuated by a military elite. In a world ruled by the logic of militarism, armed struggle becomes counterrevolutionary.

In stating this position our aim is not to condemn violent reactions to structural injustice or judge those who have felt compelled, under circumstances far more threatening than ours, to take up the gun in a liberation struggle. Nor, in using the term "nonaligned radicalism" to describe Mark's position vis-à-vis the Jewish rebellion, do I mean to imply that today we should be politically unallied. Quite the contrary! Rather, it is to say that we are searching for a political practice that will attack capitalism and militarism at their roots, and are compelled in this search by Mark's apocalyptic politics of the cross. The unity between ends and means lacking in Marxist theory and practice, and demanded by Mark, I believe can be found in Gandhian nonviolence.

Gandhi's understanding of *swaraj* (liberation, self-reliance) anticipated (by a half-century!) every cardinal theme in contemporary theologies of liberation (Jesudasan, 1984). But Gandhi insisted that

> [the poor] cannot successfully fight [the big powers] with their own weapons. After all, you cannot go beyond the atom bomb. Unless we have a new way of fighting imperialism of all brands in place of the outworn one of violent revolution, there is no hope for the oppressed [1948, II:8].

Gandhian nonviolence should not be identified with the moralism of the privileged, which imposes its abstract ethical absolutes on the situation—though admittedly it is often presented this way by First World advocates. Gandhi's experiments with *satyagraha* were forged in a context of imperial domination, and continue in such sites today. In any case, like the gospel, the truth of our commitment to nonviolence will be borne out only in practice. We are clear that our derivative practice of *satyagraha* here in the First World has a very long way to go until it is taken seriously as a revolutionary alternative by others who disagree with us.

To read and reread Mark takes us ever deeper into the ongoing struggle to promote and practice repentance and resistance in the *locus imperium*. Philip Berrigan has likened this struggle to the biblical parable of Jonah. Like that beleaguered prophet, we have been, most of us, in full flight from our vocation to "cry against the great city" (Jon 1:1). It is only when we have abandoned—or are thrown overboard from—the metropolitan "ship-of-state," so to speak, that we are able to awaken to imperial reality in the "belly of the beast." Only there do Christians realize that "those who pay allegiance to vain idols forsake their true loyalty" (Jon 2:8). Our task, in the well-known words of the nineteenth-century Cuban anti-imperialist writer José Martí, is to live "inside the monster and know its entrails."

Yet Martí's switch in biblical metaphors was also apt, for we are truly confronting an imperial Goliath (1 Sm 17). A military giant, armored to the teeth and brandishing history's deadliest spear, the metropolis stands on the hill of history, "reproaching" the people of God (17:4–11). Yet the rule of the sword today is such, and the demands of the gospel are such, that we cannot contend with this Goliath on his own terms; the armor of Saul "will not do" (17:39). Our weapon is "only the slingshot of David."

But it is to such long odds that the "mystery of the kingdom" belongs (Mk 4:30–32).

D. DISCIPLESHIP AND FAILURE: "YOU WILL ALL DESERT ME"

A few years ago, while in Australia, I was talking with a long-time advocate of radical discipleship who had just returned from an international ecumenical conference in Africa. He reported, with some indignation, that one conservative advocate of "church growth" there had rendered the following epitaph: "The radical church is the fastest-dying church in the world!" My friend shook his head, but after a moment his indignation faded, and he added, "Of course, that preacher may be right. Perhaps our movement is finished."

At the time, his words could hardly have hit home any harder. I was still recovering from the painful breakup of my own community, the loss of home and marriage. I had never expected that the "cross" would take this shape. If readers of this book still feel it is an exercise in imaginative idealism, they should be aware that Mark's vision is flesh to me, flesh seared and scarred. I have seen business-as-usual rudely disrupted by the *kairos* of the call, seen the vision of radical discipleship community realized. And more importantly, I have also seen those dreams fade, seen our best attempts to weave a fabric of hope and wholeness unravel, seen good persons bail out.

The radical discipleship movement today is beleaguered and weary. So many of our communities, which struggled so hard to integrate the pastoral and prophetic, the personal and the political, resistance and contemplation, work and recreation, love and justice, are disintegrating. The powerful centrifugal forces of personal and social alienation tear us apart; the "gravity" exerted by imperial culture's seductions, deadly mediocrities, and deadly codes of conformity pull our aspirations plummeting down. Our economic and political efforts are similarly besieged. The ability of metropolis to either crush or co-opt movements of dissent seems inexhaustible.

I know many Third World activists, courageous sisters and brothers who have risked their lives for the same vision under circumstances far more demanding than our own, who echo similar sentiment. Some have seen revolutions betrayed by those who assumed power; others have seen their modest experiments in self-determination uprooted by metropolitan-sponsored military or economic counterinsurgency. So it is that exile is replacing exodus as the central theme for many liberation theologians. At home and abroad, the empire surrounds and strangles any form of new life outside its sphere of control.

Our failures tempt us to conclude that we were simply misguided, a conclusion the current reactionary mood of both church and culture gleefully endorses. Indeed, they urge us to "come to our senses," and point knowingly to the yippie-to-yuppie pendulum that has swung inexorably from idealism to cynicism to "selfish realism" (today the 1960s do not stimulate subversive memory, only nostalgia). But we do not welcome the opportunity to reconstruct life in the mainstream; we experience only vertigo. There is no happy resocialization back into the middle-class bosom of America, for no other reason than we know too much to live the lie. It is a terrible realization that, despite experiences of miscarriage, collapse, debacle, defeat, and despair, there is still no more compelling alternative to the corruption of the age than radical discipleship.

"But if all we have to offer are the fruits of our dying," my friend insisted, "why bother?" Indeed, doubts gnaw. Is the gospel too demanding, we too frail, the world too overwhelming? What is the "good news" to those of us who have been broken by the vision, who have wept bitterly as we realized that we had both deserted and been deserted, who have good reason to question whether perhaps the "way" might not in fact be a dead end? Is it that we were wrong all along, and better that we finally realize it so we can get on with the business of life in the "real world"? Is it that we were not sober enough in "counting the cost"? Is it that we simply made too many mistakes, or were too idealistic, and that if we are to continue it must be with some scaled-down version? Or is it that we just have to keep on trying until we get it right? Please God, not that, not again. What is to be said to brothers and sisters who in good faith did the best they could, despite all the mistakes, and walked away empty-handed? Something has to be said; there is too much at stake. As the folks at Jonah House put it, "The most apostolic duty of all is to keep one another's courage up."

My most astonishing discovery in rereading Mark over and over in the course of writing this book was this: all of this anguish is anticipated by the Gospel. Mark reckoned not only with the moment of the kingdom's dawn, but the moment of failure and disillusionment. Jesus said simply, "You will all desert me" (14:27). The suggestion is that this desertion is inevitable in any and all discipleship narratives, and that means our own. Failure, in other words, does not lie outside the horizons of the narrative, but at dead center.

Mark's Jesus was certainly besieged, up against the raw power of the system with a handful of betrayal-bound companions. But he was not involved in that ancient scheme to stave off finitude by denying death's indignity. His call to "lose life in order to save it" (8:36) is an invitation not to kamikaze heroism, but to face up to the indignity—the political indignity of defeat, the personal indignity of failure. As if to say, only by facing up to death can we break its hammerlock on history, the world, and our lives. Only then can the discipleship story begin afresh, based not upon idealism but grace.

The apostle Paul, who so many radicals today think got Jesus all wrong, understood him perfectly on this point, and bet his life on its truth, and its efficacy. We forget that Paul lived to see his work crumble into apparent insignificance. Yes, he fought to preserve his vision against his ideological opponents and those who tried to co-opt it. And he struggled to prop it up where it was in decline, to rekindle it where it was flickering and going out— which, judging by his letters, was just about everywhere. But the fact is that after the initial decade of "successful" community-founding, Paul was losing ground, and knew it. Just as we do today.

Paul's great apostolic confession bears remarkable resemblance to Mark's second call to discipleship: "Always, wherever we may be, we carry with us in our body the death of Jesus, so that somehow the life of Jesus may be shown" (2 Cor 4:9). These are the words of someone who has reckoned with the cross. It puts a very different perspective upon the charge that we are a "dying movement."

Radical discipleship is, by virtue of the paradox of the gospel, a dying prospect. We would do well to consider this prospect—first, I hasten to stipulate, the dying of our poorer sisters and brothers, and all those throughout our groaning world who give their lives in the struggle "that the life of Jesus might be shown." No romanticism there; rather, torture, hunger, displacement, genocide. And secondly, our own lesser—but inevitably more real—dying. Our dreams brought down by gravity, our visions disintegrated by entropy, our finitude exposed by failure.

In the end, whether or not we will find a way to carry on with this story of biblical radicalism, this way of living and dying together, this way into a new heaven and earth, depends upon our understanding and acceptance of the tragedy and hope of our own failures. For it is there that our discipleship will either truly end or truly begin.

APPENDIX

Bringing the Gospel Down to Earth: A Review of Socio-Political Readings of the Jesus Story

New answers arise not so much from new data as from new questions, and new questions . . . arise from new theories, new hypotheses, and new assumptions.

—John Gager (1982:260)

Since the mid-1960s there have been numerous efforts to read the Gospels (and other biblical literature) from a new socio-political vantage point. I am deeply indebted to this body of work that precedes me, and have attempted to draw from its strengths and avoid its weaknesses. I will therefore briefly overview some of what I feel to be the most important works to date. Because this field is in a great deal of flux, I can only be selective, though, I hope, representative. I have divided the survey into what I take to be the four main approaches. Although these distinctions are somewhat artificial, they serve to identify general orientations and reading strategies.

A. THEMATIC POLITICAL HERMENEUTICS

Anglo-American political hermeneutics, which may be at least somewhat familiar to the reader, tends to approach the text in order to investigate a particular ethical issue that is germane to the life of the contemporary church—hence the rubric "thematic." An example would be the numerous studies focusing upon "economics" in the Bible (e.g., Gnuse, 1985; Pilgrim, 1981; see Malina's cautions, 1986b). Perhaps more than any other single theme, the moral issues of violence and nonviolence, in particular as they relate to the Jesus story, have been the object of recent investigation. This arose largely in response to the vigorous debates on the question in ecumenical circles beginning in the early 1960s.

The most well-known part of this conversation were the exchanges between S. G. F. Brandon's *Jesus and the Zealots* (1967) and its many respondents. Brandon popularized the thesis that the historical Jesus was actually a political revolutionary who was probably allied with rural Jewish insurgents. Mark's Gospel figured decisively in his theory as the first Christian attempt to cover up this true political character of Jesus practice, thus earning Brandon's label as an apologia for Rome (1967:221ff.; see above, 12,D,i). Rejoinders to Brandon came from historians and theologians alike, most notably O. Cullmann (1970) and M. Hengel (1973). G. Edwards's *Jesus and the Politics of Violence* (1972) took particular issue with Brandon's reading of Mark, though his reading of Mark's Jesus as politically disinterested was scarcely better.

This debate in turn sparked a renaissance in historical research concerning the genesis and character of the Jewish revolt. Unfortunately, as Horsley and Hanson have rightly contended, most of these studies went awry precisely because of their ideological agendas with respect to the violence question: "Many European and American scholars, responding to domestic protest and Third World movements of national liberation, attempted to ward off any implication that Jesus had advocated active resistance of any sort to the established order by contrasting Jesus with the Zealots" (1985:xiv; below, C). More recently the historical fictions associated with the "Zealots" have been overturned: not only was there no organized revolutionary movement at the time of Jesus, but the causes of and tributaries to the revolt of 66 C.E. were far more complex and varied than previously thought. New rereadings of Josephus are proving especially fruitful (ibid.; Rhoads, 1976).

Nevertheless, Brandon's "Roman apologia" hypothesis, however wrongheaded, seemed to saddle Mark with a reputation that caused it to be avoided by many who were interested in political hermeneutics. Subsequent work in political thematics thus tended to concentrate either on the Gospel of John (e.g., F. Herzog, 1972; Miranda, 1977) or, especially, Luke-Acts (see Cassidy, 1978 and 1983; J. M. Ford, 1984). These studies have certainly approached the text with important new questions derived from the modern social experience. However, they did not go on to develop new reading strategies, but remained content with the historico-critical method. Though most employ redaction analysis, T. Matura's (1984) was the best effort using form criticism to distill the "radical" core of Jesus' sayings.

John H. Yoder's epochal work, *The Politics of Jesus* (1972), deserves special mention here, for it influenced a whole generation of radical Christians in the U.S.A. This study *did* attempt a more systematic hermeneutic reconstruction, though it is more important for its theoretics than for its actual exegesis. Yoder launched a broadside attack on the conventional wisdom of modern liberal Protestant social ethics in its attitudes toward scripture. The mainstream view held that a reading of the New Testament might well yield broad ethical or political principles, such as "economic justice" or "human dignity"; it should not, however, be looked to for practical instructions on how to achieve these objectives in our modern social systems. Any *direct* appropriations were said to be naive; in fact, this meant that it was up to the modern social ethicist to "translate" the lofty abstractions of the New Testament into contemporary imperatives—not unlike the way in which the historical critic mediated the text by demythologizing it for the modern mind. Indeed, the alliance between the two "professionalist" approaches was a very real one.

For Yoder the crux of the matter was Jesus' practice of "pacifism," the New Testament evidence of which liberal scholars concede but dismiss as irrelevant to the modern situation. Jesus' injunction to nonviolence is rejected either as a "special" dispensation based upon his mistaken eschatological view of history (the so-called interim ethic), or as a well-intentioned but misguided perfectionism that could only wreak havoc in the real political world (the position of the Niebuhrian "realists"). There were of course also those who abstracted the "spirit" of the maxim from its plain meaning: we could kill our enemies, but only if we loved them. It is worth noting that liberation theologians have largely followed in the footsteps of these arguments: Jesus' renunciation of violence is seen either as "contextual" (and thus not binding) or as meaning that armed revolutionary struggle must be done with compassion in one's heart toward the class opponent.

Yoder contended that this amounted to divorcing principle from practice, or ends from means, within biblical hermeneutics, which he argued has been disastrous for the Christian church. So he turned the assumption on its head. On the one hand, the Jesus story is normative precisely on the question of *means*, or practice, providing a paradigm for redemptive, nonviolent approaches to social and interpersonal conflict. On the other hand, messianic faith has little to say concerning *ends*, or the criterion of efficacy, which it leaves in the hands of God. Further, Yoder asserted that the nonviolent "politics of Jesus" was reappropriated by each major strand of New Testament literature, and hence should be regarded as central, not peripheral or disposable, to christology and Christian ethics.

Behind the violence-nonviolence issue for Yoder was a deeper question: Would political hermeneutics take seriously the *practice* of Jesus as *specifically* articulated in the call to "take up the cross"? Equally important was Yoder's strong hermeneutical suspicion of the dominant ideologies of political efficacy—the Promethean imperative to manipulate the outcome of history—so characteristic of the intellectual legacy and ethos of modern positivism. The biblical tradition demands a historical commitment to constructing social patterns of equity and compassion. But does it assume that the only way of doing so is to seize power and thereby become "architects of our own destiny," an assumption shared by *both* Marxism and liberal democratic capitalism? I will return to these key questions below in "Evaluation" (Appendix, E).

Unfortunately, Yoder's weaknesses were several. Characteristic of a First World perspective, he tended to conceptualize the ethical problematic of violence primarily in terms of "reactive violence" ("violence number two" in Camara's spiral of violence model [1971]). Thus he seemed more interested in proving that Jesus rejected the option of armed insurrection than he was in articulating the alternative—his historical example of nonviolent resistance comes not from Jesus but from Josephus (Yoder, 1972:90ff.). A structural evaluation of the political world of the Jesus story is also lacking, as is sociological and literary analysis. In other words, Yoder failed to demonstrate the distinct and concrete political practice he claims for Jesus; because he himself is not an advocate of militant nonviolence or symbolic direct action, he could not see these elements in the stories of Jesus' engagement. He leaves us only with moralizing generalities, which do little to advance the conversation.

Standing as a sharp correction to the thematic readings is the work of Richard Horsley. His socio-historical studies of popular movements of resistance in first-century Palestine successfully shatter many of the older conceptual strait jackets concerning socially and politically subversive movements. He concludes that when the historical fiction, and ethical foil, of the "Zealot" movement is "removed from the discussion of Jesus and the question of violence . . . we must begin a fresh analysis of Jesus' ministry as well as the situation in which he worked." This Horsley himself has recently offered in *Jesus and the Spiral of Violence: Popular Jewish Resistance in Roman Palestine* (1987:xi). This book appeared just before the completion of my manuscript. It is filled with invaluable background and insight, and I heartily recommend it as an alternative approach to my own. In fact, Horsley and I have so many areas of agreement that I will simply note important points of divergence.

Because Horsley chooses a composite approach to the synoptic tradition, his conclusions, like Yoder's, tend to be exegetically synthetic; and because he relies upon a predominantly historico-critical method, his project has all the attendant difficulties (see my comments below, C). His historical and sociological framework is far superior to earlier works, but his reading strategy does not offer much improvement. Still, his treatment of the apocalyptic resistance tradition (see above, 14,F,ii) runs generally parallel to mine—up to the point, that is, of a hermeneutic translation. Ironically, after posing the violence-nonviolence question at the outset of the study, even going so far as to nuance Camara's spiral of violence model (ibid.:20ff.), Horsley sidesteps it in his conclusions.

Anxious to repudiate the image of "Jesus-as-pacifist," Horsley simply tells us that Jesus was actively engaged in resisting structural violence, although he did not advocate reactive violence. Jesus was a revolutionary, but did not really reflect upon the question of means. He was not interested in organizing armed rebellion, because his apocalyptic perspective left the task of the violent overthrow of the powers up to God: "It was his calling to proceed with the social revolution thus made possible by God's [proleptic?] rule, to begin the transformation of social relations in anticipation of the completion of the political revolution" (ibid.:324). But to take refuge in the notion of "eschatological violence" only begs several questions. Is this decisive divine intervention to be interpreted historically, or is it just an apocalyptic "fantasy"? If it is historical, when and how does it occur? If it is not historical, is it not a counterrevolutionary delusion? Or does such an understanding implicity legitimate the use of violent resistance? These questions are left unasked and unanswered.

Unfortunately Horsley appears to equate nonviolence with "apolitical" readings of the Gospel:

> Jesus opposed violence, but not from a distance. He did not attempt to avoid violence in search of a peaceable existence. He rather entered actively into the situation of violence, and even exacerbated the conflict [ibid.:319].

This explains in part why Horsley's reading tends to pay far more attention to what I have called Jesus' "constructive" program of socio-economic alternatives than to his program of resistance. Of the latter Horsley really only considers the Jerusalem conflict stories, specifically the temple action, "a prophetic act symbolizing God's imminent judgmental destruction, not just of the building, but of the Temple system" (ibid.:300). Lacking an adequate concept of militant nonviolence, and content to sidestep the question of revolutionary means, Horsley's otherwise excellent study in the end fails to answer the question of how Jesus expected to work to truly end the historical "spiral of violence," or how we might do so today.

B. LIBERATION HERMENEUTICS

A second political approach to the Jesus story, whose strong influence upon my reading I have acknowledged, is that coming from Third World liberation theologians (Latin American authors have been summarized by C. Bussmann, 1985:35ff.). Of particular significance, because it is one of the few systematic efforts, is Jon Sobrino's *Christology at the Crossroads*:

> Liberation theology has rehabilitated the figure of the historical Jesus within theology. On the one hand it seeks to overcome a highly abstract conception of Christ that is readily open to manipulation. On the other hand it seeks positively to ground Christian existence on the following of this historical Jesus [1978:6].

This accurately reflects two of the most important contributions of liberation readings: the emphasis upon the "historical practice of Jesus" in its social, economic, and political dimensions, and the insistence upon contemporary *discipleship* as liberating praxis.

Several popular liberation interpretations of Jesus are available to English readers, such as Albert Nolan's *Jesus Before Christianity* (1978), George Pixley's *God's Kingdom: A Guide for Biblical Study* (1981) and Hugo Echegaray's *The Practice of Jesus* (1984). As lay studies these books are valuable, and they provide good popular sketches of Jesus' socio-political world.

Liberation theologians have rightly disputed the traditional contention that Jesus' conflicts were religious, not political:

What they seem to forget is that the "political" life of Jesus' day in Israel depended much more on the "theology" prevalent among such groups as the scribes and Pharisees than it did on the Roman Empire and its structures. It was primarily that "theology" that organized the life of the Jewish citizenry, determined their place and position, fixed their obligation, and subjected them to oppression. . . . For that reason Jesus' counter-theology was much more political than any statements or actions directly against Rome would have been at that time [Segundo, 1979:252f.].

It is this very insight that paves the way for a properly political reading of the Jesus story as the ideological discourse of a competing social group in a wider socio-historical context. Unfortunately the exegetical work of these authors in most cases leaves much to be desired, and lacks enough depth to be taken seriously by biblical scholars. Texts are chosen quite selectively, and the way in which some jump from one evangelist to another betrays an almost "harmony of the Gospels" approach.

Ironically, the very strength of liberation hermeneutics has mired it in methodological problems. Although rightly rejecting the existentializing hermeneutics of Western biblical scholarship, their attempts to "rehabilitate the historical Jesus" have tended to repeat the mistakes of earlier historicist studies:

Our interest is focused instead on the historical project borne by Jesus and his Galilean movement, as is told in the Gospel narratives (from which we try to strip the overlay of theological justification for Jesus' death . . .). The way to discover the historical project is to look in the narrative for: (1) the strategy of the movement, (2) the organizational principles for the group of followers, and (3) the enemies of the movement [Pixley, 1981:72].

A century of historico-critical synoptic scholarship has surely demonstrated precisely such historical "quests" to be doomed projects! Yet we find both "old" and "new" questers among liberation theologians.

The "old quest" foundered on the realization that the Gospels as we have them are already so overdetermined by the ideological concerns of the early church that it is simply not credible to take them at face value as direct evidence for the historical practice or strategy of Jesus himself. It is this very problem that sinks Sobrino's otherwise brilliant liberation reading of Jesus, which hinges upon an alleged "crisis" in the course of Jesus' Galilean ministry, after which Jesus gives up on the idea of political success and determines to become a martyr (1978:365). Such a division of Jesus' public life into two distinct parts may or may not be historically accurate; all we can know for sure is that it is a narrative structure that originates with Mark. Yet Sobrino relies upon this Markan fiction as if in it we had access to the internal struggle of Jesus—blissfully ignorant of the (more demonstrable) ideological function it plays within Mark's narrative strategy.

The "new quest" in turn attempted a historical reconstruction by trying to rigorously separate "kerygma" from "history" (McArthur, 1969:3ff.). In the end, it was forced to admit that because the New Testament is not interested in history without kerygma, imposing artificial criteria derived from modern historiography upon it is neither legitimate nor appropriate. Yet so astute a scholar as Segundo, in his *The Historical Jesus of the Synoptics*, carries on the doomed project:

> It is a matter of finding a criterion of trustworthiness or reliability, or better, of priority in the reliability of the *facts* narrated. . . . And logically what seems more certain, on the basis of evangelical testimony itself, is what was attributed to Jesus *without reference* to his passion, death, and resurrection [1985:47].

Like Pixley, Segundo affirms Fernando Belo's insistence upon distinguishing the prepaschal and postpaschal traditions—the new quest in a new guise.

The problem of historicism is central to a political hermeneutics that would be historically grounded, but no real solution has been offered by liberation theology. As I have argued in this commentary, recent literary criticism has shown that the historico-critical method, insofar as it continues to dismantle narrative texts to get at the "historical traditions" behind them, is fundamentally bankrupt (see above, 1,D). The spirit of liberation theology is more than willing to interpret the Jesus story politically, but its reading strategies are weak. At the same time, the strength of Third World Christianity lies in its concrete reading site among the poor and marginal. In the final analysis, the spontaneous, intuitive interpretations of scripture by peasants in base communities bear more natural affinity to the gospel than do the ponderous intellectual apparatuses of those of us belonging to the "educated" classes.

C. SOCIOLOGICAL EXEGESIS

A third approach to socio-political hermeneutics shows keen awareness of the problems of historical methodology—in those who through rigorous use of social scientific disciplines attempt to determine the social setting of the primitive church. Unfortunately for our purposes, most of the full-fledged efforts in "sociological exegesis" have to date been directed to the nonnarrative texts of the New Testament, such as J. Elliott's fine study of 1 Peter (1981), W. Meeks's portrait of the Hellenistic urban churches of Paul (1983), R. Hock's examination of Paul's work-style as indicator of social standing and strategy (1980), and N. Petersen's search for the social-world inferred in the letter to

Philemon (1986). When it has looked at the Gospels, sociological exegesis has returned to the original goal of form criticism: the search for the "life setting" of traditions embedded in the text and the concrete social conditions of its transmission.

The German scholar Gerd Theissen has done the most to advance this method, beginning with his popular and influential work, *Sociology of Early Palestinian Christianity* (1978). There he endeavors to isolate the most "radical" sayings of Jesus, accepting the standard form-critical belief that these represent the most reliably "authentic" traditions. He then hypothesizes that these sayings (i.e., renunciation of family and possessions) could have survived oral transmission only if they were being actually practiced by a group of persons. Theissen next fashions this group for us, a special class of "wandering charismatics" who lived the radical, rootless lifestyle of Jesus, supported by local sympathetic communities. He sets this thesis within the context of a sociological portrait of the socio-economic and political conditions in Palestine in the mid-first century. More recently Theissen (1984) has offered a sociological study of the miracle story traditions, which tests his method on a wider range of texts.

Though a good deal more sophisticated than either of the two approaches mentioned so far, Theissen's hypothesis is built on dubious methodological ground. His assumption that we can identify particular strata of oral tradition with the literal practice of defined social groups raises questions about the dynamics of oral tradition (disputed by Kelber, 1983). Another problem lies in the somewhat arbitrary criteria for "authenticity," and the attendant judgments about what was and was not important to the life of the early church. And, as already pointed out, by refusing to consider the narrative as a whole, the form-critical method ignores the only truly concrete historical evidence we have: the text as it stands! Theissen offers a composite portrait of the Jesus movement based upon a random variety of texts. He does not test his portrait against the fully developed ideological statement of one gospel narrative.

Nor is Theissen's sociological methodology without problems. W. Stegemann (1984) suggests that his portrait of early Christian "vagabond radicalism" is overinfluenced by the social practice of the Cynic movement within Hellenism. J. Elliott (1986) has pointed out the severe limitations of Theissen's structural-functionalism, which focuses upon how groups adapt to hegemonic ideologies in a given social formation rather than explaining how social change comes about. Theissen is concerned primarily with the "various means [by which] the renewal movements which emerged within Judaism sought to overcome increasing tensions" (1978:98). Thus the Jesus movement, a moderate, reconciling tendency within Palestinian Judaism, simply compensated for, transferred, and internalized social aggression. As I have stated, conflict sociological models are in my opinion far more helpful for the study of subversive movements (above, 2,A,ii).

More successful are approaches that settle for a more modest goal: a social portrait not of Jesus, nor of the communities of the oral tradition, but of the "social world" of the evangelist himself. Two studies in Mark have combined sociological analysis with redaction-critical readings of the Gospel. J. Wilde's "A Social Description of the Community Reflected in the Gospel of Mark" (1974) is a valuable (though unpublished) study that concentrates primarily upon Mark 13 and the exorcism stories. It contains solid insights into the immediate historical background of the gospel text, many with which I am in agreement. Wilde is limited by the fact that as a redaction critic he still has not grasped the overall narrative strategy of Mark, and deals with only selective texts. Even more problematic, however, is the sociological side of his work. He relies heavily upon the schematic use of "constructive typologies," which he borrows from B. Wilson's sociology of sectarian religious movements (Wilde, 1978). If structural-functionalism interprets social deviancy in terms of overall systemic adjustments, sect-sociology treats it as essentially social fantasy or escapism (see above, 14,A,i).

H. C. Kee's *Community of the New Age* (1977) is still one of the most helpful compendia I have found on the many literary and historico-critical questions involved in the study of Mark, and I would particularly recommend it as a supplement to my approach. Unfortunately Kee offers only the most superficial sociological generalizations concerning the community reflected in the Gospel, and pays no real attention to the methodological problem of how to get from literary evidence to socio-historical description. Nevertheless, I have tried to expand upon several of Kee's suggestions, such as the importance of the apocalyptic literary genre, issues of social power within the community, and the geopolitical tensions between country and city reflected in Mark's "narrative avoidance" of the city.

For all the limitations of the historico-critical method and structural functionalist sociology, however, it is the lack of political hermeneutics that is the most serious drawback of sociological exegesis. This is no doubt explained in part by the fact that the preponderance of such work is being carried on in the privileged reading sites of First World scholars. As black South African theologian I. J. Mosala puts it: "The question is: on whose side, politically and socially, are these critical methods in *our* society?" (1986:22).

D. MATERIALIST CRITICISM

The last approach I will mention, "materialist criticism," is in my view the most important, for it goes the furthest in correcting the problems of the other three. First, materialist criticism, being Marxist in origin, accepts the primacy of political hermeneutics. Secondly, this method adopts a fundamentally literary analysis of entire texts, thus in principle rejecting the piecemeal approach of both the thematic and the historico-critical strategies above. But unlike formalism, which is more interested in the aesthetics of literature, materialist criticism sees the text as "a form of ideological production":

Like every other ideological production, literary production is determined by the relationship between basis and superstructure, and by class struggles. . . . A materialist theory of literature identifies types of texts and genres of texts as variations within a general social determination of literary form, and analyzes the religious, political, juridical, and other themes of a text in light of its function [Füssel, 1984:20].

In other words, rather than attributing literary conception to "ideas and inspirations," materialist theory looks for the concrete socio-economic and historical forces that determine literature as a form of cultural expression (hence the term "production" instead of "creation"—above, 1,D,ii).

As mentioned at the outset of my commentary (above, 1,B,iii), the most impressive example of this approach dealing with a biblical text is a reading of Mark's Gospel by Portuguese Marxist Fernando Belo. Belo combs backward and forward through the narrative, often finding significance in details routinely dismissed by form and redaction critics. Mark's narrative symbolism of eyes, hands, and feet, for example, represent for Belo the "powerful practice of the body," which is both the strategy of the community and the material site of practice in the world (1981:244ff.). Unfortunately, Belo's narratology, which combines the structuralist Marxism of L. Althusser with a theory of linguistic and social semiotics drawn from F. de Saussure, R. Barthes, and J. Derrida, in order to interpret the ideological signification of the various social and literary codes in the Gospel, makes particularly dense reading. Much of its considerable value is lost to the majority of North American readers, who are for the most part unfamiliar with the semantic and conceptual universes of either Marxism or structuralism. The reader may find M. Clevenot's (1985:53ff.) abridgement and reinterpretation of Belo more accessible. If one plows through the impenetrable jargon, one will find that both Belo and Clevenot extract countless fascinating socio-historical inferences from the text.

There are, however, serious flaws and inconsistencies in the way Belo applies his materialist method. For example, after spending a great deal of effort on a social description of Palestine (his structural analysis of the ideological sphere of first-century Palestine is perhaps his greatest contribution—see above, 2,E,ii), Belo tells us that Mark was written in Rome! Yet Belo makes little effort to socio-politically situate the production of the text in a Roman context. And however brilliant Belo's social analysis, and however keen his insights into the subversive character of Mark's ideological discourse, his *literary* analysis is so overdetermined by his discourse of structuralism—with its confusing array of "codes"—that it gives us very little insight into the narrative world and strategy of Mark. And until we have fully grasped the rich narrative character of the Gospel, our socio-political analysis remains purely extrinsic. Worse, it will result in a misreading, which I think is the case with Belo at several key points.

The greatest disappointment, however, lies in the fact that Belo succumbs to the historico-critical temptation of trying to determine "layers" of discourse within the text. Worse, at several points he resolves his own ideological difficulties with the text through such "deconstruction." He is particularly determined to strip away Mark's "theological discourse":

We were obliged to posit the grill of a double writing, with one writing producing a text we called prepaschal, and the other partially erasing the first and producing in its turn a text in which the paschal narrative is predicted and which we called postpaschal [1981:238].

It is interesting that Belo locates the invasion of "theological discourse" into the text at the very same point that Sobrino speaks of the "epistemological break" in the life of Jesus: namely, the moment at which Mark's Jesus announces his intention to "take up the cross." As noted (above, B), Pixley and Segundo have followed Belo in distinguishing prepaschal/postpaschal and preecclesial/postecclesial discourses (Segundo, 1985:47,60). Belo identifies this "theological discourse" as the product of the Roman church's sociopolitical powerlessness (1981:285)! It seems to me that Belo violates his own professed commitment to the "materiality" of the text by simply practicing a dismantling historicist criticism under another name, treating the text as a means to an end and so betraying the task of literary sociology. Instead we have a new project of "demythologizing," this time by historical materialism (ibid.:287). Political hermeneutics remains an orphan as far as an approach that takes seriously the whole ideology of the whole text.

E. EVALUATION: IS THE CROSS A STUMBLING BLOCK TO POLITICAL HERMENEUTICS?

This brief sketch of socio-political readings of the Gospel indicates that the field is full of problems and prospects. The first two approaches offered a perspective shaped by what I consider to be the right questions, but no distinct strategy with which to analyze the text. They suggested *what* to look for in the text but not *how* to read it. The latter two approaches offered more systematic methodologies, but in practice they reflected similar pitfalls. In my opinion the hope lies in maintaining a commitment to the political hermeneutics inherent in liberation theology, and to the disciplined use of social-scientific tools in historical research demonstrated by sociological exegesis, and the analysis of the text as ideological discourse suggested by materialist criticism. In all of this, a consistently literary approach to the narrative as a whole must be preserved.

Being explicit about one's preconceptions and political partisanship does *not*, in my opinion, grant one license to control or disregard the text. The text is never more vulnerable than when the historical critic (or literary "deconstructionist") decides to dismantle it. To do this is to silence its voice permanently, so that hermeneutics becomes a monologue instead of a dialogue. Here is where problems arise for the otherwise most promising advances in political hermeneutics: the disconcerting tendency shared by virtually all Marxist-oriented reading strategies to avoid or suppress the ideological and narrative fulcrum of Mark's Jesus story: his "strategy" of the cross.

One way of avoiding the cross, as we have seen with Belo, is to dismiss it as "theological overlay." In one sense, this simply recycles Brandon's thesis that

Mark's narrative "covers up" the truly radical Jesus. Today of course few are prepared to defend Brandon's suggestion that Jesus really *was* allied with an armed resistance in Palestine (especially because there was no such movement!); that was the romance of the "revolutionary" ethos of the 1960s. Instead, it is a matter of demurring to the implications of Jesus' choice *not* to be so allied. Jesus' execution as a political dissident is without a doubt the most historically reliable aspect of the traditions about him; with this much Marxists agree. What they wish to rid us of is the "theological discourse" of the early church in its *interpretation* of this historical fact.

But if there is a sure result of historico-critical skepticism, it is that of all the primitive traditions in the New Testament, the most firmly embedded are those that reflect upon the "meaning" of the cross. This strand cannot be simply pulled without the whole fabric of New Testament ideology unraveling ("there can be no history without interpretation"!). Political hermeneutics, therefore, cannot possibly be advanced by trivializing, suppressing, or attempting to exorcise the very heart of primitive Christian self-understanding. We must deal with it, if we wish to continue to *interpret*, and not merely exploit, the New Testament. We must make political and historical sense of the fact that the Gospels portray Jesus as opting for a nonviolent strategy of resistance, which led him in the end to refuse to defend himself, his disciples, or the oppressed poor he served against the violence of Jewish overlords and Roman imperialists.

Perhaps a more reliable way around the cross is therefore the old appeal to the "interim ethic," which can qualify the degree to which we ought to appropriate Jesus' political practice. This is the solution of Sobrino's "epistemological break"; Jesus resigned himself to martyrdom because:

> He expected the imminent end of history, the imminent arrival of God's Kingdom. The long delay in the arrival of the parousia puts the Christian in a situation that is fundamentally different from that of Jesus himself. . . . [We] must explain the following of Jesus in the context of a history that does not seem to be near its end as yet, and that therefore will require all sorts of analyses if we are to organize history on our way toward the Kingdom of God [1978:306].

Obviously, positing a distinction between the Jesus who works within the bounds of socio-political efficacy (his advocacy of the kingdom in Galilee) and the Jesus who abandons politics for the cross (the journey to Jerusalem) allows us to choose the former in our different, "noneschatological" context. Pixley is perhaps more honest in his forthrightness:

> The choice of the multitude between Jesus and Barabbas dramatizes the difference between two social analyses and two strategies of liberation, that of the Jesus movement and that of the Zealots. The crowd of the Gospels chose the Zealot option when forced to a choice between the

two. It must remain an open question whether they were right, in terms of the historical possibilities of Jesus' strategy [1981:388].

José Miranda, in a similar vein, argues that Jesus' nonviolence was simply "tactical," a streak of political realism in the face of overwhelming Roman military power (1982:57ff.). Here, it should be noted, liberation theologians are simply being faithful to their hermeneutical principle of contextuality: Jesus' choices were history-bound, so are ours, and therefore Jesus' historical commitment to nonviolence does not obligate us, his disciples.

The problem is, this returns us to the (idealist) axiom of liberal Protestantism: the Gospels offer only general principles (in this case, "liberation"), but are of no use in the consideration of specific historical means. Principle, as Yoder pointed out, has once again been wrested from practice. Moreover, the argument from context only begs the question as to what we should take as exemplary from the Jesus story in contrast to what we may discard as history- or culture-bound. If, for example, Jesus was simply practicing prudence in his *political* strategy by refusing to initiate armed struggle, as suggested by Miranda, why would this same realism not also have dictated his *social* strategy? Miranda argues that Jesus was organizing peasants against the entire apparatus of deeply entrenched socio-economic interests in Roman Palestine. Were his odds of success greater here than in a military confrontation with Roman legions? To put it more crudely, it may be commendably honest to resolve our conflict with the text by admitting, "Here the text does not agree with me, or I disagree with the text." But we must then also admit the hermeneutical consequences of such a position: namely, that it licenses our ideological opponents on the interpretive battlefield to do exactly the same!

Sobrino did much to recover a discipleship theology in which Jesus is a *normative* model of liberative praxis. Why, then, does he abandon his own thesis at the point of Jesus' choice of "love over power"? How is it that liberation theologians want the authority of a "history of Jesus" when it comes to solidarity with the poor, but not at the point of the strategy of the cross? The answer lies in the fact that they regard Jesus' choice of the cross as his abandonment of politics: "Jesus dies in total *discontinuity* with his life and his cause" (Sobrino, 1978:218). It is ironic that the most indisputable *political* fact of the gospel story is *depoliticized* by liberation theology.

One must conclude that the ambivalent relationship between Marxist political hermeneutics and the cross suggests that it has already been decided, on other grounds, that the strategy of nonviolence does not represent genuinely revolutionary politics (this also seems to be Horsley's attitude). If indeed this is not simply a preconception (i.e., critical awareness of what one is bringing to the text), but a nonnegotiable presupposition (i.e., a constraint to which the text must conform), then one can hardly criticize bourgeois theology for its domestication of the Gospel. Liberation theology insists that the God of the Bible is *not* whoever we want God to be, but God of the poor! But what if the Jesus of the Gospels is not whoever we wish him to be politically, but the Jesus of the cross? If we do not want Jesus' cross, why look to him at all? Is it even legitimate to gain access to this Jesus through texts that themselves insist that he cannot be "known *except* through the cross?"

It is for all these reasons that I have tried to offer a reading of Mark that addresses the political character of the cross head on. Yoder is right that the segregation of means and ends in hermeneutics, whether liberal or radical, is a betrayal of the Jesus story. This story *does* intend to speak to the dilemma of how to define revolutionary practice, and it *is* relevant to our own historical situation. But how can we hear the Gospel of the cross—not as an act of "discontinuity" with the messianic cause but in full continuity with its struggle to overthrow the highest and deepest systems of oppression in the historical world—unless we have a political hermeneutic that is open to it? It is with this in mind that I have suggested that such a hermeneutic may be found in the political practice of militant nonviolent struggle—what Gandhi called *satyagraha*.

In sounding these criticisms of Marxist and liberation hermeneutics, I do not mean to be glossing over the agonizing moral and political complexities and ambiguities of the problem of violence and revolutionary struggle. *Satyagraha*, like Mark's cross, has more questions than answers. But perhaps we should, as Belo put it (reflecting upon the experience of failed revolutions in Chile and Portugal), "be more alert to certain impasses in contemporary Marxism . . . and more disposed to accentuate the aspect of messianic power" (1981:xiv). It is, I suppose, some consolation that Jesus' choice to wage nonviolent struggle was no less a stumbling block for his first followers. Yet the New Testament writers labored to come to terms with it, and so I believe must we. Political readings can no longer skirt the implications of the cornerstone of New Testament faith—Jesus crucified as the *justice* of God.

References

Achtemeier, Paul.
  1970   "Pre-Markan Miracle Catanae." *JBL*, 89, pp. 265ff.
  1978   "And He Followed Him: Miracles and Discipleship in Mk 10:46–52." *Semeia*, 11, pp. 115ff.

Ahn, Byung-mu.
  1981   "Jesus and the Minjung in the Gospel of Mark," in *Minjung Theology: People as the Subjects of History*. Maryknoll, N.Y.: Orbis.

Altizer, T.
  1971   "The Dialectic of Ancient and Modern Apocalypticism." *JAAR*, 39:3, pp. 312ff.

Assmann, Hugo.
  1979   "The Power of Christ in History: Conflicting Christologies and Discernment," in *Frontiers of Theology in Latin America*. R. Gibellini, ed. Maryknoll, N.Y.: Orbis, pp. 133ff.

Bailey, Kenneth E.
  1980   *Poet and Peasant and Through Peasant Eyes: A Literary-Cultural Approach to the Parable in Luke*. Grand Rapids: Eerdmans.

Baird, J. Arthur.
  1969   *Audience Criticism and the Historical Jesus*. Philadelphia: Westminster.

Barnett, P.
  1981   "The Jewish Sign Prophets—A.D. 40–70; Their Intentions and Origin." *NTS*, 27, pp. 679ff.

Barth, Markus.
  1959   *The Broken Wall: A Study in the Epistle to the Ephesians*. Valley Forge: Judson.

Barthes, Roland.
  1957   *Mythologies*. New York: Hill and Wang.

Baum, Gregory.
  1980   *Sociology and Human Destiny: Essays on Sociology, Religion, and Society*. New York: Seabury.

Beardslee, W.
  1971   "N.T. Apocalyptic in Recent Interpretation." *Interpretation*, 25, pp. 419ff.
  1979   "Saving One's Life By Losing It." *JAAR* 47:1.

Beasely-Murray, G.
  1983   "Second Thoughts on the Composition of Mark 13." *NTS*, 29, pp. 414ff.

Beck, N.
  1981   "Reclaiming a Biblical Text: The Mark 8:14–21 Discussion about Bread in a Boat." *CBQ*, 43, pp. 49–56.

Belo, Fernando.
    1981   *A Materialist Reading of the Gospel of Mark*. Maryknoll, N.Y.: Orbis.
Bennett, W.
    1975a   "The Son of Man Must." *NovTest*, 17:2, pp. 113ff.
    1975b   "The Herodians of Mark's Gospel." *NovTest*, 17:1, pp. 7ff.
Berger, Peter.
    1969   *The Sacred Canopy: Elements of a Sociological Theory of Religion*.
             Garden City, N.Y.: Doubleday Anchor.
——and Luckmann, T.
    1967   *The Social Construction of Reality: A Treatise in the Sociology of Knowl-
             edge*. Garden City, N.Y.: Doubleday Anchor.
Berrigan, Daniel.
    1983   *The Nightmare of God*. Portland: Sunburst.
——, ed.
    1984   *For Swords into Plowshares, The Hammer Has to Fall*. Syracuse: Plow-
             shares Press.
Best, Ernest.
    1981   *Following Jesus: Discipleship in the Gospel of Mark*. *JSNT* Supplement
             Series, No. 4. Sheffield: JSOT Press.
Beuchner, Frederick.
    1977   *Telling the Truth: The Gospel as Tragedy, Comedy, and Fairy Tale*. San
             Francisco: Harper and Row.
Bilezikian, Gilbert G.
    1977   *The Liberated Gospel: A Comparison of the Gospel of Mark and Greek
             Tragedy*. Grand Rapids: Baker.
Black, Matthew.
    1967   *An Aramaic Approach to the Gospels and Acts*. Oxford: Clarendon.
Blevins, James L.
    1981   *The Messianic Secret in Markan Research 1901–76*. Washington, D.C.:
             University Press of America.
Bonhoeffer, Dietrich.
    1953   *The Cost of Discipleship*. New York: Macmillan.
Bonino, José Míguez, ed.
    1984   *Faces of Jesus: Latin American Christologies*. Maryknoll, N.Y.: Orbis.
Booth, Roger P.
    1986   *Jesus and the Laws of Purity: Tradition and Legal History in Mark 7*.
             Sheffield: JSOT Press.
Bornkamm, Gunther.
    1963   "The Stilling of the Storm in Matthew," in *Tradition and Interpretation
             in Matthew*. Bornkamm, Barth, and Held, eds. Philadelphia: Westmin-
             ster.
Bottomore, T.B. ed.
    1956   *Karl Marx: Selected Writings in Sociology and Social Philosophy*. New
             York: McGraw-Hill.
Bowker, John.
    1973   *Jesus and the Pharisees*. New York: Cambridge University Press.
Braaten, Carl.
    1971   "The Significance of Apocalyptic for Systematic Theology." *Interpreta-
             tion*, 25.

1972a   *Christ and Counter Christ: Apocalyptic Themes in Theology and Culture.*
         Philadelphia: Westminster.
1972b   "And Now—Apocalyptic!" *Dialog*, 11, pp. 21f.
Brandon, S. G. F.
1967   *Jesus and the Zealots.* New York: Scribner's.
Brown, Dale
1971   *The Christian Revolutionary.* Grand Rapids: Eerdmans.
Brown, John Pairman.
1983   "Techniques of Imperial Control: The Background of the Gospel Event,"
         in N. Gottwald, *The Bible and Liberation*, pp. 357ff.
Brown, Raymond E.
1977   *The Birth of the Messiah.* Garden City, N.Y.: Doubleday.
Budd, S.
1974   "Religion and Protest," review of B. R. Wilson's *Magic and the Millen-
         nium. Religion*, 4.
Bultmann, Rudolf.
1963   *History of the Synoptic Tradition.* New York: Harper and Row.
Burridge, Kenelm.
1969   *New Heaven and New Earth: A Study of Millenarian Activity.* New York:
         Schocken.
Buss, M.
1978   "The Idea of *Sitz im Leben*—History and Critique." *ZAW*, 90:2, pp. 157ff.
Bussmann, Claus.
1985   *Who Do You Say? Jesus Christ in Latin American Theology.* Maryknoll,
         N.Y.: Orbis.
Caird, G. B.
1956   *Principalities and Powers—A Study in Pauline Theology.* Oxford: Claren-
         don.
Camara, Helder.
1971   *The Spiral of Violence.* London: Sheed & Ward.
Caragounis, Chrys C.
1977   *The Ephesian Mysterion.* Uppsala: CWK.
Carlton, Eric.
1977   *Ideology and Social Order.* Boston: Routledge & Kegan Paul.
Carney, Thomas F.
1975   *The Shape of the Past: Models and Antiquity.* Kansas: Coronado Press.
Casalis, Georges.
1984   *Correct Ideas Don't Fall from the Skies.* Maryknoll, N.Y.: Orbis.
Cassidy, Richard.
1978   *Jesus, Politics, and Society: A Study of Luke's Gospel.* Maryknoll, N.Y.:
         Orbis.
———, ed.
1983   *Political Issues in Luke-Acts.* Maryknoll, N.Y.: Orbis.
Cave, C.H.
1979   "The Leper: Mark 1:40–45." *NTS*, 25, pp. 246ff.
Chatman, Seymour B.
1978   *Story and Discourse: Narrative Structure in Fiction and Film.* Ithaca:
         Cornell University Press.
Clevenot, Michel.
1985   *Materialist Approaches to the Bible.* Maryknoll, N.Y.: Orbis.

Cohn-Sherbok, Daniel.
1979   "An Analysis of Jesus' Arguments Concerning the Plucking of Grain on the Sabbath." *JSNT*, 2, pp. 31ff.
Collins, Adela Yarbro.
1976   *The Combat Myth in the Book of Revelation*. Missoula: Scholars Press.
1977   "The Political Perspective of the Revelation to John."*JBL*, 26, pp. 16–31.
Collins, John J.
1974   "Apocalyptic Eschatology as the Transcendence of Death."*CBQ*, 36, pp. 30ff.
1977   *The Apocalyptic Vision of the Book of Daniel*. Missoula: Scholars Press.
1981   *Daniel, 1–2 Maccabees*. Wilmington: Michael Glazier.
1984   *The Apocalyptic Imagination: An Introduction to the Jewish Matrix of Christianity*. New York: Crossroad.
Comblin, Joseph.
1979   "What Sort of Service Might Theology Render?" in *Frontiers of Theology in Latin America*. R. Gibellini, ed. Maryknoll, N.Y.: Orbis, pp. 79ff.
Cook, Michael J.
1978   *Mark's Treatment of the Jewish Leaders*. Leiden: Brill.
Corbo, Virgilio C.
1969   *The House of St. Peter at Capharnaum*. Jerusalem: Franciscan Press.
Cullmann, Oscar.
1970   *Jesus and the Revolutionaries*. New York: Harper and Row.
Culpepper, R.
1982   "Mark 10:50: Why Mention the Garment?" *JBL*, 101:1, pp. 131f.
Derrett, J. Duncan M.
1970   "KORBAN, HO ESTIN DWRON." *NTS*, 16, pp. 364f.
1972   " 'Eating up the Houses of Widows': Jesus' Comment on Lawyers?"*NovTest*, 14, pp. 1ff.
1974   "Mark 9:42 and Comparative Legal History," in *Law in the New Testament*. Leiden: Brill.
1977   *Studies in the New Testament, I*. Leiden: Brill.
1979   "Contributions to the Study of the Gerasene Demoniac."*JSNT*, 3, pp. 5ff.
1985   "*Mylosonikos* (Mk 9:42 par)."*ZeitNTWiss*, 76:3–4, p. 284.
Dewey, Joanna.
1979   *Markan Public Debate: Literary Technique, Concentric Structure, and Theology in Mk 2:1–3:6*. SBL Dissertation Series No. 48. Missoula: Scholars Press.
Dodd, Charles H.
1968   "The Primitive Christian Catechism and the Sayings of Jesus," in *More New Testament Studies*. Grand Rapids: Eerdmans, pp. 11ff.
Donahue, John R.
1971   "Tax Collectors and Sinners: An Attempt at Identification." *CBQ*, 33, pp. 39ff.
1983   *The Theology and Setting of Discipleship in the Gospel of Mark*. The 1983 Pere Marquette Theology Lecture. Milwaukee: Marquette University Press.
Douglas, Mary.
1966   *Purity and Danger: An Analysis of the Concepts of Pollution and Taboo*. London: Routledge & Kegan Paul.

1973 *Natural Symbols: Explorations in Cosmology*. New York: Vintage.

1982 "The Effects of Modernization on Religious Change," in *Religion in America*. M. Douglas and S. Tipton, eds. Boston: Beacon Press, pp. 25ff.

Douglass, James

1969 *The Nonviolent Cross: A Theology of Revolution and Peace*. New York: Macmillan.

1972 *Resistance and Contemplation*. Garden City, N.Y.: Doubleday.

1980 *Lightning East to West*. Portland: Sunburst.

Eagleton, Terry.

1976 *Criticism and Ideology: A Study in Marxist Literary Theory*. New York: Schocken.

1983 *Literary Theory: An Introduction*. Minneapolis: University of Minnesota Press.

Echegaray, Hugo.

1984 *The Practice of Jesus*. Maryknoll, N.Y.: Orbis.

Eddy, Samuel K.

1961 *The King Is Dead*. Ann Arbor, Mich.: Books on Demand.

Edwards, George R.

1972 *Jesus and the Politics of Violence*. New York: Harper and Row.

Edwards, Richard A.

1976 *A Theology of Q: Eschatology, Prophecy, and Wisdom*. Philadephia: Fortress.

Eissfeldt, Otto.

1965 *The Old Testament: An Introduction*. New York: Harper and Row.

Eliade, Mircea.

1963 *Myth and Reality*. New York: Harper and Row.

Elliott, John H.

1981 *A Home for the Homeless: A Sociological Exegesis of I Peter, Its Situation and Strategy*. Philadelphia: Fortress.

1986 "Social Scientific Criticism of the New Testament: More on Methods and Models." *Semeia*, 35, pp. 1–33.

Ende, Michael.

1983 *The Neverending Story*. London: Penguin.

Esquivel, Julia.

1982 *Threatened with Resurrection: Prayers and Poems from an Exiled Guatemalan*. Elgin, Ill.: Brethren Press.

Evans, C.A.

1985 "On the Isaianic Background of the Sower Parable."*CBQ*, 47, 464ff.

Farrer, Austin.

1951 *A Study in St. Mark*. London.

Fears, J.

1980 "Rome: The Ideology of Imperial Power." *Thought*, 55:216, pp. 98ff.

Ferm, Deane.

1986 *Third World Liberation Theologies: An Introductory Survey*. Maryknoll, N.Y.: Orbis.

Finnerty, Adam D.

1977 *No More Plastic Jesus: Global Justice and Christian Lifestyle*. Maryknoll, N.Y.: Orbis.

Fledderman, H.
1981   "The Discipleship Discourse (Mark 9:33–50)." *CBQ*, 43, pp. 57ff.
1982   "A Warning About the Scribes (Mark 12:37b–40)." *CBQ*, 44, pp. 52ff.
1983   " 'And He Wanted to Pass By Them' (Mark 6:48c)." *CBQ*, 45, pp. 389ff.
Flusser, David.
1973   "The Social Message from Qumran," in *Jewish Society Through the Ages*. H. Ben-Sasson and S. Ettinger, eds. New York: Schocken, pp. 107ff.
Ford, Desmond.
1979   *The Abomination of Desolation in Biblical Eschatology*.Washington, D.C.: University Press of America.
Ford, J. Massyngbaerde.
1984   *My Enemy Is My Guest: Jesus and Violence in Luke*. Maryknoll, N.Y.: Orbis.
Fowler, Robert M.
1981   *Loaves and Fishes: The Function of the Feeding Stories in the Gospel of Mark*. SBL Dissertation Series No. 54. Chico: Scholars Press.
Freyne, Sean.
1980   *Galilee: From Alexander the Great to Hadrian, 323 B.C.E–135 C.E.: A Study of Second Temple Judaism*. South Bend: University of Notre Dame Press.
1982   "The Disciples in Mark and the *Maskilim* in Daniel: A Comparison." *JSNT*, 16, pp. 7ff.
1985   "Our Preoccupation With History: Problems and Prospects," in *Proceedings of the Irish Biblical Association*, 9, pp. 1–18.
Fuller, Reginald H.
1971   *The Formation of the Resurrection Narratives*. New York: Macmillan.
Füssel, Kuno.
1984   "Materialist Readings of the Bible: Report on an Alternative Approach to Biblical Texts," in *God of the Lowly: Socio-Historical Interpretations of the Bible*. L. Schottroff and W. Stegemann, eds. Maryknoll, N.Y.: Orbis, pp. 13ff.
Gager, John G.
1975   *Kingdom and Community: The Social World of Early Christianity*. Engelwood Cliffs, N.J.: Prentice-Hall.
1982   "Shall We Marry Our Enemies? Sociology and the N.T." *Interpretation*, 36:3.
Gandhi, Mohandas K.
1948   *Nonviolence in Peace and War*. 2 vols. Ahmedabad: Navajivan.
Gaston, Lloyd.
1970   *No Stone on Another: Studies in the Significance of the Fall of Jerusalem in the Synoptic Gospels*. Leiden: Brill.
Geertz, Clifford.
1973   *The Interpretation of Culture: Selected Essays*. New York: Basic Books.
Gish, Arthur.
1973   *The New Left and Christian Radicalism*. Grand Rapids: Eerdmans.
Gnuse, Robert.
1985   *You Shall Not Steal: Community and Property in the Biblical Tradition*. Maryknoll, N.Y.: Orbis.

Goldmann, Lucien.
  1980   *Essays on Method in the Sociology of Literature.* W. Boelhower, ed. St. Louis: Telos Press.

Gottwald, Norman K.
  1979   *The Tribes of Yahweh: A Sociology of the Religion of Liberated Israel.* Maryknoll, N.Y.: Orbis.

————, ed.
  1983   *The Bible and Liberation: Political and Social Hermeneutics.* Maryknoll, N.Y.: Orbis.

Grayston, K.
  1974   "The Study of Mark 13." *BJRL*, 56, pp. 371ff.

Griffiths, J.
  1971   "The Disciple's Cross." *NTS*, 16, pp. 364ff.

Gross, Bertram.
  1980   *Friendly Fascism: The New Face of Power in America.* Boston: South End.

Gutiérrez, Gustavo.
  1973   *A Theology of Liberation.* Maryknoll, N.Y.: Orbis.

Hall, Douglas John.
  1976   "Toward an Indigenous Theology of the Cross." *Interpretation*, 30, pp. 153ff.

Hanson, Paul.
  1971   "Old Testament Apocalyptic Reexamined." *Interpretation*, 25, pp. 469ff.

Harrington, D.
  1985   "A Map of Books on Mark, 1975–84." *BibTheoBul*, 15:1, pp. 12ff.

Harrington, Michael.
  1977   *The Vast Majority: A Journey to the World's Poor.* New York: Simon and Schuster.

Harrison, R. K., ed.
  1985   *Major Cities of the Biblical World.* New York: Thomas Nelson.

Hartman, Lars.
  1966   *Prophecy Interpreted: The Formation of Some Jewish Apocalyptic Texts and of the Eschatological Discourse Mk 13 par.* Uppsala: Lund.

Hengel, Martin.
  1973   *Victory Over Violence.* Philadelphia: Fortress.
  1974   *Judaism and Hellenism.* Philadelphia: Fortress.
  1978   *Crucifixion.* Philadelphia: Fortress.

Herzog, Frederick.
  1972   *Liberation Theology: Liberation in Light of the Fourth Gospel.* New York: Seabury.
  1980   *Justice Church.* Maryknoll, N.Y.: Orbis.

Herzog, William.
  1982   "Pollard Lecture, 1982" (unpublished). Quoted with permission. Graduate Theological Union, Berkeley, Calif.

Hobsbawm, Eric.
  1959   *Primitive Rebels: Studies in Archaic Forms in Social Movement in the 19th and 20th Centuries.* New York: Norton.

Hock, Ronald F.
1980 *The Social Context of Paul's Ministry: Tentmaking and Apostleship.* Philadelphia: Fortress.
Hollenbach, P.
1981 "Jesus, Demoniacs, and Public Authorities: A Socio-Historical Study." *JAAR*, 49:4, pp. 573ff.
Holzner, Burkart.
1972 *Reality Construction in Society.* New York: Schenkman.
Horsley, Richard A.
1981 "Ancient Jewish Banditry and the Revolt Against Rome, A.D. 66–70."*CBQ*, 43, pp. 416ff.
1985 "Menahem in Jerusalem: A Brief Messianic Episode Among the Sicarii—Not 'Zealot Messianism'." *NovTest*, 27:4.
1987 *Jesus and the Spiral of Violence: Popular Jewish Resistance in Roman Palestine.* San Francisco: Harper & Row.
——and Hanson, J.
1985 *Bandits, Prophets and Messiahs: Popular Movements in the Time of Jesus.* Minneapolis: Winston.
Hunter, J.
1982 "Subjectivization and the New Evangelical Theodicy."*JSSR*, 21:2, pp. 39ff.
Isenberg, S. R.
1973 "Millenarism in Greco-Roman Palestine." *Religion*, 3, pp. 26ff.
Jameson, Fredric.
1981 *The Political Unconscious: Narrative as a Socially Symbolic Act.* Ithaca: Cornell University Press.
Jeremias, Joachim.
1966 *The Eucharistic Words of Jesus.* London: SCM.
1969 *Jerusalem in the Time of Jesus: An Investigation into Economic and Social Conditions during the New Testament Period.* Philadelphia: Fortress.
1972 *The Parables of Jesus*, 2d ed. New York: Scribner's.
Jesudasan, Ignatius.
1984 *A Gandhian Theology of Liberation.* Maryknoll, N.Y.: Orbis.
Johnson, E.
1978a "Mark 10:46–52: Blind Bartimaeus." *CBQ*, 40, pp. 191ff.
1978b "Mark 8:22–26: The Blind Man from Bethsaida." *NTS*, 25, pp. 370ff.
Judge, E. A.
1980 "The Social Identity of the First Christians: A Question of Method in Religious History." *Journal of Religious History*, 11:2, pp. 212ff.
Juel, Donald.
1977 *Messiah and Temple: The Trial of Jesus in the Gospel of Mark.* SBL Dissertation Series 31. Missoula: Scholars Press.
Kavanaugh, John.
1983 *Following Christ in a Consumer Society.* Maryknoll, N.Y.: Orbis.
Kealy, Sean.
1982 *Mark's Gospel: A History of Its Interpretation.* New York: Paulist, 1982.
Kee, Howard C.
1968 "The Terminology of Mark's Exorcism Stories."*NTS*, 14, pp. 242ff.
1977 *Community of the New Age: Studies in Mark's Gospel.* Philadelphia: Westminster

1980   *Christian Origins in Sociological Perspective.* Philadelphia: Westminster.

Kelber, Werner.
1973   *The Kingdom in Mark: A New Place and A New Time.* Philadelphia: Fortress.
1979   *Mark's Story of Jesus.* Philadelphia: Fortress.
1980   "Mark and Oral Tradition." *Semeia*, 16, pp. 7ff.
1983   *The Oral and the Written Gospel: The Hermeneutics of Speaking and Writing in the Synoptic Tradition, Mark, Paul, and Q.* Philadelphia: Fortress.

Kellner, D.
1978   "Ideology, Marxism, and Advanced Capitalism."*Socialist Review*, 42, pp. 37ff.

Kennedy, George A.
1984   *New Testament Interpretation Through Rhetorical Criticism.* Chapel Hill: University of North Carolina Press.

Kim, Yong-bok.
1981   "Messiah and Minjung: Discerning Messianic Politics over against Political Messianism," in *Minjung Theology: People as the Subjects of History.* Maryknoll, N.Y.: Orbis.

Lamb, Matthew.
1980   "The Challenge of Critical Theory," in *Sociology and Human Destiny.* G. Baum, ed. New York: Seabury, pp. 183ff.

Lang, F. G.
1978   "Über Sidon mitten ins Gebiet der Dekapolis. Geographie und Theologie in Markus 7:31." *ZDPV*, 94:2, pp. 145ff.

Lasch, Christopher.
1979   *The Culture of Narcissism.* New York: Norton.

Laurenson, Diana, and Swingewood, A.
1972   *The Sociology of Literature.* New York: Schocken.

Laws, Sophie.
1975   "Can Apocalytpic Be Relevant?" in *What About the N. T.?* Morna Hooker and Colin Hickling, eds. London: SCM, pp. 95ff.

Lenski, Gerhard E.
1978   *Human Societies: An Introduction to Macrosociology.* New York: McGraw-Hill.

Lightfoot, Robert Henry.
1950   *The Gospel Message of St. Mark.* Oxford: Clarendon.

Linder, R.D.
1982   "Militarism in Nazi Thought and in the American New Religious Right." *Journal of Church and State*, 24:2, pp. 263ff.

Lundquist, J.
1982   "The Legitimizing Role of the Temple in the Origin of the State," in *SBL Seminar Papers 1982.* Chico: Scholars Press, pp. 171ff.

Maduro, Otto.
1979   *Religion and Social Conflicts.* Maryknoll, N.Y.: Orbis.

Malbon, Elizabeth S.
1982   "Galilee and Jerusalem: History and Literature in Marcan Interpretation." *CBQ*, 44, pp. 242ff.
1984   "The Jesus of Mark and the Sea of Galilee." *JBL*, 103:3, pp. 363ff.
1985   "TH OIKIA AUTOV: Mk 2:15 in Context." *NTS*, 31, pp. 282ff.

1986   *Narrative Space and Mythic Meaning in Mark.* New York: Harper and Row.

Malina, Bruce J.
1981   *The New Testament World: Insights from Cultural Anthropology.* Atlanta: John Knox.
1984   "The Gospel of John from a Sociolinguistic Perspective." Unpublished lecture. Graduate Theological Union, Berkeley, Calif.
1986a   "Religion in the World of Paul." *BibTheoBul,* 16:3, pp. 92–101.
1986b   "Interpreting the Bible with Anthropology: The Case of the Poor and the Rich." *Listening: A Journal of Religion and Culture,* 21:2, pp. 148–59.

Maloney, Elliot C.
1981   *Semitic Interference in Marcan Syntax.* Chico: Scholars Press.

Martí, José
1975   *Inside the Monster: Writings on the United States and American Imperialism.* P. Foner, ed. New York: Monthly Review Press.

Marxsen, Willi.
1969   *Mark the Evangelist: Studies on the Redaction History of the Gospel.* Nashville: Abingdon.

Matera, Frank.
1982   *The Kingship of Jesus.* SBL Dissertation Series 66, Missoula: Scholars Press.

Matura, Thaddée.
1984   *Gospel Radicalism: The Hard Sayings of Jesus.* Maryknoll, N.Y.: Orbis.

May, H.
1972   *Toward a New Earth: Apocalypse in the American Novel.* South Bend: University of Notre Dame Press.

McArthur, Harvey K.
1969   *In Search of the Historical Jesus.* New York: Scribner's.

McDonald, J.
1980   "Mk 9:33–50: Catechetics in Mk," in *Studia Biblica II,* JSNT Supplement Series 2. Sheffield: JSOT Press, pp. 171ff.

McGann, Diarmuid.
1985   *The Journeying Self: The Gospel of Mark Through a Jungian Perspective.* New York: Paulist.

McKnight, Edgar V.
1978   *Meaning in Texts: The Historical Shaping of a Narrative Hermeneutics.* Philadelphia: Fortress.

Meeks, Wayne.
1983   *The First Urban Christians: The Social World of the Apostle Paul.* New Haven: Yale University Press.

Merrit, R.
1985   "Jesus, Barabbas, and the Paschal Pardon." *JBL,* 104:1, pp. 57ff.

Metzger, Bruce.
1975   *A Textual Commentary of the Greek New Testament.* New York: United Bible Societies.

Millar, William R.
1976   *Isaiah 24–27 and the Origin of Apocalyptic.* Missoula: Scholars Press.

Miller, Alice.
1981   *The Drama of the Gifted Child*. New York: Basic Books.
1983   *For Your Own Good: Hidden Cruelty in Child-Rearing and the Roots of Violence*. New York:Farrar, Straus, Giroux.
1984   *Thou Shalt Not Be Aware: Society's Betrayal of the Child*. New York: Farrar, Straus, Giroux.

Mills, C. Wright.
1960   *The Causes of World War Three*. New York: Ballantine.

Miranda, José.
1977   *Being and the Messiah: The Message of St. John*. Maryknoll, N.Y.: Orbis.
1982   *Communism and the Bible*. Maryknoll, N.Y.: Orbis.

Moiser, J.
1981   " 'She Was Twelve Years Old' (Mark 5:42); A Note on Jewish-Gentile Controversy in Mark's Gospel." *Irish Biblical Studies*, 3, pp. 180ff.

Moltmann, Jürgen.
1974   *The Crucified God*. New York: Harper and Row.
1975   "An Open Letter to José Míguez Bonino." *Christianity and Crisis*. March 29, pp. 57ff.

Montefiore, H.
1962   "Revolt in the Desert?" *NTS*, 8, pp. 135ff.

Moore, W.
1986   "Outside and Inside: A Markan Motif." *Expository Times*, 98:2, pp. 39–43.

Morrison, Clinton.
1960   *The Powers That Be: Earthly Rulers and Demonic Powers in Rom 13:1-7*. Studies in Biblical Theology I, No. 29. Naperville, Ill.: Allenson.

Mosala, I. J.
1986   "Social Scientific Approaches to the Bible: One Step Forward, Two Steps Backward." *Journal of Theology for Southern Africa*, 55, pp. 15–30.

Munro, W.
1982   "Women Disciples in Mark?" *CBQ*, 44, pp. 225ff.

Myers, Ched.
1980   "Storming the Gates of Hell: Reflections on Christian Evangelism in Nuclear Security Areas." *The Christian Century*. Sept. 16, pp. 898ff.

National Council of the Churches of Christ, USA.
1983   *An Inclusive Language Lectionary*. Atlanta: John Knox.

Neal, Marie A.
1977   *A Socio-Theology of Letting Go: The Role of a First World Church Facing Third World Peoples*. New York: Paulist.

Neusner, Jacob.
1987   *Canon and Connection: Intertextuality in Judaism*. New York: University Press of America.

Neyrey, J.
1986   "The Idea of Purity in Mark's Gospel." *Semeia*, 35, pp. 91–127.

Nickelsburg, George.
1981   *Jewish Literature Between the Bible and Mishnah*. Philadelphia: Fortress.

Nolan, Albert.
1978   *Jesus Before Christianity*. Maryknoll, N.Y.: Orbis.

1985   *The Service of the Poor and Spiritual Growth*. London: Catholic Institute for International Relations.

Obayashi, H.
1975   "The End of Ideology and Politicized Theology." *Cross Currents*, Winter, pp. 383ff.

Oppenheimer, A'haron.
1977   *The 'Am Ha-aretz: A Study in the Social History of the Jewish People in the Hellenistic-Roman Period*. Leiden: Brill.

Patte, Daniel.
1976   *What is Structural Exegesis?* Philadelphia: Fortress.

Patten, P.
1983   "The Form and Function of Parable in Select Apocalyptic Literature and Their Significance for Parables in the Gospel of Mark."*NTS*, 29, pp. 246ff.

Pavur, C.
1987   "The Grain is Ripe: Parabolic Meaning in Mk 4:26–29."*BibTheoBul*, 17:1, pp. 21–23.

Pearlman, Moshe, and Yannai, Yaakov.
1965   *Historical Sites in Israel*. Tel Aviv: PEC Press.

Perrin, Norman.
1967   *Rediscovering the Teachings of Jesus*. New York: Harper and Row.
1976   "The Interpretation of the Gospel of Mark."*Interpretation*, 30, pp. 115ff.

Petersen, Norman R.
1978   *Literary Criticism for New Testament Critics*. Philadelphia: Fortress.
1980a   "Composition of Mark 4:1–8:26." *HTR*, 73:1–2, pp. 185ff.
1980b   "When is the End not the End? Literary Reflections on the Ending of Mark's Narrative." *Interpretation*, 34:2, pp. 151ff.
1986   *Rediscovering Paul: Philemon and the Sociology of Paul's Narrative World*. Philadelphia: Fortress.

Peterson, David L.
1977   *Late Israelite Prophecy*. Missoula: Scholars Press.

Pierard, R.
1982   "Protestant Support for the Political Right in Weimar Germany and Post-Watergate America: Some Comparative Observations." *Journal of Church and State*, 24:2, pp. 245ff.

Pilch, J.
1985   "Healing in Mark: A Social Science Analysis." *Biblical Theology Bulletin*, 15:4, pp. 142ff.

Pilgrim, Walter E.
1981   *Good News to the Poor: Wealth and Poverty in Luke-Acts*. Minneapolis: Augsburg.

Pixley, George.
1981   *God's Kingdom: A Guide for Biblical Study*. Maryknoll, N.Y.: Orbis.

Pryke, E. J.
1978   *Redactional Style in the Marcan Gospel*. New York: Cambridge University Press.

Quesnell, Quentin.
1969   *The Mind of Mark: Interpretation and Method Through Exegesis of Mk 6:52*. Rome: Analecta Biblica, 38.

Rader, William.
1978   *The Church and Racial Hostility: A History of Interpretation of Eph. 2:11–22.* Tübingen: Siebeck.

Reicke, B.
1972   "Synoptic Prophecies on the Destruction of Jerusalem," in D. Aune, ed., *Studies in the NT and Early Christian Literature*, Leiden: Brill, pp. 121ff.

Remus, Harold.
1982   "Sociology of Knowledge and the Study of Early Christianity," *Sciences Religieuses*, 11:1, pp. 45–56.

Rengstorf, K. H.
1965   *"korban, korbanas."* *Theological Dictionary of the New Testament.* G. Kittel, ed. Grand Rapids: Eerdmans, pp. 865ff.

Rhoads, David M.
1976   *Israel in Revolution, 6–74 C.E.: A Political History Based on the Writings of Josephus.* Philadelphia: Fortress.

———and Michie, Donald.
1982   *Mark as Story.* Philadelphia: Fortress.

Richardson, H., ed.
1974   *Religion and Political Society.* New York: Harper and Row.

Ricoeur, Paul.
1970   *Freud and Philosophy.* New Haven: Yale University Press.
1977   "The Model of the Text: Meaningful Action Considered as Text," in *Understanding and Social Enquiry.* F. Dallmayr and T. McCarthy, eds. South Bend: University of Notre Dame Press, pp. 316ff.

Rivkin, E.
1983   "Locating John the Baptizer in Palestinian Judaism: The Political Dimension." SBL Seminar Papers. Chico: Scholars Press, pp. 79ff.

Robbins, Vernon K.
1984   *Jesus the Teacher: A Socio-Rhetorical Interpretation of Mark.* Philadelphia: Fortress.

Robinson, James M.
1982   *The Problem of History in Mark and Other Marcan Studies.* Philadelphia: Fortress.

Robinson, John A. T.
1976   *Redating the New Testament.* London: SCM.

Safrai, Samuel, and Stern, S., eds.
1977   *The Jewish People in the First Century.* Compendia Rerum Iudaicarum ad Novum Testamentum, vol. II. Amsterdam: Van Gorcum.

Sandmel, Samuel.
1978   *Judaism and Christian Beginnings.* New York: Oxford University Press.

Schaberg, J.
1985   "Daniel 7, 12 and the New Testament Passion-Resurrection Predictions." *NTS*, 31, pp. 208ff.

Schottroff, Willy, and Stegemann, Wolfgang.
1984   "The Sabbath was Made for Man: The Interpretation of Mark in 2:23–28," *God of the Lowly.* Maryknoll, N.Y.: Orbis, pp. 118ff.

Schüssler Fiorenza, Elisabeth.
1983   "The Phenomenon of Early Christian Apocalyptic: Some Reflections on

Method," in *Apocalypticism in the Mediterranean World and Near East.* D. Hellholm, ed. Tübingen: Mohr, pp. 295ff.

1985　　*In Memory of Her: A Feminist Theological Reconstruction of Christian Origins.* New York: Crossroad.

Schutz, A.

1967　　"Symbol, Reality, and Society" in *Collected Papers, Vol. I.* The Hague: Martinus Nijhoff, pp. 287ff.

Schweizer, Eduard.

1960　　*Lordship and Discipleship.* Studies in Biblical Theology No. 28. London: SCM.

1978　　"The Portrayal of the Life of Faith in the Gospel of Mark."*Interpretation*, 32, pp. 388ff.

Scroggs, Robin.

1980　　"The Sociological Interpretation of the New Testament: The Present State of Research." *NTS*, 26, pp. 164ff.

Segundo, Juan Luis.

1979　　"Capitalism Versus Socialism: Crux Theologica," in *Frontiers of Theology in Latin America.* R. Gibellini, ed. Maryknoll, N.Y.: Orbis, pp. 240ff.

1985　　*The Historical Jesus of the Synoptics.* Maryknoll, N.Y.: Orbis.

1986　　"The Hermeneutic Circle," in *Third World Liberation Theologies.* Maryknoll, N.Y.: Orbis, pp. 64ff.

Selvidge, M.

1983　　"And Those Who Followed Feared." *CBQ*, 45:3, pp. 396ff.

1984　　"Mk 5:25–34 and Lev 15:19–20: A Reaction to Restrictive Purity Regulations." *JBL*, 103:4, pp. 619ff.

Senior, D.

1987　　"With Swords and Clubs: The Setting of Mark's Community and His Critique of Abusive Power." *BibTheoBul*, 17:1, pp. 10–20.

Sherwin-White, A. N.

1963　　*Roman Society and Roman Law in the New Testament.* New York: Oxford University Press.

Smith, D.

1973　　"The Two Made One: Eph 2:14–18." *Ohio Journal of Religious Studies*, 1, pp. 35ff.

1985　　"Jesus and the Pharisees in Socio-Anthropological Perspective."*Trinity Journal*, 6:2, pp. 151–156.

Smith, George A.

1931　　*Historical Geography of the Holy Land.* London, 25th ed.

Smith, J.

1975　　"The Social Description of Early Christianity."*Religious Studies Review*, 1:1, pp. 19ff.

Sobrino, Jon.

1978　　*Christology at the Crossroads.* Maryknoll: Orbis.

Sölle, Dorothee.

1979　　"Resistance: Toward a First World Theology."*Christianity and Crisis*, 39:12, July 23, pp. 178ff.

Sowers, S.

1970　　"The Circumstances and Recollection of the Pella Flight."*TheoZeit*, 26:5, pp. 305ff.

Standaert, B.
1978   *L'Evangile de Marc, Composition et Genre Littéraire*. Zevenkerken-Brugge.

Stegemann, Wolfgang.
1984   "Vagabond Radicalism in Early Christianity?: A Historical and Theological Discussion of a Thesis Proposed by Gerd Theissen," in *God of the Lowly*. W. Stegemann and L. Schottroff, eds. Maryknoll, N.Y.: Orbis, pp. 148ff.

Stein, Robert H.
1978   *The Method and Message of Jesus' Teachings*. Philadelphia: Westminster.

Stock, A.
1986   "Jesus, Hypocrites, and Herodians." *BibTheoBul*, 16:1, pp. 3–7.

Suh, Nam-Dong.
1983   "Historical References for a Theology of *Minjung*," in *Minjung Theology: People as the Subjects of History*. Commission on Theological Concerns of the Christian Conference of Asia, ed. Maryknoll, N.Y.: Orbis.

Swomley, John.
1972   *Liberation Ethics*. New York: Macmillan.

Sykes, R.
1980   "Toward a Sociology of Religion Based on the Philosophy of George Herbert Mead," in *Sociology and Human Destiny*. G. Baum, ed. New York: Seabury, pp. 167ff.

Tannehill, Robert C.
1975   *The Sword of His Mouth*. Philadelphia: Fortress.
1980   "Tension in Synoptic Sayings and Stories." *Interpretation*, 34, pp. 149ff.

Taylor, Vincent.
1963   *The Gospel According to St. Mark*. New York: St. Martin's.

Telford, William R.
1980   *The Barren Temple and the Withered Tree*. JSNT Supplementary Series I, Sheffield: JSOT Press.

Theissen, Gerd.
1976   "Die Tempelweissagung Jesu: Prophetie im Spannungsfeld von Stadt und Land." *TheoZeit*, 32, pp. 144ff.
1978   *Sociology of Early Palestinian Christianity*. Philadelphia: Fortress.
1982   *The Social Setting of Pauline Christianity: Essays on Corinth*. Philadelphia: Fortress.
1983   *The Miracle Stories of the Early Christian Tradition*. London: T. Clark.
1984   "Lokal und Sozialkoloriet in der Geschichte von der syrophönikischen Frau (Mk 7:24–30)." *ZeitNTWiss*, 75:3–4, pp. 202ff.

Thompson, J.
1971   "The Gentile Mission as an Eschatological Necessity." *Restoration Quarterly*, 14:1, pp. 18ff.

Trinidad, Saúl.
1984   "Christology, *Conquista*, Colonization," in *Faces of Jesus: Latin American Christologies*. J. Míguez Bonino, ed. Maryknoll, N.Y.: Orbis, pp. 49ff.

Trocmé, André.
1964   *Jesus and the Nonviolent Revolution*. Scottdale, Pa.: Herald Press.

Urban, M., and McClure, J.
  1983   "The Folklore of State Socialism: Semiotics and the Study of the Soviet
            State." *Soviet Studies*, 35:4, pp. 471ff.
Van Iersel, B.
  1980   "The Gospel According to Mark: Written for a Persecuted Community?"
            NedTheoTijd, pp. 15ff.
Via, Dan O.
  1985   *The Ethics of Mark's Gospel—In the Middle of Time.* Philadelphia:
            Fortress.
Waetjen, H.
  1982   "The Construction of the Way into a Reordering of Power: An Inquiry
            into the Generic Conception of the Gospel According to Mark." Unpub-
            lished paper, quoted with permission. San Francisco Theological Semi-
            nary.
Wallis, Jim.
  1976   *Agenda for Biblical People.* New York: Harper and Row.
Walzer, Michael.
  1986   *Exodus and Revolution.* New York: Basic Books.
Weber, Hans Ruedi.
  1975   *The Cross: Tradition and Interpretation.* Grand Rapids: Eerdmans.
Weeden, Theodore J.
  1971   *Mark: Traditions in Conflict.* Philadelphia: Fortress.
Weimann, Robert.
  1984   *Structure and Society in Literary History: Studies in the History and
            Theory of Historical Criticism.* Baltimore: Johns Hopkins University
            Press.
Welch, Sharon.
  1985   *Communities of Resistance and Solidarity: A Feminist Theology of Liber-
            ation.* Maryknoll, N.Y.: Orbis.
Wengst, Klaus.
  1987   *Pax Romana and the Peace of Jesus Christ.* Philadelphia: Fortress.
Wilde, James A.
  1974   "A Social Description of the Community Reflected in the Gospel of
            Mark." Ph.D dissertation, Drew University.
  1978   "The Social World of Mark's Gospel: A Word About Method." *SBL
            Seminar Papers, II.* Missoula: Scholars Press.
Wilder, Amos.
  1982   *Jesus' Parables and the War of Myths.* Philadelphia: Fortress.
Williams, Raymond.
  1977   *Marxism and Literature.* London: Oxford University Press.
Williams, William Appleman.
  1980   *Empire as a Way of Life.* New York: Oxford University Press.
Wink, Walter.
  1973   *The Bible in Human Transformation.* Philadelphia: Fortress.
  1984   *Naming the Powers: The Language of Power in the New Testament,* vol 1.
            Philadelphia: Fortress.
Witvliet, Theo.
  1984   *A Place in the Sun: An Introduction to Liberation Theology in the Third
            World.* Maryknoll, N.Y.: Orbis.

Wright, A.
 1982 "The Widow's Mite: Praise or Lament? A Matter of Context." *CBQ*, 44, pp. 256ff.
Yoder, John H.
 1972 *The Politics of Jesus*. Grand Rapids: Eerdmans.
Zerwick, Max and Grosvenor, Mary.
 1981 *A Grammatical Analysis of the Greek New Testament*. Rome: Biblical Institute Press.
Zipes, Jack D.
 1979 *Breaking the Magic Spell: Radical Theories of Folk and Fairy Tales*. New York: Methuen.

General Index

Author Index

Scripture Index

(Includes references apart from the Gospel of Mark)